THE PRIDE OF NORTH LONDON

by Bob Goodwin

Dedicated to
Ossie

First published in Great Britain 1997 by
Polar Print Group Ltd
2, Uxbridge Road, Leicester LE4 7ST
England

Text copyright © Bob Goodwin 1997
Design copyright Polar Print Group Ltd © 1997

ISBN 1 899538 04 6

Edited by
Julian Baskcomb

Designed and Printed by
Polar Print Group Ltd
2, Uxbridge Road, Leicester LE4 7ST
Tel: (0116) 261 0800

Photographs and illustrations are courtesy of:
Sporting Pictures, Colorsport, Hulton-Getty Collection,
Press Association, Associated Sports Photography, Empics,
Popperfoto, Professional Sport International and the vast
collections of Les Gold and Bob Goodwin.
Most remaining photographs are from the private
collections of the authors or from albums owned by various
Tottenham or Arsenal supporters or former players. We
have been unable to trace the sources of all these pictures,
but any photographer involved is cordially invited to contact
the publishers in writing providing proof of copyright.

Front cover photographs:
(left) Darren Anderton challenges Paul Merson
(Colorsport)
(right) Arsenal v Spurs at Highbury 1925 (Hulton-Getty)
Alex Lindsay (Spurs) bears down on 'keeper Jock Robson.

Back cover photographs:
David O'Leary (Arsenal), Gary Mabbutt (Spurs),
Tony Adams (Arsenal) at the shared 1991 Charity Shield
(Sporting Pictures)
Main pic: Arsenal v Spurs April 1995;
Percy Hooper saves a penalty from Alf Kirchen,
Spurs v Arsenal (Jubilee Trust Fund) 1939.

Frontispage :
Charles Buchan (Arsenal) greets Arthur Grimsdell (Spurs)
at Highbury in August 1925 (Hulton-Getty)

Every summer, when the fixture list is published,
the first matches all fans look for are those against
their nearest rivals. The dream may be to carry off
one of the game's top prizes but if nothing else,
football fans are realists; they know that for the
majority the dream will remain unfulfilled.
However, if success on a national stage cannot be
achieved consolation can always be found nearer
home. It may not produce any silverware, but is the
gleam of metal any brighter than the glow of satisfaction that follows beating our neighbours?

It's a matter of pride, the local pride that the
world over has stirred the passions and made the
'derby' such a vital part of football history. Every
city has its own 'derby' but with so many clubs in
London the rivalry has become even more
localised. West London has the fight for superiority
between Chelsea, Fulham and Queens Park
Rangers, East London has West Ham, Millwall and
Leyton Orient, South London Charlton and Crystal
Palace. None of them though has such a long-
standing and fascinating history as the North
London derby between Arsenal and Spurs.

This book is intended to be a story of that derby.
It is not meant as a history of Arsenal or Spurs, or to
compare one with the other, but rather a record of
the rivalry between the two clubs through the
matches that, I hope, will provoke a flood of memories.

In compiling this book I have drawn extensively
on contemporary newspaper reports. During my
research one thing in particular has struck me. It's
only a personal view, but it seems to me there has
been a definite decline in football reporting standards. Read the old time reports and you can
almost visualise the game unfolding before your
eyes. Modern reports though seem to contain very
little about the game itself. There might be a
description of the goals but so often reporters concentrate not on what happened during the ninety
minutes that really matter but what players or managers have said afterwards. Perhaps reporters think
they do not need to describe what we may have
seen for ourselves because so many games are
shown on television these days but it does not
make it easy for the football historian. It is for that
reason practically all the reports used come from
what are now termed 'the quality papers'.
Nonetheless it is to the authors of all match reports
that I must first express my thanks. Without them
this book would not have been possible.

There are many others who have helped in various way, especially Caroline Tingay, Fred Ollier,
Gary James, Andy Porter, Andy Kelly, John
Williamson and Richard Lerman. Bobby Smith and
Joe Baker were so kind in readily agreeing to write
forewords. A particular mention must be made of
John Harris whose unquenchable thirst and enthusiasm for books on our national game provides
inspiration when the words begin to dry up. Julian
Baskcomb and Julia Byrne of Polar Print have provided help and encouragement whenever needed
and I cannot fail to mention the wonderful design
and layout of 'Clever Trevor'. My grateful thanks to
them all.

Finally, a special word of thanks must go to Les
Gold who not only made his entire photograph and
memorabilia collection available to me whenever I
wanted but also provided much invaluable encouragement.

I hope you will enjoy reading 'The Pride of North
London'. I hope there will not be too many mistakes, but if you find any please let me now. The
publishers will forward all letters on.

Bob Goodwin
Author

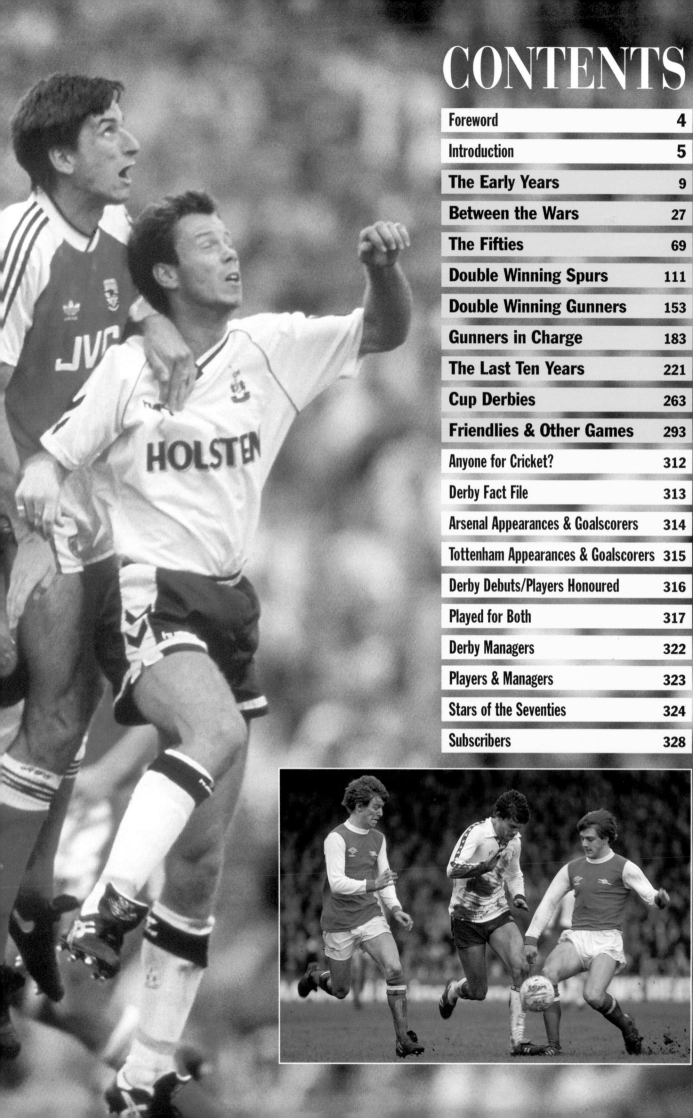

CONTENTS

Foreword	4
Introduction	5
The Early Years	9
Between the Wars	27
The Fifties	69
Double Winning Spurs	111
Double Winning Gunners	153
Gunners in Charge	183
The Last Ten Years	221
Cup Derbies	263
Friendlies & Other Games	293
Anyone for Cricket?	312
Derby Fact File	313
Arsenal Appearances & Goalscorers	314
Tottenham Appearances & Goalscorers	315
Derby Debuts/Players Honoured	316
Played for Both	317
Derby Managers	322
Players & Managers	323
Stars of the Seventies	324
Subscribers	328

FOREWORD

WHEN I first joined Arsenal I had already experienced the joys of an Edinburgh derby with Hibernian and sampled the passion of a Turin derby playing for Torino against Juventus. After leaving Highbury I was to taste the North Eastern rivalry between Sunderland and Newcastle. The Italians may have been more volatile but for me there was nothing to match the keenness and intensity of a North London derby. And nothing to match the joy of scoring in those matches.

They were always fantastic games, especially in the early sixties when Spurs had great players like Danny Blanchflower, Dave Mackay, John White and Jimmy Greaves. Pitting oneself against players like them was always a great test but to do so in the cauldron of a derby fixture added a special edge. Spurs were definitely the country's top team when I first donned the red shirt, but we had some good players too, George Eastham, Geoff Strong, George Armstrong and any fixture with Spurs was sure to bring out the best in them.

Without a doubt we always enjoyed out meetings with Spurs although the games were perhaps more important for the fans than the players. They would build them up to such an extent it was as if nothing else mattered. Of course it was different for them. If we lost we could just put everything into training and the next game, we did not have to face our mates at work or down the pub.

As a centre-forward my job was to net goals and I believe I had a pretty good record of scoring against Spurs. Certainly I will never forget the two I got at Highbury in February 1965, the only time I finished on the winning side in a North London derby, although the match that stands out most in my memory was the 4-4 draw in October 1963. To come back from two down in the last five minutes is always a great feat but to do it against Spurs just shows how much those games meant to us at Arsenal.

The Pride of North London has reminded me of some of the great matches I played in and revived some marvellous memories of wonderful players I played both with and against. I am sure you will get as much pleasure from reading this book as I have.

Joe Baker
(Arsenal & England)

BEING asked to write a foreword to The Pride of North London gives me a great deal of pleasure. I spent nine tremendously happy years at White Hart Lane playing in a very successful team, a team that, for one half of North London at least, rates with the best of all time.

During that period I played in plenty of tough matches, Cup Finals, semi-finals, championship deciders, but none of them was any harder than the twice a season meetings with Arsenal. Joining Spurs from Chelsea I had already played in London derbies and knew of Spurs' great rivalry with Arsenal but it was only when actually involved that I realised the true uniqueness of a North London derby.

The players always tried to treat each game just like any other but for the supporters they were the most important matches of the season and their desire for victory could not fail to transmit itself to those playing. For weeks before the match all the fans would talk about was the forthcoming derby. No matter how well or bad we were playing, beating Arsenal was all that mattered. It really got to you after a while and I have no doubt it made us try just that bit harder. Win and we were heroes, but lose and we just wanted the next game to come so we could make amends.

Not that the fans were the only ones to demand success. Perhaps it was because he had been with Spurs so long but beating Arsenal always meant something special to Bill Nicholson.

Even when not playing I always made a point of going to derby games. Whether at White Hart Lane or Highbury, the atmosphere was tremendous and it was impossible not to get caught up in it all. Every game was tense and hard-fought but from a player's point of view one of the most enjoyable aspects was the friendly rivalry with our opponents. We might battle each other for ninety minutes but when the game was over we were all friends.

Reading though The Pride of North London has brought the memories flooding back for me; my first North London derby, my frequent hard, but always fair tussles with Bill Dodgin, that great game in October 1963 when Arsenal battled to take a point after being two down with five minutes to go. I hope just as many come back to you.

Bobby Smith
(Tottenham & England)

INTRODUCTION

On 19th November 1887 two fledgling football clubs met for a friendly match on Tottenham Marshes. Nothing unusual about that, every Saturday was the same, local teams coming together on roughly laid out pitches for a bit of physical endeavour.

At the time it was a game of little consequence, watched by barely a handful of spectators and meriting nothing more than a brief report in the local paper; none at all where the visitors came from. Looking back though this was a game with a difference; the first meeting of what have become two of the biggest, most famous and consistently successful clubs in the country. It was the first match between Spurs and Arsenal; the start of a rivalry that was to move on from the public parks of Tottenham and Woolwich to the twin towers of Wembley, a fixture that has grown from one watched by a few onlookers with nothing better to do on a Saturday afternoon to an event where even the biggest stadium in the country cannot accommodate those anxious to attend.

Since that first meeting, brought to an end 15 minutes early because of bad light with Spurs 2-1 ahead, the north London derby has developed into one of the most eagerly awaited fixtures on the football calendar, a derby that more than stands comparison with its counterparts in Liverpool and Glasgow, Manchester and Sheffield.

Not that anyone present could ever have imagined the significance of their afternoon's entertainment. Spurs, five years old, still relied on many of the schoolboys that had formed the club while Royal Arsenal (as they were still known) had been formed little more than a year earlier from workers at the Woolwich Arsenal munitions factory.

There were many other clubs in and around London whose beginnings were equally as humble, but none of them have gone on to scale the heights reached by Spurs and Arsenal. With the benefit of maturity and ready jobs in the factory, Royal Arsenal made rapid progress.

They turned professional in 1891 (at the same time changing their name to Woolwich Arsenal) and joined the Football League two years later, the first London club in what had been an exclusively Midlands and Northern competition.

Spurs lagged well behind. It was December 1895 before they decided to pay players and although they were elected to the Southern League in July 1896 that was only after they had been rejected by the Football League, already establishing itself as the country's premier League competition.

The two clubs met in friendly matches several times after that first meeting on Tottenham Marshes but the first competitive game did not come until November 1896, a 2-1 victory for Arsenal in a United League fixture at the Manor Ground. The United League, just like the Southern District Combination and London League, was a secondary competition both clubs played in and while expected to field full strength teams reserves were frequently used. Not that these matches were without incident.

Arsenal's visit to Spurs' Northumberland Park ground on 8th April 1898 for a United League game drew fully 14,000 spectators, far more than could comfortably be accommodated. Many of them were fortunate to escape serious injury when the refreshment stand they had climbed on to get a better view collapsed. Within a year Spurs had secured a new ground.

Two years later a Southern District Combination fixture at the Manor Field was abandoned with 15 minutes left because of bad language from the crowd. Arsenal

were censured and ordered to post warning notices while the referee was heavily criticised! Despite competing in the more popular Football League Arsenal did not meet with the same success and public acclaim Spurs found.

Always near the top of the Southern League table Spurs won it only once, in 1900, but their great success came a year later when they broke the Football League's hold on the FA Cup and won it for the first time. It was a breakthrough on a national stage that thrust them to the forefront of London football and was to hold them in good stead when they applied to join the Football League seven years later.

At the same time Arsenal were struggling to make their mark. A mid-table side it was only with the appointment of Harry Bradshaw as manager that they began to look capable of promotion to the top flight. That was achieved in 1904 but Bradshaw immediately left to join Fulham, where a certain local estate agent, Henry Norris, was formulating his plans to build a London club good enough to challenge the powerful clubs of the North and Midlands.

Like Spurs' chairman Charles Roberts, Norris grew increasingly frustrated at the lack of ambition shown by the Southern League but his own plans suffered a severe setback in 1905. When Fulham refused Gus Mears' offer of moving to Stamford Bridge, Chelsea were formed and Norris had a potential rival on his doorstep. His influence no doubt played a part in letting Chelsea know they would not be welcome in the Southern League but he could do little to prevent their admission to the Football League.

In 1907 Norris masterminded Fulham's election to the Second Division but by then Chelsea had gained promotion to the First. Norris soon realised that if his ambitions were to be fulfilled in West London a club in the First Division was essential. Fulham seemed unlikely to win promotion in the near future so he looked for an alternative. He found it, or so he thought, south of the Thames, in Plumstead.

Under Phil Kelso Arsenal had reached the FA Cup semi-finals of 1906 and 1907. His successor, George Morrell, had taken them to their highest ever League position of sixth in 1909, but they were in serious financial difficulties. Just avoiding relegation in 1910 they were drawing smaller crowds than Fulham. If Norris could merge the two he would have just what he wanted, a First Division club playing in West London.

Such was Arsenal's desperate financial plight he had little difficulty taking control at Plumstead but his initial plan to merge with Fulham did not find favour with the League. They could not stop a merger, or prevent the merged club playing at Craven Cottage, but any club playing at Fulham would be more Fulham than Arsenal, and Fulham were a Second Division outfit!

Norris' back-up plan was to have both clubs play at Craven Cottage on alternate Saturdays but the League did not like this idea either. Norris had no option but to let Arsenal play on at the Manor Field, although he made it clear that would only continue as long as money was not lost.

It did not last long. With Norris and his associate, William Allen, dividing their time between Plumstead and Craven Cottage (it was not until the start of the First World War they relinquished control of Fulham), Arsenal had two poor seasons, finishing tenth each time. Poor performances attracted poor crowds, money was being lost. Norris again began to look at moving Arsenal from Plumstead. Rumours abounded but it was not until March 1913, by which time relegation was a certainty, that he announced a move was definitely on.

A new home had been found. The sports ground of St John's College of Divinity was as perfect a site for a football stadium as could be hoped for. A readily developed site, in a well populated area and with easy access by public transport.

The only possible drawback was that Highbury was right on Spurs' doorstep - only four miles away. But that did not worry Norris, by now Mayor of Fulham and with obvious political ambitions. He had clearly done his homework since the abortive attempt to move Arsenal to Craven Cottage and knew there was no way Spurs, the Football League or Football Association could thwart his plans.

Local residents were up in arms, forming the "Highbury Defence Committee", putting pressure on the Council of St John's and the Board of Education and gaining the support of Islington Borough Council at a meeting where Charles Sutcliffe, a member of the League Management Committee and later League President, spoke on behalf of Arsenal.

Again though the protestations went unheeded. Planning permission was not required and there was nothing the council, or anybody else for that matter, could do. Spurs tried. With the backing of Clapton Orient and Chelsea they protested long and loud, canvassing other clubs for support and making their feelings clear at a lengthy, and at times heated, meeting of the League Management Committee. They could not stop Arsenal's move. It was the club that was a member of the League, not the ground, and there was nothing in League rules that gave the League any say on where a club should play. Other clubs had moved grounds, although without opposition and not so as to invade a rival's territory. Only a couple of months later the League rules were changed.

At the AGM in May 1913 a proposal by Clapton Orient, seconded by Spurs, that all clubs should register their ground with the League secretary and should not be allowed to move without the prior consent of the Management Committee was carried by a big majority. By then, of course, it was too late. Spurs against Arsenal had been a "London derby". In future it would be a "North London derby".

The move to Highbury was an enormous gamble for Norris. He had six months to get the ground ready for the opening of the 1913-14 season and in that time had to lay out or guarantee payment of some £125,000 (equivalent to about £3 million today). Although only half-completed Highbury opened for business in September 1913.

The first part of his master plan achieved, Norris could now concentrate on the second stage; getting Arsenal back in the First Division.

With Spurs in the top flight, albeit struggling to stay there, promotion for Arsenal was essential. Every year they were in the Second and Spurs the First would just make it harder for Arsenal to establish themselves. The target was almost achieved in April 1914. Had it not been for Clapton Orient, of all people, taking a point from the last game of the season at Highbury, Arsenal would have gone up instead of finishing third and missing out on goal average.

The outbreak of the First World War put Norris' plans on hold. Despite public opposition to football continuing while the nation's youth were playing a far more dangerous game on foreign fields, the 1914-15 season was completed. Five years later how Spurs must have wished it had been abandoned? In an unreal atmosphere with players joining the forces and ever decreasing gates Spurs finished 20th and last in the First Division, Arsenal sixth (it was to be many years before an error was realised and their position adjusted to fifth) in the Second.

In times of war a nation pulls together, old animosities are forgotten for the common good. Football was no different. When the Ministry of Munitions announced

in September 1916 that White Hart Lane was being requisitioned for the manufacture of gas masks Arsenal were quick to offer them the Highbury facilities. Spurs spent the rest of the War playing half their games on the ground they had fought against so bitterly and the rest at Homerton, home of Clapton Orient.

Not that Arsenal were prepared to extend the hand of friendship to the field of play. Knowing it was unlikely regular goalkeeper Bill Jacques would be available for a match with Portsmouth in April 1917 and that finding a stand-in would be difficult, Spurs asked "Tim" Williamson, the Arsenal custodian, if he could put himself on standby. It was not until ten minutes before kick-off that a Spurs director arrived. He was immediately despatched to secure Arsenal's permission for Williamson to play but no Arsenal official could be found. Spurs asked Williamson to take the field sure that Arsenal would not object. They could not have been more wrong. As soon as Arsenal found out what had happened they complained to the London Football Combination. Spurs were fined five guineas for playing Williamson without Arsenal's permission.

The animosity engendered by Arsenal's move to North London may have been lessened by Spurs wartime use of Highbury but it was like nothing compared to the bitter feelings created when Norris, now Sir Henry and Conservative MP for Fulham, resumed his quest to make Arsenal London's footballing power, a quest that had taken on added urgency with Arsenal £60,000 in debt.

If Norris was to protect his investment he had to get Arsenal into the First Division, and quickly at that. Almost as soon as the war was over he was presented with the perfect opportunity to do so, but even then he would have to pull off a most audacious coup.

The Football League decided that on the resumption of normal football the First Division would be increased by two clubs. That had happened twice before. After the 1898 Test matches Blackburn were due to be relegated and Newcastle had failed to gain promotion. Both clubs were elected to Division One. In 1905 Bury and Notts County should have gone down but stayed up.

On that basis Chelsea and Spurs, who had finished 1914-15 in the bottom two positions, could reasonably hope to do likewise. Indeed the League Management Committee even told them to expect they would stay in the First Division.

Expectations are not always met though, particularly when a formidable foe like Sir Henry Norris set his sights on a target. Norris had little chance of persuading his fellow chairman to promote Arsenal at Chelsea's expense. They had finished 1914-15 one point behind Manchester United but it was subsequently proved that as part of a betting coup a late season match between United and Liverpool had been fixed to give United a 2-0 success. A reversal of that score and it would have been United not Chelsea going down.

Equally, he had no hope of depriving Derby and Preston of the place in the top flight they had won by topping the Second Division. Norris' only hope was to set up, and then win, a straight fight between Arsenal and Spurs. In seeking support for Arsenal to be promoted, Norris based their claim on the fact they had been members of the League longer than either Chelsea or Spurs.

It was a challenge Spurs, to their cost, did not take seriously. But then why should they? Never before had it been suggested length of membership gave one club a better right to promotion than another. Besides had not Barnsley, Wolves and Birmingham, third, fourth and fifth in Division Two in 1914-15, been in the League longer than Arsenal? Wolves, after all, had been founder members.

In the sporting press Norris' campaign was ridiculed, precedent and justice were in Spurs' favour. Or so they thought. When it came to the League meet-

ing in March 1919 it was soon obvious Norris had again done his homework, and in particular secured the help of his close friend, "Honest" John McKenna, chairman of Liverpool and League President.

Instead of one vote with the top four going up, McKenna suggested that the circumstances in which Chelsea had been relegated were such that they should be re-elected without a vote. That was agreed, as was his proposal that Derby and Preston should be promoted, again without a vote.

Much to the amazement of the Spurs' contingent, McKenna then urged the assembled company to vote Arsenal into the First Division, citing Arsenal's longer membership of the League. It was a transparently ridiculous argument, particularly as Barnsley, Wolves and Birmingham were also in the ballot. If length of League membership was to be the deciding factor the vote had to go in favour of Wolves.

The only point in Arsenal's favour, and it is far from clear whether it was ever advanced, was that they had been the League's standard bearers in London in its early days, the South's first professional club, ostracised by the stick-in-the-mud amateurs who controlled football in and around London and who despised the idea of paying people to play a "game". All of that was true but what had Arsenal ever achieved?

Most of the time they had struggled financially, more than half their League career had been spent in the Second Division, they had not finished higher than sixth in the First. And they had not, unlike Spurs, won the FA Cup. Even after McKenna's unprecedented plea on Arsenal's behalf, Spurs remained confident common sense would prevail.

They were sadly disappointed. Barnsley got five votes, Wolves four, Nottingham Forest three, Birmingham two and Hull one. But Arsenal collected 18 against Spurs eight.

Just how Norris managed to pull off the seemingly impossible has never been explained. There is no doubt he was a persuasive and influential force, able to call in favours owed, make a few promises here and there. But even that cannot explain how he could get almost half the clubs to support his cause.

Not surprisingly rumours circulated that money had proved a powerful weapon in Norris' campaign but nothing was ever proved, and Sir Henry never revealed his secrets. Certainly he was a ruthless man, not afraid to twist, or even break, the rules in pursuit of his dream.

He made a lot of enemies and in 1929 those enemies had their revenge when Norris was banned from the game after a series of FA inquiries and court cases revealed persistent breaches of FA rules, including the making of irregular payments to players. There was no suggestion Norris had personally gained at Arsenal's expense; after all the time and money he had invested that would have been nigh on impossible, or that he had behaved differently to any number of chairman, but he was found out and had to pay the penalty. But that was all in the future.

Back in 1919 Norris had achieved the second part of his plan. All he had to do to fulfill his dream was to make Arsenal the best team in the country. That was to take another twelve years and, of course, by then he had departed.

At the start of the decade though Arsenal were not even the top team in north London. Spurs emphasised the injustice of their relegation by almost walking away with the Second Division title, followed that up with the FA Cup in 1921 and a year later finished runners-up to Liverpool, the highest placing by a London club since the League had been formed.

Arsenal were unable to make any impression and in 1924-25 only avoided relegation by one place. They finished seven points ahead of Preston but survival was not good enough for Norris, he wanted Arsenal up at the top.

It proved the turning point in Arsenal's history. Manager Leslie Knighton was sacked, Herbert Chapman tempted away from Huddersfield, League champions for the last two years. Norris had laid the foundations for Arsenal success off the pitch, now it was for Chapman, a former Spurs' player, to finish the job on it. Chapman's first match in charge was hardly indicative of the future, Spurs winning at Highbury in the first game under the new offside rule, but by the end of the season he had lifted Arsenal to second place, behind his old club Huddersfield who thus completed the first League title hat-trick.

Chapman said it would take five years to build a trophy-winning team and so it proved, although had Cardiff not beaten Arsenal in the 1927 FA Cup final he would have done it much earlier than predicted. While Arsenal were taking the first steps towards a football domination the likes of which had not been seen before Spurs were slipping back. It all went wrong for them in May 1928.

Having completed their League programme they had 38 points and while clubs below still had games to play Spurs looked safe for another year. It would take a freak combination of results to send them down but while they were on tour in Holland that freak happened. They returned to find seven clubs one point above them and only Middlesbrough below.

Included in the seven on 39 points were Manchester United and Sheffield Wednesday, who had respectively won and drawn in Arsenal's last two home games. There were dark mutterings in some quarters that Arsenal had deliberately taken it easy in those matches to ensure Spurs' relegation but the facts suggest otherwise.

While Arsenal were playing United, Spurs were losing at Anfield and there was no way Arsenal could know how that game would turn out. The point Wednesday took from Highbury may have meant victory in their last game would ensure their safety but even if they had lost to Arsenal their superior goal average would have taken them above Spurs.

With Spurs in the Second Division Arsenal had a clear field to establish themselves as not merely masters of North London but the best club in the capital. Under Chapman and his successor George Allison they went further.

The 1930s saw Arsenal the most successful club in history. It started with their first FA Cup success in 1930 and continued with five League titles in eight years, another FA Cup success and runners-up spot in each competition once. Not only did Sir Henry Norris' dream come true, it was well and truly surpassed.

And to make it all the sweeter, while all this was happening Spurs were nowhere. In only two seasons were they even in the First Division, 1933-34 when they finished third, ten points behind Champions Arsenal and 1934-35 when they finished rock bottom as Arsenal equalled Huddersfield's record of three successive titles and demonstrated their absolute mastery of north London with a 5-1 victory at Highbury and a 6-0 stroll at White Hart Lane.

Spurs had to wait 15 years before another North London League derby on their own patch although the clubs met frequently during the Second World War when, with Highbury taken over as an Air Raid Precaution centre, Spurs were able to return the favour shown by Arsenal in the First War and allow them the use of White Hart Lane.

Arsenal's domination, at least in North London, continued immediately after the war. They won their sixth championship in 1948, while Spurs, managed for three years by Joe Hulme, one of Arsenal's brightest stars from the glorious 1930s, could not escape the Second Division. Hulme was in charge for only one competitive derby, the first FA Cup clash between the clubs in January 1949.

It was one of the freaks of the FA Cup that despite Arsenal and Spurs having entered every competition since 1894 (Arsenal had first entered in 1889) they had never before been drawn together. When they did finally meet Arsenal had a comfortable 3-0 victory. Arsenal won the FA Cup in 1950 but as the new decade opened Spurs at last looked as if they would emerge from the enormous shadow Arsenal's continued success had cast.

Arthur Rowe's "Push and Run" side won the Second Division in 1950 and followed it up twelve months later with their first League title but Arsenal were not prepared to give up their number one position lightly. FA Cup finalists in 1952, another League championship followed before Wolves and Manchester United took over as the country's top teams.

While Arsenal searched for former glories it was now Spurs turn to enjoy the most successful and acclaimed period in their history. Bill Nicholson took over as manager in 1958 and within three years led them to the fabled League and Cup "Double", a dream so many great teams had striven for, gotten so close to but never achieved. Despite the trophy winning teams of the past Spurs had never managed a period of sustained success, that changed now.

After retaining the FA Cup in 1962, the European Cup-Winners' Cup was added to the honours list a year later and the FA Cup again in 1967. George Swindin and Billy Wright both succumbed to the pressure of trying to compete with Nicholson's teams. Only once in the 1960s did Arsenal manage to finish above Spurs in the League and by then Bertie Mee had taken charge. The pendulum of North London dominance was about to swing back in favour of Arsenal.

The first sign of things to come was late in 1968 when, in their first League Cup meeting, Arsenal beat Spurs in the two-legged semi-final. They lost the final but the following year matched Spurs record by winning a European trophy, the Fairs Cup. Twelve months later they went even better becoming only the second team this century to do the "Double". And to emphasise their mastery of North London they completed the first leg of football's greatest triumph at White Hart Lane.

The early seventies were the one period when both Spurs and Arsenal were successful. While Arsenal were doing the "Double", Spurs completed a clean sweep for North London with the League Cup. Arsenal were FA Cup runners up in 1972 and second in the First Division in 1973. Spurs won the UEFA Cup in 1972, the League Cup in 1973 and were UEFA Cup finalists a year later.

It was a time of great change for football; increasing pressure, success all that mattered. Bill Nicholson decided football management was for younger men and retired in 1974, two years later Bertie Mee followed suit. They were both succeeded by the same man, Terry Neill.

The former Arsenal captain put the brakes on Spurs' decline but was unable to stop it entirely; a year after his move to Highbury they were relegated. Back on familiar territory he made Arsenal London's top team, always well placed in the League, if rarely looking like potential champions, FA Cup winners in 1979, runners up in 1978 and 1980 and losing finalists in the European Cup-Winners' Cup in 1980. Spurs' sojourn in the Second Division was short, just one year, but when they got back up they took time to make their mark.

As a new decade began though it was again their turn to lead London's challenge for the big prizes. FA Cup winners in 1981 and 1982, League (Milk) Cup finalists in 1982, regulars in Europe and UEFA Cup winners in 1984, for the first time in thirty years they posed a serious challenge for the League title, although never able to secure the one prize that really matters.

The arrival of George Graham at Highbury proved the turning point. As Spurs lost their first FA Cup final

in 1987 Arsenal secured the Littlewoods Cup to embark on a trophy-winning run to rival the days of Herbert Chapman. Another Littlewoods Cup final in 1988, the League title in 1989 and 1991, when the deduction of two points proved an incentive more than a handicap. Spurs were left to look on enviously but on the way to winning the FA Cup in 1991 they at least they had the consolation of preventing Arsenal from completing an historic second "double" by beating them in the first semi-final staged at Wembley

As football moved towards a new era with the Premier League, the increasing influence of television, multi million pound transfers and more and more high profile foreign stars gracing the British game, Graham maintained Arsenal's position of pre-eminence in London. Revenge for the 1991 Wembley defeat was secured as Arsenal completed the Coca-Cola Cup/FA Cup double in 1993 and a year later the European Cup-Winners' Cup was added to Highbury's roll of honour. If the arrival at White Hart Lane of Gerry Francis and Graham's sad departure from Highbury gave Spurs a glimmer of hope that the balance of power would shift their way their hopes were soon dashed; the team Graham left behind reaching the Cup-Winners' Cup final again in 1995.

Graham's successor, Bruce Rioch, soon showed his intention of taking Arsenal on to another plane, investing heavily in the transfer market on players who would add flair to Arsenal's legendary defensive abilities. Ever since the days of Chapman, Arsenal had been regarded as the less flamboyant of London's big two. While Spurs had the reputation for playing the more entertaining, attacking football, the off-the-cuff, unpredictable style best suited to cup competitions, Arsenal were seen as the organised and consistent team; just the qualities needed to grind out results in the demanding arena of League football.

While Rioch looked to improve Arsenal's entertainment value, his opposite number at Spurs was seeking to add a more organised approach to a reputation for producing good football that did not always achieve results. At the end of the 1995-96 season the differing approaches came together as they fought to secure the last place for European qualification. It went right to the wire as a last day victory gave Arsenal the higher placing.

Rioch did not get the chance to continue his transformation of Arsenal, being sacked before the new 1996-97 season began, but his replacement had even more of a reputation for producing exciting teams. After making his name at Monaco, Arsene Wenger had a year in Japan with Grampus Eight leading them to second place in the J League, winning the Emperors Cup and earning the Manager of the Year award. Although he could not take control until the season had started when he did arrive his impact was immediate, releasing the shackles and allowing even his defenders to exhibit attacking abilities that had been repressed for so long. The success of Euro '96 had shown the way forward was not merely to win but also to entertain, a philosophy Wenger needed no encouragement to embrace.

Over at White Hart Lane though Spurs were sliding backwards. Refusing to join the scramble for top foreign stars that followed the Bosman decision an horrendous season-long injury list provided some excuse but the fact was the tradition of entertainment was being sacrificed for a long ball, scrambling style that drew critical comparisons with Wimbledon of the 1980's. It left Spurs lagging well behind their neighbours, a fact emphasised by the final Premiership table that saw Arsenal finish third and Spurs tenth. Arsenal may have missed out on a Champions League place by goal difference but there was no doubt that, for another season at least, they could claim the title - "The Pride of North London".

The Early Years

1

WOOLWICH ARSENAL 1
Lawrence

TOTTENHAM HOTSPUR 0

Saturday 4th December 1909

Football League Division One

Manor Ground

Attendance 18,000

Woolwich Arsenal

Tottenham Hotspur

Manager
George Morrell

Manager
Directors

Hugh McDONALD	1	**John JOYCE**
Duncan McDONALD	2	**Fred WILKES**
Joe SHAW	3	**William HARRIS**
Andy DUCAT	4	**Frank BENTLEY**
Percy SANDS	5	**Danny STEEL**
Rod McEARCHRANE	6	**Jabez DARNELL**
David GREENAWAY	7	**John CURTIS**
Bob STEVENS	8	**Billy MINTER**
Gordon HOARE	9	**Ivor BROWN**
Walter LAWRENCE	10	**Bobby STEEL**
David NEAVE	11	**Bert MIDDLEMISS**

Referee **Mr H Pollitt** (Manchester)

BACKGROUND

The first meeting between Arsenal and Spurs for Football League points took place with both clubs struggling in the lower half of the First Division table. Arsenal, members since 1893, had reached their highest position in the League, sixth, the previous season, despite having sold some of their best players; Jimmy Ashcroft, Jimmy Sharp, Tim Coleman, Bert Freeman and Jackie Mordue, at the end of the previous season to help alleviate their poor financial position. They might have hoped better times were around the corner but took only five points from their first twelve games. The signs may have looked ominous but the tide had just started to turn with a draw at Owlerton against Sheffield Wednesday, followed by another draw, this time at home to Bristol City, and then an unexpected win over Bury. Percy Sands returned after missing the victory in Lancashire and David Neave was back after missing two games but Bill Buckenham was injured with Gordon Hoare taking his place. For Spurs, the First Division was new territory. Promoted only at the end of the previous season after just one year in the Second Division, they were finding the step up hard to make, conceding twenty goals as they collected just one point from seven away fixtures. To bolster the defence the directors (who had been in charge of team affairs since election to the Football League) secured Millwall's experienced goalkeeper, John "Tiny" Joyce and he was set to make his second appearance. As part of their preparations for the game Spurs had spent the week at Southend.

BEFORE THE GAME

	P	W	D	L	F	A	Pts
Spurs	14	4	2	8	18	29	10
Arsenal	15	3	3	9	15	40	9

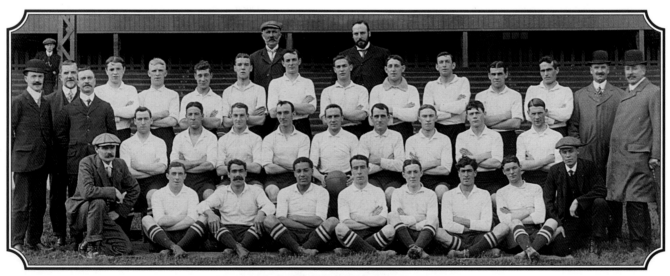

Tottenham Hotspur 1909-10 (Players only)
Back row: W.Harris, W.Williams, T.Gipps, H.Middlemiss, E.Bulling, W.Minter, F.Boreham, E.Coquet, O.Burton, F.Wilkes.
Middle row: J.Curtis, D.Brown, R.Steel, D.MacFarlane, D.Steel, T.Morris, F.Bentley, P.McConnon, T.Leslie.
Front row: C.Woodruff, J.Darnell, W.Tull, A.Lyle, D.Clark, B.Ives, J.Laydon.

SPURS STILL SINKING

I suppose it was only natural that Tottenham should desire, on the occasion of their first meeting with one of London's premier clubs under League auspices, to mark the event with a victory. Their keenness in the match at Plumstead certainly suggested it. But Woolwich were no less determined, and in the end we saw the not very edifying spectacle of two teams utterly spoiling their natural game by over zeal. This was the more unfortunate because on a turf saturated with rain, it required all the calculations of a cool and collected mind to triumph over the adverse matter. The opening play was all in favour of the Arsenal. I rather think they started with a prearranged plan of campaign fresh in their minds. They swung the ball about, and long passes helped them to maintain an attacking position in the Tottenham quarters for some time.

But there was one thing in which the forwards were deficient. They lacked the ability to complete the good work which had brought them to the jaws of the Spurs' goal. It was not so much the fault of Gordon Hoare, who was induced at the eleventh hour to play once again for the Arsenal in consequence of the breakdown of the Artilleryman, W. E. Buckenham, but rather was it due to the general weariness of Lawrence and Steven, who could make little headway on the treacherous ground. Once having found their preconceived ideas failing to bring a speedy result, the Arsenal became less methodical and more anxious. This was all in Tottenham's favour, for they were clever in a general sense in manipulating the ball, though really precious little manipulation was possible. Moreover, the 'Spurs were a much more menacing side at close quarters and only the Arsenal's unwavering defence kept them at bay.

IVOR BROWN'S LOST OPPORTUNITY

There was one occasion, however, when the 'Spurs should have scored, and I imagine Ivor Brown will never forget his failure to put the ball into a tenantless goal. The incident occurred when the game was twenty-five minutes old. Brown went between the full-backs in pursuit of a long forward pass. McDonald hesitated before leaving his goal just long enough to make his dash for the ball absolutely hopeless. When Brown tipped it to one side the custodian was left sprawling in the mud, and the goal gaped before the 'Spurs' leader. He shot, but he was far too hasty; and the ball went careering harmlessly wide of the goal. It was a fatal mistake, for it lost Tottenham at least one point.

The actual play in the second half calls for very brief description. Eight minutes after the resumption Darnell was beaten by Hoare, and Dan Steel slipped up at a critical moment, leaving the amateur to make a nice pass to Greenaway. He ran on past Harris, and centred hard and low

David Greenaway set up the first League goal in a North London 'derby'

across the goalmouth. **LAWRENCE** had followed up at top speed, and when the ball came over he instantly whipped it past the helpless Joyce. Later on only the vigilance of Joyce prevented a mistake by Wilkes from putting the Arsenal further ahead. But long prior to this accidents had had a disastrous effect on both teams. Steven in some way damaged his groin, and retired just after the Arsenal had scored, and then Brown hurt his knee and also left the field just as Sands wrenched his knee and was carried off.

None of this trio were able to resume, and the rival forces were somewhat balanced when Curtis was hurt and could only limp about. This list of casualties was the last straw. The game degenerated to such an extent that the last twenty minutes produced a more dull and dreary spectacle than I have seen for a very long time. As an exhibition of ragged and disjointed play it would have been hard to best. The players were inclined to be fractious but Mr Pollitt ruled them with a firm hand.

HOARE'S RETURN

Whatever decent football there was in the match was forthcoming before the interval when Middlemiss twice tested McDonald with splendid drives. Steven clean missed the ball when he should have troubled, if not beaten Joyce, and after Brown's great failure came a fine shot from R. Steel and a commendable effort to atone for his mistake by Brown. There was some excuse for failure but not nearly sufficient to justify condonation of all the errors that were committed. McDonald in the Arsenal goal made one mistake, but many of his clearances were masterly. He was splendidly covered by his namesake and Shaw, for while the young Scotsman had not the polish or anything like the resource of the old Accrington boy he was a stubborn defender and timed his rushes quite well.

He is built on much the same lines as Campbell, of Bradford. Ducat and McEarchrane were two capital half-backs, and the best forward work was forthcoming from Greenaway and Hoare, though they never attained a very high level. On the other hand, there was more merit in the play by Minter, who worked many openings, of which his partner Curtis could not make the best use. Middlemiss was never really happy, but he and the younger Steel were far from being poor. Dan Steel was again the best half-back, though I am inclined to think he is beginning to attempt too much, and, further behind, Wilkes still revealed traces of hesitancy, though there is no more genuine trier in the team than he. Harris showed that he is alright until he gets into a tight corner, and then he often fails, and Joyce performed his comparatively light task with credit. The crowd numbered 20,000.

'Tiny' Joyce was playing his second game in goal for Spurs.

2

TOTTENHAM HOTSPUR 1
Curtis

WOOLWICH ARSENAL 1
McGibbon

Tottenham Hotspur

Manager
Directors

Woolwich Arsenal

Manager
George Morrell

John JOYCE	1	Hugh McDONALD
Ernest COQUET	2	Duncan McDONALD
Fred WILKES	3	Joe SHAW
Tom MORRIS	4	Andy DUCAT
Danny STEEL	5	Matt THOMSON
Frank BENTLEY	6	Rod McEARCHRANE
John CURTIS	7	David GREENAWAY
Billy MINTER	8	Charlie LEWIS
Percy HUMPHREYS	9	Charlie McGIBBON
Bobby STEEL	10	Walter LAWRENCE
Bert MIDDLEMISS	11	Frank HEPPINSTALL

Referee **Mr H Pollitt** (Manchester)

BACKGROUND

Throughout the season both clubs had struggled at the foot of the table, relegation a constant worry. For Spurs the threat of a swift return to the Second Division remained a very real possibility but confidence had increased with home victories over Sunderland by 5-1 and Blackburn Rovers, 4-0, over the Easter period. After the defeat at Plumstead they had signed Percy Humphreys from Chelsea, at last securing a replacement for amateur international centre-forward Vivian Woodward who had stunned them with his retirement from top class football on the eve of the season. Humphreys had taken time to settle in but had scored on his last four outings and Frank Bentley returned after missing a one-all draw at Sheffield United. Three wins and a draw in their last four games had made financially troubled Arsenal's first division status almost secure for another season, a draw would make it certain. They were fortunate in being able to call upon the services of the Royal Artillery Sergeant, Charlie McGibbon, scorer of the winning goals on his two previous outings. White Hart Lane was said to have a capacity of 50,000, a figure that proved over-optimistic as the ground overflowed with almost 40,000 spectators anxious to see a game crucial to the future of both clubs.

BEFORE THE GAME

	P	W	D	L	F	A	Pts
Arsenal	36	11	8	17	35	63	30
Spurs	34	9	9	16	47	64	27

AT THE SEASON'S END

		P	W	D	L	F	A	Pts
15th	Spurs	38	11	10	17	53	69	32
18th	Arsenal	38	11	9	18	37	67	31

Left: Arsenal's Charlie McGibbon opens the scoring.
Below: Hugh McDonald is beaten by a powerful shot from John Curtis for the equaliser - Tottenham's first ever League goal against the Gunners.

A FATEFUL DRAW

With the points at stake almost as precious as sodium or rubber, Tottenham Hotspur and Woolwich Arsenal played a momentous game on the White Hart Lane ground last Saturday afternoon. Both sides were situated perilously near the bottom of the League table, and defeat for either would place the losing side in grave danger of relegation to the Second Division: hence public interest in the match was enormous, quite apart from the question of London rivalry. It was, therefore, not surprising to find a huge attendance at the Tottenham enclosure, estimated at fully 40,000. The stands were packed; there was talk of the gates being shut, and all round the ground faces were tier upon tier, so closely, indeed, that at the corner - particularly on the far side at the Park Lane end - the police had to allow a number of spectators to climb the barrier and arrange themselves on the turf behind the touch line.

As for the play, it was exactly what might have been expected under the special circumstances. With both sides desperately keen there was excitement enough and to spare, but the men were too anxious to do themselves full justice, and pace and earnestness had to take the place of good football. Although throughout it was a half-backs contest in which spoiling tactics played the predominant part. The 'Spurs were the better side, and had by far the bigger share of the attack, taking the match all through, but they were met by a grimly resolute defence that never wavered and never gave quarter. While both half-back lines were great as breakers up the 'Spurs' halves were the cleverer at combining attack with defence and thus Humphreys and his colleagues received more chances than fell to the share of McGibbon and Co. Luck and the Woolwich defenders were, however, against the Tottenham forwards, and though they had enough of the game in the second forty-five minutes to deserve at least a couple of goals they could do no more than counterbalance the one point which the Reds had secured during an even first half.

For Tottenham Curtis and Robert Steel were the best of a hardworking forward line, the outside right making several fine speedy runs and obtaining his side's goal with a magnificent shot, while Steel's all round work was excellent, notably the capital openings which he engineered for his fellows. Humphreys was a trier, as usual, but over-eagerness told against him, and he

was very unfortunate with one or two really good efforts to score. Danny Steel was the most conspicuous of three heroic half-backs and Coquet, in spite of being badly shaken up in a collision with Heppinstall towards half-time, played well at back in his own original way, but his partner, Wilkes, was at times very uncertain. Joyce, though only beaten once, scarcely inspired confidence, his power of anticipation being several times at fault. The Arsenal forwards compared unfavourably with those of the 'Spurs, the whole line seldom getting on the move together, and McGibbon, who tried very hard, was not supported as he deserved to be. Ducat played splendidly at half, having more idea of attack than the others, and also performing prodigies of valour in defence, one notably clever "robbery" from Humphreys saving a certain goal in the second period. The backs were safe, if not always elegant, while Hugh McDonald came creditably out of a trying ordeal.

With the spoiling tactics of the half-backs so much in evidence, the first forty five, though even and exciting, was scarcely spectacular, as that word is generally understood. There were plenty of thrilling moments and dangerous attacks on both goals, but clear-cut artistic movements were seldom allowed to develop. The scoring opened sixteen minutes after the start. McEarchrane sent Heppinstall away and the outside left swung in a centre, which Joyce misjudged, pushing the ball away to **McGIBBON**, who netted at close range. A one-goal lead for the Arsenal was the state of affairs at the interval but from the way in which Tottenham started the second half it looked odds on their equalising at any moment. Good efforts to score were made by Humphreys, R. Steel and Curtis, but still the visitors' defence held out though sorely beset. Then a great misfortune befell the Arsenal. In a melee close to the Woolwich posts McEarchrane was accidentally kicked by one of his own backs, and had to leave the field. He was away for less than a quarter of an hour, but the equalising goal came during that period as twenty-four minutes after the resumption R. Steel cleverly made an opening for **CURTIS**, who beat Hugh McDonald with a splendidly powerful shot. McEarchrane then returned, but the 'Spurs continued to be the more dangerous, despite an occasional promising breakaway, in which McGibbon was usually prominent. McDonald, though severely tested, saved his charge from further disaster, and the game ended in a draw of one goal each.

Spurs goalkeeper 'Tiny' Joyce pushes an effort over the bar.
Note the spectators perched on the roof of the stand.

3

TOTTENHAM HOTSPUR 3
Humphreys, Darnell, Minter

WOOLWICH ARSENAL 1
Chalmers

Tottenham Hotspur

Manager
Directors

Woolwich Arsenal

Manager
George Morrell

Tommy LUNN	1	Edward BATEUP
Ernest COQUET	2	Archie GRAY
Tom COLLINS	3	Joe SHAW
Frank BENTLEY	4	Andy DUCAT
Danny STEEL	5	Matt THOMSON
Jabez DARNELL	6	Rod McEARCHRANE
John CURTIS	7	Charlie LEWIS
Billy MINTER	8	Alf COMMON
Percy HUMPHREYS	9	Jackie CHALMERS
Bobby McTAVISH	10	Matt SHORTT
Bert MIDDLEMISS	11	David NEAVE

Referee **Mr H H Taylor** *(Altrincham)*

BACKGROUND

Although it was only a last match victory over Chelsea that preserved Spurs' top flight status the previous season, the summer had seen few changes in personnel. Still struggling, their new signing from Hearts, Tom Collins, was set to make his home debut for a team that had conceded nine goals in three successive defeats, the last a 0-4 hammering at Sunderland. Late in the day influential inside-forward, Bobby Steel, was forced to withdraw because of a heavy cold. His replacement was Bob McTavish, also making only his second appearance. For Arsenal the arrival of Alf Common, the first £1,000 footballer when he joined Middlesbrough from Sunderland in February 1905, had done little to improve performances with only four draws and two goals in their first seven games but a definite upturn did follow the signing of Jackie Chalmers from Clyde. He went into the match having scored six goals in eight games. The counter attraction of Fulham against Chelsea at Craven Cottage no doubt contributed to a disappointing attendance.

BEFORE THE GAME

	P	W	D	L	F	A	Pts
Arsenal	14	4	4	6	12	17	12
Spurs	14	4	2	8	17	23	10

'DERBY' STAR
★ **Percy Humphreys** ★

Headed Spurs' equaliser and, according to the 'Weekly Herald' 'gave as good a display as he has done in any match this season, and his spirited leadership was not an unimportant factor in the game'.

Humphreys spent just under two years at White Hart Lane, scoring 29 goals in 50 league and cup appearances.

'DERBY' STAR

THAT WAS THEN

★ A seat at White Hart Lane in 1910 could be reserved by sending a postal order for 2s6d (13p) to the club secretary.

★ Alf Common (pictured right) was the first ever player to be transferred for a four-figure sum when he joined Middlesbrough from Sunderland for £1,000 in 1905. Five years later he left the North East for London, joining Arsenal for £250.

Alf Common

'The Sportsman' summed the match up perfectly under the heading...

WELCOME WIN FOR THE SPURS

After losing three League matches off the reel and having nine goals scored against them, the 'Spurs gave a bright display on their own ground at Tottenham on Saturday, and scored a welcome win by three goals to one. The recent heavy rains had caused the ground to be on the soft side, but the going, which was better than might have been expected, just suited the home team who were always playing a winning game. Collins, the 'Spurs' new full back, was making his first appearance at home, while in the absence of R. Steel McTavish partnered Middlemiss. Small at the start, the crowd increased to about 20,000 at the game proceeded. The 'Spurs had the benefit of a stiffish breeze at the outset, and early in the game the Arsenal defence was tested. Play was very fast considering the conditions, but with both defences well up to their work the forwards could make little headway. It was after about fifteen minutes play that the first goal came. Darnell acted the part of a forward instead of clearing his lines, and a free kick given against him well up was turned to account by **CHALMERS**, who got the ball after Lunn had saved from Shortt and found the net. This early success was soon followed by an equalising goal. Minter sent in a fine shot, which struck the bar and rebounded into the field of play, for **HUMPHREYS** to head into the net. Exciting play followed; both goals being frequently threatened. Bateup had more to do than Lunn, the 'Spurs forwards being better together than the opposing front line. Neave spoilt a good

opening for the Reds by getting offside, and at the other end Bentley cleared when Chalmers looked like getting through. The game proceeded on fairly even lines until shortly before half-time when **DARNELL** took a long shot and to the delight of the home players saw the ball go across goal and into the net, Bateup evidently being under the impression that it was going behind. Thus at the interval the 'Spurs led by two goals to one. On resuming the Arsenal were seen to advantage, and weak play by both Collins and Coquet looked like letting the visitors through. A fruitless corner however, was all the Reds could force. Both sides played an open game, and play quickly veered from one end to the other, and exciting struggles ensued at each goal end. Chalmers was the most prominent forward for the Arsenal while Lunn also saved smartly from Neave and Shortt. Following a goal kick the 'Spurs rushed to the other end and Bateup dealt with a fine shot sent in by Middlemiss. Before his backs could come to his assistance, however, **MINTER** had got possession and, making no mistake, put the 'Spurs three up. Soon after this Darnell tried another long shot, but this time sent wide. Gray and Shaw at this period showed themselves to be a capable pair of backs, and towards the end had the satisfaction of seeing the 'Spurs' goal seriously threatened. The Arsenal forwards, however, were not so convincing at close quarters as those of the 'Spurs, and, failing to find the net, the visitors suffered defeat by three goals to one, a margin that might easily have been reduced had the visiting forwards showed a better understanding at close quarters.

Woolwich Arsenal 1910-11.

Back row (left to right): Hardy (trainer), Dick, Thomson, Bateup, Common, Rippon, Hedley. **Second row:** Gray, Ducat, Grant, McDonald, Rogers, Sands. **Third row:** Lewis, McKinnon, Greenaway, Heppinstall, Morrell (Manager), Logan, Neave, Shaw, McEarchrane.

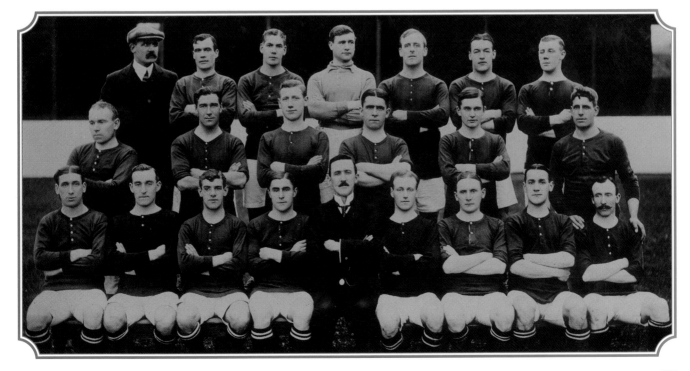

WOOLWICH ARSENAL 2
Chalmers, Common

TOTTENHAM HOTSPUR 0

Saturday 8th April 1911

Football League Division One

Manor Ground

Attendance 24,853

Woolwich Arsenal

Tottenham Hotspur

Manager
George Morrell

Manager
Directors

George BURDETT	1	Tommy LUNN
Joe SHAW	2	Tom COLLINS
Archie GRAY	3	Fred WILKES
Andy DUCAT	4	Frank BENTLEY
Percy SANDS	5	Charlie RANCE
Rod McEARCHRANE	6	Jabez DARNELL
David GREENAWAY	7	John CURTIS
Alf COMMON	8	Billy MINTER
Jackie CHALMERS	9	Darkie TULL
Gordon HOARE	10	Bobby STEEL
Charlie LEWIS	11	Bert MIDDLEMISS

Referee **Mr H H Taylor** (Altrincham)

BACKGROUND

A five match unbeaten run had taken Arsenal away from the relegation zone but their problems were of a financial, not football, nature. They were, perhaps, best summed up by a banner at the entrance to their Manor Field ground appealing to supporters to subscribe for shares in the club; "Apathy today means no football next season". Alf Common, scorer of two goals as Bristol City were beaten 3-0 at the end of March, returned after missing a 1-0 win at Newcastle. Spurs had picked up five points in three successive home games to make them safe from relegation but were unable to call on Percy Humphreys' services, 'Darkie' Tull taking his place. Spurs were just waiting for the end of the campaign but they still drew the best crowd of the season to Plumstead producing gate receipts of £746. Arsenal's money problems would have been helped even more had poor arrangements by the Great Eastern Railway on it's Wood Green to Woolwich line not meant many Spurs' supporters were unable to board a train to the game.

BEFORE THE GAME

	P	W	D	L	F	A	Pts
Spurs	34	12	6	16	50	57	30
Arsenal	32	10	9	13	33	47	29

AT THE SEASON'S END

		P	W	D	L	F	A	Pts
10th	Arsenal	38	13	12	13	41	49	38
15th	Spurs	38	13	6	19	52	63	32

Arsenal's half-back line of Andy Ducat, Percy Sands and Rod McEarchrane were very much in tune with one another.

Spurs centre-forward Daniel 'Darkie' Tull, born in Folkestone of an English mother and a West Indian father, was one of the first coloured players to appear in the Football League. He was released by Spurs in the following close-season and joined Northampton, but tragically was killed in action some seven years later during the First World War.

The Arsenal Avenged.

SPURS BEATEN AT PLUMSTEAD.

The Arsenal squared accounts with the Spurs on Saturday by winning the League match at Plumstead by 2 goals to 0. As each side has gained two points and scored three goals at the expense of the other, they can cry quits. At Tottenham, the Spurs were the better side, whereas at Manor Field the Gunners deserved to succeed. It was a happy day for the Arsenal for they established their position in the First Division beyond all question, and had their coffers enriched to the extent of £746. Many thousands of the Spurs' supporters were there, in spite of inadequate railway arrangements on the Wood Green to Woolwich line. It was really astonishing, after the G.E.R.'s many years' experience of football crowds, that the train timed to reach South Tottenham at 1.40 p.m. should have been sent off with only its usual complement of five or six carriages. The consequence was that it was packed by the time it left Seven Sisters, and at every succeeding station scores of persons were left behind.

The Arsenal won chiefly because of their undeniable superiority at half back, and also to a lesser extent because they were more thrustful in attack—two reasons which to a certain degree represented cause and effect. Ducat, Sands, and McEachrane were a powerful trio, and the Spurs' forwards were never able to get the measure of them, although they managed to keep the game pretty open. The Tottenham front men did not blend well, and their work was altogether unconvincing. Passes were so frequently ill-judged or intercepted that there were comparatively few sustained movements. Humphreys with his bustling ways would have been more effective against Sands than Tull, who was too slow, and was often beaten. Minter has rarely been seen to such little advantage, and altogether the forwards were made to appear a very moderate lot. Only once or twice did they look like scoring, and Burdett, the Arsenal keeper, had a light afternoon.

Unreliable rail service... nothing changes! "The Weekly Herald"

Charlie Lewis (above) formed an excellent understanding with Gordon Hoare on the left of Arsenal's forward line.

'The Sportsman' reported...

Neither the Arsenal nor the Hotspur need fear relegation to the Second Division of the League, but it cannot be gainsaid that Saturday's match was fraught with considerable importance to either, but anxiety was tempered by Bury, Nottingham Forest and Bristol City all succumbing. There was, nonetheless, a great deal of interest taken in the struggle at Plumstead, which in the victory of the Arsenal by two goals to nothing, had a fitting termination. Many of the 33,000 people who attended in bad weather to see a shifty wind affect play not a little will argue otherwise. But it is impossible to get over the fact that not only did the Arsenal players show better control of the ball, but they went about their work quicker, showed a more praiseworthy conception of the possibilities when in the vicinity of the goal, and performed the more creditably collectively. It was easy to notice that Shaw and Gray were in more useful sympathy with their halves than Collins and Wilkes and at few periods indeed were Ducat, Sands and McEarchrane out of concert with either of their lines. It was this happy displacement of forces which made it appear as though there were a couple of Arsenal players to one of Tottenham. Another thing disastrous to the visitors was the slowness of the work. They seemed to require more time in which to think out the problems to set their opponents, whereas the Arsenal hesitated in few things they attempted. A source of much trouble to the 'Spurs was the deportment of Tull. Now, the West Indian is clever, but he lacks the important essentials of a centre forward, speed and ability for bustling. Humphreys, whom he deputised, does not appear to one as an ideal centre forward, but he will bustle the backs which neither R. Steel, Tull nor Minter did. Time and again Shaw and Gray were clearing comfortably. A mis-kick did not appear to be attended by serious consequences, and Burdett had an easy task compared with Lunn's. Some of the latter's saves were beautifully done, but it cannot be said that because of any weakness in Collins and Wilkes his task was the harder. Bentley, Rance (who seemed slow and showed his hand too much), and Darnell were not as happy a trio as Ducat, Sands and McEarchrane, who all played well and the 'Spurs had no brainy forward like Common. The veteran may be slow, but he retains all his intuition for placing a colleague easily. He paved the way to the first goal, scored the second and was as great a source of trouble to Lunn as any attacker. The first goal of this fast but none too clever display was the direct outcome of a lovely pass of his three minutes after the start. He placed the ball ahead of Wilkes, who was beaten by Greenaway in the run up, and when the centre came along **CHALMERS** scored easily. The second point appeared three minutes from the interval. After a struggle near the line on the left the ball came back to Hoare, whose perfect pass **COMMON** took on his head and beat Lunn nicely. Meanwhile the 'Spurs forwards had given the impression they would not finish properly, and they never did, the best chance they had falling to Middlemiss, who, with only Burdett to beat, shot straight at the custodian. Lunn was a trifle lucky in saving a fine shot by Hoare, running across a yard too far to a ball turned by the wind which he just stopped with the right hand, but there was no disputing the cleverness of his second half saves from Chalmers's foot and head and Common's foot, whilst the latter put a couple of fine attempts just too high. Five minutes from the end Bentley left the field injured. Result: Woolwich Arsenal, two goals, Tottenham Hotspur, love.

5

TOTTENHAM HOTSPUR 5
Middlemiss, Minter 2, McTavish, Darnell

WOOLWICH ARSENAL 0

Tottenham Hotspur

Manager
Directors

Woolwich Arsenal

Manager
George Morrell

Tottenham	No.	Woolwich
Tommy LUNN	1	Harry CRAWFORD
Tom COLLINS	2	Joe SHAW
Fred WEBSTER	3	John PEART
Danny STEEL	4	Andy DUCAT
Charlie RANCE	5	Percy SANDS
Jabez DARNELL	6	Angus McKINNON
John McTAVISH	7	Charlie LEWIS
Ernest NEWMAN	8	Alf COMMON
Billy MINTER	9	Jackie CHALMERS
Bobby STEEL	10	Charlie RANDALL
Bert MIDDLEMISS	11	Tom WINSHIP

Referee **Mr T P Campbell** (Blackburn)

BACKGROUND

With Spurs beginning to settle to top flight football, the gates were closed on a record crowd at White Hart Lane for this Christmas morning fixture. Charlie Rance had returned after nearly two months out as Spurs lost 2-3 at home to Bradford City two days earlier but Charlie Brittan had been injured in that game, so former Gainsborough Trinity full-back Fred Webster, was called up

Debutant Fred Webster

for his debut. Arsenal made wholesale changes after only one victory in their last five games, including three successive away defeats during which they had conceded ten goals. Joe Shaw, Angus McKinnon, Alf Common, Jackie Chalmers and Charlie Randall all returned after missing the 1-3 weekend defeat at Notts County and Tom Winship came in for David Neave. They too had a player making his debut in their colours, Harry Crawford being called up in the absence of their amateur 'keeper, Dick Roose, who had only played two games after his signing from Aston Villa.

BEFORE THE GAME

	P	W	D	L	F	A	Pts
Spurs	18	8	4	6	32	27	20
Arsenal	17	5	5	7	24	29	15

'The Sportsman' reported...

THE SPURS TOO GOOD

A remarkable amount of interest was taken in the Christmas morning match at Tottenham, where, with ticket-holders, 47,109 people passed through the gates. The occasion was the meeting of London's two First League clubs, and on form Tottenham were expected to win. They did so easily, for at the close Woolwich found the score five goals to love against them. As a matter of fact, the Spurs were superior all through, and it was only when they took matters a trifle easily that Woolwich were seen to advantage. The ground was very heavy, and there were a few nasty falls, but as a game it was a capital one, the sides playing with scrupulous fairness, fouls being a rarity. Tottenham were without Brittan, whilst Woolwich lacked the services of their new goalkeeper, Roose, both having been hurt on Saturday.

For the first twenty minutes the home team did so much better that they scored three times. The first point came after nine minutes through **MIDDLEMISS**, who took a pass from McTavish, the next five minutes later by **MINTER**, who turned to equally good account a pass from R. Steel and

the third at the end of eighteen minutes, when **McTAVISH** got through by an excellent piece of individual play. Subsequently Tottenham were content to take affairs fairly easy, and in the period Woolwich had more of the game. The men from Plumstead, however, missed their opportunities, although Chalmers on one occasion had hard lines in not scoring. Common missed an open goal, whilst later Chalmers and Randall should have made better use of their chances. In the meantime Tottenham were making occasional attacks, and at times put in good work without scoring. At half time the home team led by three goals to love. After change of ends Rance was off the field for some ten minutes, but this did not affect Tottenham, who in that time added two more goals, the first through **DARNELL** by the aid of a lofty kick that swerved in, and another by **MINTER**, who, standing close up in goal easily converted Middlemiss's pass. Afterwards it was an excellent game to the end without further scoring. Woolwich had good opportunities, but found Lunn and the backs too good for them.

47,109 PEOPLE WATCH TOTTENHAM BEAT WOOLWICH AT WHITE HART LANE.

Woolwich Arsenal were badly beaten by Tottenham Hotspur yesterday, the score being 5 goals to nothing. Nearly 50,000 were present, and 10,000 were unable to gain admission. (1) Tottenham's second goal. (2) Tottenham score. The photograph shows a section of the crowd. (3) Minter, Tottenham (white jersey), and Crawford, the Woolwich goalkeeper. (4) How Tottenham scored their first goal. When Crawford (A) ran out and missed, Middlemiss (B) rushed it through.

6

WOOLWICH ARSENAL 3
Lewis, Randall, Winship

TOTTENHAM HOTSPUR 1
Minter

Woolwich Arsenal

Tottenham Hotspur

Manager
George Morrell

Manager
Directors

Harry CRAWFORD	1	Tommy LUNN
Joe SHAW	2	Tom COLLINS
John PEART	3	Fred WEBSTER
Andy DUCAT	4	Danny STEEL
Percy SANDS	5	Charlie RANCE
Rod McEARCHRANE	6	Jabez DARNELL
Charlie LEWIS	7	John McTAVISH
Alf COMMON	8	Ernest NEWMAN
Jackie CHALMERS	9	Billy MINTER
Charlie RANDALL	10	Bobby STEEL
Tom WINSHIP	11	Bert MIDDLEMISS

Referee **Mr T P Campbell** (Blackburn)

BACKGROUND

Arsenal soon had the opportunity to recover from their heaviest defeat of the season with the return fixture taking place just a day later. McEarchrane for McKinnon was the only change in the two teams, but the great difference was the weather. Wretched throughout the game, the rain fell in torrents after the interval and it would have been no surprise had the match been abandoned. Arsenal's best gate of the season would have been even better had they not increased the admission price to one shilling (5p). It proved so unpopular that some would-be spectators stood outside the ground calling on others to refuse to pay.

BEFORE THE GAME

	P	W	D	L	F	A	Pts
Spurs	19	9	4	6	37	27	22
Arsenal	18	5	5	8	24	34	15

AT THE SEASON'S END

		P	W	D	L	F	A	Pts
10th	Arsenal	38	15	8	15	55	59	38
12th	Spurs	38	14	9	15	53	53	37

'DERBY' STAR

★ **Tom Winship** ★

Woolwich Arsenal's 5ft 4in Geordie outside-left was a constant threat to the visitors, making the first and scoring the third goal.

'DERBY' STAR

THAT WAS THEN

★ No Nike, Reebok or Puma. Probably the best known football boot manufacturers of the time were Manfield & Sons of 24 & 25 Poultry in the City of London. Their top of the range boots cost 10s 6d (53p) but then they did not have to pay players to wear their products!

Billy Minter netted three times against Arsenal over the Christmas period.

ARSENAL'S REVENGE

MUD REVEL AT PLUMSTEAD

The Arsenal quickly took revenge for their Christmas morning defeat at Tottenham, for yesterday they beat the 'Spurs at Plumstead by 3-1. The teams were identical save that Arsenal included McEarchrane at left half-back in place of McKinnon.

What with pouring rain and mud ankle deep in places, the conditions were about as unpleasant as they well could be, but some 15,000 spectators attended and with a shilling charged for admission about £680 was realised. The Arsenal won well on their merits. They adapted themselves better to the mud and rain; their attack was more thrustful and their defence safer. The Arsenal forwards relied on swinging wing-to-wing passing and fast rushes, which often gave the Tottenham backs a deal of trouble. It was the game for the day, and it paid. The 'Spurs tried short passing, but it was not at all effective against a hustling defence that was so effective that Crawford was rarely called upon to deal with anything difficult. Peart played a very good game, and Winship, the Arsenal outside left, was about the most dangerous forward. In spite of the soaking wet it was a most interesting game, and the result put the Arsenal supporters on very happy terms with themselves.

The Arsenal started with sharp passing to the wings, which at once gave the 'Spurs' backs some anxiety. They relieved, and McTavish burst away and crossed to Newman, who shot across the goalmouth, but no one could take advantage of the opening. Chalmers next gave a wide pass to Winship, who centred well, and **LEWIS** scored easily in five minutes. Some neat work by the 'Spurs' right wing gave the side strong attacking position, but Shaw cleared. From Crawford's goal kick McTavish again got going, and Sands conceded a corner. Two other corners speedily followed, but nothing could be made of them.

The 'Spurs front line were clever in mid-field, but were repeatedly dispossessed when nearing goal. The defence on both sides was safe. Middlemiss made a clever run and beat Shaw. He centred nicely, but Sands fell back and cleared with Minter and Newman pressing him. A smart dribble and pass by Common to McEarchrane afforded the latter a chance, but he shot high over, and Winship and Randall gave the Tottenham backs most anxiety. When the first-named was tripped by Collins he took the free kick and placed cleverly, and **RANDALL**, close up, rammed the ball into the net, this, the second goal to the Arsenal, occurring after twenty-eight minutes play. The 'Spurs were outplayed for the remainder of the first half, and Chalmers was nearly scoring a third. Winship centred, and with his backs beaten Lunn dashed out and met Chalmers as he was in the act of shooting at an empty goal. Fortunately for Tottenham the ball just cleared the near post.

For nearly twenty minutes of the second half the 'Spurs had the better of the game. To begin with there was a capital dribble by Newman, who was robbed close in by Peart. McTavish got hold and worked across the field, but then kicked wide. R. Steel and Minter ran through, but the latter kicked too hard, and Crawford coming out punted clear. The rain pelted down, and the players had considerable difficulty in keeping their feet whenever bustled by the opposition. At this stage the 'Spurs were the stronger side, but were only permitted to take shots at long range. The best work forward was contributed by Newman and McTavish. Occasionally the 'Spurs tried the short kick and fast follow up in the hope of rushing the Arsenal backs, but Shaw and Peart held their own.

Thanks to Winship the Arsenal at length got a good opportunity and from his cross Common tested Lunn with a hard low drive. This he saved, but a moment later **WINSHIP** scored with a clipping drive, the game at that point being twenty minutes old. On resuming McTavish was brought down by Peart. He damaged his ankle and limped off. The referee awarded a free kick, and that, well placed by D. Steel, enabled **MINTER** to head through. The Arsenal played with renewed energy afterwards, and Lunn was given more to do than Crawford. A slip by Collins nearly let in Randall, and Winship had two abortive shots. The Arsenal were more aggressive and thoroughly deserved to win by 3-1.

The Return Match.

A QUESTION OF METHODS.

The two teams met again on Boxing Day at Woolwich, when the Arsenal avenged their stinging defeat of Christmas Day, and won by 3 goals to 1. The weather was wretched in the extreme, rain falling the whole time; after the interval it came down in torrents. The ground was a perfect quagmire, and water lay in pool along the touch line. It would not have been surprising had the game been abandoned, as at Leyton.

The two special trains from Enfield were well patronised in spite of the weather. A shilling gate was charged, and this was seemingly unpopular among a certain section, who stood outside the ground and called on others to refuse to pay the shilling. The teams were the same as on Monday with but one exception—McEachrane taking McKinnon's place.

To those who saw the Christmas Day match the result can hardly be imagined, but one of the causes of the Spurs undoing was their failure to adapt themselves to the prevailing conditions. The Arsenal from the commencement played with the utmost keenness, and it was quickly evident that they had made up their minds to atone for their failure of the preceding day. Four minutes from the commencement Winship, who played a fine game throughout the match, passed the ball to the opposite wing, and LEWIS opened the scoring. Inspired by this early success, the Arsenal forwards, backed by their halves, played well together, and the Spurs defence was severely taxed. The visitors got to the other end, and the right wing put in some good work, which however came to naught. Next Middlemiss cleverly beat Shaw, and put in a characteristic centre, but Minter and Steel between them failed to take advantage of this chance, and the ball was cleared by Peart. The second goal to the Arsenal came after twenty-eight minutes' play, and was the outcome of a foul on Winship by Collins just at the side of the penalty line. The free kick was taken, and RANDALL beat Lunn. A foul was given against Rance, close to the penalty line, but nothing worse than a corner followed, and two other corners in quick succession awarded to the Arsenal were fruitless. The Arsenal continued to press, and a smart shot by Lewis was safely disposed of by Lunn. At half-time they were leading by 2 goals to 0.

The rain came down in torrents when play recommenced, and one could but feel sorry for the drenched spectators. For the first nine minutes or so the Spurs played in most incisive fashion, and the Arsenal were kept well in their own territory. It looked as if the deficit would be reduced, both Newman and McTavish making determined efforts to score. The Arsenal defence, however, persisted, and their forwards raced away to the other end, where Lewis had a good opening, but shot wide. Common then tested Lunn with a shot which he got away to the right wing, where Lewis transferred to WINSHIP, who scored the third goal, which seemed to put the issue beyond doubt. The Arsenal still played with plenty of dash, and once Collins was obliged to pass back to Lunn, who safely cleared. Two corners fell to them, and the Spurs' goal had narrow escapes. The Spurs got away again, and McTavish was working the ball well in when he was fouled by Peart, and he had to retire to the side of the field for a minute or so. The free kick was taken by D. Steel, and MINTER scored his usual goal. Towards the close of the game Winship was very prominent, but neither of his shots materialised. The Arsenal retired winners by 3—1.

Not even the most rabid Tottenham partisan can deny that the Arsenal thoroughly earned the two points. They played the right game under the circumstances, and banged the ball towards the mouth of the goal every opportunity. The difference in the play of the team on successive days was strongly marked and their poor show at Tottenham seems inexplicable. The teams were:—

Woolwich Arsenal.—Crawford; Shaw, Peart; Ducat, Sands, McEachrane; Lewis, Common, Chalmers, Randall, Winship.

Tottenham Hotspurs.—Lunn; Collins, Webster; D. Steel, Rance, Darnell; McTavish, Newman, Minter, R. Steel, Middlemiss.

7

WOOLWICH ARSENAL 0

TOTTENHAM HOTSPUR 3
Steel, Cantrell 2 (1 pen)

Saturday 14th December 1912

Football League Division One

Manor Ground

Attendance 13,000

Woolwich Arsenal		Tottenham Hotspur
Manager **George Morrell**		Manager **Directors**
Harry CRAWFORD	1	John JOYCE
Joe SHAW	2	Tom COLLINS
John PEART	3	Fred WEBSTER
Edward KING	4	Finlay WEIR
Matt THOMSON	5	Charlie RANCE
Rod McEARCHRANE	6	Ed LIGHTFOOT
Freddie GROVES	7	Walter TATTERSALL
John FLANAGAN	8	Billy MINTER
David DUNCAN	9	Jimmy CANTRELL
William SPITTLE	10	Bobby STEEL
Charlie LEWIS	11	Bert MIDDLEMISS

Referee **Mr A Briggs** (Blackburn)

Spurs arrived at the ground in an excited mood a few minutes before the time to start, and had to change in a tremendous hurry.

It seems that owing to a mishap, the motor char-a-banc which was engaged to convey the Spurs to Plumstead reached Tottenham about half an hour late. The driver tried to make up for lost time on the journey to the Manor Field, but this proved to be a case of 'more haste, less speed' for within a short distance of the ground he got into a police trap, and this meant a further delay for the team of several minutes.

An extract from "The Weekly Herald"

BACKGROUND

With only one point from their last nine matches, just three draws to their credit from nine home games and a lengthening injury list, bottom of the table Arsenal were sinking fast. Reserve forwards, Freddie Groves, still an amateur, and William Spittle, who had been a professional for only three months, had been called up for Arsenal's last game, a 1-4 defeat at Derby and kept their places as Charlie Randall and George Burrell were still injured. Angus McKinnon and Percy Sands were added to the absentees after the Baseball Ground defeat. Rod McEearchrane stood in for McKinnon with full-back John Peart, who had been asked to play at centre-forward in place of another injury victim, Alf Common, at Derby replacing Sands and David Duncan, only signed from Fulham the previous day in a desperate attempt to provide urgently needed fire-power, given his debut. Spurs were unchanged, having won two of their last three games, badly needed after starting the season without a win in their first twelve matches, but had yet to win away from home. Travel problems, one of the reasons Henry Norris had decided Arsenal needed a new home, caused Spurs to arrive only minutes before the kick-off.

BEFORE THE GAME

	P	W	D	L	F	A	Pts
Spurs	15	2	3	10	14	40	7
Arsenal	16	1	4	11	9	30	6

William Spittle
- an Arsenal reserve called up for only his third game

THE GUNNERS STILL AT THE BOTTOM

The Arsenal made changes in their team for this match at Plumstead on Saturday, two reserve forwards in Groves and Spittle being called upon, while Sands was absent owing to injuries received at the previous week-end. Greenaway and Common were also resting, and the centre-forward position was occupied by Duncan, from Fulham. It did not look a too promising side to bring about the first home team victory of the season, though scratch teams have been known to succeed where the regulars failed. The weather was dull while the attendance reached 16,000. If superiority in play

Spurs' two goal hero Jimmy Cantrell

represented goals the Gunners would have been well ahead at the interval, but from this point their bad luck stuck to them, both Duncan and Spittle sustaining injuries which compelled them to go off, and for some time the Arsenal played nine men.

The Arsenal were the first to make headway, and Joyce brought off a wonderful save from Duncan, though he was knocked out in doing so. For a moment it looked a sure goal. For a few minutes the Gunners swarmed round the Hotspur goal, Collins eventually clearing. A "free" came to the Reds just outside the "area", and after Collins had again cleared Middlemiss flashed past Shaw, who recovered, and Tottenham had a free kick near the penalty line, followed by a second, which failed to produce points. Then the Reds took it up again, the Hotspur defence having a lively time, all the home forwards doing well. Joyce had to handle from Duncan, Lewis was much too speedy for Weir, though Collins proved very safe. Eventually Minter and Tattersall got away and sent across, Shaw clearing. The same pair came again with similar result. Pretty work between Groves, Flanagan, and Duncan followed, though Middlemiss soon became busy, and Cantrell lost the first chance from his pass. Steel next made a big effort, but there was no mistaking the dash of the home front rank. Again and again they got close to the Tottenham posts, only to find Joyce in the best of trim, and the visiting backs also performed well.

A long shot from Lewis almost caught "Tiny" napping, the ball swerving in, and the custodian just tipped it over the bar. Duncan ought to have turned a cross from Groves into the net; a good chance lost for the Gunners. Then Flanagan missed an opportunity, and Joyce fisted out a shot from Lewis. There was a long sustained attack on the Hotspur goal, which raised considerable enthusiasm, but goals did not come. Two minutes before the interval Duncan was carried off. Groves shot and struck the bar, and the sheet was clean when the teams crossed over.

Soon after restarting Duncan reappeared, but he limped badly, and went outside left. Joyce early saved from Flanagan, and from a well-placed corner **STEEL** scored for Tottenham. Minter nearly increased the visitors' advantage a couple of minutes later. There was a clear case of handling in the area, which the referee did not see, and the Arsenal's claim for a penalty went unheeded. They had no luck, and the 'Spurs now appeared to have the game well in hand. Spittle was obliged to leave, and though he returned, it was not for long, he and Duncan going off again, and the Arsenal continued two short. Under the circumstances they did pretty well, Lewis and King initiating a number of attacks, while McEarchrane worked hard. A penalty kick against Thomson was turned to good account by **CANTRELL** and interest in the game vanished. **CANTRELL** added a third goal, Groves gave Joyce more work to do, but the Hotspur won a lucky game by three goals to love, and, with only six points for seventeen games, the Gunners are in a bad way.

8

TOTTENHAM HOTSPUR 1
Minter

WOOLWICH ARSENAL 1
Grant

Tottenham Hotspur

Woolwich Arsenal

Manager
Peter McWilliam

Manager
George Morrell

John TATE	1	Hugh McDONALD
Tom COLLINS	2	Joe SHAW
Fred WEBSTER	3	Joe FIDLER
Finlay WEIR	4	George GRANT
Charlie RANCE	5	Matt THOMSON
Arthur GRIMSDELL	6	Alex GRAHAM
Fanny WALDEN	7	Charlie LEWIS
Billy MINTER	8	William SPITTLE
Jimmy CANTRELL	9	Steve STONLEY
Bert BLISS	10	Archie DEVINE
Bert MIDDLEMISS	11	George BURRELL

Referee **Mr A Briggs** (Blackburn)

BACKGROUND

For their last home match of the season, Spurs gave a debut to goalkeeper John Tate and their new £1,700 signing from Northampton, Fanny Walden. Special permission had to be obtained from the League for Walden to play but this was forthcoming as, whatever the result of the game, it would have no effect on the relegation issue. Spurs had again spent the season trying, but failing, to make an impact in the top flight but were, at least, safe from the drop. Arsenal were already down. A season that began atrociously had simply carried on in the same way. Nothing manager George Morrell tried could turn results around. They finished five points behind Notts County and ten adrift of 18th placed Chelsea. Three wins, 18 points and 26 goals scored were the lowest ever recorded, and it was not until 1985 that Stoke performed even worse.

BEFORE THE GAME

	P	W	D	L	F	A	Pts
Spurs	36	12	5	19	43	68	29
Arsenal	36	3	10	23	24	72	16

'DERBY' STAR

★ **George Grant** ★

The Arsenal right-half was one of the few outstanding players on the field. According to the "Athletic News" he went at it full speed from start to finish and held up the Spurs left repeatedly.

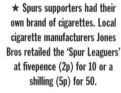

'DERBY' STAR

THAT WAS THEN

★ Spurs supporters had their own brand of cigarettes. Local cigarette manufacturers Jones Bros retailed the 'Spur Leaguers' at fivepence (2p) for 10 or a shilling (5p) for 50.

Fanny Walden, Spurs new £1,700 signing from Northampton, made his debut in this game.

LONDON RIVALS DRAW

The game between these London rivals may best be described by the hackneyed phrase - a typical end-of-the-season contest. No match at White Hart Lane this season has been productive of so much aimless kicking.

WALDEN'S ONE WEAKNESS

Having received permission from the League - which no one expected would be refused - the 'Spurs played Walden at outside-right, and this player of few inches was just himself. For the benefit of those who have not seen the ex-Northampton player much it may be added that he was wonderfully clever, passed neatly and centred well. The only fault which could be found with his play was a weakness with corner kicks.

In the first minute Middlemiss was right through, but his shot was just wide of the mark. Afterwards, thanks to shaky defensive work, the Arsenal were very much in the picture. Tate, playing in the home goal for the first time, had trouble with a dropping centre from Lewis and it was touch-and-go whether the mistake would prove fatal. A flying save on the part of McDonald which kept out the best shot of the day - from Minter - was the other event worthy of note up to the interval.

After the change over, a freak shot by Middlemiss, who put the ball into the net directly from a corner-kick, was quickly followed by a nice goal. Again Middlemiss took a corner, but this time **MINTER** helped the ball into the net with his head. This after 17 minutes play. For a long time it seemed likely that bare justice would be denied the Arsenal, for only three minutes remained when **GRANT** gained possession from a corner-kick and beat Tate.

POOR DEFENDERS

I was pleased when Grant got this goal, for whatever may be said of some of the other players he certainly went at it full steam from start to finish, and was one of the few outstanding players on the field. Grant held up the Spurs' left repeatedly, and behind him Shaw was far superior to any other back.

The 'Spurs' defenders were in so-so form, Collins and Webster made many mistakes, and as a result Woolwich would undoubtedly have won with a centre-forward who could have shot with anything like accuracy. Stonley had the speed, and it often carried him beyond the backs, but his finishing was unworthy of the rest of his play. McDonald, in the Arsenal goal, was quite good, but Tate did not inspire, and it is evident that he lacks the confidence that will come with further experience. Rance was about the best of the 'Spurs' half-back line, but even he was rather below normal. Apart from Walden there was not a shining star forward.

The Arsenal wing men tried hard but received poor support. The home left could make little headway, but on the right Minter looked after his partner quite well. Cantrell was ever ready to dash through, but like Stonley he finished none too surely.

AT THE SEASON'S END

		P	W	D	L	F	A	Pts
17th	Spurs	38	12	6	20	45	72	30
20th	Arsenal	38	3	12	23	26	74	18

New ground for the Gunners...

During the summer of 1913 Woolwich Arsenal moved into a new ground at Highbury. The match programme for the first game, v Leicester Fosse in September, included the cartoon reproduced below and the following comments from the directors...

"It is our ambition that the ground and home of the Pioneers of League Football and professionalism in London shall be second to none in the Kingdom.

The accessibility of our new home is indisputable. It can be reached from the City and places adjacent thereto in less time than any other ground, and should, therefore, prove a great boon to the cosmopolitan enthusiast who finds himself in the City during the "kick-off at 2.30pm" season, when every moment saved in travelling is valuable.

We are distinctly hopeful that, with the assistance of the football-loving public of North London, we may soon forget the depressing times we spent at Plumstead, with its poor train service and the lukewarm support received from those in the immediate neighbourhood."

Woolwich Arsenal's Highbury Scheme.

The Islington Borough Council, on Friday night, considered the question of the contemplated removal of Woolwich Arsenal's headquarters to St. John's College grounds, Highbury.

A deputation from Highbury residents, who are opposed to the scheme, attended, and Mr. H. S. Norris, Mayor of Fulham, who is one of the Arsenal directors, and Mr. C. E. Sutcliffe, a solicitor well known in football circles, were also heard, the latter being permitted to address the Council on behalf of the Woolwich club.

The Council heard speeches on both sides, and a good many extravagant statements were, no doubt, made for and against.

Alderman Saint afterwards proposed the adoption of the recommendation of the Parliamentary Committee, " that the Council of the College should be requested to refrain from granting the lease to Woolwich Arsenal, and that the Board of Education should be strongly urged not to approve the proposal." He said that he did not approach this matter as an opponent of football, whether amateur or professional. His only regard was the interests of a locality in their charge and the people for whom they were the trustees. If it were a question of restricting anything in the shape of proper physical recreation he would not be standing there moving that recommendation. He maintained that the people who lived in Highbury did not want professional football, and that if the ground were established it would do irreparable harm to the locality. He maintained that if the football club came the occupiers of houses in Highbury would have the right of appealing at once to the Assessment Committee for a reduction of their assessment. They would have hundreds of these appeals. He said this with the full realisation of the responsibility he was taking. They would say that their premises had depreciated in value and the Committee would be bound to bear them. He recognised the good that football did, but they did not want it at their doors. The Woolwich Arsenal Club wanted to improve their concern at the expense of Highbury, and the Council would be very remiss as trustees if they did not do their best to prevent the club being brought there.

Mr. Peskett seconded the adoption of the recommendation.

Mr. Wash said that the report of the Committee was liable to bias the judgment of the Council on the subject. It was a surprise to him, because he understood that they came to a decision opposed altogether to that which appeared on the agenda. (No.) He might be wrong, but if so he was wrong in association with others.

The Mayor: The Town Clerk says that the report records what took place.

Mr. Walsh, Exercise man; the Town Clerk was not present. We passed a resolution not compromising the Council in any way.

On a division the recommendation of the Committee was carried by 36 votes to 16.

Dr. Highbury—A very narrow escape indeed. Another twelve months under my colleague here and it would have been all up with you. His treatment would have killed anyone with a less robust constitution. However, I have been called in in time, and with a change of air and plenty of visitors to cheer you up there is no reason why you should not regain all your former vigour.

9

TOTTENHAM HOTSPUR 2
Cantrell, Bliss

ARSENAL 1
Rutherford

Saturday 15th January 1921

Football League Division One

White Hart Lane

Attendance 39,221

Tottenham Hotspur

Arsenal

Manager
Peter McWilliam

Manager
Leslie Knighton

Bill JACQUES	1	Ernie WILLIAMSON
Tommy CLAY	2	Frank BRADSHAW
Bob McDONALD	3	Arthur HUTCHINS
Bert SMITH	4	Alf BAKER
Charlie WALTERS	5	Jack BUTLER
Arthur GRIMSDELL	6	Angus McKINNON
Fanny WALDEN	7	Jock RUTHERFORD
Jimmy SEED	8	Henry WHITE
Jimmy CANTRELL	9	Fred PAGNAM
Bert BLISS	10	Billy BLYTH
Jimmy DIMMOCK	11	James PATERSON

Referee **Mr A Pellowe** (Oldham)

"Arsenal lacked the touch of football magic which for the lack of a better word we call mastery. This the Spurs did not lack." - Daily News

"The present Tottenham side is about the best that have yet represented the club; at least, it is equal to the eleven that included Tait and Erentz, and were led by Sandy Brown... From a practical point of view, they were no better than the Arsenal on Saturday.. They carried prettiness too far." - Daily Telegraph

"Spurs played the close-passing, skilful game. Arsenal played the full-steam-ahead game, booting the ball hard, and dashing after it at top speed. At the end no-one could say which was the more effective." - Daily Mail

BACKGROUND

The first North London League derby took place with both clubs comfortably placed in mid-table. Spurs, runaway winners of the Second Division the previous season, had four survivors from the last League meeting, Bliss, Cantrell, Grimsdell and Walden, and the previous week had set out on what was to prove a successful FA Cup campaign with a 6-2 drubbing of Bristol Rovers. They were unchanged for the sixth successive match. None of the Arsenal eleven had played in that last encounter and in their previous outing they had gone out of the FA Cup to Third Division Queen's Park Rangers. Frank Bradshaw deputised for injured Joe Shaw, Alf Baker returned at the expense of Clem Voysey and Dr Paterson returned in place of Joe Toner. Arsenal had won only one of their last five games but had picked up both points in three of their last four away games; 4-0 at Huddersfield, 2-1 at Chelsea and 4-2 at Everton.

BEFORE THE GAME

	P	W	D	L	F	A	Pts
Spurs	22	10	4	8	49	31	24
Arsenal	22	8	8	6	33	29	24

Bert Bliss scored Spurs' winner.

SPURS DRAMATIC DECIDER, FOG FOILED AS SPOILSPORT

Arsenal goalkeeper Ernie Williamson 'effected more than one brilliant save'

It must have been with a certain amount of trepidation that the gates at White Hart Lane were opened on Saturday for mist had been in evidence from about 10 a.m., and promised to develop in density. Happily matters did not become bad enough to warrant a postponement, and fully 40,000 spectators saw what they could of a spiritedly contested encounter, which, thanks to referee Pellows's determination - he dispensed with an interval, too - was played through, and resulted in a narrow victory for the 'Spurs by the odd goal of three. As they had already decisively defeated Chelsea twice, and the Pensioners had also conceded three points to The Arsenal, the London Championship may rightly be regarded as theirs, though a great struggle should be forthcoming at Highbury this weekend.

Fog, as usual, played its pranks. There were periods, notably early in the second half, when it was comparatively easy to follow the course of the play, at others it was little more to the occupants of the grand stand than a spectre show when the game was on the opposite side of the ground, whilst during the stoppage caused through the injury to Grimsdell before the free kick awarded was taken, with about 15 minutes to go, the fog descended and blotted out the greater portion of the football. Frost - the grime was still in evidence - had somewhat stiffened the surface of the arena, and the football, if more scrambling towards the end, was of a really good standard, notably as regards the display of the rival sets of half-backs, and the excellent kicking of the last line of defence. The 'Spurs had their usual side, and the Arsenal welcomed back Dr Paterson - who was not, however, very much in the picture - and Baker, as usual excellent, whilst Butler shifted to centre half in the continued absence of Graham, and greatly improved upon his showing in the Cup-tie at Shepherd's Bush.

There was very little to choose between the teams, although the 'Spurs undoubtedly did most of the attacking in the first half and caused Williamson to effect some brilliant saves, notably one from Seed, to which he just managed to bring himself within reach. Thirteen minutes remained to half time when a spirited attack on the right forced a corner. Walden dropped the ball nicely in front of goal, there was a bit of a melee following Williamson's punch away, and then a roar as the ball passed into the net off

CANTRELL's head, his identity being further established by the customary handshake. This roused the Gunners, who twice directed hot shots which the defence rather luckily cleared, and on a third a fine opportunity went begging. Following change of ends the visitors again exerted prolonged pressure. Baker took a free kick for hands from which nothing tangible accrued, and then at the end of 14 minutes from the restart came an equaliser, also the outcome of a well directed corner-kick. It was "Jock" RUTHERFORD, just previously hurt, who got in one of his clever corners. It evidently beat the crowd around goal, and Jacques in trying to deal with it pulled it into his net (as far as could be distinguished!). Then for a while the 'Spurs held the upper hand, and Williamson, despite a nasty collision with Cantrell, effected more than one brilliant save. Bliss at this point being especially energetic, Walden a worker, as usual.

About 15 minutes remained when the decider was registered. Grimsdell made one of his brilliant efforts to take the ball through himself - he is a trifle too fond of it, maybe - and had worked into a good position when he was badly fouled and hurt. BLISS took the kick after a stoppage, and from pretty long range - over 20 yards - drove the ball hotly into the net amid a prolonged roar of applause. Played continued desperate to the end, but instead of the draw which had appeared probable the 'Spurs secured victory by two goals to one.

THAT WAS THEN

★ The official Spurs programme cost a penny for four pages. There was a cartoon by Fred Perry on the cover, editorial on page 2, teams and league tables on page 3 and fixtures and results on the back.

★ Seats at White Hart Lane could be reserved for five shillings (25p).

Cartoon from the Weekly Herald.

10

ARSENAL 3
Rutherford 2, White

TOTTENHAM HOTSPUR 2
Cantrell, Smith

Arsenal

Tottenham Hotspur

Manager
Leslie Knighton

Manager
Peter McWilliam

Arsenal		Tottenham Hotspur
Stephen DUNN	1	Bill JACQUES
Frank BRADSHAW	2	Tommy CLAY
Arthur HUTCHINS	3	Bob McDONALD
Alf BAKER	4	Bert SMITH
Jack BUTLER	5	Charlie WALTERS
Angus McKINNON	6	Arthur GRIMSDELL
Jock RUTHERFORD	7	Fanny WALDEN
Henry WHITE	8	Jimmy SEED
Joe NORTH	9	Jimmy CANTRELL
Billy BLYTH	10	Bert BLISS
James PATERSON	11	Jimmy DIMMOCK

Referee **Mr A Pellowe** (Oldham)

BEFORE THE GAME...

	P	W	D	L	F	A	Pts
Arsenal	23	8	8	7	34	31	24
Spurs	23	11	4	8	51	32	26

AT THE SEASON'S END...

		P	W	D	L	F	A	Pts
6th	Spurs	42	19	9	14	70	48	47
9th	Arsenal	42	15	14	13	59	63	44

"Boundless energy and praiseworthy pluck enabled the Arsenal to turn the tables on the Spurs. Just that extra shade of dash and pace gave the Arsenal the verdict" - Athletic News

BACKGROUND

For the first few seasons after the Great War the Football League decreed that return fixtures should take place the following week, so Arsenal only had seven days to wait for the opportunity for revenge. When Highbury was built it was claimed a crowd of 60,000 could be accommodated. That claim was put to the test by supporters keen to see a repeat of the previous week's great battle and Spurs' first senior visit to Highbury. Fully 60,600 spectators were crammed in. Arsenal were without Ernie Williamson and top scorer Fred Pagnam, both injured at White Hart Lane, and called up Stephen Dunn and Joe North, whereas Spurs were able to field their full strength eleven.

An attack on the Arsenal goal showing Jimmy Dimmock of Spurs (nearest the camera) and Arsenal's Stephen Dunn (goalkeeper), Angus McKinnon and Arthur Hutchins (falling).

GUNNERS TURN THE TABLE - A RECORD FOR HIGHBURY

There was a record crowd at Highbury on Saturday, a remarkable game, marked at the close by a scene of the greatest enthusiasm on the part of a most orderly and delighted gathering. The Arsenal atoned for their rather unlucky defeat in the mist at White Hart Lane the previous week-end, and few would be found to begrudge them their victory, which was only secured after a grandly contested struggle by the odd goal in five. As at Tottenham, the 'Spurs were slightly the cleverer team, but this was neutralised by the sterling work of the home side, who, if anything lasted rather better and special praise must be bestowed on the Arsenal centre line, who in spite of the fact that Baker has done better, never gave the "Spurs" front line any respite. Seldom has "Fanny" Walden been less in the picture; on the other hand, the Gunners' right wing worked together admirably and to good purpose.

Whereas the visitors were able to play full strength - there had been rumours before the start that Bliss might have to stand down - the Arsenal lacked Williamson, Graham and Pagnam. Dunn, however, proved an able substitute for the first-named in goal, and Butler gave an heroic display in the second stage as pivot. He had retired not long before the interval with his left collar-bone badly bruised, at first it was feared there was a fracture. On restarting, however, he turned out again, his left arm hanging by his side and in evident pain. In spite of this and several falls that must have added to his agony, he stuck grimly to his work, and was the recipient of a well deserved ovation. North had to deputise as the leader of the Arsenal attack vice Pagnam, and displayed plenty of energy and pluck, but the ordeal was rather too great for him, and he frequently lacked cleverness, which was not compensated for by extra earnestness.

An hour before the start it was evident that the ground would not accommodate the thousands who poured towards it. Every endeavour was made to "pack", but the gates had to be closed before the start, and the more youthful spectators were allowed to scale the rails and sit on the ground round the fringe of the field of play. Although the exact figures could not be given, the official's rough return was 57,000, constituting a record for the ground. It was an enthusiastic but most orderly crowd, appreciative to the full of a fast, fine display of football, vigorous but clean as well as clever.

In the opening stage the 'Spurs elected to defend the northern or Finsbury Park goal with the wind favouring, only to find the sun make appearance to bother them. In the first few minutes Dimmock, after beating Baker and Bradshaw, had a fine chance, practically an open goal, but he dallied, allowed the home defence to intervene and Dunn to clear. About 18 minutes had elapsed without score when **RUTHERFORD** received following an effort on the left wing. He was unmarked and had a splendid opening. His shot was low and straight towards Jacques, but there must have been more pace in it and some spin; at any rate, as the 'Spurs custodian shaped to take the gall it passed through his hands and bounced into the net. With half an hour gone the Reds had a golden opportunity of increasing their lead, for Grimsdell conceded a penalty for handing in that area - from the grand stand it certainly appeared that the decision was a correct one, for there was a distinct downward movement of his arm. It, however, sadly disconcerted the International for a while. Bradshaw took the kick, but shot too far towards his left and Jacques got his right hand to the ball and glanced it wide of the upright. Eight minutes of the first half remained when **CANTRELL**, with the home defence in a tangle placed the 'Spurs, on terms with a capital shot, and the Spurs left the field with the score one all.

The Arsenal applied strong pressure on resuming and so far "shook up" the rival defence that they registered a couple of goals in the first 16 minutes. One, at the end of nine, was from a cross by "the Doctor", Paterson's centre going going past North to **WHITE**, who promptly utilised the opportunity, and the second, also after an effort on the home left, being credited to **RUTHERFORD** (who was at his best) following a neat pass by his partner. The 'Spurs never relaxed effort, but all they could register was one goal, midway through the half, by **SMITH**, that half-back beating Dunn with a good drive after the custodian had fisted out from a well-placed corner by Dimmock, and the visitors thus lost the day by 3 goals to 2.

'DERBY' STAR

★ Jock Rutherford ★

Scored twice and was 'at his best' in this game. Made nearly 600 league and cup appearances for Newcastle, Arsenal and Clapton Orient. Still holds the record as the oldest player to represent Arsenal in a League match at the age of 41 years 159 days.

11

TOTTENHAM HOTSPUR 2
Grimsdell, Seed

ARSENAL 0

Tottenham Hotspur			Arsenal
Manager **Peter McWilliam**			Manager **Leslie Knighton**

Herbert BLAKE	1	Ernie WILLIAMSON
Tommy CLAY	2	Frank BRADSHAW
Bob McDONALD	3	Arthur HUTCHINS
Bert SMITH	4	Alf BAKER
Charlie WALTERS	5	Alex GRAHAM
Arthur GRIMSDELL	6	Tom WHITTAKER
Fanny WALDEN	7	Jock RUTHERFORD
Jimmy SEED	8	Henry WHITE
Jimmy CANTRELL	9	Andy YOUNG
Andy THOMPSON	10	Reg BOREHAM
Jimmy DIMMOCK	11	Joe TONER

Referee **Mr S Rothwell** (St.Annes-On-Sea)

BACKGROUND

Strengthened by the return of Fanny Walden, second in the table Spurs, two defeats in twenty-five games, still had a mathematical chance of winning the League title although Liverpool, five points ahead, were the odds-on favourites. Their last two games had both been at White Hart Lane and had been won 2-1 against Birmingham and 3-1 against Oldham. Arsenal were again fighting relegation and even though Tom Whittaker and Andy Young returned the fact they had tasted defeat in their last six away games meant Spurs were expected to win this Easter Saturday fixture comfortably.

BEFORE THE GAME

	P	W	D	L	F	A	Pts
Spurs	37	19	8	10	60	35	46
Arsenal	36	11	6	19	38	52	28

'DERBY' STAR
★ Bob McDonald ★

"The full-back play on both sides touched a very high level, and it is handing out real praise to McDonald to suggest he was the best of the four" - how the Athletic News rated Spurs Scottish defender's performance.

'DERBY' STAR

Arsenal's Alf Baker.

Tom Whittaker — returned to an Arsenal team fighting against relegation.

SPURS BEAT THE ARSENAL

Arsenal skipper Frank Bradshaw

Had it not been for the high wind, there is little doubt some fine football would have been witnessed at White Hart Lane, Tottenham on Saturday, when the first of the battles which meant so much to the Highbury team attracted a crowd officially given as 42,000. On the previous day, whilst the Reds were resting, the 'Spurs were doing them a good turn by lowering the colours of Oldham Athletic at the same enclosure, but on Saturday, showing little signs of fatigue, they played "all out" in a keen contest with their local rivals and deservedly won by a margin of two goals to love. They had in the field the same side as on Good Friday, except that Walden was able to resume at outside-right, and he it was who played no small part in sealing the fate of the Gunners.

The latter were a goal down on change of ends, but, with the diagonally-blowing wind in their favour, they applied strong pressure for about twenty minutes. Then the Spurs reasserted themselves and Walden, lying well out in midfield, broke away with a clever dodgy run, despite the fact that he was tackled by a couple of the opposition, one of whom conceded a corner. Walden took it himself, and ably directed the leather to which **SEED** (who in the first half had certainly not been seen at his best) applied his head and with remarkable force the ball passed into the net out of Williamson's reach.

GRIMSDELL'S GREAT GOAL

On good Friday it was Cantrell's day, on the morrow the victory may be associated with the captain, Arthur **GRIMSDELL**, whose poor effort against his club right wing at Craven Cottage probably cost him his place in the last two Internationals, in which most people would have liked to have seen him included. His goal on the present occasion, with the match sixteen minutes old, was one that will long be remembered. Securing the ball not very far from the half-way line, he cleverly made his way with it towards goal, controlling it admirably. He must have worked to about thirty yards range and then let fly, a lightning shot with the precision of a real gunner, driving the ball into the net with terrific force, a feat deservedly greeted with tumultuous applause.

MISTAKEN TACTICS BY THE LOSERS

Arsenal's captain, Bradshaw, played a great game for his side, McDonald being easily the better of the 'Spurs' couple, but the majority of the visiting team failed to do themselves justice, and their tactics were frequently at fault. Rutherford for the first fifteen minutes did not touch the ball - two attempts by White went sadly astray - but he persisted in hugging the touch-line on the grand stand side. Walden started doing likewise on change of ends but wisely well into midfield, and was far more in the picture. It could scarcely be said that the teams as a whole displayed great cleverness in their battle with the breeze, but the home halves gave little rope to the opposing front line, of which White was the pick, Young promising well but to fade away. Their half-backs, however, gave then few openings, the spaces covered by Grimsdell possibly tempting them to try long shots at Blake - whose goal kicks upfield are a source of wonder - as preferable to feeding the forwards. In defence they were stubbornness personified and, there may have been method, but they were inclined to overdo matters.

Cantrell, as already hinted, was not in the limelight as on the previous day, but just after the opening score of the day he got so much "powder" behind a drive to Williamson that the Arsenal custodian grasped his right hand in pain after effecting an able clearance. In the melee in which the second item was added the home centre-forward received a kick that led to him shifting to outside, and a little later he broke down and had to be assisted off the field. But the victory had then been won. Rutherford did not have a shot into goal until the last minute or so of the opening moiety, but during the period following the resumption, when the Arsenal applied strong pressure, and with better understanding and finish, ought to have drawn level, he was more in evidence, and two or three corner kicks were a pattern of accuracy.

Arthur Grimsdell's goal was one that will long be remembered... "a lightning shot with the precision of a real gunner, driving the ball into the net with terrific force."

ARSENAL 1
Graham (pen)

TOTTENHAM HOTSPUR 0

Arsenal

Tottenham Hotspur

Manager
Leslie Knighton

Manager
Peter McWilliam

Arsenal		Tottenham Hotspur
Ernie WILLIAMSON	1	Herbert BLAKE
Frank BRADSHAW	2	Tommy CLAY
Arthur HUTCHINS	3	Bob McDONALD
Alf BAKER	4	Jimmy SKINNER
Alex GRAHAM	5	Charlie WALTERS
Tom WHITTAKER	6	Arthur GRIMSDELL
Jock RUTHERFORD	7	Fanny WALDEN
Henry WHITE	8	Jimmy SEED
Andy YOUNG	9	Jimmy CANTRELL
Reg BOREHAM	10	Andy THOMPSON
Billy BLYTH	11	Jimmy DIMMOCK

Referee **Mr S Rothwell** (St.Annes-On-Sea)

BACKGROUND

In the seven days between the season's two fixtures Arsenal had practically escaped the threat of relegation. With the return of Billy Blyth they took three points from West Bromwich Albion, leaving them clear of Bradford City, their opponents in their last two games, and relegated Manchester United. For Spurs, their slim hopes of winning the championship vanished with defeat at Oldham on Easter Monday whilst Liverpool were beating third placed Burnley to secure their third title. Jimmy Cantrell, Andy Thompson and Arthur Grimsdell all missed the game at Oldham but were not fit to return while Jimmy Skinner stood in for Bert Smith.

BEFORE THE GAME

	P	W	D	L	F	A	Pts
Spurs	39	20	8	11	62	36	48
Arsenal	39	12	7	20	43	56	31

AT THE SEASON'S END

		P	W	D	L	F	A	Pts
2nd	Spurs	42	21	9	12	65	39	51
17th	Arsenal	42	15	7	20	47	56	37

Spurs owed much to Herbert Blake's fine goalkeeping

THAT WAS THEN

★ Three months before this game the Duke of York (later King George VI) ceremoniously cut the first turf for a new football stadium in North London. Construction of the Empire Stadium, Wembley was underway.

ENGLISH LEAGUE.
WON BY A PENALTY.
CLOSE GAME AT HIGHBURY.

At half-time, at Highbury, on Saturday, the Arsenal were leading by 1—0, Grimsdell was crippled into incapability, and Bradford City were a goal down at Birmingham. Arsenal supporters discerned a break in the clouds of relegation which have hovered above them for months, and when the end came, after a few rude shocks, with no change in the positions, they gave vent to their feelings of relief by prolonged cheering. Arsenal won, and they may be congratulated upon their victory, but what a close thing it was. Despite having to face only ten men, Arsenal could only win by an accident. Had Grimsdell remained on the field, a different tale might have to be unfolded, and the Arsenal might be less hopeful of escaping relegation. Arsenal have been most unfortunate in respect of the weather for their big home matches this season. On Saturday, it rained throughout the game, and the pitch was in a treacherous state. Sometimes the ball would strike an ordinary patch and bounce like a respectable ball should. At other times it would skim over the watery surface with the players at sea, in more senses than one. It was Alec Graham's benefit, and 42,000 enthusiasts attended.

From the "Tottenham and Edmonton Weekly Herald"

THE ARSENAL AVENGED

SPURS LOSE AT HIGHBURY
Graham's Gratifying Benefit

The Arsenal's avoidance of relegation was rendered much brighter on Saturday at Highbury by the reversal of the verdict of the previous week-end in opposition to their North London rivals, the 'Spurs. It is true that the margin was only a successful penalty kick rather unluckily (though according to the rules) awarded against Dimmock, who had tried to reach the ball from a pass by Rutherford to White - and brought down the latter. The 'Spurs player had taken the risk and paid the penalty, though just previously there had appeared to be a case at the opposite end far more deserving of disaster. **GRAHAM** took the penalty shot himself and got the ball wide of Blake's left hand amid tumultuous applause. It sufficed to secure the verdict.

This score occurred when thirty nine minutes had elapsed in the course of a contest in which the Arsenal were all out for the points, their visitors none the less eager. The fixture had been set apart as a benefit for Alec Graham, the Scottish International, who had been associated with the "Gunners" in their disastrous pre-War days at Plumstead, and he has cause to look back on it with pleasure. He was paid the compliment of captaining the home side, enjoyed an enthusiastic reception from a crowd that, in spite of a wet, miserable afternoon, numbered 48,000, and, as seen, had the satisfaction of scoring the solitary goal. The fate of the Londoners depends on their outstanding games with Bradford City. One or the other is practically certain to go down, and two of the four points should render them safe.

'SPURS' SERIOUS HANDICAP

As already indicated the struggle was a strenuous one - a typical cup-tie -and the Arsenal threw such zeal into their work that it made one regret that it had not been displayed on other occasions. Only at one period, viz, for about a quarter of an hour after the interval, did the play flag: what followed made ample amends. Each had one alteration from the combination engaged at the White Hart Lane match. For the visitors Skinner was at right half vice Bert Smith, crocked during the Easter holidays, for the Reds Blyth was outside left in place of Toner, indisposed. But the 'Spurs were most seriously handicapped midway through the opening half through a mishap that befell their leader, Grimsdell, was was badly bruised on the top of his left thigh in a heavy charge. He returned after a few minutes' absence but limped, and was in evident pain. He went outside left and did his best but was naturally of little service. He did not resume after the interval though it required much persuasion to cause him to remain away, and the ex-FA Cup-holders had to struggle on with ten men, which they did in most plucky fashion. In the first few minutes of the match Clay was off for a brief period during which the Arsenal, who, losing the toss, first defended the College goal, all but scored. There were other mishaps, for the battle was waged with much earnestness.

Play prior to the interval was unquestionably in the Arsenal's favour as a whole, and the 'Spurs owed much to Blake's fine "keeping", the ability of Clay and the failure of the home attack to avoid being pulled up for offside. Cantrell early on got in a stinger from long range, the ball, after strik-

Alex Graham scored the only goal of the game from the penalty spot on his benefit.

ing the bar, going over and there were several narrow escapes from close quarters, notably from Boreham, who gave unquestionable evidence of his ability more than once. But Blake effected a great save - one of many. Rutherford, on the other hand, though he did some clever things, was not so much in the picture as usual; for one thing he was too carefully watched by McDonald. The 'Spurs' attack was not seen to it's usual advantage on the greasy surface, notably the wing men. Midway through the second stage the visitors' goal had two narrow escapes, first from Boreham and then following a rebound off McDonald when Blake had to run out to Young, who got his foot to the ball but caused it to trickle just the wrong side of the upright. Not long before the end the 'Spurs all but equalised. Williamson was drawn and Dimmock appeared to have the goal at his mercy but somehow Baker, who was a tower of strength, nipped in the way and averted a score, being damaged in saving for his side an invaluable point.

13

TOTTENHAM HOTSPUR 1
Lindsay

ARSENAL 2
Boreham 2

Saturday 23rd September 1922

Football League Division One

White Hart Lane

Attendance 40,582

Tottenham Hotspur

Manager
Peter McWilliam

Arsenal

Manager
Leslie Knighton

Tottenham Hotspur	No	Arsenal
Herbert BLAKE	1	Stephen DUNN
Tommy CLAY	2	Frank BRADSHAW
Bob McDONALD	3	Arthur HUTCHINS
Bert SMITH	4	Alf BAKER
Charlie WALTERS	5	Clem VOYSEY
Arthur GRIMSDELL	6	Alex GRAHAM
Fanny WALDEN	7	Jock RUTHERFORD
Jimmy SEED	8	Henry WHITE
Alex LINDSAY	9	Andy YOUNG
Bert BLISS	10	Reg BOREHAM
Jimmy DIMMOCK	11	Billy BLYTH

Referee **Mr C Austin** (Kidderminster)

BACKGROUND

Arsenal arrived at White Hart Lane determined to improve a record that had seen them lose their opening three away games, 2-5 at Liverpool and 1-4 at both Burnley and Cardiff. Such heavy defeats had cost Ernie Williamson his place, Stephen Dunn, at only five foot eight, given the chance to show size was not everything and helping Arsenal beat Cardiff in the return fixture. Spurs had lost one game, 1-3 at home to Burnley, but got revenge a week later with a 1-0 victory at Turf Moor. Alex Lindsay took over from Jimmy Cantrell, injured at Burnley, and even though Tommy Clay was suffering from influenza and Charlie Walters with a carbuncle, Spurs went into the match with confidence high. The match was to prove one of the most acrimonious between the two clubs.

BEFORE THE GAME

	P	W	D	L	F	A	Pts
Spurs	5	3	1	1	8	6	7
Arsenal	6	2	1	3	8	15	5

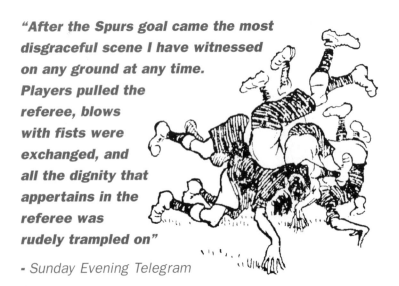

"After the Spurs goal came the most disgraceful scene I have witnessed on any ground at any time. Players pulled the referee, blows with fists were exchanged, and all the dignity that appertains in the referee was rudely trampled on"

- Sunday Evening Telegram

36 *THE PRIDE OF NORTH LONDON*

ANGRY SPECTATORS AT TOTTENHAM

Mr C Austin suffered an unpleasant experience at Tottenham on Saturday. Really, he got through an awkward refereeing job exceedingly well. He encountered several disturbing episodes during a super-keen League match and, by way of a wind-up, the responsible official was literally mobbed by excited players desirous of knowing why he allowed a goal on the stroke of time and, apparently, after the whistle had sounded the cessation of hostilities. A mistake was made somewhere without any shadow of doubt; perhaps, a foolish spectator blew a whistle instead of the referee; anyway that disputed point made no difference to the actual result, for the Arsenal had scored twice prior to the end of the tale incident, and Tottenham Hotspur found themselves beaten at home by two goals to one.

SOME HARD KNOCKS

First Division League encounters never are drawing room affairs; the knocks come hard and frequently, and, in the old days, the same were borne without either complaint or advertisement. Seemingly, the modern demand is for the cutting out of the plain shoulder to shoulder charge with, naturally, the weaker vessels faring second best, and, upon this occasion, veterans could not understand why spectators and referee took strong exception to the things that happened, notably, to Lindsay, Seed and Bliss. Tackling, even if somewhat heavy, is part and parcel of the "Soccer" business and, as Bradshaw and Hutchins only did their duty in defending their side and their club, the spleen of a bigoted crowd - the attendance numbered about 40,000 on a dull and damp afternoon - was both uncalled for and unnecessary.

Reckoning everything, with Tottenham more sinned against then sinning, including the paltry attempts at, and actual perpetration of, fouls that crept into the proceedings, it was not a completely nice game to watch. The quality of football fell below the high standard usually associated with White Hart Lane, the main reason being that both sets of forwards were almost subjugated by magnificent half-backs among whom Grimsdell, Smith, Voysey and Graham shone superlatively. The 'Spurs, undoubtedly, were the finer artists as a whole, their extreme daintiness recalled the distinguished difference between the billiard playing of Stovenath and Dawson, but Tottenham lost because they had nearly all the bad luck that was going in an amazingly strenuous contest. An accidental injury to Walden reduced the home forces to ten men about a quarter of an hour from the start and, subsequently, Lindsay and Bliss were hurt to further complicate matters. Still, Tottenham did more attacking than their opponents and yet one could not help feeling impressed by the sledge-hammer opposition of the Arsenal when using an over-light ball on slippery turf.

Before Walden's retirement the 'Spurs did a lot of pressing for the Arsenal front line kept on falling into the off-side trap set by Clay and McDonald. The visitors' understanding improved gradually, with Voysey supplying beautiful passes to Rutherford, and from one of the latter's centres, Young, Boreham and Blyth all missed a reasonable opening. Lindsay distinguished himself with admirably straight dashes and shots, and Dunn stopped a long, nastily bouncing ball from Grimsdell while, at the other end, Boreham faltered and failed at another chance accruing from a perfect Rutherford middle. With Walden and Lindsay both off the field - the last-named for a few minutes only - Tottenham held their own with even nine men and, from Dimmock's centre, Seed headed just wide of the post. The first half was drawn blank, but the Arsenal secured the lead four minutes following the change of ends.

SCORING THE GOALS

Both a Tottenham back and Blake miskicked, the custodian conceding a corner on the left. Blyth's effort from the flag went to Rutherford, who had a bare chance with little room. Rutherford preferred making a certainty of it and passed to **BOREHAM** for the amateur to easily beat Blake from short range. Bliss and Dimmock changed places and Lindsay might have equalised with a shade more quickness. Smith headed over the top and Seed up against the bar and, about this period, the 'Spurs were terribly unlucky. About ten minutes from the finish Young supplied a clever pass to **BOREHAM** who dribbled along before firing a long shot from a sharp angle which surprised Blake - he should have stopped the ball - by passing into his net and, practically in the last second **LINDSAY**, from perilously near off-side, broke through and scored a fine goal for Tottenham. In this way the Arsenal won by two goals to one.

THE AFTERMATH...

As a result of the referee and both teams coming in for a lot of criticism from press and public alike an FA Commission of Inquiry was held on 5th October to investigate events during the match. Having heard evidence from officials and players of both clubs, Spurs' Bert Smith was found to have used "filthy language" and suspended for a month. Alex Graham was censured for retaliating instead of reporting matters to the ref and Stephen Dunn for his conduct after Spurs goal had been allowed to stand.

Pictured arriving at the FA Enquiry are (left) Spurs' Jimmy Seed and Bert Bliss and (right) Arsenal manager Leslie Knighton, captain Billy Blyth and goalkeeper Stephen Dunn.

14.

ARSENAL 0

TOTTENHAM HOTSPUR 2
Dimmock 2

Arsenal

Tottenham Hotspur

Manager
Leslie Knighton

Manager
Peter McWilliam

Arsenal		Tottenham Hotspur
Stephen DUNN	1	Herbert BLAKE
Frank BRADSHAW	2	Tommy CLAY
Arthur HUTCHINS	3	Bob McDONALD
Alf BAKER	4	Bert SMITH
Clem VOYSEY	5	Charlie WALTERS
Alex GRAHAM	6	Arthur GRIMSDELL
Jock RUTHERFORD	7	Alex LINDSAY
Henry WHITE	8	Jimmy SEED
Andy YOUNG	9	Charlie WILSON
Reg BOREHAM	10	Jimmy DIMMOCK
Billy BLYTH	11	Sammy BROOKS

Referee **Mr W E Russell** (Swindon)

BACKGROUND

After the controversial events of a week earlier the eyes of the football world were focussed on Highbury. Arsenal fielded the same eleven, but with Walden and Bliss failing to recover from injuries sustained at White Hart Lane and Jimmy Cantrell still out with a thigh injury, Spurs were forced to call up Charlie Wilson and former England winger Sammy Brooks for his debut. Mr C Austin, a linesman in Spurs' 1921 FA Cup final success, had been heavily criticised for his handling of the first meeting. Due to take charge of the return fixture, the Football League decided it was best to replace him with another official.

BEFORE THE GAME

	P	W	D	L	F	A	Pts
Arsenal	7	3	1	3	10	16	7
Spurs	6	3	1	2	9	8	7

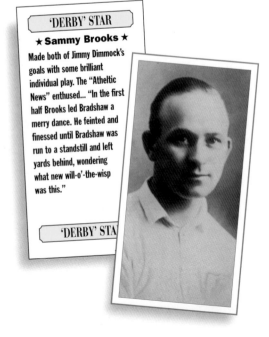

THE CALM AFTER THE STORM.

SPURS AVENGED.

The Spurs gained their revenge over the Arsenal at Highbury on Saturday in a game of parlour football. What would have happened if Mr. Austin had been there is another story. Another referee, Mr. W. E. Russell, of Swindon, had charge of the game, and in an atmosphere at first tense and of suppressed anxiety, and later of tranquillity, he discharged his functions worthy of a knight of the whistle. A suggestion—even the shadow of a ghost of a suggestion—of a foul met with condign punishment. The Highbury cynics may say this reduced the game to an absurdity. Tottenham folk will reply that it prevented Bradshaw, Hutchins and Graham from transgressing, and from this assumption they will tell you that was why the Spurs won. But let memories of the game at Tottenham be buried with the hatchet in a deep grave. Recrimination will not do the clubs any good, and what is of more concern to everybody, it will do harm to the game.

The Spurs' two goals were indirectly the outcome of brilliant play by Brooks, and immediately due to two superlative shots by Dimmock, who, in the second half seemed to be content to stroll along till the end satisfied that he had won more laurels. I frankly admit, however, there was precious little difference between the teams.

From the "Tottenham and Edmonton Weekly Herald"

THAT WAS THEN

★ At its AGM the Football League decided to revise its cup-tie bonuses. In future players would get £8.00 for winning the FA Cup – a reduction of £2.00!

'DERBY' STAR

★ **Sammy Brooks** ★

Made both of Jimmy Dimmock's goals with some brilliant individual play. The "Athletic News" enthused... "In the first half Brooks led Bradshaw a merry dance. He feinted and finessed until Bradshaw was run to a standstill and left yards behind, wondering what new will-o'-the-wisp was this."

'DERBY' STAR

SPURS BEAT ARSENAL
DIMMOCK'S SHOOTING AT HIGHBURY

Tottenham Hotspur accomplished the table-turning trick and beat the Arsenal by two goals to love at Highbury on Saturday. The North Londoners thus took considerable compensation for a defeat sustained at White Hart Lane a week previously, when delicate folk shuddered at super-keen methods, and both spoke and wrote accordingly. Nothing in the least shocking happened during the course of this return engagement, witnessed by a huge assembly, officially returned at 55,000; and it was just a good First Division League match, with the result quite properly favouring the side showing the superior Soccer football under ideal conditions.

"The Arsenal flattered and then disappointed sadly. They gave much promise in the first quarter of an hour, but then they dropped their oars and began to flounder, and have never been seen to less advantage in any home game."
- The Athletic News.

INEFFECTIVE FORWARDS

The Arsenal played the same eleven as at Tottenham, and the side as a whole failed to reproduce the form that secured a couple of valuable points seven days earlier. The reason is not far to seek. Walters dominated Young to such an extent that the latter's ineffectiveness ultimately spread to the other home inside forwards. Blyth, on the left wing, made a brave show with the few passes he received from Boreham, but Rutherford obtained most of his openings from Baker and Voysey. White tried desperately hard at inside right, but he was out of luck, and suffered an indifferent match. The difference between the two front lines really determined the verdict.

The 'Spurs are singularly happy in their stock of reserves; every position apparently is understudied. The Tottenham management appeared in a pretty pickle with Walden, Banks, Bliss and Cantrell under doctor's orders, but Peter McWilliam solved the problem by placing Lindsay outside right, Dimmock inside left to Brooks, and Wilson leading the attack. The freshly-constituted line fitted in like a glove, Brooks and Lindsay were the success of the match, Seed and Wilson we know, and it might be worth while persevering with Dimmock and Brooks as a left wing. Dimmock scored both goals for his side in this match, and on shooting alone he is an asset at inside left. One thing is certain - Tottenham Hotspur are not short of the necessary class forwards; the shoe must pinch on that account with the Arsenal. Both defences are excellent, particularly Bradshaw and Clay. Voysey would be a great centre half if he parted with the ball instead of beating so many men as he does now; the later policy, clever as it is, beats itself because of wasted time in attack. At the finish Bradshaw and Grimsdell, the rival captains, ran up and shook hands, a pretty spectacle that might be overlooked by those so ready to find fault with everything transpiring in professional "Soccer".

Jimmy Dimmock - both goals at Highbury.

DIMMOCK'S TWO GOALS

The quality of the early football reached a very high standard; it was all so fast, bright and clean. The 'Spurs were the most finished experts - this criticism applied a week earlier - but on this occasion the luck switched into their direction. Exciting moments at both ends entered into the proceedings - Dunn made one marvellous save from Lindsay - and twenty-eight minutes of the first half had passed away when Grimsdell, a master in attack, supplied Brooks with the sublime pass. Brooks swerved his way along, keeping control of the ball until he saw his partner favourably placed. DIMMOCK then got a perfect pass and, clearing a space for himself, scored a grand goal with a long shot with which Dunn had not the ghost of a chance. Just on half-time DIMMOCK repeated the dose with even a more brilliant shot than before, succeeding a similar movement, and at the interval the Arsenal were two goals down.

Subsequently the 'Spurs, possessing a long lead, did not trouble much about scoring; they played more for safety than anything else, and consequently the second half suffered by comparison with the first. The Arsenal missed the few chances that came their way, and eventually Tottenham Hotspur won comfortably by two goals to love.

AT THE SEASON'S END

		P	W	D	L	F	A	Pts
11th	Arsenal	42	16	10	16	61	62	42
12th	Spurs	42	17	7	18	50	50	41

ARSENAL 1
Townrow

TOTTENHAM HOTSPUR 1
Seed

Arsenal

Manager
Leslie Knighton

Tottenham Hotspur

Manager
Peter McWilliam

Jock ROBSON	1	George MADDISON
Alex MACKIE	2	Tommy CLAY
Tom WHITTAKER	3	Matt FORSTER
Alex GRAHAM	4	Bert SMITH
Jack BUTLER	5	Harry LOWE
Billy BLYTH	6	Arthur GRIMSDELL
Jock RUTHERFORD	7	Fanny WALDEN
Frank TOWNROW	8	Jimmy SEED
Bobby TURNBULL	9	Alex LINDSAY
Henry WOODS	10	Jack ELKES
James PATERSON	11	Charlie HANDLEY

Referee **Mr H W Andrews** *(Prestwich)*

BACKGROUND

What a difference a year makes! Only eight players survived from the corresponding fixture the previous season; Graham, Blyth and Rutherford for Arsenal; Clay, Smith, Grimsdell, Seed and Lindsay for Spurs. Substantial changes, but for neither club had performances improved with Spurs in mid-table and Arsenal, thanks to only two defeats in their last ten games, just below. Arsenal welcomed back Jock Rutherford and James Paterson, while Bobby Turnbull returned in place of Andy Young; Spurs kept the same team that had beaten Nottingham Forest seven days before, their first victory in eight games. A sodden pitch and strong winds did not provide the best of conditions.

BEFORE THE GAME

	P	W	D	L	F	A	Pts
Arsenal	14	5	3	6	13	16	13
Spurs	14	5	5	4	14	12	15

Jimmy Seed equalised with his first goal of the season.

COLOURS
RED SHIRTS
WHITE KNICKERS

MR A. LESLIE KNIGHTON, MANAGER.
MR H. J. PETERS, SECRETARY.

ARSENAL·FOOTBALL·CLUB·L.TD

DIRECTORS:-
WM. HALL, ESQ., L.C.C., (Vice-Chairman); Colonel SIR HENRY NORRIS, D.L., (Chairman);
Major SIR SAMUEL HILL-WOOD, BART., J.P., D.L.; Lt.-Col. C. D. CRISP, J.P., O.B.E.;
G. W. PEACHEY, ESQ., O.B.E. J. W. HUMBLE, ESQ.;

Telegraphic Address:
"GUNNERETIC &
FINSPARK LONDON."

Registered Offices
AVENELL ROAD,
GILLESPIE ROAD.

VOL. XII. No. 22.

SATURDAY, NOVEMBER 17th, 1923.

[Price, TWO-PENCE.

OUR EDITORIAL NOTE

BY "THE GUNNERS' MATE."

Welcome "Spurs." In the lengthy list of attractive dishes, which figure on the Highbury menu, I venture to say that none tickle the palate more than the clash with Tottenham Hotspur. In the big world of football there is room for all of us and the season's programme is the richer because of the thrills our encounters with the White Hart Lane boys provide. After all there is a lot in local rivalry and the great game, as a spectacle and a popular attraction, would be the poorer if deprived of what we are pleased to call these "Derbies." The Tottenham team is one for which we have the highest respect and admiration. Like ourselves they have not enjoyed the best of fortune this season. Injuries have been a handicap to progress but I believe they will be at something like full strength for to-day's encounter. They have some players of high repute, who need little introduction to the Highbury crowd. Clay, Grimsdell, Smith, Walden and Seed are men of international fame and we give them a hearty welcome. We look with confidence to a game that will grip the attention and thrill the onlooker and it is only a natural hope that our boys will reveal a superiority that will receive its due reward.

A Point well-earned. By the time you read these notes you will be aware of the constitution of our team. I have reason to hope that we will be at full strength, which was not the case when we faced the determined forces of Middlesbrough at Ayresome Park. There Kennedy, Dr. Paterson and Rutherford were not able to play, but, even with such notable absentees, our boys, as a combination,

revealed their sterling worth and earned a point that was richly deserved. Middlesbrough played with the determination inspired by a knowledge of their precarious position in the League table. They were all out, and it is to the lasting credit of our defence that it never wavered. Drastic but by no means weakening changes in the Tee-siders combination failed to achieve the desired result, and Robson was ever on the spot when the thrustful Middlesbrough vanguard crashed the ball at the goal. Admirable defensive work was done by our middle men, among whom Jack Butler deserves commendation for his herculean efforts. The forwards worked hard, and to some purpose, for the Middlesbrough goal was not without its escapes, but they met a dour defence and in fairness to the Yorkshiremen, I am bound to say that a goal-less draw was quite a reasonable reflex of the play.

Baker and a Big Win. The reserves were very much in form last week-end, too, and a four—nil victory over Millwall gave the second stringers a lift in the League table. If only we could get our casualty list brought down a bit, I believe the reserve eleven would very soon be making a fight for a leading position, but the calls made by the first team have been specially heavy during the past few weeks. Baker was out again a week ago with the reserves, and did enough to suggest that we may confidently look forward to the day when the energetic little half back will report as sound as a bell. He is not quite that yet, of course. Did you notice that Dr. Paterson is to play at outside right for the F.A. team against Cambridge on the 29th of this month?

TOTTENHAM DRAW AT HIGHBURY - CLEAN AND WELL FOUGHT GAME

As was only to be expected the meeting of the Arsenal and Tottenham Hotspur at Highbury on Saturday attracted the biggest crowd of the season so far, fully 45,000 being crowded into the enclosure. Those among them who expected to see a "rough and tumble" must have gone away disappointed, as at no time did the players get unduly excited, and the outcome of a keen and well-contested game, in which there were fewer fouls than usual, was a draw of one goal each. It took the Arsenal just an hour to secure the lead, but they only held this eight minutes, a well-placed corner kick enabling Seed to draw level, a goal that ended the scoring. It was a satisfactory result on the run of the game, neither side being able to show any distinct advantage over the other on a ground rendered soft by recent heavy storms of rain.

STORY OF THE GAME

The Arsenal had the advantage of a stiffish breeze in the first half, and the 'Spurs kicked off with a slanting sun at their backs. Lindsay was the first to get a shot at goal, but Robson cleared, and on play being taken to the other end Paterson beat Smith, and centring gave Townrow a chance that was not accepted. Tottenham were showing the better combination, but their standard of play was not so good as usual, the Reds playing a good spoiling game. Good work by Rutherford and Paterson on the wings failed to bring any result, nor could the 'Spurs drive home their attack. The home goal looked like falling after play had been in progress 30 minutes, Handley sending in a fine shot, only to see Robson effect an equally fine clearance. A foul against Smith led up to some exciting play in the 'Spurs' goal, but although the Arsenal made strong efforts the defence of Clay and Forster prevailed. Some ten minutes before half-time Clay

went off with a damaged shoulder, and he was shortly followed by Blyth, who limped off lame in the right leg, but, fortunately, their injuries were not serious and both returned before the interval. In the meantime Walden had put Seed in a position to have a shot at goal, and a fine effort by Paterson caused Maddison to concede a corner. Half-time, however, came without a score to either side.

REDS TAKE THE LEAD

The first incident in the second half was a foul by Whittaker on Lindsay. The 'Spurs were applying some pressure and the Arsenal left back in stopping Lindsay brought him down unfairly. Both came down inside the penalty area, but the foul was given just outside the line. Grimsdell took the kick, and the ball was cleared by Mackie, who had to go on his knees to get his head to the ball. He was stunned by the blow, but soon recovered. Turnbull, who was playing a more subdued game than usual at centre forward, made many efforts to get through, but did not meet with success, and the first goal was credited to Townrow 15 minutes after changing over. It was Paterson who gave him the chance, as the doctor, who had more than once beaten Smith and Clay, got in a lovely centre which got Maddison in two minds, and in the scramble TOWNROW had an easy goal. This aroused the players, and some fast play ensued. Success at last rewarded the 'Spurs efforts, Seed scoring his first goal of the season and equalising matters. Elkes had looked like running through but he was tackled by Mackie and the ball went out, a corner being awarded the 'Spurs with the result stated, SEED heading into the net from a well-placed kick. There were many exciting incidents before the game ended but at the close little fault could be found with a division of the honours.

'DERBY' STAR

★ **Dr James Paterson** ★
Throughout the game 'Dr Pat' played extremely well, and with Woods was responsible for several exhibitions of classic football.

A tussle in front of Arsenal's goal.

TOTTENHAM HOTSPUR 3
Lindsay 2, Elkes
ARSENAL 0

Saturday 24th November 1923

Football League Division One

White Hart Lane

Attendance 31,624

Tottenham Hotspur

Arsenal

Manager
Peter McWilliam

Manager
Leslie Knighton

George MADDISON	1	Jock ROBSON
Tommy CLAY	2	Alex MACKIE
Matt FORSTER	3	Tom WHITTAKER
Bert SMITH	4	Alex GRAHAM
Harry LOWE	5	Jack BUTLER
Arthur GRIMSDELL	6	Billy BLYTH
Fanny WALDEN	7	Jock RUTHERFORD
Jimmy SEED	8	Frank TOWNROW
Alex LINDSAY	9	Andy YOUNG
Jack ELKES	10	Alf BAKER
Charlie HANDLEY	11	James PATERSON

Referee **Mr H W Andrews** *(Prestwich)*

BACKGROUND

While Spurs fielded the same team for the return match, Arsenal were able to recall Andy Young in place of Bobby Turnbull but that was offset by the loss of Henry Woods, whose place was taken by Alf Baker. The most notable absentee, though, was off the pitch, Arsenal manager Leslie Knighton deciding his search for new inside-forwards had to take priority.

BEFORE THE GAME

	P	W	D	L	F	A	Pts
Spurs	15	5	6	4	15	13	16
Arsenal	15	5	4	6	14	17	14

AT THE SEASON'S END

		P	W	D	L	F	A	Pts
15th	Spurs	42	12	14	16	50	56	38
19th	Arsenal	42	12	9	21	40	63	33

'DERBY' STAR
★ Alex Lindsay ★
Scored two and, according to "The Athletic News"... "he opened out the game, kept the wings in touch with him, and showed courage and command of the ball at critical moments. No one need wish to see more brilliant goals than he got - and both the reward of that touch of individualism which in its place and at the right moment is the crying need of latter-day football."

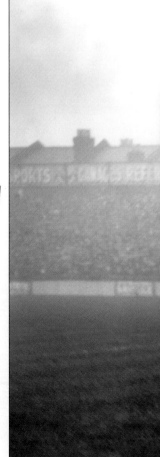

ALL RIGHTS RESERVED.
COPYRIGHT.
Tottenham Hotspur Football & Athletic Company, Limited.
Official Programme
And Record of the Club.
PRICE ONE PENNY.
Issued every Match Day.
NOVEMBER 24, 1923.
Vol. XVI. No. 18.

IF THE REF
HAD'NT STOPPED
THE FIGHT, I'D ★
★ ★ ★ ★

IF I'D HAD
FIVE MINUTES
MORE WITH
YER, I'D ★★★

STOPPIT!

TOTTENHAM WIN THE RETURN - EXCITING LAST TEN MINUTES

As was only to be expected there was a big crowd to witness the return match between Tottenham Hotspur and Arsenal on the ground of the 'Spurs on Saturday, and they were rewarded with another good game. This time, however, the efforts of the 'Spurs prevailed, and instead of a division of the spoils Tottenham claimed both points at stake by virtue of a three goals to love victory. It must be said at once that the winners were by no means the superior side as the score would appear to indicate. The first half was contested without either side being able to claim any advantage, and it was not until shortly after the change of ends that anything was scored. Then Lindsay gave the 'Spurs the lead. They held on to this advantage, but it was anyone's game, and it was with great relief that the home team's supporters saw Lindsay, by a brilliant single-handed effort, put on a second and practically made the issue safe. To crown all, Elkes found the correct direction just on time, and the big crowd of 'Spurs supporters went home in a happy frame of mind.

RUN OF THE GAME

The Arsenal started the game in the presence of some 40,000 people. Both sides took some time to settle down, and there was little to enthuse over for the first quarter of an hour. Both goalkeepers had shots to deal with, but they were easily dealt with. Later Seed gave Walden a good opening but the wingman failed as did Paterson when he tried at the other end, his shot hitting an upright. An injury to Butler led to the re-arrangement of the Red's team, Baker going right half and Graham centre half. The rival defenders played

Spurs players Alex Lindsay (left) and Charlie Handley attack the Arsenal goal.

a sound game, but there was a lot of unnecessary offside play prior to the interval, at which period neither side had scored.

LINDSAY OPENS THE SCORING

After change of ends the 'Spurs set up the first attack, and Mackie did well to relieve Elkes of the ball when a score seemed likely. The first corner kick of the game came in this half, and from it Smith shot over. It was not long, however, before Tottenham met with success, LINDSAY, who had been very active, getting through the defence of Whittaker to score a good goal some five minutes from the resumption. Robson had to save another fine shot sent in by Lindsay shortly afterwards, and then the Reds had a turn, but to no purpose, corner kicks and shots by Young and Butler all failing to produce anything. Walden caused Whittaker a lot of trouble but the 'Spurs outside right was rather apt to overdo his tricky work. With seven minutes to go a great change came over the game, as Lindsay got possession and made tracks for the Arsenal goal. There was an appeal for offside, but LINDSAY proceeded and although brought down by Mackie he had got in a direct shot that beat Robson, who had been drawn and was out of reach. Three minutes from the end ELKES made success doubly sure as he completely beat the opposing back and scored with a shot that left Robson helpless. The better team won, but it was not such a decisive win as the final score would indicate.

17

ARSENAL 1
Brain

TOTTENHAM HOTSPUR 0

Saturday 25th October 1924

Football League Division One

Highbury

Attendance 51,000

Arsenal		Tottenham Hotspur
Manager **Leslie Knighton**		Manager **Peter McWilliam**

Jock ROBSON	1	Bill HINTON
Alex MACKIE	2	Matt FORSTER
Andy KENNEDY	3	Cecil POYNTON
Billy MILNE	4	Bert SMITH
Jack BUTLER	5	Harry LOWE
Bob JOHN	6	Sid WHITE
Jock RUTHERFORD	7	Frank OSBORNE
Jimmy BRAIN	8	Jimmy SEED
Henry WOODS	9	Alex LINDSAY
Jimmy RAMSEY	10	Jack ELKES
Joe TONER	11	Jimmy DIMMOCK

Referee **Mr J W D Fowler** (Sunderland)

BEFORE THE GAME

	P	W	D	L	F	A	Pts
Arsenal	11	5	2	4	11	11	12
Spurs	11	3	4	4	11	10	10

Joint League leaders at that time were Huddersfield and Notts County, ahead of West Bromwich Albion, Sunderland and Birmingham. Also in the top division were Bury, Cardiff, Burnley, Sheffield United and Preston North End.

"Despite the fact that the Election is claiming the attentions of so many of us, we venture to think that such an attractive event as our match with the 'Spurs' today will provide a pleasant break in a week of high political tension. At least football knows no politics and, if it engenders partisan feeling, it is a healthy condition of rivalry and a welcome distraction from the more serious phases of life."

An extract from the official programme...
'football knows no politics' - those were days!

BACKGROUND

Victory in the opening three matches of the season had given Arsenal their best start since before the Great War, but they had been unable to maintain such form and slipped to a mid-table position. Goalscoring was the problem. They had failed in a bid to sign Preston's England centre-forward, Tom Roberts and against Aston Villa a week earlier had recalled transfer-listed Bobby Turnbull while manager Knighton was away on another scouting mission. For Spurs' visit Henry Woods was recalled and Jimmy Brain given his debut. Alex Mackie continued in place of Alf Baker, still injured. Spurs had also started well with victory in their first two games, but only tasted success once in the next nine outings as they too found scoring a major problem. Tommy Clay was still out, as were long-term injury victims Arthur Grimsdell and Buchanan Sharp. Jimmy Seed was only passed fit shortly before a kick-off that had looked in doubt until an hour before the start when fog lifted.

B Bennison in '**The Daily Telegraph**' reported...

ARSENAL BEAT TOTTENHAM

From the beginning to the end of the game, watched by 50,000 people at Highbury on Saturday afternoon, Tottenham Hotspur against the Arsenal courted disaster. They were all wrong, no more than half a team, all lop-sided; and they were fortunate not to be beaten by more than the only goal scored. Tottenham were a side with but one forward of outstanding ability. Their half-backs were inferior to the local three, and, of course, Clay's absence meant ever so much. The Arsenal may urge that their visitors were only as good as they were permitted to be, but although they improved tremendously upon recent displays, the little cleverness shown by the Spurs was to me at least surprising. They failed to pull all together; they lacked confidence in themselves; had it not been for Elkes their attack would have been without character, for Dimmock, at outside left, was no more than a very plain and obvious footballer, mastered by Milne, a half-back of high quality. Lindsay against Butler was completely out of it, and only occasionally did Seed and Osborne do anything out of the ordinary. Tottenham were made to appear as unlike their traditional selves as it was possible to make them. They failed to give finality to whatever ideas they had, and I may only congratulate them upon coming out of the match with but the loss of a goal. It could not have been that the occasion and the excitement of it all were too much for them; they were simply not good enough to beat or to draw with the Arsenal.

Having ventured so much, it may be inferred that the game was so one-sided as to be disappointing; it was not that. It was an affair in which, although one side was markedly superior to the other, they had many arresting features, and as a fight between near neighbours it was, in that there was no serious departure from the spirit of sport, one that I

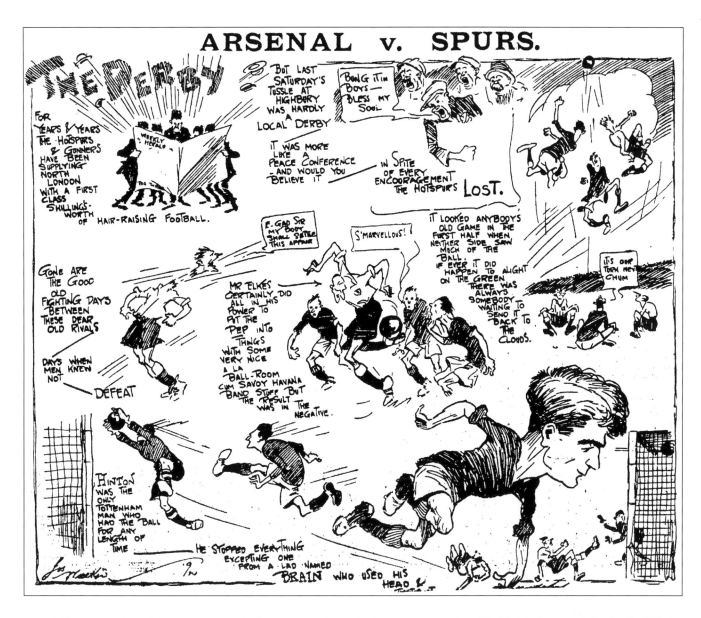

ARSENAL v. SPURS.

enjoyed. There was nothing of the win, tie or wrangle about it. The goal which decided the match was got shortly after the change of ends by Brain, who was making his first appearance in League football as partner of Rutherford. There was, I found, among the camp followers of Tottenham more than a suspicion that this score should not have been allowed because of off-side. My opinion is that it was a perfectly good goal. It came about in this way. Rutherford, taking a sweeping pass, outpaced Poynton, who was apparently under the impression that the Arsenal forward would be pulled up by the referee, and centring the ball perfectly, offered to **BRAIN** an opportunity to head it into the net. And this the young man did, Hinton, as good a goalkeeper as I have seen this season, being helpless to save.

NEWCOMER TO FOOTBALL

Brain, apart from capturing the Tottenham goal, convinced me that he has much football in him. He was not always correct in his passing at the start, and I feared that the ordeal would be too much for him, but he so got the hang of things as to serve Rutherford and his side admirably. I would not have it thought that Brain is a genius, and that it is certain that he will work wonders. He is a very promising novice, and, if I am not mistaken, has a natural aptitude for the game. Now and then he controlled the ball very well, and gave the impression that he has got more than an elementary notion how best to build the kind of combination that makes for progress. I will not say that he is a better player than Neil, whose place he took; there is much that Brain may only learn by experience, but he has so surely the ways of a footballer of uncommon kind as to warrant a generous trial alongside Rutherford. And of Rutherford I must say that he was,

remembering his long service, entirely wonderful. I doubt whether there is a more expert corner-kicker, and his centres remain a model of accuracy. Given the right type of retriever, and Rutherford may not fear comparison with any other outside right in the game.

Woods returned to the Arsenal attack to make it more of a decided force than it was against Aston Villa; and Ramsey and Toner also played as well as I have ever seen them play. I liked the Arsenal forwards in this game, and Milne, Butler and John were in nearly ever particular better than Tottenham's Smith, Lowe and White. Butler I thought to be one of the most improved centre-halves of the season. He appears to have learned the wisdom of keeping the ball on the ground, and is more enterprising, more daring than he used to be. He gave unto Lindsay, the leader of the Spurs, not one little bit of rope; I do not remember Lindsay when he has been so ineffective as he was on Saturday. It was as if he were playing in hobbles. Only Elkes of the visiting forwards distinguished himself; the rest, for the most part, had a very bad day. There was a weakness in the Tottenham half-back line and of the two full backs I preferred Poynton. Forster was given to kicking too hard. As I have suggested, the Spurs have in Hinton a brilliant goalkeeper. He had no such backs as the Arsenal pair, Kennedy and Mackie (these two did splendidly); but one always felt that it would only be an exceptional shot that beat him.

'DERBY' STAR

★ Jimmy Brain ★

Scored the only goal of the game on his League debut for Arsenal, the first of many for the club.

18

TOTTENHAM HOTSPUR 2
Dimmock, Elkes

ARSENAL 0

Saturday 28th February 1925

Football League Division One

White Hart Lane

Attendance 29,457

Tottenham Hotspur

Arsenal

Manager
Peter McWilliam

Manager
Leslie Knighton

Tottenham Hotspur		Arsenal
Bill HINTON	1	Jock ROBSON
Matt FORSTER	2	Alex MACKIE
Bob McDONALD	3	Andy KENNEDY
Bert SMITH	4	Alf BAKER
Harry SKITT	5	Jack BUTLER
Jimmy SKINNER	6	Bob JOHN
Andy THOMPSON	7	Sid HOAR
Jimmy SEED	8	Andy NEIL
Bill LANE	9	Jimmy BRAIN
Jack ELKES	10	Billy BLYTH
Jimmy DIMMOCK	11	Sammy HADEN

Referee **Mr J W D Fowler** (Sunderland)

BEFORE THE GAME

	P	W	D	L	F	A	Pts
Spurs	29	9	10	10	38	33	28
Arsenal	28	10	4	14	32	37	24

AT THE SEASON'S END

		P	W	D	L	F	A	Pts
12th	Spurs	42	15	12	15	52	43	42
20th	Arsenal	42	14	5	23	46	58	33

Jack Butler

BACKGROUND

Without a victory in the new year and knocked out of the FA Cup by West Ham in a first round second replay, five successive League defeats had plunged Arsenal into the midst of the relegation battle. Having lost 0-5 at home to Huddersfield in their last game and with Andy Kennedy and Jack Butler available again, Leslie Knighton made wholesale changes. Jock Robson was restored in place of Dan Lewis, Alf Baker tried at half-back and Billy Blyth at inside-forward. Jimmy Brain was asked to lead the line with Andy Neil recalled and Sammy Haden replacing Joe Toner. Beaten only once in their last eight games mid-table Spurs were in the middle of their best run of the season. The only setback had been a disappointing FA Cup third round replay defeat at Blackburn two days earlier in which Tommy Clay and Arthur Grimsdell had both been injured.

ARSENAL FORWARDS FAIL.
POINTS FOR TOTTENHAM.
BY OUR SPECIAL CORRESPONDENT.

For half the game between the Hotspur and the Arsenal the spectators at Tottenham saw a fine contest which was played in excellent spirit. The Hotspur forwards were just so good as to make it essential that the Arsenal backs should kick the ball as quickly as possible in whatever direction they were running. That is why the home team deserved their 2—0 victory. It was in the second half when Tottenham got their first goal. Some fine work by Seed was ended with an excellent pass to Thompson, who had the way clear for a centre to the front of the goal-mouth. The ball dropped at the feet of Dimmock, who had no difficulty in scoring from an inside-right position. After that Brain, who was at centre forward for the Arsenal, had an easy chance of equalising, but he shot straight at Hinton from a distance of about eight yards. Then Elkes got a goal with a splendid shot after a clever dribble, and so the Hotspur secured the two points.

Forward inability was the cause of the Arsenal's failure. There was enough looseness about Forster and Macdonald at back for the Hotspur to be taken advantage of had the Arsenal possessed an attack which could have been looked upon as efficient. Brain is far better at inside right than he is in the centre of the forwards, and Neil appears to have lost nearly all the good form he used to display when with Brighton. Hoar was the one forward on the losers' side who showed excellence. Still, he could not do all that he might have done, for he got the ball so seldom, and often it was sent to him in such a manner that only a really clever forward could have made use of it.

On the other hand, the Hotspur forwards were a fast and tricky set. They seemed to be playing well within themselves all through. Thompson has established himself at outside right, for so long as he maintains the form he displayed in this game there is no need to hurry Osborne out of his enforced retirement. Lane did one or two clever things at centre forward, but the best-watched forward in the winners' team was Seed, who seemed likely to score every time he received the ball. Elkes was always dangerous, and he gave Dimmock quite an easy time of it, because he did not always pass the ball out to his partner when to do so would have been good football. Hinton made some smart saves, but ran out of goal on several occasions with poor judgment, as if he could not quite trust his backs to do their work.

Report from the "Daily Telegraph".

SPURS TOO GOOD FOR ARSENAL

Tottenham deserved to beat the Arsenal at White Hart Lane on Saturday because they were easily the better of two moderate sides but they did so little shooting - and that little was very feeble - that until Dimmock scored midway through the second half there was every indication that the Spurs would repeat their exasperating habit of outplaying a team yet not winning. It was a surprise when they finally won by two clear goals.

It was not a good game - but that is usual nowadays when big London clubs clash. The first half, indeed, was a dull affair, though greatly fought. Each side endeavoured to put a strangle-hold on the other, and out of a hurly-burly of fierce and frequently aimless kicking, of defensive tactics and constant throw-ins due to the Arsenal's over-cautious backs, and with a full measure of offside added there came just one real thrill - when Dimmock gave Elkes a fine chance, and the inside left lofted the ball against the bar.

ONLY ONE TEAM

But when the 'Spurs settled down to thoughtful football in the second half, concentrating on the ball and not too closely on opposing players, there was only one team to look at.

Jack Elkes scored Spurs' second with a great dribble and finish.

The Arsenal's reorganised side had a bad time, and that it did not collapse altogether was due to some terribly bad finishing by the Tottenham forwards.

The Arsenal had practically a new forward line. For ten minutes after the kick-off it promised to do big things; then it deteriorated rapidly until it became really bad. Brain was a poor leader because he never made proper use of his wings, and when the ball came to him in the penalty area he preferred to pass rather than take the responsibility of shooting. Neil was another who made such a fetish of passing that his shooting suffered.

Blyth, tried once again at inside left, was just the fearless sort of player who might have been dangerous, but a leg injury, received early in the game, took all the fire out of him. The wing forwards, Hoar and Haden, were clever, one could see, but they were starved.

With an inefficient attack, a big strain naturally was thrown upon the Arsenal defence - and it often cracked up. Baker, restored to the half-back line after a long term of service as a back, worked like a hen, but his ardour sometimes led him to stray from his real duties. It will take time before he becomes thoroughly accustomed to his change of work. John found the task of holding Seed and Thompson a bit too much for him, and that the new back formation of Mackie and Kennedy was not strong was evident from the great amount of kicking out indulged in, which frequently spoiled the game as a spectacle.

ATTEMPTED TOO MUCH

Tottenham really should have done better. They were superior in each line of defence, and this meant that their forwards saw quite a lot of the ball. In the second half, indeed, they always seemed to have it. But their attacks broke down one after another because the inside men would attempt too much. When the ball was swung about the Arsenal defence got into nasty tangles, and it was puzzling why Tottenham did not always make use of a more open style of attack when they had in Thompson and Dimmock two wing forwards who by their speed and cleverness could beat the defence on two occasions in every three.

Dimmock, in fact, was the outstanding player - the only one to play a great game all through. He was absolutely fearless, very fast and versatile, and had such fine control of the ball, even when going at top speed, that he did almost what he liked with Baker and Mackie. Not only did he get past and centre in first class style, but he frequently cut in with the ball in a most dangerous manner. After he had got the first goal he made one glorious dribble beating man after man until only Robson, the goalkeeper was left. Very unselfishly, but also unwisely, he passed across the goal enough to give another the honour of scoring, but the chance was not taken, and a brilliant piece of work thus came to nothing.

Dimmock's goal, however, was really due to Seed, although the wing man showed fine anticipation in running into the centre when Seed charged out to the left with the ball at his feet. When the ball came across to the opposite wing Thompson sent it back to **DIMMOCK** who, from an ideal position, scored an easy goal. Dimmock then gave a simple chance to Elkes after cleverly drawing the defence, but this was not taken, and the scoring seemed to have ended when, a minute from time, **ELKES** made amends by making a great dribble and finishing with a shot that well beat Robson.

19

ARSENAL 0

TOTTENHAM HOTSPUR 1
Dimmock

Arsenal

Manager
Herbert Chapman

Tottenham Hotspur

Manager
Peter McWilliam

Jock ROBSON	1	Bill HINTON
Alex MACKIE	2	Tommy CLAY
Andy KENNEDY	3	Matt FORSTER
Billy MILNE	4	Jimmy SKINNER
Jack BUTLER	5	Harry SKITT
Bob JOHN	6	Arthur GRIMSDELL
Sid HOAR	7	Andy THOMPSON
Charlie BUCHAN	8	Jimmy SEED
Donald COCK	9	Alex LINDSAY
Jimmy RAMSEY	10	Charlie HANDLEY
Joe TONER	11	Jimmy DIMMOCK

Referee **Mr D Hitson** (West Bromwich)

BACKGROUND

The summer of 1925 saw major changes both at Highbury and in the rules of the game. Leslie Knighton was dismissed as Arsenal manager and replaced by Herbert Chapman, a former Spurs forward who had just led Huddersfield Town to their second successive League championship. He immediately set about imposing his style on Highbury, signing Charlie Buchan from Sunderland for £2,000 plus £100 for every goal he scored and installing the ex-England forward as captain. For the opening game of the season Chapman paired Buchan with Donald Cock, signed from Notts County for £4,000 immediately after Arsenal's defeat at White Hart Lane in February but victim of a broken leg against his former club on only his second outing. Despite five defeats in their last six games that left Spurs with nothing better than a mid-table finish they had made no change in personnel. The major point of interest for the new season was the change in the off-side rule. Only two, instead of the previous three, defenders between the foremost attacker and goal were now required. Arsenal seemed to have devised no new tactics for such a radical change but Spurs played centre-half Harry Skitt deep, more a third full-back than an attacking midfielder.

BEFORE THE GAME

	P	W	D	L	F	A	Pts
Arsenal	0	0	0	0	0	0	0
Spurs	0	0	0	0	0	0	0

What a great picture as the legendary Charlie Buchan leads Arsenal out on his debut - the opening match of the 1925/26 season.

The introduction to the "Daily Telegraph" report on the game makes you think when you look at what the spectators and players were wearing...

'The 53,000 onlookers who saw Tottenham Hotspur defeat the Arsenal by 1-0 at Highbury sweltered and perspired in the scorching sun. But they we all very happy, and they had much to enthuse over, for the game abounded in thrills'.

GREAT DUEL AT HIGHBURY

There was only one goal in the game at Highbury when the Arsenal met Tottenham Hotspur and as this was scored by Dimmock, the outside left for the visitors, both points were taken away by the Spurs.

The result was a great disappointment to the supporters of the home club, who had confidently counted on Buchan leading his men to victory.

When Buchan, the appointed captain of the Arsenal club, led his men on the field there were fully 50,000 present, and they gave him a tremendous welcome. The turnstiles were still clicking merrily, and later in the afternoon it was officially announced that the attendance was 53,000, a great send-off from a financial point of view.

The game was worthy of so great an assembly, for there were ninety minutes of football played in a spirit that proved the keenest rivalry was compatible with the finest sportsmanship. Only once in the hour and a half did the referee's whistle blow for a foul, and that was for a technical offence against a Tottenham player that might well have been passed over.

It was not, however, a milk-and-water match. There was plenty of hefty charging, but it was all scrupulously fair, and the referee did right not to penalise it. It is the more pleasurable to be able to write in terms of unstinted praise of both teams in the matter of sportsmanship because so often when local rivals are in opposition there are incidents that could well be spared.

Judging the game from the point of view of the average spectator, who wishes to see a non-stop match, there is no doubt that the alteration to the off-side law must be rated a success, so far as Saturday's game proves anything. The stoppages were few in number and the off-sides that were given were mostly following attacks on the goals, when a player happened to be slow in returning to his position.

That they did not score was not altogether their fault. They made many praiseworthy attempts, but Hinton was in an unbeatable mood, and he greatly enhanced his reputation not only by what he did but by the manner in which he did it. He had in front of him a fine pair of backs, Clay being the best on the field, while at half the work of Grimsdell and his colleagues was of high quality. There was a sustained duel between the rival captains, and the determination and anticipation of Grimsdell brought him out on top. It was due to him that not more was seen of Buchan, although the latter by his strategy and adroit passes was of great value to his side.

The Tottenham forwards were slow in getting together, but they were thrown somewhat out of gear by an early accident to Handley which set him limping, and in the second half he changed places with Dimmock. Lindsay was a trier but finished poorly, his ball control being disappointing and it was Seed and Thompson on the right who were the more dangerous Tottenham wing.

A heading the duel between Arsenals' Charlie Buchan and Tottenham's Tommy Clay.

NOT GIVEN TIME

As against this there was not so much combination as usual, but then there were two reasons for this. In the first place there is often very little of this when two local teams face each other, and in the second place there were two tenacious sets of defenders, neither of whom stood upon ceremony, and the forwards were not allowed time to work out their plans, nor were they afforded the necessary room in which to manœuvre.

Tottenham were the better side so far as there was any combination, but this was amply compensated for by the vim and determination of the home side, whose forwards gave a whole-hearted display that was in welcome contrast to so many of their unconvincing games last season.

STURDY DEFENCE

There was not a weak spot in the Arsenal side. In the enforced absence of Baker, Mackie and Kennedy were the backs, and they stood up in sturdy fashion to the onslaughts of their opponents. The Arsenal were also well served by their middle line players, and of the forwards Cock, who was a most industrious leader, was ever prominent, excellent work also being done by Hoar and Toner.

There was no scoring in the first half, but Lindsay and Dimmock should have found the net for Tottenham. After ends were changed the Arsenal put on severe pressure and the Tottenham goal had numerous narrow escapes. There were twenty-five minutes to go when **DIMMOCK**, receiving from Seed, defeated three opponents who sought to arrest his progress and then drove the ball squarely between the posts with a great shot.

20

TOTTENHAM HOTSPUR 1
Thompson

ARSENAL 1
Baker

Saturday 2nd January 1926

Football League Division One

White Hart Lane

Attendance 43,221

Tottenham Hotspur / Arsenal

Manager		Manager
Peter McWilliam		**Herbert Chapman**

Bill KAINE	1	Bill HARPER
Tommy CLAY	2	Alex MACKIE
Matt FORSTER	3	Bob JOHN
Bert SMITH	4	Alf BAKER
Harry SKITT	5	Jack BUTLER
Jimmy SKINNER	6	Billy BLYTH
Andy THOMPSON	7	Sid HOAR
Alex LINDSAY	8	Charlie BUCHAN
Frank OSBORNE	9	Jimmy BRAIN
Jack ELKES	10	Andy NEIL
Jimmy DIMMOCK	11	Sammy HADEN

Referee **Mr D H Asson** (West Bromwich)

BACKGROUND

By the time of Herbert Chapman's second derby he had already turned Arsenal from relegation candidates to championship challengers. Top of the table, Donald Cock and Jimmy Ramsey had been discarded after the opening game of the season to be replaced by Jimmy Brain and Andy Neil. The move had paid dividends with Brain, top scorer, striking up an immediate rapport with Charlie Buchan. Chapman had begun to construct a team to his liking and in November 1925 persuaded Henry Norris to follow the investment in Charlie Buchan with the £4,000 signing of goalkeeper, Bill Harper from Hibernian. Both Buchan and Blyth were doubtful right up to kick-off. Spurs were well up the table but already beginning to suffer from the loss of inspirational captain Arthur Grimsdell who had broken his leg at Leicester in October 1925. Jack Elkes and Jimmy Dimmock were able to return after missing the Boxing Day fixture with Birmingham. Dimmock was far from over the effects of tonsillitis, but with Jimmy Seed injured his inspirational wing play was urgently needed.

BEFORE THE GAME

	P	W	D	L	F	A	Pts
Arsenal	23	13	4	6	52	36	30
Spurs	23	11	4	8	45	47	26

AT THE SEASON'S END

		P	W	D	L	F	A	Pts
2nd	Arsenal	42	22	8	12	87	63	52
15th	Spurs	42	15	9	18	66	79	39

Spurs' Jimmy Dimmock rushes Arsenal goalkeeper Bill Harper after the latter had saved a shot.

'The Sporting Life and Sportsman' reported...

SPURS CONTENT WITH DRAW
- ARSENAL'S RALLY IN SECOND HALF
- FOULS TOO FREQUENT AT TOTTENHAM

Tottenham Hotspur were not able on Saturday, in their return match at White Hart Lane with the Arsenal, to repeat their victory of the opening Saturday of the season at Highbury. The points were shared, a result with which Tottenham should be well satisfied in view of the superiority of their opponents in the second half of the game.

While the visiting club was at full strength, the Spurs were without Seed, who was injured the previous Saturday, and, of course, Hinton and Grimsdell, but the latter was one of the most interested of the 44,000 spectators of the match, and he is making excellent progress towards recovery from the broken leg caused at Leicester in October.

Lindsay deputised for Seed, and in the first half he did exceedingly well, but before the interval he was injured in a collision, and although he kept on the field he was severely handicapped, and the effectiveness of the right wing, the best on the field before he was hurt, largely faded away.

The spirit in which the game was fought was not so satisfactory as at Highbury in August. There was not anything to complain about in the first half, but after ends were changed there were far too many fouls, and it was obvious that some of the players were rattled.

There was also a vast difference in the quality of the play in the two periods. The first forty-five minutes provided delightful football, in which science was the distinguishing feature, but in the closing three-quarters of an hour there was a marked falling-off, and the game developed to a large extent into a kick and rush business, and in this method the Arsenal were unquestionably the more effective side. They also served up at times very smart combination, and as they were splendidly supported by their half-backs they put great pressure on the Tottenham goal.

SELDOM DANGEROUS

Their chances for scoring, however, were not nearly so numerous as those presented to the Spurs in the first half hour, when the visitors were outplayed. They could not get together and it was seldom that they were dangerous, although a couple of rushes might well have led to concrete successes but for the style in which Clay and Forster covered their goal, and the coolness shown by Kaine, who gave a satisfactory display between the posts.

It was, however, Harper, the Scottish international, the Arsenal's last line defender, who took the eye most. He was a busy man in the first twenty minutes, and he rescued his side from threatened disaster on several occasions, added to which he had good fortune in shots which beat him just missing their intended billet.

Mackie and John were a determined pair of backs, and the Arsenal half-backs, after a poor first half, came out in great style, and largely kept the Tottenham attack in subjection. While the Spurs were well on top their backs and middle line players were most impressive, but when their opponents were making such desperate efforts to get the lead there was a lot of miss-kicking and much weak clearing.

Skinner was prominent at half, but Skitt destroyed much of his possible usefulness by playing throughout as a third back with the result that the opposing inside men found their path of advance much more easy than it should have been, added to which the home inside-forwards did not get the ball nearly so often as they should have done.

This cartoon appeared in the following week's Tottenham programme.

OFF-SIDE DECISIONS

There were many off-side decisions, all but one against the Spurs, and in some of them the referee was not at all happy, nor was he in giving free kicks for hands from obviously accidental handling. He certainly adopted the right course in giving a foul for anything that even approached an infringement of Law 9, as leniency would have been a mistake in view of the evident feeling there was in the game.

Tottenham opened the scoring four minutes from the start, Thompson leading up to the goal by a smart run and centre which Harper fisted away, but it went to Lindsay, who got his head to it, and simultaneously he came into collision with the goalkeeper, who had followed the ball up. Mackie partially cleared almost from under the bar, but the ball went to **THOMPSON**, who banged it into the net, Mackie making a fruitless attempt to save, while Harper was on the ground when the ball passed between the posts.

The Spurs should have had two more goals in the next five minutes, but Osborne and Lindsay both missed fine openings, and there was no more scoring until the twelfth minute of the second half, when an absurd decision against Clay for hands was converted into a goal by **BAKER**, who shot hard and true into the net with a powerful low drive.

Osborne headed over at the other end with Harper beaten, but generally from this point the Arsenal were on top, and the home goal had many narrow escapes.

ONE FOR THE REFEREE...

"Probably the coolest man on the field was the referee. His face gives the impression of his being deferential even if it does not suggest he is too easy going. But he had a smile that would not come off. He ruled the final at Wembley in 1923 - the Invasion Final - when crowd and passions broke loose. Mr Asson had my confidence and if I did not agree with hime on certain occasions I would bow to his decision, appreciating he was in a better position to judge than I was."

- The "Weekly Herald" reporter records his respect for the West Bromwich official.

STAKES DIVIDED.

At the local Derby on Saturday last, some well-known horses were entered. "Offside Tactics" ridden by Gunner, and "Finesse" ridden by Cocky, dead heated, "Muddy" and "Push and Go" were second and third. Owing to the recent rains it was very heavy going.

21

ARSENAL 2
Butler, Brain

TOTTENHAM HOTSPUR 4
Osborne 2, Seed, Handley

Saturday 18th December 1926

Football League Division One

Highbury

Attendance 49,429

Arsenal		Tottenham Hotspur
Manager **Herbert Chapman**		Manager **Peter McWilliam**
Bill HARPER	1	Jimmy SMITH
Tom PARKER	2	Tommy CLAY
Bob JOHN	3	Matt FORSTER
Bill SEDDON	4	Bert SMITH
Jack BUTLER	5	Jack ELKES
Billy BLYTH	6	Alex LINDSAY
Joe HULME	7	Andy THOMPSON
Jimmy BRAIN	8	Jimmy SEED
Charlie BUCHAN	9	Frank OSBORNE
Jimmy RAMSEY	10	Charlie HANDLEY
Sammy HADEN	11	Jimmy DIMMOCK

Referee **Mr H W Sykes** (Northampton)

BACKGROUND

The promise Arsenal showed finishing second to Huddersfield Town in 1925-26 did not continue the following season but Chapman was still building a team to his liking. Joe Hulme had arrived from Blackburn for £3,500 in February 1926, Tom Parker from Southampton a month later. They had started with four points from their first two games but were always likely to concede a goal, their goalless draw at Birmingham the week before Spurs' visit was only their second clean sheet of the season, and too often had to settle for one point when two were needed. Top scorer Jimmy Brain returned after missing the game at St Andrews. Spurs were an average team, capable of stunning football at times, as when they beat Sheffield Wednesday 7-3 and Birmingham 6-1, but at others, likely to collapse, particularly away from home as evidenced by a 1-4 defeat at Derby and a 0-5 trouncing at Burnley. With only one point from their last four games they could have done with their top scorer, Jimmy Blair, but he was out injured.

BEFORE THE GAME

	P	W	D	L	F	A	Pts
Spurs	19	8	5	6	42	35	21
Arsenal	19	6	8	5	35	36	20

"The meeting of the Arsenal and the Spurs at Highbury on Saturday proved a veritable battle of giants, and although there was no mistaking the superiority of the Spurs after the early stages, the Arsenal stubbornly contested every inch of the way, and were always giving promise of pulling the game out of the fire." - The Sporting Life.

Tottenham's Matt Forster and Tommy Clay race for possession with Charlie Buchan.

Jack Butler (hidden behind Spurs goalkeeper Jimmy Smith) scores Arsenal's first goal with Charlie Buchan looking on.

'Wayfarer' in 'The Athletic News' under the headline...

SPURS MAKE ARSENAL LOOK SMALL
- SPURS BRILLIANT RALLY AGAINST THE ARSENAL

When rivals clash the football is not always of the best and purest, but Highbury staged a match on Saturday which will linger long in the memories of the 53,000 spectators who witnessed it. It was a game which created 53,000 football missionaries, so high was the standard of play, so admirable was the sportsmanship of the 22 players engaged.

The pace was so terrific that few dreamed it could be maintained, yet there was no flagging right up to the finish. There were plenty of hard knocks, but not one really bad foul, plenty of goals, a penalty kick which gave Harper a chance to strengthen his claim to be one of the world's best goalkeepers, and minor thrills in plenty.

The 'Spurs, overwhelmed at first by wave after wave of fiercely directed attacks, were two goals down after fifteen minutes play, but they remained true to 'Spurs' tradition. They did not lay aside the rapier for the bludgeon. They continued according to plan - the best McWilliam plan - and ultimately they gained the victory by 4-2.

They won because their forward play was superior to that of their rivals, for whom Buchan played a lone hand. The Arsenal badly need the help of at least one more class inside forward. Their weakness was thrown up into bold relief by the brilliance of the 'Spurs.

FOUR MINUTES, THREE GOALS

J. Smith, in the Tottenham goal, left the impression that a big crowd and a big occasion had a tendency to unsettle him. He made a present of the first goal to Butler, who so rarely figures among the scorers that no doubt this reasonable gift was appreciated. BUTLER, having dribbled to the right of goal, sent in a swerving shot which Smith allowed to slip through his hands. Brain was at hand to make sure, but it was Butler's goal.

The first three goals came in a period of four minute's play. Hulme placed a corner which was only half cleared and Ramsey headed goalwards. BRAIN, standing only a yard from the line, neatly headed the ball on into the net.

MASTERS IN CONFLICT

From this point the 'Spurs began to shape like winners. There was method in everything they essayed, and behind a well-balanced line stood the veteran Tom Clay, engaging that other master, Charlie Buchan, in a series of epic duels and winning most of them.

Seed paved the way for OSBORNE to score the 'Spurs' first - a goal that showed that the Tottenham centre's reputation for not liking to be bustled is not deserved. With Blyth on the ground, a temporary casualty, Osborne sent Thompson away and Harper was prevented from getting the centre clear. First Dimmock's shot was charged down and then SEED drove the ball hard into the net.

Dimmock a minute or two later was seen weaving his way towards goal. He hopped nimbly over Seddon's legs, swerved round Parker, and was making for goal when the ex-Southampton back brought him down from behind - a technical rather than a malicious foul perhaps, but unquestionably a case for a penalty kick.

Dimmock's shot Harper saved with a full length dive and whilst still on the ground he saved two more "close up" drives from Handley in a manner which brought his colleagues clustering round with congratulations. This rung the curtain down on the most thrilling forty-five minutes football I have seen for a long time.

THE REAL SPURS

It took the 'Spurs only ten minutes in the second half to consolidate the position already half won. OSBORNE scored after very nearly bungling the opening and the fourth and last goal came from HANDLEY, who got under control an awkwardly bouncing ball, following a throw-in by Smith, and a centre by Thompson.

When the Spurs are in this mood they are good enough for anything, there was not a weakness fore or aft, with Clay, Elkes, Bert Smith, Dimmock and Osborne the outstanding men.

For the Arsenal only Buchan was a forward success. Butler was the most useful of the half-backs for Seddon was immature, though promising, and Blyth would wander out of position. Parker has got back to the form which first drew the attention of the F. A. Selection Committee to the Dell, and Harper did other feats of valour besides the penalty miracle.

22

TOTTENHAM HOTSPUR 0

ARSENAL 4
Brain 2, Tricker 2

Saturday 7th May 1927

Football League Division One

White Hart Lane

Attendance 29,555

Tottenham Hotspur

Manager
Billy Minter

Arsenal

Manager
Herbert Chapman

Jock BRITTON	1	John MOODY
Matt FORSTER	2	Tom PARKER
Cecil POYNTON	3	Andy KENNEDY
Harry SKITT	4	Herbie ROBERTS
Jack ELKES	5	Jack BUTLER
Arthur GRIMSDELL	6	Bob JOHN
Frank OSBORNE	7	Joe HULME
Taffy O'CALLAGHAN	8	Billy BLYTH
Arthur SANDERS	9	Reg TRICKER
Charlie HANDLEY	10	Jimmy BRAIN
Jimmy DIMMOCK	11	Harry PEEL

*Referee **Mr H W Sykes** (Northampton)*

'DERBY' STAR

★ Reg Tricker ★

India-born Tricker became a hero by scoring two goals in only his fourth game for Arsenal. He played only another eight League games for the Gunners, taking his goals total to five, before moving on to Clapton Orient.

'DERBY' STAR

THAT WAS THEN

★ Billy Minter's elevation to manager in February 1927 left Spurs seeking a new trainer. They did not need to look far taking on George Hardy, 16 years with Arsenal but sacked by Herbert Chapman after shouting tactical instructions to the players during a game.

BACKGROUND

The last match of the season saw beaten FA Cup finalists Arsenal field three reserves in Herbie Roberts, Reg Tricker and John Moody. With Charlie Buchan injured Tricker, recently signed from Charlton, was tried at centre-forward and top-scorer Jimmy Brain moved inside. Spurs were able to field their strongest eleven, most interest being shown in the re-appearance of captain Arthur Grimsdell, playing his second game after returning from a broken leg. A mid-table clash that was only of relevance to the clubs in deciding which would finish with the higher League placing, at least Herbert Chapman had something resting on the outcome. He would get a £250 bonus if Arsenal finished in the top half of the table.

BEFORE THE GAME

	P	W	D	L	F	A	Pts
Spurs	41	16	9	16	76	74	41
Arsenal	41	16	9	16	73	86	41

AT THE SEASON'S END

		P	W	D	L	F	A	Pts
11th	Arsenal	42	17	9	16	77	86	43
13th	Spurs	42	16	9	17	76	78	41

SPURS' HUMILIATION.

DASHING ARSENAL'S BIG WIN.

That direct methods are often more profitable in football was proved again on Saturday, when in the "Local Derby" between Spurs and Arsenal at Tottenham, the home team suffered a humiliating defeat by the big margin of 4—0. On the one side we had a team making football as difficult as it was possible, frittering away chances and making themselves hot and bothered by trying to weave patterns but merely tying themselves into knots; and on the other hand, there were the Arsenal with direct methods, encouraged by mistakes in a perplexed defence and securing an apparently runaway victory. I asked a Spurs' director after the match what he thought of it all and he shook with merriment. He said that he could not take the game seriously. His team had had as much, if not more, of the play than Arsenal, had forced the play for the greater part of the time, and the other side had coolly walked off with the plums.

From "The Weekly Herald"

ARSENAL'S BIG WIN
- TOTTENHAM HOTSPUR SOUNDLY BEATEN IN FINE GAME

The last game of the season at White Hart Lane was played in beautiful weather, and before about forty thousand people, who saw Tottenham Hotspur well and truly beaten by the Arsenal, who scored four goals without reply.

This victory was all the more meritorious by reason of the fact that Buchan, owing to injury, was not able to turn out for the visitors. In his absence Tricker played at centre-forward, Brain at inside-left and Blyth at inside-right, and the result was in every way most satisfactory. Also the Arsenal were without Lewis, whose place in goal was taken by Moody.

Winning the toss, Tottenham made the Arsenal face a strong sun, but they themselves had to play against a gusty wind. The start was quite sensational, for only about six minutes had gone before **BRAIN**, from a centre by Peel, headed through to give Arsenal the lead, and a few minutes later unaccountable hesitancy on the part of the Tottenham defenders led to **TRICKER** making the visitors two goals up. Then for a period Tottenham showed their best form during the match, and after Handley had shot just over, the home side forced two corners, but without success, for AW

Sanders, the centre-forward, also shot too high when well placed. All things considered, however, the Arsenal were the more impressive side, and close on half-time another centre by Peel enabled **BRAIN** to rush the ball into the net.

After the interval the play was not so interesting. In many ways Tottenham showed cleverness, but against a resolute defence their finishing was woefully weak, though on one occasion Dimmock got in a mighty shot which crashed against the cross-bar. About fifteen minutes from the end **TRICKER** got the Arsenal's fourth goal in clever fashion, he heading into the corner of the net from a centre by Hulme, and in the time remaining the visitors, though not all out, had no difficulty in preventing Tottenham from scoring. It was a thoroughly interesting game, and fought out in the best possible spirit.

SPURS v. ARSENAL.

23

ARSENAL 1
Hoar

TOTTENHAM HOTSPUR 1
O'Callaghan

Monday 2nd January 1928

Football League Division One

Highbury

Attendance 13,518

Arsenal

Tottenham Hotspur

Manager
Herbert Chapman

Manager
Billy Minter

John MOODY	1	Cyril SPIERS
Tom PARKER	2	Matt FORSTER
Eddie HAPGOOD	3	Jock RICHARDSON
Alf BAKER	4	Darkie LOWDELL
Jack BUTLER	5	Harry SKITT
Bob JOHN	6	Arthur GRIMSDELL
Joe HULME	7	Charlie HANDLEY
Charlie BUCHAN	8	Taffy O'CALLAGHAN
Jimmy BRAIN	9	Alex LINDSAY
Billy BLYTH	10	Jimmy ARMSTRONG
Sid HOAR	11	Jimmy DIMMOCK

Referee **Mr A W Lamacraft** *(Exeter)*

BACKGROUND

Postponed in November because of fog, the lowest crowd in derby history saw a match that could well have been postponed again for, with rain pouring throughout, the pitch was little better than marsh land. Right up to kick off the groundsmen were forking the pitch in an abortive effort to clear it of surface water. Both teams showed several changes. For Arsenal, four wins in their last five games, John Moody replaced the injured Dan Lewis, Eddie Hapgood, recently signed from Kettering, stood in for Horace Cope and their forward line was strengthened by the return of Joe Hulme and Charlie Buchan. By comparison Spurs, three successive defeats, 1-6 at Leicester, 1-4 at Bolton and 2-3 at Birmingham, left it to the last minute before announcing

Eddie Hapgood

their line-up. Still without Jack Elkes, whose place was taken by their recent signing from Chelsea, Jimmy Armstrong, at least Arthur Grimsdell was able to return allowing Alex Lindsay to move up front in place of Frank Osborne, out with kidney trouble. Jock Richardson was back with Matt Forster moving to right back in place of injured Tommy Clay.

BEFORE THE GAME

	P	W	D	L	F	A	Pts
Arsenal	21	10	5	6	45	40	25
Spurs	22	9	4	9	41	47	22

B Bennison reported in **The Daily Telegraph**...

ARSENAL AND HOTSPUR DRAW - SOME IMPRESSIONS

On something like a huge slab of mud and in incessant rain, with banks of decaying snow all around, the Arsenal and Tottenham Hotspur, at Highbury, yesterday decided their League match which a few weeks ago was not possible owing to fog. If the idea of football in such deplorable conditions had been reduced to an extravagant burlesque there would have been no surprise; it was expected. But, remarkable to relate, the game, which resulted in a draw, the score one goal all, was from every point of view one of the best seen on the North London enclosure this season - pace high, the skill of the players undoubted, and an enthusiasm that rebounded to the credit of all concerned. And better, since the affair was one between near neighbours, a regard for the spirit of the game was both splendid and close; it was free from pettiness; it was a thing all hard and healthy and clean in it's hardness. And it was a

match in which to the impartial onlooker the result did not really matter, for each side might have won without leaving any room for squealing; it was one of the best examples of professional "Soccer" that I have witnessed for many a long day. Even the old campaigner was roused and thrilled by it.

From the kick off it was touch and go. Away went the Arsenal, Buchan leading the way after the manner of dictator; it seemed as if the Spurs were to be taken by storm, but the defence of the visitors proved equal to a series of raids. Spiers, the goalkeeper, quick to decide, Forster and Richardson, his backs, making even a next to impossible ball responsive to their bidding, and thereafter, until the interval, Tottenham had decidedly the pull. On three or more occasions the Arsenal goal escaped by the merest inches; often did Moody, who deputised for Lewis, save with the odds all against him. Parker,

SPURS v. ARSENAL

his right full-back, was wonderfully safe; Hapgood, a youth, fitted in, Baker, Butler and John carried themselves gallantly; but Brain was the leader of an attack that did not knit together in the same purposeful way as that led by Lindsay, a Scot, who supplanted Osborne.

A DISALLOWED GOAL

As a team Tottenham carried most guns, and they well deserved to begin the scoring, **O'CALLAGHAN** finding the net with an unstoppable shot. The Arsenal, by comparison with the opposition, were mostly plodders, but they will, perhaps, have it, and with sound reason, that they should have been on a level footing before half-time, that a shot by Brain, which found the net, should have counted; that the referee was unduly harsh on them when, instead of awarding a goal, he ordered the ball to be thrown up in the penalty area. What happened was this: Brain, ploughing his way through the slush, ran on until Spiers was the only opponent to confront him. Spiers left his charge, Brain shot, the ball hit the goalkeeper, who fell as if hurt, perhaps seriously. The whistle went at the moment that Brain shot, and so there was no goal. But if the rules had been interpreted literally that shot would have been allowed to count. The Hotspur were decidedly lucky, and, as if by way of appreciation of their good fortune, they played so well and with such purpose as to dominate the game until the change of ends. If all had gone their way they would, perhaps, have been in a winning position when ends came to be changed instead of being only a goal in front.

It was **HOAR** who equalised and insisted upon a division of the spoils; and his goal told of the schemer and the efficient marksman; it represented his highest achievement, for he was not a consistently good performer. I was the more impressed by the football of Tottenham. Their tactics were sounder; they were less inclined to hug to the ball, and, remembering their very poor holiday, their football in every respect was surprisingly good. Dimmock, at outside left, was the least distinguished member of the team, being casual in his ways. The most notable visitor was Grimsdell; nothing better was seen than a dribble by him. Always did he revel in the heavy going. But there was no passenger among the Tottenham defence. Unquestionably Spiers is a goalkeeper of prime quality; the best, I should say, that Tottenham have had for many seasons. Forster and Richardson were worthy backs, and Lowdell, the right-half, improved enormously on his displays during the early days of the season. O'Callaghan was the bright particular star among the forwards; much of a football genius is this young man. Lindsay was an intelligent centre, and Armstrong, who came in for Elkes, did passably well at inside left.

Except in the matter of method, I saw little wrong with the Arsenal; they would have found an open game more profitable. I am quite decided that Moody is the best goalkeeper in the employ of the club; Parker remains one of our most competent backs; Hapgood is more than promising; the half-backs were good enough for any purpose, but there was an unevenness about attack; it was in turn good, moderate, and indifferent; rather lopsided at times.

24

TOTTENHAM HOTSPUR 2
O'Callaghan 2
ARSENAL 0

Saturday 7th April 1928

Football League Division One

White Hart Lane

Attendance 39,193

Tottenham Hotspur

Manager
Billy Minter

Arsenal

Manager
Herbert Chapman

Cyril SPIERS	1	Danny LEWIS
Matt FORSTER	2	Tom PARKER
Cecil POYNTON	3	Bob JOHN
Bert SMITH	4	Alf BAKER
Harry SKITT	5	Herbie ROBERTS
Arthur GRIMSDELL	6	Billy BLYTH
Charlie HANDLEY	7	Joe HULME
Taffy O'CALLAGHAN	8	Jimmy SHAW
Frank OSBORNE	9	Jimmy BRAIN
Alex LINDSAY	10	Jack LAMBERT
Jimmy DIMMOCK	11	Sid HOAR

Referee **Mr A W Lamacraft** (Exeter)

'DERBY' STAR

★ **Taffy O'Callaghan** ★

'The best footballer on view' said the "Daily Telegraph". The "Athletic News" described the two goal hero as 'enthusiastic', 'prominent' and 'always in the right place during an attack'. A Welsh international, Taffy – real name Eugene, was adored by the Spurs crowd. He was good with both feet and packed a powerful shot.

'DERBY' STAR

BACKGROUND

On the last day of March Spurs stood seventh on the First Division table with 35 points from an equal number of games. They lost at Sheffield United that day and on the following Friday former Spurs' star Jimmy Seed inspired a Sheffield Wednesday team that had already been written off as relegation certainties to a 3-1 win at White Hart Lane. After two dismal displays manager Billy Minter recalled Charlie "Tich" Handley and the veteran Bert Smith for an Easter Saturday fixture that was to provide Spurs last First Division victory for over five years. With a heavy run-in, Jack Butler and Charlie Buchan were both rested from Arsenal's team of the previous day team against Cardiff, their last victory of the season. Herbie Roberts and Jimmy Shaw deputised.

BEFORE THE GAME

	P	W	D	L	F	A	Pts
Arsenal	34	13	9	12	73	74	35
Spurs	37	14	7	16	67	74	35

Herbie Roberts deputised for Jack Butler in the Arsenal eleven.

HOTSPUR BEAT ARSENAL

Tottenham Hotspur, on their ground at White Hart Lane, won their League match with the Arsenal by two goals to none. There were 50,000 spectators.

In games between near neighbours unusually good and well-ordered football is seldom seen; this was not a notable exception. Its outstanding feature was the high rate at which it was played, and an extravagant, mostly futile, expenditure of physical energy. The ball was light and flighty, given to strong capering; the ground was hard. But more than average teams would have risen superior to the conditions; as it was the sides were no more than moderately good, and for the most part we saw what was little better than a scramble, in which individual and collective skill was largely at a discount. Only the white-hot partisan could have found joy in it; the unbiased onlooker was left cold.

The match, however, served to introduce two strangers, both of the Arsenal, to big football - Shaw, an inside right, and Roberts, a six-footer at least, at centre-half. Neither was an unqualified success, for Shaw was given to describing circles, a stranger he was, apparently, to direct methods, with the result that Hulme, his distinguished partner, received no sort of help. Roberts was only conspicuous when the ball was in the air; then he profited by his considerable height. Both recruits showed that they have much to learn; Buchan and Butler, who were rested, would perhaps have made a world of difference.

As it was the Arsenal, their experiments notwithstanding, with just a little luck, would at have least escaped defeat, for in the second half when they were but a goal behind only a gigantic fluke kept them from scoring, a shot made at a moment when Spiers was in no position to save striking Grimsdell and knocking him out; and had Hoar been less erratic and not so obviously overwrought by the occasion, he must have captured the Tottenham goal once, if not twice.

MODERATE FORWARDS

Few matches have I seen this season in which forwards counted for so little. Their attempts to build up combination were quite frightful to see. All save O'CALLAGHAN were as a job lot. And this Welsh boy, with a gorgeous Irish name, scored the goals, the first from a corner kick by Dimmock a few minutes after the start, the other late in the second half after about the one and only concerted movement during the afternoon. Neither Brain nor Osborne was a successful centre; Skitt mastered the Arsenal leader; Osborne, like the rest, was sadly lacking in ball control; Hulme, because of the small service rendered by Shaw and the unremitting attention paid to him by Grimsdell, was not his usual self; for one of his undoubted ability he had a bad match. Lambert played wholeheartedly, but to little purpose, and Hoar was apt to be foolishly and inexcusably petulant in his various tussles with Forster.

The Arsenal had only one consistently good half back - Blyth. But in John, full back with Parker, they had, next to O'Callaghan, the best footballer on view. Which was as well, for Parker, especially in the early stages, was far from reliable. Lewis, the goalkeeper, in making a desperate dive for the ball, and by which he prevented the irrepressible O'Callaghan from getting a third goal, hurt his

back so severely some ten minutes before the end that he had to be carried off. Baker, who filled the breach, was not troubled by any shot. All things considered Tottenham deserved their victory. Their defence was sounder than that of Arsenal; as a pair I preferred Forster and Poynton to Parker and John; and had it not been for Blyth the Highbury side would have been completely out of it at half-back, for Smith returned to the Tottenham middle line to demonstrate that he is by no means at the end of his tether; Skitt was so good as to make Roberts appear to be very poor; and if Grimsdell is no longer sprightly, his defence was scarce without a flaw, his captaincy priceless.

The 4-page official Spurs programme for the day

25

TOTTENHAM HOTSPUR 1
Felton (pen)

ARSENAL 1
Bowden

Saturday 16th September 1933

Football League Division One

White Hart Lane

Attendance 56,612

Tottenham Hotspur

Manager
Percy Smith

Arsenal

Manager
Herbert Chapman

Joe NICHOLLS	1	Frank MOSS
Bill FELTON	2	George MALE
Bill WHATLEY	3	Eddie HAPGOOD
Tom EVANS	4	Frank HILL
Arthur ROWE	5	Herbie ROBERTS
Tom MEADS	6	Bob JOHN
Jimmy McCORMICK	7	Ray PARKIN
Taffy O'CALLAGHAN	8	David JACK
George HUNT	9	Ray BOWDEN
Willie HALL	10	Alex JAMES
Willie EVANS	11	Cliff BASTIN

Referee **Mr J H Perks** (Tipton)

BACKGROUND

For the first North London derby in over five years, the gates were closed an hour before kick-off on a record White Hart Lane crowd, originally returned as 57,246 but subsequently amended to 56,612, that had started to build up as early as nine o'clock. Spurs had started their first season back in Division One in fine form, winning their home games against Wolves and Aston Villa 4-0 and 3-2 respectively, drawing at Sheffield United and winning 3-1 at Leicester with a hat-trick from Jimmy McCormick. They were at full strength but, deprived of the services of Joe Hulme since the first match of the season, League champions Arsenal tried occasional half-back or inside-forward Ray Parkin at outside-right after Ralph Birkett and Tim Coleman, signed as a centre-forward, had failed to compensate for the loss of the former England winger. Coleman was now injured, as was Jack Lambert, but at least David Jack was fit to return, allowing Ray Bowden to lead the line. Bob John was also back after missing the midweek defeat at West Brom.

BEFORE THE GAME

	P	W	D	L	F	A	Pts
Spurs	5	3	1	1	10	4	7
Arsenal	5	2	2	1	7	5	6

'The Daily Telegraph' reported...

Arsenal Team Booed Before Start of Match

The great North London duel at White Hart Lane, watched by a record crowd, had a prelude which must be unique in football - the booing of the visiting team before a ball was kicked!

As the Arsenal players ran onto the field a section of the onlookers demonstrated against them in no uncertain manner. I am at a loss to understand why, for no team in the country plays cleaner or more attractive football.

The 'Spurs' crowd is notorious for its partisanship, which no one minds. But to boo an opposing side before the game begins is disgraceful.

From "The Weekly Herald"

IF NOT A CLASSIC, A FOOTBALL TREAT.

SPURS—ARSENAL MATCH PROVIDES FEAST.

RECORD GATE.

DRAW A FAIR RESULT.

Will the Spurs—Arsenal match at Tottenham be remembered by posterity as a classic match? If it did not reach the distinguished heights of a classic, it was a football treat. The ninety minutes were crowded with ninety thrills.

The play provided a contrast in styles—Spurs' speed versus Arsenal's guile as demonstrated by that prince of football jugglers, Alec James.

While the Spurs enjoyed three-fourths of the attack in the first half, Arsenal rose superior after the interval.

A draw is universally regarded as a fair and fitting result, although the Spurs got their goal by a penalty-kick.

Remarkable scenes were witnessed, though after congratulating the two teams on their magnificent fight, we might congratulate also the crowd upon their general behaviour.

The attendance was 57,246, which is a record. The takings were £3,483.

The previous record was that set up by the Villa match (a cuptie) on March 5th, 1921, when the attendance was just under 55,000 —no actual figures has ever been officially issued. The takings then amounted to £6,956, this being due to the prices of admission being higher.

THRILLS, SPILLS AND A RECORD CROWD

A crowd of 57,000 - more than had ever packed into the White Hart Lane enclosure before - swayed and cheered and received full value for their money throughout an exciting game, played at a breakneck pace: a game as full of thrills as of skill. Tottenham's only score was from a penalty, and Jack in the first half headed the ball into the angle of the post and bar without getting it into the net; but although Tottenham shot far more often than Arsenal, they lacked precision, and a draw was a fair reflex of the game's changing fortunes.

When Arsenal appeared someone in the stands took it into his head to throw handfuls of ready-made confetti over the Press box. The huge crowd quivered with excitement and anticipation, and the game soon had them screwed up to an even higher pitch of enthusiasm. Clever things were done by almost every player, in lightning succession and at lightning speed.

James marked his sense of the occasion by firing in a shot just wide of the post, Jack was admonished by the referee for

Frank Moss (left) played a wonderfully skilful and daring game in the Arsenal goal, Ray Bowden (right) scored Arsenal's equaliser.

using his elbow instead of his shoulder, and then Roberts headed out a dangerous dropping shot, but in doing so knocked poor Moss into the net.

MOSS'S "MONKEY TRICKS"

Hunt, always on the ball, drove in a fierce shot from the right towards the nearer post - the most difficult of all shots to intercept - but Moss sprang across and beat it down. Then McCormick put in a low shot from close range. It glanced off the foot of an Arsenal defender, and Moss had almost to dislocate his backbone in changing direction as he plunged to stop it. A first-class save!

And then only the fates prevented an Arsenal score. Parkin, who had been neglected, centred and Jack flicked the ball with his forehead so that it crashed venomously into the left corner of bar and post - and against all probability shot out again. Nicholls stood blinking and thankful!

But at the other end Hunt chased a ball running to the right, and miraculously hooked it back at an acute angle, very fasy. Moss, not to be outdone, tipped the surprise drive over the bar, and a few seconds later fell to take a shot from Hunt's toe delivered from only three yards out.

Then Hill very foolishly tripped W. Evans as he was going through. **FELTON** took the penalty kick and left Moss a spectator. But the 'Spurs did not hold their lead for long. Against the run of the play **BOWDEN** scored with a hard ground shot after Jack had gone through and seen his drive charged down. Nicholls appeared to have his view obstructed, for Bowden's shot, though hard and well placed, came from thirty yards out.

THEIR SECOND BREATH

The 'Spurs began the second half as sprightly as ever. Hunt turned a centre across the goal as he fell, and W. Evans worked inwards, only to shoot wide. Hill tripped Hunt just outside the penalty area, but the free kick brought nothing to the 'Spurs. Gradually the Arsenal defence, which had been rattled till the cracks showed, began to work effectively again, and Hall was forced to shoot from a long way out. It was a fierce ball, however, from a pass taken on the half-volley, and Moss did well to fall and scoop the swerving ball round the post.

The Arsenal began to attack in earnest, after James had anxiously consulted his watch. The Arsenal captain took a pass before it touched the ground and drove only a foot wide. Nicholls fisted out a centre from Parkin past Bastin's oncoming nose, and a moment later caught a header from Bowden. the game ended with a tired Arsenal attacking an even more tired Tottenham.

Moss, his confidence regained, played a wonderfully skilful and daring game in the Arsenal goal. But Tottenham should have had at least three goals out of their innumerable assaults in the first half. Their forwards were all fervour and no finish. Rowe demonstrated the craft of defensive half-back play even better than Roberts, and took the ball to the other end in his spare time. But not a man in this thrilling, fast, clever game let up for one second.

26 ARSENAL 1
Bastin

TOTTENHAM HOTSPUR 3
Evans 2 (1 pen), Howe

Arsenal

Manager
George Allison

Tottenham Hotspur

Manager
Percy Smith

Arsenal		Tottenham
Frank MOSS	1	Joe NICHOLLS
George MALE	2	Bill FELTON
Eddie HAPGOOD	3	Bill WHATLEY
Charlie JONES	4	David COLQUHOUN
Herbie ROBERTS	5	Arthur ROWE
Bob JOHN	6	Wally ALSFORD
Ralph BIRKETT	7	Jimmy McCORMICK
Ray BOWDEN	8	Les HOWE
Jimmy DUNNE	9	George HUNT
Cliff BASTIN	10	Willie HALL
Pat BEASLEY	11	Willie EVANS

Referee **Mr W P Harper** *(Stourbridge)*

BEFORE THE GAME

	P	W	D	L	F	A	Pts
Arsenal	25	14	7	4	43	23	35
Spurs	26	13	4	9	47	29	30

AT THE SEASON'S END

		P	W	D	L	F	A	Pts
1st	Arsenal	42	25	9	8	75	47	59
3rd	Spurs	42	21	7	14	79	56	49

BACKGROUND

Spurs' share of the points in September had taken them to the top of the table but by the return fixture, delayed for four days as both clubs were involved in the fourth round of the FA Cup, Arsenal were heading for their second successive title and third in four years. Four points clear at the turn of the year the illness and subsequent death of Herbert Chapman led to a dip in performances and only two points out of a possible six had allowed Derby County to close the gap. However Arsenal went into the match fortified by a 7-0 FA Cup thrashing of Crystal Palace and the return of Frank Moss who had been forced to miss the cup-tie because of a thumb injury sustained in the last League game at Manchester City. Spurs had performed just as well in the Cup, beating West Ham 4-1, to give them 12 goals in their last four games, although they had failed to score in their last League game at Leicester. Again Spurs drew a record crowd to Highbury with the gates being closed over an hour before kick-off.

Some of the huge crowd that gained admission to the ground but could not see the game. In the background, behind the gates, is seen the vast number of people who were locked out altogether.

Arsenal Lose League Leadership
BEATEN AT HOME BY SPURS

WINNER'S THREE GOALS IN HALF-HOUR - CROWD OF 70,000

After leading the way in the First Division for two months, Arsenal were deposed yesterday. They lost their home match against the 'Spurs before a 70,000 crowd - a record for the ground - and while this was happening Derby County, their chief rivals for the leadership, were winning at Leeds. The positions at the head of the table now read:

	P	W	D	L	F	A	Pts
Derby County	26	14	7	5	50	26	35
Arsenal	26	14	7	5	44	26	35
Huddersfield T.	26	12	9	5	57	29	33
Tottenham H.	27	14	4	9	50	30	32

Arsenal's defeat does not come as a surprise to close followers of the game. The writing has been on the wall for some time; their attack is not good enough to carry them along. So long as their wonderful defence stood up to a gruelling in match after match there was hope of a breakaway goal and a snap victory. But sooner or later the defence was bound to crack.

It cracked in this match at Highbury - ominously. A penalty was conceded in less than five minutes, and at the end of twenty-five minutes Hapgood and Male, the backs, had blundered fatally. Three goals down, Arsenal fought back magnificently in the second half - actually the 'Spurs were overplayed then - but it was too much to hope that the damage done could be repaired.

WAS IT A PENALTY ?

The penalty award was very unfortunate from Arsenal's standpoint. Hunt, having beaten Roberts, was almost on the dead-ball line when Hapgood tackled him. It was a perfectly fair attempt to get the ball. Hapgood, however, missed it. He brought Hunt to the ground and the referee (Mr W.P. Harper of Stourbridge) decided that a penalty was justified. A great number of people disagreed with him.

W. EVANS took the kick and scored. The incident had a thoroughly upsetting effect on Arsenal's defence, particularly on Hapgood. At the twenty-second minute - and after Bowden and Birkett had missed reasonable chances of equalising - Hapgood made a complete miskick, and presented a goal to **HOWE**. And before the crowd had recovered from this shock Male, the right back, was guilty of a faulty tackle, which let **W. EVANS** through to put the 'Spurs on the high road to victory.

The score was still 3-0 at the interval. I must confess I was unprepared for what followed. On the first half form the 'Spurs looked to be romping away with the game, and my mind went back to a February afternoon of 1925, when, on the same ground, Huddersfield routed Arsenal by 5-0. That was their last decisive home defeat, and there seemed good reason for believing that the score would be repeated.

NICHOLLS THE HERO

Instead the second half was 80 per cent Arsenal, and they would have pulled the game out of the fire but for some amazing goalkeeping by Nicholls, who made save after save at point blank range. He made mistakes, too, but the fates were very kind to the Tottenham goal.

A quarter of an hour from time **BASTIN** at last got the ball into the net. This, too, was a lucky goal, as the ball was diverted from it's true course through striking a defender. But Bastin well deserved to score. The outstanding Arsenal forward, he was also a lion-hearted worker.

Beasley and Dunne were also dangerous Arsenal attackers, but there was a definite weakness on the right wing. Bowden's passes were nearly always going wrong, and Birkett missed some first-class scoring openings.

The 'Spurs were a grand team in the first half. The speed of their forwards upset Arsenal's defensive machinery, and once again I was enormously impressed with the Hall - W. Evans partnership. No club in the country has a better left wing than this. Hunt was held safe by Roberts, but Howe was frequently too quick for John and Hapgood.

After that disastrous opening half-hour Arsenal's defence settled down to it's normally sound game.

27

ARSENAL 5
Drake 3, Beasley, Evans.T (og)

TOTTENHAM HOTSPUR 1
Hunt

Saturday 20th October 1934

Football League Division One

Highbury

Attendance 70,544

Arsenal		Tottenham Hotspur
Manager **George Allison**		Manager **Percy Smith**

Frank MOSS	1	Joe NICHOLLS
George MALE	2	Fred CHANNELL
Eddie HAPGOOD	3	Tom EVANS
Jack CRAYSTON	4	David COLQUHOUN
Herbie ROBERTS	5	Arthur ROWE
Bob JOHN	6	Tom MEADS
Pat BEASLEY	7	Jimmy McCORMICK
Ray BOWDEN	8	Les HOWE
Ted DRAKE	9	George HUNT
Alex JAMES	10	Willie HALL
Cliff BASTIN	11	Willie EVANS

Referee **Mr H E Hull** (Burnley)

BACKGROUND

Champions Arsenal had made a great start in their pursuit of a hat-trick of League titles - particularly at home. Five games had produced victories over Liverpool 8-1, Blackburn 4-0, West Brom 4-3, Birmingham 5-1 and Manchester City 3-1. Their latest big-name signing, Wilf Copping, was injured but they had the perfect replacement in stalwart Bob John. The high hopes Spurs started the season with after finishing third the previous campaign had proved misplaced and they knew they would have to be at their best to get a result but drew heart from their last game, a 2-1 victory at Sunderland. However, a knee injury forced full-back Bill Whatley to stand down at the last minute and although specialist full-back George Goldsmith, a summer signing from Hull, was fit and ready to play, manager Percy Smith preferred to give Tom Evans, a half-back who had never played at the back before, the unenviable task of replacing Whatley. Amid pre-match reports, and strenuous Arsenal denials, that Spurs had tried to sign Arsenal's out of favour winger Joe Hulme, Highbury's gate record again fell.

BEFORE THE GAME

	P	W	D	L	F	A	Pts
Arsenal	10	5	4	1	30	13	14
Spurs	10	3	3	4	13	13	9

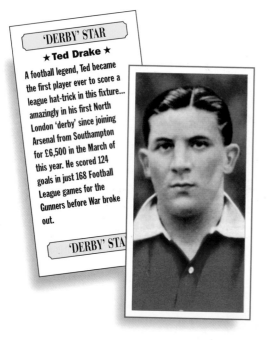

'DERBY' STAR

★ **Ted Drake** ★

A football legend, Ted became the first player ever to score a league hat-trick in this fixture... amazingly in his first North London 'derby' since joining Arsenal from Southampton for £6,500 in the March of this year. He scored 124 goals in just 168 Football League games for the Gunners before War broke out.

'DERBY' STA

SPURS WEAKNESS EXPOSED
ANOTHER HAT-TRICK BY ARSENAL CENTRE

With a full team out, the 'Spurs would most likely have lost the North London duel at Highbury, but if Whatley had been in his usual place at left-back Arsenal would not have won so emphatically.

Whatley's eleventh-hour defection was a terrible drag on the Tottenham wheels. Tom Evans, a wing-half, converted into an emergency left-back, was so obviously in deep water that, at half-time, he surrendered the job to Meads, another half-back.

Now both Evans and Meads suffer from lack of speed, and Arsenal, quick to seize on the weakness plied Beasley, their right winger, with more passes than he could reasonably expect to receive in two matches.

This handicap down the left flank was bound to be fatal to the 'Spurs. They were heavily defeated; nevertheless I extend congratulations to Channell and Rowe on their fine defensive play in discouraging circumstances.

Congratulations also to Hunt, Howe and Hall, of the forwards, for their plucky second half fight. Four goals down was a hopeless plight to be in, but the 'Spurs struck back gallantly. But for atrocious luck in finishing their reward of one goal by Hunt would have been greater.

It took Arsenal half an hour to find the first loophole in Tottenham's improvised defence, but from the moment Beasley volleyed through Bastin's centre the gap was ever widening. Poor Evans had the wretched misfortune to put the ball in his own net - he did not realise that Nicholls had advanced from goal - and then Drake completed another hat-trick.

WILLIE EVANS MASTERED

The marked difference between the teams was, of course, in defence. Arsenal enjoyed some very lucky escapes in the second half, it is true, but in the early stages Roberts and his colleagues were as steady as a rock.

Crayston was an outstanding player, the best half-back on the field, in fact. It has taken Crayston the better part of two months to attune himself to the Highbury atmosphere; now it can be safely said he has "arrived". This powerfully built right-back thoroughly mastered Willie Evans, and in addition, played a big part in Arsenal's right-wing attacks.

On the left flank John just as surely held McCormick, and with both their wingers tied down it was remarkable that the 'Spurs were able to claim so much of the second half exchanges. Once reason was that Hunt again proved himself a brilliant individualist, and another that Howe (in spite of missed openings) was in such splendid form.

The match was one more personal triumph for Alex James. His was the tactical mind that sensed the flaw in the 'Spurs defence and he exposed it unmercifully. Bowden was almost as elusive as James, and Drake showed what a dangerous leader he is when given freedom of action.

The goals were scored in this order: 28min, BEASLEY; 40min, T.EVANS (own goal); 42min, DRAKE; 50min, DRAKE; 85min, DRAKE; 86min, HUNT.

28

TOTTENHAM HOTSPUR 0
ARSENAL 6

Kirchen 2, Drake 2, Dougall, Bastin (pen)

Tottenham Hotspur

Manager
Percy Smith

Arsenal

Manager
George Allison

Alan TAYLOR	1	Frank MOSS
Fred CHANNELL	2	George MALE
Bill WHATLEY	3	Les COMPTON
Ernie PHYPERS	4	Jack CRAYSTON
Les HOWE	5	Norman SIDEY
Wally ALSFORD	6	Wilf COPPING
Jimmy McCORMICK	7	Alf KIRCHEN
Almer HALL	8	Bobby DAVIDSON
George HUNT	9	Ted DRAKE
Doug HUNT	10	Peter DOUGALL
Archie BURGON	11	Cliff BASTIN

Referee **Mr H E Hull** (Stockport)

BACKGROUND

An injury-ravaged season for Spurs was about to reach it's lowest point. Willie Hall damaged his knee at the start of November 1934 and did not play again until the final few matches of the season. Arthur Rowe was injured in early December and missed the rest of the season. Without their two most influential performers they always struggled and one win in twelve games had seen them sink to a relegation spot. As if they did not have enough problems already, injuries ruled out Tom and Willie Evans forcing manager Percy Smith to give a debut to Ernie Phypers and try Archie Burgon at outside-left. Not that top of the table Arsenal were without problems. Alex James and Herbie Roberts were injured four days earlier as West Ham knocked them out of the FA Cup and Eddie Hapgood was also missing. They were at least able to give their new £6,000 signing from Norwich, Alf Kirchen, his debut as their season long battle with Sunderland for the championship moved towards it's conclusion. Cliff Bastin took over as captain for the first time.

BEFORE THE GAME

	P	W	D	L	F	A	Pts
Spurs	30	8	7	15	41	62	23
Arsenal	30	16	8	6	85	37	40

AT THE SEASON'S END

		P	W	D	L	F	A	Pts
1st	Arsenal	42	23	12	7	115	46	58
22nd	Spurs	42	10	10	22	54	93	30

Arsenal goalkeeper Frank Moss catches a header from Tottenham's George Hunt. Les Compton is the player between the two.

SPURS CAUGHT IN THEIR OWN TRAP - OFFSIDE PLOT A FAILURE ARSENAL FORWARDS' GOAL HARVEST

The 'Spurs touched rock-bottom in this match at White Hart Lane. Outplayed in every phase of the game, they might as easily have lost by 10 goals as six.

Everybody sympathises with the club in their unprecedented troubles. For months they have been pursued by atrocious luck in the matter of injuries to players, and against Arsenal they were compelled to field a skeleton team.

Phypers, brought in at right-half, was making his First Division debut, and Burgon, an emergency outside-left, has rarely played in that position before in the reserve side. In the circumstances they would have done well to save a point, even if these experiments had been successful.

But, as though they were not handicapped enough, the 'Spurs tried a type of game entirely foreign to them. Someone must have told them that the way to stop Arsenal's attack was through the off-side trap. The referee's whistle was heard every few minutes, but the 'Spurs' strategy was a miserable failure.

There were bound to be many occasions when Arsenal's forwards kept behind the ball, with the result that there were more clean breaks-through from near the half-way line than one expects to see in any three matches. Channell and Whatley were on the run most of the afternoon, and the half-backs were completely at a loss to hold Arsenal's lively wings.

ARSENAL'S CLEVER RESERVES

For Arsenal the match was a walk-over. They were without James, Roberts and Hapgood, but none of the regulars was missed. Dougall, deputising for James, controlled the ball delightfully, and was forever bringing Drake and Bastin into scoring positions. Sidey showed all the Roberts' soundness, and Compton's form at left-back was most impressive.

Naturally all eyes were on Kirchen, the £6,000 newcomer from Norwich City. These are early days and the opposition was weak, but unless I am much mistaken Kirchen has solved Arsenal's right-wing problem. He has speed, is a quick thinker, and is not afraid to shoot. Two goals in his first match should give this young man all the confidence he may have needed.

Arsenal scored three times in each half. **DRAKE** got the opening goal at the 6th minute. It was typical of several that followed - a long upfield kick by Dougall and only one defender there to tackle the centre-forward. Taylor had no chance with Drake's left-foot shot.

Kirchen increased the lead after 24 minutes with a splendid low drive - he cut in from the wing and **DOUGALL** scored the third following a dazzling interchange of passing with Bastin that bewildered the defence.

A good deal of the second half play was farcical. Midway through it **DRAKE** and **KIRCHEN** netted twice in less than a minute, and **BASTIN**, eight minutes from the end, converted a penalty awarded for hands against Alsford.

I prophesy that it will be a long time before the 'Spurs try the offside manœuvre again.

Alf Kirchen (below) scored twice on his Arsenal debut following a £6,000 move from Norwich City.

> "Streets ahead of the Spurs in craftsmanship and all that counts for football ability, Arsenal made them appear an inferior - even indifferent - combination."
> - Tottenham and Edmonton Weekly Herald.

The Fifties

TOTTENHAM
FOOTBALL AND ATHLETIC
Official Pro
AND RECORD OF
F.A. Cup Winners 1930, 1936, 1950.
Arsenal
FOOTBALL CLUB
Football
FOOTBALL LEAGUE D
Arsenal v. Tottenha
SATURDAY, 26th AUGUST
KICK-OFF 3.15 p.m.
Season 1950-1
League Champions 1931, 1933, 1934, 1935, 1938, 1948, 1953
Season 1959-60
Football League Division I
ARSENAL v. TOTTENHA
Season 1955-6
COPYRIGHT
TOTTENHAM HOTS
FOOTBALL AND ATHLETIC COMPANY LIMITE
Official Programme
AND RECORD OF THE CLUB
Chairman: FRED. J. BEARMAN
SATURDAY, OCTOBE
VOL. XLVI. No. 17
RECORD BLOTTED AT BOLTON
14th January, 1956
HOTSPUR
Arsenal
FOOTBALL CL
Season 1952-3
F.A. Cup Winners 1930, 1936, 1950. League Champions 1931, 1933
ALL RIGHTS RESERVED
TWOPENCE
SATURDAY, JANUARY 15th, 1955
ME TO THE "GUNNERS"
A win by 4—0 to-day would therefore put us all
ARSENAL v. TOTTENHAM HOTSPUR
Saturday, 7th February, 1953
KICK-OFF 3 p.m.

29

ARSENAL 2
Roper, Barnes (pen)

TOTTENHAM HOTSPUR 2
Burgess, Walters

Saturday 26th August 1950

Football League Division One

Highbury

Attendance 64,638

Arsenal

Tottenham Hotspur

Manager
Tom Whittaker

Manager
Arthur Rowe

George SWINDIN	1	Ted DITCHBURN
Walley BARNES	2	Alf RAMSEY
Lionel SMITH	3	Arthur WILLIS
Arthur SHAW	4	Bill NICHOLSON
Les COMPTON	5	Harry CLARKE
Joe MERCER	6	Ron BURGESS
Freddie COX	7	Sonny WALTERS
Jimmy LOGIE	8	Peter MURPHY
Peter GORING	9	Len DUQUEMIN
Doug LISHMAN	10	Eddie BAILY
Don ROPER	11	Les MEDLEY

Referee **Mr E W Baker** *(Stoneleigh)*

BACKGROUND

Arsenal, the FA Cup holders, welcomed Spurs, the Second Division champions, to Highbury for their first Football League meeting in fifteen years having beaten Burnley at home 1-0 and drawn 0-0 at Chelsea. With Alex Forbes injured at Stamford Bridge Arthur Shaw was called. Spurs had started their return to the top flight with a 1-4 defeat at home to Blackpool but bounced back with a reversal of that score at Bolton. Injuries deprived them of two of their recognised "Push and Run" team, Arthur Willis replacing Charlie Withers who had been injured at Bolton and Peter Murphy, signed from Coventry in the close season, continuing in place of Les Bennett who had been injured in the opening game of the season. There was only one survivor from the last League encounter on show; Les Compton, almost 38 but yet to win his first England cap.

BEFORE THE GAME

	P	W	D	L	F	A	Pts
Arsenal	2	1	1	0	1	0	3
Spurs	2	1	0	1	5	5	2

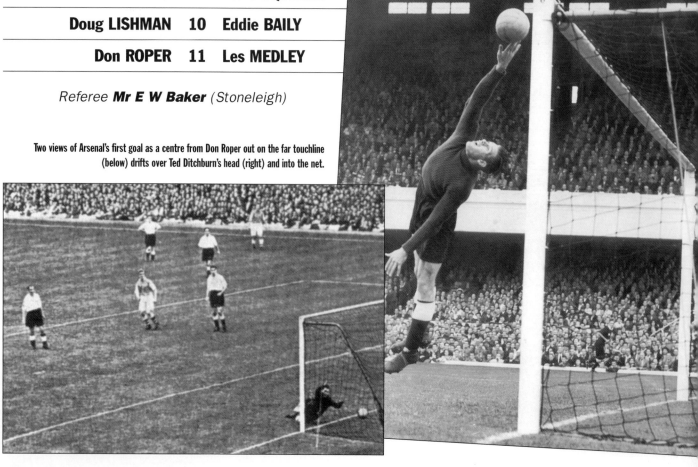

Two views of Arsenal's first goal as a centre from Don Roper out on the far touchline (below) drifts over Ted Ditchburn's head (right) and into the net.

Spurs No.7 Sonny Walters turns away after putting his side 2-1 up.

Tony Horstead in '*The Sunday Despatch*' under...

TWO GIFT GOALS FOR ARSENAL

This match had everything - good football despite a high wind, thrills, excitement, and non-stop action. A draw was a fair result, although the Spurs should have taken both points, for they gave Arsenal their two goals.

Number one was when **ROPER** took a haphazard swing at the ball with a general idea of lobbing it into the goalmouth, only, to his patent amazement, to see it swerve, get caught in the wind, and drop quietly into the back of the net way out of the reach of Ditchburn who had advanced to anticipate the centre.

Number two was the penalty, when Nicholson made an unnecessarily despairing rush. **BARNES**, of course, made no mistake from the spot.

Spurs provided the football - particularly in the first half when they produced stuff of which we dream; Arsenal produced the thrust and threat. An ideal recipe for a Soccer feast.

It was quite against the run of play when Roper lobbed the ball in after 26 minutes. but Spurs were not worried and five minutes later equalised.

IMPECCABLE RAMSEY

Lishman brought Baily - who had a wonderful match - down just inside the Arsenal half, and the impeccable Ramsey placed the free kick perfectly for **BURGESS** to leap and head the ball in off the far post.

On the resumption, with the wind at their backs, Arsenal tore into the Spurs, and Roper kept Ditchburn busy with several of his rocket-like drives. The defence held firm and the Spurs attack got into it's stride. Medley shot just wide from a fine pass from Duquemin; next minute Ditchburn was tipping over a Goring pile-driver; then Logie hit the bar, and, before you could blink, Swindin was saving brilliantly at the expense of corners from Baily and Duquemin.

Then the indefatigable Ron Burgess, at his brilliant best, went right through alone and saw his shot go inches wide of the post. After 25 minutes of the second half Medley beat Leslie Compton, lobbed the ball into the goalmouth, and **WALTERS**, after stumbling, tapped the ball into the net with the Arsenal defence spreadeagled. Six minutes later came the Barnes penalty.

Saved by the crossbar

WILLIS

RAMSEY

REFEREE G.W. BAKER

DITCHBURN

Spurs full-back Willis leaps too late as goalkeeper Ditchburn stands helplessly by. But the crossbar trapped this Arsenal shot from Logie and it was scrambled away

Penalty Foils Spurs

By BERNARD JOY

BEFORE 64,500 spectators at Highbury today, the London Derby between Arsenal and Spurs ended all-square.

Arsenal led with a goal by Roper after 27 minutes. Burgess equalised five minutes later. In the second half Walters gave Spurs the lead, but a penalty by Barnes saved Arsenal.

Both Forbes (Arsenal) and Withers (Spurs) failed in fitness tests early today and were unable to play, so Shaw was right-half for Arsenal and Willis left-back for Spurs.

Arsenal kicked off into a strong breeze, and Logie and Cox immediately forced a corner off Burgess. Clarke beat Goring to the kick to head well up field.

Apparently thinking Willis might be a weakness, Arsenal concentrated their early attacks on the right, but he was in complete command.

Arsenal's attack could make little headway against the strong wind. The close-passing game of Spurs was more suited to the conditions and they had more of the play.

Usually the Arsenal rearguard kept them out of the penalty area, but when Mercer and Shaw collided at a corner taken by Walters, Duquemin was left clear. He shot wildly across the face of the goal. Then Medley screwed well wide from 15 yards range.

After 27 minutes ROPER gave Arsenal the lead with a goal which Ditchburn should have saved.

Roper put in a centre from the wing, but so far forward that it seemed to be going over the bar. But it caught in the wind and dipped into goal as Ditchburn, who had advanced, was trying vainly to get back.

Roper was the most surprised man on the field as his colleagues rushed to congratulate him. Five minutes later Spurs were level through Burgess.

Ramsey took a free kick from the halfway line and BURGESS ran in to time his header perfectly.

The ball went in off the right hand post with Swindin full length in a vain endeavour to save.

Newcomer Peter Murphy was finding the pace—and the close marking of Mercer—too much for him. In contrast, Logie, the other inside-right, was the best forward, but too often passes to him were in the air.

A heavy shower just before the interval had the ball skidding off the pitch at great speed. Roper took advantage with a fierce 30-yard drive that was only inches wide, but Spurs nearly went in front with a header from Medley that Swindin just managed to turn over the bar.

Half-time : Arsenal 1 Spurs 1

With the wind now behind them after the restart, and a greasy top surface, Arsenal were trying long shots, and Goring and Roper twice tested Ditchburn.

A Lishman - Mercer - Logie move opened up the Spurs defence and Logie slipped the ball past Clarke. Goring ran on to it, but Ditchburn made a brilliant save to push the drive over the bar.

From the corner Logie hit the crossbar, and as the ball bounced on the line, Ditchburn flung himself on it to clear.

Arsenal's open game and willingness to shoot kept Spurs on the run. Spurs had the more classic touches but found the Arsenal middle line too well organised.

After having been on the defensive for 15 minutes, Spurs hit back. Swindin could only push out a corner, near in, from Medley and Baily hooked the ball wide as he fell. Then Duquemin got in a back header which Swindin turned over the bar with a flying leap.

Although it did not touch the heights, it was an interesting, exciting game, and it was fought in the best possible spirit, despite the obvious desire of many spectators to make it a "blood" match.

Burgess made a great effort with a solo run from the halfway line past Shaw and Compton, but his final shot was pulled well wide of the right-hand post.

Murphy and Baily switched and immediately Spurs got a goal. Murphy charged down Compton's clearance—Arsenal appealed for hands—and put Medley away.

Medley sent over a long centre which Walters did not trap cleanly and the ball ran past Mercer and Smith. That left WALTERS with the simple task of side-shooting past Swindin. It was 24 minutes after the restart.

Roper had one great drive another struck Willis. Then just outside a post and then Shaw hit the side netting after dribbling right into the area.

Thirty-four minutes after the restart BARNES equalised for Arsenal from a penalty. The kick was awarded when Nicholson brought down Lishman as he was going through to a pass from Logie.

Arsenal now had Roper, who was limping on the left knee, in the middle with Cox outside left and Goring on the other wing.

Result : Arsenal 2, Spurs 2.

30

TOTTENHAM HOTSPUR 1
Baily
ARSENAL 0

Saturday 23rd December 1950

Football League Division One

White Hart Lane

Attendance 54,898

Tottenham Hotspur

Manager
Arthur Rowe

Arsenal

Manager
Tom Whittaker

Ted DITCHBURN	1	**George SWINDIN**
Alf RAMSEY	2	**Laurie SCOTT**
Arthur WILLIS	3	**Walley BARNES**
Bill NICHOLSON	4	**Alex FORBES**
Harry CLARKE	5	**Les COMPTON**
Ron BURGESS	6	**Joe MERCER**
Sonny WALTERS	7	**Ian McPHERSON**
Les BENNETT	8	**Jimmy LOGIE**
Len DUQUEMIN	9	**Peter GORING**
Eddie BAILY	10	**Doug LISHMAN**
Les MEDLEY	11	**Freddie COX**

Referee **Mr E W Baker** (Stoneleigh)

Baily's goal was a winner

BACKGROUND

It took Spurs "Push and Run" team a little while to adapt to First Division football but by the Christmas matches they had climbed to fourth in the table, three points behind leaders Middlesbrough with a game in hand. They had been propelled from mid-table to title challengers by a run of eight victories on the trot, including home successes over Stoke by 6-1 and Portsmouth 5-0 and climaxed by a stunning 7-0 thrashing of third-placed Newcastle. Huddersfield had brought the run to an end but two draws and a 1-0 win at Blackpool soon had Spurs back on track. Ron Burgess had missed that last game but was back for Arsenal's visit. Nine games without defeat had taken Arsenal to the top of the table at the half-way stage but defeat at Burnley in their last game dropped them down to second. Laurie Scott continued to deputise for Lionel Smith while former Spurs' winger Freddie Cox replaced Don Roper.

BEFORE THE GAME

	P	W	D	L	F	A	Pts
Arsenal	22	13	5	4	49	24	31
Spurs	21	12	5	4	51	28	29

AT THE SEASON'S END

		P	W	D	L	F	A	Pts
1st	Spurs	42	25	10	7	82	44	60
5th	Arsenal	42	19	9	14	73	56	47

Spurs Win A Thrilling Game

Few League matches in recent years have caught the imagination, weeks before it took place, like yesterday's match at White Hart Lane. Queues began in bitterly cold weather before midnight on Friday. Interest, working up from a steady hum, reached the crescendo of a dynamo as the time for the kick-off drew near, and whole districts outside the ground, for this meeting of two most remarkable teams, nearest of neighbours, seemed drained of all other life.

After all this the match might easily have been an anti-climax, but in fact, throughout it's whole length it was a tense, thrilling drama, played at top speed if not with classic skill. Tottenham were the more polished side, but there were moments in the second half when the flow of their forward movements was broken and Arsenal emerged from their battering to crowd on pressure in the failing light.

Then anything might have happened; but Tottenham weathered the storm, though some of their close passing in defence must have nearly given their supporters heart failure, and towards the end the ball was again moving smoothly from line to line and breaking like waves on the Arsenal goal.

The first half was nearly all Tottenham. Arsenal's defence, unusually nervous, made a considerable number of mistakes early on, and the Spurs were both beating them to the ball and robbing them in possession. Compton recovered from his mistakes to play a fine solid game, saving two or three certain goals, but the others did not. Barnes and Scott never got the measure of Walters and Medley, and the only relief Arsenal had before half-time were the quick breakaways of Logie and Forbes.

These were, in fact, the only two of Arsenal's team to emerge from this match with credit, for Clarke, rising to new heights, played Goring out of the game, and Cox and McPherson on the wings were given neither time nor room. Willis, Nicholson and Ramsey were never shaken out of control, and they set attacks going time after time with exact passes made under pressure.

The ground's surface was always difficult, slippery on top and hard underneath, but the footwork of the Spurs' forwards, Medley, Baily and Bennett, who got through a lot of work, was rarely less than remarkable. Burgess, who had a quiet match, was nevertheless always covering his more mercurial colleagues, and early on a long through pass from him, which Walters chased and Swindin dropped, nearly gave Spurs a snap lead.

The winning goal, however, came after some 35 minutes. Bennett took the ball upon the right and flicked it to Walters, who put it back diagonally through the centre. His pass hit Compton's heel as he tried to turn and recover, and rebounded to BAILY, who instead of shooting first time, half swivelled and shot left-footed into the right hand corner of the net. It was a beautifully taken goal and it was the measure of Tottenham's superiority.

Arsenal 'keeper George Swindin falls injured and referee Baker attends.

31

ARSENAL 1
Holton

TOTTENHAM HOTSPUR 1
Murphy

Arsenal

Tottenham Hotspur

Manager
Tom Whittaker

Manager
Arthur Rowe

Arsenal		Tottenham Hotspur
George SWINDIN	1	Ted DITCHBURN
Walley BARNES	2	Alf RAMSEY
Lionel SMITH	3	Arthur WILLIS
Alex FORBES	4	Bill NICHOLSON
Ray DANIEL	5	Harry CLARKE
Joe MERCER	6	Ron BURGESS
Arthur MILTON	7	Sonny WALTERS
Jimmy LOGIE	8	Peter MURPHY
Cliff HOLTON	9	Sid McCLELLAN
Doug LISHMAN	10	Tommy HARMER
Freddie COX	11	Les MEDLEY

Referee **Mr B M Griffiths** *(Newport)*

BACKGROUND

For fifth-placed Arsenal, one point and one place behind defending League champions Spurs, the combination of Cliff Holton and Doug Lishman was proving devastating. Between them they had scored thirteen of Arsenal's sixteen goals, Lishman two and Holton the other three as Arsenal had beaten Derby and Manchester City on their last two outings. Spurs first title success had been achieved with a settled, almost injury-free, line-up but the 1951-52 season had started with one absentee after another. Harry Clarke had played his first game of the season the previous week as leaders Manchester United were beaten 2-0, Eddie Baily had not played since the first week of the season, Len Duquemin had played only once in the last six games and now Les Bennett was injured. Under such a heavy handicap Arsenal were clear favourites.

BEFORE THE GAME

	P	W	D	L	F	A	Pts
Spurs	10	6	2	2	21	15	14
Arsenal	10	5	3	2	16	8	13

Alan Hoby's Column

THIS WAS A GAME TO REMEMBER

I HAVE seen American baseball with its fanatical zealots hooting and screaming. I have watched big fights in London, Paris, and New York. I have glowed with patriotic pride as British athletes smash world records. BUT— There is no atmosphere in the world quite like the tingling, electric tension which radiates from a great Soccer match. It clutches the crowd by the throat. It is essentially British—and essentially CLEAN.
At Highbury yesterday I saw such a game—the first real Soccer classic of the season.
Frankly, it was one of the finest displays of football I have watched.

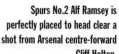

Spurs No.2 Alf Ramsey is perfectly placed to head clear a shot from Arsenal centre-forward Cliff Holton.

Spurs Hold Arsenal

Cliff Holton heads Arsenal's equaliser.

Tottenham Hotspur, with a somewhat scratch forward line, did well to hold Arsenal as long as they did at Highbury yesterday. A beautifully taken goal after five minutes, when **MURPHY** placed a ground shot from 20 yards into the left-hand corner of the net, put Tottenham a goal up, a lead they held against mounting pressure till half-time. But soon after a long intricate dribble by Logie forced one of several corners for Arsenal, each of which had looked dangerous, and **HOLTON** equalised with a well-angled header.

A warm sun broke through heavy early mist, and the ground was green and fast. Arsenal were soon moving smoothly, with Logie flicking passes to each wing in turn. Only the perfect positioning of Ramsey and Willis, and the linked approach work of Ramsey, Nicholson and Walters, were keeping the fast and heavy Arsenal forwards out. Twice Ditchburn saved at full stretch from Holton, and once Ramsey, after a corner headed out a fierce header by Lishman with Ditchburn truly beaten.

After the interval Medley tested Swindin in quick succession with searching shots. Then, engineered by Logie and with Milton switching to the left, came Arsenal's onslaught. When it gradually began to spend itself, Tottenham came back with cool triangular movements, but their forwards, without Baily and Bennett, were never properly in touch, or fast or powerful enough to outwit Barnes and Smith.

RUTHLESS PRESSURE

Arsenal stormed into the attack again, Logie edging himself through time and again, but Tottenham's defence in depth, the quick covering of Nicholson and Burgess, and the precision with which Ramsey started counter attacks under ruthless pressure, kept the match open. It was fast, individual attacking play against classical positional defence, with Clarke rivetting down the middle.

Medley, roving on his own, made occasional dashes in the late sunshine, but Harmer, McClellan and Murphy, the Spurs inside forwards, were too slow in moving into openings, and were frequently rattled off the ball with plenty of room to move in. Tense and exciting though it was, a draw, not without its object lessons, grew increasingly inevitable. For Logie, as for the whole Spurs defence, it was nevertheless something of a triumph.

High-kicks from Arsenal inside-left Doug Lishman in the autographed photograph as the ball evades Spurs centre-half Harry Clarke. Looking on are Bill Nicholson, Arthur Milton, Ron Burgess and (extreme right) Tommy Harmer.

32

TOTTENHAM HOTSPUR 1
Walters

ARSENAL 2
Roper, Forbes

Tottenham Hotspur

Manager
Arthur Rowe

Arsenal

Manager
Tom Whittaker

Ted DITCHBURN	1	George SWINDIN
Alf RAMSEY	2	Walley BARNES
Charlie WITHERS	3	Lionel SMITH
Bill NICHOLSON	4	Alex FORBES
Harry CLARKE	5	Roy DANIEL
Ron BURGESS	6	Joe MERCER
Sonny WALTERS	7	Freddie COX
Eddie BAILY	8	Jimmy LOGIE
Len DUQUEMIN	9	Reg LEWIS
Tommy HARMER	10	Doug LISHMAN
Les MEDLEY	11	Don ROPER

Referee **Mr G W Tedds** (Nottingham)

BACKGROUND

The band played "Abide With Me", the players wore black armbands and the crowd observed a minute's silence before the game in memory of King George VI. Spurs were sixth but their last League match had seen them lose 0-2 at leaders Manchester United and seven days earlier Newcastle had dumped them out of the FA Cup with a 3-0 victory at White Hart Lane. Five points behind United, Spurs were desperate for a victory if they were to maintain any hope of retaining their title. Unbeaten in five games since the turn of the year, Arsenal had continued to dispute the title race with Portsmouth, Manchester United and Newcastle but were missing Cliff Holton, injured at Old Trafford early in December. Peter Goring had initially replaced Holton but Reg Lewis had been called up for the FA Cup fourth round tie with Burnley and responded with a hat-trick.

BEFORE THE GAME

	P	W	D	L	F	A	Pts
Arsenal	29	15	7	7	57	41	37
Spurs	29	14	5	10	52	44	33

TOTTENHAM HOTSPUR
FOOTBALL AND ATHLETIC COMPANY, LIMITED
President: The Right Hon. LORD MORRISON, P.C., D.L., J.P.

Official Programme
AND RECORD OF THE CLUB

Secretary: R. S. JARVIS
Team Manager:
ARTHUR S. ROWE
Medical Officer:
Dr. A. E. TUGHAN

Chairman: FRED J. BEARMAN
Directors: F. JOHN BEARMAN, Wm. J. HERYET, E. DEWHURST HORNSBY, G. WAGSTAFFE SIMMONS, F.J.I., HARRY TAYLOR, FREDK. WALE

PRICE
TWOPENCE

VOL. XLIV. No. 39. SATURDAY, FEBRUARY 9th, 1952

NEWCASTLE WIN A GREAT MATCH

Last Saturday, much to the regret of all—Directors, Management, Players and Supporters, the Spurs had to say farewell to the F.A. Cup for another season. After Scunthorpe we had hoped to go far in this season's competition. When the draw for the fourth round gave us Newcastle as opponents at Tottenham, although we knew it would be a hard match, we felt we could go into the hat again on the following Monday. But it was not our lucky day. The ground churned up badly, and became a sea of mud, which enabled the weight and height of the Newcastle players to overcome the conditions far better than our own boys.

Again they moved the ball about so that their two wingers came right into the game and were a menace during the whole 90 minutes' play. Still, in spite of this we had quite as many shots at goal as Newcastle did, but Simpson played an inspired game and kept out many efforts that should have been goals. Twice the crossbar saved Newcastle, a splendid header by Harmer

and a shot by Medley looked goals all the way, but the goalie saved when it looked impossible for him to do so.

For the first ten minutes it was all Newcastle and in the thirteenth minute they opened the score when G. Robledo seized on an opening and scored from a few yards out leaving Ditchburn no chance of saving. We made several good attempts to draw level but midway through the first half Mitchell, the visitors' outside left, hit the ball hard from about 25 yards out, and sailed into the net off the far post, and so they led at half time by two goals.

In the second half we had much of the play but goals would not come and when mid-way through this half G. Robledo added a third for Newcastle it was evident that our exit from the cup was certain. However, our boys never gave up trying to beat Simpson, but the mud beat them all the time. Summing up, we feel that the Newcastle wingers, who both had a good game, and saw much of the ball, won the match for their side as Milburn, in the centre, was well held by Clarke.

The match was fought out in splendid spirit and all the twenty-two players deserve every credit for giving the 69,000 spectators such a sporting game in the appalling conditions, and we can only say good luck to Newcastle as they go on the way to Wembley once more.

The Nation's Great Loss

The passing of King George has evoked world-wide tribute to his memory. This afternoon on every football ground where a match is played under the jurisdiction of the Football Association a simple but sincere tribute will be paid to the memory of our late, beloved Patron. In the minds of us all at this hour must dwell a tender thought for the Queen's Mother and the Royal Family.

TO-DAY'S ARRANGEMENTS. Prior to the match this afternoon the Enfield Central Band will play two verses of the hymn "Abide with Me." The players of both teams will then line up in front of the West Stand, and there will be a Minute's Silence followed by the National Anthem.

Printed by Thomas Knight & Co. Ltd., The Clock House Press, Hoddesdon, Herts.

Players, officials and the huge crowd observe a minute's silence in memory of King George VI. The Tottenham programme (right) was printed in black ink instead of the usual blue and on the front page was a tribute headed 'The Nation's Great Loss'.

Roland Allen in 'The Sunday Times' under...

ARSENAL STRENGTHEN THEIR "DOUBLE" BID

The chief thought of the 66,438 people who saw Tottenham defeated by Arsenal today may well have been whether Manchester United (who beat Preston and remain on top) or Arsenal will take the place of Spurs as League Champions at the end of this season.

Arsenal moved up to second place in the League table because of this victory. They are still interested in the Cup. Manchester United have no such distraction. It is entirely a matter of choice whether that is accepted as a clue.

All the goals at Tottenham today came "out of the blue", and they were all out of the ordinary. In five minutes, Logie, who seemed to be well covered and not a bit dangerous, suddenly back-heeled the ball from the inside-left position. **ROPER** raced in and scored.

WALTERS leaned far back and just slipped the ball past Swindin, to bring the Spurs level after a further seven minutes of extremely scrappy stuff.

MISSED THEIR CHANCE.

It was then that the Spurs, even if they hardly ever looked quite like champions, missed their chance of going on to make sure of winning. The Arsenal defence did not know a lot about a free kick which, taken by Ramsey, went a foot or so wide.

Baily, who seems to be a little out of touch with his various tricks nowadays, shot first too high, and then with an extremely vague sense of direction. In the second half he made the miss of the match from a few yards out.

Then, just to show us that he still does know a thing or two about shooting, Baily lofted a shot over the heads of Arsenal defenders so cunningly that it beat Swindin, but struck the crossbar. It was a masterly bit of work. If he had scored it would have been a wonderful goal. Allowing all that, it nevertheless was the Arsenal whom we were expecting to score most of the time. They did, and it was at the same time a queer, casual and an impudent goal.

It happened early on in the second half. Roper pushed the ball in towards the middle. We had the impression that the referee got rather in the way of

Clarke, the Spurs centre half-back, as he moved in to clear - and that Clarke told him so.

Anyhow, a short clearance went to **FORBES**, Arsenal Scottish international wing half-back. He paused for a second to look around, then, standing quite still, sent in a swerving shot with his left foot of the sort to which there is no known answer.

There was not much else in this dullish affair except these three strange goals.

WHAT IS WRONG?

It is inevitable that people soon will be asking what is wrong with the Spurs. It could be that, having been beaten at home on two successive Saturdays, they have lost some of their confidence. What can be said is that, on their own pitch, which is all against their precise style of football in its present condition, they have lost some of their pinpoint accuracy.

They should not yet, however, be counted out of this complicated scramble for the Football League championship. And they have that remarkable young forward, Harmer, who has added a sort of chipped and floating pass to his repertoire of tricks. Even so accomplished a player as Forbes eventually gave up trying to tackle this elusive person.

Eddie Baily couldn't miss - but he did!

An open goal, a slow rolling ball - and not a soul to dispute the right of way. Give my eight-year-old kid these sort of chances and he'd eat a dozen of them before breakfast. I doubt that England's Eddie Baily will ever forget that 55th minute picture - especially the sequel. From penalty spot range Eddie side-footed this gift outside the Arsenal posts! It was an incredible miss.
- Pat Collins

Spurs No.7 Sonny Walters slips the ball past George Swindin for the equaliser.

AT THE SEASON'S END

		P	W	D	L	F	A	Pts
2nd	Spurs	42	22	9	11	76	51	53
3rd	Arsenal	42	21	11	10	80	61	53

33

TOTTENHAM HOTSPUR 1
Harmer

ARSENAL 3
Goring, Milton, Logie

Tottenham Hotspur

Arsenal

Manager
Arthur Rowe

Manager
Tom Whittaker

Ted DITCHBURN	1	Ted PLATT
Alf RAMSEY	2	John CHENHALL
Arthur WILLIS	3	Lionel SMITH
Bill NICHOLSON	4	Arthur SHAW
Harry CLARKE	5	Roy DANIEL
Ron BURGESS	6	Alex FORBES
Les MEDLEY	7	Arthur MILTON
Tommy HARMER	8	Jimmy LOGIE
Len DUQUEMIN	9	Peter GORING
Eddie BAILY	10	Doug LISHMAN
George ROBB	11	Don ROPER

Referee **Mr R J Burgess** (Reading)

BACKGROUND

After losing to Arsenal in February 1952 Spurs had gone to the end of the season unbeaten, just pipping Arsenal for the honour of being runners-up to Manchester United. The good run did not carry over to the new season, West Brom winning 4-3 at White Hart Lane on the opening day, but even with Bill Nicholson out injured six points from the next four games was no cause for concern. Defeat at leaders Liverpool and bottom-of-the-table Sheffield Wednesday though showed how much Spurs were missing wingers Les Medley and Sonny Walters. Les Bennett and Ron Burgess, injured at Hillsborough, were unable to take their places for the visit of unbeaten Liverpool but George Robb and Nicholson return. Tommy Harmer was called up and Vic Groves, an amateur with Leytonstone given his debut. Harmer scored once and Groves twice as the Merseysiders were beaten 3-1. It was just the boost Spurs needed for Arsenal's visit and the picture looked even rosier with Burgess and Medley back to fitness. Arsenal had started the season with two victories, but even with Cliff Holton replacing injured Don Oakes only two points followed from their next three games. The return of Jimmy Logie and Gloucestershire cricketer Arthur Milton inspired a 3-1 defeat of Portsmouth but three days later Charlton left Highbury with a 4-3 victory under their belt. Injuries dictated mass changes for the return with Portsmouth but two Holton goals gave Arsenal an early lead before they allowed the home team to retrieve a point. With Doug Lishman and Logie recovering Dave Bowen and Holton stood down.

BEFORE THE GAME

	P	W	D	L	F	A	Pts
Arsenal	8	3	3	2	14	12	9
Spurs	8	3	2	3	14	14	8

JIMMY LOGIE.

... Capped for Scotland.

Ted Ditchburn is unable to stop Peter Goring's shot and Arsenal go one up after just 10 minutes.

Alan Ross in 'The Observer' reported on how...

ARSENAL UPSET THE SPURS

Taking even longer to settle down than usual, Tottenham Hotspur were well beaten 3-1 by Arsenal at White Hart Lane yesterday. On the most golden of afternoons, with the relaid pitch billiard-table green, the Tottenham machinery looked strangely clogged.

There were, it is true, moments when the juggling genius of Harmer, and early on of Baily, managed to catch the Arsenal defence on the wrong foot, but even when open spaces had been created the Spurs forwards, because of their hesitancy near goal and of the close Arsenal covering, never seemed dangerous.

Arsenal, on the other hand, were quicker on the ball, more elastic in method and firmer in defence. Logie and Milton on the right wing had a fluency and understanding neither Spurs wings approached, and it was through them that Arsenal first upset the Tottenham defensive balance, and later exploited it.

CLEVER PASSES

Harmer began the match with two dazzling demonstrations of killing a high bouncing ball, and then made angled passes that left the backs standing. Robb drove one only just over the bar, but then a series of bad passes by the backs and halves let the Spurs rhythm slacken. Not till the last minutes of the match did they find their touch again.

After 10 minutes Logie intercepted a weak pass from Ditchburn to Willis, and **GORING**, unmarked scored from his centre. From now on, except for one superb run by Baily and a fine header by Robb saved at full length by Platt, Arsenal did more or less as they liked. Roper headed against the bar with Ditchburn nowhere near, and Milton, reached by a series of deep diagonal passes from Forbes and Logie, beat Willis at will. Clarke, fortunately, was holding Goring with some ease or Arsenal must have scored half a dozen in the first half.

OLD MAGIC LACKING

At no time in the match did the Spurs forward line move with any of its old magic. Baily and Robb made little progress on the left, and Harmer and Medley barely exchanged a pass. Duquemin, in the centre, gave Daniel the idlest of days.

This Spurs lethargy in attack has been transformed before by the classic accuracy and positional play of the defence. Yesterday, however, Ramsey and Willis were sadly inaccurate with their passes and were frequently outpaced. **MILTON** and **LOGIE** early in the second half ran through the whole Spurs defence to score in quick succession with lovely shots to the corner of the net.

Three goals down, Tottenham recovered a little when, with 10 minutes to go, **HARMER** sold a perfect dummy and beat Platt from 25 yards. But the result had long been decided.

Above: Arsenal's Peter Goring is crowded out as the Spurs rearguard keep him out.

Left: Arthur Milton drives the ball wide of Ted Ditchburn for the Gunners' second goal.

34

ARSENAL 4
Holton 2, Lishman, Logie

TOTTENHAM HOTSPUR 0

Saturday 7th February 1953	
Football League Division One	
Highbury	
Attendance 69,051	

Arsenal

Manager
Tom Whittaker

Tottenham Hotspur

Manager
Arthur Rowe

Arsenal		Tottenham Hotspur
Jack KELSEY	1	Ted DITCHBURN
Joe WADE	2	Alf RAMSEY
Lionel SMITH	3	Arthur WILLIS
Alex FORBES	4	Bill NICHOLSON
Ray DANIEL	5	Harry CLARKE
Joe MERCER	6	Colin BRITTAN
Arthur MILTON	7	Sonny WALTERS
Jimmy LOGIE	8	Les BENNETT
Cliff HOLTON	9	Len DUQUEMIN
Doug LISHMAN	10	Eddie BAILY
Don ROPER	11	Les MEDLEY

Referee **Mr R J Burgess** (Reading)

BACKGROUND

Arsenal stood fifth in the table but had games in hand on all the clubs above them, including four on leaders Wolves who were only three points ahead. Beaten once in twelve games, they had won 5-1 at Liverpool and 6-4 at Bolton and in their last three home games had found the net 15 times, four against Doncaster in the FA Cup, five against Wolves in the League and another six a week earlier against Bury in another FA Cup-tie with the goals spread around the forward line. Not surprisingly no changes were deemed necessary for Spurs' visit. Spurs had experienced a poor time in comparison to previous seasons. In the lower half of the table, one defeat in five League games including three wins over the Christmas/New Year period had moved them up to a position where they were not going to have a say in the destination of the League title but equally were well clear of the relegation places. In midweek they had overcome Preston in a fourth round FA Cup replay. Ron Burgess had been injured in that game but at least Les Medley was ready to return after missing the two games with Preston.

BEFORE THE GAME

	P	W	D	L	F	A	Pts
Arsenal	24	12	7	5	54	38	31
Spurs	27	11	7	9	49	34	29

AT THE SEASON'S END

		P	W	D	L	F	A	Pts
1st	Arsenal	42	21	12	9	97	64	54
10th	Spurs	42	15	11	16	78	69	41

THAT WAS THEN...

★ The Arsenal programme advertised a supporters trip to the following Saturday's FA Cup 5th Round tie at Burnley... return rail fare 35 shillings (£1.75). Arsenal had been allocated 11,500 match tickets for Turf Moor at 2/6d each (13p).

Ted Ditchburn is unable to stop a shot from Cliff Holton (out of picture) and Arsenal take the lead.

*Alan Ross in '**The Observer**' under...*

Arsenal Team Prove Their Mettle

Arsenal, beating Tottenham Hotspur at Highbury by four goals to none, once again showed that when put to it there is no finer all-round side in the country. The ground was much harder and faster than of late, but the sun shone from a thin blue sky and there was so little wind that the smoke-stacks to the east, like steamers run aground, smoked straight up in the air.

Nearly 70,000 watched the game which, if it petered out as a struggle early in the second half, was always an interesting contrast in styles. Tottenham worked to a close, intricate design, leaving little margin for error, while Arsenal, moving the ball sooner and further, gave their strong, fast forwards plenty of room.

The score, of course, speaks for itself; yet Tottenham completely controlled the opening 25 minutes of the match, and during this period, moving on the Arsenal goal with perfectly timed central attacks, the ball being flicked from forward to forward with the Arsenal defence groping, they might have been at least two goals to the good - and the first goal in a match of this kind usually makes all the difference.

As it was, the Arsenal defence was opened three times in quick succession, but Duquemin, Walters, and Bennett all made their shots slightly off balance. Then a neatly linked move between Duquemin and Bennett let Duquemin clean through the centre, but his rising shot hit the bar and skidded over. That, as it happened, was the end of Tottenham's fluency.

Milton raced the length of the field in the next minute, his centre ricocheted to HOLTON a few yards from goal, and Ditchburn had no chance at all. Tottenham nevertheless remained the more subtle side until the interval, but they were no longer finding the gaps. Wade, greatly poised now at full-back, kept Baily and Medley well out on the touchline; and Forbes was always racing back to hurry them more than they like.

The second half began with Milton again racing clear of Willis and giving HOLTON a second chance to pick his spot in the back of the net. This, in fact, was the pattern of the rest of the game, for Milton, perfectly fed by Logie, who consistently lobbed Willis, now made raid after raid. His quick acceleration took him clear of the Spurs defence and Holton, Logie and Lishman, tore down the centre to meet a stream of accurate passes from the by-line. LISHMAN drove in a pass from Logie 10 minutes later, and soon after LOGIE was unmarked to flick Milton's centre wide of Ditchburn.

Four goals up, Arsenal were moving now with a sweep and speed that left the Tottenham defence ragged and ineffectual. The Spurs held no more threat, and while they were pressed to increasing and sadly undignified mistakes, Arsenal acquired a fearsome majesty.

Below: Jimmy Logie and Doug Lishman (nearest the camera) are seated as the latter's shot finds the back of the net to put Arsenal three up.

Bottom: Arsenal's Jack Kelsey saves. Joe Wade provides the cover.

35

TOTTENHAM HOTSPUR 1
Robb

ARSENAL 4
Logie 2, Milton, Forbes (pen)

Tottenham Hotspur

Arsenal

Manager
Arthur Rowe

Manager
Tom Whittaker

Tottenham	No.	Arsenal
Ted **DITCHBURN**	1	Jack **KELSEY**
Alf **RAMSEY**	2	Len **WILLS**
Charlie **WITHERS**	3	Dennis **EVANS**
Bill **NICHOLSON**	4	Alex **FORBES**
Harry **CLARKE**	5	Bill **DODGIN**
Ralph **WETTON**	6	Joe **MERCER**
Sonny **WALTERS**	7	Arthur **MILTON**
Les **BENNETT**	8	Jimmy **LOGIE**
Len **DUQUEMIN**	9	Tommy **LAWTON**
Tommy **HARMER**	10	Doug **LISHMAN**
George **ROBB**	11	Don **ROPER**

Referee **Mr N C Taylor** (Westbury)

BACKGROUND

Spurs started the season as if it were they, not Arsenal, defending the title. Four wins in five games, albeit three of them at home, kindled hopes of a serious challenge for the championship but it did not last and by the time of Arsenal's visit they were back in the middle of the table, seven points behind leaders, West Brom. Tommy Harmer continued in the absence of Eddie Baily and while they were pleased to welcome back Sonny Walters and Bill Nicholson the return of the future Spurs' manager was offset by the loss of his half-back partner, Ron Burgess, who was playing for Wales against England at Cardiff. Arsenal had begun the campaign in atrocious fashion, losing six and drawing two of their first eight games, the last a 1-7 defeat at Sunderland that saw George Swindin finish his last game for Arsenal on a stretcher. In desperation, manager Tom Whittaker signed Tommy Lawton, a month short of his 34th birthday, from Brentford for £10,000. By the time of his arrival Arsenal had secured their first victory of the season, they got a draw on his debut and won the next two games without him but he returned for the derby in place of Cliff Holton. Arsenal's had problems, though, at full-back. With Wally Barnes also playing for Wales and regular choices Joe Wade and Lionel Smith injured, they were forced to rely on youngsters Dennis Evans and, making his debut, Len Wills.

BEFORE THE GAME

	P	W	D	L	F	A	Pts
Spurs	12	6	1	5	20	19	13
Arsenal	12	3	3	6	16	22	9

THAT WAS THEN...

★ The Tottenham programme carried the following warning to the occupants of the Boys' Enclosure...
" We all fully recognise that boys will be boys but if, as we trust, they are young sportsmen we must ask them to refrain from throwing rubbish such as apple cores, half-oranges, and bad fruit on to the adult supporters who have taken up positions in front of this enclosure... Now, boys, remember your duty to the Club and let us hear of no further complaints."

Sonny Walters goes full length to head the ball back across the Arsenal goal.

ARSENAL IN LEAGUE RACE BY XMAS?

A swaying, tip-toed, hanging-on-for-dear-life crowd of 70,000, in constant danger of spilling over the barriers, saw at Tottenham the most complete and decisive ending of one of Soccer's most mysterious slumps.

Arsenal, I can report, are back in full production.

I say this not merely because Arsenal scored four goals, but because there was throughout the team a thrilling surge and sense of purpose, a determination which brushed aside at last all doubts and criticisms.

Opposed to such a swell of team spirit and endeavour, Spurs went under, struggled, and finally sank. But this much, too, must be said. That old imp, the luck of the Arsenal, was back on the field playing his puckish part in bringing Arsenal so much nearer to the task of defending their championship.

Arsenal survived a non-stop onslaught by Spurs in the first ten minutes, themselves scored four goals within 24 minutes, then defended with cool heads and kind fortune against all the desperation of Tottenham's counter-attacks.

Kelsey, the Arsenal goalkeeper, was brilliant and courageous in these situations. Every Spurs forward can testify to a succession of most daring saves.

But the truth is Tottenham had no inside forwards capable of bringing Robb and Duquemin effectively into these attacks, and without Burgess their defence was ill-organised and guileless, despite the skill and effort of Ramsey.

I sum up the significance of this game thus:

A continuation of football like this will put Arsenal into the League race by Christmas; a few more weeks of football like this and the Spurs will be looking around them to see if there are any teams still behind them.

Arsenal's revival was not driven along by Lawton, who contributed very little to the match, but by Logie, now master of all his team's attacks, scoring goals and playing as well as ever.

The refereeing of the match was confusing. Arsenal were given a first half penalty for which I could see no justification, and each side was refused a penalty in the second half which I think should have been awarded.

Arsenal were 4-0 at half-time in this way: **LOGIE** (9min.), **MILTON** (22min.), **FORBES** (penalty, 34min.), and **LOGIE** (39min.). Spurs goal was scored by **ROBB** nine minutes from the end.

A shot from Arthur Milton bounces off the post and Jimmy Logie (No.8) is on hand to score his second and Arsenal's fourth goal.

Top of the page: Sonny Walters and Joe Mercer struggle for possession.

'DERBY' STAR

★ Jimmy Logie ★

"Master of all his team's attacks, scoring goals and playing as well as ever", said the 'Sunday Despatch'. Another report read... "Logie was terrific, a pint-sized tornado in a red shirt. Arsenal's other forwards were no better than they have been all season, but Jimmy achieved the status of a giant with his first-half destruction of Spurs' defence."

'DERBY' STAR

"**Football grounds throughout the country had a great shock on Saturday when the half-time scores went up on the board - Tottenham 0 Arsenal 4**"

36

ARSENAL 0

TOTTENHAM HOTSPUR 3
Robb 2, Walters

Arsenal

Tottenham Hotspur

Manager
Tom Whittaker

Manager
Arthur Rowe

Jack KELSEY	1	Ted DITCHBURN
Len WILLS	2	Alf RAMSEY
Walley BARNES	3	Arthur WILLIS
Alex FORBES	4	Tony MARCHI
Bill DODGIN	5	Harry CLARKE
Joe MERCER	6	Ralph WETTON
Brian WALSH	7	Sonny WALTERS
Jimmy LOGIE	8	Les BENNETT
Cliff HOLTON	9	Dave DUNMORE
Doug LISHMAN	10	Eddie BAILY
Don ROPER	11	George ROBB

Referee **Mr N C Taylor** (Westbury)

BACKGROUND

With both teams in mid-table, apparently safe from relegation and out of the championship race, it says a lot for the lure of a derby that a crowd of over 64,000 still attended a match that was of little more than local interest. Since the first meeting Arsenal had continued to repair the damage caused by their early season misfortunes, the only setback coming with a surprise FA Cup exit at the hands of Norwich. Without a game on fifth round day they had played a friendly against the Brazilian tourists Portuguesa de Desportos and won 7-1 with Cliff Holton netting five. They had then won 1-0 at Preston without Joe Mercer and Jimmy Logie who were now fit to return. Spurs were still in the Cup, having just beaten Hull City in a replay to set up a sixth round clash at West Brom, but most attention was focussed on their new £10,500 centre-forward, Dave Dunmore. He had scored 25 goals in 48 matches for York and was called up to make his debut in place of the injured Len Duquemin while Tony Marchi stood in for Bill Nicholson.

BEFORE THE GAME

	P	W	D	L	F	A	Pts
Arsenal	30	11	10	9	53	51	32
Spurs	30	12	4	14	46	50	28

AT THE SEASON'S END

		P	W	D	L	F	A	Pts
12th	Arsenal	42	15	13	14	75	73	43
16th	Spurs	42	16	5	21	65	76	37

★ The top five in the First Division on the morning of the game were West Bromwich Albion (45 points from 31 games), Wolves (43/31), Huddersfield (39/31), Burnley (38/31) and Bolton (37/30). Liverpool were two points adrift of Middlesbrough at the bottom! Wolves eventually pipped their Black Country neighbours to the title but the bottom two remained the same.

In '**The Observer**' AJ Ayer reported...

SPURS REVENGE

On a sunny afternoon at Highbury, Tottenham Hotspur took their revenge for the heavy defeat which Arsenal had inflicted on them at Tottenham earlier this season.

It was a good-humoured, if not brilliant, game which the Spurs thoroughly deserved to win. Except for the first quarter of an hour they always looked to be the better side. They played a more open game than usual, and were quicker on the ball than the Arsenal who, by comparison seemed lackadaisical. It was as if the Arsenal had assumed a superiority which they proved not to possess.

Much interest attached to the first appearance of Dunmore, Tottenham's new recruit from York City, who deputised at centre-forward for the injured Duquemin. Though his play deteriorated in the second half, he showed some promising touches, and it was he who put **ROBB**

through after 30 minutes to score the Spurs' first goal. The second was also scored by **ROBB** 10 minutes later with a remarkable overhead kick following a corner by Walters, and the third came shortly after half-time when **WALTERS** headed in Robb's well-placed centre.

Apart from Robb, Ramsey, who captained the side in Burgess's absence, was outstanding for the Spurs, whose forwards showed more cohesion than they have for most of this season, though Baily is still somewhat out of touch.

As always, the Arsenal were dangerous in occasional breakaways, but the Spurs' covering was sound, and Ditchburn had only three difficult shots to save. The Arsenal were handicapped in the second half by an injury to Walsh, their outside-right, but by the time it occurred they were already a beaten side.

Spurs go two up as Arsenal goalkeeper Jack Kelsey is well beaten by a fine shot from George Robb (out of picture). Wally Barnes is the Arsenal player nearest the goal-line.

Ted Ditchburn saves bravely at the feet of Arsenal's Jimmy Logie. Ralph Wetton looks on.

37

ARSENAL 2
Logie, Lishman

TOTTENHAM HOTSPUR 0

Arsenal		Tottenham Hotspur
Manager **Tom Whittaker**		Manager **Arthur Rowe**

Jack KELSEY	1	Ted DITCHBURN
Len WILLS	2	Alf RAMSEY
Walley BARNES	3	Charlie WITHERS
Peter GORING	4	Ralph WETTON
Alex FORBES	5	Harry CLARKE
Dave BOWEN	6	Colin BRITTAN
Derek TAPSCOTT	7	Sonny WALTERS
Jimmy LOGIE	8	Les BENNETT
Tommy LAWTON	9	Dave DUNMORE
Doug LISHMAN	10	Eddie BAILY
Don ROPER	11	George ROBB

Referee **Mr W Clements** (West Bromwich)

BACKGROUND

On 10th April 1954 Joe Mercer was carried from the Highbury pitch having broken his leg in a collision with team-mate Joe Wade whilst playing against Liverpool. It brought his career to an end. The loss of the former England international was immediately felt with Arsenal losing their first three matches of the new season. Four days before the derby they picked up their first points with a 2-0 home defeat of Everton. It was not only Arsenal that lost one of their most influential, driving forces. Just a month after Mercer announced his retirement, Ron Burgess left Spurs to join Swansea. His departure did not seem to be so keenly felt, but victory in the opening two games of the season was to prove deceptive, as Spurs went to Highbury on the back of two defeats.

BEFORE THE GAME

	P	W	D	L	F	A	Pts
Spurs	4	2	0	2	9	9	4
Arsenal	4	1	0	3	4	7	2

Two views of Jimmy Logie's goal, netting from an acute angle despite the efforts of Spurs No.4 Ralph Wetton and goalkeeper Ted Ditchburn.

No sign of Arsenal decline

'The Sunday Times' *Special Correspondent reported...*

Although North London was some way from being as deserted as Goldsmith's village, there were at least some 54,000 good Londoners - and one broad Aberdonian whom I took pleasure in escorting to the ground - inside Highbury yesterday. They saw Arsenal beat their old foes Tottenham Hotspur comfortably enough by two goals to none, and in seeing must have realised that there need be few fears of the Arsenal decline that so many seize upon at the flimsiest hint.

Whether Arsenal would have coasted home without being fully stretched had not an injury to Withers' right knee forced a re-adjustment of Tottenham's forces after 25 minutes must remain one of those imponderables. That is the way of football: but with the full-back hobbling at outside-left, Robb, the individualist, out of place at inside-right, Bennett in the half-back line and Wetton as Ramsey's partner, the Spurs lost their smooth look of the opening phases.

MERE FORMALITY

And from the moment **LOGIE** cheekily flicked Arsenal into the lead at the half hour, after Lawton's header to a corner by Roper had brought Ditchburn full length, there were never any serious doubts about the final answer. Indeed, the first minute of the second half made all that remained a mere formality.

Lawton, not for the first time, was rudely toppled by a worried Clarke, and from Goring's well-angled free-kick **LISHMAN** headed home a great second goal from some 12 yards to leave Ditchburn helpless.

There it was. And there was a full crowd, its face resembling banks of gravel in the sunshine, enjoying a typical Englishman's Saturday afternoon after a morning of typical English rain. They may not exactly have been left gasping at any Magyar mysteries; perhaps there was no superb Uruguyan artistry. But it was good enough entertainment even if, like the proverbial curate's egg, it was not all palatable.

The first half was good; later standards declined. But one gained a very clear impression that real efforts are now being made at a greater degree of ball skill and accuracy at the grammar of the game. In fact, there was a sense of both sides trying to work out their moves ahead, like chess players. Things at last may be moving in the right direction after the recent proddings from overseas.

So the first of this season's "London Derbies" has come and gone. In it one noticed especially the red head of Forbes as an Arsenal centre-half not entirely wedded to defence - a fine player; the gyrations of Logie at inside-right, and the balance that Lawton brought at centre-forward as he linked the Arsenal line together.

His thunderous shot and his last degree of pace have gone, but he is still a thinking footballer and he can still climb the sky for his headwork. This last quality of his leads Arsenal into a major fault. Too often they try to find that head of his in the final assault.

As for the Spurs, one must be tempered on this occasion. Misfortune knocked their machine out of shape, but Ramsey's cultured touches still remained, even if Roper's strength worried him. Baily, too, full of tricks and verve, played himself into the ground.

But the old smooth approach of their Championship year has gone and their close passing brought too much bunching at the crucial moment. Still, it was good enough fun. And now Arsenal must be feeling happier about the approaching trip to Moscow.

Ted Ditchburn punches clear of Tommy Lawton. Harry Clarke and Alf Ramsey are the Spurs defenders in attendance.

Ted Ditchburn is beaten by a header from Doug Lishman (out of picture) and Arsenal go 2-0 in front.

38

TOTTENHAM HOTSPUR 0

ARSENAL 1
Lawton

Tottenham Hotspur

Manager
Arthur Rowe

Arsenal

Manager
Tom Whittaker

Ron REYNOLDS	1	Jack KELSEY
Alf RAMSEY	2	Walley BARNES
Mel HOPKINS	3	Dennis EVANS
Danny BLANCHFLOWER	4	Peter GORING
Harry CLARKE	5	Jim FOTHERINGHAM
Tony MARCHI	6	Dave BOWEN
Johnny GAVIN	7	Arthur MILTON
Eddie BAILY	8	Derek TAPSCOTT
Dave DUNMORE	9	Tommy LAWTON
Johnny BROOKS	10	Doug LISHMAN
George ROBB	11	Cliff HOLTON

Referee **Mr W Ling** (Stapleford)

BACKGROUND

In a season of rebuilding that had seen Johnny Brooks, Dave Dunmore, Johnny Gavin, Mel Hopkins and Ron Reynolds all become first team regulars, a mini-revival of six unbeaten games, five in the League, following the signing in December 1954 of Danny Blanchflower had taken Spurs clear of the relegation places. They were five places above bottom club Sheffield Wednesday, who already looked doomed, but still very much part of a battle already developing to avoid the dreaded drop. Arsenal, too, were in the middle of that battle, only three points ahead of Leicester, who occupied the other relegation place. Like Spurs they were in a period of transition trying to replace aging stars who had brought so much success with new talent such as Dave Bowen, Jim Fotheringham, Derek Tapscott, Danny Clapton and Joe Haverty.

BEFORE THE GAME

	P	W	D	L	F	A	Pts
Spurs	25	8	6	11	41	49	22
Arsenal	25	7	6	12	42	46	20

SPURS v ARSENAL ON ICE!

"Now I've seen it all. The show of the century. Colossal. Superb. Stupendous. Spurs v Arsenal on Ice. The Soccer spectacle to end all Soccer spectacles...

Ninety minutes of spills and thrills. Ninety minutes of breath-taking North Pole - sorry, North London - local Derby. All served up without skates at the Ice Drome, Tottenham, otherwise popularly known as White Hart Lane.

Spectacle Soccer. Pantomime Soccer. Soccer with a purpose - and the inevitable light relief...

Like when a linesman running down the blue-painted 'white' line goes a-sliding non-stop like some kid in a playground.

Novelty Soccer. A Christmas card with a kick."

- Maurice Smith reporting in 'The People'

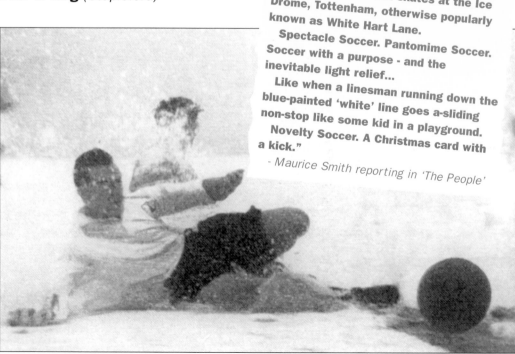

In *'The Observer'* JL Weinstein reported...

Spurs' Run Ended

White Hart Lane was aptly named yesterday afternoon for the seasonal battle between the rivals of North London. Arsenal's victory, their fourth on the trot on this ground, takes them above Tottenham Hotspur in the championship, at least on goal average, and ended a long Spurs' run of six matches without defeat. Indeed, Tottenham before this game had lost only once - at home to Everton - since the second week in November.

That the game was played at all was a credit to the groundstaff. The pitch was prepared by the ingenious use of scaffolding planks. These were laid out across the surface and stamped down, then turned over, and the process was repeated the length of the field.

The result was that the snow was compressed until a carpet of about two inches instead of the original four or five covered the playing area, and though at times the scene was like an ice rink, there was an abundance of good football.

Ramsey and Blanchflower, on the Spurs right flank, set the example. Their artistic and thoughtful distribution of the ball cannot fail to inspire the youngsters of Tottenham, who are settling into the side.

Holton, Arsenal's outside-left, who had already made an opening for Bowen, nearly opened the scoring in the fifth minute with a thundering free kick which shuddered the angle of Reynold's crossbar and left-hand post. Gavin almost at once raced away from Baily's pass and his cross, which Barnes cunningly allowed to slip through his legs, ran just wide of Robb. The general pattern of the game was as had been expected. Tottenham preferred the shorter pass frequently made and continuous contact between players. Baily and Blanchflower combined well with Marchi and Brooks on the left. Arsenal attacks were developed down the flanks.

If **LAWTON** sometimes saddened with reminders that his greatness is past, he nevertheless made enough good passes to give his side most of the chances missed. Besides, he did score the goal that mattered. This came a quarter of an hour after the interval, following a scrimmage in which both Lishman and Tapscott took part. From that point on Arsenal played with greater confidence.

The arrival of a new ball, which the hovering fog made necessary, did not help Tottenham. They pressed hard, but Barnes and Evans at full back were equal to all efforts. Behind them, Kelsey saved brilliantly at Gavin's feet, and then deflected a fine shot by Robb for a corner. Though Tottenham forced four more corners before the end - the entire team, except for the goalkeeper, Reynolds, and the left-back, Hopkins, advanced for one of them into the Arsenal penalty area - they did not seem likely to score.

MATCH FACTS *(by 'Fact Finder' in 'The People')*

	Spurs	Arsenal
➤ **Shots at goal**	18	11
➤ **Corners**	8	1
➤ **Good passes**	14	13
➤ **Off-course passes**	18	8
➤ **Dispossessed of ball**	9	8
➤ **Good tackles**	10	11

➤ *Arsenal goalkeeper Jack Kelsey was credited with 2 brilliant saves, 5 good saves and 7 interceptions.*

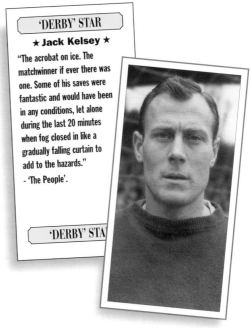

'DERBY' STAR

★ Jack Kelsey ★

"The acrobat on ice. The matchwinner if ever there was one. Some of his saves were fantastic and would have been in any conditions, let alone during the last 20 minutes when fog closed in like a gradually falling curtain to add to the hazards."
- 'The People'.

'DERBY' STA

AT THE SEASON'S END

		P	W	D	L	F	A	Pts
9th	Arsenal	42	17	9	16	69	63	43
16th	Spurs	42	16	8	18	72	73	40

Tommy Lawton (extreme right) scores the only goal of the game.

39

TOTTENHAM HOTSPUR 3
Baily, Stokes 2

ARSENAL 1
Roper

Saturday 10th September 1955

Football League Division One

White Hart Lane

Attendance 51,029

Tottenham Hotspur

Arsenal

Manager
Jimmy Anderson

Manager
Tom Whittaker

Ted DITCHBURN	1	Jack KELSEY
Charlie WITHERS	2	Walley BARNES
Mel HOPKINS	3	Dennis EVANS
Danny BLANCHFLOWER	4	Peter GORING
Harry CLARKE	5	Jim FOTHERINGHAM
Tony MARCHI	6	Dave BOWEN
Sonny WALTERS	7	Danny CLAPTON
Johnny BROOKS	8	Derek TAPSCOTT
Alfie STOKES	9	Tommy LAWTON
Eddie BAILY	10	Don ROPER
George ROBB	11	Brian WALSH

Referee **Capt. A W Smith** (Aldershot)

BACKGROUND

Bottom of the table with only one point out of twelve, Spurs' decline since winning the League title in 1951 continued unabated. Unable to re-create his great "Push and Run" team Arthur Rowe's health suffered and after continual problems he resigned in July 1955 to be replaced by his assistant Jimmy Anderson. Spurs also lost Alf Ramsey during the summer when he took the first step on a managerial career with Ipswich. Anderson though made few changes to the team that had only managed to finish 16th the previous season. Ted Ditchburn was re-instated as first choice 'keeper, the veteran Charlie Withers recalled to replace Ramsey and 5'9" Alfie Stokes, who had not appeared in the League side since March 1954, installed at centre-forward. Arsenal's start had not been much better, one win and three draws, but at least Tommy Lawton, six goals in four games, was showing that even at 35 he still knack that goal-scoring ability. With summer signing Jimmy Bloomfield injured Brian Walsh was given a rare outing.

BEFORE THE GAME

	P	W	D	L	F	A	Pts
Arsenal	6	1	3	2	8	11	5
Spurs	6	0	1	5	6	12	1

OH! ARSENAL - GO OUT AND BUY

"Tottering Hotspur? Feeble, down-dropping, Doddering Hotspur? Not Likely! Not on this sample. Relegation Tottenham? Forget it!

I speak as I find. And yesterday I found Spurs back to their old best - back, at least, to within a hackle's width of it. Gilt-edged, perkily-confident Spurs once more. Even the old cockerel on the grandstand seemed to have a new glint in his eye...

...The deep depression that had settled over Tottenham is moving off south-west to Highbury. I make this forecast: The Arsenal, unless they go player-shopping soon and in a big way, will find themselves in the dampening cold of the Second Division!

No, Tottenham needn't worry. BUT ARSENAL MUST!"

- *Maurice Smith in 'The People'*

The ball hits the back of the net as Eddie Baily puts Tottenham ahead.

'The Daily Telegraph and Morning Post' reported...

BAILY PEPS UP THE SPURS
– IN ENGLAND FORM AGAINST ARSENAL

Tottenham manager Mr Jimmy Anderson will walk into his office this morning feeling light of heart probably for the first since the season began.

His refusal to change a side which had scraped only one point from six games has been amply justified by their winning the seventh in most handsome fashion. And what more appropriate first victims than their next-door neighbours and closest rivals?

True, Tottenham are still at the bottom of the First Division table. But on this form, which particularly in the second half revived memories of their past glories, they will soon rise to more respectable heights. A great deal may well depend upon **BAILY**, who inspired this much-needed success.

INSPIRING DISPLAY

The former England inside-left was right back to his exuberant best, placing his passes with guile and accuracy, chivvying colleagues whose enthusiasm did not match his own, and heading an all-important confidence-boosting goal from Walters' centre in the tenth minute.

It was not the fault of Baily, nor of Brooks, the second-best forward afield, that a shapeless, tired-looking Arsenal were allowed to come back into the game with a goal by **ROPER** 15 minutes from the end of an entertaining first half.

Robb, Walters and Stokes began to make full use of their team-mates efforts only after the interval, when **STOKES** wiped out all previous misdemeanours by scoring two excellent goals.

Eddie Baily (extreme right) celebrates as as shot from Alf Stokes evades Walley Barnes to put Spurs 2-1 up.

Above: Arsenal winger Danny Clapton beats Spurs' 'keeper Ted Ditchburn in the air.

Left: Walley Barnes comes in to tackle as Johnny Brooks prepares to shoot.

'DERBY' STAR

★ **Alfie Stokes** ★

Playing his first League game for 18 months the Spurs centre-forward won the match with two excellent second-half goals.

40

ARSENAL 0

TOTTENHAM HOTSPUR 1
Robb

Arsenal

Tottenham Hotspur

Manager
Tom Whittaker

Manager
Jimmy Anderson

Jack KELSEY	1	Ron REYNOLDS
Len WILLS	2	Maurice NORMAN
Dennis EVANS	3	Mel HOPKINS
Alex FORBES	4	Danny BLANCHFLOWER
Jim FOTHERINGHAM	5	Harry CLARKE
Cliff HOLTON	6	Tony MARCHI
Danny CLAPTON	7	Micky DULIN
Derek TAPSCOTT	8	Johnny BROOKS
Vic GROVES	9	Len DUQUEMIN
Jimmy BLOOMFIELD	10	Bobby SMITH
Gordon NUTT	11	George ROBB

Referee **Capt. A W Smith** *(Aldershot)*

BACKGROUND

Arsenal's form throughout the first half of the season is perhaps best summed up by their two matches preceding the derby, a 2-2 draw at home to non-League Bedford in the FA Cup and a fortunate 2-1 extra-time win two days earlier in the replay, where only a Vic Groves equaliser five minutes from the end of normal time prevented a giant-killing act to match their 1933 defeat at Walsall. Jack Kelsey had returned at Bedford after a seven game absence with a broken finger but Peter Goring, Stan Charlton and Mike Tiddy were missing with Alex Forbes, Len Wills and Gordon Nutt replacing them. Spurs had remained at the bottom of the table until Christmas but their form had improved in the last few weeks although they were still relegation candidates. Maurice Norman, signed from Norwich, was settling in at right-back, Ron Reynolds had been recalled in goal and the evergreen Len Duquemin discovered a new lease of life with the December arrival of Bobby Smith from Chelsea. They had also met non-League opposition in the Cup seven days earlier but had found the task somewhat easier than Arsenal, beating Boston 4-0 at White Hart Lane.

BEFORE THE GAME

	P	W	D	L	F	A	Pts
Arsenal	25	8	8	9	34	41	24
Spurs	25	8	3	14	32	42	19

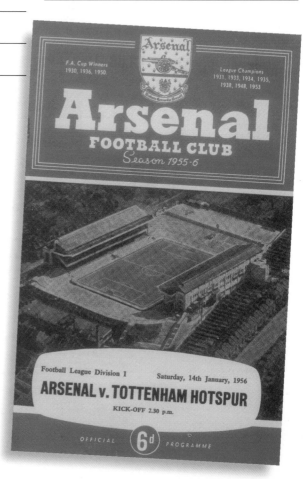

The only goal of the game is turned in by No.11 George Robb.

'The Sunday Times' reported on...

TWO POINTS FOR SPURS

Tottenham Hotspur continued their improved League form at the expense of their near neighbours Arsenal at Highbury.

Nearly 60,000 spectators saw these two once great teams, who are now sharing the First Division shadows, produce a game remarkable for its lack of guile. The result was justice insomuch as Tottenham did display a few ideas, even if their fussiness in the mud sometimes brought them trouble.

Arsenal gave an impression of unharnessed power. Yet they should have equalised. In the closing minutes they flung in wave after wave of attack which, if they beat a firm Tottenham defence, invariably collapsed through lack of steadiness or inspiration.

Between victors and vanquished there was little to choose in defence, although Tottenham's Norman was the pick of the full-backs. He showed his versatility when Arsenal's pressure was at its greatest by racing 60 yards down the wing and bringing Kelsey sprawling to save his shot.

In attack Tottenham were superior because in Robb and Brooks they had two forwards determined not to get involved in the general edginess of the match. They defied the ferocious tackling of Arsenal wing-halves Forbes and Holton with the consequence that, after the opening exchanges, Tottenham were always more menacing.

It was their coolness that brought the all-important goal after 31 minutes. Centre-forward Duquemin pushed the perfect through-pass down the middle. Brooks calmly squared it across goal and ROBB had to do no more than tap the ball into the net.

Arsenal's worst piece of luck came with 10 minutes to go. After a series of atrocious misses Groves beat goalkeeper Reynolds and a defender with a shot, only to see it roll an inch wide.

SPURS IN CLEAR BUT ARSENAL...

Arsenal ......0 Spurs 1

NO one expects stately Soccer this time of year, when mud makes fools of the finest players. All the more credit, then, to four Spurs, who dreamed up a wonderful winning goal in the 33rd minute.

Skipper Danny Blanchflower started it with a piercing through pass on the right wing.

Centre-forward Len Duquemin trapped the ball and rapped it onwards to inside-right Johnny Brooks, hovering near goal.

Arsenal defenders, including goalkeeper Kelsey advanced on Brooks, anticipating a shot.

Tricked ! With masterly calm and canny sizing-up of the situation, wavy-haired Brooks pushed the ball across the goalmouth mudpatch to Robb, racing in from the other side.

All he had to do was tap it home. Not an Arsenal man had touched the ball after Blanchflower collected it just inside the half-way line.

Just the once

Spurs tried this classy approach all through the first half. It never clicked again. Perhaps they were foolish to persevere with the delicate arts on a pitch crying out for the brute-force boot.

Perhaps . . but not even in the thickest mud would you ask a side to emulate a raw, ragged bunch of runabouts, which, sorrowfully, is all Arsenal's attack amounted to.

Part of Arsenal's trouble is that leader Vic Groves is still expending energy recklessly, doing most of his fetching and carrying.

Inside-left Bloomfield has apparently been told to hang back and concentrate on scheming. But he found the job beyond him.

The return of Alex Forbes, after ten months out of the League team, promises well when he gets the feel of present conditions. He tackled heftily as ever and won some half-hearted booing, most of which was for old times' sake.

"Spurs are no relegation team" —that is what I wrote a fortnight ago after they had beaten Charlton at The Valley. I see no reason to hedge.

But as for Arsenal, I only wish I could be half as optimistic.

Arsenal.—Kelsey ; Wills, Evans ; Forbes, Fotheringham Holton ; Clapton, Tapscott, Groves, Bloomfield, Nutt.
Spurs.—Reynolds ; Norman, Hopkins ; Blanchflower, Clarke, Marchi ; Dulin, Brooks, Duquemin, Smith, Robb.

Top: Spurs goalkeeper Ron Reynolds win an aerial duel with Arsenal's Derek Tapscott.

Above: Tony Marchi (left) and Vic Groves have eyes fixed firmly on the ball.

Right: Spurs centre-half Harry Clarke clears just in time as Vic Groves stretches to get an effort on goal.

AT THE SEASON'S END

		P	W	D	L	F	A	Pts
5th	Arsenal	42	18	10	14	60	61	46
18th	Spurs	42	15	7	20	61	71	37

41

ARSENAL 3
Herd 2, Haverty

TOTTENHAM HOTSPUR 1
Smith

Saturday 20th October 1956

Football League Division One

Highbury

Attendance 60,588

Arsenal | Tottenham Hotspur

Manager
Tom Whittaker

Manager
Jimmy Anderson

Arsenal	No	Tottenham Hotspur
Con SULLIVAN	1	Ted DITCHBURN
Stan CHARLTON	2	Peter BAKER
Dennis EVANS	3	Ron HENRY
Len WILLS	4	Danny BLANCHFLOWER
Bill DODGIN	5	Harry CLARKE
Cliff HOLTON	6	Tony MARCHI
Danny CLAPTON	7	Micky DULIN
Derek TAPSCOTT	8	Tommy HARMER
David HERD	9	Bobby SMITH
Jimmy BLOOMFIELD	10	Alfie STOKES
Joe HAVERTY	11	George ROBB

Referee **Mr R P Hartley** (Burnley)

Ted Ditchburn takes a tumble after saving at the feet of David Herd. Spurs centre-half Harry Clarke is also on the scene.

BACKGROUND

For what proved to be Tom Whittaker's last match as Arsenal secretary-manager (he was to pass away four days later) both clubs were hit by injury and international calls. Arsenal's Jack Kelsey and Spurs' Mel Hopkins and Terry Medwin were all playing for Wales against Scotland while Arsenal also had to make do without the injured Peter Goring, Dave Bowen and Vic Groves. Len Wills replaced Goring while Cliff Holton, who only two weeks earlier had scored four of Arsenal's goals in a 7-3 demolition of Manchester City, was moved into the half-back line with third choice centre-forward, David Herd, given a rare outing. Maurice Norman was a long-term absentee for Spurs but the loss of Johnny Brooks had been compensated for by the form of his replacement Alfie Stokes, eight goals in the last five games while Ron Henry and Micky Dulin replaced Spurs' Welsh stars. On the back of six straight wins Spurs had climbed to second in the table although they were three points behind Manchester United.

BEFORE THE GAME

	P	W	D	L	F	A	Pts
Spurs	12	9	1	2	39	16	19
Arsenal	13	6	1	6	28	24	13

HA Pawson in '**The Observer**'
reported...

Raiding Arsenal Put Emphasis on Speed

The loudspeaker announced: "There are three changes in the Arsenal side, one of them positional. Wills comes in for Goring at right-half, Holton moves to left-half and Herd comes in at centre-forward." A good part of the 60,000 crowd at Highbury was loud in its disapproval. Two hours later no one was dissatisfied at anything: for Arsenal supporters there was a solid 3-1 victory and the happy memory of the incessant raids of their small swift forwards, and for the Tottenham section there remained the excitement of a challenging game, in balance till the closing moments.

Throughout the match the two forward lines bore purposefully down on goal. Tottenham's approach was more intricate but slower, with short passes changing the direction of attack and probing for the opening.

Two-goal David Herd.

Right: Arsenal goalkeeper Con Sullivan is well beaten by Bobby Smith's shot as Spurs take a 33rd minute lead.

Below: Within a minute Arsenal are level as David Herd's header gets past Ted Ditchburn.

Arsenal's emphasis was on directness and speed; speed with the ball, in making the pass, and, still more important, in running into position.

Exemplar of all these virtues was Haverty on the left wing, a restless, intelligent player who was beautifully poised in all he did. His passes were stabbed swiftly along the ground, and he rarely made a conventional centre. He would feint to lob the ball over and, instead, slip it back hard to the advancing inside or wing half; it was his sense of opportunity that sent him racing over to the right to start the final decisive thrust.

FATAL WEAKNESS

But the whole Arsenal line moved so purposefully, and interchanged with such understanding, that the defence had no respite. In the end the contrast was not between dash and delicacy but between a line that was well balanced and one that had a fatal weakness on the right where Medwin's absence was sadly felt.

At the start it was the clever distribution of Harmer and Blanchflower that sent the ball flowing towards Arsenal's goal. But the first chance was fashioned by Smith, when he beat Dodgin and sent a pass inside the back for Robb to run through only to shoot wide.

Soon it was apparent that the decisive battle was between the two former amateur internationals, Robb and Charlton. In the end the tackling of Charlton won;

but he was always at full stretch, and it was not long before Robb eluded him and, turning inwards, dribbled into the centre to slip the ball through to **SMITH** who hit it home from close range.

There was scarcely time for congratulations before Tapscott chased a ball to the goal-line and lobbed it back to **HERD** who jumped high to head it over Ditchburn into the net.

CUT AND THRUST

Now it was cut and thrust. Just before half-time Ditchburn made an unprofitable sally to the edge of his area and Clarke had to head off the line. Then Sullivan made a fine diving save as Stokes shot low and hard for the corner.

At last Arsenal broke through. Herd and Tapscott swept the ball smoothly from the right to **HAVERTY**, who nonchalantly evaded a sliding tackle before scoring with ease.

Tottenham fought fiercely and Smith twice came near to scoring; but the final goal was fair comment on the game. At one end Robb's shot was saved. Immediately Arsenal were on the attack, with Haverty gathering the ball unmarked on the right. Two quick passes and Clapton had given **HERD** the chance to settle the game with a simple shot.

'DERBY' STAR

★ Joe Haverty ★

'The Observer' described Arsenal's 20-year-old Dubliner as "a restless, intelligent player who was beautifully poised in all he did"

42
TOTTENHAM HOTSPUR 1
Medwin
ARSENAL 3
Bowen 2, Tapscott

Wednesday 13th March 1957

Football League Division One

White Hart Lane

Attendance 64,555

Tottenham Hotspur

Manager
Jimmy Anderson

Arsenal

Manager
Jack Crayston

Ron REYNOLDS	1	Jack KELSEY
Peter BAKER	2	Len WILLS
Maurice NORMAN	3	Dennis EVANS
Danny BLANCHFLOWER	4	Cliff HOLTON
John RYDEN	5	Bill DODGIN
Tony MARCHI	6	Dave BOWEN
Terry MEDWIN	7	Danny CLAPTON
Tommy HARMER	8	Derek TAPSCOTT
Bobby SMITH	9	David HERD
Johnny BROOKS	10	Jimmy BLOOMFIELD
George ROBB	11	Joe HAVERTY

Referee **Mr R J Leafe** (Nottingham)

BACKGROUND

From almost the start of the season Spurs had shadowed Manchester United as the defending champions battled for the ultimate "treble" of League title, FA Cup and European Cup. The challenge all but evaporated following defeat at Third Division (South) Bournemouth in the fifth round of the FA Cup. In the next three games Chelsea left White Hart Lane with both points and Spurs could do no better than return from Leeds and West Brom with 1-1 draws. If any hope of catching Matt Busby's side was to be maintained two points against Arsenal were essential, but Spurs were not helped by the absence of top scorer Alfie Stokes, playing for the Football League against their Scottish counterparts. Arsenal, with Len Wills standing in for Stan Charlton, needed no greater incentive. Jack Crayston had been appointed to succeed Tom Whittaker and he immediately promoted David Herd from the reserves. A run of ten games without defeat took Arsenal to third place at the turn of the year but Manchester United were the outstanding team and the FA Cup soon became the only hope of Crayston starting his managerial career with a trophy. They looked a good bet for it after drawing at the Hawthorns in the sixth round but a disappointing performance in the replay saw West Brom go through to the semi-final.

BEFORE THE GAME

	P	W	D	L	F	A	Pts
Spurs	31	17	8	6	81	44	42
Arsenal	32	16	5	11	69	59	37

'DERBY' STAR

★ Dave Bowen ★

Dave was the only player, apart from goalkeeper Jack Kelsey who had not scored for Arsenal this season, but he made up for it with a vengeance with two goals to seriously dent Tottenham's championship dream. It was a great night for the 'London Welsh' as all four goals were scored by Welsh internationals. After his second goal, Bowen's team-mates knocked him flat on his face and almost trampled on him.

'DERBY' STAR

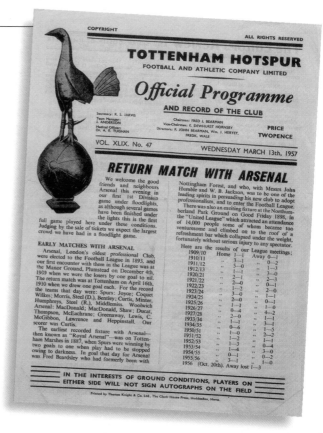

ARSENAL DEFENCE CHECKS SPURS - TWO SURPRISE GOALS BY BOWEN

White Hart Lane is one of those courses for horses where Arsenal are concerned. Until last night they had won there four times out of six in the Championship, quite apart from two successful F.A. Cup semi-finals against Chelsea since the war. Now they won again before a crowd over 65,000 strong, the biggest attendance yet at any League match under floodlights. The crush was powerful and the traffic congestion almost chaotic. One man arriving an hour before the kick-off found himself having to park his car at Walthamstow.

But if anybody drew a great sigh of relief it must have been Manchester United. With 10 Championship matches, a Cup semi-final, perhaps even a Cup Final itself, and two semi-final ties against Real Madrid in the European Cup within the next seven weeks, they have their plate full, beside the added worry of injuries. This means two games and perhaps even three a week from now until the end of the season. If anyone has doubted the task that lies before them of bringing off the double those figures should set it in high relief. And now Arsenal came very much to their rescue at a timely moment.

The position in the Championship at the moment is this. Tottenham with this defeat are now seven points behind Manchester United with an equal number of games played. Preston, with one match more, are five points in the rear, so that the United for the moment at least can breathe more freely. In addition their goal average is better than both pursuers.

LET FLY

It was a great match last night. Even if it had not been, three of the four goals alone were worth talking about. The first came in the twenty-fifth minute to put Tottenham ahead. Norman, who played finely at left-back, put Medwin away out on the left flank, out of his position. But **MEDWIN** cared not a jot. Selling the dummy, accelerating outside Wills and reaching the corner of the penalty area he let fly a terrific left-foot shot from an angle to hit the roof of Kelsey's net like a thunderbolt. But 10 minutes later Arsenal had drawn level, to go in at the interval to work out their plans for the second half.

Their goal, too, was a beauty and it came, of all people, from **BOWEN**, their left-half, who showed any watching schoolboy how retreating defence can be beaten. Taking a mid-field pass from Clapton he ran on some 25 yards looking to left and right for an opening pass. Instead he was confronted with a defence funnelling back into the penalty area. As he looked up once more one could almost hear his brain tick over. Going another yard or so he picked his spot in the top left-hand corner and shot from some 20 yards. The arrow went home like a flash, and the Arsenal roars rose from this vast North London crowd.

TURNING POINT

Immediately after half-time there came the turning point. From Tottenham's point of view it was a tragedy. Baker, caught with the ball in an awkward spot, swivelled backwards and passed towards Reynolds. **TAPSCOTT** was on the ball in a flash, and there he was whacking home left-footed beyond a defence now left wide open. From that moment, for all Tottenham's spirit and drive and clever approach, the stars above took on a red glow, and with half an hour left Arsenal settled things. Once more it was **BOWEN** who beat his man, moved forward some five yards and this time chose the right-hand top corner of Reynolds' goal for his own special pleasure. Another 25-yard shot fizzed home and that was that.

For Tottenham Norman, Ryden and Blanchflower were masters in their way. Robb and Medwin showed pace and thrust down the flanks, while Brooks began in a way that might have dazzled any selector. But none of these units could finally be threaded into a positive whole by the artistry and passing of Harmer. Time after time his chips and flicks went to the last inch as if on a thread, but Dodgin, Bowen and company played it all as if they had played it for most of their lives.

Above: Len Wills heads clear from under the Arsenal crossbar as Bill Dodgin and Johnny Brooks (left) look on.

Below: Derek Tapscott intercepts a back pass from Peter Baker to slam Arsenal's second goal past Ron Reynolds.

AT THE SEASON'S END

		P	W	D	L	F	A	Pts
2nd	Spurs	42	22	12	8	104	56	56
5th	Arsenal	42	21	8	13	85	69	50

43

TOTTENHAM HOTSPUR 3
Smith, Medwin 2

ARSENAL 1
Holton

Tottenham Hotspur

Manager
Jimmy Anderson

Arsenal

Manager
Jack Crayston

Ted DITCHBURN	1	Jack KELSEY
Peter BAKER	2	Stan CHARLTON
Mel HOPKINS	3	Dennis EVANS
Danny BLANCHFLOWER	4	Cliff HOLTON
John RYDEN	5	Bill DODGIN
Jim ILEY	6	Dave BOWEN
Terry MEDWIN	7	Derek TAPSCOTT
Tommy HARMER	8	Vic GROVES
Bobby SMITH	9	David HERD
Alfie STOKES	10	Jimmy BLOOMFIELD
Johnny BROOKS	11	Mike TIDDY

Referee **Mr R P Hartley** (Burnley)

BACKGROUND

Spurs may have finished second in 1956-57 but they started the next season more like relegation candidates than championship hopefuls, only one point from their first four games leaving them propping up the table. Continual injury problems did not help with Maurice Norman, Bobby Smith, George Robb and Micky Dulin all suffering but the weakness was in defence, only one clean sheet in 12 games. 13 goals conceded in the last three games saw Ted Ditchburn recalled just two weeks short of his 36th birthday. While Spurs were losing, Arsenal were winning their last three games to put them well up with the championship pacesetters and were strengthened by the return of Stan Charlton and Vic Groves. Manager Jack Crayston did take something of a gamble though, replacing flu victim Danny Clapton with Derek Tapscott, still recovering from a cartilage operation.

BEFORE THE GAME

	P	W	D	L	F	A	Pts
Arsenal	11	7	1	3	21	13	15
Spurs	12	3	2	7	25	34	8

A NEW LIFE SPURS OUTPLAY ARSENAL

BLANCHFLOWER BLOTS OUT GUNNERS

A Special Correspondent for 'The Sunday Times' reported...

Harmer Prompts Spurs to a Confident Victory

This match was full of the unexpected, even to the extent that pre-match predictions were justifiably swept aside by a Tottenham side which produced both pretty and effective football.

The match had just started when **SMITH** scored the important Spurs' goal from which stemmed their confidence. Not that the newly-returned Ditchburn was idle. But it seemed to be his own whims which caused most trouble, as when he wandered to the touchline and scrambled back just in time to see Tapscott's shot sail over his crossbar.

However, the football of this Arsenal team does not flow, and it was the more intelligent play of the Spurs which resulted in Harmer being free and able to pass to **MEDWIN** for this habitual opportunist to beat Kelsey.

A REVIVAL

The second half threatened to develop unpleasantly, especially when Brooks had to leave the field to join the already injured and unlucky Groves. Soon both returned, and as if to celebrate, Spurs now played their best football. Blanchflower, studious both in looks and in football demeanour, was one architect, and the little general Harmer, was the other.

To these two Arsenal had no adequate response, for the injury to Groves had robbed them of their best forward, and the upfield sallies of Charlton, virtually unaided as they were, achieved little. It was thus no surprise when **MEDWIN** scored again and Spurs showed their superiority with a move from Ditchburn to Brooks which went the length of the field.

Very near the end **HOLTON**, amid discouragement from the spectators, followed up his penalty kick which had been parried by Ditchburn, and gave Arsenal their sparingly justified goal.

Above: Prostrate on the White Hart Lane turf are Ted Ditchburn (left) and Vic Groves. Ditchburn was soon back on his feet but Groves was off the field for half-an-hour before returning as a passenger on the right wing with his knee heavily bandaged.

Below: How one of the newspapers captured the 40th minute 'Was it over the line?' controversy when Johnny Brooks' header hit the underside of the bar before being pushed out by Jack Kelsey.

Right: Terry Medwin scores Tottenham's second goal.

HE'S MISSED IT

Left is the incident which caused the day's biggest crowd to argue all the way home from the Tottenham ground. Arsenal's Jack Kelsey hurtles after the ball which Spurs fans say crossed the goal-line. But the referee didn't agree. Kelsey scooped the ball away for a corner.

Right: Tottenham's outside-left Johnny Brooks gets the better of Stan Charlton.

Below: Bobby Smith opens the scoring after just five minutes.

44.

ARSENAL 4
Henry (og), Clapton, Nutt, Herd

TOTTENHAM HOTSPUR 4
Smith 2, Harmer 2 (1 pen)

Saturday 22nd February 1958

Football League Division One

Highbury

Attendance 59,116

Arsenal		Tottenham Hotspur
Manager **Jack Crayston**		Manager **Jimmy Anderson**

Jack KELSEY	1	Ted DITCHBURN
Stan CHARLTON	2	John HILLS
Dennis EVANS	3	Ron HENRY
Gerry WARD	4	Danny BLANCHFLOWER
Jim FOTHERINGHAM	5	Maurice NORMAN
John PETTS	6	John RYDEN
Danny CLAPTON	7	Terry MEDWIN
Vic GROVES	8	Tommy HARMER
David HERD	9	Bobby SMITH
Jimmy BLOOMFIELD	10	Johnny BROOKS
Gordon NUTT	11	Cliff JONES

Referee **Mr R J Leafe** (Nottingham)

BACKGROUND

By the time Spurs visited Highbury they had climbed to a mid-table position overtaking an Arsenal side whose season had effectively come to an end over the Christmas/New Year period. Successive Christmas defeats at Aston Villa and Luton were followed by the lowest point of the season, a third round FA Cup exit at Third Division Northampton. Blackpool won at Highbury and while two points were collected at Leicester, the next two games resulted in home defeats to Manchester United and Bolton. Arsenal needed new blood but the board was reluctant to sanction big money signings; a policy made all the more unpalatable as ever-improving Spurs, the switching of Maurice Norman from full-back to centre-half proving inspirational, paraded their new £35,000 signing Cliff Jones; a long time target of Jack Crayston's.

BEFORE THE GAME

	P	W	D	L	F	A	Pts
Spurs	30	13	6	11	65	63	32
Arsenal	29	12	3	14	48	54	27

AT THE SEASON'S END

	P	W	D	L	F	A	Pts
3rd Spurs	42	21	9	12	93	77	51
12th Arsenal	42	16	7	19	73	85	39

Tommy Harmer makes it 2-2 as Arsenal's Gerry Ward and Dennis Evans look on helplessly. Terry Medwin is the Spurs player behind the goal-line on the left of the picture

SPURS LATE FIGHTBACK

3 mins	**1-0**
38 mins	**1-1**
53 mins	**2-1**
62 mins	**2-2**
72 mins	**3-2**
77 mins	**4-2**
86 mins	**4-3**
87 mins	**4-4**

*John Sellers in '**The Sunday Times**'...*

CLIFF JONES GIVES GLIMPSE OF HIS QUALITY

Above: Jumping desperately to clear a centre by Arsenal winger Gordon Nutt, Spurs left-back Ron Henry heads into his own net. 1-0 to the Gunners after just three minutes.

Left: Spurs debutant Cliff Jones.

Below: Bobby Smith shoots past Jack Kelsey to level the scores at 4-4 with three minutes to go.

How can any man show in one game that he is worth a transfer fee of £35,000? Cliff Jones, making his entry into the strife of the First Division on Spurs' left wing at Highbury yesterday, saw too little of the ball to offer any kind of answer.

But his quality was obvious. He did not use all of his few opportunities quite as well as he can, nor did he move the ball as finely as he clearly will learn to do. But his value to Spurs' forward line should be immense.

With Jones and Brooks on one wing, and Medwin and Harmer on the other, switching places, running into the open spaces, with each man fast, elusive, inimical, and Smith, that sturdy warhorse, on his mettle, it looked as though Arsenal would be swallowed whole. And for most of the first half Spurs' flowing line of attack made the Arsenal defence appear clumsy.

It took Spurs half an hour to equalise through **SMITH**, after Arsenal had led from the third minute, when **HENRY**'s clearance unluckily found his own net.

Early in the second half a defensive error allowed **CLAPTON** to make it 2-1 for Arsenal. But, **HARMER** equalising, it still promised to be Spurs' game. Then, alas, as the fog began to give place to snow, Spurs' backs wilted, their forwards began to starve the wings, and Arsenal took command.

So it was that Norman, now a veritable giant among centre-halves showed how very good he has become. Time and again he broke up attacks by getting his head to the ball at angles that would have beaten lesser men.

But, even with Ditchburn supporting Norman like a master, the Arsenal pressure was too great. Within five minutes of each other **NUTT** and **HERD** scored and at 4-2 with five minutes left to play Arsenal's points looked secure. Then a penalty, which **HARMER** netted, and a chancy goal by **SMITH** brought Spurs level - justly I think.

But Arsenal: I wish I could say something encouraging but, really, as a team they depress me, their craftmanship is so poor. Though more spirited than a few weeks back, they still finish deplorably, and only Kelsey, Nutt and Groves, who played his heart out, showed some kind of football wisdom.

Like any other Three Wise Men they cannot control the prodigalities of their fellows.

45

ARSENAL 3
Nutt, Herd 2

TOTTENHAM HOTSPUR 1
Clayton

Arsenal

Tottenham
Hotspur

Manager
George Swindin

Manager
Jimmy Anderson

Jack KELSEY	1	John HOLLOWBREAD
Len WILLS	2	Peter BAKER
Dennis EVANS	3	Mel HOPKINS
Gerry WARD	4	Danny BLANCHFLOWER
Bill DODGIN	5	Maurice NORMAN
Tommy DOCHERTY	6	Jim ILEY
Danny CLAPTON	7	Terry MEDWIN
Vic GROVES	8	Tommy HARMER
David HERD	9	Bobby SMITH
Jimmy BLOOMFIELD	10	Eddie CLAYTON
Gordon NUTT	11	George ROBB

Referee **Mr H Horner** (Coventry)

BACKGROUND

Jack Crayston's frustrations at being unable to prise open the Highbury purse strings resulted in his departure in May 1958, after nearly a quarter of a century's service. His successor, George Swindin, fared much better at getting money released for signings, returning from the opening game of the season at Preston without any points, but with £27,000 half-back, Tommy Docherty. Four of the next five games were won, the last two 6-1 victories over Everton and Bolton. While Arsenal were second to newly-promoted West Ham, Spurs were only two places off the bottom. The season had started abysmally with Cliff Jones breaking his leg in pre-season training and continued that way with just one win to their credit prior to the trip to Highbury.

BEFORE THE GAME

	P	W	D	L	F	A	Pts
Arsenal	6	4	0	2	22	8	8
Spurs	6	1	1	4	10	16	3

Right: Gordon Nutt (out of picture) hooks his shot over John Hollowbread from an acute angle for Arsenal's opening goal.
Below: Jimmy Bloomfield celebrates as David Herd's shot whizzes past Hollowbread for the second.

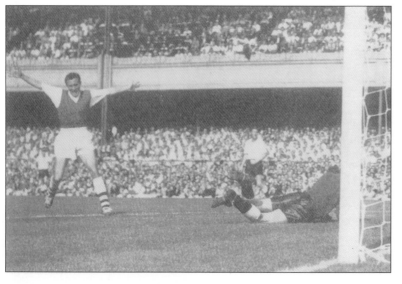

Jim Wilson in *'The Sunday Times'* under...

PURPOSEFUL ARSENAL GIVE SPURS A LESSON

"Arsenal fans," said my choleric and obviously dyspeptic neighbour in the tube, "are only the fair weather type." Only a thought-reader could have guessed if he meant the weather or was talking in a football sense; yesterday, however, the supporters he maligned certainly had it both ways.

For yesterday, in Autumn sunshine that would not have disgraced Capri, Arsenal gave a truly fine performance. There is these days a sense of purpose and urgency about all they do; it extends throughout the team from Kelsey's magnificent clearances to Herd's power-shooting at centre-forward.

The forwards certainly play closer, more patterned football than the great Arsenal teams of the past, but there is no slavish adherence to any particular style, the occasional long ball forming an effective contrast to their normal linked passing. The secret of their success, in fact, is fitness and team spirit; every player seems to want the ball and to be prepared to run into an open space to receive it.

LACK-LUSTRE SPURS

Tottenham, by contrast, were largely a team of talented individuals, and on the day no match for their neighbours' combination and enthusiasm. Spurs forwards have always depended greatly on an effective service from behind; yesterday Blanchflower lacked the time and Harmer, seemingly, the inclination to provide it.

The defence worked hard enough to keep Arsenal under control; but with both Blanchflower and Iley inclined to neglect the defensive side of their duties, Norman and his backs found themselves often with too much on their plates. Bloomfield and Herd were quick to take advantage of the inevitable gaps down the middle.

Arsenal's first attacks showed the pattern of what was to come. Once, Iley was forced to handle just outside the penalty area, next Bloomfield raced through on the left, drew Hollowbread from his goal, for Herd to head his cross just over the bar.

DEFENCE IN PANIC

Spurs' attacks built up altogether more slowly, though Iley once found Medwin on the other wing with a cross-pass worthy of their palmiest days: Docherty and Ward thus soon established a grip in midfield they were never, save for a short period in the second half, to relax.

Clapton soon made it clear that he not only had the legs of Hopkins but also the footwork to throw the rest of the defence into a panic whenever he got the ball. For 40 minutes only Hollowbread, luck and moderate finishing, especially by Herd, kept Tottenham's goal intact. Finally, just as one was beginning to wonder if Arsenal had missed the bus, Clapton chipped a centre neatly across the goal for **NUTT** rather luckily to beat Hollowbread with a half-hit low volley.

The second half began as if it would be merely a continuation of the first, and Docherty and Ward, a fine player with something of Joe Mercer's ability to sidefoot the ball forward to his forwards, were soon again close up behind the forwards.

Suddenly, after a fine move by Bloomfield, the ball ran loose: **HERD**, who had evidently had his shooting boots re-zeroed during the interval, slammed an unstoppable ground-shot past Hollowbread from 20 yards. The Tottenham defence was now in tatters.

It is, however, fatal to relax in a Derby match. After 60 minutes, slackness in Arsenal's defence let in **CLAYTON** who beat Kelsey with a neat groundshot. Suddenly Spurs were back in the game and Clayton nearly equalised with a terrific right-foot shot that hit the bar with Kelsey hopelessly beaten. Spurs were playing with something of their old rhythm and confidence, and Iley was once only stopped by some tactics borrowed for the occasion from Twickenham.

CALM RESTORED

At last, 15 minutes from the end, Docherty restored calm and confidence to his defence and Arsenal began once more to move with their method of the first half. Fourteen minutes from the end, after Bloomfield had seemed to fritter away a good chance, the ball ran loose to **HERD** who hit a powerful drive into the corner of the goal from the right-hand edge of the penalty area.

Spurs fought hard to the end, but lacked the inspiration to pull the game out of the fire against an Arsenal who had made things needlessly hard for themselves by falling back on defence.

Nevertheless, this was a fine display by Arsenal. They will, it is true, face stronger, better-balanced teams than yesterday's Tottenham. Nevertheless, on this form, they well deserve their position at the top of the table and it will take a truly fine team to remove them.

46

TOTTENHAM HOTSPUR 1
Smith

ARSENAL 4
Groves, Herd, Henderson 2

Tottenham Hotspur

Manager **Bill Nicholson**

Arsenal

Manager **George Swindin**

John HOLLOWBREAD	1	Jack KELSEY
Peter BAKER	2	Len WILLS
Mel HOPKINS	3	Dennis EVANS
Bill DODGE	4	Tommy DOCHERTY
Maurice NORMAN	5	Bill DODGIN
Jim ILEY	6	Dave BOWEN
Johnny BROOKS	7	Danny CLAPTON
Tommy HARMER	8	Vic GROVES
Bobby SMITH	9	David HERD
Dave DUNMORE	10	Len JULIANS
Cliff JONES	11	Jackie HENDERSON

Referee **Mr L J Hamer** (Bolton)

BACKGROUND

In just six months George Swindin had halted Arsenal's decline and taken them back to the top of the table, even if they were just a point ahead of Wolves having played two games more. The signing of Docherty had been followed by the arrival of Jackie Henderson from Wolves and just before Christmas, Arsenal had again opened the cheque book to secure Len Julians from Leyton Orient. Unbeaten in six games they were favourites to come out on top in Bill Nicholson's first North London derby as Spurs' manager. His reign had begun in October 1958 with a startling 10-4 victory over Everton but he had been unable to halt Spurs' slide. In the seven games before the new year they had collected only one point and were firmly entrenched in the relegation zone. A desperate situation called for desperate measures and Nicholson responded by dropping Danny Blanchflower and calling up the more defensive Bill Dodge. Nicholson's decision looked to be vindicated with three successive victories before Arsenal's visit.

JULIANS IS SENT OFF!

The dramatic scene just before Arsenal's Len Julians was sent off by referee Les Hamer. Julians appeared to kick Spurs centre-half Maurice Norman, who goes down in the mud. Spurs No.2 Peter Baker signals the incident and the referee comes ovet to talk to Julians.

| Baker | Herd | Norman | Julians | Groves | Ref. Hamer |

Laurence Kitchin in
'The Observer' *described...*

Chess by Arsenal

Before they were reduced to 10 men and a holding action for most of the second half, Arsenal had already shown themselves, before 60,000 people, to be the better side. After the second goal against them Spurs turned on the heat for a quarter of an hour, but they had Kelsey's anticipation and the run of the ball to cope with. Disastrously, they were a fraction too slow in shooting.

That was the difference between the teams at top pressure when Spurs were still in the hunt. Another, which came more and more into focus, was Arsenal's great directness. Whereas their three inside men could be seen streaking into the open spaces by the straightest route, Spurs worked crossfield fast enough but were too deliberate in the middle.

Especially in the second half, Docherty set the tone. Often in line with Wills and Dodgin, he would pounce into the tackle with grim precision. Evans, too, did as much as anyone to keep Spurs out in the danger period, when Bowen was unhappy against the switches of Brooks and Smith.

The vital first two goals were mainly the work of Groves. After five minutes his was the through-pass which sent Herd clear on the left, and **GROVES** put in the rebound when Hollowbread partially saved. Boring in four minutes later on a thrust started by an innocent-looking pass from Docherty, Groves set **HERD** free to score with a low shot well out of reach.

MISSED A SITTER

During the Spurs' counter-attack, Dunmore and Iley shot wide, Iley, Brooks, and Jones drew great saves from Kelsey, and Smith missed a sitter. When Julians coaxed Hollowbread wide and pulled back a pass to **HENDERSON**, who shot calmly into an empty goal, Arsenal took charge again and Spurs grew ragged and dispirited.

Eight minutes after the change of ends, Julians was sent off after a collision with Norman, and the match became a chessboard demonstration of Arsenal cunning. Groves lay back, Docherty darted to and fro, and **HENDERSON** came into his own.

During the first half he had kept in the rear, acting as a link in Bloomfield's absence. Now he crossed over to help the subdued Clapton and be a general nuisance. He succeeded so well that he scored his second goal, with a long shot wickedly dipping on the swerve.

In the closing minutes **SMITH** scored for Spurs from a centre floated to the inch by Harmer. But by that time Arsenal had beaten them, both as athletes and tacticians.

Vic Groves drives home a rebound to make it 1-0 to Arsenal.

Jackie Henderson's shot is on its way in. 3-0 to Arsenal.

Bobby Smith scores Tottenham's consolation goal in the closing minutes.

BEFORE THE GAME

	P	W	D	L	F	A	Pts
Arsenal	27	15	3	9	64	44	33
Spurs	26	8	5	13	49	61	21

AT THE SEASON'S END

		P	W	D	L	F	A	Pts
3rd	Arsenal	42	21	8	13	88	68	50
18th	Spurs	42	13	10	19	85	95	36

ARSENAL 1
Barnwell

TOTTENHAM HOTSPUR 1
Medwin

Arsenal

Tottenham Hotspur

Manager
George Swindin

Manager
Bill Nicholson

Jim STANDEN	1	Bill BROWN
Len WILLS	2	Peter BAKER
Billy McCULLOUGH	3	Mel HOPKINS
Mel CHARLES	4	Danny BLANCHFLOWER
Bill DODGIN	5	Maurice NORMAN
Tommy DOCHERTY	6	Tony MARCHI
Danny CLAPTON	7	Terry MEDWIN
John BARNWELL	8	Tommy HARMER
David HERD	9	Bobby SMITH
Jimmy BLOOMFIELD	10	Dave DUNMORE
Joe HAVERTY	11	Cliff JONES

Referee **Mr L J Tirebuck** (Halifax)

BACKGROUND

In March 1959 Bill Nicholson tried to sign Mel Charles from Swansea but the Welsh international choose Arsenal instead. Nicholson turned his attention back to a player he had tried to sign earlier, Dave Mackay, and this time was successful, securing the Scot's signature on transfer deadline day for £32,000. Mackay played his part in ensuring Spurs' top flight survival and many in the crowd were looking forward to comparing the two powerful half-backs. They were to be disappointed though, as Mackay had to stand down at the last minute due to a boil on his leg. Tony Marchi, who had rejoined Spurs in the summer after a spell in Italy, took his place. Spurs began with a 5-1 win at Newcastle, drew home games with West Brom and Birmingham and in midweek won the return fixture at the Hawthorns. George Swindin had spent his first season in charge drastically overhauling Arsenal's playing staff. Apart from Docherty and Charles he brought in Billy McCullough, Len Julians and Jackie Henderson and promoted Jim Standen and John Barnwell from the reserves. Beaten by Sheffield Wednesday on the opening day, a Danny Clapton hat-trick gave Arsenal the points at Nottingham Forest but they could only draw their next games against Wolves and Forest.

BEFORE THE GAME

	P	W	D	L	F	A	Pts
Arsenal	4	1	2	1	7	5	4
Spurs	4	2	2	0	9	4	6

A gift goal for Terry Medwin (second right) as Arsenal 'keeper Jim Standen deflects a shot from Dave Dunmore (left) into his path.

THAT WAS THEN...

★ "Spurs and Arsenal are both heavy spenders in the transfer market. Tottenham's team of all talents are indeed the most expensive in football history"... was an interesting statement in one of the match reports. So how much did the Spurs team cost to build? £161,000! Jones £35,000, Blanchflower £30,000, Norman £28,000, Medwin £25,000, Brown £16,500, Smith £16,000 and Dunmore £10,500. Baker, Hopkins, Marchi and Harmer were all home grown. £32,000 Dave Mackay was out injured.

TWO TEAMS BUT ONLY ONE IDEA

"For 50 minutes this was a chessboard classic – an all-London masterpiece. As the hot September sun poured down, Spurs and Arsenal, representing nearly £300,000 of the country's top talent, plotted a breath-taking series of moves and counter-moves.
From man to man, and foot to foot, from goal to goal and end to end, the ball flashed at shimmering speed before the eyes of 60,000 spellbound spectators...
... It was superb, scintillating stuff. Any result other than a draw would have been a blazing injustice to one team."
– Alan Hoby

Arsenal right-back Len Wills heads clear under pressure from Cliff Jones, Dave Dunmore and Bobby Smith.

It will tax the longest football memory to recall an occasion when Arsenal and the Hotspur played so evenly, so amiably and, above all, so similarly as in this straightforward, unexciting draw. The players began as if someone had hypnotised them into the belief that a blazing sun and a hard, fast grassy pitch were, in fact, the proper setting for their game. Arsenal moved quickly along the normal main roads of footballing advance, and Haverty, springing up surprisingly on the left, sent a finely-angled shot narrowly behind Brown and even more narrowly across the front of his goal.

Within a few minutes, too, Bloomfield returned a pass at rattling speed to Herd, who shot as well on the turn as any man might hope to do - so well, indeed, that Brown, in saving, demonstrated that he is not merely an International-class goalkeeper but possibly worth even the money Tottenham paid for him.

SHORT CUTS

While Arsenal ran along the wider roads, Harmer steered the Tottenham forwards through some alleyways of his own discovery. These routes, however, proved such remarkable short cuts that his colleagues, finding the Arsenal goal suddenly open to them, were apparently too surprised to step in.

So, more straightforwardly, Harmer sent Dunmore in on the right and his half-cross half-shot bounced off Standen so simply that **MEDWIN** had only to kick it to score.

Tottenham led by that goal until the first movement of the second half, when Baker let in Haverty for a quick exchange of passes with Herd which left **BARNWELL** time to control the ball before he planted it well out of Brown's reach.

Now the two teams settled to play football so alike that it was small wonder their defences found adequate counters to it. Blanchflower and Marchi hovered half-deep in the mid-field belt, just as Docherty and Charles did; with Docherty and Blanchflower inventive, Marchi and Charles pedestrian.

Marchi is entitled to some weeks of reacclimatisation before it can be said that Italian football has made a player who does his own job and leaves others to do theirs; but certainly on this form he is not the driving force he was.

HARMERISMS

Mel Charles played hard in demonstrating that he is not his brother. He has, apparently, done the work himself for so long that he is not disposed to make the ball do it; whence it may be argued that he might make Arsenal a powerful stopper centre-half or a bludgeoning centre-forward - but not a top-class wing-half-back.

The second half of the game consisted of a number of half-chances from which many tried to score, only for everyone to be the crucial fraction of a second behind the bounce of the ball.

There was a fair scattering of Harmerisms, Haverty wise-cracked his way down the left wing - and elsewhere - while Blanchflower, Bloomfield and the quick, intelligent Wills worked out some good ideas. But the advance forwards - with Clapton and Jones determined one-stringed fiddles - never could outwit or outpace two defences which covered with good discipline, tackled quickly and disposed of the ball before it could become an embarrassment to them.

These teams will play better on a wetter day; and the wet days may find them both in good League positions.

48

TOTTENHAM HOTSPUR 3
Allen 2, Smith

ARSENAL 0

Tottenham Hotspur

Manager
Bill Nicholson

Arsenal

Manager
George Swindin

Bill BROWN	1	Jim STANDEN
Peter BAKER	2	Eddie MAGILL
Ron HENRY	3	Dennis EVANS
Danny BLANCHFLOWER	4	Len WILLS
Maurice NORMAN	5	John SNEDDEN
Dave MACKAY	6	John BARNWELL
John WHITE	7	Danny CLAPTON
Tommy HARMER	8	David HERD
Bobby SMITH	9	Len JULIANS
Les ALLEN	10	Jimmy BLOOMFIELD
Cliff JONES	11	Joe HAVERTY

Referee **Mr L Callaghan** (Merthyr Tydfil)

BACKGROUND

After their opening day defeat at Hillsborough, Arsenal went nine games unbeaten and were hot on the heels of First Division pacesetters, Spurs. They then won only two of the next 13 games to plummet down the table, while Spurs maintained their bid for a first League title since 1951. The cause was injuries; Kelsey, Evans, Herd, Groves, Charles and Docherty were all out for long periods, the loss of Docherty being the most heavily felt. Even his return for the FA Cup had not improved performances though. Twice held to a draw by Rotherham United, the second replay was due to take place at Hillsborough two days after the visit to White Hart Lane. Docherty was injured again with 17-year old John Snedden thrown in for his debut. In comparison nothing could go wrong for Spurs. Even when Mel Hopkins was injured playing for Wales, Ron Henry stepped in to prove himself a more than capable deputy, and Nicholson's latest signings, John White and Les Allen, took no time to settle in. Three points clear of Burnley and Preston, the title was a definite possibility.

BEFORE THE GAME

	P	W	D	L	F	A	Pts
Spurs	25	13	8	4	54	30	34
Arsenal	25	8	6	11	42	53	22

AT THE SEASON'S END

	P	W	D	L	F	A	Pts
3rd Spurs	42	21	11	10	86	50	53
13th Arsenal	42	15	9	18	68	80	39

'DERBY' STAR

★ **Tommy Harmer** ★

Harmer began one of the most fantastic dribbles I have seen. Down the left he jinked, twisting and turning on the skating-rink surface in a magician's maze of his own making. One, two, three, four men Harmer beat. Then drawing the entire Gunners defence towards him as if he were a mobile magnet, he calmly juggled the ball to Bobby Smith, whose shot skidded off a lunging foot into goal." - Alan Hoby.

'DERBY' STAR

An aerial duel between Arsenal centre-forward Len Julians and Spurs left-back Ron Henry.

POOR OLD ARSENAL - IT IS INDEED

Tottenham's first goal...

Les Allen sends No.4 Len Wills the wrong way...

...then shoots past the off-balance Wills as goalkeeper Jim Standen comes out...

...Standen drops to his knees and centre-half John Sneddon moves across to cover him...

...but Allen has chosen his spot well and the ball flashes past the despairing Standen and Sneddon into the empty net.

Outside White Hart Lane, the newspaper sellers were shouting "Paper! Poor old Arsenal! Paper! Arsenal for the Second Division!" Poor Arsenal, indeed. Deprived of Docherty and Dodgin; forced to throw a 17-year old centre-half in at the deep end of a London "derby"; reduced to ten men for all the second half; a goal down when Evans slipped on the snow; five times within an ace of a goal by Julians, their cup was full long before Allen scored Tottenham's third.

On a murderously difficult pitch - a snow-rink first, then a quagmire of sand and slush, the floodlights winking in its puddles - the football was of astonishing quality. Spurs played most of it; poised, fluid and methodical, moving the ball out calmly from a constructive defence.

Blanchflower, after a dominant first half, withdrew to let Mackay take up the running. Jones darted and dashed, Harmer was inspired throughout. The pitch seemed less a difficulty to him than a challenge; he was ubiquitous, now turning past a floundering opponent, now pushing a short ball to an unmarked man.

PICKED HIS WAY

When, after 12 minutes of the second half, he trundled the ball to the penalty area, picked his way meditatively past three men, and saw the ball run loose for **SMITH** to score, it was the consummation of his afternoon: though even so, Spurs' embraces seemed vulgar and exaggerated.

The odd thing was that the fair-haired Barnwell, his immediate opponent, contrived to be the best man in Arsenal's side. His determination, the elegance of his ball control, his precise distribution, must surely, if he maintains them, bring him into the England team.

Arsenal began as if they intended to mock at vicissitude. Within the first three minutes, Barnwell's high shot forced Brown to soar across goal to save. But it was only summer lightning. Almost at once Spurs took control, and when Snedden, the young centre-half, kicked wildly at the ball and missed, Smith went through alone, to land flat on his back, missing the easiest of chances.

Two headers from Smith - one pushed against the bar, one just over - another by Norman, which Evans headed gallantly off the line, and Arsenal's defence was tottering. Snedden, happily, seemed unperturbed by his mistake. He is dark haired, tall and upright, powerful in the air, and clearly the possessor of a splendid temperament.

To waste a ball after winning a tackle is obviously repugnant to him, and to see him taking it past opponents with the outside of his foot is a joy. His future may well be brilliant.

When Spurs scored at last, after 22 minutes, it was because Evans slipped, giving White all the time in the world to pass to Allen, and **ALLEN** equal leisure to score.

Arsenal responded with a cross-shot by Haverty (generally disappointing) which hit Brown's feet in mid-air, a header by Julians against the crossbar, and a drive by the same player which rebounded from Brown's chest. Jones was temporarily on the right wing, plaguing Evans, but just before half-time Evans limped painfully away from a tackle, and Arsenal's hopes had gone.

STRANDED AND AGONISED

He was at centre-forward for the second half, in which Bloomfield, Barnwell, Wills, Herd and Clapton kept Arsenal bravely in the game. Thrice Julians nearly scored, but five minutes from time Smith's fine shot hit the bar, flew into the air, and Standen could only watch stranded and agonised as **ALLEN** headed in.

Allen has indeed given Spurs the thrust they've been lacking; but this further demonstration of it was more than Arsenal deserved.

Double Winning Spurs

49

ARSENAL 2
Herd, Ward

TOTTENHAM HOTSPUR 3
Saul, Dyson, Allen

Saturday 10th September 1960

Football League Division One

Highbury

Attendance 59,868

Arsenal

Tottenham Hotspur

Manager
George Swindin

Manager
Bill Nicholson

Jack **KELSEY**	1	Bill **BROWN**
Len **WILLS**	2	Peter **BAKER**
Billy **McCULLOUGH**	3	Ron **HENRY**
Gerry **WARD**	4	Danny **BLANCHFLOWER**
John **SNEDDEN**	5	Maurice **NORMAN**
Tommy **DOCHERTY**	6	Dave **MACKAY**
Danny **CLAPTON**	7	Terry **MEDWIN**
Jimmy **BLOOMFIELD**	8	John **WHITE**
David **HERD**	9	Frank **SAUL**
Peter **KANE**	10	Les **ALLEN**
Jackie **HENDERSON**	11	Terry **DYSON**

Referee **Mr J G Williams** (Nottingham)

BACKGROUND

In less than two years Bill Nicholson had turned Spurs from relegation candidates to potential champions. But for a late season collapse that saw them win only one of seven games, leaving them two points behind Burnley, they could have won the title in 1959-60. To ensure any repeat would not prove so costly, they started the new season as if determined to wrap up the title race before Christmas. Even with Bobby Smith and Cliff Jones injured, six straight wins took them to Highbury confident of returning with both points for the first time in five years. Arsenal had come in for a lot of press criticism as George Swindin continued the search for his ideal team. Mike Everitt and John Snedden had been installed as first choice half-backs and Peter Kane, a summer signing from Northampton, had come in for the last two games in place of John Barnwell. They were still fourth in the table, though, and had won their three home games without conceding a goal.

BEFORE THE GAME

	P	W	D	L	F	A	Pts
Spurs	6	6	0	0	18	5	12
Arsenal	6	3	1	2	8	5	7

SPURS ARE STREETS AHEAD
They can score goals almost to order

"Let me tell you about Frank Saul. When you've been involved in the tempestuous world of soccer as long as I have you become a little cautious about hailing youngsters as future stars. So often you have to eat your words later on. But at Highbury yesterday I watched a boy who's going to reach the heights. Yes you can quote me as forecasting full international honours for 17-year-old Spur, Frank Saul. I'll tell you why – he's a natural, he does the right things without having to work them out and I'll bet he's not even aware he's doing them."

– Joe Hulme

Young Frank Saul fires Spurs into an early lead with his first League goal.

Spurs Scheme their Way to Victory

As an aperitif to watching two clubs at the foot of the Division on television later in the day, 60,000 Londoners turned up in the flesh at Highbury and witnessed the wide gap in quality between the clubs currently lying first and eighth. It was a gap that remained throughout for all to see, while the leaders strolled into a two-goal lead which should have been greater, lost it, scored again, and then kept the ball in possession or out of play until the referee declared the game at an end.

They then shook hands with one another and their opponents and trotted down the tunnel as good as new. Their hosts followed them, flattered by the narrowness of the recorded defeat, and the local derby was over.

DEDICATION

Had the teams been in the same class, we might have had the traditional fights and fouls by the players, and threats and warnings by the officials, that we all pretend to abhor. As it was we had football of considerable quality with 22 men behaving for all the world as if their lives had been spent in or around the better class tea-shops of a cathedral city.

Without a shadow of a doubt Tottenham's success flows from their half-backs. The scheming of Blanchflower, the impressive covering of Norman, the full-blooded dedication of Mackay, have no counterpart in the Arsenal contingent.

For the first half, Spurs' superiority was not only the result of the fact that man for man they have the better side: whenever you saw the ball there were more white than red shirts in attendance.

After 10 minutes **SAUL** scored his first League goal, from an overhead pass by Allen. It was an opportunist goal, well taken from a lucky bounce.

It is of course possible that Saul sustained some injury from the fervent congratulatory hugs of his team-mates, but apart from this goal and a back header that found Dyson he did little more to justify the custody of a No. 9 white shirt.

It was **DYSON**, then, who headed in the second goal, Saul whose left foot missed the next, and Kelsey in Arsenal's goal making up for a defence whose day this was not.

When the only remaining question appeared to be the margin of victory, **HERD** collected a Clapton corner and shot it hard and low into the net.

The applause for this goal was restrained, for it seemed no more than a gesture; five minutes later, to the longest and loudest cheer of the afternoon, Henderson backheeled the ball, and **WARD** (of all people) with a Mackay-like drive scored the equaliser from all of 25 yards.

For the next few minutes each move was greeted with tense anticipation; but even with their lead gone, Spurs looked the better, calmer side.

We didn't have to wait long; five minutes after Ward's goal, Blanchflower, who shines less brightly as the game advances, returned from temporary rustication and upfielded a ball to **ALLEN**, who lobbed immaculately over Kelsey for his bonus money.

Below: Terry Dyson heads Spurs' second goal.

Bottom: David Herd's hard low shot following a corner beats the Spurs rearguard with Ron Henry helpless on the goal-line.

50

TOTTENHAM HOTSPUR 4
Allen (2), Blanchflower (pen), Smith

ARSENAL 2
Henderson, Haverty

Saturday 21st January 1961

Football League Division One

White Hart Lane

Attendance 65,251

Tottenham Hotspur

Manager
Bill Nicholson

Arsenal

Manager
George Swindin

Tottenham		Arsenal
Bill BROWN	1	John McCLELLAND
Peter BAKER	2	Eddie MAGILL
Ron HENRY	3	Billy McCULLOUGH
Danny BLANCHFLOWER	4	Terry NEILL
Maurice NORMAN	5	Allan YOUNG
Dave MACKAY	6	Tommy DOCHERTY
Cliff JONES	7	Danny CLAPTON
John WHITE	8	George EASTHAM
Bobby SMITH	9	David HERD
Les ALLEN	10	Jackie HENDERSON
Terry DYSON	11	Joe HAVERTY

Referee **Mr A E Ellis** (Halifax)

BACKGROUND

Ten points clear of Wolves, Spurs were expected to return to winning ways five days after sustaining only their second defeat of the season at Old Trafford, particularly as the return of Peter Baker and Cliff Jones from injury enabled them to field their first choice eleven. Arsenal were not so lucky. Jack Kelsey had injured his hand in the previous week's 5-4 defeat of Manchester City and his deputy, John McClelland, was making his League debut. Mel Charles and Vic Groves were also missing, but at least George Eastham, a £47,500 signing from Newcastle in November, and David Herd were able to take their places. Herd had scored 24 goals in 26 games, seven in the last three, and that included two hat-tricks.

BEFORE THE GAME

	P	W	D	L	F	A	Pts
Spurs	26	22	2	2	81	30	46
Arsenal	26	12	4	10	52	50	28

AT THE SEASON'S END

		P	W	D	L	F	A	Pts
1st	Spurs	42	31	4	7	115	55	66
11th	Arsenal	42	15	11	16	77	85	41

A touching moment as Terry Dyson congratulates
Bobby Smith on his goal.

'DERBY' STAR
★ Dave Mackay ★
"His was the greatest personal performance I have seen this season. And if there is any other logical claimant to the title of Footballer of the Year he must be superhuman if not supernatural."
— Bob Pennington

...

Tottenham Back in The Groove

So consistently successful have Tottenham been this season that it has been a relief lately to find them sometimes human after all. However great a team's ability, football is such a matter of confidence and timing that bad patches are inevitable: it is a measure of Tottenham's talent that such crises have hitherto been met as they occur by bursts of individual or collective brilliance.

Today, Spurs were once again properly in the groove. Arsenal kept going gamely, but never looked likely to win once Tottenham had taken the lead.

It was an entertaining match, with much more good football for the 65,000 crowd to savour and enjoy. Not all of it came from Tottenham, for Arsenal's forwards, despite being handicapped after the first half-hour by having Clapton a limping cripple on their right-wing, were always dangerous.

Eastham, working the ball neatly with his left foot, had a touch of class about all his work, while Henderson and Haverty both had good matches.

Yet Tottenham always carried the bigger guns, and once they had fully settled to their proper rhythm were altogether too much for an inexperienced Arsenal defence.

MAGICAL MOVES

Tottenham's third goal, just before the interval, was a typical example of their football at it's best and fittingly crowned a 20-minute sequence of magical moves. Mackay, retrieving a ball bobbing like a cork from a ruck of players in midfield, began it with an overhead kick back to his centre-half Norman.

A push to Henry, back again to Mackay, out to Jones on the left wing and the Arsenal defence was now in tatters. As three defenders, including the goalkeeper, converged on Jones, the ball ran loose to **SMITH**, who tapped it in.

Arsenal's first goal, to give them the lead after nine minutes, was, however, nearly as good. McCullough worked the ball out of defence before passing square to Docherty. A through pass found **HENDERSON**, intelligently positioned to take advantage of Blanchflower's forays upfield, and a flashing shot completely beat Brown.

ALLEN, inevitably from a pass by Mackay, equalised almost at once, but Arsenal were a little unlucky to find themselves behind after 23 minutes. There was no real danger to their goal when Neill, completely mistiming his tackle, floored Dyson, who had wandered hopefully to the right, just inside the area. The resulting penalty, from which **BLANCHFLOWER** scored easily, was condign, if doubtless inevitable, punishment.

SPURS CONTENT

The second half, less eventful than the first, saw Tottenham content to take things easily. **ALLEN** increased their lead - a greatly improved player.

HAVERTY's goal for Arsenal - a fantastic screw which may have touched a Tottenham defender en route - was a just reward for his industry and determination.

Once again Spurs' strength stemmed from their superb play in midfield. Mackay can never have played better, Blanchflower's inventiveness made up for the occasional defensive mistake, while White, the link in so many of their moves, as usual hardly put a foot wrong.

The sequence of pictures above show how Les Allen tightropes along the line and sends the Arsenal defenders the wrong way before driving the ball past debutant 'keeper John McClelland to make it 4-1.

Below: McClelland clears from the head of Spurs No.8 John White.

51

TOTTENHAM HOTSPUR 4
Allen, Dyson 3

ARSENAL 3
Skirton, Charles 2

Tottenham Hotspur

Manager
Bill Nicholson

Arsenal

Manager
George Swindin

Bill BROWN	1	**John McCLELLAND**
Peter BAKER	2	**Eddie MAGILL**
Ron HENRY	3	**Billy McCULLOUGH**
Danny BLANCHFLOWER	4	**Laurie BROWN**
Maurice NORMAN	5	**John SNEDDEN**
Tony MARCHI	6	**Terry NEILL**
Cliff JONES	7	**John MacLEOD**
John SMITH	8	**George EASTHAM**
Bobby SMITH	9	**Mel CHARLES**
Les ALLEN	10	**Jackie HENDERSON**
Terry DYSON	11	**Alan SKIRTON**

Referee **Mr R J Leafe** *(Nottingham)*

BACKGROUND

Mel Charles

Spurs' defence of the "Double" started with a 2-1 win at Blackpool but they were immediately struck by a problem they had rarely faced in sweeping all before them; injuries. Both Dave Mackay and John White were injured, unable to take their places in the 2-2 draw at West Ham which followed and still unavailable for Arsenal's visit. Arsenal had begun with a home draw against Burnley and then collected two points at Leicester. Having been moved up front to replace David Herd, sold during the summer to Manchester United, Mel Charles had scored both goals against Burnley. His place in defence had been taken by Laurie Brown, only signed from Northampton the day before the season opened. Another newcomer to the Arsenal ranks was John MacLeod, a summer signing from Hibernians.

BEFORE THE GAME

	P	W	D	L	F	A	Pts
Spurs	2	1	1	0	4	3	3
Arsenal	2	1	1	0	3	2	3

With Bill Brown on the floor it looks a certain goal but Danny Blanchflower gets back to block Alan Skirton's shot.

Brian Glanville in 'The Times' under headline...

DYSON GIVES SPURS A SCRAMBLED VICTORY

A Derby indeed, all passion and upheaval! If Tottenham won, it was by the nearest of near things; a match snatched out of the fire by two late goals in two minutes, when their home record seemed to lie in pieces before us. They were two up, all square, one down (two headers by Mel Charles that his brother might have envied), and then, with the minutes slipping away, two goals by little Dyson gave them victory.

It was a match for the partisan, rather than the purist. Neither team was at full compliment; Spurs lacked Mackay and White, Arsenal Kelsey and Groves. As a team there was no doubt of Spurs' superiority, but Charles, Eastham and MacLeod pulled Arsenal round making up for their poor goalkeeping, their dreadful backs, their lack of cunning at wing-half, so that by the end there was nothing in it. But in these Male and Hapgood-less days Arsenal's defence is less of a rock than a pumice stone.

IMPRESSIVE START

Tottenham began impressively; their opening goal was fine. Blanchflower pushed the ball to Jones, splendid throughout, who began one of his endless, intricate, astonishing cross-field runs. His pass found John Smith on the right wing, Smith's centre floated across Arsenal's defence and **ALLEN** got up to head it in.

In the very next minute plump young Smith, once, at left-half, the toast of the East End, should really have headed another. A passing exchange of calm impertinence between Blanchflower and Allen - on the right wing - ended with Snedden, the Arsenal centre-half, flat-footed and the ball drifting over goal to Smith, unmarked at the far post. He had all the goal to aim at - and he hit the side net.

But it hardly mattered. Within two minutes Blanchflower had lofted a free-kick into the goal area, and Dyson, rising like a jack-in-the-box, got his head to it. McClelland turned it onto the bar - **DYSON** headed it in.

That should have been the end of Arsenal, who had scarcely begun as it was. But Eastham, with that agonising double-piston run of his, was beginning to move about dangerously, and in 25 minutes came a goal. **SKIRTON**, their lank-haired outside-left scored it, with a coolness and confidence he had given one no reason to suspect. Taking a pass from Neill, he turned across two Spurs' defenders, and with his right foot and on the turn, banged his shot past Brown.

The second half opened with a flurry of near misses. First Eastham put Skirton clear, but Brown dived like lightning at his feet. Then, at the other end, Jones scooped up a ball with his back to goal, and flicked it over his head like a white Pele, only for it to hit the cross-bar and go over. Next, a five-man assault by Arsenal took Spurs by storm, only to end with Charles' goal-bound shot striking Henry on the heel.

In the 67th minute Charles and Arsenal had their consolation. McLeod, ridiculing the cries of "Henry for England", passed the left-back with an admirable dummy, which he followed with an equally admirable cross. **CHARLES** leapt high by the far post - even above Norman - and the ball was in. Five minutes later he had done it again - Eastham's cross this time - from the same spot with a more majestic leap still.

There was an Arsenal roar that could be heard from here to Highbury, and the red-and-white embraces put even Tottenham's to shame. Arsenal were rampant now, MacLeod appearing now on one wing and now on the other, like a scourge; Eastham masterfully probing. But with seven minutes left Allen took a corner, the ball came back to **DYSON** from a defender's body and he hooked it into goal.

Two minutes more and Blanchflower found the little winger alone and forgotten with a calm, immaculate pass. **DYSON**'s left foot struck again, and the ball went in off the post. Arsenal had shot their bolt; they even lost their goalkeeper before the end. If only they'd a defence!

Above: Terry Dyson celebrates the first of his goals after heading in at the second attempt having first hit the crossbar.

Right: Bobby Smith has his arms raised but Tony Marchi's long-range shot is ruled out for offside.

52

ARSENAL 2
Charles, Skirton

TOTTENHAM HOTSPUR 1
Mackay

Arsenal

Tottenham
Hotspur

Manager
George Swindin

Manager
Bill Nicholson

Jack KELSEY	1	Bill BROWN
Dave BACUZZI	2	Peter BAKER
Billy McCULLOUGH	3	Ron HENRY
Eddie CLAMP	4	Danny BLANCHFLOWER
Laurie BROWN	5	Maurice NORMAN
John SNEDDEN	6	Dave MACKAY
John MacLEOD	7	Terry MEDWIN
John BARNWELL	8	John WHITE
Mel CHARLES	9	Les ALLEN
George EASTHAM	10	Jimmy GREAVES
Alan SKIRTON	11	Cliff JONES

Referee **Mr F P Clarke** *(Coventry)*

BACKGROUND

Although Arsenal maintained a place in the top half of the table, even the signing of Wolves' half-back, Eddie Clamp, failed to solve their season long problem - inconsistency. Just a month before Spurs' visit they had won 3-2 at Wolves, but followed that up with a draw at home to West Ham and a defeat at struggling Sheffield United. Now they had inflicted the first Turf Moor defeat on leaders Burnley. Could they maintain that form against a Spurs' team that had won it's last three games and was reinforced by the signing of Jimmy Greaves, scorer of a hat-trick on his debut seven days earlier?

BEFORE THE GAME

	P	W	D	L	F	A	Pts
Spurs	21	12	3	6	42	32	27
Arsenal	22	8	7	7	38	37	23

AT THE SEASON'S END

	P	W	D	L	F	A	Pts
3rd Spurs	42	21	10	11	88	69	52
10th Arsenal	42	16	11	15	71	72	43

Arsenal goalkeeper Jack Kelsey has no chance as Dave Mackay's pile-driver puts Spurs one up.

'DERBY' STAR John White... "that slender, unwearying perfectionist, was their guiding spirit, always moving or passing into the open space" – Sunday Times.

TALENTED ARSENAL SCORE SHOCK WIN OVER SPURS

For all the bitterness of the wind, all the magnetic pull of Christmas shopping, Greaves, the North London Derby and Arsenal's revival today brought 63,000 to Highbury; plain enough evidence that football retains it's magic. And the crowd had it's reward; a fine fast game, three exciting goals and a victory which finally went where it morally belonged. If they had a disappointment too, it lay in the absolute eclipse of Greaves, a yard behind the play where he was not two, without a single goal to atone for it.

Kelsey's brave dive a few minutes from time, saw to it that he should buy no eleventh hour redemption. But if there was nothing to be seen of Greaves, one could appreciate instead the opportunism of Skirton, that goal scoring enigma.

Arsenal's performance on this frozen and difficult pitch was controlled and impressive. Kelsey, unlike Bill Brown, was giving nothing away, the half-backs were solid, Eastham tirelessly inventive, Charles revitalised, a terrible handful for Norman.

Yet, perhaps, the real hero was Snedden, impressively converted from centre-half to left-half, where his unshakable nonchalance, his compulsion to beat a man, his loathing of the first time clearance, became assets rather than liabilities. His distribution was splendid, and there was a delightful passage in the second half, down by the corner flag, when he elegantly picked his way past two players.

The goal with which Tottenham took the lead after 17 minutes was so good that it could scarcely be begrudged, and yet, on the run of play, it was very hard on Arsenal. Blanchflower sent over a long expert cross from the right which was duly headed away.

Ninety-nine times out of 100 that would have been that. But this was the 100th. **MACKAY** came racing in to catch the ball with a magnificent left-footed half volley. Kelsey flew across his goal, but there's no stopping those; the shot went home like a meteor.

Thus encouraged, Tottenham proceeded to make the running for the rest of the half. White, that slender, unwearying perfectionist, was their guiding spirit, always moving or passing into the open space, marvellously precise, as sure footed as any proverbial mountain goat. He was here one moment, yards away the next - always where he could be most effective.

CLOSE SHAVE

Behind him Blanchflower, relatively subdued, and Mackay exploited every ball. But Arsenal's defence was more solid than it has been for a long time, and the best opening we saw was made not by Spurs, but by Arsenal.

Five minutes from half time, the remarkable Skirton, so dangerous precisely because he looks so unwieldy, almost equalised. Charles beat Norman in front of goal and the ball ran loose. Suddenly Skirton was on it, awkward as ever taking it across goal, then turning painfully to hit it off balance, an insidious shot which beat Brown and came back from the far post.

In the ninth minute of the second half the Spurs goal first miraculously escaped - then at long last fell. It's survival was from Barnwell's shot, a crisp one from well out which that erratic fellow Brown somehow contrived to dive on, scoop into the air, and catch most fortunately just on the right side of the line.

But Arsenal now had their tails up. Back they came. Eastham to Clamp, Clamp a lob to Charles, and **CHARLES** hustling the ball past Norman managed to keep control as it bounced, and force it past Brown as well. Such was the fervour of the embraces that they might almost have been Tottenham's own.

NEAR MISS

Three minutes later Arsenal were within an ace of taking the lead, when Skirton (always Skirton) deflected McCullough's low fast centre wide of Brown, only for Henry to clear off the line by the far post.

Eleven minutes from time Barnwell pushed the ball out to Skirton, now on the right, no real danger it seemed - but you never know with **SKIRTON**. Taking the ball on a few yards he beat Brown with a sudden ferocious shot into the top right-hand corner, then jumped up and down in the penalty box arms upheld like a child delighted by it's Christmas box.

He had every right to be.

53

TOTTENHAM HOTSPUR 4
Mackay, White, Jones 2

ARSENAL 4
Court 2, MacLeod, Strong

Saturday 6th October 1962

Football League Division One

White Hart Lane

Attendance 61,749

Tottenham Hotspur

Arsenal

Manager
Bill Nicholson

Manager
Billy Wright

Bill BROWN	1	John McCLELLAND
Peter BAKER	2	Eddie MAGILL
Ron HENRY	3	Billy McCULLOUGH
Danny BLANCHFLOWER	4	John SNEDDEN
Maurice NORMAN	5	Laurie BROWN
Dave MACKAY	6	Vic GROVES
Terry MEDWIN	7	John MacLEOD
John WHITE	8	Geoff STRONG
Les ALLEN	9	David COURT
Eddie CLAYTON	10	George EASTHAM
Cliff JONES	11	Alan SKIRTON

Referee **Mr G D Roper** (Cambridgeshire)

BACKGROUND

Having dropped three points to Wolves with defeat at White Hart Lane and a draw at Molineux, Spurs occupied third place in the table, four points behind the Midlanders and two adrift of Everton. In their last game they had hammered close rivals Nottingham Forest 9-2 with Jimmy Greaves scoring four. It was just the type of performance they needed to set them up for the meeting with Arsenal, although the buoyant mood was somewhat tempered by the news that Greaves had not recovered from an injury sustained in England's mid-week draw with France. Under new manager Billy Wright, and with a new centre-forward in Joe Baker, Arsenal had started the season with two wins but, beset by injury problems that had deprived them of captain Terry Neill, John MacLeod, Eddie Magill and Geoff Strong at various times, they had collected only one more win and were just a point off the bottom. Now Joe Baker was injured, with 18-year old David Court taking his place.

BEFORE THE GAME

	P	W	D	L	F	A	Pts
Spurs	11	7	1	3	37	18	15
Arsenal	11	3	2	6	15	20	8

Above: Jubilation after one of David Court's goals.
Right: A tangle between Spurs' Maurice Norman and Gunners' Alan Skirton.

Max Marquis in 'The Sunday Times' under headline...

TOTTENHAM, THREE AHEAD, JUST CLING TO POINT

It was unbelievable. At half-time Arsenal were two goals down against a vastly superior side who deserved to have a lead of six - and had made more than enough chances to score them comfortably. At the end there was nothing to choose between the two teams; and in fact no one would have been surprised if Arsenal had won.

True, Arsenal had the rub of the green and more than a shade of tolerance from the referee for some strategic pushes by defenders. But they handsomely deserved their point for gritting their teeth and blindly refusing to admit they were beaten.

Spurs contributed to their shattering second half change of the course of events; but if Arsenal's transformation was at all due to Billy Wright's half-time homily, his remarks must have been as effective as the Gettysburg Address.

Spurs started with the same elan and deadly efficiency as they showed in annihilating Nottingham Forest 9-2 last week.

A comparable score seemed highly likely as early as the fourth minute when **MACKAY** crashed home the ball from the edge of the penalty area after it had gone from wing to wing and back to the centre.

IRRESISTIBLE LOOK

Spurs' forward line - in which Clayton worked hard to fill the great gap left by Greaves - looked irresistible. It went through the rude Arsenal defence like a tidal wave through a torn fishing net. Time after time a Spurs forward was left in a wide open space.

More despatch in shooting by Spurs and less inspired goalkeeping, both good and lucky, by McClelland, and they would have scored again before the 16th minute, when Blanchflower started a movement which ended in **WHITE** running through alone to put the ball in the net.

Another ten minutes of superb attacking play then Jones and White passed the ball back and forth as casually as if at practice around wooden posts before **JONES** cracked home a handsome goal.

Only a minute later, Norman juggled the ball onto his chest and lost it to **COURT**, who thumped it unceremoniously into Brown's goal. Oh well - accidents will happen. Spurs seemed to smile tolerantly.

LUDICROUS SITUATION

The smile grew a little strained in the 33rd minute when Skirton sent across a centre as powerful as most shots. Brown got a fingertip to the ball; it went to Strong, whose muffed shot turned out to be a perfect pass to **COURT**. Again the centre forward took his chance and thumped the ball home.

It was ludicrous really. The score should have been 6-1 yet Spurs were only 3-2 ahead. Still, seven minutes Blanchflower again chipped an immaculate through ball which went from White and Allen before **JONES** scored with another bullet-like shot.

There had been a dozen clear chances but only four goals. Even so, when Tottenham trotted off at half-time there was no doubt in anyone's mind that they would soon put things right in the second half.

Instead, the sacrificial Arsenal lamb - albeit an obstinate one - turned and snapped at the executioners. In the 53rd minute Eastham, who had been labouring shrewdly and intelligently, at last saw that his colleagues had found open spaces.

He started a move carried on by MacLeod and Court before **MacLEOD** scored as handsome a goal as anything Spurs had done.

TIDE TURNS

The tide turned slowly, then gathered impetus. The Tottenham forwards confidence ebbed, they tried to tee up the ball before shooting.

The Arsenal wing-halves, who had looked on the point of collapse at half-time, found new strength and ability to find their forwards, who were at last running intelligently off the ball.

Incredibly, it was now the Tottenham defence which was in a horrible tangle of uncertainty; a brilliant Eastham did as well as White had done earlier; Brown had to make a near miraculous save from MAcLeod, the teenage Court was giving the experienced Norman a terrible time of it.

With 17 minutes left, **STRONG** ran on to a perfect pass to score. The incredible, the astonishing, the unbelievable had happened - Arsenal were level and even scenting victory.

Mackay played like three strong men, trying to prop up a cracked and tottering Spurs' defensive wall. Spurs fought back grimly but superb football brains were clouded by the fever of excitement. They tried to hammer instead of slice their way through Arsenal's defence.

Spurs were attacking at the final whistle but they were a clumsy shadow of the formidable looking team of only 45 minutes earlier.

A draw. It was unbelievable.

Below: John McClelland, hidden behind the three challengers, punches clear.

John McClelland lies helpless as Dave Mackay's shot finds the net to give Spurs an early lead.

ARSENAL 2
Strong, Baker

TOTTENHAM HOTSPUR 3
Smith, Jones, Marchi

Saturday 23rd February 1963

Football League Division One

Highbury

Attendance 59,980

Arsenal   ## Tottenham Hotspur

Manager
Billy Wright

Manager
Bill Nicholson

John McCLELLAND	1	Bill BROWN
Eddie MAGILL	2	Peter BAKER
Billy McCULLOUGH	3	Ron HENRY
John BARNWELL	4	Tony MARCHI
Laurie BROWN	5	Maurice NORMAN
John SNEDDEN	6	Dave MACKAY
John MacLEOD	7	Terry MEDWIN
Geoff STRONG	8	John WHITE
Joe BAKER	9	Bobby SMITH
George EASTHAM	10	Jimmy GREAVES
George ARMSTRONG	11	Cliff JONES

Referee **Mr H G New** (Portsmouth)

BACKGROUND

Arsenal went into the match with a record of seven wins in the last eight games stretching back for three months, much of that due to the continual postponements caused by the arctic weather. Spurs, without skipper Danny Blanchflower, who was recovering from a cartilage operation, had played only two competitive games in the year, losing their grip on the FA Cup they had held for two years with a 0-3 defeat at home to Burnley, and beating Blackpool.

BEFORE THE GAME

	P	W	D	L	F	A	Pts
Spurs	25	15	5	5	75	34	35
Arsenal	24	10	5	9	46	46	25

AT THE SEASON'S END

		P	W	D	L	F	A	Pts
2nd	Spurs	42	23	9	10	111	62	55
7th	Arsenal	42	18	10	14	86	77	46

Cliff Jones scores Tottenham's second goal (below) and Joe Baker nets Arsenal's second (above).

Talented Spurs are blessed with luck

More talented, more methodical and more inventive than Arsenal, Spurs were also, on the day, considerably more fortunate. They deserved to win, but two of the goals they scored came straight from the theatre of the absurd; or out of the realm of belated Christmas presents.

Eastham troubled them at times, little Armstrong played with his usual industry and courage, MacLeod had his illuminated moments, but their defence, with Norman imperturbable, made Arsenal work desperately for their two goals, while Arsenal's defence gave them recklessly away.

Spurs still miss Blanchflower - though Marchi was solid, Mackay full of fluency and power - and their recent eagerness to buy Scott was quite comprehensible. Greaves and White had no more than sporadic moments. Smith scored a beauty and missed a sitter, and it was left to Jones, with reindeer virtuosity to give dash to a forward line which would have looked quite feeble without him.

SUPREME BALANCE

For over half an hour defence had the better of the game on a surface which grew increasingly more difficult as time went on. It was 10 minutes from the break before we had a goal, and when it came, it was as spectacular as it was surprising. White gave a short pass to Jones, out on the left, Jones made himself space for an accurate but unexceptional low centre, and **SMITH**, with unusual dexterity, moved to the ball before the back, to turn it beautifully past McClelland on the volley, just inside the near post.

This was the signal for an astonishing ten minutes by Jones, flitting across the snow with supreme balance and absolute poise, as though he alone of the 22 players had been equipped not with football boots but snow shoes.

Greaves put him clear - though he looked offside to me - and only McClelland's nimble dive prevented a goal. Next, wandering into the middle and setting himself, Jones took a fine left-footed shot which brought from McClelland a still finer save. Best of all, the little Welshman came racing across the field from the left, leaving in his wake a line of mesmerised, red shirted statues, and at last, when a goal seemed the inevitable and poetic end, letting fly a shot which McClelland turned wide of the post.

But McClelland remains the least predictable of goalkeepers. Scarcely had the game restarted than he dived on a through ball, after which Smith was plodding in heavy pursuit, and fumbled it entirely, to give the centre-forward a chance ten times easier than the one he had previously taken. But Smith, lunged, slipped, ultimately fell, and the ball flew over the empty goal.

ATROCIOUS DEFENCE

Thus, it was a sustained passage of atrocious defence which ten minutes later gave Tottenham their second goal. At least three Arsenal players should have tackled Greaves as he ferreted for the ball on the right-hand edge of the penalty area. But carelessly they let him through, carelessly they left Jones unmarked, and **JONES**, on this sort of day and at this sort of range, was not going to miss this sort of chance.

Arsenal - one could understand it - looked a little dispirited after that. Their attack, when all was said and done, had built up some pretty first half movements, without coming near to a goal since Strong's fine header after a mere five minutes, a header which Brown gymnastically turned over the bar.

It was on **STRONG**, plainly, that Arsenal based their firmest hopes of a goal: nor does he seem to be in the attack for any other purpose. He is good in the air, he has a useful right foot, and he moves with determination. In linking play, alas, he is virtually non-existent. But when Eastham slid him a classical through pass across the snow, after 70 minutes, he did not need to link, merely to score: and this he did.

ANOTHER GIFT

Alas, for Arsenal, they almost at once presented Tottenham with another goal when **MARCHI**'s slow, soft shot from the edge of an over-populated penalty area, slipped through everybody's legs and into the corner of the goal. Marchi laughed incredulously. McClelland retrieved the ball miserably. As Groucho himself might have said "I've heard of goals, but this was ridiculous".

With eleven minutes left Arsenal, still gamely refusing to lie down, scored another hard-earned goal, when Armstrong turned back a long cross from the right and **BAKER** shot home from a hard pressed position and a difficult angle.

Too late: the presents had been made, the die cast, the match won. Arsenal pressed on regardless, but they had set themselves altogether too cruel a handicap.

BOBBY SMITH WINS THE DUEL

BOBBY SMITH of Tottenham Hotspur, MUST lead England against France when the two countries meet in Paris on Wednesday in the vital second leg of the European Nations Cup. (The first match at Sheffield last year ended in a 1—1 draw.)

This is my verdict after watching the controversial and under-rated Smith, with his odd mixture of craft and ruggedness, win his personal duel with Arsenal's Joe Baker for the vacant England centre forward spot.

...Alan Hoby reporting in the 'Sunday Express'.

Bobby Smith shakes off a challenge from Arsenal left-half John Sneddon to score Spurs' first goal.

55

ARSENAL 4
Eastham 2 (1 pen), Baker, Strong

TOTTENHAM HOTSPUR 4
Greaves, Smith 2, Mackay

Tuesday 15th October 1963

Football League Division One

Highbury

Attendance 67,857

Arsenal

Manager
Billy Wright

Tottenham Hotspur

Manager
Bill Nicholson

Ian McKECHNIE	1	Bill BROWN
Eddie MAGILL	2	Peter BAKER
Billy McCULLOUGH	3	Ron HENRY
Laurie BROWN	4	Danny BLANCHFLOWER
Ian URE	5	Maurice NORMAN
Vic GROVES	6	Dave MACKAY
John MacLEOD	7	Cliff JONES
Geoff STRONG	8	John WHITE
Joe BAKER	9	Bobby SMITH
George EASTHAM	10	Jimmy GREAVES
George ARMSTRONG	11	Terry DYSON

Referee **Mr D H Howell** (Birmingham)

BACKGROUND

Held over from the Saturday to Tuesday because of international calls, it was some years since the two clubs had met with both of them riding high at the top of the League. Spurs were second, one point and four places above Arsenal who, reinforced by the signing of Ian Ure, had dropped only two points in the first six home games, and those in an opening day defeat by Wolves. George Eastham had missed Arsenal's victory at Stoke but was fit to return, as was Spurs' Peter Baker who had missed a 3-3 draw at Sheffield United. While the reward of top spot was enough to attract the fans, they also had the prospect of watching the most free-scoring attacks in the League, Geoff Strong had already scored 13, Joe Baker and Jimmy Greaves, 15.

BEFORE THE GAME

	P	W	D	L	F	A	Pts
Spurs	11	8	1	2	40	21	17
Arsenal	12	8	0	4	31	24	16

Tottenham's Peter Baker stops a goal-bound shot.

'The Times' Association Football correspondent reported...

LAST ARSENAL FLICK ROBS TOTTENHAM
STORMING GAME LIFTS LEAGUE FOOTBALL FROM THE RUT

This was one of those matches that every now and then lift League football away from the humdrum. This was a match which neither, in the end, deserved to lose, although in truth it was Tottenham who should have won on all things artistic and pure. As it was they were robbed of their victory with virtually the last flick of a storming game, a header by Strong to the top corner from MacLeod's corner kick - taken as injury time ran out it's last few seconds.

Still, Spurs and their cockerel are now roosting again at the top of the First Division tree. They may not exactly be the cock of North London - postal district N.5 will these days refuse to bow to N.17 - but none the less Tottenham maintain their pedigree at Highbury where they have lost only

once in the past five years. A throbbing match indeed, it was consistent with the two highest scorers in the league - Spurs now with 44 goals, Arsenal with 35.

THOUSANDS LOCKED OUT

It is many years since there were such crowd scenes at Highbury. Some three-quarters of an hour before the kick-off the gates were shut on a 68,000 crowd. Thousands of others were locked out and there were moments outside the ground when one felt that we were near to disaster as solid walls of humanity heaved like a billowing sea. This might have been part of the original Wembley scene, a thought that was heightened when a mounted policeman on a white horse found him-

self in the centre of a stampede.

All this had set the high temperature of a thrilling match, and especially of a great first half in which all but two of the goals were fashioned. Later the furious pace told, and for the last 20 minutes Greaves was a limping passenger. One can only hope that he will be fit to take his place in England's shirt next week against the Rest of the World.

RAGING NAPOLEON

Here were 90 minutes of aggressive football. Here was power and skill and some flowing poetry of Tottenham movement, fired by the immaculate White and Mackay, a raging Napoleon in midfield in Tottenham's new 4-2-4 pattern. But if Spurs had

UPROAR AT HIGHBURY

Arsenal and Spurs fight out their greatest battle

Smith booked

Strong makes it 4–4 in last 20 seconds

By KEN JONES   Arsenal 4, Spurs 4

SENSATION and anger swept over Highbury last night as Arsenal and Spurs fought out their greatest and grimmest battle.

The tension was breathtaking as Spurs fought to hold on to their 4—3 lead with just 20 seconds and a corner-kick left.

Arsenal right winger Johnny McLeod's kick flashed to the corner of the six-yard box. A bullet header from inside right Geoff Strong beat a despairing dive by Bill Brown and the Gunners were level with time only to restart the match

And that sent a stream of Spurs men swarming after Birmingham referee Denis Howell in angry protest claiming that Arsenal's dramatic equaliser should have been disallowed for a foul on Brown.

Wouldn't Shut Up

Centre-forward Smith was booked by referee Howell, the Birmingham MP, who then pushed away other Spurs stars as they followed him angrily to the players' tunnel.

Howell told me afterwards: "I booked Smith because he disagreed with a perfectly good goal and wouldn't shut up."

But Smith said: "I was not disputing the goal. I was just pointing out to the referee that Brown was on the floor injured.

"The referee said: Get out of my way, and I told him he needn't talk to me like that, and then he booked me.

"If he wants to take me to the F.A. I'm quite prepared to go with him."

Brown commented on that last goal: "I thought I was on the receiving end of a cavalry charge."

HELPING HAND . . . Bobby Smith helps attend to a young fan who fainted in the crush just before the match began. It was quite a night for Bobby. He scored twice for Spurs and had his name taken for arguing with the referee after the final whistle.

---

the refined grain it was Arsenal, with their never-say-die spirit, who somehow or other stayed with them to the last breath, though one felt that they were helped by two doubtful decisions on the part of the referee which probably robbed Tottenham of an unassailable position before half time.

As it was, Spurs led 4-2 at the interval and all their goals were great. In terms of boxing, here, indeed, was counter-punching with the viciousness, timing and speed of a Joe Louis. Within three minutes they were ahead as **GREAVES**, with a remarkable sideways flick over his shoulder, turned in a free-kick by Blanchflower, the 198th goal this little man of the remarkable reflex action has scored in first class football. At 20 minutes Spurs were two up when **SMITH**, turning on a cross from Henry after Jones had decoyed the whole defence with a duck of the head, thundered his shot into the roof of McKechnie's net.

Then, at the half-hour, came a harsh penalty given for a tackle by Dyson, deep in defence, on Armstrong, his opposite number. It is not often that 11 meets 11 in such close contact, and now one felt it was the slippery, greasy pitch, shimmering under a drizzle, that was the real culprit in Dyson's attempted tackle. Anyway, a penalty said the referee and **EASTHAM**'s subtle left foot did the trick. But, as so often before, Spurs produced one of their master counter-punches.

Straight from the kick-off **MACKAY** moved some 40 yards, took a lovely diagonal pass from White, was through a gap like a steam engine and

all McKechnie could do was to pick the ball out of the his. One-three and shortly it should have been 1-4 when, after a flowing movement between Blanchflower, Dyson, Greaves and Jones, a sizzling shot to the top corner was strangely disallowed.

LURKING FIGURE

Perhaps it was the lurking figure of Smith near the far post that was the trouble, but certainly he did not seem to have interfered with the play. This, it seemed, was the letter rather than the spirit of the law being interpreted. It was harsh on Tottenham, and harsher still when, 60 seconds later, **EASTHAM** seized on a defensive error to find the top corner of Brown's net.

Two-three now instead of 4-1 to Spurs. That is football; but before the interval Spurs had got their men by the throat once more when a smooth movement of great speed, precision, and artistry down the right by White and Jones ended with **SMITH** thumping in White's cross with his head. There it remained, 4-2 until the last desperate seconds as Arsenal thundered away in frontal attack, striving to upset the poise and experience of their foe.

INVISIBLE LADDER

In all this the Arsenal wingers, MacLeod and Armstrong, fed by the subtleties of Eastham, were always posing questions of Baker and Henry. Strong, who seems to carry an invisible ladder around with him, was always dangerous in the air,

but until the last five minutes the Arsenal assault was countered by Mackay and Norman, with Blanchflower putting in a wise word now and then deep in defence as an auxiliary cover. And there too was White, with the ball bouncing off him from man to man as if he were some Telstar, always ready to mount a riposte though now the flashing heels of Greaves were reduced to quarter-speed.

Those last five minutes were made only for strong men with strong hearts. With the match apparently under their control Spurs were playing out time with a quiet authority. Then suddenly **BAKER,** with a sideways slant, evaded Norman's tackle and shot left-footed and low past Brown's dive. Only 4-3 to Spurs, and now Highbury Stadium was like some giant pot on the boil, banners waved and the roar was incessant. With two successive corners in the last few seconds of injury time, and the referee looking at his watch, **STRONG** rose on his spring heels and headed the second of the kicks, from MacLeod, home off the belly of the bar.

Tottenham were robbed. But it was high drama worth, I am sure, every penny and all the discomfort endured by that great company.

56

TOTTENHAM HOTSPUR 3
Greaves (pen), Jones 2

ARSENAL 1
Strong

Saturday 22nd February 1964

Football League Division One

White Hart Lane

Attendance 57,261

Tottenham Hotspur

Manager
Bill Nicholson

Arsenal

Manager
Billy Wright

Tottenham	No	Arsenal
John **HOLLOWBREAD**	1	John **McCLELLAND**
Peter **BAKER**	2	Fred **CLARKE**
Mel **HOPKINS**	3	Billy **McCULLOUGH**
Phil **BEAL**	4	Vic **GROVES**
Maurice **NORMAN**	5	Ian **URE**
Tony **MARCHI**	6	John **SNEDDEN**
Cliff **JONES**	7	John **MacLEOD**
John **WHITE**	8	Geoff **STRONG**
Laurie **BROWN**	9	Joe **BAKER**
Jimmy **GREAVES**	10	George **EASTHAM**
Terry **DYSON**	11	George **ARMSTRONG**

Referee **Mr T W Dawes** (Norfolk)

BACKGROUND

With Spurs top, three points ahead of third-placed Arsenal, both club's early season form had been maintained - in the League. In cup competitions they had not fared so well. Manchester United had ended Spurs' defence of the European Cup-Winners' Cup in the first round, Arsenal's first venture into Europe had come to a disappointing end at the hands of Standard Liege in the second round of the Inter-Cities Fairs Cup. In the FA Cup Spurs had gone out to Chelsea in the third round, Arsenal to Liverpool in the fifth. Billy Wright had continued his Highbury rebuilding with the signing of Jim Furnell from Liverpool in November, but Bill Nicholson had stayed out of the transfer market despite losing Danny Blanchflower to the knee injury that was to end his career and Dave Mackay with a broken leg sustained at Old Trafford in December. That all changed the day before the derby. Spurs may have been heading the table, but they had collected only one point, and of more concern only one goal, in their last three games. In a surprise move, Nicholson signed Arsenal's out of favour centre-half Laurie Brown for £40,000 - installing him at centre-forward in place of Bobby Smith, the England no 9. It was, said Nicholson, "a calculated gamble".

Geoff Strong (left) scores for Arsenal. Joe Baker and George Armstrong celebrate.

BEFORE THE GAME

	P	W	D	L	F	A	Pts
Spurs	30	17	6	7	75	53	40
Arsenal	31	15	7	9	78	62	37

AT THE SEASON'S END

	P	W	D	L	F	A	Pts
4th Spurs	42	22	7	13	97	81	51
8th Arsenal	42	17	11	14	90	82	45

THAT WAS THEN...

★ The official Tottenham programme for this game cost threepence for 12 pages, five of which were taken up by teams, tables and fixtures and another three with photographs.

Max Marquis in 'The Sunday Times' under...

BROWN INSPIRES JADED SPURS

If this game proves to be typical, the £40,0000 for Brown's transfer from Highbury to Tottenham was a bargain. He inspired and revitalised a jaded Spurs' forward line until it reached nearly the heights of it's golden days.

As everyone expected, Brown had the beating of Ure in the air. What was so dumbfounding was his control on the ground and his use of the ball. As the game progressed he grew in stature, skill and influence. Less ably supported, Baker was most impressive for Arsenal. He, Strong and Eastham gave the Tottenham defence a second-half pounding that was worth more than a single goal.

The game started at a tremendous pace with Tottenham showing a greater sense of decision and urgency than in some of their recent matches; while Arsenal contributed to their own difficulties by being astonishingly dilatory in clearing the ball.

Arsenal's goal had two uncomfortably close calls in the first quarter of an hour. McClelland missed a shot from White, but the ball was cleared off the line...to Brown, who side-footed it against a post. Shortly afterwards, Brown out-jumped everyone to head the ball to Greaves, but his header lacked direction. A minute later Baker broke away, darted through a spreadeagled defence and his thunderbolt of a shot hit a post.

GREAVES' SPIRITS RISE

The game's frenetic pace and tremendous excitement were maintained. It was too fast for craftsman like Eastham and White, although Eastham once again did an unbelievable amount of work, plugging holes at one end and trying to force them at the other.

As Brown's touch and confidence grew, so did Greaves's spirits, and he set off on a series of electrifying runs. Arsenal's defence was finding it hard going.

Yet Arsenal were the first to score. A long pass from Snedden accurately found Baker on the right wing. He prodded the ball to MacLeod, who lobbed the ball casually into the centre. **STRONG** managed to beat off two defenders and score with a header in the 42nd minute.

In first-half injury time Spurs forced two quick corners. From the second Brown headed over McClelland - always ready to leave his goal-line - and Clarke had to punch the ball over the bar to save a goal. **GREAVES** scored from the penalty, but the goal was morally Brown's.

If anything, the pace and excitement increased in the second half. Arsenal had their fair share of the opening minutes, and in the 57th minute Baker broke away. He put over a hard, low centre, which somehow evaded everyone, including Strong - only feet from the goal-line.

A minute later Brown gave Greaves a handsome pass. He burst through, drew McClelland, and squared the ball to **JONES**, who could have blown it into the net.

"RAILED IN"

Three minutes after this - in the 61st minute - White centred from the right-wing. Brown was standing on the penalty spot with Arsenal players round him like railings round a tall tree. Almost unnoticed, **JONES** ran in to score again with a header.

Arsenal, to their credit, fought back hard and skilfully, shrewdly prompted from behind by that knowledgeable old war horse, Groves. Baker and Strong made it clear that even if the Spurs' forward line was looking as nearly as dangerous as ever, the defence was just as uncertain. But Spurs held out and in the closing moments McClelland saved at full-length a cracking header from Brown, who dived headlong at Jones' centre. So the game ended at as high a pitch as it started.

Arsenal No.2 Freddie Clarke 'saves' Laurie Brown's header (above) but Jimmy Greaves scores from the resultant penalty (left).

57

TOTTENHAM HOTSPUR 3
Robertson, Greaves, Saul

ARSENAL 1
Baker

Saturday 10th October 1964

Football League Division One

White Hart Lane

Attendance 55,959

Tottenham Hotspur

Manager
Bill Nicholson

Arsenal

Manager
Billy Wright

Tottenham		Arsenal
Pat JENNINGS	1	Jim FURNELL
Cyril KNOWLES	2	Don HOWE
Ron HENRY	3	Fred CLARKE
Alan MULLERY	4	Frank McLINTOCK
Maurice NORMAN	5	Gordon FERRY
Tony MARCHI	6	Peter SIMPSON
Jimmy ROBERTSON	7	Terry ANDERSON
Jimmy GREAVES	8	Geoff STRONG
Frank SAUL	9	Joe BAKER
Cliff JONES	10	George EASTHAM
Terry DYSON	11	George ARMSTRONG

Referee **Mr E Crawford** (Doncaster)

BACKGROUND

Throughout Spurs history a period of success had always been followed by a sharp decline as aging stars proved difficult to replace. With Danny Blanchflower's knee injury forcing his retirement, Dave Mackay still recovering from a broken leg and the tragic death of John White, struck down by lightning on a golf course, Bill Nicholson moved into the transfer market in a determined bid to keep Spurs at the top. Alan Mullery and Jimmy Robertson were signed in March 1964, Pat Jennings and Cyril Knowles in the close season. At home, at least, the new signings proved a success, six victories in six games. On their travels though it was a different story. Two points out of a possible twelve left Spurs in the pack chasing leaders Chelsea. Arsenal had suffered an early set-back with the loss of Ian Ure but had won their last three away games, and were now reinforced by the arrival of the country's most expensive half-back, Frank McLintock, an £80,000 buy from Leicester. With Terry Neill and Alan Skirton absent, youngsters Peter Simpson and Terry Anderson were given another chance to stake a claim to a regular place.

BEFORE THE GAME

	P	W	D	L	F	A	Pts
Spurs	12	6	2	4	23	19	14
Arsenal	11	5	2	4	18	18	12

Jimmy Robertson puts Spurs into a 10th minute lead.

Jimmy Greaves makes it 2-0 to Tottenham with his club's 100th League goal against Arsenal.

Max Marquis in 'The Sunday Times' explained...

Arsenal left floundering by Greaves's skill

Tottenham won comfortably and indisputably; for 20 minutes or so in the first half, inspired by Greaves, they even provoked flashes of memory of the team they once were. But their victory and the manner of it must be seen in the context of the opposition which Arsenal provided them - and this was unconvincing and lack-lustre.

McLintock, who is still feeling his way with strange colleagues, was forced to curb his natural instinct for attack to help an uncoordinated and uncertain defence; while the delicate craftsman Eastham was forced to labour like a navvy.

It is difficult to understand how some of his team-mates can be so lacking in compassion and conscience to allow him to carry such a disproportionate burden of work.

That Arsenal were always floundering against the brilliant Greaves is understandable; but Saul, who is the sort of centre-forward who vigorously charges at goalkeepers, also caused them more trouble than was reasonable.

Tottenham had in Norman and Marchi two great defensive rocks on which the often-apathetic Arsenal forward line broke time and time again, liberating Mullery to give more attention to attack than he has in some recent matches.

And then, of course, there was Greaves, who dominated the scene whenever he had the ball or was near it.

Arsenal started with verve and power; and for ten minutes were the better and more dangerous side. In the second minute Eastham hit a post with a shrewd shot. and two minutes later Anderson hit Jennings with a shot rather than the goalkeeper saving it.

FINDING HIS TOUCH

But already Greaves was finding his touch, already Tottenham were combining well and running intelligently off the ball to rip great gaps in the Arsenal defence. In the 11th minute Marchi sent a long pass to Dyson. From him the ball went to Jones, and on towards Robertson. Clarke, who should have had the ball, did not, and **ROBERTSON** scored from fairly close in.

Twelve minutes after this Saul put the ball to Greaves on the edge of the penalty area. It came to him awkwardly while he was being harried by two defenders - yet **GREAVES** performed one of his minor miracles to control it and hit it hard on the turn past Furnell.

Eastham and Baker combined well just before the interval, but Jennings came out to smother Baker's shot; and the goalkeeper held a fine shot from Strong after Eastham had put him through with a brilliant pass.

The second half was scrappy and dull by comparison, coloured by brief moments of Greaves's performance, a long hard shot by Knowles, and two goals. The first of these, in the 61st minute, was Tottenham's, when Furnell failed to hold Robertson's shot giving **SAUL** an easy chance to score.

Five minutes before the end Strong emerged from obscurity to send Anderson away. **BAKER** rushed in to meet the winger's centre two yards from goal to score.

In these days of so much indifferent refereeing it is good to see Mr E Crawford from Yorkshire control the game with such accuracy, the right degree of firmness, and an excellent understanding of the advantage rule.

58

ARSENAL 3
Radford, Baker 2

TOTTENHAM HOTSPUR 1
Gilzean

Arsenal

Manager
Billy Wright

Tottenham Hotspur

Manager
Bill Nicholson

Tony BURNS	1	Bill BROWN
Don HOWE	2	Cyril KNOWLES
Billy McCULLOUGH	3	Ron HENRY
Terry NEILL	4	Alan MULLERY
Ian URE	5	Maurice NORMAN
David COURT	6	Tony MARCHI
Brian TAWSE	7	Jimmy ROBERTSON
John RADFORD	8	Jimmy GREAVES
Joe BAKER	9	Alan GILZEAN
George EASTHAM	10	Eddie CLAYTON
George ARMSTRONG	11	Cliff JONES

Referee **Mr J K Taylor** (Wolverhampton)

BACKGROUND

Stuck in mid-table throughout the season, Arsenal's only hopes of success rested on the FA Cup, but those hopes were dashed by an embarrassing defeat at Third Division Peterborough. Defeats by top of the table Chelsea and Leeds followed, with the gloom over Highbury only slightly lessened by a 2-0 victory over Fulham three days before Spurs' visit. Despite their poor form Arsenal still went into the the games as favourites. While Arsenal were beating Fulham, Chelsea had knocked Spurs out of the Cup, but Spurs' major concern was their away form. Only six points had been secured on 15 visits to opponents grounds and even the December signing of Alan Gilzean, a former team-mate of Ian Ure at Dundee, had done little to improve their atrocious record.

BEFORE THE GAME

	P	W	D	L	F	A	Pts
Arsenal	31	14	4	13	54	59	32
Spurs	30	14	6	10	58	49	34

AT THE SEASON'S END

		P	W	D	L	F	A	Pts
6th	Spurs	42	19	7	16	87	71	45
13th	Arsenal	42	17	7	18	69	75	41

The first goal of the night goes in as Spurs 'keeper Bill Brown is beaten by a deflection to John Radford's shot.

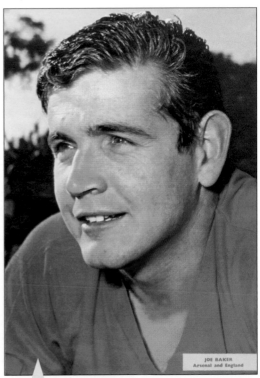

'DERBY' STAR **Joe Baker…** "Going like the wind, feet coaxing the ball with feathery touch, again looked one of Britain's best centre-forwards." – David Miller.

ARSENAL SHOW SOME ABILITY IN MIDFIELD

Joe Baker scores Arsenal's second goal, something of a present from Spurs No.6 Tony Marchi.

For all the disappointments the two teams have given their supporters in recent weeks, a crowd of 48,367 turned up to see this north London derby last night. None the less, the Highbury floodlights clearly showed why Arsenal and Spurs are now lying in the shadows of their western neighbour, Chelsea. Except for the more rabid Arsenal supporters, it was another disappointment; so many names of note together produced a match of nothingness.

It is always easy, of course, for criticism to be destructive, but how else can it be in a match of so little construction. What there was came mostly from Arsenal and that, as well as the result, gives them some cause for satisfaction.

Arsenal, at least, had some ability in midfield, although Eastham, their guiding light without the assistance of McLintock, was subdued for long periods. And no wonder, for of those behind him only Howe showed any skill in playing the ball out of defence. Apart from Howe, the Arsenal rearguard was big, strong and uninteresting.

BETTER PROPOSITION

However, they succeeded in limiting Spurs to four attacks of note and one goal, so presumably they earned their crust. That goal, scored by **GILZEAN** from Robertson's diagonal cross from the byline and which made the score 2-1, two-thirds of the way through the second half, showed the value of Robertson's speed and in doing so exposed McCullough's lack of it.

The Arsenal attack, however, was a better proposition. **BAKER**, after muddling through early on, in the end had a fine evening. He scored two of the goals, Arsenal's second and third, and if his first was something of a present from

Marchi, who, from behind Norman, headed the ball into Baker's path, his second, near the end, was a beauty. It came from Tawse's cross, which was half cleared. In a flash Baker was on to the ball. He pulled it back with the side of one boot and lashed it into the corner of the goal with the instep of the other.

Tawse, only 18, had a comparatively quiet evening after his performance of last Saturday, but one or two of his thoughts offered promise for the future and in the first half he was not helped by colleagues who failed to run where he expected they would. **RADFORD**, who got the first goal thanks to a deflection by Norman, formed a sort of battering ram and he and Baker often succeeded in leaving Marchi and Norman guessing as to who should be marking whom. On the left, Armstrong was a live wire of intermittent current. At times he left Knowles standing.

NEAT TOUCHES

The Spurs defence dithered often and panicked occasionally. There were times when first Henry and then Norman stood alone, but Norman always looked vulnerable when drawn from the middle. In midfield there was nothing. In attack we were left with one goal, one move involving Mullery, Robertson, Greaves and Gilzean, some neat touches by Gilzean, notably one beautiful back heel which almost put Greaves through, and one run past three men in 30 yards by Greaves himself. But in 90 minutes that was all, and for Spurs and those who follow them, it was not enough. Judged on the night's performance, they must surely take the opportunity to experiment.

59

TOTTENHAM HOTSPUR 2
Saul, Gilzean

ARSENAL 2
Brown L (og), Baker

Tottenham Hotspur

Manager
Bill Nicholson

Arsenal

Manager
Billy Wright

Tottenham		Arsenal
Bill BROWN	1	Jim FURNELL
Maurice NORMAN	2	Don HOWE
Cyril KNOWLES	3	Billy McCULLOUGH
Alan MULLERY	4	Frank McLINTOCK
Laurie BROWN	5	Terry NEILL
Dave MACKAY	6	David COURT
Jimmy GREAVES	7	George ARMSTRONG
Eddie CLAYTON	8	John RADFORD
Alan GILZEAN	9	Joe BAKER
Frank SAUL	10	Jon SAMMELS
Derek POSSEE*	11	George EASTHAM
Roy LOW (11)	12	Ian URE

Referee **Mr L Callaghan** (Merthyr Tydfil)

BACKGROUND

By their own high standards both clubs had a disappointing season in 1964-65 but neither of them ventured into the summer transfer market, preferring to rely on the development of home-produced talent. Arsenal had promising youngsters like Bob Wilson, Tommy Baldwin, John Radford, Jon Sammels, Peter Storey and Peter Simpson, Spurs the likes of Derek Possee and Keith Weller, looking for their chance as Cliff Jones was injured pre-season. With a midweek victory over Leeds taking Spurs to the top of the table it looked a good policy, but the fact was they were not playing well, not a shadow of the great team of the so-recent past. Arsenal had started poorly but a fine midweek win at Nottingham Forest gave them confidence.

BEFORE THE GAME

	P	W	D	L	F	A	Pts
Spurs	5	4	1	0	15	6	9
Arsenal	5	2	2	1	7	7	6

"The army of Spurs supporters who jammed the damp bowl of White Hart Lane yesterday endured 90 minutes of 'cliff-hanging' as this savagely criticised Arsenal, playing like giants 12ft tall, had lofty Tottenham struggling and scrambling for the luckiest of draws." – The Sunday Express.

Above: Joe Baker finishes off a fine move to put Arsenal two up.
Right: Alan Gilzean celebrates after making it 2-2.

Max Marquis in 'The Sunday Times' reported...

Arsenal find their feet

In a lusty game where a sense of local occasion provoked an excitement when the football flagged, Arsenal, their morale visibly uplifted and the resolve stiffened by their mid-week away win, succeeded in taking one point from Tottenham.

Only Tottenham's well-known talent for scoring an unexpected goal after a period of anonymous mediocrity enabled them to save the game and push their run of unbeaten home performances to 29.

With the rugged but unflagging Neill at centre-half, Arsenal looked a much better-integrated team than in their recent matches in London: high, floating balls no longer sent ripples of uncertainty through the defence. There was too, a recognisable pattern about their play.

True, Tottenham had only two attackers who needed to be watched unremittingly: Greaves - who usually saw the ball only when he went and fetched it for himself - and Gilzean, who has added bite to his elegant play. Saul was grotesquely out of touch, Clayton played deep, making valuable interceptions; Possee started with a strapped-up thigh and a limp, to be replaced at half-time by Low.

So, after two early Tottenham bursts when Furnell snatched a handsome pass by Gilzean from Possee's feet and Greaves missed by centimetres - unaccountably - from close in, Arsenal were allowed to settle down. For once there were more Arsenal players than opposition at any given time and place.

In the 11th minute McCullough thundered down the left wing like a tribal uprising, passed to Eastham and took a return pass. His pulled back centre hit the honest ploughman **BROWN (L)** and ricocheted into the net.

MAJOR THORN

Although Greaves came close to scoring twice, and perhaps really ought to have done so, Arsenal quickly established a strong sense of superiority. Baker, a fast-moving, shrewd and determined player, looking nearly every inch an England centre-forward, was the major thorn in the Tottenham heavy-footed defence. Supporting him well were Court and McLintock in midfield, and Eastham on the wing, who made Norman's size look like a handicap.

In the 22nd minute **BAKER** charmed the ball past Brown (L), leaving him on the ground like a toppled crane before shooting with complete aplomb into the narrow space left him by the advancing Bill Brown.

It was Arsenal's half, yet 10 minutes before the interval Possee chipped over a speculative centre from what looked suspiciously over the by-line. Gilzean back-headed the ball on, and **SAUL** clumped in to bundle the ball into the net without grace.

The second half was a much less interesting business. Players of both sides made bad passes on a surface made suddenly treacherous by heavy rain; Mackay understandably ran out of steam, and Arsenal out of rhythm. One astonishing collective aberration by the Tottenham defence, and a magnificent shot by Greaves, spectacularly saved by Furnell, were the only high points of a long stretch of animated suspension.

A quarter of an hour before the end the perceptive Bill Brown called for the ball and quickly sent one of his long kicks well into the Arsenal half, where Gilzean had only Neill near him. Gilzean judged his jump and the bounce of the ball with minute accuracy and squeezed past Neill. Furnell, caught midway between the players and his goal line, could not reach **GILZEAN**'s perfectly-lobbed scoring header.

This sparked off a final quarter of an hour of urgent endeavour when either side could have won the game. Tottenham had the best chance when Greaves fought for and won the ball, then crossed it in front of Arsenal's empty goal, where Saul was running in. Predictably, he missed unequivocally with an ungainly header.

"We nicked a point," commented Greaves after the match. Graphic, and just.

Derek Possee is stopped in his tracks by Jim Furnell.

HISTORICAL NOTE...

Roy Low became not only the first substitute used in a North London League 'derby' but also the first used by Spurs in any League fixture.

A snap shot from Spurs No.10 Frank Saul is watched over the bar by all present.

60

ARSENAL 1
Court

TOTTENHAM HOTSPUR 1
Possee

Tuesday 8th March 1966

Football League Division One

Highbury

Attendance 51,805

Arsenal

Tottenham Hotspur

Manager
Billy Wright

Manager
Bill Nicholson

Jim **FURNELL**	1	Pat **JENNINGS**
Peter **STOREY**	2	Alan **MULLERY**
Billy **McCULLOUGH**	3	Cyril **KNOWLES**
Terry **NEILL**	4	Eddie **CLAYTON**
Ian **URE**	5	Laurie **BROWN**
David **COURT**	6	Dave **MACKAY**
Alan **SKIRTON**	7	Jimmy **ROBERTSON**
Jon **SAMMELS**	8	Jimmy **GREAVES**
John **RADFORD**	9	Frank **SAUL**
George **EASTHAM**	10	Alan **GILZEAN**
George **ARMSTRONG**	11	Derek **POSSEE**
Peter **SIMPSON**	12	Neil **JOHNSON**

Referee **Mr G Martin** (Whitchurch)

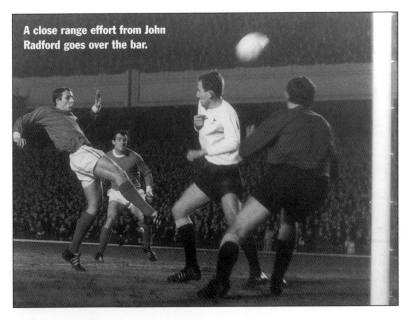

A close range effort from John Radford goes over the bar.

BACKGROUND

In the last match of 1965 Arsenal beat Sheffield Wednesday 5-2 with George Eastham scoring two and Joe Baker one. Only once more did they take both points from a game before Spurs' visit, four straight defeats culminating in an FA Cup third round exit to soon to be relegated Blackburn, victory at Stoke followed by three draws. The ending of their interest in the FA Cup saw Baker and Eastham dropped but with Frank McLintock victim of a gashed shin David Court moved to half-back and the transfer-listed Eastham was recalled. To add to their worries full-back Don Howe broke his leg against Blackpool three days earlier. If Arsenal had their problems, Spurs were not faring much better. Maurice Norman had broken his leg in November and Jimmy Greaves had missed much of the season with hepatitis. In their last outing the lowest point for many years had been reached with Preston dumping then out of the FA Cup. That defeat cost Phil Beal his place. Alan Mullery was asked to play at full-back, Eddie Clayton moved to midfield and Derek Possee was recalled up front.

BEFORE THE GAME

	P	W	D	L	F	A	Pts
Spurs	29	14	8	7	61	43	36
Arsenal	29	10	9	10	49	51	29

'The Times' staff reporter under...

DETERMINATION RETURNS TO ARSENAL

Those spectators who came to cheer Eastham stayed to applaud the greater determination of the whole Arsenal team. They came to see Tottenham's army in retreat from that spiritless thrashing at Preston and stayed to see them learn from the enemy's example how to fight. In the end they, the supporters of Arsenal and Tottenham, had been given good enough value for two average teams - and that is all they are at the moment - produced, under Highbury's floodlights last night, a match in keeping with these North London derbies.

It was supposed to be match between two teams in the doldrums, searching for their pride; it became instead a story of two men who once played together at Dundee - Gilzean, about whom many kind things have been said in the past - and Ure, of whom the reverse is true.

Last night Highbury saw Ure as near to his best as they have seen him. For 45 minutes they saw Gilzean at what, one would hope, was his worst. But after the interval some Scottish blood returned to Gilzean's pallid face. He made the goal which rescued Tottenham's pride - and that quality in

POSSEE TO THE RESCUE..

Shaky Spurs hit back to equalise in a blazing Highbury duel

Arsenal 1, Spurs 1

ARSENAL and Spurs, two teams on trial, fought themselves to a standstill in a blazing duel of strength at Highbury last night.

In the end they found equality and perhaps satisfaction out of thundering tackles and bombarding long ball assaults.

But in the fire shutters dropped on the power on the theories of 4-2-4 coaching concern and rubbish and class.

The substance he had poured last night is now perhaps a means to an end.

In the matter of the point Gilzean for the Spurs and Arsenal's George Eastham nodded a sense of inspiration to it.

Two little men of great skill symbolising for a second their search for a place in a duel where artistry was at a premium and seldom wanted.

By KEN JONES

Hard

Eastham set one in a thundering duel with the fact that he had demanded his reward. He tried as hard as any of them and as much as the full frame could stick.

Greaves producing one looked shot that was at last a flash of his old self

was willing to plunge himself into tasks that had played no part in his game until now.

Ambition governs this type of team planning but on the night it was beyond the capabilities of the men who had to play.

Spurs setting in a new strategy after their shame in Cup exit at Preston on Saturday moved wing half A an M ery to right back and ranged three men in midfield.

But almost immediately they were under fire with tension tugging at their tactics.

A wicked half volley from Arsenal left winger George

Spurs left winger Derek Possee (left) hooks a shot just wide of the post, watched by team-mate Frank Saul, Arsenal's Ian Ure and goalkeeper Jim Furnell (right). Possee later won his spurs by hitting the equaliser.

Armstrong was brilliantly pushed over one-handed by Pat Jennings.

After two flashes of Eastham skill, Arsenal went in front in the ninth minute.

A mix-up and Spurs defence allowed Alan Skirton two bites at the ball. At his second attempt he sent it to David Court who flashed a fierce shot past an unsighted Jennings.

Arsenal piled it on and Spurs seemed unsure of themselves and of their football.

Command

It wasn't until the second half that a note of command came into their game as Arsenal lost their grip in midfield.

Dour defensive play by Ian Ure and Terry Neill kept Spurs at bay but confidence began to flow into their football.

Greaves shot inches wide

Alan Gilzean forced a fine save out of Jim Furnell and then in the 62nd minute Spurs were level.

The more began deep in their own half. The ball went on via Eddie Clayton to Gilzean and when Saul tried a shot the ball bobbled free for hard working left winger Derek Possee to hit it home.

Chance

Arsenal might have won it when Eastham breaking fast with Ure on his right gave the Scottish international a chance, but Jennings made a good save.

Spurs might have won it when Saul with a chance made by Greaves hammered the ball high over the bar.

They both might have won it but deep down apart from their efforts I don't think either of them really deserved to.

The frailty of Spurs defence was underlined by Preston's equaliser after 30 minutes. Centre forward Alex Dawson was completely unmarked when he was permitted to nod in a ball that should have been the sole property of either Laurie Brown or goalkeeper Pat Jennings.

The second goal followed an equally bad defensive error. Francis Lee crossed the ball over. Jennings failed to hold a shot from Alan Spavin. The rebound was a gift goal for Ern: Hannigan.

> "I knew as soon as I connected that the ball was going in.
> "You couldn't blame the Arsenal goalkeeper. He was caught in two minds and it all happened so quickly." – Derek Possee

AT THE SEASON'S END

		P	W	D	L	F	A	Pts
8th	Spurs	42	16	12	14	75	66	44
14th	Arsenal	42	12	13	17	62	75	37

both teams is always on trial in these affairs - and then forced Furnell to atone for the error that produced the draw. In the train of Gilzean's revival came Tottenham's. It was far from complete but at least the passenger became one of the engineers.

TOOK CONTROL

The first half, from the first minute when Armstrong's half volley left Jennings' gloved hand stinging and Radford headed the resulting corner past a post, belonged to Arsenal. Their defence took control and with the confidence gained from the knowledge of the seeming solidity behind them their limited attack often left Tottenham groping. That confidence spread from the half-back line and Ure was in command at it's helm.

Eastham had a quiet game, but his presence indirectly improved the performance of the team. Armstrong, for one, benefited from his return, Sammels did as well to a lesser extent, and Court, moved back, looked a better player in a wing half's jersey.

But it was Court, moving forward, who got the Arsenal goal after 10 minutes. Skirton crossed at the third attempt: Brown, Knowles and Mackay were all pulled to Tottenham's left, and Court, with a drive, hit hard and true found a gap to Jennings' right. It was a deserved lead, and Radford and Skirton should have increased it before the interval.

Tottenham just could not get going, Mullery looked wasted at full back, and with Mackay mostly to be found as the sweeper in the rear of the defence, there was no power in

midfield to drive Gilzean and Greaves. And the inside men needed to be fed. Clayton looked an honest worker but no more. Knowles often committed himself too soon and the attack was completely disjointed.

The start of the second half saw little change until Furnell gave Tottenham the bit of luck they needed. Gilzean found Saul with a fine pass down the middle but Ure was there and the shot was blocked. But the ball only ran clear to **POSSEE** who, from an angle, found an opening to Furnell's right as the goalkeeper went to his left. Now, with a little under half an hour to go, Tottenham led the race and Arsenal's house looked a little tinny, particularly at full back.

David Court's shot beats Pat Jennings to put Arsenal ahead.

61

TOTTENHAM HOTSPUR 3
Jones, Greaves 2
ARSENAL 1
Sammels

Saturday 3rd September 1966

Football League Division One

White Hart Lane

Attendance 56,271

Tottenham Hotspur

Manager
Bill Nicholson

Arsenal

Manager
Bertie Mee

Pat JENNINGS	1	Jim FURNELL
Joe KINNEAR	2	David COURT
Cyril KNOWLES	3	Peter SIMPSON
Phil BEAL	4	Frank McLINTOCK
Mike ENGLAND	5	Ian URE
Dave MACKAY	6	Terry NEILL
Jimmy ROBERTSON	7	Tommy COAKLEY
Jimmy GREAVES	8	Tommy BALDWIN
Alan GILZEAN	9	John RADFORD
Terry VENABLES	10	Jon SAMMELS
Cliff JONES	11	George ARMSTRONG
Eddie CLAYTON	12	Jimmy McGILL

Referee **Mr W G Handley** (Cannock)

BACKGROUND

Arsenal's fall to 14th place in the First Division, their lowest placing since 1930, and their failure to escape Spurs' shadow cost Billy Wright his job in the summer of 1966. While the football world expected a big name replacement, Arsenal sprung a surprise by appointing physiotherapist Bertie Mee as his successor. Mee realised football was changing, flair and artistry alone were no longer enough, hard work and commitment allied to organisation were needed. Any misgivings at George Eastham being allowed to leave for Stoke before the new season began were soon dispelled with victory in the opening three games followed by a draw at West Ham. Spurs, reinforced by £95,000 Mike England had started almost as well, defeat at Stoke the only points they had dropped.

BEFORE THE GAME

	P	W	D	L	F	A	Pts
Spurs	4	3	0	1	7	3	6
Arsenal	4	3	1	0	8	4	7

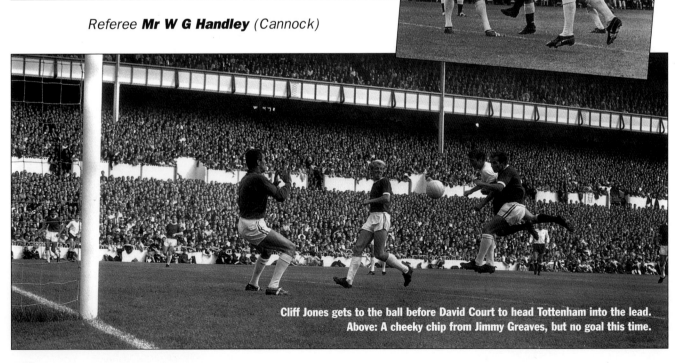

Cliff Jones gets to the ball before David Court to head Tottenham into the lead.
Above: A cheeky chip from Jimmy Greaves, but no goal this time.

Jimmy Greaves nets his second and his side's third goal.

*David Miller in **'The Sunday Telegraph'** reported...*

Greaves double ends Arsenal run

Spurs predictably punctured the new Arsenal balloon this afternoon. They should, by the end, have left it completely deflated instead of just sagging, for 6-2 would have been a more correct score.

Sad to say, at a time when London has no European representative, Spurs lacked the killer instinct, while Arsenal, in several positions, lacked any instinct at all. Not that you could claim to be surprised, for Coakley, Baldwin, Radford and Armstrong is hardly the quartet to put fear into any self-respecting defence.

SLIPSHOD CHANGE

Over the last half-hour, Robertson, Greaves and Jones backed by Venables and Mackay, and possessing the kind of skill that Arsenal saw disappear down the road with Baker and Eastham, washed through the Arsenal defence like the tide through sandcastles. Only the prodigious squandering by Greaves of three sitting targets prevented a rout.

Arsenal began almost as brightly as the sun shone, McLintock for a while looked the best player on the field, always in possession and moving forward, but Arsenal's transition from 4-4-2 in defence to 4-2-4 in attack was slip-shod and soon McLintock's preoccupations were more to the rear than in front of him.

Mackay, brimming with experience, calmed a nervy Spurs with a couple of audacious back passes to Jennings, who had badly missed a centre, and things began to move, though more by individual ability than collective rhythm.

The referee missed - did he really see them and ignore them? - a trip on Robertson on the edge of the area at one end and another on Baldwin inside it at the other.

Court, having fouled Jones, was obviously troubled by his conscience and nearly beat his own goalkeeper with a lobbed back pass, but Jones soon got his own back with a superb goal.

HABITUAL POACHER

Venables and Greaves opened the way for Robertson, who raced past Simpson, flashed across a dipping centre, and there was **JONES** tumbling in headlong like some Eastern European acrobat to meet the ball with perfect timing and glance it beyond Furnell's reach.

Arsenal tentatively replied with two efforts by Baldwin, a diving header by Radford and a shot-cum-centre by Simpson but Venables, with for him surprising power, grazed the angle of the posts from more than 30 yards to restore Spurs' authority.

Soon after half-time Greaves began the torment of Ure which grew steadily for the rest of the game, then Ure obstructed Jones. Mackay's free kick curled over to Gilzean, an acute shot was only parried by Furnell and there was **GREAVES**, the habitual poacher, stabbing the ball home.

GREAVES was able to get his second after he and Furnell had stood looking at each other for what seemed like a minute after a corner.

More chances followed, with Arsenal now bemused, but it was **SAMMELS** who had the final say.

'DERBY' STAR

Jimmy Greaves

62

ARSENAL 0

TOTTENHAM HOTSPUR 2
Gilzean, Robertson

Arsenal

Tottenham Hotspur

Manager
Bertie Mee

Manager
Bill Nicholson

Jim FURNELL	1	Pat JENNINGS
Bob McNAB	2	Phil BEAL
Peter STOREY	3	Cyril KNOWLES
Frank McLINTOCK	4	Alan MULLERY
Peter SIMPSON	5	Mike ENGLAND
Ian URE	6	Eddie CLAYTON
Gordon NEILSON	7	Jimmy ROBERTSON
John RADFORD	8	Jimmy GREAVES
George GRAHAM	9	Alan GILZEAN*
Jon SAMMELS	10	Terry VENABLES
George ARMSTRONG	11	Keith WELLER
Tom WALLEY	12	Frank SAUL (9)

Referee **Mr K Dagnall** *(Bolton)*

BEFORE THE GAME

	P	W	D	L	F	A	Pts
Spurs	24	12	3	9	43	37	27
Arsenal	24	8	7	9	31	31	23

AT THE SEASON'S END

		P	W	D	L	F	A	Pts
3rd	Spurs	42	24	8	10	71	48	56
7th	Arsenal	42	16	14	12	58	66	46

BACKGROUND

Following the defeat at Spurs in September, Mee continued his rebuilding programme, allowing Alan Skirton to leave Highbury for Blackpool and signing Colin Addison, George Graham and Bob McNab. Talented individuals all, they took time to settle and in 23 games Arsenal collected just six wins, one of those a second replay victory over Gillingham in the League Cup. Terry Neill had missed the last three games with a head injury and not trained for two weeks but with Peter Simpson doing well in his place, Mee resisted the temptation to recall the Irishman. Addison was out with a heavy cold but John Radford was fit to resume having missed the last game, a one goal win at Aston Villa. Spurs, too, had gone through a difficult period but with Jimmy Greaves recovered from illness, his goals ensured they remained in the upper reaches of the First Division. They had beaten Newcastle 4-0 on their last outing but were forced to make one change, Eddie Clayton coming in for Dave Mackay, who had a damaged ankle.

Jim Furnell saves as (l to r) Bob McNab, Frank Saul, Ian Ure and Keith Weller look on.

THAT WAS THEN...

★ Reserved seats at Highbury in the 1966/67 season could be booked for 12/6d (63p), 15/- (75p) and 20/- (£1).

★ The Gunners match programme cost sixpence (3p) for 16 small pages.

Above: Pat Jennings gathers comfortably as Mike England holds off a challenge from John Radford.

Bruce Barber in 'The Observer'...

Arsenal battle in vain

That dictum about the ability to deserve success being worthier than achieving success is the most improbable in the language. It was surely hatched by a curmudgeon cheated of victory's feast.

Certainly Arsenal will not inscribe it on their Coat of Arms after this defeat. For the reward of a storming second half, in which they carried the fight to the enemy, was precisely nil.

True, the skills and science of Spurs merited their two goals lead at half-time. Equally, the dash and the spice that transformed Arsenal's game thereafter pointed to shared spoils.

For 45 minutes, Greaves was at his irrepressible best and that meant a Spurs' side enjoying mastery. Arsenal's defence was repeatedly split.

In only seven minutes Spurs flared into flame after a spluttering start.

Mullery held off a couple of challenges as he forced his way in from the right. His pass found **GILZEAN** astutely stationed alongside the near post. It was half a flick, half a lob that steered the ball past Furnell.

SKIMMING SHOT

For a space, Arsenal's penalty area resembled a shooting gallery, three or four marksmen trying their luck in turn. Finally, Greaves did hammer the ball into the net. The goal seemed perfectly legal but referee Dagnall apparently detected an unpermitted hampering of Furnell.

By contrast Arsenal's breakaways lacked at this stage purpose or thrust. Sammels hit a 20-yarder straight into Jennings' arms. Coolly Tottenham regained control. **ROBERTSON** swept smoothly down the wing and his left foot skimmed the ball past Furnell's dive and inside the far post.

Whatever fighting words were addressed to the Arsenal players during the interval possessed galvanic force. They swung the ball about with rare gusto.

Shot after shot was blocked more by accident than design. Spurs defenders were aligned like a colonnade, with all of the pillars stood in the right spot.

It could be contended that Spurs accepted a defensive role rather than having it forced upon them. If so, the greater the pity their tactics worked.

Below: Alan Gilzean nips in ahead of Peter Simpson to steer a pass from Alan Mullery past Jim Furnell for Tottenham's first goal.

63

ARSENAL 4
Radford, Neill (pen), Graham, Addison

TOTTENHAM HOTSPUR 0

Saturday 16th September 1967

Football League Division One

Highbury

Attendance 62,936

Arsenal

Tottenham Hotspur

Manager
Bertie Mee

Manager
Bill Nicholson

Jim FURNELL	1	Pat JENNINGS
Peter STOREY	2	Joe KINNEAR
Peter SIMPSON	3	Cyril KNOWLES
Frank McLINTOCK	4	Alan MULLERY
Terry NEILL	5	Mike ENGLAND
Ian URE	6	Phil BEAL
John RADFORD	7	Jimmy ROBERTSON
Colin ADDISON	8	Jimmy GREAVES
George GRAHAM	9	Alan GILZEAN
Jon SAMMELS	10	Terry VENABLES
George ARMSTRONG	11	Frank SAUL
David SIMMONS	12	Cliff JONES

*Referee **Mr L Hamer** (Bolton)*

John Radford opens the scoring with a header.

BACKGROUND

After two wins, two defeats and a draw in their opening five games Arsenal began to find their form just in time for the first derby of the season; victories at West Bromwich Albion and Sheffield United and Coventry in the League Cup, putting them in buoyant mood. Spurs, second in the table, had started by dropping only one point in their first four games but in their last away game had been hammered 1-5 at Burnley. They had recovered with successive home wins over Wolves and Sheffield Wednesday but a good result at Highbury would set them up nicely for the start of their European Cup-Winners' Cup campaign against Hadjuk Split in Yugoslavia four days later.

BEFORE THE GAME

		P	W	D	L	F	A	Pts
2nd	Spurs	7	5	1	1	15	11	11
6th	Arsenal	7	4	1	2	12	8	9

*Tony Pawson in **'The Observer'**...*

Arsenal's speed shatters Spurs

An annihilating win over Tottenham confirmed that Arsenal have a side that will make a serious challenge for the championship. You had to be a very early bird to find parking space within earshot of Highbury for this enthralling clash.

Inevitably there was more to this match than the usual interest of a local derby, for this was a real test of Arsenal's resurgence. How splendidly they met the challenge and what a wonderful game this was until Spurs disintegrated under the pressure.

It was only seconds before the interval that the first goal came and yet the first half had enough incident to fill a normal 90 minutes. From the first whistle Arsenal exploited their main asset - a killing pace of attack in which skill was not submerged by speed.

Spurs struggled vainly to slow the game to their own more leisurely concepts. Always they were a stride too late as the bubbling enthusiasm of the red shirts undermined their calculated poise. Soon their defence was as helpless as a ping-bong ball on a waterspout, bouncing about without any control of their own destiny.

DESPERATE

Yet somehow they survived the initial onslaught. Graham pounced on a bad back pass to shoot narrowly over, then saw Jennings arch back to turn another dipping drive over the bar. Sammels, clipping his long passes with precise certainty, was controlling the attack with subtle changes of pace and direction. Graham challenging fiercely for every ball was a constant threat in the centre.

But Tottenham were soon to show themselves equally

George Graham gets to the ball before Alan Mullery to score Arsenal's third goal.

penetrating on the break. Robertson had gone weaving through on his own for Furnell to fumble his low shot, then clutch it back as Greaves leapt over him. Now Furnell's desperate leap swept a free kick away from England's forehead. As the play flickered from end to end Greaves was nearly through with a mazy dribble, then missed by a fraction as he swung at Robertson's volley across the face of goal.

At last, like the drip of water on stone, Arsenal's remorseless pressure began to wear Tottenham down. Graham made Knowles lose his temper and control. Before Knowles had recovered from the angry exchange he left Radford unmarked as Armstrong turned back to send a right-foot centre curling cunningly behind the defence. **RADFORD** moved confidently in to nod it home.

As a match the contest died a few minutes after the interval. Beal, going for a loose ball on the edge of the area, was balked by Addison and bowled him over.

The lenient tenor of the refereeing suddenly changed to award a penalty that can be kindly described as harsh. **NEILL** hammered it home off the underside of the bar and Tottenham's self-control was swept aside, the rhythm of their play finally destroyed.

Ill-tempered exchanges completed their own downfall for Arsenal remained physically dominant, mentally in command. One was left to admire only the forceful determination of their team. Billy Wright collected together all of these

players but never succeeded in moulding them into such a powerful side.

Ure's defensive skills barely sufficed to hold Greaves in check. But Neill's swift interceptions exposed Gilzean as pitifully slow in movement and anticipation. This central dominance gave the base from which McLintock roved upfield carefree and confident.

Yet part of the defensive solidity was due to the tireless energy of the forwards. Perhaps Armstrong is most typical of the new Arsenal, chasing back relentlessly, tackling with a power of inverse ratio to his height, yet using the ball in attack with cold precision. It was another of his curving right-foot centres that again caused havoc at the far post as **GRAHAM** squeezed past Knowles to slide it in.

Then Radford, breaking through, lost the ball which ran loose to **ADDISON**; with contemptuous calm he chose his time and place to slide the ball wide of Jennings into the net.

In the crowd a bugler played the "Last Post" and only a drive from Greaves that brought Furnell to his knees and a shot pulled wide of the post by Venables indicated that there was any life left in Tottenham.

64

TOTTENHAM HOTSPUR 1
Gilzean

ARSENAL 0

Tottenham Hotspur

Manager
Bill Nicholson

Arsenal

Manager
Bertie Mee

Tottenham Hotspur	No	Arsenal
Pat JENNINGS	1	Jim FURNELL
Joe KINNEAR	2	Peter SIMPSON
Cyril KNOWLES	3	Bob McNAB
Alan MULLERY	4	Frank McLINTOCK
Phil BEAL	5	Terry NEILL
Dave MACKAY	6	Ian URE
Jimmy ROBERTSON	7	John RADFORD
Alan GILZEAN	8	David JENKINS*
Martin CHIVERS	9	George GRAHAM
Terry VENABLES	10	Jon SAMMELS
Jimmy GREAVES	11	George ARMSTRONG
Eddie CLAYTON	12	Pat RICE (8)

Referee **Mr J Finney** (Hereford)

BACKGROUND

New signing Martin Chivers

A worrying slump in form from late November to the end of the year had not only seen Spurs trailing behind Manchester United, Leeds and Liverpool in the championship race, but also going out of the Cup-Winners' Cup to the little-fancied French club, Olympique Lyonnais. Bill Nicholson reacted positively, signing Martin Chivers from Southampton for a record £125,000. He made a great start, scoring a midweek winner at Sheffield Wednesday and was set for his home debut. Arsenal were going through one of those periods when they seemed to pick up draws far more easily than victories, six in the last ten League games. Three days earlier though they had secured a 3-2 victory to carry into the second leg of the League Cup semi-final with Huddersfield.

BEFORE THE GAME

	P	W	D	L	F	A	Pts
Spurs	25	11	6	8	39	40	28
Arsenal	25	10	7	8	40	31	27

AT THE SEASON'S END

		P	W	D	L	F	A	Pts
7th	Spurs	42	19	9	14	70	59	47
9th	Arsenal	42	17	10	15	60	56	44

Above: Jim Furnell punches clear as Jimmy Greaves challenges.
Right: Greaves again, this time outpacing Arsenal's Peter Simpson.

It's a close shave... In the picture are Spurs' Alan Gilzean and Jimmy Roberston (grounded) and Arsenal's Terry Neill, George Armstrong (in the background) and Jon Sammels.

Max Marquis reported in **'The Sunday Times'** *under...*

Elegant Arsenal run out of luck

Excitement in this game was to be expected; the tension could be felt all the way from White Hart Lane station through the carpet-peddling atmosphere of the kerbside ticket market to the ground. Less predictable was the high quality of the football - and the major share of that came from Arsenal.

The only jarring element was that the score had little relationship to the play. Arsenal were faster, stronger and much more determined and should have won about 4-2. In the closing stages Spurs played out time with a dedicated professionalism as their defence clutched at enough straws to thatch a modest home.

The outstanding player was Ure. He had the dubious privilege, which he turned to his advantage, of having to mark Chivers, whose personal direct threats on the Arsenal goal amounted to two shots, two headers, two beautifully judged crosses and two prodigious throws in. Somehow, it seemed less.

In defence, Arsenal played man to man as closely as if they were handcuffed to their opposite numbers and when Venables had the ball in midfield, he could rarely see anyone free to pass to.

Arsenal, on the rather hand, ran ceaselessly. In the first half-hour Armstrong, in particular, had Spurs in serious trouble. When Radford's header from his cross hit the base of the post with Jennings praying, the odds seemed heavily on their scoring. However, Beal at least played firmly and calmly to subdue Graham.

From the start incidents proliferated. McNab headed away from Greaves at one end, then made Jennings hop, at the other; McLintock hurled himself at one of Armstrong's many crosses; next Greaves was robbed near the penalty spot by Simpson while being too deliberate. Sammels thundered in a 30-yard shot and the hard-working Mullery drew a tremendous save from Furnell.

The half closed with Jenkins, set free by a rare Beal error, hooking his shot wide.

So far, then, Arsenal, their defence tight, their attack eager, had looked the more dangerous team.

Jenkins wound up the excitement again five minutes after the interval when McLintock sent him away, kept on side by someone over the far side. But Jennings' hopeful foot diverted his shot. Then Chivers was off, let in by Neill. The wave of expectancy broke as Ure robbed him without fuss.

Back to the Spurs' penalty area, where Graham headed Armstrong's right-wing corner against a post. It seemed that Tottenham's best defensive weapon was the crowd's psychokinesis.

On the hour Chivers at last drove in a handsome shot at Furnell who saved - and held - the ball superbly.

Less than a minute later there was disappointment or delight, according to one's sympathies. Jennings hit a long, awkwardly bouncing ball upfield, and a close-packed line of players of both persuasions chased it. Simpson tried to head the ball towards his goalkeeper, but instead gave **GILZEAN** a perfect pass from which he scored elegantly.

Arsenal's enthusiasm lasted for a while longer, but gradually ran down as Spurs checked the impetus of the game and finally strangled Arsenal's hopes.

'DERBY STAR'

Ian Ure –
came out on top in his battle with Martin Chivers.

65

TOTTENHAM HOTSPUR 1
Greaves

ARSENAL 2
Beal (og), Radford

Saturday 10th August 1968

Football League Division One

White Hart Lane

Attendance 56,280

Tottenham Hotspur

Arsenal

Manager
Bill Nicholson

Manager
Bertie Mee

Pat JENNINGS	1	Bob WILSON
Phil BEAL	2	Peter STOREY
Cyril KNOWLES	3	Bob McNAB
Alan MULLERY	4	Frank McLINTOCK
Mike ENGLAND	5	Terry NEILL
Peter COLLINS	6	Peter SIMPSON
Jimmy ROBERTSON	7	John RADFORD
Jimmy GREAVES	8	Jon SAMMELS
Martin CHIVERS	9	George GRAHAM
Terry VENABLES	10	David COURT
Jimmy PEARCE	11	David JENKINS
Cliff JONES	12	Bobby GOULD

Referee **Mr J Finney** (Hereford)

BACKGROUND

For the first time, Spurs entertained Arsenal in the opening fixture of the season. A guide to the form of both clubs came from their pre-season games. Spurs had beaten Glasgow Rangers 3-1 at White Hart Lane, Arsenal had drawn 2-2 at Ibrox. With Dave Mackay having left for Derby in the summer young Peter Collins, a £5,000 buy from non-League Chelmsford City, was given his chance in defence and Jimmy Pearce, a product of the youth ranks, made his debut in the absence of suspended Alan Gilzean. Arsenal had been on the receiving end of a lot of criticism for a lack of activity in the transfer market, but it was not for lack of trying. According to the board they had tried to sign four players, each at a transfer record, but clubs were just not prepared to sell.

BEFORE THE GAME

	P	W	D	L	F	A	Pts
Spurs	0	0	0	0	0	0	0
Arsenal	0	0	0	0	0	0	0

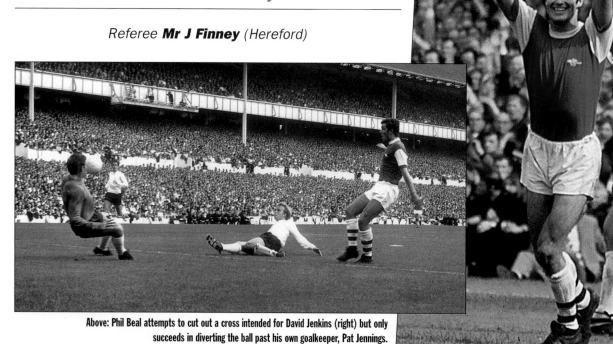

Above: Phil Beal attempts to cut out a cross intended for David Jenkins (right) but only succeeds in diverting the ball past his own goalkeeper, Pat Jennings.
Right: George Graham celebrates Beal's misfortune as Arsenal go one up.

Spurs miss Mackay's energy

Spurs debutant Jimmy Pearce pictured before the game.

Tottenham, in extreme moods, offered 20 minutes of flowing soccer, and finally surrendered to boisterous Arsenal at White Hart Lane yesterday.

A crowd of 56,000 in shirt sleeve order reflected happily on Tottenham's competent start to the new season. They saw Arsenal stumbling into tackles, looking far too slow, and hardly touching the ball for a quarter of an hour. But Tottenham's work was dramatically undone by an own goal after 21 minutes. The goal altered the character of Arsenal's play. They moved more directly, and found one another quickly with short passes.

Tottenham were looking around for the energetic Mackay. Nobody on this opening day of the season threatened to fill his shoes. Young Collins shirked nothing, but is understandably short of experience at this level. They could also have done with the suspended Gilzean.

Greaves was blocked by two, and sometimes three, Arsenal players and Chivers was unsuccessful in trying to take the weight off Greaves.

Arsenal's success sprung from their strength at half-back where McLintock and Neill made light of Ure's absence. They encouraged Radford and Jenkins to play as conventional wings. On the retreat they had the assistance of Simpson, whose positional sense was most uncanny.

Robertson and 20-year-old Pearce, making his League debut, were drawn into the middle too often.

Arsenal having survived Tottenham's early erratic bombardment, turned on their opponents. Sammels found Radford scampering up the right wing. Radford's cross was intended for Jenkins, closing in on the left. **BEAL** arrived first, but could only frantically turn the ball past a confused Jennings.

Sammels was off balance when another goal was in the offing a moment later. Tottenham were noticeably disheartened, but were still sharp enough to induce some panic around Arsenal's penalty area. Pearce cut inside McNab, forcing Wilson to leap high and late. The unpredictable Greaves, believed to be offside by Arsenal's defence, carried on running, but lost his footing inside the penalty box. He recovered nimbly, and outwitted Wilson, only to find Simpson rushing back and heading off his goal line.

Arsenal could have regarded themselves as unlucky early in the second half when Beal brought Jenkins down inside the box. The crowd and Arsenal were convinced it was a deliberate trip. Referee Jim Finney, closer to the incident, thought differently.

Arsenal's second goal, on the hour, was superbly executed. Sammels fired an accurate low centre from the right and Graham fooled Tottenham's full backs by running over the ball. **RADFORD** completed the tricks, coming in behind and ramming the ball in from twelve yards.

Desperately, Mullery ordered England to move up as an extra centre forward. Not even his strength and height could alter the course of the game. England was involved in one or two over-robust exchanges with Neill. In one of these his elbow crashed into Neill's face and while the Arsenal player lay dazed on the ground Finney spoke to a linesman and then lectured England.

GREAVES scored Tottenham's solitary goal with nine minutes left, rounding off a move which involved Pearce and England. Vainly, Tottenham pursued a second goal and one point but Arsenal, tight at the back, stifled their orthodox football.

Jimmy Robertson challenges Bob Wilson in the air but the Arsenal 'keeper just manages to clear the danger

66

ARSENAL 1
Sammels

TOTTENHAM HOTSPUR 0

Arsenal   *Tottenham Hotspur*

Manager   Manager
Bertie Mee   **Bill Nicholson**

Bob WILSON	1	Pat JENNINGS
Peter STOREY*	2	Ray EVANS
Bob McNAB	3	Tony WANT
Frank McLINTOCK	4	Alan MULLERY
Ian URE	5	John PRATT
Peter SIMPSON	6	Peter COLLINS
John RADFORD	7	Jimmy PEARCE*
Jon SAMMELS	8	Jimmy GREAVES
David COURT	9	Alan GILZEAN
Bobby GOULD	10	Terry VENABLES
George ARMSTRONG	11	Neil JOHNSON
George GRAHAM (2)	12	David JENKINS (7)

Referee **Mr J R Osborne** *(Ipswich)*

BACKGROUND

If there was any match to revive the morale of Arsenal and their supporters only nine days after losing the League Cup Final to Third Division Swindon Town, it was the fourth meeting of the season with Spurs. Apart from their opening day success, Arsenal had beaten Spurs in the two-legged League Cup semi-final and for this Monday evening game mid-table Spurs were badly hit by injuries. Martin Chivers was a long-term absentee, Mike England and Phil Beal were both injured in a weekend defeat of Chelsea and flu caused Roger Morgan to make a late withdrawal. To make matters worse Cyril Knowles was out through suspension. Almost an entire new defence had to be fielded with Tony Want given a rare outing, Ray Evans and John Pratt their debuts. Fourth-placed Arsenal, in need of the points if they were to stay in touch with Leeds and Liverpool, were able to field the team defeated at Wembley.

Spurs debutant John Pratt

BEFORE THE GAME

	P	W	D	L	F	A	Pts
Arsenal	31	18	8	5	44	18	44
Spurs	32	10	15	7	49	41	35

A cross clears Bob McNab to leave Jimmy Pearce with a free header, but Bob Wilson keeps Spurs at bay.

Geoffrey Green in '**The Times**' under...

ARSENAL MARCH ON AS SPURS RUN OUT OF IDEAS

By this victory at Highbury last night, Arsenal not only nestled into third place in the League championship, but also clearly earned themselves the title of champions of North London.

Four times this season they have met Tottenham Hotspur. Twice have they won in the League - completing the double on this occasion; they beat Spurs 1-0 at Highbury in the first leg of the League Cup semi-final and then drew the return to reach the climax of their competition at Wembley with sad consequences.

However, there is no disputing who are now the cock of the Metropolitan north and by the look of this much-changed Spurs side last night, with Knowles missing on suspension, Beale and England injured and Morgan in bed with influenza, there seems little in reserve at White Hart Lane. They were now shapeless, frenzied and with scarcely a constructive idea. I little thought I would one day have to say that about a Tottenham side.

I wonder what Blanchflower, the late John White or even the watching Mackay would have been able to make of this fast running rabble. It would certainly have needed their collective genius to bring some imagination, creative instinct and change of tempo to affairs.

Not that Arsenal were much better in the first half when at least they did manage to decorate the night with it's single goal. It was a move between Storey, Gould and McLintock which **SAMMELS** lashed home - a low swerving daisycutter past Jennings' dive from fully 20 yards. That was the end of the ration, though Arsenal completely dominated the second half and should have added to the score through Armstrong, Gould and McLintock.

In the main, however, it was a hapless, haphazard match that brought to memory the speed of those old Charlie Chaplin and Mack Sennett comedies of the early days of silent films; or even those Keystone Cops. All that seemed to be missing now were a few custard pies.

All of which leaves us with one curiosity of the season. None of the sides still alive in any knock-out competition at home or abroad are in the top half of the First division table. Manchester United, semi-finalists in the European Cup lie thirteenth, West Bromwich Albion and Leicester, yet to contest their semi-final in the FA Cup are fourteenth and twenty-first respectively; Manchester City, already at Wembley in the Cup Final stand fifteenth; and Newcastle, virtually in the semi-final of the Fairs Cup, lurk in sixteenth place.

This leaves a scramble for the crumbs at the head of the table. Assuming Leeds win the title and enter the European Cup next season, then Liverpool and Arsenal as the leading clubs of Merseyside and London, should move into the continent with a passport to the Fairs Cup. The spare place, remembering the rules of this competition, which precludes two sides entering from the same city, may yet go to someone like Southampton.

ARSENAL TAKE THE NORTH LONDON CHAMPIONSHIP

ARSENAL 1, SPURS 0

ARSENAL have taken the North London soccer championship by beating Spurs three times out of four in their encounters this season. But Tottenham, with injuries reaching crisis peak, can claim to have gained a moral victory at Highbury on Monday night.

Fielding virtually a reserve team defence they restricted Arsenal to one goal—a fine low swerving 20 yard drive by Jon Sammels which flashed just inside the upright five minutes before the interval.

Because of injuries to Phil Beal and Mike England, Ray Evans and John Pratt made their first team debuts. Strangely enough when Arsenal visited Spurs on the opening day of the season Jimmy Pearce and Peter Collins were given their first senior outings.

Another absentee on Monday was Cyril Knowles, starting a seven day suspension after receiving his third booking of the season at Manchester, Tony Want deputised.

With Roger Morgan still recovering from the effects of flu Neil Johnson kept his place on the week.

UNCONVINCING

With such a psychological advantage Arsenal should have been far more convincing than they were. Instead, although they were successful in pinning Spurs into their own half for long periods, there was too much slipshod passing and ineffectual positioning to make this a satisfactory performance by the Gunners.

Peter Simpson played Jimmy Greaves right out of the game but Ian Ure did not look so happy against the wily Alan Gilzean. Up front Sammels seemed to have the best appetite for action and when George Graham deputised for Storey 20 minutes from the end he too provided some nimble touches.

Radford had a hard night against the tough tackling Want. The game never rose to wildly exciting heights and the main interest lay—for Tottenham fans at any rate—in finding out whether the Spurs youngsters could live in the top grade of soccer.

Tony Want, with some iron-boot tackling, certainly showed he could stand in for Cyril Knowles at any time. In fact he looked the most effective and efficient defender on the field.

Ray Evans stood up to the pace well and on a couple of occasions overlapped effectively to cause a moment of panic in the Arsenal defence.

John Pratt also played strongly although the speed of events around him obviously began to tell in the later part of the game.

Although Peter Collins wore a number six shirt his position was centre-half and here again he proved to be a very capable deputy for Mike England. He headed one certain goal off the line.

BEST CHANCE

Despite the problems in defence Spurs broke out on attack quite frequently. Perhaps their best chance was midway through the first-half when Pratt slipped the ball through to Jimmy Greaves who moved forward but the ever alert Bob Wilson came out smartly to repel the danger.

For a Arsenal v Spurs derby clash this was a disappointing game. But for a few of the young bloods at Tottenham it was a night to remember.

Arsenal: Wilson; Storey (Graham), McNab; McLintock, Ure, Simpson; Radford, Sammels, Court, Gould, Armstrong.

Spurs: Jennings; Evans, Want; Mullery, Pratt, Collins; Pearce (Jenkins), Greaves, Gilzean, Venables, Johnson.

MATCH FACTS

Arsenal

Offside	...	...	1
Free-kicks	...	...	16
Throw-ins	...	...	15
Corners	...	...	7
Shots at goal	...	9
Goals	...	...	1

Spurs

Offside	...	...	6
Free-kicks	...	...	8
Throw-ins	...	...	22
Corners	...	...	2
Shots at goal	...	4

Jon Sammels – scored the only goal of the game and appeared to have the best appetite for action.

AT THE SEASON'S END

		P	W	D	L	F	A	Pts
4th	Arsenal	42	22	12	8	56	27	56
6th	Spurs	42	14	17	11	61	51	45

67

ARSENAL 2
Robertson, Radford

TOTTENHAM HOTSPUR 3
Gilzean, Pratt, Chivers

Tuesday 16th September 1969

Football League Division One

Highbury

Attendance 55,280

Arsenal

Tottenham Hotspur

Manager
Bertie Mee

Manager
Bill Nicholson

Malcolm WEBSTER	1	Pat JENNINGS
Peter STOREY	2	Phil BEAL
Bob McNAB	3	Cyril KNOWLES
Frank McLINTOCK	4	Alan MULLERY
Terry NEILL	5	Mike ENGLAND
Peter SIMPSON	6	Peter COLLINS
Jimmy ROBERTSON	7	Martin CHIVERS*
Charlie GEORGE	8	Jimmy GREAVES
John RADFORD	9	Alan GILZEAN
George GRAHAM	10	John PRATT
Jon SAMMELS	11	Roger MORGAN
George ARMSTRONG	12	Tony WANT (7)

Referee **Mr G W Hill** (Leicester)

BACKGROUND

Whilst defensively Arsenal had the makings of title contenders, the lack of a regular goalscorer was holding them back. Unable to secure anybody on the transfer market, Bertie Mee turned to youth at the start of the season with the introduction of an eighteen-year-old Islington lad with flair and a talent for the unexpected, Charlie George. George had enormous potential but needed time and was not an immediate answer to Arsenal's problems. They had won only one of their four games at Highbury but tuned up for Spurs visit with victory at Burnley three days earlier. Strengthened by the return of John Radford and George, Bob Wilson was out injured with another eighteen-year-old, Malcolm Webster, called up for his debut. Spurs had started the season with defeat at Leeds, won their next three away games but were beaten 0-3 at home by Manchester City in their last match. Martin Chivers had returned from injury at the start of the season but with only two goals in seven games had been dropped. Told by Bill Nicholson to study the centre-forward play of West Ham's Geoff Hurst, he was recalled in place of injured Jimmy Pearce.

BEFORE THE GAME

	P	W	D	L	F	A	Pts
Spurs	9	5	1	3	14	11	11
Arsenal	9	3	4	2	7	6	10

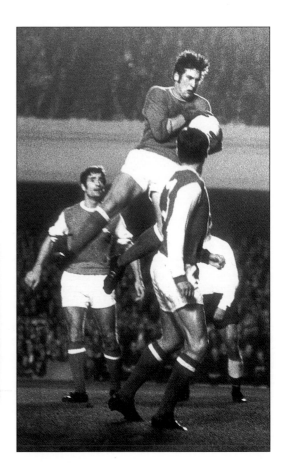

Above: Arsenal full-backs Bob McNab and Peter Storey close in as Jimmy Greaves (second left) gets a shot in.
Right: Arsenal's 18-year-old debutant goalkeeper Malcolm Webster shows a safe pair of hands.

Geoffrey Green in 'The Times'...

Spurs' slender margin as Arsenal hit back

If there is no business like show business, there is also no business like football for producing the unexpected. When Arsenal and Tottenham met at Highbury last night, one would have expected a taut, arid struggle with little or nothing given away and perhaps no more than one effective strike. But the 55,000 crowd was given non-stop action and almost a flood of goals. In the end Tottenham were the victors.

But how close a finish it was. With only a quarter of an hour left, Spurs were three goals in the clear and a press extract quoted in the programme was looking slightly foolish.

Referring to last week's Glentoran match in the Fairs' Cup, the extract read: "After all, the elite of the English First Division would find it difficult to crack the Arsenal defence three times in one game, yet that is what the part-timers from the Irish League must do to earn a play-off in the second leg." Here were Spurs three goals clear through Gilzean, Pratt and Chivers and apparently coasting home.

Arsenal, however, at that point rolled up their sleeves and with goals by Robertson and Radford in the closing stages, almost rescued their lost cause.

Once the twilight had faltered into dusk, the struggle began to throb. For half an hour the match hovered between reality and impersonation only suddenly to explode as Beal began a move down the Tottenham right. Greaves dummied sideways beating two men and just as he was drawing back his left foot for a shot **GILZEAN** beat him to the draw, virtually shooting off the little man's toe to put a low right-foot shot past young Webster, an 18-year-old making his bow - impressively.

Spurs led by that at the interval and then proceeded to fling up a giant shield, with England at the heart of it, as Arsenal battered their defences for the first quarter of an hour of the second half. England was magnificent, finely helped, among others, by little Pratt.

Suddenly the siege was raised and **PRATT**, a bundle of energy, exploded from one end of the field to the other. It was with a fine instinct that he moved, swiftly and confidently exchanged two return passes with Chivers, won three sharp rebounds from hard tackles finally to find himself picking his spot coolly beyond Webster. For a moment Pratt seemed not to know what he had done.

From then on, the tempo rose and nearly every movement held the germ of possibility. For Tottenham, Greaves and Gilzean were always dangerous in the quick break. At the back, England leaping to head away cross after cross held the defence together. For Arsenal, McLintock and Graham drove their forces on. But Tottenham scored again as **CHIVERS** turned in a corner by Pratt. A quarter of an hour remained and now the great Arsenal challenge arrived.

ROBERTSON at last found a way through as he volleyed in a long cross from the right. With five minutes still left a long free kick by Simpson on the left was nodded in by **RADFORD** after McLintock had decoyed the defence.

Though Arsenal appealed strongly for a penalty, when Radford was hooked up just inside the area, their pleas were in vain. It was a free kick to them a yard outside leaving them, no doubt, with a sense of grievance and futility.

Arsenal pull one back as Jimmy Robertson's shot leaves Pat Jennings rooted to the ground...

... and John Radford brings it back to 3-2 with five minutes still to play.

Cocky Spurs 3 up then relax

By STEVE CURRY

Arsenal 2 Tottenham 3

3 **A**RSENAL'S defence, the rock on which they have built a reputation, crumbled last night under the incisive raiding of the Tottenham attack.

But as Spurs relaxed to survey the wreckage they had caused, they were almost made to pay the penalty for their arrogance.

68

TOTTENHAM HOTSPUR 1
Gilzean

ARSENAL 0

Saturday 2nd May 1970

Football League Division One

White Hart Lane

Attendance 46,969

BACKGROUND

The very last match of a season compressed to end in mid-April so England could prepare for their defence of the World Cup, Arsenal had originally been scheduled to visit White Hart Lane on 15th April but the match had been delayed because of their progress in the Fairs Cup. The second leg of the final against Anderlecht had taken place only four days earlier when goals from Eddie Kelly, John Radford and Jon Sammels produced a 4-3 aggregate victory and the first trophy at Highbury for 17 years. With the exception of captain Frank McLintock, a cup winner at last after four losing finals, two in the League Cup with Arsenal following two in the FA Cup with Leicester, they were at full strength. Spurs had not played for nearly three weeks since beating Manchester United, but were at least able to call on a full squad although Steve Perryman was rested after helping Spurs' Youth team win the FA Youth Cup. Both clubs were in mid-table but the result would determine which club finished higher.

Tottenham Hotspur

Arsenal

Manager
Bill Nicholson

Manager
Bertie Mee

Pat JENNINGS	1	Bob WILSON
Ray EVANS	2	Peter STOREY
Cyril KNOWLES	3	Bob McNAB
Alan MULLERY	4	Eddie KELLY*
Mike ENGLAND	5	John ROBERTS
Phil BEAL	6	Peter SIMPSON
Alan GILZEAN	7	George ARMSTRONG
Jimmy PEARCE	8	Jon SAMMELS
Martin CHIVERS	9	John RADFORD
Martin PETERS	10	Charlie GEORGE
Roger MORGAN	11	George GRAHAM
Peter COLLINS	12	Ray KENNEDY (4)

Referee **Mr J Finney** (Hereford)

BEFORE THE GAME

	P	W	D	L	F	A	Pts
Arsenal	41	12	18	11	51	48	42
Spurs	41	16	9	16	53	55	41

AT THE SEASON'S END

		P	W	D	L	F	A	Pts
11th	Spurs	42	17	9	16	54	55	43
12th	Arsenal	42	12	18	12	51	49	42

John Radford gets clear of Spurs full-back Ray Evans.

Alan Gilzean – his 70th minute header preserved this fixture's proud record of 68 games without a goalless draw.

John Moynihan in 'The Sunday Telegraph' on...

GILZEAN DECIDER

Games between these old rivals can seldom have been as tepid as this one, with a near 50,000 crowd slow-hand clapping in the spring sunshine.

But at the end of a long, gruelling season, with three of the cast off to Mexico tomorrow, the general apathy was understandable.

Alan Gilzean, with a fierce header after 70 minutes, gave Tottenham the double and made sure that not one of these two club's 68 meetings have ended in a goalless draw.

Arsenal could have conceded a goal as early as the third minute - their minds obviously still savouring their midweek European Fairs Cup success. A poor punch by Wilson gave Chivers a chance to head against the bar and McNab kicked off the line. Then Mullery shot a foot wide from a Gilzean flick.

Arsenal's more co-ordinated, businesslike combination was shown with a fluid passing movement between Armstrong and George, with a Tottenham defender bravely deflecting George's shot.

Arsenal came forward with more purpose and Graham should have scored twice. But Tottenham goalkeeper Jennings blocked both his shots, leaving Graham to show his disgust.

Much of the earlier promise disappeared, the game disintegrating into a choppy, niggly affair. It seemed that Arsenal might win the game with their sporadic attacks and a splendid shot by Radford, from Sammels' pass, sped just over.

Tottenham scored through an act of generosity by Roberts, who allowed Morgan to cross to the far post where **GILZEAN** met it decisively.

Mullery, Peters and McNab, members of England's World Cup squad, came through without injury. But they are unlikely to talk about this game on the plane going to Mexico.

Tottenham's Welsh international defender Mike England challenges Jon Sammels.

THAT WAS THEN...

★ In this, the last programme of the season, Spurs announced increased admission prices for the 1970-71 season. Reserved seats would cost 15/- (75p), unreserved seats 12/- (60p), ground admission 6/- (30p). Season ticket prices ranged from £15 for a seat in the North Stand to £22 for the best seats in the West Stand.

Arsenal pair John Roberts (left) and Peter Simpson keep out Spurs forward Martin Chivers.

69

ARSENAL 2
Armstrong 2

TOTTENHAM HOTSPUR 0

Arsenal · Tottenham Hotspur

Manager **Bertie Mee**

Manager **Bill Nicholson**

Arsenal	No.	Tottenham Hotspur
Bob WILSON	1	Ken HANCOCK
Pat RICE	2	Joe KINNEAR
Bob McNAB	3	Tony WANT
Eddie KELLY	4	Alan MULLERY
Frank McLINTOCK*	5	Mike ENGLAND
John ROBERTS	6	Phil BEAL
George ARMSTRONG	7	Alan GILZEAN
Peter STOREY	8	Steve PERRYMAN
John RADFORD	9	Martin CHIVERS
Ray KENNEDY	10	Martin PETERS
George GRAHAM	11	Roger MORGAN
Sammy NELSON (5)	12	Jimmy PEARCE

Referee **Mr D W Smith** (Stonehouse)

BACKGROUND

Before the season started Bertie Mee looked to have problems. John Roberts was a ready-made replacement for Peter Simpson, recovering from a cartilage operation, but compensating for the absence of midfield creator Jon Sammels looked more difficult. Pat Rice, eight senior appearances to his credit, was given the right-back spot with Peter Storey moved into midfield. A 2-2 draw at champions Everton provided a good start to the campaign but it was not without cost as Charlie George was injured. Ray Kennedy, like George a product of Arsenal's youth policy but even less experienced with just six senior outings to his name, was paired up front with John Radford. It was not until the fifth game that Arsenal were beaten by Chelsea and four days before Spurs' visit they held Leeds to a goalless draw despite playing for over an hour with ten men after Eddie Kelly had been dismissed. Spurs, too, had suffered only one defeat but Pat Jennings, Cyril Knowles and Peter Collins had all been injured at Huddersfield. The experienced Phil Beal was recalled in place of Collins but Nicholson was forced to give Ken Hancock and Tony Want rare outings.

BEFORE THE GAME

	P	W	D	L	F	A	Pts
Arsenal	6	2	3	1	8	4	7
Spurs	6	2	3	1	7	5	7

Goal number one... George Armstrong fends off a challenge from Joe Kinnear (grounded) to make sure a goal-bound effort from John Radford (left) reaches its intended destination.

Deryk Brown in *'The Sunday Times'*...

For 30 minutes Arsenal played as though all the prophecies of a new Jerusalem in N.5 were about to come true. For the other 60 they showed even more forcibly that they are not quite ready to live with the Leeds Uniteds of this world.

They have immense potential. Kelly, their most famous young name, played in the middle of a 4-3-3 but ran forward and back with such skill and drive that he proved he is capable of upsetting any equation.

Rice and Nelson, a second half substitute for the injured McLintock, demonstrated they are full-backs of increasing versatility. Roberts, riding shotgun at McLintock's elbow whenever trouble came, is a powerful deputy for the injured Simpson.

But it was Kennedy, another alleged tyro, who caused Tottenham most trouble. He often outran and outjumped England and Beal. In itself, this was telling enough but it left Radford and Armstrong to play tricks of their own.

Both sides looked at one another shiftily for a quarter of an hour and then Arsenal scored. Radford chased a clearance down the right and touched it past the oncoming Hancock. It might have been a goal anyway, but **ARMSTRONG**, challenged by Kinnear, flicked it home.

Arsenal had tasted honey and went on to have a brief feast. In the 23rd minute Graham put a sneaky pass to Kelly on the right. Kennedy and Hancock jumped for the centre, and the ball ran loose for **ARMSTRONG** to whip it into the empty net.

Kennedy glanced a header just over and Hancock prevented a third goal by robbing Radford after he had rounded England. Everything Tottenham tried ended with the sound of breaking glass. Only Gilzean, lurking here and ghosting in there, gave them credibility. Meanwhile, Arsenal were everywhere.

That was the wine and what followed was taproom spit and sawdust. Arsenal found their rhythm for only a few minutes of the second half. Tottenham had lost theirs in the journey across north London and the match became a scramble. Tempers were short, too, and Graham was booked for fouling Mullery.

A race for the ball between Mike England (left) and John Radford.

THAT WAS THEN...

★ The Arsenal programme advertised a 2-day jet trip to Rome for the forthcoming Fairs Cup game with Lazio at £28!

★ Spurs fans could fly to Scotland for a Texaco Cup game with Dunfermline for £15.

Goal number two... George Armstrong blasts a George Graham cross into the roof of the net.

70

TOTTENHAM HOTSPUR 0

ARSENAL 1
Kennedy

Tottenham Hotspur

Manager
Bill Nicholson

Arsenal

Manager
Bertie Mee

Pat JENNINGS	1	Bob WILSON
Joe KINNEAR	2	Pat RICE
Cyril KNOWLES	3	Bob McNAB
Alan MULLERY	4	Eddie KELLY
Peter COLLINS	5	Frank McLINTOCK
Phil BEAL	6	Peter SIMPSON
Alan GILZEAN*	7	George ARMSTRONG
Steve PERRYMAN	8	George GRAHAM
Martin CHIVERS	9	John RADFORD
Martin PETERS	10	Ray KENNEDY
Jimmy NEIGHBOUR	11	Charlie GEORGE
Jimmy PEARCE (7)	12	Jon SAMMELS

Referee **Mr K Howley** *(Middlesbrough)*

BACKGROUND

The most important match in North London derby history? Well, certainly for Arsenal. The situation was simplicity itself. Victory or a goalless draw would give Arsenal the title, anything else and the championship trophy would be on it's way to Elland Road. And that was not all. Success would leave Arsenal just five days and an FA Cup final against Liverpool away from the "Double". Not surprisingly interest in the game was enormous. North London was brought to a stop, the gates closed an hour before kick-off on a crowd of over 50,000 with five times that number locked out. With Alan Mullery fit to return, Spurs were able to field their first choice eleven, the same team that had won the first trophy of the season, the League Cup, nine weeks earlier, determined to preserve their record as the only club to achieve the "Double" in the 20th century. Arsenal were without Peter Storey, injured in the weekend defeat of Stoke.

BEFORE THE GAME

	P	W	D	L	F	A	Pts
Arsenal	41	28	7	6	70	29	63
Spurs	40	18	14	8	53	32	50

AT THE SEASON'S END

		P	W	D	L	F	A	Pts
1st	Arsenal	42	29	7	6	71	29	65
3rd	Spurs	42	19	14	9	54	33	52

Above: The amazing scene outside White Hart Lane with an estimated 50,000 fans locked out.
Right: Arsenal goalkeeper Bob Wilson punches clear of Alan Gilzean.

'DERBY STAR **Ray Kennedy** – his goal clinched the championship.

Kennedy gives Arsenal the title

Geoffrey Green in 'The Times' under..

Arsenal halfway to League and FA Cup double

Arsenal are the champions. With their fine victory over Tottenham Hotspur at White Hart Lane last night, they finished like true champions, on a top note; surpassing Leeds United at the top of the table by one point in the last stride after a long, gruelling season. They have set a new record by winning the title for the eighth time in history to surpass the feats of Manchester United, Everton and Liverpool.

So at the end poor Leeds, again, are left to face stark reality. That the destination of this title should hang on the concluding match was itself exciting enough. That it should involve also one of the Cup Finalists who will be at Wembley but few days hence, added to it all. That the match should be decided a mere three minutes from the end, with a goal from Kennedy - with Arsenal already almost there with a goalless draw - was more than nerve could stand.

The goal itself was dramatic enough. It began when Kinnear was pressed into an unwise dribble across his penalty area. George, seeing the thread of events, suddenly intervened on the right, found space to centre, and as Radford tried desperately to force the ball home, there was Jennings to dive full length and punch away at the far post. But the ball only went as far as Armstrong, outside the penalty area to the left. He in turn centred once more, and this time there was **KENNEDY** to rise powerfully and send home a blitz of a header underneath the crossbar.

At that, Arsenal knew they were home and all North London - or at least half of it - suddenly seemed to catch fire. At that moment, Leeds United died and are now left holding an unenviable record: runners-up who have scored most points in that position.

It was worthy that Arsenal should win by a clear margin and not rely on mathematicians. But for Kennedy's goal at that last breath Arsenal were heading with a 0-0 draw for the title by one hundredth part of a goal on goal average. But in the end there was no lapse from the straight and narrow.

Here was a magnificent battle in which, thankfully, attack from both sides was the order of the day. Not for one second, from the very kick-off, did Arsenal show any inclination to hide behind their defensive shell and drag out a blank night. This was indeed a magnificent battle, hard but fair, with no quarter expected. Both sides went at it hammer and tongs. It was check and counter-check all the way with action flowing the length and breadth of White Hart Lane.

In spite of Arsenal pressure which showed in a first-half advantage of seven corners to one it was Peters who actually came nearest to breaking the shell of the night. Near the half hour, he ended a quick open move between Knowles and Chivers by putting a 25 yard, instant volley just onto the roof of the angle of crossbar and upright. That was a mere matter of inches, and before the interval, it was he again who forced Wilson to a great diving save as he finished a move between Mullery and Gilzean with a right foot shot.

In the second half the action, if possible, found a new dimension and pace. With half an hour left, Tottenham produced the best move of the match when Mullery, Neighbour and Knowles linked fast down the left. Knowles flashed a low cross first time across the heart of the Arsenal defence and there was Gilzean diving in full-length and only failing by a whisker to touch home the ball. Next, Graham headed on to the top of the Tottenham crossbar from an Armstrong corner; Peters saw his header blocked on the goal-line by Rice, and then, at the other end, there was Kinnear to almost put the ball into his own goal as a back pass to Jennings flew just wide of the Spurs post.

With time nearly ended and Arsenal virtually there on goal average, the decisive goal was scored. The field was flooded with the Arsenal supporters. One could almost lean against the noise, which stood up like a wall. Both sides had fought it out toe-to-toe; both sides had been on the very brink and all this after White Hart Lane itself had been completely ringed by the crowds, six deep, three-and-a-half hours before the kick-off.

The gates were shut on a 52,000 assembly one hour before the start with thousands left outside, even the referee, Kevin Howley, officiating at his very last League match was forced to walk the last mile to the ground having abandoned his car, and the Arsenal players had to fight their way in.

The sunny evening had slipped into night with not a cloud in sight, except in the end for poor Leeds United, beaten on the post but with six successive great seasons behind them, which have seen them champions in 1969, fourth on two occasions and now runners-up for a third time. Perhaps their day will come again.

For Arsenal their duty is not yet finished. For them the double now lies ahead at Wembley on Saturday with the shadow of Liverpool standing massively across their path. The one man now left on a knife-edge is Storey, unfit to play at right-half for Arsenal last night. His next few days, as he fights for fitness, could bring some sleepless nights.

71

TOTTENHAM HOTSPUR 1
Chivers

ARSENAL 1
Kennedy

Tottenham Hotspur

Manager
Bill Nicholson

Arsenal

Manager
Bertie Mee

Pat JENNINGS	1	Bob WILSON
Ray EVANS	2	Pat RICE
Cyril KNOWLES	3	Bob McNAB
Ralph COATES	4	Peter STOREY
Mike ENGLAND	5	John ROBERTS
Phil BEAL	6	Frank McLINTOCK
Jimmy NEIGHBOUR	7	George ARMSTRONG
Steve PERRYMAN	8	Eddie KELLY
Martin CHIVERS	9	John RADFORD
Martin PETERS	10	Ray KENNEDY
Alan GILZEAN	11	George GRAHAM
John PRATT	12	Sammy NELSON

Referee **Mr K Walker** (Ashford)

BACKGROUND

Third place in the League and success in the League Cup may have taken Spurs back into European competition but Bill Nicholson knew it would take a lot more to climb out of the massive shadow cast by Arsenal's garnering of both League Championship and FA Cup. Within days of the season ending he splashed out £190,000 on Burnley winger Ralph Coates, and with Martin Chivers establishing himself as the country's best centre-forward Spurs began the season well, at least at home where they were unbeaten in 14 games. Arsenal began their defence of the title with two wins but this was followed by three defeats and as attention turned to the European Cup so their League form faltered. Coach Don Howe had been tempted away to West Bromwich Albion and his influence was missed as the defence lost the meanness on which success had been achieved. They went into the derby beaten in the last four games, going out of the League Cup to Sheffield United and culminating in a 1-5 defeat at Wolves. Changes were needed and Bob McNab and Eddie Kelly were recalled in place of Sammy Nelson and Charlie George.

Eddie Kelly - back in favour

BEFORE THE GAME

	P	W	D	L	F	A	Pts
Spurs	17	8	5	4	35	23	21
Arsenal	17	9	0	8	26	23	18

MARKSMAN CHIVERS MAKES ARSENAL PAY FOR RICE SLIP

Tottenham's equaliser – the headline and Pat Rice's face (left) say it all.

ARSENAL HALT TIDE OF MISFORTUNE WITH CHARACTER

Arsenal at last stemmed the cruel tide against them in a frantic and full blooded match at White Hart Lane last night. And had it not been for a back pass from Rice 10 minutes from time that fell short of it's target and presented Chivers with Tottenham's equaliser, the night would have left Arsenal with many more of the same joys of that championship winning evening on this same ground last spring.

As it is, the run of Arsenal defeats has been halted on the ground where they would have wanted to halt it. Their character and their competitiveness remained intact. Had those qualities not been there in the fullest measure last night Arsenal would surely have collapsed in the face of crushing Tottenham pressure throughout the whole of the second half.

During that period nobody was braver nor more totally committed in this frenzied arena than Wilson in the Arsenal goal. It had become the time to look for scapegoats, perhaps, after four successive defeats, and Wilson had not escaped that gaze, but now his courage and timing were never bettered and his flying save from Peters' close-range header and a flick over from a difficult volley from Perryman in the final minute saved the match for Arsenal.

Arsenal had first shown their hand early in the day when George, who had not shown enough hard work of late to balance his great skills, was left out. Clearly it was to be a night of running and fighting for Arsenal, and soon it became equally clear that it was to be a night of caution too.

Rarely were fewer than nine red shirts in midfield and defence. It was a shield, held together by McLintock and Roberts, that Spurs scarcely seemed likely to pierce. Storey added his usual fiery quota to the action - and had his name taken for a heavy tackle on Coates - and the longer Arsenal held out the greater their confidence grew. They began once more to look like champions.

At the other end, Kennedy and Radford were never simply a token attacking force and in the first half, offered the more menacing prospect than Chivers and company.

KENNEDY's first warning shot was a blistering one that just cleared the Tottenham bar, and his goal 10 minutes before half-time came from that same fearsome right foot. It was a masterpiece of nerve and timing by the big man as he took Graham's pass, turned swiftly inside Beal - in itself an achievement - and let fly with a cross shot that had Jennings groping but without much hope of making contact.

Had Graham connected with a header a moment later from Armstrong's sweetly measured cross, it would surely have put Arsenal far enough clear to have made Tottenham's second half assault a lot less relevant.

As it was, Tottenham came out for the second half as men stung, as most certainly they would have been by Bill Nicholson's words during the interval. Now they flung more men forward, they quickened their pace and they presented Arsenal with a much more formidable proposition.

So often now they were searching for the head of the mighty Chivers or seeking to capitalise on those delicate flicks from Gilzean. So much so that it almost caught Arsenal out when Coates, his stuttering form still far below his best, swept across a fine centre for Peters to come in unmarked like a thief and thunder a close range header that Wilson miraculously parried with one hand before a friendly boot did the rest.

Now as Spurs fought for their pride and the equaliser, and the crowd turned up the volume still more, Evans, England and Knowles were all thrown into more and more attacks. At times the game resembled one for five-year-olds, with perhaps 15 pairs of boots swinging in close proximity of the ball, and it all added to the intense excitement.

At last Spurs were rescued with only 10 minutes remaining and through an agonising error by Rice. All night he and the returning McNab had been model full backs, swift to the tackle and intelligent with the clearance, but now Rice cost his side the game. His back pass was short of Wilson - not for the first time over the years that Arsenal have been vulnerable in this area - and it left **CHIVERS**, of all people, to pounce. Though the angle was sharp his aim was sure.

Ray Kennedy volleys home a marvellous goal to put Arsenal in front.

72

ARSENAL 0

TOTTENHAM HOTSPUR 2
Mullery, Coates

Arsenal

Manager
Bertie Mee

Tottenham Hotspur

Manager
Bill Nicholson

Arsenal	No.	Tottenham Hotspur
Geoff BARNETT	1	Pat JENNINGS
Pat RICE	2	Joe KINNEAR
Bob McNAB	3	Cyril KNOWLES
Sammy NELSON	4	Alan MULLERY
Frank McLINTOCK	5	Mike ENGLAND
John ROBERTS	6	Phil BEAL
George ARMSTRONG	7	Alan GILZEAN
Peter SIMPSON*	8	Steve PERRYMAN
John RADFORD	9	Jimmy PEARCE
Ray KENNEDY	10	John PRATT
George GRAHAM	11	Ralph COATES
Peter MARINELLO (8)	12	Roger MORGAN

Referee **Mr J Hunting** (Leicester)

BACKGROUND

After the excitement of twelve months earlier the second derby of the season, again the last of the First Division fixtures, was never going to be one to live long in the memory. Like so many clubs before and since, Arsenal found trying to retain their title even harder than winning it. Lagging behind the early pacesetters, Leeds, Derby and the two Manchester clubs, Bertie Mee paid £220,000 to Everton for Alan Ball in December 1971, too late for the fiery little World Cup winner to play in the European Cup clash with holders Ajax. A 2-1 defeat in Amsterdam looked enough to take Arsenal into the semi-final but a George Graham own goal in the return put them out and left them with just the FA Cup to battle for. And battle they had to. Three games against Derby and two against Stoke in the semi-final took them to Wembley and a meeting with a Leeds team themselves chasing the "Double". An Allan Clarke goal gave Leeds the Cup but two days later, as Arsenal were drawing with Liverpool to stop them taking the title, Leeds failed to collect the one point they needed at Wolves. Spurs were mid-table throughout the season but enhanced their reputation as Cup fighters, going out to Leeds in the sixth round of the FA Cup and to Chelsea in the League Cup semi-final. Less than a week before the trip to Highbury they had returned from Molineux with a 2-1 lead in the first leg of the UEFA Cup final. Both teams were weakened by England's weekend clash with West Germany, Ball, Storey, Chivers and Peters all in the squad for the European championship quarter-final. Arsenal were also without Bob Wilson, injured in the first FA Cup semi-final with Stoke.

BEFORE THE GAME

	P	W	D	L	F	A	Pts
Arsenal	41	22	8	11	58	38	52
Spurs	41	18	13	10	61	42	49

Awaiting a left-wing corner are (in the foreground) Pat Rice, Alan Gilzean and John Radford.

David Miller in 'The Daily Telegraph'

Spurs twist knife in drab derby

Despite the presence of 14 full and three Under-23 internationals - the injured George, and England men Ball, Storey, Peters and Chivers were absentees - this North London derby closed the First Division programme on a disappointing note.

Only the goals, by Mullery and Coates, enlivened a match which, with nothing at stake but local prestige, predictably lacked finesse.

On Monday, when Arsenal drew with Liverpool, the FA Cup Winners flag had been lowered and last night those proclaiming League Champions had gone, too. To add insult to injury, the fifth place, of which Arsenal were assured before the kick-off, is not enough to gain UEFA Cup admission.

HERO McLINTOCK

Spurs, though more coherent than their opponents in an often stumbling match, can still remain in the UEFA Cup by holding their lead over Wolves in next week's second leg of the final.

Man of this lack-lustre match was the so-professional Frank McLintock.

In the first half, Radford and Nelson had shots saved by the unflappable Jennings, while Pratt twice went close for Spurs. With 26 minutes to go, **MULLERY** blasted home from 20 yards and two minutes from the end, **COATES** ran through from the halfway line to twist the knife for Arsenal.

AT THE SEASON'S END

		P	W	D	L	F	A	Pts
5th	Arsenal	42	22	8	12	58	40	52
6th	Spurs	42	19	13	10	63	42	51

'DERBY' STAR

Ralph Coates – brought down the curtain on the League season with a goal to remember.

THAT WAS THEN...

★ The Arsenal programme boasted that the total attendances for the 62 home and away games played by the Gunners was 2,366,128. As this figure didn't include the previous Saturday's FA Cup Final or this game with Tottenham the final total for the season topped 2.5 million. That's an average of 39,000 for all games — League, FA Cup, League Cup, European Cup and three pre-season friendlies.

Coates classic floors Arsenal

By NORMAN GILLER

Arsenal 0   Tottenham 2

RALPH COATES chose the last minute of this final First Division game of the season to score a goal that has not been bettered during all the shooting of the past nine months.

Even Arsenal fans applauded in appreciation of what I will remember as one of the greatest goals of the season. It deserves this detailed description.

Coates collected the ball 10 yards outside his own penalty area. He was in no-man's land, out on the left.

Only two defenders were in the Arsenal half because their team-mates were pressing forward in eager search of an equaliser.

Coates seemed in two minds what to do as he stood over the ball like a retriever who had lost his way. Then he set off on a 70-yard run along the left touchline, with team-mate John Pratt racing parallel with him down the middle.

PRETENCE

A posse of Arsenal players set off in pursuit, their attention divided between Coates and Pratt.

But Coates was only using Pratt as a decoy as he cut inside and made a pretence at a pass.

Goalkeeper Geoff Barnett came off his line and left only the smallest of gaps for Coates to aim at. But he squeezed the ball in as low and true as a Jack Nicklaus putt for only his second League goal of the season.

What a way to bring down the curtain on this seemingly endless League season!

If Coates can promise to carry on where he left off, I just can't wait for NEXT season to start.

The match, played in a swirling wind and in driving rain, had been anything but a classic.

Arsenal were showing the strain of playing their third match in six days, and it was a lack of concentration that let in **Alan Mullery** for a smash-and-grab goal in the 61st minute.

Sammy Nelson was Arsenal's most effective player— as a marauding midfield man. He went closest to scoring for them with a close-range shot that was blocked by his Northern Ireland team-mate, Pat Jennings.

Alan Ball, Peter Storey, Martin Peters, and Martin Chivers all missed this devalued match because of their England commitments in Berlin.

None of them—not even Chivers—could have bettered the goal created by Coates, and it puts Tottenham in just the right mood for the second leg of their EUFA Cup final against Wolves next Wednesday.

For the record, this was the 72nd League game between the two London sides. Spurs have now won 30, and Arsenal 27, with the rest drawn.

A shot from Steve Perryman goes over the bar.

73

TOTTENHAM HOTSPUR 1
Peters

ARSENAL 2
Storey, Radford

Saturday 9th December 1972

Football League Division One

White Hart Lane

Attendance 47,515

Tottenham Hotspur

Manager
Bill Nicholson

Arsenal

Manager
Bertie Mee

Pat JENNINGS	1	Bob WILSON
Ray EVANS	2	Pat RICE
Cyril KNOWLES	3	Bob McNAB
John PRATT	4	Peter STOREY
Mike ENGLAND	5	Jeff BLOCKLEY
Terry NAYLOR	6	Peter SIMPSON*
Jimmy NEIGHBOUR*	7	George ARMSTRONG
Steve PERRYMAN	8	Alan BALL
Martin CHIVERS	9	John RADFORD
Martin PETERS	10	Ray KENNEDY
Jimmy PEARCE	11	Eddie KELLY
Ralph COATES (7)	12	Frank McLINTOCK (6)

Referee **Mr R Capey** (Madeley Heath)

BACKGROUND

Although only the halfway stage of the season Arsenal's visit was Spurs' 33rd competitive match. In the previous two weeks they had played five games; two League Cup ties with Liverpool, a UEFA Cup tie with Red Star Belgrade and League games with Liverpool and Southampton. Cup success had not adversely affected their League performances, they were fifth, two points behind second-placed Arsenal with a game in hand. The one problem so many games did cause though was injuries, Alan Gilzean being absent after the midweek League Cup defeat of Liverpool. Under Bertie Mee, Arsenal's success had been built on a strong defence, a hard-working midfield and the long ball game. It earned them a "boring" tag and Mee tried to change that with the inclusion of Charlie George and Peter Marinello and the signing of £200,000 centre-half Jeff Blockley. The experiment came to an end when a 3-0 League Cup defeat at home to Norwich was followed by a 5-0 hammering at Derby, Bob Wilson's first game back after the cartilage injury he had suffered in the FA Cup semi-final against Stoke. Ray Kennedy and George Armstrong were recalled, the effect immediate; a 2-1 defeat of Leeds.

BEFORE THE GAME

	P	W	D	L	F	A	Pts
Arsenal	21	11	5	5	27	21	27
Spurs	20	9	5	6	27	21	23

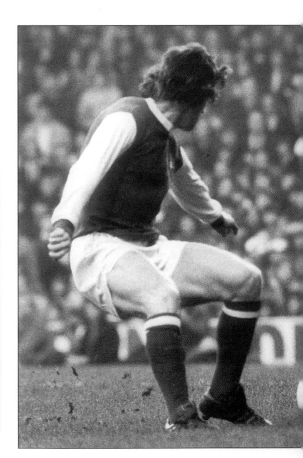

Peter Storey rises majestically to head Arsenal in front after 64 minutes.

John Radford slips the ball past Pat Jennings for Arsenal's second goal.

Bob Wilson saved Arsenal in injury time with a glorious mid-air catch from Ralph Coates' shot.

Below: Jimmy Neighbour (right) takes on Peter Storey.

Brian Glanville in **'The Sunday Times'**...

Coates revives Spurs but Wilson saves the day

At the end of a week tormented by such questions as whether Best should sign for Bournemouth, and whether Mr Denis Follows should be admitted to youth matches, Spurs and Arsenal gave us the thousand natural shocks of their famous North London derby. Arsenal, with a debatable second goal carried the day, but a draw would have been more equitable. Perhaps Spurs would have got it had they brough Coates on earlier.

The immense value to their team in general and Chivers in particular of Gilzean could scarcely have been better illustrated than by his absence. Without him Chivers had no "shoulder" and was but half the player in consequence. There was no one to play off, no tall companion gliding, flicking and lurking with intent. Neighbour, like Pearce and still more than Pearce, is essentially a winger doing what he does (and yesterday it was very little) not in the middle but out on the flank.

In these circumstances it's doubtful whether Tottenham could have hoped effectively to use a three-man attack, the less so with Blockley and Simpson so commanding in Arsenal's central defence. From midfield, moreover, there was little invention, Perryman, Peters and Pratt remaining obscure figures for most of the game. It was only when Coates came on and the team, stung by Arsenal's dubious second goal hurled themselves into attack, that Arsenal at last looked vulnerable and anxious.

Arsenal's own midfield scarcely bubbled with ideas. Kelly was the most active and enterprising. Storey at least scored an admirable goal (and seemed to persuade the linesman to change his mind about the second) but Ball had another sadly anonymous match. In the firing line, Kennedy again looked cool and powerful.

There were but three chances in the first half: all Arsenal's, two of them Ball's. After 18 minutes a move between Rice, Simpson and Radford flowered with a nice square pass from Kennedy. Ball, neither quick nor incisive enough, shot wide. Three minutes later, he might have got a touch to Armstrong's right-wing free-kick, when it passed tantalisingly across the whole defence. The kick, given for a foul by Knowles on Rice, led to the Spurs' left-back being booked for arguing, evidently upset that the referee had allowed play to go on, with an Arsenal man manifestly offside.

The second-half began with two splendid interceptions by England first on Radford, then on McNab, who had both been indulgently allowed to break through on the left.

It was a cross from the right, however, which at last brought Arsenal a goal, at once simple and spectacular, but a little too simple to exonerate a static Tottenham defence. Little Armstrong, from far and deep out on the right, made on the run a centre of impeccable length and trajectory. Over the whole Tottenham goalmouth it flew, to be met with equal effectiveness on the far post with a header into the opposite corner of the goal by **STOREY**; who had beautifully timed his blind side run.

Four minutes later, with the linesman's flag waving for offside on the right against Storey, the Tottenham defence momentarily and fatally stopped, the referee let play go on, the linesman's flag went down, and Radford had the vital couple of yards which made Evans' pursuit hopeless. Jennings advanced but **RADFORD** shot precisely past him. He who hesitates is lost, indeed, even if the incident did seem to drive one more nail into the coffin of that strange concept, interfering with play.

Spurs, two goals down and only three days distant from a hard midweek game, brought Coates on for Neighbour and rose gallantly from the canvas.

With 10 minutes left they struck back with a notable goal. Confusion on the right flank of Arsenal's defence, where Blockley was for once at fault, allowed Chivers to break majestically through. Wilson dashed out boldly to meet him and blocked the ball as he shot, only for it to run to **PETERS**. He, with unhesitating accuracy, struck it high into the unguarded net.

Tottenham continued to hammer Arsenal with a will. Coates too vigorous for McNab, England massively up with the attack. In injury time, Coates shot true and hard, but Wilson saved gloriously in mid-air, and Arsenal just survived.

74

ARSENAL 1
Storey

TOTTENHAM HOTSPUR 1
Chivers

Saturday 14th April 1973

Football League Division One

Highbury

Attendance 50,863

Arsenal

Tottenham Hotspur

Manager
Bertie Mee

Manager
Bill Nicholson

Arsenal	No.	Tottenham Hotspur
Bob WILSON	1	Pat JENNINGS
Pat RICE	2	Joe KINNEAR
Bob McNAB	3	Cyril KNOWLES
Peter STOREY	4	Ralph COATES*
Jeff BLOCKLEY	5	Mike ENGLAND
Peter SIMPSON	6	Phil BEAL
George ARMSTRONG	7	Alan GILZEAN
Alan BALL	8	Steve PERRYMAN
John RADFORD	9	Martin CHIVERS
Ray KENNEDY	10	Martin PETERS
Eddie KELLY*	11	John PRATT
Charlie GEORGE (11)	12	Ray EVANS (4)

Referee **Mr R C Challis** (Tonbridge)

BACKGROUND

Back to the tried and tested after the embarrassment at Derby, one defeat in 22 games had seen Arsenal battling with Liverpool at the top of the table and through to the FA Cup semi-final. But in the space of eight days dreams of another "Double" were shattered. First Derby left Highbury with both points; seven days later at Hillsborough, Second Division Sunderland ended hopes of a third consecutive FA Cup Final. Arsenal desperately needed a return to winning form if they were to keep the pressure on Liverpool. One point behind Bill Shankly's team, they still had to meet Everton, Southampton, West Ham and Leeds, but they were all away, Spurs' visit their last home game of the season. Spurs were again inconsistent in the League, hovering around mid-table, but again showing their liking for knockout competitions. Having won the League Cup for the second time in three seasons, they had high hopes of retaining the UEFA Cup after nothing worse than a one goal defeat at Anfield in the first leg of the semi-final four days earlier.

BEFORE THE GAME

	P	W	D	L	F	A	Pts
Arsenal	37	22	8	7	51	33	52
Spurs	36	14	10	12	48	39	34

AT THE SEASON'S END

		P	W	D	L	F	A	Pts
2nd	Arsenal	42	23	11	8	57	43	57
8th	Spurs	42	16	13	13	58	48	45

Above: Martin Chivers thumps the ball to Bob Wilson's right and high into the roof of the net. 1-0 to Spurs.

Left: Steve Perryman attacks, Alan Ball shadows.

★ This was the first North London 'derby' in which admission prices were subject to Value Added Tax. However supporters did not have to pay any more on this occasion – Arsenal agreed to foot the tax burden for this, the only game of the current season to be affected by the new tax which had been introduced on April 1st.

Brian Glanville in 'The Sunday Times' under...

ARSENAL DROP A POINT AS SPURS CROWD THEM OUT

Arsenal, these days, are finding goals horribly hard to come by. In their last three League games at Highbury, they have managed only two, bringing with them a mere three points, when they so badly needed all six if they hoped to win the Championship. Yesterday, in the North London derby, their old rivals, Tottenham, pegged them to a 1-1 draw with no excessive difficulty, even though they have neither hope nor fear in the League themselves. They solidly packed their defence around the dominant England, and Arsenal, as we know, find a packed defence as acceptable as a vampire finds garlic.

Neither Ball nor Peters, incumbents of the present England midfield, had any continuous influence on the game, though in Peters' defence it might be said that he tends to do good by stealth; that his value lies in his very unexpectedness. His part in the Tottenham goal was characteristic, though he might have done better with an early chance of his own.

Gilzean was one of the major consolations of the afternoon, particularly in the first half, when all around him was tedium. Like Altafini, whose dazzling goals one admired last Wednesday in Turin, 34 years seem no burden on him. His celebrated head flicks were as much in evidence as always - one of them should certainly have produced a goal - but he was also polished and precise in his control and distribution, ready as ever to accept the bumps and bangs which ensure that a strikers' life is not a happy one. There were even moments when he was to be seen clearing, providentially,

from his own goal area, providing that in these work-obsessed days, he can work with the most industrious; even if he glides rather than gallops.

Jennings, in the Spurs goal, gave a performance of casual authority, absolute master of his own area, once seizing a high free-kick with one powerful arm. In front of him, England, though he had his uneasy moments against the forceful Radford, and was lucky once not to be booked for tripping him, stuck to his task with dogged strength.

After a first half which was mostly a desert of non-event, the early second half gave two fine goals in a minute. Pratt, jumping surprisingly high for a little man, won a ball inside the Arsenal half, **CHIVERS** played a smooth one-two with Peters and there he was, clean through and free as air, to smash his right-footed shot past Wilson.

Arsenal's response was instant. They went straight to the Tottenham end, where a glorious diagonal pass by Armstrong, momentarily in the middle, split the Spurs defence, and allowed the cunningly positioned **STOREY** to steal in from the left and score. Just after that, Blockley's header from a right-wing corner flew just wide of the right-hand post. The game was suddenly, vigorously and transiently alive.

Eight minutes from the end, Arsenal brought on George for Kelly and soon afterwards forced Jennings to make his first true save of the match; one to authenticate his newly-won title as Footballer of the Year. Kennedy headed an excellent pass to Radford, in full flight down the left. The big centre forward easily negotiated Beal - who had a fallible sort of match - but Jennings was out like lightning to cut down his angle, dive on his hard low shot, and keep a point for Tottenham.

Alan Ball steps up to strike the ball as Tottenham defend a free kick.

75

TOTTENHAM HOTSPUR 2
Gilzean, Chivers

ARSENAL 0

Tottenham Hotspur

Manager
Bill Nicholson

Arsenal

Manager
Bertie Mee

Tottenham		Arsenal
Barry DAINES	1	Bob WILSON
Ray EVANS	2	Pat RICE
Cyril KNOWLES	3	Bob McNAB
John PRATT	4	Peter STOREY
Mike ENGLAND	5	Peter SIMPSON
Phil BEAL	6	Eddie KELLY
Alan GILZEAN	7	George ARMSTRONG
Steve PERRYMAN	8	Charlie GEORGE
Martin CHIVERS	9	John RADFORD*
Martin PETERS	10	Ray KENNEDY
Chris McGRATH	11	Liam BRADY
Joe KINNEAR	12	Brendan BATSON (9)

Referee **Mr J P Jones** (Treharris)

BACKGROUND

Spurs' cup successes of the early 70's could not disguise the fact they were on the decline; too many players reaching the end of their top flight careers at the same time. Bill Nicholson knew fresh blood was needed but finding it was a problem. One of the richest clubs in the country, never afraid to spend big, could not find the new players desperately needed. Five of the first eight games had been lost, three of them at home and Pat Jennings had been injured at Liverpool three weeks earlier. The first home victory of the season over Derby had been followed by a draw at Ipswich but in their last outing Spurs had surrendered the League Cup at the first hurdle to Queens' Park Rangers. With Ralph Coates injured in that game, 18-year old striker Chris McGrath was called up for his debut. Arsenal had started the season even worse than Spurs but four victories in the last five League fixtures had seen them move up the table. They too had gone out of the League Cup, embarrassingly beaten at Highbury by Tranmere. Alan Ball had been injured and was not risked with England's crucial World Cup qualifier against Poland at Wembley on the coming Wednesday. It meant Arsenal also gave a full debut to a young Irishman, 17-year old Liam Brady.

BEFORE THE GAME

	P	W	D	L	F	A	Pts
Arsenal	10	5	1	4	13	12	11
Spurs	10	3	2	5	11	15	8

GILLY GOAL WINS IT FOR TOTTENHAM

Spurs' young debutant Chris McGrath (left) congratulates Alan Gilzean on shooting his side ahead. Martin Peters is the other player in the picture.

LIGHTS GO DIM IN NORTH LONDON

What makes a good player play badly, I thought as I stood in Spurs' car park, full of excitement yet fear. Poor Blockley and Armstrong seem lost this season, now that the threats of McLintock and Marinello have gone. Chivers gets worse yet there's still not a rival in sight. Has W.Nicholson lost his nerve after Roger Morgan and Coates? With all their loot, surely they could find one new striker in three years.

Yesterday they unveiled 18-year-old Chris McGrath (in place of Coates) from the reserves. He showed touches but no confidence. Arsenal too brought in an Irish teenager, Liam Brady (in place of Blockley), but they never gave him the ball. Neither looked a threat to the off-colour stars. It does, alas, seem a sad fact that some players need a rival to play well.

What makes a team play is a fight against the old enemy. If these two couldn't have produced some action, despite each having a draggy season, then the lights might well have gone out all over North London. Spurs at least scored twice and managed some reasonable group excitement.

Spurs always had the edge and played much better than of late, though they looked like gaining nothing from their supremacy until their two goals in the last ten minutes, both from Knowles free kicks. **GILZEAN** got the first - catching the bounce and lobbing Wilson - and **CHIVERS** headed the second. Until then, the best shots had been from long range and neither goalie had been in much danger apart from a Peters header at the far post.

Arsenal on this showing have most problems. Tranmere have crept into their soul. Even at their best, they have only one exciting player, a player capable of exciting any crowd, and that's Mister C.George. Yesterday he was good for a laugh, but what a luxury. He had three wild shots, the first 20 yards wide, the next ten yards wide and the third eight yards high, so he was getting better.

When he fell dramatically, the Spurs crowd naturally cheered, being good sportsmen. Then up he jumped, grinning like the bloke in Mad magazine, and gave the crowd a suitable gesture. Later, he did get hurt and had his ankle and boot bandaged, bobbling like the ailing thoroughbred which he's now become.

Arsenal's main trouble is midfield. Pratt, Perryman and most of all Peters, who had an excellent game, never gave them a chance. Yet they usually had four in the middle with Armstrong staying back only to get in the way. Behind them Simpson and Storey looked sullen. Only McNab and Rice realised it was a derby game.

Radford and Kennedy, who together are capable of excitement, played isolated games. Radford did try hard but achieved nothing except a booking, along with Beal, then limped off injured - after which Spurs scored their goals.

Spurs have currently three exciting players (four if you count the missing Jennings) though the level of their supporting players is normally less than Arsenal's. There's Cyril Knowles, currently the country's most talented left-back. Unlike Mike England, whose fouls are so blatantly child-like even a TV commentator can see them, Knowles can be rather nasty when things go badly. Yesterday he kept nice - and laid on the two goals.

Gilzean's famous flicks are still there, though flickering fast and even the smallest bully can knock him over. But he too was on form. Which brings us to Chivers, about whom it has been said. That goal will give him great confidence for Wednesday, but he still won't put himself out for a 50-50 ball. He holds back when he must know that every defence is wetting itself whenever he approaches.

But enough of this criticism. Peters is definitely on top form for Wednesday, and harping on at Chivers isn't at this stage going to make him come good. He, like Arsenal's fading stars, must have had a bellyful these last few weeks. Until both managers find some first class rival reserves or they discover psychologically how to handle their guilty players there's only one thing left. Let us now praise famous men. Charlie George, what a blinder. And Martin Chivers, phew, what a scorcher. (Thank you, Sir Alf. That'll be ten guineas).

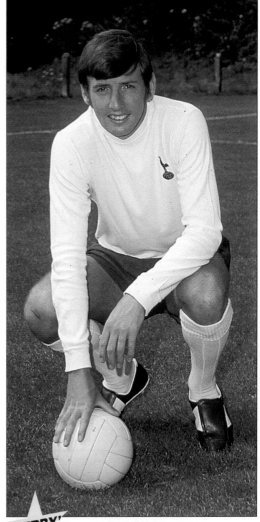

'DERBY' STAR **Martin Peters** – on top form.

Arsenal's young Irish starlet Liam Brady in full flight on his full league debut.

THAT WAS THEN...

★ Fierce fighting between hundreds of Spurs and Arsenal supporters broke out on the White Hart Lane terraces before the game and again during half-time. Police ejected a number of youths.

76

ARSENAL 0

TOTTENHAM HOTSPUR 1
McGrath

Arsenal

Tottenham Hotspur

Manager
Bertie Mee

Manager
Bill Nicholson

Bob WILSON	1	Pat JENNINGS
Pat RICE	2	Ray EVANS
Sammy NELSON	3	Terry NAYLOR
Peter STOREY	4	John PRATT
Peter SIMPSON	5	Mike ENGLAND
Eddie KELLY	6	Phil BEAL
George ARMSTRONG	7	Chris McGRATH
Alan BALL	8	Steve PERRYMAN
John RADFORD	9	Martin CHIVERS
Ray KENNEDY	10	Alan GILZEAN
Liam BRADY	11	Ralph COATES
David PRICE	12	Matt DILLON

Referee **Mr G C Kew** (Amersham)

BACKGROUND

For two clubs that had won so much so recently, the 1973-74 season was one both would rather forget. In the eight games since Christmas Spurs had lost only once, at Leicester, but that was enough to see them wave goodbye to the FA Cup for another year. Four of the eight had been drawn, including their last three away League outings, but at least the best run of the season had pulled them clear of strugglers, Norwich, Manchester United, Birmingham and West Ham. And there was still the UEFA Cup. Their quarter-final first leg clash with Cologne was less than three weeks away. With Martin Peters injured Alan Gilzean made a welcome return for his first match of the year. Arsenal had won only two of their last twelve League games but draws in half of them had kept them out of the relegation zone. They had also made an early exit from the FA Cup, going out to Aston Villa in a fourth round replay. A great game was not in prospect.

BEFORE THE GAME

	P	W	D	L	F	A	Pts
Arsenal	29	9	9	11	32	37	27
Spurs	28	9	9	10	32	38	27

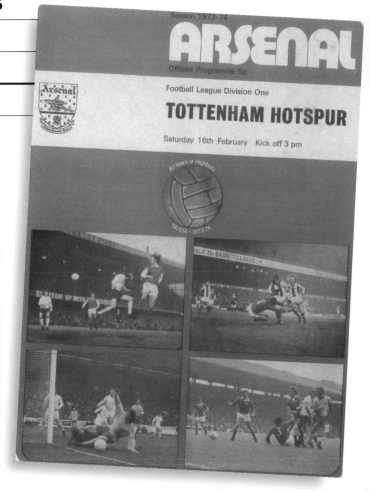

The only goal of the game – scored by Chris McGrath (right).

Howard Fabian in 'The Sunday Telegraph' reported...

Arsenal and Spurs salvage some pride

It is strange to find these two famous North London clubs left with only a respectable place in the League to play for, but this made little difference to the zest and vigour with which they contested this match.

There was skill to be admired, too, notably the wonderful timing of Gilzean with his accurate headed passes and the fine dribbling of young Brady. Incidentally, one felt Brady should aim at getting in his shots and passes a little quicker and then he might be devastating.

Arsenal were unlucky to lose and only an "out-of-this-world" save by Jennings thwarted them. Playing with the wind in the second half they subjected Spurs to almost ceaseless pressure, but all credit to the embattled Spurs defence which resisted superbly.

ARMSTRONG'S AWARD

The proceedings opened with a presentation to George Armstrong to commemorate his 500th competitive appearance for Arsenal. This was done by Arsenal chairman, Denis Hill-Wood, on behalf of the directors.

Grim determination now took the place of sunny smiles as Arsenal, even playing against the wind, surged into the attack, Kennedy twice going very close and it came as a surprise when Spurs took the lead in only their second attack. A long throw by Chivers was headed on by England to **McGRATH**, who slammed it into the net. Kennedy again shot just wide after prolonged Arsenal pressure, while in a Spurs attack Wilson saved well from Pratt's header.

Arsenal swarmed to the attack in the second half and Jennings soon had to save on the line from Nelson's header. Kennedy should have scored when he seized on a bad Tottenham back pass and then came the wonderful Jennings save from Simpson's tremendous shot from 14 yards.

Top: Mike England foils John Radford.

Centre: Steve Perryman makes a spectacular overhead clearance.

Bottom: Liam Brady shoots just wide.

AT THE SEASON'S END

		P	W	D	L	F	A	Pts
10th	Arsenal	42	14	14	14	49	51	42
11th	Spurs	42	14	14	14	45	50	42

77

TOTTENHAM HOTSPUR 2
Perryman, Chivers

ARSENAL 0

Tottenham Hotspur		Arsenal
Manager **Terry Neill**		*Manager* **Bertie Mee**
Pat JENNINGS	1	Jimmy RIMMER
Ray EVANS	2	Peter STOREY
Cyril KNOWLES	3	Sammy NELSON
John PRATT	4	Eddie KELLY
Mike ENGLAND	5	Richie POWLING
Terry NAYLOR	6	Peter SIMPSON
Jimmy NEIGHBOUR	7	George ARMSTRONG
Steve PERRYMAN*	8	Alan BALL
Martin CHIVERS	9	John RADFORD
Martin PETERS	10	Liam BRADY
Chris JONES	11	Brian KIDD
Ralph COATES (8)	12	John MATTHEWS

*Referee **Mr J Hunting** (Leicester)*

BACKGROUND

Spurs' worst League position since Bill Nicholson's first season in charge merely confirmed drastic changes were called for. Still unable to secure the quality players he wanted in the transfer market, he began the new season by introducing two home-grown youngsters, centre-half Keith Osgood and striker Chris Jones. Their potential was obvious, but so was their inexperience. After losing the opening two games 0-1 Osgood was omitted, another 0-1 defeat, at First Division newcomers Carlisle, and Jones was left out. Martin Chivers was recalled for the visit of Manchester City but another defeat proved too much for Nicholson. After almost 16 years in charge he resigned. The players re-inforced their campaign for Nicholson to stay with a 2-0 defeat of Derby but Nicholson would not be swayed. The most successful period in Spurs' history ended with a 2-5 defeat at Anfield and a 0-4 League Cup thrashing at home to Middlesbrough. The surprise replacement was Hull and Northern Ireland manager, and ex-Arsenal star, Terry Neill. His first two games in

Former Arsenal player Terry Neill was now in the manager's seat at White Hart Lane.

charge produced four points but three defeats followed and it was only a poor 1-1 draw with Carlisle that took Spurs off the bottom of the table on goals scored. Neill's first signing, John Duncan, a striker from Dundee, was signed too late to make his debut but watched from the stands. The one team below Spurs was Arsenal, three points from the last 18 and knocked out of the League Cup by Leicester. Like Nicholson, Bertie Mee had set about rebuilding his team; Jimmy Rimmer replacing the retired Bob Wilson, Brian Kidd signed from Manchester United to take over from Ray Kennedy, John Matthews given his chance. Mee's plans were almost wrecked before the season began when Alan Ball, who had broken his leg in the final match of the last campaign, broke his ankle in a pre-season friendly but victory in two of the first three games gave rise to a misplaced sense of optimism.

BEFORE THE GAME

	P	W	D	L	F	A	Pts
Spurs	12	3	1	8	14	20	7
Arsenal	12	2	3	7	12	18	7

Celebrations after Tottenham's second goal, scored by No.9 Martin Chivers.

Tony Pawson in 'The Observer'...

Joke's on Arsenal

There have been few echoes this season of Tottenham's glory days, but at least they could say a hallelujah or two for the defeat of fellow-strugglers Arsenal. It was Tottenham's remembered skills from set pieces that gave them the two goals in a match nicely balanced when play was flowing free. Control of the air was the decisive factor as Peters, Chivers and England left Arsenal grounded.

It's tough at the bottom, but the desperation was well masked and there was even a pleasant hint of humour from Kelly. He was a joker at large, enjoying himself hugely in a game that everyone else took seriously. Kelly's party piece, which baffled opponents, was to bend down as if about to pick up the ball. As they turned in hopeful appeal, he would accelerate past them without touching it with his hand. Like all his jokes, it was practical and purposeful.

Spirit and skill indeed enlivened a game that might well have degenerated into anxious running and harsh tackling. The solitary booking of Kidd was fair indication that both sides strove to be poised to play rather than fight their way out of trouble.

After 12 successive games without a win, Arsenal are no doubt tired of looking for a silver lining in the cloud of defeat. But Kelly was not alone in catching the eye, for Radford and Kidd were always harassing the defenders with their courageous readiness to take on any four.

Brady's frail talents hardly seemed suited to the fierce struggle in midfield. And it was here that Tottenham took control with the bustling energy of Perryman and Pratt. But whenever they pressed upfield, Arsenal were quick and direct in their counter. Kidd was left clear only to try an over-subtle flick through the legs when the simple was so much more likely to succeed. And Jennings had to save with his legs when Evans passed back under pressure. Rimmer was soon following his example with a sliding tackle on Peters which would have pleased a centre-half.

Yet the threat of the high ball was playing persistently on Arsenal's nerves as Chivers decoyed away Simpson, the only tall defender. When Knowles' corner drifted beyond the far post it was England who towered over the others to head it back. As Ball hesitated to clear, **PERRYMAN** surged in behind him to hit an instant shot cleanly into the corner.

Tottenham carried their scars bravely in the second half, with Pratt nursing an injured arm and Perryman needing repairs after ducking into Brady's kick. But Pratt continued to press through and curl across his threatening centres from either wing. And it was Perryman's free kick that Peters headed back for **CHIVERS** to bend low and nudge in despite a flying boot. Rimmer's swift reaction cheated Chivers of another goal, and Jennings arching save of Radford's header had killed Arsenal's challenge.

TOTTENHAM'S GOALS... Steve Perryman fires the first (top) and Martin Chivers is set for the second (below).

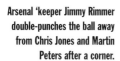

Arsenal 'keeper Jimmy Rimmer double-punches the ball away from Chris Jones and Martin Peters after a corner.

78

ARSENAL 1
Kidd

TOTTENHAM HOTSPUR 0

Saturday 26th April 1975

Football League Division One

Highbury

Attendance 43,762

Arsenal

Manager
Bertie Mee

Tottenham Hotspur

Manager
Terry Neill

Arsenal		Tottenham Hotspur
Geoff BARNETT	1	Pat JENNINGS
Pat RICE	2	Joe KINNEAR
Sammy NELSON	3	Cyril KNOWLES
Peter STOREY	4	Phil BEAL
Terry MANCINI	5	Keith OSGOOD
Peter SIMPSON	6	Terry NAYLOR
Alan BALL	7	Alfie CONN
Liam BRADY	8	Steve PERRYMAN
Brian HORNSBY	9	Chris JONES
Brian KIDD	10	John DUNCAN
George ARMSTRONG	11	Jimmy NEIGHBOUR*
Wilf ROSTRON	12	John PRATT (11)

Referee **Mr R W Toseland** (Kettering)

BACKGROUND

Following defeat at White Hart Lane Bertie Mee moved swiftly to arrest the slide. Terry Mancini was signed from Queen's Park Rangers, Pat Rice and Bob McNab recalled and Arsenal climbed away from the relegation places. Alex Cropley from Hibernian was added to the Highbury payroll in December but played only seven games before sidelined by a broken leg. Inconsistency kept Arsenal in the lower reaches of the table but the FA Cup provided welcome, although hard earned, relief. Struggling Second Division York took them to extra-time in a Bootham Crescent replay, two games were needed to overcome Coventry and three to see off Leicester before West Ham put them out in the sixth round, the first London club to beat Arsenal in an FA Cup-tie at Highbury. One defeat in eight games following John Duncan's arrival had taken Spurs out of the relegation zone but it did not last. In three months from mid-December they collected only five points from 28 and with eight defeats in nine games plunged back into the relegation battle. Don McAllister's signing from Bolton to bolster the defence was offset within three weeks when Mike England announced his retirement. With seven games left the situation looked desperate but, inspired by Bill Nicholson's last signing, Alfie Conn, Spurs took eight points from five games, including crucial victories over fellow strugglers Chelsea and Luton. Any result at Highbury would be more than welcome, for Spurs last match was at home to the European Cup finalists Leeds.

BEFORE THE GAME

	P	W	D	L	F	A	Pts
Arsenal	40	12	11	17	46	46	35
Spurs	40	12	8	20	48	60	32

Brian Kidd slides in to score the only goal of the game... would it be the goal to send Spurs down?

Deryk Brown in 'The Sunday Times' under...

PASSION, FRENZY AND STILL HOPE

THEY DO NOT make football matches like this any more, just as they do not make those roaring Westerns where the US Cavalry storms in to save the beleaguered homesteaders. However, when all the magnificent hurly-burly was done, the fact remains that Tottenham Hotspur must take a point from Leeds United tomorrow night to stay in the First Division. If they fight like this, they will surely do it.

The passion and the frenzied pace of yesterday's match, a true derby, pushed any failings of Tottenham, and indeed Arsenal, far into the background and underneath it all there was a grim humour: as when the darting Conn sat on the ball after being fouled, Mancini laughed back at an ironic cheer, and Perryman clapped a bit of jiggery-pokery on the ball.

On the surface, there was little pattern but Arsenal just deserved to win. In the first half Armstrong gave them the upper hand, his fine dribbling troubling a bad Tottenham defence. And throughout Brady, that claw-like left foot working overtime, Kidd, and sometimes Ball, looked that shade more likely to create a goal.

Kidd it was who scored the goal after 16 minutes. Already Mancini had shown Arsenal's own nasty shortcomings in defence with a couple of unhappy fouls. But his opposite number, the young Osgood, was likewise unsteady, and when Brady hit a short cross, **KIDD** nipped in too fast for a wondering defence to turn the ball under Jennings.

But for Kidd's goals, of course, Arsenal could easily be going down themselves. They have had one bad season and cannot really afford another. The latent promise of their youngsters, yesterday evident in the performance of Hornsby as well as Brady, is not enough.

Tottenham could so easily have scored. Perryman typified their effort as much as anyone, running with a worried courage which showed in his face. Tottenham had a potential match winner in Conn and twice in the second half he came so close to scoring. Somehow, however, Tottenham could not harness his effort into that of their team and now they must wait until tomorrow night.

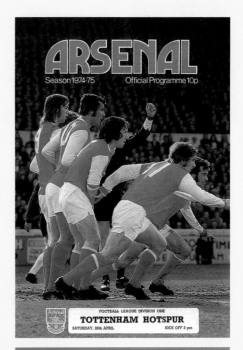

THAT WAS THEN...

★ For season 1974-75 Arsenal doubled the price of their programme from 5p to 10p. Although the number of pages remained at 16 there was extra colour, with a full colour action photograph on the cover. Tottenham's programme rose from 5p to 7p although it broke the 10p barrier in 1975-76!

Alfie Conn misses a golden opportunity to the horror of team-mate John Duncan. Spurs lost, but won their last game to survive relegation by one place. Luton, Chelsea and Carlisle went down.

AT THE SEASON'S END

		P	W	D	L	F	A	Pts
16th	Arsenal	42	13	11	18	47	47	37
19th	Spurs	42	13	8	21	52	63	34

79

TOTTENHAM HOTSPUR 0

ARSENAL 0

Saturday 27th September 1975

Football League Division One

White Hart Lane

Attendance 37,064

Tottenham Hotspur

Arsenal

Manager
Terry Neill

Manager
Bertie Mee

Pat JENNINGS	1	Jimmy RIMMER
Terry NAYLOR	2	Pat RICE
Cyril KNOWLES	3	Sammy NELSON
John PRATT	4	Eddie KELLY
Willie YOUNG	5	Terry MANCINI
Keith OSGOOD	6	David O'LEARY
Neil McNAB	7	Alan BALL
Steve PERRYMAN	8	Alex CROPLEY
John DUNCAN*	9	Frank STAPLETON
Chris JONES	10	Brian KIDD
Jimmy NEIGHBOUR	11	Wilf ROSTRON*
Martin CHIVERS (9)	12	Liam BRADY (11)

Referee **Mr P N Willis** (Meadowfield)

BACKGROUND

78 League derbies and never a goalless draw. It was a remarkable record but one that had to end one day. And with both teams struggling so early in the campaign never was there a more likely day. Terry Neill had stayed out of the transfer market during the summer, preferring to give Spurs' promising youngsters the opportunity to replace experienced stars like Mike England, Ray Evans, Martin Peters and Phil Beal. The season started with a home win over Middlesbrough but while Chris Jones, Keith Osgood and 18-year-old Neil McNab brought a refreshing sense of optimism to a club that had begun to look stale and lethargic, results did not match performances. One victory in the next eight games, and that at Fourth Division Watford in the League Cup, left Spurs just one place off the bottom. Going forward, Spurs always looked likely to score, but when put under pressure it was the defence that let them down. Willie Young, not the prettiest of footballers but big and strong, was signed from Aberdeen and made a solid debut in a 1-1 draw at Leeds. Bertie Mee too, had placed his faith in youth, introducing David O'Leary and giving further opportunities to Brian Hornsby, Alex Cropley and Frank Stapleton. Inconsistent was the only way to describe their start, a 3-1 win at Sheffield United followed by a one goal defeat at home to Stoke, a 1-1 draw with Leicester at Highbury followed by a two-all draw at Everton in the League Cup. Four days before the meeting with Spurs they had gone out of the League Cup, beaten 0-1 at home by Everton in the replay.

BEFORE THE GAME

	P	W	D	L	F	A	Pts
Arsenal	8	2	4	2	8	8	8
Spurs	8	1	3	4	11	14	5

"Some of those players looked as if they'd never kicked a ball before in their lives. I'm ashamed. I want to apologise to the fans. It was an absolute disgrace."

– Spurs' boss Terry Neill speaking at the post-match press conference.

The game was a milestone for two Tottenham players. **Pat Jennings** (left) equalled the club record of 418 Football League appearances, held by Ted Ditchburn since 1958, and **Cyril Knowles** (above) played his 500th Spurs game in League and Cup competitions.

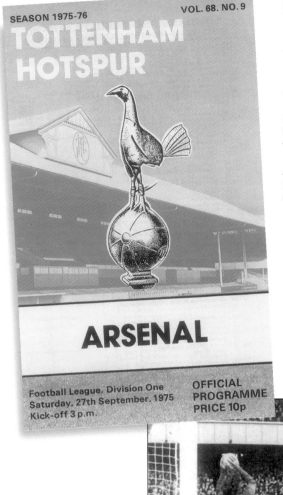

SEASON 1975-76   VOL. 68. NO. 9

TOTTENHAM HOTSPUR

ARSENAL

Football League, Division One
Saturday, 27th September, 1975
Kick-off 3 p.m.

OFFICIAL
PROGRAMME
PRICE 10p

Deryk Brown in 'The Sunday Times' under...

History was bunk

In one sense this match was historic, being the first goalless draw between these two teams in their long league history. In every respect, it was eminently unhistoric and forgettable. A very poor 90 minutes entertainment.

There was no pattern, only a frenzied close-passing game as Tottenham's white and Arsenal's red converged in midfield for a nervy confrontation. The wind was a nuisance making some of Rimmer's goal kicks drop like stones in the first half and Jennings' too in the second. But that is no excuse.

Both sides are limited enough without having to produce the extra something which the artificial brouhaha surrounding these derby matches demands. Tottenham, certainly, did not match their performance of a week ago when they counter attacked a stuttering Leeds side with youthful vigour. For long one has suspected that the top London teams, especially Arsenal, played a much more relaxed game away from the capital. Little that happened yesterday disproves the theory.

Jennings was equalling a Ted Ditchburn goalkeeping record of 418 league matches for Tottenham. Until Brady, Arsenal's substitute, hit a shot in the closing minutes, Ditchburn today could have stopped much of what Arsenal aimed at the Tottenham goal. Knowles also was at a milestone - his 500th appearance - but he spoiled it by being booked along with Rostron as frustration took over.

Overall, Tottenham had just the better of it. Their defence was adequate with their new player Young effective if not always delicate. Pratt, in midfield, had as good an afternoon as any and produced two well struck shots in the first half which Rimmer did well to stop.

Ball began as though he might give some order to Arsenal with his intelligent short passes; then he faded and Kelly, despite taking at least one knock, worked well. And in defence, Arsenal could take consolation from the play of O'Leary, a leggy young number 6, who seems to have the intuition of Simpson, his clever predecessor.

From the front runners there was little coherence. Arsenal's looked marginally the better, with Kidd showing his vision (although it was lost on the crowd) and with Stapleton a fair jumper. At the end, Terry Neill, the Tottenham manager, had some hard things to say about it. Fortunately football fans are a forgiving lot and next Saturday soon comes round.

**Below and right:
Two assaults on the Tottenham goal from Brian Kidd.**

80

ARSENAL 0

TOTTENHAM HOTSPUR 2
Pratt, Duncan

Saturday 3rd April 1976

Football League Division One

Highbury

Attendance 42,031

Arsenal

Manager
Bertie Mee

Tottenham Hotspur

Manager
Terry Neill

Arsenal		Tottenham Hotspur
Jimmy RIMMER	1	Pat JENNINGS
Pat RICE	2	Terry NAYLOR
Sammy NELSON	3	Don McALLISTER
Trevor ROSS	4	John PRATT
Terry MANCINI	5	Willie YOUNG
Richie POWLING	6	Keith OSGOOD
George ARMSTRONG	7	Chris JONES
Alan BALL	8	Steve PERRYMAN
John RADFORD	9	Martin CHIVERS
Brian KIDD	10	John DUNCAN
Liam BRADY	11	Jimmy NEIGHBOUR
Alex CROPLEY	12	Glenn HODDLE

Referee **Mr R Tinkler** (Boston)

BACKGROUND

No matter what Bertie Mee tried he could not halt Arsenal's slide towards the lower reaches of the First Division. Terry Mancini and Eddie Kelly were dropped, Peter Storey recalled and Richie Powling given his chance. Another veteran, George Armstrong, replaced the injured Alex Cropley but still they could not string together a decent run of results. Half-way through the season Arsenal were four off the bottom, firmly entrenched in a battle with Birmingham, Burnley and Wolves to avoid joining Sheffield United, who were to spend the whole season propping up the table, in relegation. It was only with the recall of another veteran, John Radford, in late February that any consistency was achieved. Three consecutive victories, with Radford scoring the winner in two of them, followed by two draws and the best result of the season, a 6-1 hammering of West Ham, almost assured survival and two days later Mee announced he would retire at the end of the season. The unbeaten run came to an end with a 0-3 defeat at Leeds a week before the return with Spurs. While Arsenal were flirting with relegation for the first time since the arrival of Herbert Chapman, Terry Neill was steadily taking Spurs in the opposite direction. Beaten by Newcastle in the League Cup semi-final, too many draws kept them in mid-table but on the back of four consecutive wins they went to Highbury with hopes of finishing high enough to qualify for the UEFA Cup.

BEFORE THE GAME

	P	W	D	L	F	A	Pts
Spurs	37	12	14	11	56	56	38
Arsenal	36	12	9	15	42	43	33

John Radford goes close for the Gunners.

'DERBY' STAR **Willie Young** – "some of his touches of skill were unbelievable in so big a man".

Alun Rees in 'The Sunday Telegraph' reported...

SPURS GAZE AT EUROPE

Spurs kept their hopes of European football next season burning with their fifth win a row. Their transformation from a ragged side hovering on the brink of disaster has been remarkable. Yesterday they shone with pride and the will to win.

Apart from a natural desire to walk tall in North London Arsenal didn't have a lot to play for and it showed. Brady, neat and possessing great vision, had a good first half but only Ball kept going flat out until the end. He found himself slightly outnumbered.

Spurs current revival is based on collective enthusiasm. Perryman and Pratt, as hard and composed a pair as you will see in a month of Sundays, constitute a tremendous mid-field engine room, and the support is magnificent.

From Jennings, returning after a two game absence with calf damage, to Jones, replacing the injured Coates, they all did their bit. If one man could be singled out for special praise it would have to be Young.

Young brought sheer physical strength to the defence when he was signed from Aberdeen for £100,000 in September, but he is developing into a fine all-round player. Some of his touches of skill were almost unbelievable in so big a man.

Naylor, McAllister and Osgood had excellent games too and Arsenal lacked the craft and drive to get within testing range of Jennings. In contrast Arsenal's defensive flanks were suspect and never rivalled Spurs in cohesion.

Yet Arsenal should have gone ahead within 30 seconds. Jennings could only palm away Brady's shot but Kidd, in glorious isolation, missed the rebound completely. Thereafter, Kidd's grasp of affairs was never better than tenuous.

It took Spurs 10 minutes to get going, and 15 to score, when **PRATT** curled his corner wickedly under the bar. A committed Rimmer could do no more than claw it against the woodwork from which it fell over the line.

DUNCAN missed a couple of chances but made up for that with a glorious header from Naylor's cross after 38 minutes. In the meantime Rimmer had saved a phenomenal twisting shot from McAllister and Pratt had hit the post.

The second half was quieter though Rimmer had to save smartly from Duncan and Perryman and Jones went close. Nelson, Rice and Powling tried fitfully to help Ball get something going but Spurs, bursting with energy, had matters well under control.

AT THE SEASON'S END

		P	W	D	L	F	A	Pts
9th	Spurs	42	14	15	13	63	63	43
17th	Arsenal	42	13	10	19	47	53	37

Above: John Pratt's swerving corner is pushed onto the bar by Jimmy Rimmer, but the ball rebounds onto the Arsenal 'keeper's legs and into the net for Spurs' first goal.

Left: John Duncan rises and nods a looping header from Terry Naylor's cross in off the far post for Spurs second goal.

THE PRIDE OF NORTH LONDON **177**

81

TOTTENHAM HOTSPUR 2
Young, Duncan

ARSENAL 2
Macdonald 2

Monday 27th December 1976

Football League Division One

White Hart Lane

Attendance 47,751

Tottenham Hotspur

Arsenal

Manager
Keith Burkinshaw

Manager
Terry Neill

Tottenham		Arsenal
Pat JENNINGS	1	**Jimmy RIMMER**
Terry NAYLOR	2	**Pat RICE**
John GORMAN	3	**Richie POWLING**
Glenn HODDLE*	4	**Trevor ROSS**
Willie YOUNG	5	**David O'LEARY**
Keith OSGOOD	6	**Peter SIMPSON**
Alfie CONN	7	**Peter STOREY**
Steve PERRYMAN	8	**Liam BRADY**
John DUNCAN	9	**Malcolm MACDONALD**
Ralph COATES	10	**Frank STAPLETON**
Peter TAYLOR	11	**Wilf ROSTRON**
John PRATT (4)	12	Pat HOWARD

Referee **Mr B H Daniels** (Brentwood)

Willie Young gets down low to head Peter Taylor's free-kick past Jimmy Rimmer to level the scores at 1-1.

BACKGROUND

Bertie Mee's retirement led to enormous speculation as to who his successor would be. The prestige attached to managing one of the most famous clubs in Europe saw every manager of standing mentioned; and not only British managers; at one time the Yugoslav, Miljan Miljanic of Real Madrid was favourite. Brian Clough and Terry Venables were hotly tipped but when it came to a decision Arsenal settled for a manager much nearer home, an ex-Arsenal player with only two years experience at the top level - Terry Neill. Despite the progress made at White Hart Lane, Neill had never been accepted by the Spurs' faithful and had only a lukewarm relationship with the Board. He resigned in June 1976 and within a fortnight took over the Highbury hot seat, making an immediate impact with the signing of Malcolm Macdonald from Newcastle for a third of a million pounds. The England centre-forward, signed in the face of fierce competition from Spurs, was needed to replace Brian Kidd, who had joined Manchester City before Neill's arrival. Neill's reign could not have got off to a worse start as newly-promoted Bristol City won the opening game of the season at Highbury by the only goal. Changes were needed and Neill was not afraid to make them. Happy to rely on the youthful talent of Ross, O'Leary and Stapleton, Cropley, Radford and Ball were allowed to move on, Pat Howard signed from Newcastle. Consistency was found and were it not for three straight defeats in October Neill's first derby as Arsenal manager would have taken place with Arsenal challenging Ipswich and Liverpool at the top of the table, not in sixth place. While Neill was enjoying his new job, the same could not be said for his replacement at White Hart Lane. Keith Burkinshaw, first team coach for just a year under Neill, inherited a squad weakened by the departure of Martin Chivers and the retirement of Cyril Knowles. Apart from Macdonald, he lost out in the chase for David Johnson, the Ipswich man preferring to join Liverpool, and then saw John Duncan and Pat Jennings injured in pre-season games. With untried Gerry Armstrong starting the season at centre-forward, the first two games were lost, the third drawn. The arrival of Ian Moores from Stoke was followed by League Cup victory at Middlesbrough and League wins at Manchester United and home to Leeds, but even the return of Jennings could not prevent Spurs returning to losing ways, going out of the League Cup 2-3 to Third Division Wrexham at White Hart Lane. England winger Peter Taylor was signed from Crystal Palace and in his first two games Spurs were thrashed 2-4 at West Bromwich and 2-8 at Derby. John Gorman's capture was greeted by defeats at home to Bristol City and away to Sunderland. By Christmas Spurs were among the favourites for relegation, only West Ham and Sunderland having less points.

BEFORE THE GAME

	P	W	D	L	F	A	Pts
Arsenal	18	9	4	5	34	27	22
Spurs	18	4	4	10	23	38	12

Steve Curry in 'The Daily Express' reported on...

Young sent off

Willie Young, of Tottenham, already banned for life from playing for Scotland, was sent off in the second half of a Christmas derby with as much good will as a guerrilla war.

Young had been cautioned by Essex referee Brian Daniels, who was always struggling to control the neighbourly tension, in the 47th minute for a foul on Arsenal's improving Frank Stapleton.

DELIBERATE

Daniels choose to view further indiscretions by the Tottenham centre half leniently until the 66th minute. But when Young used his knees to force off a challenge from Stapleton to a 66th minute corner, the referee had no choice but to show the red card.

Even Young's manager, Keith Burkinshaw, was forced to admit: "It was the only thing the referee could do. Willie claimed he went for the ball, but it did look as though it was a deliberate foul."

It was sad that this incident should detract from a two-goal performance from Arsenal's Malcolm Macdonald, bringing his tally to seven in the last four league matches.

In the fifth minute **MacDONALD** left the Spurs contingent in stunned silence with a left-foot volley from a Liam Brady free kick, which gave even Pat Jennings little chance.

The equaliser came from **YOUNG** in the 20th minute - a low header at the far post from a free-kick superbly flighted by Peter Taylor.

But in the 32nd minute Arsenal resumed their lead when yet another foul by Young on Stapleton gave Brady the chance to sidestep a free kick for **MacDONALD** to fire another left foot shot passed Jennings' left hand.

And as the second half threatened to get out of referee Daniels' control, and with Young dismissed, Arsenal seemed ready to consolidate their improving First Division position.

But with 15 minutes left Tottenham got a surprise equaliser, a cross by Ralph Coates from the left being swept home by John **DUNCAN**.

Arsenal manager, Terry Neill, said: "I thought that we did well, and that if anyone was going to win the game it was us. I was the man who brought Willie Young to Tottenham.

"When I was manager at the club he was booked only a couple of times, but I was surprised at his behaviour today."

The incident which led to Willie Young receiving his marching orders. Young, already booked, used his knees to force off a challenge from Frank Stapleton.

Tottenham's second equaliser, turned in by No.9 John Duncan.

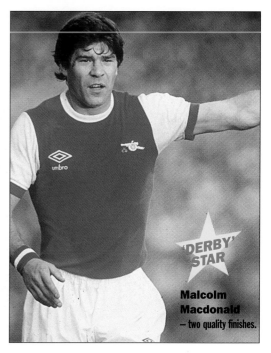

'DERBY' STAR

Malcolm Macdonald – two quality finishes.

82

ARSENAL 1
Macdonald

TOTTENHAM HOTSPUR 0

Monday 11th April 1977

Football League Division One

Highbury

Attendance 47,432

Arsenal

Manager
Terry Neill

Tottenham Hotspur

Manager
Keith Burkinshaw

Arsenal		Tottenham Hotspur
Jimmy RIMMER	1	Barry DAINES
Pat RICE	2	Terry NAYLOR
John MATTHEWS	3	Jimmy HOLMES
David PRICE	4	John PRATT
David O'LEARY	5	Keith OSGOOD
Willie YOUNG	6	Steve PERRYMAN
Graham RIX*	7	Chris JONES
Alan HUDSON	8	Glenn HODDLE
Malcolm MACDONALD	9	Gerry ARMSTRONG
Frank STAPLETON	10	Ralph COATES
George ARMSTRONG	11	Peter TAYLOR
Liam BRADY (7)	12	Andy KEELEY

Referee **Mr C B White** *(Harrow)*

BACKGROUND

The Christmas draw at White Hart Lane was the start of a miserable three months for Arsenal. One win in 14 League games destroyed any hopes of finishing high enough to qualify for a spot in the UEFA Cup and although they saw off Notts County and Coventry a comprehensive 1-4 fifth round defeat at Middlesbrough, one of nine successive defeats, put them out of the FA Cup. Alan Hudson, signed from Stoke before Christmas, was called up in the new year but produced the talent that had made him such a favourite at Chelsea far too rarely. Pat Howard had not proved the success Neill expected, and when Willie Young became available he was quick to sign the big Scot for the second time in 18 months. It was, however, only with the introduction of young Graham Rix that Arsenal began to get back on track; a 3-0 Highbury defeat of Leicester on his debut followed by a 2-0 win at West Brom restoring confidence. While Arsenal had been slipping down the table, Spurs had slowly clawed their way up and had the better record of the two since the last meeting. Although Cardiff had knocked them out of the FA Cup in the third round, two victories in January gave them heart, but it was all too short-lived with defeat in all four February matches. Rock bottom and with Jennings injured again, a desperate situation demanded desperate measures. Willie Young was dropped and with Steve Perryman moved to central defence, Norwich and Liverpool beaten. Jimmy Holmes was signed to play alongside Osgood but instead had to replace the injured Gorman. Four points from the next five games were not enough and although Spurs entered the Easter games two points and four places off the bottom, three of the clubs below had games in hand. Maximum points from the three Easter fixtures were essential if Spurs were to avoid the drop for the first time in 42 years and they had started well with a 3-0 defeat of QPR.

BEFORE THE GAME

	P	W	D	L	F	A	Pts
Arsenal	34	12	9	13	53	53	33
Spurs	34	10	7	17	41	61	27

Below: Malcolm Macdonald steers the ball past Barry Daines for the only goal of the game.

> "Once again Arsenal's victory leaves Spurs in a major quandary over their chances of staying in the First Division"

*Norman de Mesquita reported for **'The Times'** on...*

Brady the man of the hour as destiny again stalks Spurs

Above: Ex Spurs defender Willie Young, now in the red of Arsenal, heads clear of Chris Jones, despite losing a boot.

Right: Gunners substitute Liam Brady evades a challenge from Steve Perryman.

In 84 previous encounters these north London rivals have only once failed to score at least one goal between them. For an hour at Highbury yesterday we could have been forgiven for thinking that it would be another 84 before a goal would come. It was a shapeless match, with Arsenal seemingly reluctant to move at full speed and Tottenham not good enough to dictate matters.

Then, on the hour, Brady replaced Rix, and a transformation came over Arsenal. This is not to belittle the efforts of Rix, a young midfield player of immense promise; but with Hudson playing deeper than ever and just not getting involved where it mattered most, the home side needed to add incisiveness to their unimaginative build-up. Brady proved to be the man and, within 10 minutes of his appearance, he had set up MacDonald for the only goal of the game.

There was an element of luck about the way in which Brady got the ball, but there was nothing lucky about his first-time lobbed pass which sent **MacDONALD** on one of his typical bursts through the middle. In spite of the attentions of two Tottenham defenders he kept his concentration and that, allied to his well known determination, enabled him to work the ball on to his favourite left foot and score his twenty-sixth goal of the season and to plunge Spurs deeper into relegation trouble.

Only the brilliance of Daines had earlier denied MacDonald, and the Tottenham reserve goalkeeper had two more opportunities to show just how good he is. First, he did well to block a diving header by Price; then, when O'Leary headed a corner by Armstrong into the goalmouth, Daines was at his best to palm away MacDonald's header from no more than two yards out.

If Spurs are to gain any comfort from this troubled season, it must lie in the fact that Daines has emerged, during the prolonged absence of Jennings, as a goalkeeper of the highest class. He may not dominate the goal in quite the same way as Jennings (who does?), but his reflexes are superb.

There was not much else of comfort to emerge from Tottenham's point of view. Their one truly skilful player, Hoddle, was rarely able to impose himself on the game, and there were far too many unforced errors. Arsenal were not a great deal better until Brady's arrival. Hudson's influence was once again minimal, and Stapleton had an unhappy afternoon.

Highbury's biggest league crowd of the season did not have a very entertaining bank holiday afternoon. Arsenal are still short of confidence after their recent dismal spell, although this third successive win will at least send them to Anfield on Saturday with a degree more confidence. As for Spurs, they still have an awful lot to do, and even a win at Ashton Gate this evening will not see them out of the wood.

AT THE SEASON'S END

		P	W	D	L	F	A	Pts
8th	Arsenal	42	16	11	15	64	59	43
22nd ▼	Spurs	42	12	9	21	48	72	33

Tottenham Hotspur

Football League, Division One
Saturday, 23rd December, 1978. Kick-off 3

ARSENAL

Season 1980–81
Saturday 30 August

Football Leag
TOTTENHAM
Kick-off 3.00 p

AR

Season 1981-82

10

Football League
Division One
TOTTENHAM H

TOTTENHAM HOTSPUR

...AMME
...rved
...il 1980
...
...23 Price 25p
...all

1

2

Arsen

Official Programme 20p
Season 1978-79

Football League
Division One

Tottenha

**TOTT
HOTS**

ARSENAL
OFFICIAL PROGRAM

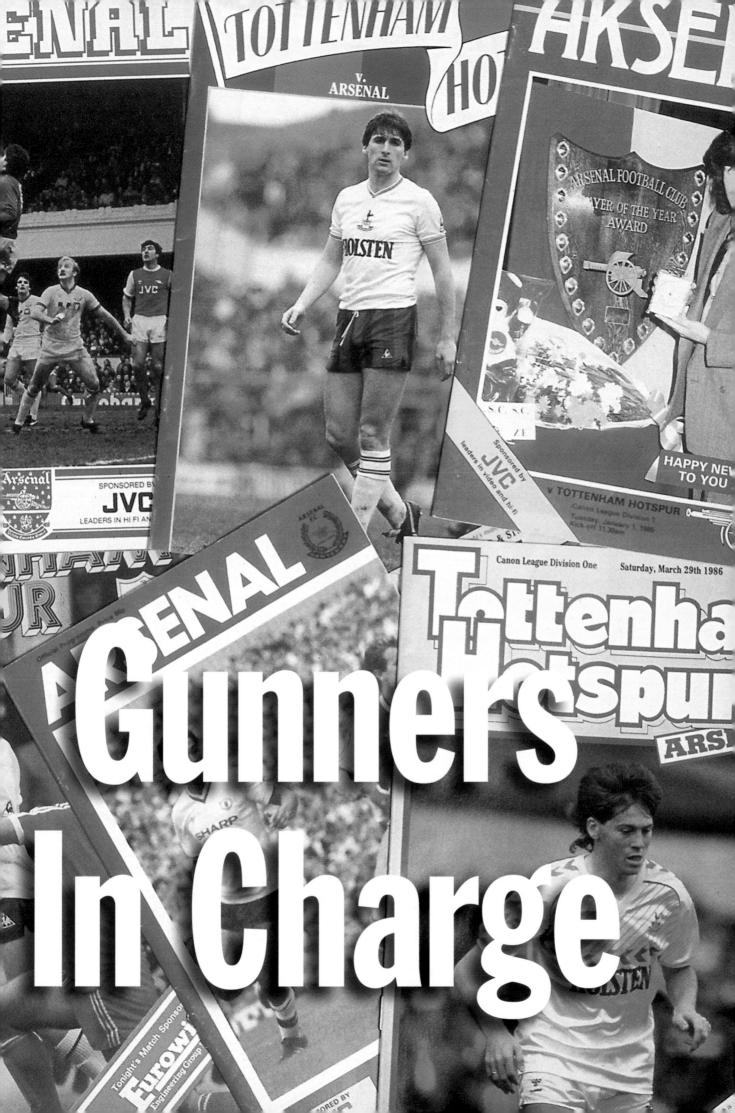

83

TOTTENHAM HOTSPUR 0

ARSENAL 5
Sunderland 3, Stapleton, Brady

Tottenham Hotspur

Manager
Keith Burkinshaw

Arsenal

Manager
Terry Neill

Mark KENDALL	1	Pat JENNINGS
Terry NAYLOR	2	Pat RICE
John GORMAN	3	Steve WALFORD
Jimmy HOLMES	4	David PRICE
John LACY	5	David O'LEARY
Steve PERRYMAN	6	Willie YOUNG
John PRATT*	7	Liam BRADY
Ossie ARDILES	8	Alan SUNDERLAND
Colin LEE	9	Frank STAPLETON
Glenn HODDLE	10	Steve GATTING
Peter TAYLOR	11	Graham RIX
Chris JONES (7)	12	John KOSMINA

Referee **Mr T D Spencer** (Salisbury)

BEFORE THE GAME

	P	W	D	L	F	A	Pts
Arsenal	19	9	7	3	30	17	25
Spurs	19	8	6	5	22	28	22

**Hat-trick hitter
Alan Sunderland.**

BACKGROUND

Spurs climbed out of the Second Division with the same players who had seen them relegated, but Keith Burkinshaw knew that if any impression was to be made in the top flight the squad had to be strengthened. A new centre-half was the priority but when Burkinshaw was told that Ossie Ardiles, midfield star of Argentina's 1978 World Cup campaign, was available he lost no time jetting out to South America. Glenn Hoddle, Neil McNab and John Pratt had looked the perfect midfield trio in the Second Division but no club with ambition could afford to ignore the best midfield player in the world. Burkinshaw returned not only with Ardiles but also Ricky Villa, another midfielder; not a member of the World Cup winning team but rated by many judges every bit as good as Ardiles. It was a transfer coup that shook the football world. Although the pair cost £700,000, money was still found to sign the Fulham centre-half, John Lacy. The two Argentinians made Spurs the biggest attraction in the country but early results made the bold move look decidedly risky. The season started well enough with a draw at Nottingham Forest but Aston Villa left White Hart Lane with both points and Chelsea one before Spurs drew at Swansea in the League Cup. In the next game Spurs were given a lesson by European Cup holders, Liverpool; the 0-7 defeat the biggest in Spurs' first class history. Burkinshaw kept faith with the Hoddle-McNab-Villa-Ardiles midfield for the League Cup replay with Swansea but when the Third Division club won 3-1 changes had to be made. John Pratt and Jimmy Holmes replaced McNab and Hoddle, Colin Lee the soon to depart John Duncan. Results improved immediately, Hoddle won his place back, young Mark Kendall retained his after injury to Barry Daines had given him his chance and Spurs moved up the table. The defeat at Manchester United a week before Arsenal's visit was only the third since the Anfield debacle. With Spurs' relegation Burkinshaw had decided Barry Daines offered the better long-term prospect and released Pat Jennings. Neill quickly moved for his former international team-mate and also secured promising reserve defender, Steve Walford, but perhaps his most important "signing" was Don Howe. Bertie Mee's right-hand man had not enjoyed the best of times in his four years at West Brom and was coaching Leeds when Neill persuaded him to return to Highbury. Fifth in the League, runners-up in the FA Cup and League Cup semi-finalists, Neill's second season in charge may not have produced any silverware but tangible reward for his efforts seemed just around the corner. Early season form, though, made such optimism look misplaced. The first three games produced two draws and a defeat, the fourth saw interest in the League Cup ended with defeat by Rotherham at Millmoor. Malcolm Macdonald had clearly not recovered from a knee injury and needed further surgery that all but finished his season. Neill was forced to rethink his formation. Rix was recalled, Sunderland and Stapleton left to forage up front. Results immediately changed and Pat Jennings made his first return to White Hart Lane with Arsenal unbeaten in nine games, behind pacesetters Everton and Liverpool, but close enough to have the Merseysiders worrying.

Colin Malam in 'The Daily Telegraph' under...

Whitewash Hart Lane

Christmas came two days early for Arsenal at White Hart Lane yesterday. Having been made a gift of a goal after only 38 seconds they went on to enjoy themselves hugely at the expense of a Spurs side which was generous to a fault throughout the 90 minutes.

Considering the importance of the occasion and the passion this North London confrontation generates it was an astonishingly slack performance by Spurs. In no department were they convincing and the defensive work was particularly poor.

This was Spurs heaviest defeat by Arsenal at home since the war, and it reflected accurately the Gunners' clear superiority in every area of the field. On yesterday's evidence, Arsenal are much the sounder of the two old rivals at the moment.

The pre-match publicity had, with good reason, billed this match as a duel between those two fine midfield players, Ardiles and Brady. For a long time, however, both of them looked on unhappily as the play passed them by in a frenzied swirl.

Ardiles never did really get into the game, but Brady eventually got its measure to such an extent that he supplied the passes for two of Arsenal's goals, and scored another one himself.

Even so, the impish little Irishman was overshadowed by his England team-mate Sunderland. He scored three of the goals, hit the bar and generally made life miserable for a lackadaisical Spurs defence with his waspish running and stinging finishing.

Stapleton also struck the woodwork. He did so near the end of a second half in which Arsenal seemed to score whenever they felt like it against totally demoralised opponents. By the finish, the Spurs defence had practically ceased to exist.

By then, too, the heat had gone out of a match which had threatened earlier to run out of control. Many of the tackles exceeded the bounds of simple enthusiasm, and the failure of the referee to resort to the yellow card provoked innumerable private feuds.

All that was still to come, however, when Pratt found himself in possession just inside the Arsenal half less than a minute after the kick-off. But finding his way blocked, the Spurs midfield player turned and, inexplicably aimed a reckless pass back towards Lacy, his centre half.

The ball never reached its target, because **SUNDERLAND**'s alertness and electric speed enabled him to get there first, outpace the tall, gangling Lacy and drive a shot home off Kendall's foot and the underside of the bar.

Thrusting runs from defence by Walford and Young, two of Arsenal's three former Spurs players, confirmed that the defensive misunderstanding which had led to Sunderland's early goal was no accident. Yet the industry of Perryman and the guile of Ardiles kept Spurs moving forward purposefully enough to suggest the deficit could be made good.

However, their attack, in which Hoddle looked out of place and ill at ease, lacks a cutting edge. In the 26th minute, for instance, Lee put the ball out for a throw-in on the far side of the pitch after Perryman's pass and Young's slip left him in the clear.

It was in the 38th minute that Brady first made his considerable presence felt. His crossfield pass to the right wing

was measured to perfection and **SUNDERLAND** cut past Holmes to thump the ball into the net, this time off Kendall's hands, and the underside of the bar.

In the first 11 minutes of the second half Arsenal almost scored three more goals. Sunderland headed against the underside of the bar, Kendall blocked a far-post header by the completely unmarked Price and Sunderland very nearly beat the young Spurs keeper with a wickedly swerving shot.

Nothing would go right for Ardiles, as we saw on the hour, when he stabbed Lee's centre high over the bar in what was to be Spurs only really dangerous attack of the second half. Two minutes later it was 3-0 to Arsenal as **STAPLETON**, as unmarked at the far post as Price had been, headed in the glorious centre with which Brady climaxed a clever dribble along the by-line.

Full of confidence now, **BRADY** took the ball off Taylor at the corner of Spurs penalty area and lashed it into the far corner of the net on the rise three minutes after providing Stapleton with his goal. In the circumstances Brady's victory jig in front of the Arsenal end was perfectly understandable.

Brady's goal prompted Spurs to take off Pratt, pull Hoddle back into midfield and bring on their substitute, Jones, a striker. It was too little, too late, though.

Eight minutes from the end Stapleton flicked the ball on and **SUNDERLAND**, going wide to the left, steered his shot accurately into the far corner of Spurs' bulging net.

Liam Brady (top) celebrates after netting Arsenal's fourth goal, and Alan Sunderland makes it 5-0 in completing a hat-trick.

'DERBY' STAR **Liam Brady** — he stamped his class all over the proceedings and scored a memorable goal in front of the TV cameras.

84

ARSENAL 1
Stapleton

TOTTENHAM HOTSPUR 0

Tuesday 10th April 1979

Football League Division One

Highbury

Attendance 53,896

Arsenal

Tottenham Hotspur

Manager **Terry Neill**

Manager **Keith Burkinshaw**

Pat JENNINGS	1	Barry DAINES
Pat RICE	2	Terry NAYLOR
Steve WALFORD	3	Don McALLISTER
Brian TALBOT	4	Jimmy HOLMES
David O'LEARY	5	Paul MILLER
Willie YOUNG	6	Steve PERRYMAN
Liam BRADY	7	John PRATT
Alan SUNDERLAND	8	Peter TAYLOR
Frank STAPLETON	9	Chris JONES
David PRICE	10	Glenn HODDLE
Graham RIX	11	Ricky VILLA
Steve GATTING	12	Colin LEE

Referee **Mr T D Spencer** (Salisbury)

BACKGROUND

Re-inforced by the signing of Brian Talbot, Arsenal got as high as second in the League by the middle of February but they were never going to catch Bob Paisley's great Liverpool team. Arctic conditions decimated the fixture list but Highbury's undersoil heating allowed them to continue playing, climbing the table but leaving their rivals with games in hand. Interest in the UEFA Cup had been ended by Red Star Belgrade in the third round but there was still the FA Cup. After the poor performance against Ipswich in the 1978 Final, Neill had promised Arsenal would be back and the determination to fulfill that promise was shown in the five games it took to dispose of Third Division Sheffield Wednesday in the third round. Notts County, Nottingham Forest and Southampton proved somewhat easier to overcome and nine days before Spurs' visit Neill's promise was kept with the semi-final defeat of Wolves. At one stage Spurs had looked like joining Arsenal at Wembley but Manchester United ended that dream in the sixth round. In the League Spurs could not climb above mid-table. The two Argentinians were still drawing the crowds, particularly Ardiles who had settled to the English game somewhat quicker than Villa, but Spurs' pattern of play had to be changed to accommodate them and the other players were finding it hard to adapt to a more continental style. On the back of three straight defeats Barry Daines was recalled, Ardiles rested and Paul Miller called up for his debut.

BEFORE THE GAME

	P	W	D	L	F	A	Pts
Arsenal	34	15	10	9	51	36	40
Spurs	34	11	11	12	37	51	33

Frank Stapleton heads Arsenal's late, late winner.

Robert Oxby in 'The Daily Telegraph' under...

STAPLETON SEALS IT FOR ARSENAL IN INJURY TIME

Arsenal completed the double over Spurs, their North London rivals, with a goal by Frank Stapleton in injury time at Highbury last night. Earlier in the season, the FA Cup finalists had won 5-0 at White Hart Lane.

The last-gasp goal was a tragedy for Paul Miller, 19, who was given his League debut for Spurs at centre-back. The youngster played superbly until he misjudged an inswinging cross from Brady and **STAPLETON** headed home.

The introduction of Miller, who clearly has a great future, was only one example of the boldness of Keith Burkinshaw, Spurs' manager, who dropped Ardiles, the Argentinian international, because he was "stale".

Mr Burkinshaw also brought back Daines in goal for the first time in nearly six months, and he played remarkably well, bringing stability to the defence and making one brilliant save from Stapleton in the first half.

DAINES OVERSHADOWED

For much of Daines' career at White Hart Lane he was deputy to Pat Jennings, and last night the Northern Ireland international again overshadowed him when it seemed that Spurs, who had made a slow start, would run riot in the second half.

The huge crowd of 54,051 helped to produce a tense atmosphere which affected the players, and the first half was one of the least memorable I have seen.

There was far too much frantic running, and centres whizzed across each goalmouth without much accuracy or intention of finding their men.

The first half ended, however, with Naylor being shown the yellow card for bringing down Stapleton, who had just beaten him. From the free-kick on the edge of the penalty area, Daines saved magnificently from Brady.

The second half was completely different, with Spurs at last finding some cohesion in attack, and Hoddle, Taylor and Villa thrusting through.

A fierce Holmes shot was saved by Jennings, and when Hoddle sent Taylor racing through, the ball skimmed wide of the advancing Jennings and a post.

The Arsenal goalkeeper was at full stretch when he saved an effort from Taylor with his foot and, later in the half, he dived bravely at the feet of Villa.

Towards the end, however, Arsenal took control, but even they could not have expected that late winner - which delighted their supporters and infuriated the visiting Tottenham fans.

Paul Miller had performed immaculately on his debut until his last minute stumble let in Frank Stapleton for the winner.

AT THE SEASON'S END

		P	W	D	L	F	A	Pts
7th	Arsenal	42	17	14	11	61	48	48
11th	Spurs	42	13	15	14	48	61	41

THAT WAS THEN...

★ The Arsenal programme, now 20p for 16 pages, advertised trips to the following Saturday's away game at West Bromwich Albion at £4.00 by rail and £3.40 by coach.

Peter Taylor (left) shoots past Pat Jennings but wide of goal as Arsenal's Steve Walford and Brian Talbot chase back.

85

ARSENAL 1
Sunderland
TOTTENHAM HOTSPUR 0

Wednesday 26th December 1979

Football League Division One

Highbury

Attendance 44,560

Arsenal

Tottenham Hotspur

Manager
Terry Neill

Manager
Keith Burkinshaw

Pat JENNINGS	1	Milija ALEKSIC
John DEVINE	2	Chris HUGHTON
Pat RICE	3	Don McALLISTER
Brian TALBOT	4	Terry YORATH
David O'LEARY	5	Gordon SMITH
Willie YOUNG	6	Steve PERRYMAN
Liam BRADY	7	Ossie ARDILES
Alan SUNDERLAND	8	Chris JONES
Frank STAPLETON	9	Gerry ARMSTRONG*
John HOLLINS	10	Glenn HODDLE
Graham RIX	11	John PRATT
Steve WALFORD	12	Tony GALVIN (9)

*Referee **Mr B H Daniels** (Brentwood)*

BACKGROUND

Although forced to call up the last survivor of the "Double" winning team, Pat Rice, in place of Sammy Nelson for this Boxing Day 11.30 kick off, Arsenal were strengthened by the return of Willie Young. Third in the table, they were five points behind the leaders but with just two or three more goals would have been right up with Liverpool and Manchester United. Too many games had been drawn, four in the last five, ten all together, and in six of those Arsenal had failed to score. A couple of weeks earlier their interest in the League Cup had been brought to an end by their old foe, Swindon, but they were still in the European Cup-Winners' Cup having beaten Fenerbahce and Magdeburg. Despite signing Terry Yorath to add bite in midfield Spurs had started the season with three defeats. John Lacy, Gordon Smith, Ricky Villa and young Mark Falco were all dropped, Chris Hughton given his chance, Gerry Armstrong and Paul Miller recalled. Two defeats in 14 games followed and Spurs got to within two points of leaders Liverpool before defeat at Anfield started a run of only one win in six games, culminating in defeats at home to Aston Villa and away to Ipswich.

BEFORE THE GAME

	P	W	D	L	F	A	Pts
Arsenal	21	7	10	4	26	16	24
Spurs	21	8	5	8	28	34	21

Gerry Armstrong gets past Willie Young's lunge.

A HUNGRY SUNDERLAND DINES OUT ON A MORSEL

Keith Burkinshaw... "If only we could score goals".

A feast was expected yesterday morning but the feeding of the 48,000 fell far short of fulfilment. Although the hosts, Arsenal, were offered a large morsel before noon, the fare thereafter consisted of crumbs scattered across an untidy table. Arsenal will be content with the result, a 1-0 victory over their north London rivals, Tottenham Hotspur, but not with the way it was achieved.

The morsel was brought in on a platter after 15 minutes. Rix danced over the flailing legs of Hughton and curved an early, delicate cross into the wind. As it hung teasingly in the air, Aleksic and McAllister were tempted to clear. Both attempts failed and **SUNDERLAND** hungrily cleared up the mess. Even the decisive goal was scrappy.

The conditions did not help. Heavy going does not suit the likes of Brady, Rix, Hoddle and Ardiles. The wind, however, did help Spurs to push forward and create three chances for Pratt, Smith and Jones before the interval. Jennings, or inaccuracy, prevented them from equalising.

Aleksic, in turn, also prevented Arsenal from stretching their lead. First he used an unorthodox method - an unlikely combination of head, chest and shoulders - to clear from Sunderland. Then, in more orthodox fashion, he caught Talbot's close-range header after Brady had curled in another cross.

Glenn Hoddle is the centre of attention for Graham Rix and John Devine.

Like the canopy above, there were only fleeting glimpses of brightness in the second half. Most was grey matter. Indeed the highlight came near the end when Pratt volleyed towards the clock and struck some railings. When Jennings retrieved the ball, it was as flat as the contest.

Spurs brought Perryman forward to add strength, if only in numbers, to their front line. They threatened once when Ardiles, again trying to flit over the mud, was tackled heavily in the penalty area. Furious appeals were raised, not least by Ardiles himself, but Mr Daniels waved them all away. He might have waved goodbye as well for, like a man dying of old age, the game drifted to a quiet, peaceful end.

As Terry Neill, Arsenal's manager, said afterwards: anticipation is often bigger than the event himself. "Take Christmas presents". he said. "I didn't get my Lambourghini. I did get some handkerchiefs, though, initialled with the letter T. At least my mother got that right. But, seriously, both teams can play better than that".

They will have to if they hold any hopes of catching the two above them. An ominous gap is opening up and Arsenal's next visit is to Old Trafford on Saturday. No one looks forward to going there. For Spurs there was no joy over the holiday period but at least their next two games are at home. As their manager Keith Burkinshaw, said: "If only we could score some goals....".

86

TOTTENHAM HOTSPUR 1
Jones

ARSENAL 2
Vaessen, Sunderland

Tottenham Hotspur		Arsenal
Manager **Keith Burkinshaw**		Manager **Terry Neill**

Barry DAINES	1	Paul BARRON
Paul MILLER	2	Pat RICE
Chris HUGHTON	3	Steve WALFORD
Terry YORATH	4	Brian TALBOT
Don McALLISTER	5	David O'LEARY
Steve PERRYMAN	6	Willie YOUNG
Ossie ARDILES	7	Liam BRADY*
Chris JONES	8	John DEVINE
John PRATT	9	Paul VAESSEN
Glenn HODDLE	10	John HOLLINS
Tony GALVIN	11	Paul DAVIS
Gerry ARMSTRONG	12	Alan SUNDERLAND (7)

Referee **Mr R Toseland** (Market Harborough)

BACKGROUND

Beaten by Manchester United in the sixth round of the FA Cup a month earlier, Spurs' season had effectively come to an end and by the Easter fixtures it was just a case of playing out the season and looking to the future. Two days earlier Tony Galvin had been given only his second League outing and had proved the star of the show as Spurs won at Wolves. For Arsenal the situation was exactly the opposite. Well up with the leaders, although no threat to Liverpool's twelfth League title, they were just two days away from the first leg of their European Cup-Winners' Cup semi-final with Juventus and at the weekend were due to meet Liverpool in what was to become a marathon, four game FA Cup semi-final. With such a heavy schedule Terry Neill made full use of his squad, resting Pat Jennings, David Price, Graham Rix, Frank Stapleton and Alan Sunderland and replacing them with Paul Barron, Pat Rice, John Hollins, Paul Vaessen and debutant Paul Davis.

BEFORE THE GAME

	P	W	D	L	F	A	Pts
Arsenal	35	15	13	7	45	27	43
Spurs	36	14	8	14	45	53	36

AT THE SEASON'S END

		P	W	D	L	F	A	Pts
4th	Arsenal	42	18	16	8	52	36	52
14th	Spurs	42	15	10	17	52	62	40

Above: Paul Vaessen headed Arsenal's first goal.
Left: Chris Jones heads Tottenham's consolation.

Spurs No.2 Paul Miller outjumps Arsenal's Paul Vaessen (No.9) and Willie Young (hidden) as the home side launch an attack.

Norman Fox, Football Correspondent of 'The Times' reported...

Arsenal have enough in reserve to handle Tottenham

Being preoccupied with tomorrow's European Cup Winners' Cup tie against Juventus and next Saturday's FA Cup semi-final, Arsenal risked defeat and possible admonishment from the Football League by fielding an "under-strength" team at White Hart Lane yesterday. They then destroyed all the evidence by winning with two late goals.

They gave nothing away by their action. The visiting Juventus team and their manager would have gained little instruction and Arsenal lost nothing in league or local status. Such selectional action may have altered their tactics and not improved the attractiveness of the game, but Tottenham, least of all, had reason for complaint.

Arsenal's reluctance to play yesterday had met with no sympathy from Spurs, so it was not surprising that they began with six reserves including a complete newcomer, Davis, a 17-year old who strolled into the game with almost veteran assurance. Tottenham, however, did not make it difficult for anyone.

Arsenal were liberally staffed with midfield players, successfully anticipating that this was where they could contain the game. Rice also found himself there, Devine having retained the right back position, and with

Chris Jones is watched by David O'Leary.

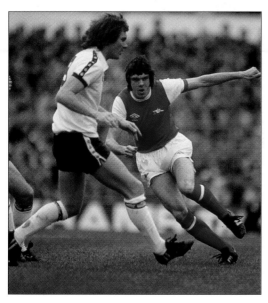

Talbot, Hollins and Davis also operating behind Brady and Vaessen, the numerical advantage overwhelmed Tottenham.

Brady was allowed to leave the game early in the second half and Sunderland replaced him. By this time Arsenal were probably satisfied that they had little to fear from a lethargic Tottenham side which eventually capitulated and were never a cohesive force.

From beginning to end Arsenal created the distinct opportunities, but especially in the end, scoring their first goal after 84 minutes, and their second two minutes later. Tottenham made token apology with their goal another two minutes later at a time when spectator attention was being diverted to terrace violence of frightening proportions as three Molotov cocktails burst against a wall beneath packed crowds.

Most of the action, wanted and otherwise, occurred in these last six minutes. Until then the game followed a course that was no more exciting than an Easter Day trip to the Dartford tunnel.

Arsenal would have been satisfied with a point but when O'Leary risked leaving his defence to meet Talbot's corner his volley across goal was headed in by **VAESSEN**. As Tottenham tried to move forward to salvage local pride, **SUNDERLAND** took advantage of the space they left and when seeing Daines off his line, lobbed a 30-yard shot over his head. The fact that **JONES** headed in an attractive goal from Hoddle's cross two minutes from time was not to make Tottenham's defeat any more palatable for those of their supporters who prefer to keep ahead of the Joneses.

87

ARSENAL 2
Price, Stapleton

TOTTENHAM HOTSPUR 0

Saturday 30th August 1980

Football League Division One

Highbury

Attendance 54,045

Arsenal

Tottenham Hotspur

Manager
Terry Neill

Manager
Keith Burkinshaw

Pat **JENNINGS**	1	Mark **KENDALL**
John **DEVINE**	2	Gordon **SMITH***
Kenny **SANSOM**	3	Chris **HUGHTON**
Brian **TALBOT**	4	Terry **YORATH**
David **O'LEARY**	5	John **LACY**
Willie **YOUNG**	6	Steve **PERRYMAN**
John **HOLLINS**	7	Ossie **ARDILES**
Alan **SUNDERLAND**	8	Steve **ARCHIBALD**
Frank **STAPLETON**	9	Ricky **VILLA**
David **PRICE**	10	Glenn **HODDLE**
Graham **RIX**	11	Garth **CROOKS**
Paul **VAESSEN**	12	Peter **TAYLOR (2)**

Referee **Mr C Thomas** *(Porthcawl)*

BACKGROUND

Arsenal went into the last ten days of the 1979-80 season with the prospect of picking up two major trophies. They ended with neither, beaten by West Ham in the FA Cup Final and then losing on penalties to Valencia in the Cup-Winners' Cup Final. The season was not over though, two League games left and four points would at least qualify them for the UEFA Cup. They beat Wolves but ended the season with a miserable display at Middlesbrough where they were lost 0-5. As if that was not enough Liam Brady, along with Glenn Hoddle the most gifted midfielder of his generation, was off to Juventus, a fact known for almost a year but none the easier to accept. The Italians got an absolute bargain. £600,000, the maximum under UEFA rules for a player at the end of his contract, not even half the fee paid for Clive Allen, the QPR striker exchanged for Kenny Sansom only two months after signing. The loss of Brady was painfully obvious at the start of the new campaign; four games, four goals and all of them from Stapleton. For two years Ardiles and Hoddle had dazzled in midfield but Spurs did not have the strikers to take full advantage of their talents. Burkinshaw remedied that with the summer signings of Steve Archibald from Aberdeen and Garth Crooks from Stoke. An investment of almost £1.5m paid immediate dividends with victories over Nottingham Forest and Crystal Palace and a draw with Brighton putting Spurs top of the table.

BEFORE THE GAME

	P	W	D	L	F	A	Pts
Arsenal	3	1	1	1	3	4	3
Spurs	3	2	1	0	8	5	5

Garth Crooks (left) and Kenny Sansom – two newcomers to the North London 'derby'.

"It is becoming embarrassing now for Tottenham to play Arsenal. They have not beaten their neighbours in a League game for five years – and the blushes get even more red when Pat Jennings is mentioned.

Jennings, the goalkeeper Spurs virtually gave away to Arsenal, turned in another acrobatic display to rob his old club of any reward for their first-half superiority.

Mark Kendall, one of the many goalkeepers Spurs have tried since Jennings left, allowed his inexperience to shine through again with with two second-half errors, and it was all over."
– 'Sunday People'.

The Jennings and Rix show

Alan Sunderland (right) congratulates Frank Stapleton on his goal.

A local derby is possibly the best place to test early season aspirations, and Tottenham's were shredded. Their defensive frailty was their undoing against an Arsenal side they had outplayed emphatically for an exciting half an hour.

The irony, not lost on Spurs' supporters, was that it was their former goalkeeper Jennings who stopped Arsenal disappearing down the plughole, in a manner that must have made his former employers curse the day that someone decided he was past it. But although the day was Arsenal's, the quality of much of Spurs' forward play was such that the season might still be theirs.

The defensive culpability which cost Spurs their unbeaten League record was collective but neither the most recent of Jennings' successors, Kendall, nor the ambling Lacy reeked of the kind of competence it's nice to have behind you when the advance troops are busy laying siege. Within five minutes Kendall had misjudged a Rix cross without punishment but the laconic Arsenal forward turned the game with two movements which destroyed the Spurs defence.

Rix's emergence as the day's decisive influence was far from predictable in a first half in which he had loitered elegantly on the edge of the action, standing aside as Highbury's latest love object, Sansom, dribbled down the left flank, and Hollins' venerable lungs and legs struggled to fulfil the midfield role vacated by Brady - a task that most would think more within Rix's scope. Ardiles and Hoddle had kneaded the flow in Tottenham's favour, and the last twenty minutes of the first half became Jennings versus the rest.

A memorable series of saves started in the twenty-ninth minute when Villa brushed past Hollins, kneed the ball casually into Crooks' stride, and the well-struck shot was saved one-handed, at full stretch on the ground. Archibald, whose readiness to go where the going was toughest gave O'Leary a troubled spell, had a volley stopped by Jennings four minutes later, and the Scot's subtle touch to Crooks had the goalkeeper performing miracles again. But even Jennings should have been helpless seconds before half-time when Archibald steadied himself to pick his spot after the ball dropped to him from the goalkeeper's instinctive beating out of a Villa volley. But the shot, for all the deliberation, flew wide.

Perhaps Spurs were still congratulating themselves for this purple patch as the second half kicked off, for in seconds Rix's cross was allowed to travel the width of the penalty area to an unmarked **PRICE**, whose stooping header beat Kendall. Fifteen minutes later Rix robbed Hughton in the Arsenal half, and casually lofted a 40-yard pass into **STAPLETON**'s path, as the striker left Lacy standing for pace, and speed of reaction. Kendall came, hesitated, and was lobbed for the second goal.

Tottenham's willingness to go forward after falling to two sucker punches was confirmed when Taylor replaced the full-back Smith, and the substitute came closest to scoring six minutes from the end; but Devine cleared after the intimidating obstacle of Jennings' presence had been beaten for once. Fittingly, the final seconds belonged to the afternoon's heroes - Jennings cooling down a dangerous Taylor cross in classic style, and Rix shaving the bewildered Kendall's left-hand post with a teasing swerver.

TOTTENHAM HOTSPUR 2
Archibald 2

ARSENAL 0

Tottenham Hotspur   *Arsenal*

Manager
Keith Burkinshaw

Manager
Terry Neill

Barry DAINES	1	**Pat JENNINGS**
Don McALLISTER	2	**John DEVINE**
Paul MILLER	3	**Kenny SANSOM**
Graham ROBERTS	4	**Brian McDERMOTT**
John LACY*	5	**Steve WALFORD**
Steve PERRYMAN	6	**Willie YOUNG**
Garry BROOKE	7	**John HOLLINS**
Steve ARCHIBALD	8	**Alan SUNDERLAND**
Tony GALVIN	9	**Frank STAPLETON**
Glenn HODDLE	10	**Steve GATTING**
Garth CROOKS	11	**Graham RIX**
Terry YORATH (5)	12	Paul DAVIS

*Referee **Mr L C Shapter** (Torquay)*

BACKGROUND

The loss of their unbeaten record at Highbury knocked Spurs back. Five League games without a win and only one goal was not title winning form but then Spurs were not a title winning team. Frustratingly inconsistent their home form was good enough, only one defeat, but on their travels they were always vulnerable. As the Archibald-Crooks partnership developed scoring was no longer a problem but despite Keith Burkinshaw's shuffling of his men they remained suspect in defence and could not get back into the title race. There was always the FA Cup though and just ten days earlier they had embarked on what was to prove another successful march to Wembley with a third round replay defeat of Queens Park Rangers. They might have been strengthened by the return of Ardiles, released to play for Argentina in the Gold Cup, but he was omitted as the penalty for returning late from Uruguay. Knocked out of the League Cup by Spurs, Paul Vaessen's last minute winner at Everton a week earlier; sweet revenge for the Goodison club's FA Cup victory seven days before, had taken Arsenal to fourth in the League. Too often forced to settle for one point when two were needed, they had slipped behind pacesetters Ipswich and Aston Villa but a good run would soon put them back in contention. Reinforced by the return of Graham Rix and Alan Sunderland, Vaessen was left out and Paul Davis demoted to the substitutes' bench.

BEFORE THE GAME

	P	W	D	L	F	A	Pts
Arsenal	26	11	10	5	39	29	43
Spurs	26	10	8	8	50	47	28

Steve Archibald fires Spurs into a sixth minute lead.

Arsenal on short time

Brian Glanville in 'The Sunday Times' under...

THAT WAS THEN...

★ Rather surprisingly, the gate for this 'derby' was smaller than that for a game played between non-league Enfield and Barnsley in an FA Cup replay at White Hart Lane less than three weeks later when an attendance of 35,244 was recorded!

TO ERR is human: to forgive... Devine! Only a minute remained of a game in which Arsenal, strangely languid and a goal down at half-time, had utterly dominated the second half without managing to break a Tottenham defence in which Daines had played heroically.

Suddenly, as so often and perversely happens in football, Tottenham broke away. Hoddle, always capable of the occasional, remarkable thing, neatly found Archibald, scorer of the opening goal after five minutes. Devine, Arsenal's blond Irish right back, showing slight signs of strain after a previously excellent half, made a sad hash of his attempted back pass to Jennings and **ARCHIBALD**, that snapper-up of unconsidered trifles, tucked the ball away inside the right hand post.

It was a cruel blow to an Arsenal team which would not have been flattered had it won; though to tell the truth, there was not at this stage any real prospect of their forcing a draw.

Perhaps, for Arsenal, the moral of the afternoon was that one should play for 90 minutes rather than 45. In the first half they were slightly too bad to be true. Tottenham caught them with Archibald's early goal, a very good one indeed after the alert Daines had kicked clear in turn from Stapleton and Sunderland; but Arsenal were scarcely brought to life. It wasn't until after the interval, when stern, cogent words must have been said to them, that they found, at last, a rhythm and simply played Tottenham off the park.

Pat Jennings saves bravely at the feet of Spurs No.2 Don McAllister.

That goal came thanks in no small measure to the 20-year old Spurs newcomer, Brooke. Bravely, he challenged Walford and won a bouncing ball, which he then gave to Hoddle. Hoddle studiously moved it to the quicksilver **ARCHIBALD**, whose beautifully angled shot from the right gave Jennings not a hope in a hundred.

A cunning and accomplished free kick by Hoddle completely deceived Arsenal's defence, and almost enabled McAllister to beat Jennings; but there was pathetically little else to remember in that drab first half.

Spurs have made a number of interesting changes; and a further change was thrust on them when Lacy dropped out with a pulled hamstring, Perryman taking his place in defence, Yorath coming into midfield. Brooke, keeping his place in preference to the late home Ardiles, is full of energy and skill, Roberts makes a competent left back, but Galvin did not repeat yesterday his recent, lively form on the left wing.

Part of his problem is that he is clearly one of nature's right-footers; and that right foot delivered Tottenham's only real shot of the second half, before Archibald's, when he drifted across Devine and struck a drive which Jennings held at the near post.

Arsenal's second half was a catalogue of near misses. When Stapleton, quiet in the first half but rampant in the second, beat Miller out on the left and crossed, Roberts blocked Gatting's shot and Yorath just beat McDermott to the loose ball. Stapleton played a ball to the incisive Sunderland, whose drive Daines kept out with his legs; later, he saved a thundering shot by Gatting and a header by Stapleton from Rix's cross.

By now Rix was immensely more influential in midfield than ever he had been before half-time.

Ironically, one of Daines' best saves did not count. When Hollins struck a free kick rolled to him by Rix, Daines turned it splendidly over the bar, only for the kick to be retaken. Not that this would much have worried Daines; or Tottenham.

AT THE SEASON'S END

		P	W	D	L	F	A	Pts
3rd	Arsenal	42	19	15	8	61	45	53
10th	Spurs	42	14	15	13	70	68	43

'DERBY' STAR

Steve Archibald – his 'derby double' took his tally to 19 in his first season in England. Manager Keith Burkinshaw boasted "I have no doubt he will end up as the First Division's top marksman."

89

TOTTENHAM HOTSPUR 2
Archibald, Hughton

ARSENAL 2
Sunderland 2

Monday 29th March 1982

Football League Division One

White Hart Lane

Attendance 40,940

Tottenham Hotspur

Arsenal

Manager
Keith Burkinshaw

Manager
Terry Neill

Ray CLEMENCE	1	George WOOD
Chris HUGHTON	2	John HOLLINS
Graham ROBERTS	3	Kenny SANSOM
Paul PRICE	4	Brian TALBOT
Ricky VILLA	5	David O'LEARY
Steve PERRYMAN	6	Chris WHYTE
Ossie ARDILES	7	Raphael MEADE
Steve ARCHIBALD	8	Alan SUNDERLAND
Tony GALVIN	9	Paul DAVIS*
Glenn HODDLE	10	Stewart ROBSON
Micky HAZARD	11	Graham RIX
Paul MILLER	12	Peter NICHOLAS (9)

Referee **Mr R Lewis** (Great Bookham)

BACKGROUND

Postponed in late December because of arctic weather conditions, about the last thing Spurs needed was to meet an Arsenal side not only battling with them near the top of the table but also looking to gain revenge for their third round FA Cup defeat at White Hart Lane. Five days later Spurs were due to continue their defence of the FA Cup with a Villa Park semi-final against Leicester and just four days after that Barcelona would visit for the first leg of their European Cup-Winners' Cup semi-final. Such was the price of success. Challenging for four trophies, Spurs had played 19 games in just ten weeks including extra-time as they lost to Liverpool in the League (Milk) Cup Final and although eight points adrift, the first season of three-points-for-a-win meant they had more than enough games in hand to overhaul leaders, Southampton. Paul Miller was rested, Glenn Hoddle and Micky Hazard fit to return after the weekend defeat at West Brom but Garth Crooks was still missing. In contract, Arsenal's one remaining hope of success lay with the League. Liverpool had knocked them out of the League Cup, Spartak Moscow the UEFA Cup. Early season form had been erratic but results improved as veteran John Hollins, signed from QPR, settled in and Chris Whyte replaced Willie Young. Pat Jennings had been out since injured in the FA Cup-tie but Arsenal's weakness was up front. Brian McDermott, Ray Hankin, John Hawley, Paul Vaessen, Raphael Meade and Paul Gorman had all been given the chance, but none of them came near to replacing Frank Stapleton who had departed for Manchester United during the summer. Only once had they managed to score more than two goals in a match, and that two days earlier as they beat Aston Villa 4-3 at Highbury.

BEFORE THE GAME

	P	W	D	L	F	A	Pts
Arsenal	31	15	8	8	29	24	53
Spurs	27	15	5	7	45	26	50

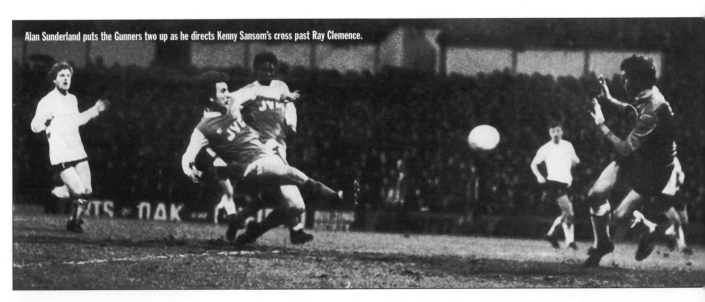

Alan Sunderland puts the Gunners two up as he directs Kenny Sansom's cross past Ray Clemence.

Sunderland hero and villain of an epic night

Tottenham's Graham Roberts is crowded out by Arsenal trio Chris Whyte, Graham Rix and David O'Leary.

For the second time in three days Arsenal were involved in an epic match. Last night they threatened to lay claim to the first division title on the ground where they clinched the championship 11 years ago. But Tottenham Hotspur, displaying stirring resilience, came back from a two-goal deficit to share the points in a dramatic finish that in the end improved the hopes of neither club.

Encouraged by their free scoring victory over Aston Villa last Saturday, Arsenal wore a cloak of confidence rather than the threadbare garment that has covered them for most of the season, particularly in the penalty area. In midfield, they now have a neat mixture of skill, in Rix and Davis, and determination, in Talbot and the impressive youngster, Robson. Sunderland, as usual, foraged ahead more or less on his own.

They took the lead after 25 minutes. Sansom intercepted a pass from Hoddle and invited Sunderland to free Davis on the left. With Miller dropped and absent for the first time this season, the new central partnership of Roberts and Price was nowhere to be seen for the cross that **SUNDERLAND** headed home.

Clemence saved superbly from O'Leary, a glancing header from Rix's free kick, before being beaten for the second time on the stroke of the interval. Ardiles this time was forced into yielding possession. Sansom took advantage again and crossed for **SUNDERLAND** to score once more with a firm volley from close range.

So at half-time Arsenal stood third on the table, and seemingly on the threshold of a glorious challenge. For an hour their covering was supreme. Each Tottenham move was wrapped securely in chains, each Tottenham player was tied to at least one red shadow. Like escapologists unaccustomed to such tight restrictions, Spurs struggled to break free.

Referee Ray Lewis books David O'Leary.

Galvin signalled the start of their recovery, shooting into the side netting, and then against Wood's legs. Yet, it was perfectly placed for **ARCHIBALD** and his drive could scarcely have been more emphatic. Ten minutes later, Spurs were level, Hazard's cross bouncing off the heads of Galvin and Roberts for **HUGHTON** to squeeze in at the far post.

Nicholas came on for Davis with ten minutes remaining but Sunderland and Hughton were soon to depart, sent off after scuffling on the touchline. The referee, seemingly now obsessed with discipline, then took the names of Hazard, O'Leary, Hollins and Robson, for leaving the pitch without permission.

At least Ardiles did not leave his home ground on the losing side before his return to Argentina, and World Cup training. Indeed, but for Wood's fine save from Galvin in the final minute, Spurs might have won.

90

ARSENAL 1
Hawley

TOTTENHAM HOTSPUR 3
Hazard, Crooks 2

Arsenal

Manager
Terry Neill

Tottenham Hotspur

Manager
Keith Burkinshaw

Arsenal		Tottenham Hotspur
George WOOD	1	Ray CLEMENCE
John HOLLINS	2	Graham ROBERTS
Kenny SANSOM	3	Paul MILLER
Brian TALBOT	4	Paul PRICE
David O'LEARY	5	Micky HAZARD
Chris WHYTE	6	Steve PERRYMAN
Raphael MEADE	7	Ricky VILLA
John HAWLEY	8	Chris JONES
Peter NICHOLAS	9	Tony GALVIN
Stewart ROBSON*	10	Glenn HODDLE
Graham RIX	11	Garth CROOKS
Brian McDERMOTT (10)	12	Garry BROOKE

Referee **Mr C Thomas** *(Porthcawl)*

BACKGROUND

Arsenal effectively dropped out of the title race with a draw at Wolves and defeat at Brighton following their visit to White Hart Lane but Highbury's biggest crowd of the season still assembled for this Easter Monday fixture. With Alan Sunderland suspended after his sending off two weeks earlier John Hawley was called up and while Graham Rix was fit to return, Peter Nicholas continued in midfield because of injury to Paul Davis. Spurs had continued their assault on an unprecedented treble despite Ossie Ardiles returning home to help Argentina prepare for their defence of the World Cup and Ricky Villa being left out of the FA Cup semi-final after the Falkland Islands invasion. Garth Crooks had returned to help book Spurs' place at Wembley and Villa was back in the team for a 1-0 defeat of Ipswich that kept Spurs close on the heels of Liverpool, who had now moved to the top of the table. Only in the Cup-Winners' Cup had Spurs faltered, a one all draw leaving Barcelona favourites with the second leg in their Nou Camp Stadium. Paul Price stood in for the suspended Chris Hughton and Chris Jones got a rare first team outing with Steve Archibald injured.

BEFORE THE GAME

	P	W	D	L	F	A	Pts
Arsenal	34	15	10	9	33	29	55
Spurs	29	16	6	7	48	28	54

AT THE SEASON'S END

		P	W	D	L	F	A	Pts
4th	Spurs	42	20	11	11	67	48	71
5th	Arsenal	42	20	11	11	48	37	71

Garth Crooks heads his first as goalkeeper George Wood (left of the picture) is stranded.

Sheer joy for goalscorer Garth Crooks and the Spurs fans packed behind the goal.

Gerald Sinstadt reported for **'The Times'** *on…*

SPURS ON COURSE TO SCALE THAT MOUNTAIN

'DERBY' STAR Ricky Villa
— vigorously booed fom the North Bank, the Argentinian used this as his incentive for a fine performance of strength and skill, setting up Spurs' first and third goals.

Whatever scepticism there may be in other parts, there was no sign in north London yesterday that Tottenham Hotspur's many-sided ambitions will be self-defeating.

Spurs beat Arsenal at Highbury with a light-footed, imaginative display that gave no hint of a team bewildered by too many targets or burdened by too many fixtures. Arsenal themselves played a full part in an entertaining derby match that was won, as their manager, Terry Neill, readily conceded afterwards, by the better team.

Tomorrow Tottenham will be back at White Hart Lane to receive Sunderland. Three more points then and even Merseyside may cast an anxious eye towards the capital. The task still looks formidable, but the way it is being tackled is undeniably impressive.

Arsenal made at least as many chances as their opponents, but it was Tottenham who contributed the genuine invention and menacing thrusts.

Hoddle, once again in the form that raises World Cup hopes, was at the heart of so much that was both graceful and thrilling. Late in the game, he flicked up the ball with his right foot and wafted a pass with the outside of his left with a nonchalance that would have earned an ovation in Brazil.

Villa was looking for his touch early in the game, but when he found it, in the tenth minute, the outcome was a stunning goal. The Argentine wrong-footed Arsenal's defence with a delicate pass that gave Hazard a couple of yards of room. A quick shuffle across the edge of the penalty area opened the shooting angle and **HAZARD**'s left-foot drive flew past Wood.

Arsenal's response was typical. Rix began to produce diagonal passes that Hoddle would not have been ashamed to claim. Talbot, Nicholas and Robson rolled up their sleeves to add effort and stamina, but the finishing touch was lacking. Arsenal's most dangerous moment of the half followed a Meade header that Clemence fumbled. Only some quick closing of ranks prevented an equaliser.

From less possession, though, it was Tottenham who threatened most. Hazard struck a half volley just wide, Hoddle fired in a fierce shot that struck Wood, off balance and stumbling, somehow manage to kick away. Then Hazard's left foot, letting fly from 25 yards, extracted from Wood the best save of the match.

The quality of the second half was equally admirable, with the bonus of three goals in five minutes. Hazard showed a shrewd head in running through an advancing offside trap, and even though **CROOKS'** position was doubtful as he took the pass to score, it was a deserved goal. Within seconds **HAWLEY** reduced the margin with a thumping first-time shot from Rix's pass.

Spurs, however, were not to be denied. Roberts opened Arsenal's right flank, Galvin and Villa carried the move sweetly across the penalty area, and **CROOKS** scored his second goal.

Hoddle and Sansom both had good shots well saved, and just as it seemed the game might dwindle to a quiet close, a woman did for Highbury what Erika Roe did for Twickenham. It was not an afternoon when anyone could have felt justified in asking for his money back.

91

ARSENAL 2
Sunderland, Woodcock

TOTTENHAM HOTSPUR 0

Arsenal

Tottenham Hotspur

Manager
Terry Neill

Manager
Keith Burkinshaw

Arsenal		Tottenham Hotspur
Pat JENNINGS	1	Ray CLEMENCE
John HOLLINS	2	Chris HUGHTON
Kenny SANSOM	3	Gary O'REILLY
Brian TALBOT	4	Graham ROBERTS
David O'LEARY	5	Micky HAZARD
Stewart ROBSON	6	Steve PERRYMAN
Paul DAVIS	7	Gary MABBUTT
Alan SUNDERLAND	8	Steve ARCHIBALD
Peter NICHOLAS	9	Tony GALVIN*
Tony WOODCOCK	10	Glenn HODDLE
Graham RIX	11	Garth CROOKS
Lee CHAPMAN	12	Garry BROOKE (9)

*Referee **Mr L C Shapter** (Torquay)*

Linking arms are
Peter Nicholas and
Micky Hazard.

BACKGROUND

Despite four victories and a draw in the last five matches of the 1981-82 season allowing Arsenal to finish in fifth place, Terry Neill knew he had to do something about Arsenal's chronic lack of a regular goalscorer. In the summer he spent £500,000 each on Lee Chapman from Stoke and England international Tony Woodcock from Cologne but the infusion of new blood did little to improve performances. Chapman was dropped after only one goal in eight League games and two against Spartak Moscow as the Russians, 5-2 winners at Highbury, dumped Arsenal out of the UEFA Cup in the first round. They were not their usual miserly selves, especially at home, Liverpool, West Ham and Watford all taking away three points. In their last game at Highbury they had at least beaten second placed Aston Villa, and that having played the last half-hour with only ten men after goalkeeper George Wood had been sent off for a professional foul. Woods' dismissal saw the return of Pat Jennings but even he could do little as the last game before Spurs' visit ended in a 0-3 defeat at bottom-of-the-table Sunderland. With Chris Whyte absent, fit-again Peter Nicholas was called up for his first game of the season. Spurs' assault on four trophies the previous campaign had ended with just one, the FA Cup, the sheer volume of games and attendant injuries proving too much. Keith Burkinshaw had also dipped into the summer transfer market but on a far smaller scale than Neill. Despite the fact he was going to be without Ossie Ardiles who had decided it would not be wise to return after the Falklands conflict and gone on loan to Paris St Germain, his only signing, for £105,000, was the promising young Gary Mabbutt. Expected to start his Spurs' career in the reserves, Mabbutt was thrust straight into the first team because of injuries, a continual problem that saw Tony Galvin, Glenn Hoddle, Paul Miller, Graham Roberts, even Steve Perryman out for long spells. The inability to field the same team in successive games was reflected in results, especially away from home where Spurs had collected just one point in six games.

BEFORE THE GAME

	P	W	D	L	F	A	Pts
Arsenal	19	6	5	8	21	26	23
Spurs	19	8	3	8	30	27	27

THAT WAS THEN...

★ The official programme for this game cost 40p for 24 pages, 2 of which were adverts.

★ A coach trip for Arsenal fans to the forthcoming away game at Southampton was advertised at £6.60 return, INCLUDING a match ticket for the terraces.

ARSENAL OUTPLAY SPURS DESPITE ROBSON DISMISSAL

Alan Sunderland is mobbed after slotting Arsenal's opener past Ray Clemence (below).

A crowd of 51,497 - Highbury's biggest for two seasons - saw Arsenal gain a magnificent victory over their North London rivals despite having Stewart Robson sent off in the 55th minute.

Robson, 18, was dismissed for a foul on Galvin five minutes after he had gone into referee Lester Shapter's notebook for bringing down Roberts. Though the second offence seemed more an error of timing, the referee was left with no alternative.

Arsenal were leading by Sunderland's 40th min. goal, but each man seemed determined to make up for Robson's absence and, indeed, they remained the superior side, scoring again through Woodcock in the 87th min.

Up front, Woodcock and Sunderland, helped by a splendid service from Davis and Rix, were a formidable partnership and their supremacy contrasted sharply with the more laboured efforts of Crooks and Archibald.

The opening goal was a classic. Davis cleared a Hoddle corner to Rix, who drew the defence and served Woodcock.

The England striker saw Sunderland overlapping on the right, and an accurate pass enabled **SUNDERLAND** to dribble around Hazard and drive home from an acute angle.

Spurs replaced the injured Galvin with Brooke in the 59th minute and Arsenal's spirit enabled them to maintain pressure on Clemence's goal. With three minutes remaining a long goal kick by Jennings went straight to **WOODCOCK** who controlled the ball, turned past O'Reilly and fired into the net.

92

TOTTENHAM HOTSPUR 5
Hughton 2, Falco 2, Brazil

ARSENAL 0

Tottenham Hotspur

Manager
Keith Burkinshaw

Arsenal

Manager
Terry Neill

Tottenham	No.	Arsenal
Ray CLEMENCE	1	George WOOD
Chris HUGHTON	2	Stewart ROBSON
Gary O'REILLY	3	Kenny SANSOM
Graham ROBERTS	4	Chris WHYTE*
Paul MILLER	5	David O'LEARY
Terry GIBSON	6	Peter NICHOLAS
Gary MABBUTT	7	Brian TALBOT
Steve ARCHIBALD	8	Paul DAVIS
Tony GALVIN	9	Alan SUNDERLAND
Alan BRAZIL	10	Tony WOODCOCK
Mark FALCO	11	Graham RIX
Micky HAZARD	12	Vladimir PETROVIC (4)

Referee **Mr A Robinson** (Waterlooville)

BACKGROUND

Spurs injury problems did not let up throughout the season. Even when Ossie Ardiles returned from France he played only four games before a broken shin sidelined him for the rest of the season. Those games included the lowest point of the season, a 1-4 defeat at home to a Burnley team struggling at the bottom of the Second Division in the fifth round of the Milk Cup. With resources stretched to the limit and Steve Archibald joining the injured list, Keith Burkinshaw decided he had to strengthen his squad and paid out £450,000 to sign Alan Brazil from Ipswich. Brazil made his debut at Watford as Spurs won 1-0 to record their first away League win since mid-September but in the same game Steve Perryman was sent off and was suspended for two games, the second of which was this Easter Monday fixture. Just two days earlier Spurs had lost at bottom of the table Brighton. Despite the arrival of Yugoslav midfielder Vladimir Petrovic, Arsenal, too, had found the going tough in the League but at least solace was found in the cup competitions. Defeated by Manchester United in the Milk Cup semi-final their opportunity for revenge was just twelve days away, with an FA Cup semi-final at Villa Park against United.

Spurs' Terry Gibson takes on Arsenal's Yugoslav Vladimir Petrovic (right).

Below: Tony Woodcock shields the ball from Gary Mabbutt.

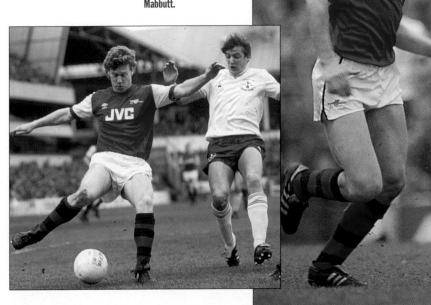

BEFORE THE GAME

	P	W	D	L	F	A	Pts
Spurs	33	13	8	12	44	43	47
Arsenal	33	12	10	11	44	41	46

AT THE SEASON'S END

		P	W	D	L	F	A	Pts
4th	Spurs	42	20	9	13	65	50	69
10th	Arsenal	42	16	10	16	58	56	58

Cannons silenced in 1912 overture

In **'The Times'** Stuart Jones reported...

Alan Brazil scored his first goal in Tottenham colours.

It was not so much a famous victory for Tottenham Hotspur, more an embarrassing humiliation for Arsenal. They were three down within 18 minutes, fortunate that the total was not doubled by the interval, conceded two more afterwards and lost their captain, O'Leary, with an ankle injury midway through the second half.

Only once before, in 1912, have Arsenal suffered a similarly heavy defeat at White Hart Lane. Keith Burkinshaw, the Spurs manager, more readily recalled the score five years ago. "They did us 5-0 here in my first year as manager in the first division and it hurt a bit. You don't sleep easily after results like that".

Burkinshaw was also in despair after Saturday's late collapse at Brighton but one particular moment yesterday delighted him. **FALCO**'s stunning volley, a Brazilian dream, from Gibson's early cross in the thirteenth minute was "the best goal I've seen for a long time and pleased me more than anything else this season because they're both home-grown players."

Tottenham, without the suspended Perryman and the injured Hoddle, Villa and Ardiles, lined up effectively with five strikers, an adventurous move that was perhaps too alien for Arsenal to comprehend. Even so it was a full back, **HUGHTON**, who began the rout, the ball bobbling in from his second wild miskick.

HUGHTON added the third as well and, if **BRAZIL** had not scorned several opportunities to score his first goal for his new club until after the hour, Arsenal's defence would have been in even deeper chaos. As it was, the uncertain Whyte was replaced during the interval and the ebullient Robson was booked yet again.

Wood, cruelly taunted throughout by Tottenham's biggest crowd of the season (43,642), was at fault only for the fourth. Although Miller's free-kick was launched from a distance of 60 yards, **FALCO** was left unchallenged, with the equally generous permission of Talbot, to volley home with less spectacular precision.

The only threat to Tottenham's defence, not surprisingly in the one-sided circumstances, was provided by their captain, Roberts. Unaware that his goalkeeper was exercising at the other extremity of his area, he inadvertently tested Clemence's sprinting ability. The audience merely laughed.

Not so Terry Neill, Arsenal's manager. In clearly restraining his criticism of a side that yielded "total control", he described their performance as "simply not good enough and something will have to be done." More poignantly, he added "We haven't a moment to lose".

O'Leary damaged the ankle that kept him out for several weeks recently. Last night it was encased in plaster. Neill was more concerned about the player's fitness for Saturday. The subsequent FA Cup semi-final against Manchester United a week later was almost too much for him to contemplate.

'DERBY' STAR

Mark Falco — scored with two stunning volleys.

93

TOTTENHAM HOTSPUR 2
Roberts, Archibald

ARSENAL 4
Nicholas 2, Meade 2

Tottenham Hotspur — Arsenal

Manager
Keith Burkinshaw

Manager
Don Howe

Tottenham	No	Arsenal
Ray CLEMENCE	1	Pat JENNINGS
Chris HUGHTON*	2	Colin HILL
Richard COOKE	3	Kenny SANSOM
Graham ROBERTS	4	Stewart ROBSON*
Gary STEVENS	5	David O'LEARY
Steve PERRYMAN	6	Tommy CATON
Ossie ARDILES	7	Raphael MEADE
Steve ARCHIBALD	8	Paul DAVIS
Alan BRAZIL	9	Tony WOODCOCK
Glenn HODDLE	10	Charlie NICHOLAS
Ally DICK	11	Ian ALLINSON
Mark FALCO (2)	12	David CORK (4)

Referee **Mr R Lewis** (Great Bookham)

Pat Jennings punches clear as
Steve Perryman challenges.

BACKGROUND

Among the pre-season favourites for the title, Spurs began in disappointing fashion. Without a win in their first four games, new signing Danny Thomas, Steve Archibald, Paul Miller and Glenn Hoddle were all hit by injury and, even worse, Archibald was transfer-listed after Keith Burkinshaw questioned his commitment. With Archibald determined to prove his manager wrong and hitting a hot streak, results improved in time for the UEFA Cup and although Arsenal put them out of the Milk Cup, Spurs had climbed to fourth place in the league by the start of December. Victory over Bayern Munich took them through to the fourth round of the UEFA Cup but defeat at Norwich, a goalless draw at home to Southampton and a live televised 2-4 defeat at Manchester United left them well behind leaders Liverpool. Archibald and Chris Hughton were fit to return after missing the game at Old Trafford but Steve Perryman had to revert to full-back in place of the injured Thomas while Burkinshaw called up Ossie Ardiles for his first start in almost a year as Tony Galvin was also injured. Although Arsenal reached the semi-final of both cup competitions, finishing tenth in the League was just not good enough for Terry Neill, the Arsenal board or the fans. Tony Woodcock had proved a success but the same could not be said of Lee Chapman. Extra firepower was essential and in the summer Neill laid out another £650,000 to secure Celtic's exciting young star, Charlie Nicholas. A crowd pleaser of the first order, Nicholas became the fan's favourite immediately but he found it difficult to adapt to the faster pace of the English game and found scoring much harder than in his last season in Scotland when he had scored over fifty goals. Inconsistency marked Arsenal's season as a couple of good wins would be followed by two or three defeats. The pressure began to build on Neill, Tommy Caton was signed from Manchester City to strengthen the defence but on his first day at Highbury he could only sit and watch as Third Division Walsall humbled Arsenal for the second time in their history with a 2-1 Milk Cup victory. Two more defeats and Neill was sacked, Don Howe appointed caretaker-manager. Howe pulled Nicholas back into a deeper position and called up the more physical Raphael Meade to partner Woodcock. The result was immediate, a 3-1 win at Watford with Meade scoring all three. Now came the big test.

BEFORE THE GAME

	P	W	D	L	F	A	Pts
Spurs	18	8	5	5	30	27	29
Arsenal	18	8	0	10	30	26	24

St Nicholas's Day is late this year

Nicholas became the patron saint of Arsenal yesterday. And if the namesake of the original Santa Claus and one of the most popular saints in Christendom arrived some 12 hours late at White Hart Lane, the devoted of Arsenal will not give a fig about that. They will be relieved that their vigil is at long last ended.

For four months they have been waiting to greet a League goal from the young Scot and he kept them waiting for only another 26 minutes, after which he added a second just after the interval and, like a man blessed, helped to create two more in the closing quarter of an hour.

For Terry Neill the timing could scarcely be less apt. Don Howe, the caretaker-manager, admitted that "had this happened a fortnight ago Terry would still be in charge". Yet it is Howe's lone change - bringing back Meade - that has lifted the fortunes of Arsenal in general and Nicholas in particular.

Howe explained the reason why: "Meade is a strong runner and he's determined in the box, the sort of qualities that front players need nowadays. Nicholas and Woodcock were too similar in style. Both of them were dropping back and wanting the ball at their feet. We were becoming too stereotyped."

So, Keith Burkinshaw would add, is Tottenham's defence. They are taking the season of good will too far. After presenting several gifts to Manchester United at Old Trafford (coincidentally on the day that Neill was dismissed) they handed Arsenal at least three more. By subtle implication Burkinshaw laid most of the blame on Hughton but, Perryman apart, all have been wearing red coats and white beards.

Meade, for instance, was allowed to open up the right flank and invite **NICHOLAS** to give Arsenal the lead. Even then Nicholas needed a second chance. As though with a double-barrelled shotgun, he fired first with his right foot, seized the rebound and let go with his left. His joy, understandably, was unconfined.

When Tottenham's back four felt drawn to either touchline in the 48th minute, **NICHOLAS** merely accelerated from the deep, ran on to Allinson's chip and lobbed gently over Clemence. No one challenged Davis, either, when he exchanged passes with Nicholas and crossed for **MEADE** to head home at the near post.

After Tottenham had further stretched their own rearguard by replacing the hapless Hughton with Falco, Woodcock took advantage of a slip by Roberts to set up another opportunity for Nicholas. Clemence could only parry his bobbling effort and **MEADE** prodded in the rebound to claim his fifth goal in two games.

In spite of their alarming defensive frailties Tottenham might still have gained revenge for their Milk Cup defeat by their North London rivals six weeks ago. Stevens, for example, chose to head against the same piece of woodwork, the angle between post and bar, in the first and 30th minutes.

The profligacy of Brazil was even more embarrassingly apparent. Put through by Dick in the first half and Stevens in the second, he failed to beat Jennings on either occasion and, with only one League goal to his name since he arrived from Ipswich Town he is entering the wilderness from which Nicholas has so gleefully emerged.

On either side of the interval Tottenham managed to score from free kicks. Hughton's was bundled in by **ROBERTS** and Hoddle's was cleanly struck by **ARCHIBALD**. Burkinshaw commented: "We get most of our injuries cleared up and then this happens." The dark clouds seem to have rolled a few miles across north London.

'DERBY STAR' Charlie Nicholas – Don Howe's decision to give Charlie a deeper role and push Raphael Meade (left) into the firing line paid dividends with both players bagging a brace.

Above right: An acrobatic routine from Graham Roberts.

94

ARSENAL 3
Robson, Nicholas, Woodcock

TOTTENHAM HOTSPUR 2
Archibald 2

Saturday 21st April 1984

Canon League Division One

Highbury

Attendance 48,831

Arsenal

Manager
Don Howe

Tottenham Hotspur

Manager
Keith Burkinshaw

Arsenal		Tottenham Hotspur
John LUKIC	1	Tony PARKS
Colin HILL	2	Danny THOMAS
Kenny SANSOM	3	Chris HUGHTON
Brian TALBOT	4	Graham ROBERTS
David O'LEARY	5	Paul MILLER
Tommy CATON	6	Steve PERRYMAN
Stewart ROBSON	7	Gary MABBUTT
Charlie NICHOLAS	8	Steve ARCHIBALD
Paul MARINER	9	Tony GALVIN
Tony WOODCOCK	10	Ian CROOK*
Graham RIX*	11	Garth CROOKS
Paul DAVIS (11)	12	Gary STEVENS (10)

Referee **Mr K Baker** (Rugby)

BACKGROUND

Arsenal's improvement continued under the caretaker management of Don Howe, seven League games without defeat spoilt only by an early exit from the FA Cup at Middlesbrough, and it seemed certain Howe would get the post on a permanent basis come the end of the season. Any doubts a run of three defeats with only one goal may have cast were soon dispelled as the Arsenal board backed Howe's judgment with a £150,000 cheque to secure Paul Mariner from Ipswich. The arrival of the England centre-forward brought immediate rewards; the eight games leading up to Spurs' visit including just one defeat. The only setback was an eye injury sustained by Pat Jennings in a 4-1 win at Coventry which meant he would miss Spurs' visit. December's run of two points from six games ended any hopes Spurs may have harboured of making an impact on the title race and when Norwich put them out of the FA Cup in the fourth round all they had to play for was the UEFA Cup. Injuries had continued to stretch Spurs' resources to the limit. Ray Clemence had not fully recovered from an injury sustained at Fulham in January, Gary Mabbutt and Tony Galvin had been on and off the treatment table and Glenn Hoddle was out for the rest of the season. With the second leg of the UEFA Cup semi-final against Hadjuk Split only four days away, Keith Burkinshaw decided not to risk Mark Falco and Micky Hazard, calling up Garth Crooks and giving Ian Crook a rare first team outing. Just as Arsenal's directors had an end of season decision to make on the managerial front, so did their counterparts at Spurs. Burkinshaw, the most successful Spurs' manager after Bill Nicholson but disenchanted with the plans of Spurs' new owners Irving Scholar and Paul Bobroff, had announced at the beginning of April he was resigning once the season was over. FA Cup final referee, John Hunting, had been due to take charge of Burkinshaw's last North London derby but pulled out late in the day to be replaced by Ken Baker.

BEFORE THE GAME

	P	W	D	L	F	A	Pts
Spurs	37	16	9	12	58	54	57
Arsenal	36	15	7	14	61	50	52

AT THE SEASON'S END

		P	W	D	L	F	A	Pts
6th	Arsenal	42	18	9	15	74	60	63
8th	Spurs	42	17	10	15	64	65	61

Charlie Nicholas makes it 2-1 to Arsenal with a brilliant goal.

Welcome to Arsenal, home of fine arts

Don't be deceived by the score. Arsenal were streets ahead of Spurs, dominating the 100th North London derby to an extent that at times it was embarrassing. Here, crystallised in ninety minutes of football, was the reason why Tottenham's manager is leaving, and why Arsenal's board of directors would be insane not to appoint their caretaker manager Don Howe on a permanent basis.

And what rich irony for Howe, branded a defensive coach, that it was Arsenal who were slick, and fast, and polished: and that Spurs, equally unnaturally, were simple big-hearted battlers, short of ideas, at times outclassed.

Howe has done a very simple and clever thing with the Arsenal attack. He bought Mariner to play alongside Woodcock up front, and withdrew Nicholas into a free-ranging role in midfield.

Yesterday Mariner had a zest that has been missing from his game for months. Woodcock looked as enthusiastic as ever and yards faster than the Tottenham central defenders, and Nicholas managed to combine general authority with moments that were breathtaking - his goal was pure Celtic Nicholas.

The strange thing was that the first half, in which Spurs appeared to react to events while Arsenal anticipated them, should only produce one goal. After the game both managers, one putting on a brave face, the other unable to stop smiling, reckoned that Arsenal were worth a two or three-goal interval lead.

If anything that was an underestimation. As

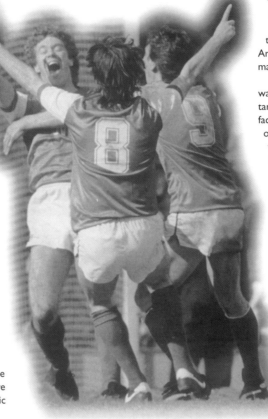

Celebrations after Tony Woodcock's goal for Arsenal.

well as **ROBSON**'s goal, deflected off Mabbutt from the edge of the area, Woodcock had one disallowed, Talbot missed two, and Parks made three heart-stopping saves.

For much of the second half, Arsenal purred quite nicely showing off how easily their back four

were dealing with Crooks and Archibald. But at least Spurs, with Stevens replacing young Crook in midfield, were making an occasional thrust. Then in the space of seven minutes Arsenal twice made the game safe, and twice made it interesting by giving away careless goals.

The first of the four goals was so good that it was forgivable that the Arsenal defence momentarily took leave of their senses. **NICHOLAS**, facing the North Bank, beat one Spurs defender on the edge of the area, and then another, and then a third, the ball spinning kindly into space, and then he went round the goalkeeper, and then, for all this was unfolding like a dream sequence, he threaded the ball between two defenders standing on the goal-line.

So ecstatic and prolonged were the crowd's celebrations that the realisation that the game had been restarted came as a surprise, particularly for O'Leary and Caton in the centre of the Arsenal defence. Both missed chances to clear the ball, and with Crooks and **ARCHIBALD** for once combining well, Spurs scored within 30 seconds of the restart.

In a way that was excusable - but it happened again. **WOODCOCK**, put in the clear down the left courtesy of Mariner's flick, sprinted clear of Miller and easily beat Parks with his left foot. Tottenham immediately replied with a fine strike by **ARCHIBALD**, who managed to find pace and accuracy with a left foot shot at full stretch.

Two sleepy moments - for O'Leary was also at fault in not heading clear before Tottenham's goal - had contrived to put Spurs back in the game, and they almost made a draw of it when Roberts thundered into the penalty area in the closing seconds, forcing a brave catch by Lukic, who was then kicked - Roberts' second unnecessary act of violence in the match.

Spurs could point to Parks' brilliant goalkeeping, to Roberts' fine all-round display, and to Archibald's two viperish strikes. But they should not delude themselves. Even allowing for the absence of Hoddle, the suspension of Falco, and assorted injuries, they are a collection of talented bits and pieces rather than a cohesive side.

If, as Spurs directors insist, they are to challenge for the First Division Championship (something Keith Burkinshaw never managed), then much is to be done.

Perhaps we should not read too much into one match, however symbolic, but Arsenal may have the basis of a consistently successful side. They probably need another central defender, and a top class midfielder to play with Rix and Nicholas. A few nuts and bolts: for yesterday they had all the flair they'll need.

The first goal for Steve Archibald as he beats John Lukic in a crowded goalmouth.

95

ARSENAL 1
Woodcock

TOTTENHAM HOTSPUR 2
Crooks, Falco

Tuesday 1st January 1985

Canon League Division One

Highbury

Attendance 48,714

Arsenal

Tottenham Hotspur

Manager
Don Howe

Manager
Peter Shreeves

John LUKIC	1	Ray CLEMENCE
Viv ANDERSON	2	Gary STEVENS
Tommy CATON	3	Gary MABBUTT
Brian TALBOT	4	Graham ROBERTS
David O'LEARY	5	Paul MILLER
Tony ADAMS	6	Steve PERRYMAN
Stewart ROBSON	7	John CHIEDOZIE
Ian ALLINSON	8	Mark FALCO
Paul MARINER	9	Tony GALVIN
Tony WOODCOCK	10	Glenn HODDLE*
Charlie NICHOLAS*	11	Garth CROOKS
Steve WILLIAMS (11)	12	Clive ALLEN (10)

Referee **Mr T D Spencer** (Salisbury)

BACKGROUND

Confirmed as Arsenal's permanent manager shortly after their success in the April 1984 derby, Don Howe had resisted the temptation to plunge into the summer transfer market, his only signing England full-back Viv Anderson from Nottingham Forest. The season began inauspiciously, a Highbury draw with Chelsea and defeat at Nottingham Forest, but seven victories in the next eight games saw Arsenal heading the table. Successive defeats at West Ham and Manchester United, sandwiching a Milk Cup exit at Second Division Oxford, ended the best run of the season but good home form kept Arsenal in touch with the leaders. It was their away form that let them down, five successive defeats on the road only brought to an end two days before meeting Spurs with a 3-1 win at Newcastle. A good win, but Howe knew his midfield lacked a player with battling qualities and the next day he paid out £550,000 to sign Steve Williams from Southampton. Although Keith Burkinshaw left the Spurs' board with the UEFA Cup sitting in the trophy cabinet, he also left them with the problem of who to appoint as his successor. Many names were mentioned but following Burkinshaw was not an attractive proposition and eventually they settled on his assistant, Peter Shreeves. Shreeves immediately set about making his mark, signing Clive Allen and John Chiedozie, selling Steve Archibald to Barcelona. Even without Glenn Hoddle, the season started well and by the end of September Spurs were top of the table, ahead of Arsenal on goal difference. Arsenal took over for a while but with Hoddle returning and Garth Crooks and Mark Falco finding the back of the net regularly, Spurs entered the New Year back on top, through to the fourth round of the UEFA Cup and defeated only once in 14 games.

BEFORE THE GAME

	P	W	D	L	F	A	Pts
Spurs	22	13	4	5	45	22	43
Arsenal	22	12	3	7	42	28	39

Skippers Tony Woodcock and Steve Perryman line-up with match officials and mascots for the pre-match formalities.

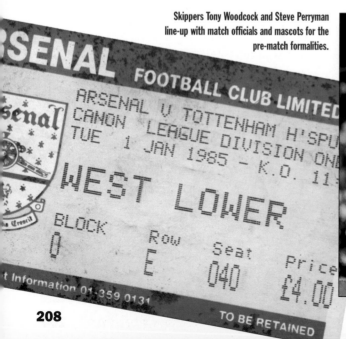

Spurs revel in new resolution

It was a stiff, biting wind that blew both sides some good at Highbury yesterday, but it was Tottenham Hotspur who turned it significantly to their advantage to sail seven points clear of their North London rivals. More importantly, though, it keeps them at the head of an unpredictable championship.

When played into the wind the ball was conveniently held up for both sets of forwards but it was the "battling" Hoddle, a delightful surprise not only to his manager, Peter Shreeves, who made devastating use of it on one particular occasion to turn the match Tottenham's way.

Whether this fixture, the 101st between the clubs, signalled a parting of the ways in the race for the League title this season, it is too early to say. But Tottenham again displayed a toughening in their character and camaraderie away from home while Arsenal again showed a disturbing lack of resolution, more so on this first day of the new year.

Tottenham have failed to win only once - at Coventry and only through a late goal - in their last five away games. They had to come from behind on superiority and a goal yesterday. Arsenal, buoyed up by their handsome victory at Newcastle and the presence of another expensive stimulant on the substitutes' bench in the shape of Williams, played in the first half with an enthusiasm for the morning derby that would have left any new year reveller, as well as those from Tottenham, feeling sick.

Their pre-match training, in order to stir mind and muscle, looked beneficial as Anderson's lively late runs caught Tottenham still sleeping at the back. Roberts was required to call upon his well-known heroic qualities (though some might describe them as villainous) to keep Tottenham in the game. Clemence, too, was drawing on familiar strengths, such as experience and athleticism. But Nicholas, whose performance withered along

with that of his team, should have beaten Clemence before Woodcock did three minutes before half-time. Anderson sharply avoided Falco's lunge near the byline and crossed for **WOODCOCK** to turn it in with equal sharpness.

The transformation which overcame Tottenham after the interval was obvious from the initial determined attempt by Perryman, the captain, to finish off a one-two. Hoddle, who had been forced deeper and deeper by the excellent Robson, showed how difficult it is to nullify players who can strike a long ball with precision. In the 59th minute Hoddle, from left back, hit a deep one that cut into the wind just long enough to confuse Caton and Lukic, who left his line and then retreated. **CROOKS**, single-mindedly, stole in to score his fifth goal in five matches from a fine angle.

The story-line was now clearly defined and Tottenham, assuming the role of aggressor, kept faithful to it until they were rewarded in the 73rd minute when the supporters' displeasure at a short ball by Galvin to **FALCO** quickly changed as they saw this sturdy, unfussy forward's shot humming home. Williams, who was at the time stretching his legs down the touchline, came on for Nicholas to take a closer look at his new club and vice versa. Certainly Arsenal liked what they saw.

Garth Crooks climbs higher than Steve Williams and Stewart Robson to direct a header at goal.

Falco shrugs off broken nose to keep Spurs top

By ALEX MONTGOMERY: Arsenal 1, Spurs 2

MARK FALCO scorched into the New Year with a goal, a resolution — and a broken nose.

The big, brave Spurs striker hit a superb winner in this meeting of the big two North London tribes.

And he left Highbury with the rest of his Tottenham mates determined that 1985 will be the year they bring the title back to White Hart Lane.

Falco won't score a more satisfying goal in the year

Viv Anderson and Tony Galvin give chase.

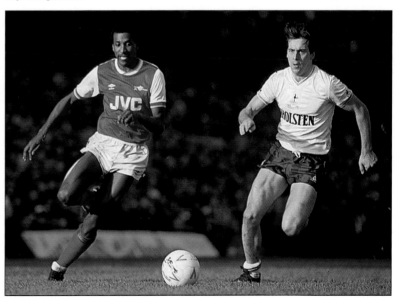

96

TOTTENHAM HOTSPUR 0

ARSENAL 2
Nicholas, Talbot

Wednesday 17th April 1985

Canon League Division One

White Hart Lane

Attendance 40,399

Tottenham Hotspur

Manager
Peter Shreeves

Arsenal

Manager
Don Howe

Tottenham	No.	Arsenal
Ray CLEMENCE	1	John LUKIC
Danny THOMAS	2	Viv ANDERSON
Mark BOWEN	3	Kenny SANSOM
Graham ROBERTS	4	Steve WILLIAMS
John CHIEDOZIE	5	David O'LEARY*
Steve PERRYMAN	6	Tommy CATON
Ossie ARDILES	7	Stewart ROBSON
Mark FALCO	8	Graham RIX
David LEWORTHY	9	Ian ALLINSON
Glenn HODDLE	10	Brian TALBOT
Tony GALVIN*	11	Charlie NICHOLAS
Micky HAZARD (11)	12	Paul MARINER (5)

Referee **Mr C Downey** (Hounslow)

BACKGROUND

Despite bad weather causing the postponement of Spurs' three scheduled home League fixtures in January and February, they continued to dispute top spot with Everton, but come March it all began to go wrong. Beaten at home for the first time in European competition by Real Madrid, six days later they dropped three points to Manchester United, and, worse, lost the services of Gary Stevens for the rest of the season. They bounced back with victory at Anfield, ample revenge for defeat in the FA Cup, but John Chiedozie was injured and a week later he was joined on the injury list by Chris Hughton as Southampton were beaten 5-1. Aston Villa then won at White Hart Lane and even though there were still ten games left the destination of the title was all but decided when Everton returned to Merseyside with another three points. Spurs did not give up hope, drawing at West Ham and winning at Leicester, but anything less than victory over Arsenal would make the task of overhauling Everton nigh on impossible. With Garth Crooks looking jaded Peter Shreeves gave a surprise League debut to reserve striker David Leworthy. Arsenal had continued to pick up points at home but away from Highbury they could do little right, the lowest point of the season coming with defeat at Fourth Division York in the FA Cup. They, too, had suffered with injuries, losing Paul Davis, Tony Woodcock and Raphael Meade just when they needed all their resources if they were to finish high enough to qualify for the UEFA Cup.

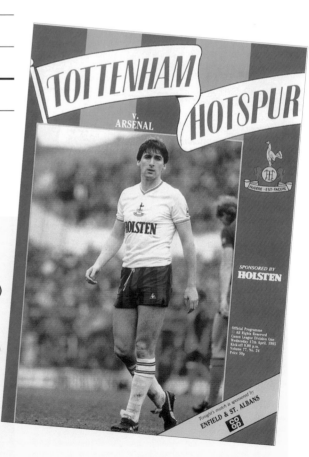

BEFORE THE GAME

	P	W	D	L	F	A	Pts
Spurs	34	19	7	8	64	36	64
Arsenal	36	16	8	12	54	43	56

AT THE SEASON'S END

		P	W	D	L	F	A	Pts
3rd	Spurs	42	23	8	11	78	52	77
7th	Arsenal	42	19	9	14	61	49	66

★ The match programme cost 50p for 28 pages, 5 of which were adverts. Season tickets for the following season (1985/86) were advertised, with prices ranging from £63 in the standing enclosure (juniors & OAPs half price) to £260 for the best seats in the West Stand. Matchday admission prices would be £3 for standing and £5, £7, £8 and £10 to sit down.

Clive White in *'The Times'* reported on...

Tottenham denied title by old rivals

Arsenal could not have wished for the League championship challenge of their great North London rivals to have finally expired at a better time. Arsenal, whose chase for one of the remaining UEFA Cup places had been reduced to an embarrassing crawl in recent weeks, chose last night at White Hart Lane to claw their way back into the reckoning with their first away win of the year.

Their heroes performed in unlikely roles: Nicholas as match winner, Mariner as match saver. When Arsenal lost their captain, O'Leary, in the 43rd minute, Mariner, who had only just recovered from an ankle injury, came on as substitute to give a heartily courageous performance at centre back as Tottenham pressed for an equaliser without great conviction or invention.

Though this Derby had lost some of it's appeal, coming at a time when most of the season's prizes had already been reserved, the atmosphere was as intimidating as ever. The first 20 minutes of play was fringed by a cordon of police leading away Arsenal "supporters" who had infiltrated the Tottenham end and caused disturbances.

It was nothing though to the disturbance the Arsenal team caused after 21 minutes when they scored their first away goal since January 19. It was an uncommonly well taken goal by Nicholas that owed it's inception to a mistake further upfield by Bowen, the inexperienced young Welshman. A neat triangular movement broke down on his poor pass and Rix swept the ball up to Williams. His short pass found **NICHOLAS** accelerating into space as he had done earlier when pulled back by Perryman. This time he succeeded in getting behind the Tottenham defence and scored.

Tottenham, who were giving Leworthy, a 22-year old, his debut in place of the jaded Crooks, had looked the brighter side in attack throughout the first half but managed to manufacture little of consequence. Leworthy, however, settled in quickly and played with the confidence a manager can only hope for from a forward who scored 22 goals in 29 reserve games. Twice in the first 12 minutes he set up Falco. From their first association Lukic pushed Falco's shot over the crossbar and the next time the big man turned sharply to strike a post.

Whether or not Arsenal's objective to defend was determined by the injury to O'Leary (following a tackle with Chiedozie of all people) or their winning position, the pattern of play was monotonously one way in the second half. Arsenal's midfield protected their defence with considerable effort, guile and sometimes outrage: Ardiles was pushed and pulled by Williams and Robson, who in quick succession were both booked to join Rix and Perryman. The best Tottenham could summon was from Hoddle, were two long-range strikes and a rasping drive from Leworthy which narrowly cleared the bar.

With 10 minutes to go a shot by Hazard produced a wild scramble in the Arsenal penalty area out of which Anderson emerged like a scrum half with the ball but only after he had handled it. Arsenal protested furiously the penalty and Anderson, before the kick and Sansom, for some strange reason, after it incurred further cautions. Roberts made such behaviour quite unnecessary by driving his spot kick ferociously against the crossbar and out of play.

With seconds left, **TALBOT** completed Tottenham's humiliation with a well taken breakaway goal. If all this was a sad end to Tottenham's season a sadder one still was to follow as spectators at the Paxton road end tore up seats and hurled them down on the heads of opposing supporters.

Brian Talbot (below) completed the scoring with seconds left.

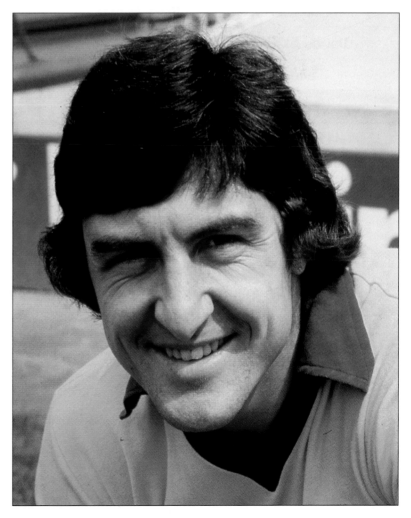

Charlie Nicholas races clear of Mark Bowen to open the scoring.

97

ARSENAL 0

TOTTENHAM HOTSPUR 0

Arsenal

Manager
Don Howe

Tottenham Hotspur

Manager
Peter Shreeves

Arsenal		Tottenham Hotspur
John LUKIC	1	Ray CLEMENCE
Viv ANDERSON	2	Gary STEVENS
Kenny SANSOM	3	Chris HUGHTON
Paul DAVIS	4	Graham ROBERTS
David O'LEARY	5	Gary MABBUTT
Martin KEOWN	6	Steve PERRYMAN
Ian ALLINSON	7	Ossie ARDILES
David ROCASTLE	8	Mark FALCO
Charlie NICHOLAS	9	Clive ALLEN
Niall QUINN*	10	Glenn HODDLE
Graham RIX	11	Chris WADDLE
Tony WOODCOCK (10)	12	Paul ALLEN

Referee **Mr J Moules** (Ingatestone)

BACKGROUND

Following a poor start to the season, Arsenal climbed to third place in mid-September with four successive victories but they could not keep the run up and gradually slipped further behind runaway leaders Manchester United. A 1-6 defeat at Everton early in November convinced Don Howe his established stars were not doing the business and he looked to a promising crop of youngsters to resurrect a season that was drifting nowhere. Martin Hayes, Niall Quinn and Martin Keown were all given their chance and Howe's faith in them seemed to be rewarded as Arsenal prepared for Spurs' visit with home victories over Liverpool and Queens' Park Rangers sandwiching a surprise win at Old Trafford. Another youngster, Gus Caesar, had played in the last two of those games but with Viv Anderson back from suspension he stepped down. Peter Shreeves had again been busy in the transfer market in the summer paying out £600,000 to sign Chris Waddle and another £400,000 on Paul Allen. They shared three goals as Watford were beaten 4-0 in the opening game but a draw at Oxford and three straight defeats followed. 15 goals in the next four games, all won, suggested the corner had been turned but with injuries again taking their toll Spurs began to struggle and it was only with the return of Clive Allen after nine months out injured that they began to move up the table. Four wins in five games took Spurs into the top half of the table but four days before the visit to Highbury they had lost 0-2 at Chelsea. With Danny Thomas injured Gary Stevens moved to full-back and Graham Roberts, absent from the last three games to avoid any further bookings putting him out of the FA Cup third round clash with Oxford, returned.

BEFORE THE GAME

	P	W	D	L	F	A	Pts
Arsenal	23	12	5	6	28	26	41
Spurs	23	10	4	9	39	28	34

HODDLE'S A BOBBY DAZZLER

Glenn stars on ice

Arsenal 0, Spurs 0

GLENN HODDLE skated into 1986 yesterday with a performance that must have warmed England manager Bobby Robson on a freezing day in North London.

Hoddle kept his feet while others slipped and slid and the Tottenham star almost left Arsenal with a big New Year's Day hangover.

High-flying Glenn Hoddle is watched by Charlie Nicholas.

The morning-after men struggle to find their feet at Highbury

Below: Graham Roberts clears the danger. Bottom: Gary Mabbutt gains the advantage over Niall Quinn, Viv Anderson and Chris Hughton.

It was an ill-opportune moment to record the first goalless draw at Highbury between these famous rivals in 77 years of healthy, productive activity. An encouraging crowd of 45,109 had dragged themselves out for the morning kick-off after the night before only to witness a performance which had all the vigour of a New Year's Eve reveller who had celebrated to excess.

The performance, however, was undermined by conditions which were more difficult than the crowd, perhaps, realised. The glorious morning sun had only thawed the surface, making foothold as precarious as that for a novice ice skater.

The stalemate brought a run of three consecutive, good quality victories to a close for Arsenal, who have capitalised recently on the enthusiasm of their youngsters. But yesterday Quinn and Rocastle found the conditions more intimidating than Tottenham and the long-legged Quinn was eventually substituted.

Despite spurts of genius from Ardiles, Hoddle and Nicholas, it was regrettably true that the game would be best remembered for one horrendous tackle by Roberts on Nicholas which carried both players off the field, through an advertising hoarding and into the laps of ringside spectators.

Roberts "tackle" had all the finesse of a charging rhino but though hopelessly ill-timed - as so many of his challenges this season have been - I do not believe it was malicious. For a moment it threatened to spark a riot as Arsenal players reacted furiously to the referee's decision merely to warn Roberts. Peter Shreeves, the Tottenham manager, commented: "Roberts was totally committed. Charlie never complained. And he's an honest lad. Situations in front of the main stand always do tend to flare up".

Fortunately tempers cooled before any real damage could be done, the hoarding apart. The least affected seemed Roberts who 10 minutes later went in a trifle roughly on Davis as if to prove his mental well-being and was booked by the referee with a keenness that suggested he had had self-recriminations about his earlier decision to absolve Roberts. Hughton was also booked for a later foul on Allinson.

The football came in fits and starts. Tottenham seemed to take an early hold in midfield though they had nothing tangible to show for it. Arsenal supporters were quick to forget the team's recent strides and Rix was not the only player to sense dissatisfaction among the audience. Yet Arsenal's Nicholas, a prolific scorer in these derbies produced the only first half strike of note, turning a header on to the bar then post with Clemence well beaten.

Tottenham squeezed their grip a little harder soon after the interval and Arsenal were thankful that at least Lukic had not forgotten his good form of 1985, recovering to save a close range shot by Falco that seemed to have eluded him. The Arsenal defence, in which O'Leary was outstanding, for the most part looked encouragingly secure and confident.

Arsenal, desperately missing the driving force of Robson, who was absent with a groin strain, did not catch sight of the Tottenham goal again until the 78th minute when a move, which had it's origins in a neat pass by Rocastle, Robson's replacement, almost produced a match-winning goal for Quinn. But his goalbound shot was blocked by the loitering body of his friend and confidant Rix.

98

TOTTENHAM HOTSPUR 1
Stevens

ARSENAL 0

Tottenham Hotspur

Manager
Peter Shreeves

Arsenal

Manager
Steve Burtenshaw

Ray CLEMENCE	1	John LUKIC
Paul ALLEN	2	Viv ANDERSON
Danny THOMAS	3	Kenny SANSOM
Graham ROBERTS	4	Steve WILLIAMS
Paul MILLER	5	David O'LEARY
Gary STEVENS	6	Martin KEOWN
Gary MABBUTT	7	Martin HAYES
Mark FALCO	8	David ROCASTLE
Tony GALVIN	9	Charlie NICHOLAS
Glenn HODDLE	10	Niall QUINN*
Chris WADDLE*	11	Graham RIX
Ossie ARDILES (11)	12	Paul MARINER (10)

Referee **Mr P Vanes** (Warley)

BACKGROUND

After the New Year's Day draw at Highbury Spurs went four League games, three of them at home, without a single goal, let alone a point. The story was similar in the ill-fated Screen Sport Super Cup, a 0-2 defeat at the hands of Liverpool and a goalless draw with Everton, both at White Hart Lane. The monotony was broken only in the FA Cup, but even then replays were needed to overcome Oxford and Notts County. The writing was already beginning to appear on the wall for Peter Shreeves. He had taken over a club that had just won a major European trophy, received all the financial backing he could hope for but had failed to produce a successful team and attendances were down. 18-year old David Howells grabbed the winner against Sheffield Wednesday as he made a surprise debut at Hillsborough but Spurs were soon back in the all too familiar routine as first Liverpool in the League and then Everton in the FA Cup departed North London victorious. Tony Galvin returned from long-term injury against doomed West Bromwich Albion and Spurs at last rediscovered some of their early season form with a 5-0 victory. A win at Birmingham and draw at Newcastle lifted confidence just in time for Arsenal's visit. In comparison, in the League at least, Arsenal's fortunes appeared to be on the up. Only one defeat since the turn of the year and winners of their last four games they had climbed to fifth in the table, well behind the two Merseyside clubs and Manchester United but close enough to challenge Chelsea as London's top club. All was not well though. In the Milk Cup they had lost to Aston Villa in a Highbury replay and had gone out of the FA Cup in a second replay to Luton. Rumours were rife that the Highbury board were keen to replace Don Howe with Terry Venables who had taken Barcelona to the Spanish title in his first season and was now leading a successful campaign that would take them to the European Cup final. Howe decided to jump before he was pushed. Just a week before the visit to Spurs Arsenal beat Coventry 3-0. After the game he asked to be released from his contract and the board agreed. Chief Scout Steve Burtenshaw was given the job of looking after the first team till a new man was appointed.

BEFORE THE GAME

	P	W	D	L	F	A	Pts
Arsenal	31	17	7	7	42	32	58
Spurs	33	13	6	14	51	41	45

AT THE SEASON'S END

		P	W	D	L	F	A	Pts
7th	Arsenal	42	20	9	13	49	47	69
10th	Spurs	42	19	8	15	74	52	65

Celebrations after Gary Stevens nets the winner.

Brian Glanville for 'The Sunday Times'...

Another fine mess

A BRUISING, hectic, mile-a-minute north London derby between these two troubled clubs was won by a solitary, rather scrappy first half goal. Stevens scored it for Tottenham, who might have had others in a vigorous 10-minute period, when Hoddle inspired them. But the virtue went out of the Spurs in the second half, when only three resourceful saves by Clemence saved his team the points.

The sheer frenzy of the proceedings prevented any player with less magical skill than Hoddle from doing very much but survive; that Quinn, the lanky

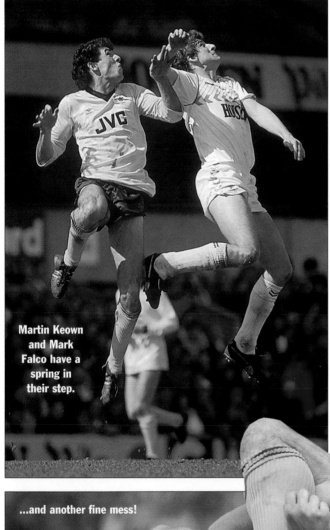

Martin Keown and Mark Falco have a spring in their step.

...and another fine mess!

Arsenal striker, should manage to do so until 11 minutes to the end was, given the ill treatment he received from Roberts and Miller, but a surprise and a tribute to his durability.

Certainly neither he nor anybody else had real protection from the referee, Mr Paul Vanes.

Two second half incidents will serve to show what I mean. They took place in close proximity, at least in terms of area. First, Allen barged Williams off a ball he made no effort to reach; and Allen was given the foul. Subsequently, when Allen came racing through on a fine, sustained overlap, and Sansom flagrantly fouled him, Mr Vanes simply let play go on. The combination of a heated match like this and a referee like that could well have been much more combustible.

So in their first game of the season without Don Howe, Arsenal were somewhat unluckily defeated. Their reputation as a great club which handles things with patrician dignity has scarcely survived the 1950s, let alone the latest confusion. It was in the fifties, when Arsenal's devoted left back captain, Eddie Hapgood, was down on his luck, and asked for help that they offered him £30.

In the sixties came the messy affair of Billy Wright, sacked as manager after the chairman had expressed full confidence in him. As for Howe, the wonder of it was that he stayed when Terry Neill went. For all Howe's fervent protest, his central role in Neill's regime was undeniable, and it was a divided Arsenal board that appointed him.

While, Terry Venables would be a marvellous catch for either Arsenal or Tottenham; as would the remarkable Paris St Germain manager, Gerard Houllier, so vast a success in his very first season there. Houllier, who once taught English in schools and university, speaks it perfectly, and has an ambition to manage an English club.

If it be true that Juventus want him, Spurs and Arsenal could never match the money. If it isn't, why not go for him? At Tottenham whatever happened yesterday, the likeable Peter Shreeves had had the kind of season which has seen him walking a tightrope for weeks. Transfers have gone wrong, weaknesses have been left untouched, team selection has been criticised.

In this game, Tottenham's finest spell lasted from the 25th minute, when Mabbutt's header from Hoddle's corner was saved by Lukic, to the 35th, when Hoddle struck a second long, low right-footed shot against the post.

A minute earlier, Hoddle had sent over a splendid cross from the right. Galvin returned it to the middle, Lukic badly mis-punched, and **STEVENS** drove the ball in, despite the lunging legs on the line.

Apart from a close thing in the 50th minute, when Keown, getting in between Waddle and Hoddle's long pass, under-hit his back pass, and Waddle shot wide, Tottenham created surprisingly little after the interval. Arsenal themselves were scarcely a creative team, and it was significant that their finest double chance arrived when, after 63 minutes, Mabbutt lamentably missed the ball, and the sporadic Hayes, running in from the right, had his drive blocked by Clemence, who proceeded to block Nicholas's follow-up with his legs.

Nicholas was the same old fits and starts Nicholas; a maddening enigma. In the closing minutes when Anderson's cross skidded to him off a Tottenham head, he spurned a glorious chance, merely nodding the ball forward.

But then, receiving from the always busily inventive Rix, three minutes from the end, Nicholas danced across two defenders from the left, and pivoted to strike a shot which Clemence blocked again.

99

ARSENAL 0

TOTTENHAM HOTSPUR 0

Saturday 6th September 1986

Football League Division One

Highbury

Attendance 44,707

Arsenal

Tottenham Hotspur

Manager
George Graham

Manager
David Pleat

John LUKIC	1	Ray CLEMENCE
Viv ANDERSON	2	Gary STEVENS
Kenny SANSOM	3	Mitchell THOMAS
Stewart ROBSON	4	Graham ROBERTS
David O'LEARY	5	Richard GOUGH
Tony ADAMS	6	Gary MABBUTT
David ROCASTLE*	7	Clive ALLEN
Paul DAVIS	8	Mark FALCO*
Niall QUINN	9	Chris WADDLE
Charlie NICHOLAS	10	Glenn HODDLE
Graham RIX	11	Tony GALVIN
Martin HAYES (7)	12	Ossie ARDILES (8)

Referee **Mr A Gunn** (Burgess Hill)

Niall Quinn (left) faces up to a corner with Tottenham's summer signings Mitchell Thomas (centre) and Richard Gough (right).

BACKGROUND

Spurs dispensed with Peter Shreeves' services at the end of the 1985-86 season and joined Arsenal in the search for a new manager. Terry Venables was widely tipped for both jobs but when he decided to stay in Spain they looked closer to home. Arsenal settled on Millwall manager George Graham, a member of their 1970-71 "Double" team while Spurs appointed the Luton manager, David Pleat. Graham allowed Tony Woodcock to return to Germany, but despite losing Martin Keown to Aston Villa when he and the player were unable to agree a new contract, he decided not to re-inforce his playing staff, preferring to give those on the books a chance to impress. Pleat was far more active, taking Mitchell Thomas from Luton and, quickly recognising that with Steve Perryman having left in March 1986 Spurs were in desperate need of a leader on the pitch, signing Richard Gough from Dundee United. Both clubs made a mixed start to the season. Arsenal beat Manchester United at home, lost at Coventry and Liverpool and then returned to winning ways with a 2-0 Highbury victory over Sheffield Wednesday. Spurs won their first game at Aston Villa with three goals from Clive Allen, drew with Newcastle, beat Manchester City at home and then lost at Southampton.

BEFORE THE GAME

	P	W	D	L	F	A	Pts
Spurs	4	2	1	1	5	3	7
Arsenal	4	2	0	2	5	4	6

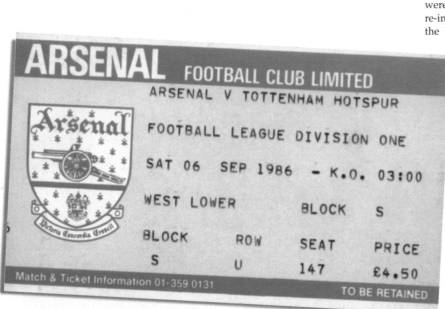

ARSENAL FOOTBALL CLUB LIMITED
ARSENAL V TOTTENHAM HOTSPUR
FOOTBALL LEAGUE DIVISION ONE
SAT 06 SEP 1986 - K.O. 03:00
WEST LOWER   BLOCK   S
BLOCK   ROW   SEAT   PRICE
S   U   147   £4.50
Match & Ticket Information 01-359 0131
TO BE RETAINED

A derby without a flicker

Neither of these North London giants could establish an early season supremacy over the other at Highbury yesterday in a match that did little for football's appeal as a spectator sport.

A crowd of more than 44,000 undoubtably deserved better, but all the attacking intentions of the club's new managers, George Graham and David Pleat, could not alter the fact that high-powered local derbies of this kind are more often than not dull, sterile affairs.

In a game packed with international footballers past and present, not one of them could rise above the suffocating level of mediocrity all around to provide something that was decisive or even memorable.

Since Spurs succeeded in drawing with their old rivals away from home, this was technically a better result for them than for Arsenal, a concession made willingly afterwards by Graham.

"It's a couple of points lost at home as far as I am concerned." said the Arsenal manager. "That was the poorest we've played at home so far. We were very poor today."

"There are very few good local derbies between these clubs. I've played in a few, and there's very little good football played. Today, everyone cancelled everyone else out. It never got off the ground, although perhaps that was the trouble, it was too much off the ground."

That was a pretty fair assessment of a rather tedious afternoon although it did overlook the fact that if anyone deserved to win, it was Arsenal. They certainly made what few real chances there were.

Robson, for instance, nearly celebrated his promotion to England's senior squad with a thrilling goal in the 11th minute. Nicholas split the Spurs defence for him with a lovely, instinctive back-heel, but Robson still had to get past Roberts to hit a fierce right-footer that Clemence kept out only by hurling himself across goal.

There is no doubt that Robson is a vigorous, determined young midfield player who times his runs into the penalty area well. Often, though, he lacks composure when he gets there, as we saw when he headed a centre from the impressive hardworking Quinn over the bar after 35 minutes.

Matters deteriorated so much after the interval that when the referee halted the game to complain about the whistlers in the crowd, it was tempting to believe he had decided to save everyone from further punishment.

Only once in the entire second-half did either goal come under serious threat. That was in the very last second when Rix's low centre from the left struck both Roberts and Nicholas in turn, before running across the face of the Spurs goal and out of play.

Until then the only moments of note had been the introductions of the substitutes. Hayes came on for Rocastle after 77 minutes and Ardiles replaced Falco, four minutes later.

The Arsenal substitution was a tribute to the defensive work of Thomas, England's new deputy left back, who allowed Rocastle, a member of the Under-21 squad going to Sweden this week, little scope. On the whole, however, Arsenal looked the more convincing both individually and collectively.

> ## "Today, everyone cancelled everyone else out. It never got off the ground, although perhaps that was the trouble, it was too much off the ground"
> ### George Graham

A more elegant jump you couldn't wish to see... Kenny Sansom challenges Richard Gough as Gary Stevens, Niall Quinn and Graham Rix look on.

TOTTENHAM HOTSPUR 1
Thomas M

ARSENAL 2
Adams, Davis

Tottenham Hotspur — Arsenal

Manager
David Pleat

Manager
George Graham

Tottenham		Arsenal
Ray CLEMENCE	1	John LUKIC
Danny THOMAS	2	Viv ANDERSON
Mitchell THOMAS	3	Kenny SANSOM
Ossie ARDILES*	4	Steve WILLIAMS
Richard GOUGH	5	David O'LEARY
Gary MABBUTT	6	Tony ADAMS
Clive ALLEN	7	David ROCASTLE
Paul ALLEN	8	Paul DAVIS
Chris WADDLE	9	Niall QUINN*
Glenn HODDLE	10	Charlie NICHOLAS
Tony GALVIN	11	Martin HAYES
Nico CLAESEN (4)	12	Graham RIX (9)

Referee **Mr R G Milford** (Bristol)

The programme for this Centenary derby was a bumper souvenir issue which included a reprint of the programme from the very first league meeting.

The 36-page main programme included photographs of players (and the two managers) of both clubs dressed in early 20th century gear and on the cover (reproduced here) was a combined team group entitled 'friendly foes'.

The programme cost 80p.

BACKGROUND

David Pleat continued his rebuilding programme with the October signing of striker Nico Claesen, expecting the Belgian international to take some of the pressure off Clive Allen who had been responsible for nine of Spurs' ten League goals. Ironically Claesen's arrival resulted in the worst run of the season. After winning at Liverpool on his debut a draw followed by three defeats dropped Spurs from third to mid-table. Pleat soon got things back on track and with the addition of Steve Hodge Spurs were back up to fifth after a New Year's Day victory at Charlton. Hodge was injured at Selhurst Park and unable to take his place but Mitchell Thomas, absent for two games, returned. After the goalless draw at Highbury Arsenal had gone another three games without scoring, but only the last had been lost. They then set out on an unbeaten run of 18 games, 14 wins and four draws, and arrived for the centenary derby leading the title race, one point ahead of Everton with a game in hand. In six months George Graham had turned them from also-rans to championship favourites and had done that with only one signing, Perry Groves, a bargain £50,000 capture from Colchester.

BEFORE THE GAME

	P	W	D	L	F	A	Pts
Spurs	23	11	5	7	37	27	38
Arsenal	23	14	6	3	39	12	48

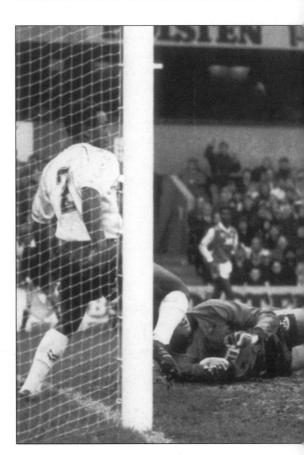

Centenary stakes spur Arsenal to a memorable win

Arsenal boldly underlined their nationwide supremacy, not forgetting that of North London, in their hundredth League derby against Tottenham Hotspur at White Hart Lane yesterday. It was a pulsating match that graced the presence of so many famous names from bygone derbies between these two great clubs.

As the lepers of European club football, it was the sort of game you wished that the Continent could have been there to see, so that they could view the vibrantly healthy competition they are missing. It had all the finest English qualities; strength, pace, spirit and not least of all, delicate skill, that made you wonder how it could survive in such a vigorous environment.

It was a compliment to the players and the referee that only one player from either side was booked, Hoddle, of Tottenham, surprisingly, and Williams of Arsenal, not so surprisingly, though it took 71 minutes for his petulance and cynicism to be punished.

The introduction of a host of former "champions" from either side stretching down the years helped create further a "big fight" atmosphere. If this Arsenal team have yet to be crowned champions themselves, they opened with the channelled aggression of Mike Tyson, another heir-apparent to undisputed supremacy.

They swarmed over the challengers, catching them cold in the fifth minute before stunning them again five minutes before half time. Tottenham picked themselves up off the floor four minutes later but thereafter, were always running into Arsenal's rigid defence, the deep-lying strength of this team.

David Pleat, the Tottenham manager said: "They have great stickability. We half gifted them two goals but you can't take any credit away from them. The test will come when they've been beaten." And he added a warning which one sensed was on behalf of both clubs when he said: "Sooner or later we will get it away from Merseyside. I don't think there's any doubt about that."

Tottenham were still reeling from a shot by Anderson which Danny Thomas stopped short of the line when Sansom crossed back into Quinn. This time, the young giant stooped to head into space and **ADAMS,** marginally quicker to the ball than Clemence, forced a ricochet over the goalkeeper's head for his sixth and probably most significant goal of the season.

Arsenal continued to force the blistering pace as Rocastle struck a post and Hayes sprinted half the length of the field with a run which must have un-nerved Tottenham supporters even if the finish was unthreatening. Then, seven minutes before half time, Nicholas played a fine ball through the gap to Hayes and Danny Thomas pursued him and brought him down on the fringe of the penalty area. Rocastle back-heeled the free kick to **DAVIS,** who slotted it home through the Tottenham wall with no great power.

Mitchell Thomas, returning after a two match absence with an ankle injury, limped out of the action after nine minutes following a scything tackle by Adams, but returned two minutes later to play an important part in the occasion. In the midst of the mounting frenzy, Clive Allen plucked out a moment's relief to stroke a pass calmly out to Hoddle, who clipped in a diagonal ball which comprehensively defeated the Arsenal defence; Mitchell **THOMAS** converted at the far post.

Ardiles, deputising for the injured Hodge, submerged himself in the derby with great commitment until substituted by Claesen in the 76th minute, as was Quinn by Rix for his first game since September 23.

The action remained hypnotic but for all Tottenham's pressure in the second half, one felt that there was little they could do to give a twist to the tale that was unfolding. There was an inevitability about Arsenal's nineteenth game without defeat which was confirmed in the final minute, when Paul Allen, fighting free of Adams' clutches, crossed into the penalty area and Claesen was flattened by Anderson in a most convenient collision.

Tony Adams causes a moment of panic in the Spurs goalmouth.

101

TOTTENHAM HOTSPUR 1
Claesen

ARSENAL 2
Rocastle, Thomas

Sunday 18th October 1987

Barclays League Division One

White Hart Lane

Attendance 36,680

Tottenham Hotspur

Manager
David Pleat

Arsenal

Manager
George Graham

Tottenham		Arsenal
Tony PARKS	1	John LUKIC
Gary STEVENS	2	Michael THOMAS
Mitchell THOMAS	3	Kenny SANSOM
Ossie ARDILES	4	Steve WILLIAMS
Chris FAIRCLOUGH	5	David O'LEARY
Gary MABBUTT	6	Tony ADAMS
Shaun CLOSE*	7	David ROCASTLE
Paul ALLEN	8	Paul DAVIS
Chris WADDLE	9	Alan SMITH
Steve HODGE*	10	Perry GROVES*
Nico CLAESEN	11	Kevin RICHARDSON
Vinny SAMWAYS (7)	12	Martin HAYES (10)
Clive ALLEN (10)	14	Gus CAESAR

Referee **Mr J E Martin** (Waterlooville)

BACKGROUND

David Pleat had taken Spurs to the FA Cup Final in his first season but even before losing to Coventry at Wembley knew he would have to replace the Monaco-bound Glenn Hoddle. Johnny Metgod was signed from Nottingham Forest, as was centre-half Chris Fairclough, but hopes of a settled start to the season were shattered as Richard Gough, reportedly homesick, returned to Scotland early in October and Steve Hodge was said to be unhappy in London. Despite the unsettling effect of such matters Spurs had extended their home record to 16 wins out of 18 since Arsenal's visit on 4th January. The only defeats had been in the Littlewoods Cup semi-final; against Arsenal. Young striker Shaun Close kept his place at the expense of Clive Allen, but another youngster, Vinny Samways, gave way to fit again Chris Waddle. A groin strain kept Ray Clemence out, giving Tony Parks his first White Hart Lane outing since his penalty heroics had won the UEFA Cup in May 1984. George Graham had also taken Arsenal to a cup final in his first season, a Charlie Nicholas double beating Liverpool in the Littlewoods Cup, but the Wembley hero was now out of favour. Alan Smith, signed after the March 1987 transfer deadline had remained on loan with Leicester till the end of the season but now reported to Highbury where he joined up with other new boys, Kevin Richardson and Nigel Winterburn. After only one point in their first three games Nicholas was dropped and replaced by Perry Groves. Of the next nine games Arsenal had won eight, drawn the other and climbed to third in the table. They had not conceded a goal in seven games. Six days later Frank Bruno and Joe Bugner were due to meet at White Hart Lane and prior to the match between London's football heavyweights the boxing heavyweights were paraded.

BEFORE THE GAME

	P	W	D	L	F	A	Pts
Arsenal	10	6	2	2	18	5	20
Spurs	11	6	2	3	15	8	20

THAT WAS THEN...

★ The cover of the Spurs programme showed a picture of boxing heavyweights Joe Bugner and Frank Bruno together as part of the pre-fight publicity for the following Saturday's 'Big Bang' at White Hart Lane. Bruno stopped Bugner in the eighth round.

David Rocastle strokes home Arsenal's equaliser. Tony Parks and Gary Mabbutt look on helplessly.

'DERBY' STAR **Kenny Sansom** — the Arsenal skipper was in outstanding form, surging down the left flank to link with the front runners.

Stuart Jones, Football Correspondent of 'The Times'...

Arsenal display the class of title contenders

If there is to be a significant threat to Liverpool's potentially overwhelming supremacy in England, it will be posed in the south by Arsenal. Their dominance in North London, confirmed in between an explosively attractive start and a tempestuously unattractive finish at White Hart Lane yesterday, is beyond dispute.

But George Graham. who consistently stated last season that his side was incapable of winning the League title, was not ready to utter any wild claims in spite of their recent record. The victory, which lifted them into third place, was their eighth in a row.

"Some of our attacking play in the first half might have surprised some people," he said. "It looked like we were at home rather than away. There were some lovely patches, which was very encouraging, but we have to learn to perform like that over the full 90 minutes."

Although Arsenal's captain, the outstanding Sansom, puffed out his chest and stated that "there is no better team than us in the country", his manager disagreed. "He is entitled to his opinion but I don't feel that way," he added. Without mentioning Liverpool directly, it was obvious which stronger club he had in mind.

Tottenham Hotspur, beaten twice in their own home by their neighbours in last season's Littlewoods Cup semi-final, even had the benefit of an unlikely slice of generosity. Arsenal, who had not conceded a goal in the previous 11 hours and 43 minutes, extended their resistance for only another 41 seconds.

Williams immediately opened up his own almost impregnable defence with an imprecise back pass. Adams, surprised by the waywardness of his colleague, hesitated. So did Lukic. But **CLAESEN** did not. He promptly hooked in his ninth goal of the season, his fifth in his last four appearances.

"It was a bad mistake," Graham admitted, "but we then showed some character." David Pleat felt that his rearguard, in turn, committed two elementary and crucial errors. "We needed to hold on longer to that lead to give us time to get going." Mitchell Thomas was the guilty party.

Twice, in the fourth and fourteenth minutes, he allowed the territory that he should have been protecting to be invaded. **ROCASTLE**, released by Williams, and Mike **THOMAS**, freed by Smith, punished him and Tottenham's square back four with similarly clean strikes. No matter that Parks, rather than Clemence, was in goal.

The subsequent balance before the interval was unmistakable. Arsenal's pressure was sustained. Tottenham's threats were isolated. After it, as the game subsided into a display of increasingly childish petulance, Pleat's men almost maintained their admirable sequence at home. Not since January 4, 14 fixtures ago, had their own crowd seen them even held.

Williams, who continually betrays his talent through his inability to restrain his malicious spite, eventually had his name taken. So later were those of Ardiles, who is equally given to petty verbal comments to officials and opponents alike, and Waddle, for dissent. Others might also have been booked.

Tottenham became more and more infuriated with Arsenal's offside trap - which was more convincingly secure than their own - and with a linesman's interpretation of the law. One decision in particular, which ruled out a seemingly legitimate effort by Mabbutt, irritated them and their supporters.

Pleat conceded that his view of the incident was obscured but he believed the version of the culprit, Mabbutt, who was convinced that he was onside.

"The rule should be changed anyway," Tottenham's manager suggested. "Anyone who is adjudged to be level with the last defender should be all right."

If so, the comparatively dull second half of the show presented live on television would doubtless have been immeasurably more appealing. Yet it would not have disguised the gap that exists between a solid and confident unit and a set of restless individuals who are neither in form or at full strength.

Tottenham's Gary Mabbutt and Paul Allen struggle to keep tabs on Perry Groves.

102

ARSENAL 2
Smith, Groves

TOTTENHAM HOTSPUR 1
Allen C

Arsenal

Manager
George Graham

Tottenham Hotspur

Manager
Terry Venables

Arsenal	No.	Tottenham Hotspur
John LUKIC	1	Bobby MIMMS
Nigel WINTERBURN	2	Brian STATHAM
Kenny SANSOM	3	Mitchell THOMAS
Michael THOMAS	4	Terry FENWICK
Gus CAESAR	5	Chris FAIRCLOUGH
Tony ADAMS	6	Gary MABBUTT
David ROCASTLE	7	Clive ALLEN
Martin HAYES	8	Paul ALLEN
Alan SMITH	9	Ossie ARDILES
Perry GROVES	10	Vinny SAMWAYS
Kevin RICHARDSON	11	Paul WALSH
Paul DAVIS	12	Nico CLAESEN
Niall QUINN	14	Neil RUDDOCK

Referee **Mr V Callow** (Solihull)

BEFORE THE GAME

	P	W	D	L	F	A	Pts
Arsenal	28	14	6	8	43	26	48
Spurs	30	10	9	11	30	32	39

AT THE SEASON'S END

		P	W	D	L	F	A	Pts
6th	Arsenal	42	18	12	13	58	39	66
13th	Spurs	42	12	11	17	38	48	47

BACKGROUND

On the last day of October Arsenal beat Newcastle to take top spot from Liverpool. They stayed there till the middle of November but from then till February only managed to collect the three points in one of eleven games as the Merseysiders marched towards another title, although progress was made in the Littlewoods and FA Cups. Not helped by Paul Davis being injured it was ironically the loss of his midfield partner, Steve Williams, that saw the end of their bad run. Michael Thomas was switched to midfield for the first leg of the Littlewoods Cup semi-final with Everton won by a Perry Groves goal. In the next four games, all at Highbury, Luton and Charlton were beaten in the League, Manchester United in the FA Cup and Everton in the Littlewoods Cup semi-final second leg. A season Spurs had expected so much from totally collapsed before October was out. It was not the fourth straight 1-2 home defeat by Arsenal that did it but the loss of manager David Pleat, left with little alternative but to resign after newspaper allegations about his private life. In the month before Terry Venables arrived to take over the managerial reins Spurs scored only one goal as they collected just two points from five games and went out of the Littlewoods Cup. Venables first two games were lost but his organisational abilities were soon apparent as results gradually improved. Terry Fenwick was signed to strengthen the defence but it was not until Port Vale knocked Spurs out of the FA Cup that Venables really entered the transfer market, signing Bobby Mimms from Everton and Paul Walsh from Liverpool.

Clive Allen is mobbed by his Spurs teammates after netting the equaliser.

'The Times', reported...

Spurs succumb to forwards under threat

Alan Smith and Perry Groves have responded to the threat posed by the probable arrival at Highbury of Kerry Dixon from Chelsea. The pair, selected to lead the attack in 25 of Arsenal's 38 previous fixtures this season, had never before each scored in the same game.

Yesterday, in doing so, they won the unofficial North London Championship, although it was partially handed to them, and to Smith in particular, by the Tottenham goalkeeper. Mimms, himself a new acquisition, was alone and inexcusably responsible for allowing Arsenal to take a significant early lead within a couple of minutes.

Terry Venables, the Tottenham manager, described it as "a cruel blow". Yet it was entirely avoidable. **SMITH**, in clearing up an untidy mess that typified the rain-soaked afternoon, volleyed on the turn. Mimms, who had failed to clear the initial danger from a corner, merely dived across it's path without diverting it.

It may have been the most blatant error of the goalkeeper, who was brought from Everton for £375,000, but it was not the only mistake he committed. Tottenham were far from flawless as well before the interval, by which time they should have been further behind.

A header from Adams, appointed captain instead of Sansom, was scrambled off the line by Samways and Groves was guilty of embarrassing profligacy. Put through by Rocastle, the calmest and most elegant individual amid the predictable frenzy, he pulled his effort not so much inches as yards wide.

George Graham admitted that his first purchase, who cost no more than £70,000 should have "hit the target", but he added that Groves was "arguably the man of the match" for the regularity and timing of his runs. That he should have claimed the winner was presumably a bonus.

Walsh was instead officially voted the outstanding figure. One of the three fresh players Venables has so far introduced, he was principally responsible for a recovery that was sensed apparently by Tottenham's followers - who persisted

in singing in the rain at the start of the second half - but had seemed utterly unlikely.

After a typically spritely turn, Walsh invited Clive **ALLEN** - who had claimed only four goals before Venables took over - to increase his total since to nine with the crispest of drives from the edge of the area. "For 25 minutes we lost it," Graham conceded. "and they dominated us."

So fiery had been Tottenham's response that Arsenal's decisive strike was in turn unexpected. A throw from Sansom, whose future at Highbury is now the subject of some debate, bounced over Smith and Fairclough to **GROVES**. His shot in the 75th minute bisected the gaps between Fenwick's legs and between Mimms and the far post.

"Local derbies are always tight," Graham said, "and this was no exception, but it was unusual in that the four strikers were outstanding." He preferred not to comment on speculation concerning Dixon, one of the viewers watching the occasion on television.

Perry Groves is congratulated by Michael Thomas after scoring what proved to be the winner.

Top left: Tony Adams heads clear of Mitchell Thomas and Ossie Ardiles.

103

TOTTENHAM HOTSPUR 2
Waddle, Gascoigne

ARSENAL 3
Winterburn, Marwood, Smith

Saturday 10th September 1988

Barclays League Division One

White Hart Lane

Attendance 32,621

Tottenham Hotspur

Manager
Terry Venables

Arsenal

Manager
George Graham

Bobby MIMMS	1	John LUKIC
Brian STATHAM*	2	Lee DIXON
Mitchell THOMAS	3	Nigel WINTERBURN
Terry FENWICK	4	Michael THOMAS
Chris FAIRCLOUGH	5	David O'LEARY
Gary MABBUTT	6	Tony ADAMS
Paul WALSH	7	David ROCASTLE*
Paul GASCOIGNE	8	Paul DAVIS
Chris WADDLE	9	Alan SMITH
Vinny SAMWAYS*	10	Paul MERSON
Paul ALLEN	11	Brian MARWOOD*
David HOWELLS (2)	12	Perry GROVES (11)
Paul MORAN (10)	14	Kevin RICHARDSON (7)

*Referee **Mr L C Shapter** (Torquay)*

BACKGROUND

A place in the bottom half of the table was not good enough for Spurs and Terry Venables spent the close season rebuilding his team with a vengeance, twice breaking Spurs' transfer record. First to arrive was Manchester City centre-forward Paul Stewart for £1.7 million, hotly followed by Newcastle's outstanding young midfielder Paul Gascoigne for £300,000 more. Both played as Spurs were beaten 0-4 by Arsenal in the Wembley International tournament but the embarrassment of that defeat was nothing compared to the fiasco of the League's opening day. Due to entertain Coventry, the game was called off at the last minute when the local council refused a safety certificate because of continuing work on the refurbishment of the East Stand. It meant Gascoigne's Spurs' debut took place on familiar territory, St James' Park, where goals from Terry Fenwick and Chris Waddle secured Spurs a 2-2 draw. Paul Stewart was absent from that game, as he was for Arsenal's visit, a four game suspension a legacy of his time at Maine Road. George Graham had completed his rebuilding of Arsenal in the summer with the signing of Steve Bould from Stoke, although he was disappointed to lose out on West Ham's Tony Cottee who preferred to join Everton. Brian Marwood had been secured from Sheffield Wednesday in late March 1988 and with Lee Dixon and Nigel Winterburn making the full-back spots their own he had a team capable of bringing the championship trophy back to London for the first time since 1971. They made a cracking start to the season with a 5-1 win at Wimbledon but surprisingly lost 2-3 at home to Aston Villa in the next game, Smith netting his fourth goal of the campaign and Marwood his second.

BEFORE THE GAME

	P	W	D	L	F	A	Pts
Spurs	1	0	1	0	2	2	1
Arsenal	2	1	0	1	7	4	3

PAUL DAVIS surely forced himself into the England side on the day that Paul Gascoigne socked it to 'em in a tremendous North London derby.

Arsenal midfielder Davis and his Gunners took the honours, but Gazza signalled his Spurs home debut with a goal from his stockinged right foot when he lost his boot.

It was Arsenal's fifth win in a row at White Hart Lane since George Graham became manager, but his opposite number Terry Venables was left talking of what might have been at the end of this five-goal thriller.

Spurs had two goals ruled out by offside in a second half fightback and Venables claimed: "I have seen the video and Vinny Samways' effort on the hour should have

Nigel Winterburn salutes his goal.

Above: John Lukic gathers safely from Paul Allen.

Rob Hughes in 'The Sunday Times'...

GAS COOKING

Below: Paul Gascoigne celebrates his goal — 'the Mars bar kid was on a different plane'!

The message from White Hart Lane is that Gascoigne is ready to begin the meaningful period of his career that should lead to him assuming the mantle of England midfield creator. The weather was Brazilian, the pace British, the tactics neither one thing nor the other, and the skill - split level. Gascoigne, and to a lesser degree Waddle, were above the ordinariness.

The afternoon turned on an extraordinary 18 minutes of tissue-thin defences offering up gift goals. First, after 21 minutes, Mimms was to blame. **WINTERBURN** was allowed to make tracks down the left and then, seeing the goalkeeper standing like a rabbit caught in headlamps, the Arsenal left-back was able to score with a long, low-angled shot which Mimms appeared to think was going wide.

Three minutes later Tottenham were level when Arsenal's back four, standing idly square, allowed Allen to penetrate them, and, from his pass, **WADDLE** to use his left foot to beat Lukic.

Then came two soft Arsenal goals within the space of 90 seconds. After a free-kick, Davis lobbed the ball into the heart of the Tottenham defence, nobody was capable of blocking out **MARWOOD** and he was able to score from six yards. **SMITH** plucked out another goal from Winterburn's accurate centre.

What was clear, at least in the first half, was the distinctive quality of Gascoigne. Though he later faded, he managed to eclipse the midfield Arsenal trio of Davis, Thomas and Rocastle who will vie with him for an England place on Wednesday. They were efficient but the Mars bar kid was on a different plane.

When Waddle offered the chance to score, **GASCOIGNE** strode through the inside right channel, produced a matador's swerve which put Lukic on the seat of his pants and finished the scoring.

Shining amidst the disorder, he excelled. Ironically, when his effort was spent, Tottenham swept forward and might have saved the match, not least in the dying moments when Mabbutt headed in, but from an offside position.

104

ARSENAL 2
Merson, Thomas

TOTTENHAM HOTSPUR 0

Arsenal

Tottenham Hotspur

Manager
George Graham

Manager
Terry Venables

John LUKIC	1	Bobby MIMMS
David O'LEARY	2	Guy BUTTERS
Nigel WINTERBURN	3	Mitchell THOMAS
Michael THOMAS	4	Terry FENWICK
Steve BOULD	5	Chris FAIRCLOUGH
Tony ADAMS	6	Gary MABBUTT
David ROCASTLE	7	Paul WALSH
Kevin RICHARDSON*	8	Gudni BERGSSON
Alan SMITH	9	Chris WADDLE
Paul MERSON	10	Paul STEWART
Brian MARWOOD*	11	Paul ALLEN
Paul DAVIS (8)	12	Chris HUGHTON
Perry GROVES (11)	14	Paul MORAN

Referee **Mr A Seville** (Birmingham)

BACKGROUND

George Graham's shrewd transfer dealings added to the young home-grown talent he inherited had made Arsenal amongst the championship favourites before the season began. When 1989 arrived they were red hot favourites, eleven points ahead of Liverpool and with only Norwich looking a threat. Television demands meant a five o'clock kick-off and with Norwich having drawn with QPR, Arsenal knew victory over Spurs would take them two points clear of the East Anglians. Everything had gone right for Graham's men, the defence solid in the best Arsenal tradition, Smith and Merson finding the target regularly, injuries few and far between. The only set-back had come a week after beating Spurs at White Hart Lane when Paul Davis was caught by the TV cameras punching Southampton's Glenn Cockerill in an off-the-ball incident. Davis received a nine game ban but in Kevin Richardson Arsenal had a more than adequate replacement. Even when Lee Dixon was injured David O'Leary, a central defender all his career, proved a revelation at full-back. If everything in the Highbury garden was rosy the same could not be said of life at White Hart Lane. One win in the first ten games had left Spurs propping up the First Division. Gascoigne was fulfilling all expectations but Stewart disappointed, just one goal in his first nine games. The turning point had come in a Littlewoods Cup replay at Blackburn when Stewart got the winner in extra-time. A 3-2 win over Wimbledon three days later took them off the bottom of the table and only one defeat in the next eight League games gave them mid-table security. Changes had been made; young centre-half Guy Butters replacing the unfortunate Gary Stevens, injured again, the giant Norwegian Erik Thorstvedt just waiting for Bobby Mimms to make the mistake that would let him in and Icelandic international Gudni Bergsson making his debut in a Boxing Day draw with Luton and retaining his place for the 2-0 defeat of Newcastle two days before the game at Highbury. Before the match Graham and Venables unveiled the famous Arsenal clock in it's new position above the new Clock End stand. The clock had first been erected in September 1930 - the first season Arsenal had won the League Championship.

BEFORE THE GAME

	P	W	D	L	F	A	Pts
Arsenal	18	11	4	3	40	20	48
Spurs	19	6	7	6	30	28	25

AT THE SEASON'S END

		P	W	D	L	F	A	Pts
1st	Arsenal	38	22	10	6	73	36	76
6th	Spurs	38	15	12	11	60	46	57

Steve Bould heads clear of a crowded goalmouth.

Arsenal go back on top without scaling heights

THAT WAS THEN...

★ Seat ticket prices for this Highbury 'derby' ranged from £5.50 for an adult member in the Family Enclosure (£2.75 children) up to £12.00 for a centre block position.

★ The match programme was 80p for 32 pages.

Norwich City experienced surely the shortest residence of any team at the top of the League yesterday when Arsenal, kicking off two hours behind the East Anglian club, did just enough to regain the lead by two points and confirm their position as championship favourites.

As derbies between the two north London giants go, this one at Highbury was not one of the better ones. But then they are seldom classics.

Arsenal, having asserted their authority in the first half when Merson gave them the lead with his eighth goal of the season, kept Tottenham at bay during a more evenly contested second half.

Despite the presence of ITV cameras, Arsenal's biggest League crowd of the season, 45,129, turned up to acclaim their champions-elect. But if it was not one of Arsenal's more impressive performances, they again, displayed the strength, skill, and perhaps not least the luck necessary to take the title back to Highbury for the first time in 18 seasons.

Tottenham's supporters will point to the valid appeals for a penalty just before half-time, when Lukic brought down Waddle with his legs, and to the second-half chances scorned by Waddle and Stewart. The England winger failed to hit the target with two free headers and Stewart, similarly unattended, shot straight at Lukic in the 89th minute.

For all that, I never felt that Tottenham were deserving of a draw, even if the outcome was in doubt until the last minute, when Merson put Michael **THOMAS** through for a simple second goal.

One cannot deny that Arsenal have finally shaken off the "boring" tag as Peter Hill-Wood, the club chairman, was at pains to emphasise in the programme.

"There was a time, a few years ago, when even I feared the tag might be appropriate." he said. "Not now. We don't go away and play defensively, not even at Liverpool."

"We are an adventurous team now. That's a great tribute to George Graham's leadership, because managers are in a precarious profession and it's much safer to opt for an unimaginative approach."

Hill-Wood made it clear that the club has no intention of following Tottenham's commercial route. He said: "Success on the pitch is vital before you can market commercial schemes. We don't see Arsenal becoming a leisure company. We see ourselves as a well-run football club, playing attractive and successful football into the 21st century."

It was Tottenham who started the more enterprising. The old clock, which was unveiled before the kick-off in it's more elevated position above the £6.5 million ground development, told us the game was eight minutes old when Tottenham made the first threatening move.

Lukic, coming to meet a free kick from Fenwick, punched the ball weakly and straight at Butters. He looped a header back over the goalkeeper and it was only the defensive vigilance of Smith which avoided an embarrassing start for Arsenal.

It proved to be a momentary aberration on the part of the Arsenal defence who, apart from the odd moment in the second half, held the menace of Stewart and Walsh in check. Stewart was fortunate to see out the game after going in with his boot up on Adams.

Tottenham's attempt to take the initiative was disappointing. It was to be hoped that the clear-cut victory against Newcastle United had removed any suggestion that Gascoigne was all-important to Tottenham. Without the

Michael Thomas and Paul Davis line up the Arsenal wall. Spurs' Paul Walsh tags onto the end.

precocious young midfield talent, Tottenham were sadly lacking in initiative and variety in their attacking play.

Arsenal, by contrast, were the epitome of pure, free-flowing football. Even before they had taken the lead they played with the confidence one might expect from a side who have not been beaten by their great rivals in four seasons of League encounters.

A cheer went up from the terraces as Davis went through his warming-up exercises on the touchline, but Arsenal did not call upon their midfield player until the 74th minute, when he made his first appearance since the start of his nine match suspension on October 12.

It was another sound reason why Arsenal look the team most likely to succeed Liverpool; strength and depth could be decisive over the remaining months of the season.

Arsenal's goal in the 24th minute was a good example of the intelligent and unselfish way in which they combined.

Marwood, bubbling nicely on the wing, cut inside a defender and crossed for Smith to nod the ball cleverly on to where he knew Merson lurked. With great composure, despite the attention of Fairclough, **MERSON** managed to pull his shot around the defender and wide of Mimms, who conceded his first goal in four matches.

'DERBY' STAR **Paul Merson** — scored the first and set up the second for Michael Thomas.

105

TOTTENHAM HOTSPUR 2
Samways, Walsh

ARSENAL 1
Thomas

BACKGROUND

Terry Venables continued his big spending, investing £750,000 on midfielder Steve Sedgley from Coventry and agreeing to pay £1.5 million to Barcelona to secure England's premier goalscorer, Gary Lineker, and make permanent the signing of Nayim, who had been at White Hart Lane on loan since October 1988. Despite injuries in pre-season games Spurs started by beating Luton but Venables was still looking to strengthen his squad and after a defeat at Everton in the next game at last tied up a £600,000 deal for their experienced Welsh international defender Pat Van Den Hauwe. A draw and two defeats left Spurs with only Sheffield Wednesday below them and it was not until his sixth game that Lineker notched his first League goal for Spurs. A hat-trick against QPR followed and four days before the derby Lineker scored again in a 3-1 win over Charlton although Nayim suffered a knee injury that put him out of Arsenal's visit. Paul Walsh took his place. Arsenal had won the championship in the most dramatic fashion with Michael Thomas scoring the last minute winner at Anfield. Graham decided to remain loyal to the men who had secured their ninth title, his only signing Icelandic international Siggi Jonsson from Sheffield Wednesday for a tribunal fixed £475,000. The defending champions learnt in their opening match of the season the truth of the old adage that it is harder to retain the title than to win it and opponents raise their game against the title-holders, losing 1-4 at Manchester United. They soon got back to the old routine, winning seven and drawing two of their next nine games to know that victory over Spurs would put them on top of the table. Fresh from a 4-0 hammering of Manchester City, Martin Hayes replaced the injured Brian Marwood and Perry Groves was called up for his first start of the season with Paul Merson taking a seat on the bench.

Tottenham Hotspur		Arsenal

Manager **Terry Venables**		Manager **George Graham**

Tottenham		Arsenal
Erik THORSTVEDT	1	John LUKIC
Mitchell THOMAS	2	Lee DIXON
Pat VAN DEN HAUWE	3	Nigel WINTERBURN
Terry FENWICK	4	Michael THOMAS
Paul ALLEN	5	David O'LEARY
Gary MABBUTT	6	Tony ADAMS
Paul WALSH	7	David ROCASTLE
Paul GASCOIGNE	8	Kevin RICHARDSON*
Vinny SAMWAYS*	9	Alan SMITH*
Gary LINEKER	10	Perry GROVES
Steve SEDGLEY	11	Martin HAYES
Guy BUTTERS	12	Siggi JONSSON (8)
David HOWELLS (9)	14	Paul MERSON (9)

Referee **Mr R Milford** (Bristol)

BEFORE THE GAME

	P	W	D	L	F	A	Pts
Arsenal	8	5	2	1	15	5	17
Spurs	8	3	2	3	13	15	11

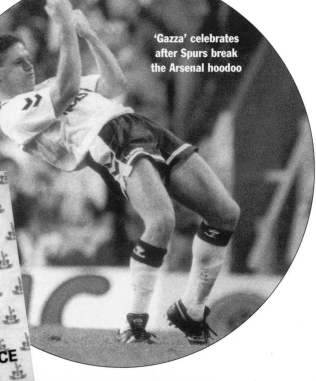

'Gazza' celebrates after Spurs break the Arsenal hoodoo

Patrick Barclay in
'The Independent' *reported...*

Spurs achieve a rare triumph over tension

Tottenham, who had twice let slip leads of two goals in recent weeks, held on to the match that mattered to their supporters at White Hart Lane last night.

A rolling, thunderstorm of relief greeted Spurs' success in the North London confrontation, all the sweeter for its rarity, and for once their defence took a major share of the honours, even if a late lapse forced Erik Thorstvedt to make a breathtaking save from Perry Groves's header.

With 10 points now secured from a possible 12, Terry Venables professed himself: "Very encouraged," adding: "We have waited for a long time for this, Arsenal have outfought us in the past, but it didn't happen tonight."

This was nevertheless far from a glory, glory night: gory, gory was more like it as fouls proliferated on the turf once graced by Blanchflower and White. Those among the 34,000 who had come merely to see Spurs win, however, after five successive home defeats by Arsenal, went home satisfied, courtesy of first-half goals from Vinny Samways and Paul Walsh.

The champions, though, were not at their best, especially in defence during what George Graham called the "crazy spell" that cost them the goals. A victory would have given them the League leadership, yet had Gary Lineker made more of his chances defeat might have rivalled Arsenal's last, by 5-1 at Old Trafford on the opening day of the season.

So much for football. The tension was no excuse for so much crass ferocity. After only a couple of minutes Steve Sedgley had to go off for stitches in his head after tangling

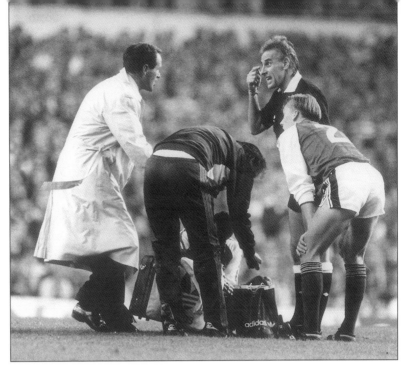

with Groves. He returned to play impressively. But for 34 minutes, as the contest clattered on, Arsenal seemed in no serious trouble.

Then the pattern dramatically altered after Tony Adams committed one foul too many. The free kick was partly cleared to **SAMWAYS**, who shot through a line of defenders, the ball taking a deflection as it sped beyond John Lukic.

Three minutes later, after Adams, in pulling back Walsh, had been booked for persistent fouling, Spurs scored again. Another free kick, wide on the right, was floated into the middle by Paul Gascoigne and **WALSH**, loosely marked, put a delicate header inside the far post.

The rough and tumble continued after the interval with bookings for Terry Fenwick, Gascoigne, Michael Thomas and Kevin Richardson.

The drama was fed in the 53rd minute when Arsenal reduced Spurs' lead. Thorstvedt let a long drive from David Rocastle bounce off his chest and the ensuing corner was backheaded by David O'Leary. Rocastle could not quite force the ball in at the far post but it broke to **THOMAS** and was in the net in a flash.

Now Arsenal surged forward in numbers, Lee Dixon's overlaps giving Rocastle space on the right, but several times they were caught short at the back. A superb reverse pass by Gascoigne gave Lineker one opportunity, which he put wide as Lukic came out. The substitute David Howells then played a fine through pass that let the England striker veer away from Adams, only to miss the target again. But, thanks to Spurs' Norwegian goalkeeper, there was no need for sombre reflection.

A game littered with fouls saw Arsenal boss George Graham race onto the pitch after a challenge on Perry Groves. "I saw it!" said referee Roger Milford (above).

Below left: Paul Walsh falls to the ground after a clash with Lee Dixon.

TOTTENHAM used the temper of Tony Adams to their advantage last night as they turned the tables on their illustrious North London neighbours.

For five crucial minutes of a frantic and frenetic White Hart Lane derby Arsenal skipper Adams let a red mist obscure his usually phlegmatic spirit.

He gave away critical free kicks on the edge of his own area — and both resulted in the goals that ultimately decided the issue.

Adams, who has been a Titan in these

TOTTENHAM emerged at last from the shadow of their great rivals to achieve their most important result under Terry Venables.

This hard-earned victory could prove a vital brick in Venables's rebuilding at White Hart Lane, laying the North London hoodoo which Arsenal have maintained ever since his arrival.

106

ARSENAL 1
Adams

TOTTENHAM HOTSPUR 0

Arsenal

Tottenham Hotspur

Manager
George Graham

Manager
Terry Venables

Arsenal		Tottenham Hotspur
John LUKIC	1	Erik THORSTVEDT
Lee DIXON	2	Mitchell THOMAS
Paul DAVIS	3	Pat VAN DEN HAUWE*
Michael THOMAS	4	Paul ALLEN
David O'LEARY	5	David HOWELLS
Tony ADAMS	6	Gary MABBUTT
David ROCASTLE	7	Vinny SAMWAYS*
Kevin RICHARDSON	8	John POLSTON
Alan SMITH	9	Paul STEWART
Steve BOULD	10	Gary LINEKER
Perry GROVES	11	Steve SEDGLEY
Brian MARWOOD	12	Paul WALSH (3)
Paul MERSON	14	NAYIM (7)

Referee **Mr V Callow** (Solihull)

BACKGROUND

By the middle of November Arsenal were leading the title chase but three defeats in the four games since Christmas had left them four points behind Liverpool and Aston Villa. Having lost their last match at Wimbledon, three points were essential if they were not to give up all hope of retaining the title. David Rocastle was recalled after four games on the bench and Paul Merson again found Perry Groves preferred for a North London derby. Spurs had done little since beating Arsenal, hovering around mid-table but never likely to get in amongst the pacesetters. Knocked out of the FA Cup by Southampton, their only hope of any silverware lay in the Littlewoods Cup where they had drawn at Nottingham Forest in the fifth round three days before the game at Highbury. Paul Gascoigne, who had broken a bone in his arm at Coventry on New Year's Day was still absent

BEFORE THE GAME

	P	W	D	L	F	A	Pts
Arsenal	22	12	3	7	37	24	39
Spurs	22	9	6	7	32	29	33

AT THE SEASON'S END

	P	W	D	L	F	A	Pts
3rd Spurs	38	19	6	13	60	47	63
4th Arsenal	38	18	8	12	54	38	62

AN emphatic contribution from the much-maligned Tony Adams determined the right outcome of a frenetic North London clash.

The third goal in five games from the young Arsenal captain confirmed that, despite the anxieties of manager George Graham about alarming fluctuation in form, it's not impossible that the League Championship will stay at Highbury for a further season.

Hopefully, however, the blustering claim of Tottenham that a title tilt remains one of their ambitions will be laid to decent rest.

David Rocastle leaves Spurs sub Nayim on his backside (right) and Paul Davis shrugs off a challenge from Mitchell Thomas (far right).

Adams moves in for the skill

Some of the few neutral observers at a packed Highbury felt that this match needed all its brimming aggression and exciting incident to compensate for the painful scarcity of imagination and coherence.

The two managers, however, saw it differently. Terry Venables and George Graham are among the most informed of insiders but the tributes they tossed towards their men at the finish seemed, to say the least, slightly lacking in objectivity. Perhaps the key is to be found in Graham's declaration that the game was a marvellous advertisement for English football. All such a claim can do is to make us wonder about the qualities English football has to advertise these days. Certainly, on this evidence, they rarely include players with the ability to impose a thoughtful shape on the play from midfield, to look at the big picture and set about altering it to their own design. Much of the action in that area was confined to a spirited swirl. Even when such as Rocastle and Thomas were making telling contributions it was generally with brief forward surges on the ball, seldom in the form of intelligent probing. It was all about as cerebral as a hailstorm.

Nostalgic mutterings about the not-so-distant days when Arsenal could call on a Brady, Tottenham on a Hoddle, may be out of place but the mere fact that the term "playmaker" has the ring of cliche does not mean the function it describes has lost its validity.

'DERBY' STAR Tony Adams — Arsenal's young captain scored the winner with a deadly volley that crashed in off the far post.

Naturally the Arsenal majority in a crowd of 46,000 (which was under capacity yet apparently left many milling around miserably outside) would be happy with a victory that was undoubtably much more more deserved than Mr Venables acknowledges and should do something to nourish

faltering belief that the League title can be retained. And there is no doubt that the club's captain, Adams, will have fond memories of how he settled this sometimes bitter North London derby with his fourth goal of the season.

Such a scoring rate isn't bad for a central defender and he has the additional satisfaction of knowing that his volley in the 63rd minute was struck with a killing certainty that would have done credit to a specialist finisher.

Arsenal should have scored an hour earlier when, in their first attack, Rocastle gave Thomas the chance to pass into the net. Thomas responded with too much vigour and too little accuracy and the ball spun high and wide of the goal. Groves, too, should have hit the net (and more than once) before half-time but the best he could do was hook a right-foot shot against the bar.

There was early evidence of a harsh edge when Van den Hauwe and Rocastle were involved in a brief but nasty skirmish that prompted the referee to take the names of both.

More palatable excitement came from an electric Lineker. He had that old air of the hunting greyhound about him.

All he needed was the right encouragement and that was provided when Sedgley made a smooth, perceptive run out of defence and, having been fed by Samways, perfectly delivered the kind of pass Lineker has always loved to exploit. The England forward stabbed in an instant shot and he had a right to clutch his head in frustration when the ball rammed against the foot of Lukic's right-hand post and bounced harmlessly across the face of the goal.

There was no shortage of hectic activity around both goals during a second half in which Spurs replaced Samways and the injured Van den Hauwe with Nayim and Walsh but what counted was the response of **ADAMS** when a Richardson corner from the right was headed on by Bould. As the ball rose conveniently from the ground he swung his right leg with precise venom to score off Thorstvedt's left-hand post.

107

ARSENAL 0

TOTTENHAM HOTSPUR 0

Arsenal   Tottenham Hotspur

Manager
George Graham

Manager
Terry Venables

David SEAMAN	1	Erik THORSTVEDT
Lee DIXON	2	Gudni BERGSSON
Nigel WINTERBURN	3	Pat VAN DEN HAUWE
Michael THOMAS	4	Steve SEDGLEY
Steve BOULD	5	David HOWELLS
Tony ADAMS	6	Gary MABBUTT
David ROCASTLE	7	Paul STEWART
Paul DAVIS	8	Paul GASCOIGNE*
Alan SMITH	9	NAYIM
Paul MERSON*	10	Gary LINEKER
Anders LIMPAR	11	Paul ALLEN
Perry GROVES (10)	12	Paul WALSH
Andy LINIGHAN	14	Mitchell THOMAS (8)

Referee **Mr J Worrall** (Warrington)

BACKGROUND

In his four years in charge George Graham had not been averse to spending Arsenal's money in the transfer market but he had resisted the temptation to really splash out on big buys. Having finished one point and one place behind Spurs that changed in the summer of 1990 when he paid £1.3 million to secure QPR's England 'keeper, David Seaman, and another £1 million to sign Sweden's Anders Limpar from Cremonese. The Limpar signing was looked upon in some quarters as something of a gamble, a flair player, unpredictable, not the normal steady player Graham would usually go for. He did not look out of place as Arsenal won their first two games, 3-0 at Wimbledon and 2-1 against Luton at Highbury. Terry Venables had never been afraid to back his judgment with big money but, perhaps a sign of things to come, his summer transfer dealings had been modest by any standards. Justin Edinburgh, a £150,000 capture from Southend and John Hendry, £50,000 from Dundee, both youngsters signed with the future in mind, were the only new arrivals. Neither of them figured in the first team as Spurs started with a home 3-1 victory over Manchester City and a goalless draw at Sunderland.

BEFORE THE GAME

	P	W	D	L	F	A	Pts
Arsenal	2	2	0	0	5	1	6
Spurs	2	1	1	0	3	1	4

THAT WAS THEN

★ Admission prices for this game ranged from £8 to £16 for seats and £7 (half price for senior citizens and juniors) to stand on the terraces.

★ The 32-page Arsenal programme cost £1.

EXECUTIVE BOXES

BARCLAYS LEAGUE – DIVISION 1

ARSENAL
v
TOTTENHAM HOTSPUR
SATURDAY 1st SEPTEMBER 1990
KICK-OFF 3.00

ARSENAL FOOTBALL CLUB LIMITED
BARCLAYS LEAGUE DIV. ONE
ARSENAL V TOTTENHAM HOTSPUR
01 SEP 1990 03:00

Above: Nigel Winterburn gets a toe to the ball despite Gary Lineker's efforts to fend him off.

Below: David Seaman punches the ball clear of Paul Stewart as Lee Dixon guards.

In 'The Sunday Telegraph' Colin Malam reported...

Spurs spike Arsenal guns

Tottenham suggested yesterday that they may be more durable now than in the past. Though definitely second-best in the second half of a frenzied north London derby, their defence stood up well to the pounding it received from Arsenal.

A match of few incidents was notable for the substitution, two minutes from the end, of Spurs' national hero, Paul Gascoigne. Although the England star had not played well, the introduction of Mitchell Thomas for him was probably intended principally to secure a valuable away point.

Not surprisingly, in view of the tribal passion aroused by the pre-match hype there was a violent beginning. Only a minute had gone when Adams was booked for clattering into Stewart from behind, leaving the Spurs striker writhing in agony.

Just as predictably, Arsenal did most of the early pressing, with Davis settling in mid-field quicker than Gascoigne. Thorstvedt had to field an awkward, bouncing shot from Davis after the Arsenal man had dribbled himself cleverly into shooting range.

Spurs just could not get going and their frustration showed when Stewart, flagged offside, said something to the linesman that earned him a lecture from the referee.

Nearly 25 minutes had gone when Seaman first had to exert himself in Arsenal's goal. Anticipating the danger well, he snatched the ball off Allen's head at the edge of the area.

Little had been seen of Gascoigne but he reminded the

North Bank of his presence after 28 minutes with a swerving free-kick that had Seaman diving anxiously across goal as the ball flew narrowly wide of the far post.

Like Davis's dribbling and passing, Seaman's fine anticipation was one of the first half's redeeming features. Arsenal's expensive new goalkeeper read the play expertly again to snatch the ball away from Allen once more as the Spurs forward exchanged passes with Nayim.

Depressingly, the second half began in exactly the same manner as the first. This time, the yellow card was shown to Bergsson for bringing down Winterburn as the opposing full-back threatened to get away.

Arsenal's Swedish winger was more involved in the play in the first few minutes of the second half than he had been throughout the first. It was his return pass that Davis was going for in the 55th minute when he went down under a challenge from Howells.

Arsenal and their fans appealed loudly for a penalty, but the referee was unconvinced. A few minutes later, Mr Worrall again refused to respond to Arsenal's appeals when Bould collapsed in a heap with Van den Hauwe as they challenged for a Winterburn centre.

Roused, perhaps, by feelings of injustice, the Gunners opened up with everything they had and nearly scored in the 65th minute. Given some space for the first time in a suffocating match, Smith slid Thomas's astute pass wide of the far post.

108

TOTTENHAM HOTSPUR 0

ARSENAL 0

Tottenham Hotspur

Manager
Terry Venables

Arsenal

Manager
George Graham

Erik THORSTVEDT	1	David SEAMAN
Mitchell THOMAS	2	Lee DIXON
Justin EDINBURGH	3	Nigel WINTERBURN
Terry FENWICK	4	Michael THOMAS
David HOWELLS	5	Steve BOULD
Gary MABBUTT	6	Andy LINIGHAN
Paul STEWART	7	David O'LEARY
Paul GASCOIGNE	8	Paul DAVIS*
Paul WALSH	9	Alan SMITH
Gary LINEKER	10	Paul MERSON*
Paul ALLEN	11	Anders LIMPAR
Paul MORAN	12	David HILLIER (8)
Steve SEDGLEY	14	Perry GROVES (10)

Referee **Mr A Buksh** *(London)*

BACKGROUND

Having spent much of the season in third place, always behind Liverpool and Arsenal, Spurs had slipped up after Christmas with three defeats on the trot, a run brought to an end seven days earlier with a third round FA Cup victory at Fourth Division Blackpool. In their last game before the holiday season they had beaten Luton 2-1 despite having Nayim and Pat Van Den Hauwe sent off but they were now suspended, Paul Walsh replacing Nayim and Justin Edinburgh getting a rare chance to show what he could do. Terry Fenwick, who had broken his leg fourteen months earlier, retained his place at Steve Sedgley's expense after his first outing of the season at Blackpool. Arsenal were second, a position they had occupied nearly all season, one point behind Liverpool having played a game more but with two points deducted after a mass brawl at Old Trafford in October. Unbeaten in the League all season, Arsenal's great strength, as always, lay with their defence, only ten goals conceded, and that despite losing captain Tony Adams. Convicted before Christmas of a drink-driving offence, he was in the middle of a three month prison sentence but Andy Linighan, a summer signing from Norwich, was proving a more than adequate deputy. Stopping goals was not their only forte for they were joint top scorers with Liverpool and Alan Smith had scored six in the last four games.

BEFORE THE GAME

	P	W	D	L	F	A	Pts
Arsenal*	21	14	7	0	41	10	47
Spurs	21	9	6	6	34	27	33

*Two points deducted

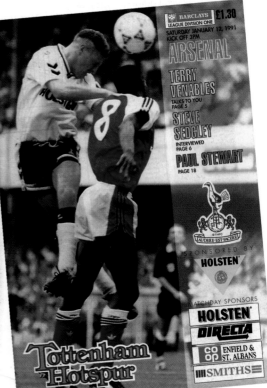

ARSENAL are still unbeaten after 22 League games this season — courtesy of England skipper Gary Lineker.

Crackshot Lineker is ⬚⬚⬚⬚⬚ ⬚⬚⬚⬚⬚ean spell, with only one goal from ⬚⬚⬚⬚⬚ ⬚⬚⬚he last seven games.

He should have had a ⬚⬚⬚⬚⬚⬚⬚⬚⬚ No wonder Gary shook his head in dis⬚⬚⬚⬚ ⬚⬚⬚manager Terry Venables afterwards.

It's true Lineker didn't have much luck. In the 15th minute he looked to be pulled back by David O'Leary ⬚⬚⬚ odds-on to score.

And, in the ⬚⬚⬚ stages, he was ⬚⬚⬚⬚⬚ a brilliant ⬚⬚⬚ David Seam⬚⬚⬚ ball sailing ⬚⬚⬚⬚ corner o⬚⬚

Arsenal remain unbeaten after a hard struggle

The earth moved in the 100th north London derby but, alas, there were no goals. It leaves Arsenal undefeated after 22 games, and still second in the championship.

And to those American orientated FIFA lords who deem a goalless match to be anathema, let it be said defences also earn a crust, and Arsenal were this time taken to the depths of their competitiveness in a season which for endurance must rank with any in their history.

One had wondered about Lineker's pre-match statement that this is more intense even than a Merseyside derby. But when did he ever lie? The master of understatement was pitched in the thick of it from the opening moment of a match which exploded into action, in which the often reckless pace and bruising commitment was such that one was reminded of fighting cocks.

Gascoigne, hysterically booed by the Arsenal section, was playing his last match before suspension, and though his lip was buttoned he certainly was physically putting it about. In the first minute he clattered into Winterburn, and after several more fouls he was fortunate to be at least booked for a flailing two-footed jump tackle at Limpar.

Yet in between this both Gascoigne and his team flickered through the attrition with some moves burning with vivacity. In the eighth minute Mitchell Thomas and Gascoigne opened up the Arsenal defence. And when Gascoigne exchanged a final one-two with Lineker, the half-chance fell to Gascoigne, who, from 10 yards, rolled his shot wide.

The signal, if anything, was to inject even more ferocity of pace. Walsh suddenly found Lineker with a diagonal through-ball struck with the outside of his boot. Lineker swept past Bould but shot high. Then, after 18 minutes, Lineker, with his searing acceleration, coursed through once more. The move had swept from Thorstvedt, Fenwick and Howells. Lineker passed O'Leary, was held back by the Arsenal defender tugging at his shirt sleeve, but after Seaman had deflected his shot wide referee Buksh ignored the clear penalty.

However, during this period of whole-hearted Tottenham running, it is doubtful if any other side in the land could have stood so resolute for so long as did Arsenal. Sometimes we overlook the fact that their defence, with the exception of O'Leary, had known rejection in the early years of their careers. George Graham evidently, looks for that, and turns hunger into resolve.

And, almost as if it were timed with swift precision, Arsenal began after 25 minutes to get their full-backs into forward positions, and to release Merson and Limpar for swift counter-attacks.

Merson was particularly elusive. With one audacious body-swerve he proved so tricky that Gazza, no less, was left in a crumpled heap on the turf.

In another Merson break, Stewart, adapting well to his midfield duties, tracked back to dispossess the Arsenal forward close to the penalty spot. And Edinburgh twice showed the sort of calm with his interceptions in dangerous situations that make him most unlike a Tottenham defender.

The unremitting hardness was reflected in yellow cards for harsh fouls by Winterburn and Linighan, but the thirst for daring forward runs was still more than evident in the sec-

ond half. (In fact Arsenal appealed after the match that Winterburn's yellow card was mistaken identity, that Limpar had made the trip.)

Paul Allen battled his way forward, tussled around Winterburn, ignored the challenge which put him on his knees, and scuffled back on to his feet to attempt a shot which deflected off O'Leary.

Within 30 seconds Limpar was retaliating in kind. He took the ball straight at Mabbutt, somehow performed slight of foot to lose the Spurs captain, and then persuaded Thorstvedt to use every inch of his 6ft 3in frame to palm Limpar's crafty shot over.

Limpar wanted more. He was quick as a lizard in spotting Mabbutt had dwelt on the ball. The Swede was upon him but Thorstvedt, an excellent sweeper, raced out of his area to block-tackle the ball to safety.

One more thrust of hope from Spurs, one more superlative example of denial by Arsenal. Walsh, desperately seeking "one for the nipper", a celebration for the birth yesterday morning of a son, Alfie, sped where the tackles hurt into Arsenal's penalty box.

From the corner of his eye, he spotted a white shirt, inevitably Lineker. And from 12 yards, a distance which is meat and drink to England's captain, the famous left foot let fly.

Seaman reacted as if a button had been pressed, moving like lightning across his line and palming away the last chance for either side.

David Seaman
— Gunners boss George Graham commented after the game... "We survived today because of resilience and because of Seaman - showing that if you pay for the best then you get the best"

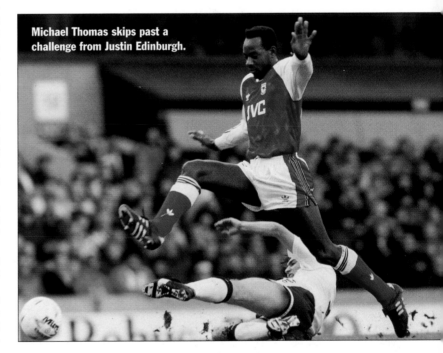

Michael Thomas skips past a challenge from Justin Edinburgh.

AT THE SEASON'S END

		P	W	D	L	F	A	Pts
1st	Arsenal*	38	24	13	1	74	33	83
10th	Spurs	38	11	16	11	51	50	49

*Two points deducted

109

ARSENAL 2
Wright, Campbell

TOTTENHAM HOTSPUR 0

Arsenal

Tottenham Hotspur

Manager
George Graham

Manager
Peter Shreeves

David SEAMAN	1	Erik THORSTVEDT
Lee DIXON	2	Terry FENWICK
Nigel WINTERBURN	3	Pat VAN DEN HAUWE
David HILLIER	4	Gudni BERGSSON
Steve BOULD	5	David HOWELLS
Andy LINIGHAN	6	Gary MABBUTT
David ROCASTLE*	7	Paul STEWART
Ian WRIGHT*	8	Gordon DURIE
Alan SMITH	9	Vinny SAMWAYS*
Paul MERSON	10	Paul WALSH
Kevin CAMPBELL	11	Paul ALLEN
David O'LEARY (7)	12	NAYIM (9)
Anders LIMPAR (8)	14	Steve SEDGLEY

Referee **Mr K Redfern** (Whitley Bay)

BACKGROUND

The Terry Venables/Alan Sugar takeover brought to an end possibly the most traumatic period in Spurs' history. With Sugar becoming Chairman and taking on responsibility for financial affairs, Venables was made Chief Executive, charged with the day to day running of the club. He knew he would have little time for team affairs so Peter Shreeves, who had been working with Steve Perryman at Watford, was re-appointed manager. The financial position was still precarious but money was found for Shreeves to break the club's transfer record with the signing of Gordon Durie from Chelsea. The loss of Paul Gascoigne was always going to be a serious blow but Spurs started well with only five points dropped in their first seven games. They climbed to third place but in the next seven games collected only four points although they were through to the third round of the European Cup-Winners' Cup. The weakness was in front of goal where they were over-reliant on Gary Lineker, scorer of 15 of their 22 League goals. It was already known Lineker would be leaving at the end of the season to join Nagoya Grampus Eight of Japan but he was unable to take his place against Arsenal when it was found his baby son George was suffering from Leukaemia. At least Paul Stewart was fit to return after missing two games through injury and Terry Fenwick replaced Justin Edinburgh two weeks after being released from a prison sentence for drink-driving. Arsenal began their title defence with no new signings but with only one point from their first three games George Graham began the search for extra fire-power which was concluded at the end of September with the £2.5 million arrival of Ian Wright. The former Crystal Palace star was an immediate hit with eight goals in his first ten matches but had been signed too late to play in the early rounds of the European Cup and could only watch from the stands as Arsenal, after a fine 1-1 draw in Lisbon, were outplayed by Benfica in the second leg before going down 1-3. Apart from the Benfica debacle Arsenal had lost one and drawn two of their last three League games, were 13 points behind leaders Leeds and had gone out of the Rumbelows Cup to Coventry. Graham abandoned his three centre-half line-up, dropping Colin Pates and calling up striker Kevin Campbell.

BEFORE THE GAME

	P	W	D	L	F	A	Pts
Arsenal	16	7	5	4	31	21	26
Spurs	14	6	2	6	22	19	20

Ian Wright gets past Paul Walsh and Paul Stewart.

IAN WRIGHT, the Arsenal striker who faces an FA charge of misconduct over an alleged spitting incident, featured in another X-certificate mini production at Highbury yesterday.

Millions of ITV viewers must have been mystified that referee Ken Redfern didn't caution him after an amazing incident in the 32nd minute of an unspectacular North London derby. Brought down by Gudni Bergsson, Wright was clearly seen grabbing the Icelandic defender by the throat as the Tottenham player lay on the ground. Wright was on top of him with his knee in Bergsson's chest and his hands around his throat.

Terry Fenwick, the Spurs right back, who came out of prison just over a fortnight ago, dived in to pull Wright off and he too could have been punished for violent play. But Redfern only reprimanded Wright, who scored the 68th minute goal which prevented the

Tottenham glimpse a grisly future

Tottenham Hotspur yesterday caught a glimpse of their future without Gary Lineker and it was not a cheering sight. Twisted into defensive contortions, they meekly filled the subservient role at Highbury in a north London derby described by George Graham as the most one-sided in his experience.

Unable to raise a single genuine blow of their own Tottenham endured an afternoon of almost unremitting anxiety. The defeat, their sixth in eight games, might have been their heaviest of the season and heightened still further the gloom that enveloped the club after the news of Lineker's misfortune.

The presence of Lineker alone would have posed a threat to Arsenal. Enjoying his most productive start to any season, he had scored 19 goals, 15 of them in the League, before he was granted indefinite compassionate leave. Without him, as they promise to be after May, Tottenham lacked penetrative power.

Nor is their rearguard any more reliable. Having collected only four points out of a possible 24, Shreeves admitted: "We are losing too many silly goals and contributing to our own downfall. That was the case again today, although we defended well for 60 minutes."

Nevertheless, Tottenham needed several large slices of luck to avoid being overwhelmed before the interval. In attacking Fenwick, who was released from prison a fortnight ago and still carried the effects of his confinement, Arsenal fashioned a host of openings. "We could have been quite a few up." Graham said.

Nor was he exaggerating. Dixon and Smith missed the clearest of opportunities before combining to foil each other, Hillier's drive was deflected on to the foot of a post and Bergsson was twice to clear hastily from underneath his own bar. The first half closed with Thorstvedt's spectacular save from Smith.

Graham, in spite of claiming that no forward line in the country is stronger than Arsenal's, conceded that "We didn't take a high percentage of chances." In the end, they had to rely on errors, mentioned by Shreeves and committed by Bergsson, to climb up to fourth place, ten points behind the leaders.

Wright, one of three Arsenal players charged with misconduct by the Football Association on Friday, was the first to benefit. Bergsson needlessly yielded possession near his own area and Hillier, rewarded for his relentless midfield artistry by being voted as the player of the match, released the England forward.

In scoring his ninth goal in 11 games, by squeezing the ball through the legs of Thorstvedt, **WRIGHT** tore a groin muscle and later withdrew. His departure allowed **CAMPBELL** to move to the central position he prefers and add the second himself.

Escaping from Bergsson, who had momentarily lost concentration, he swept in Limpar's through-ball. Later, he was honest enough to appease the complaints on the North Bank by indicating that Thorstvedt had not brought him down inside the area. His sporting example was not matched elsewhere on the pitch.

Rocastle, who tweaked his knee, escaped punishment for assaulting the back of Stewart's legs. So did Bergsson, Durie, Wright and Winterburn, all of whom were involved in unseemly scuffles during the game. Fenwick alone was cautioned for a late tackle on Limpar to complete his and Tottenham's miserable afternoon.

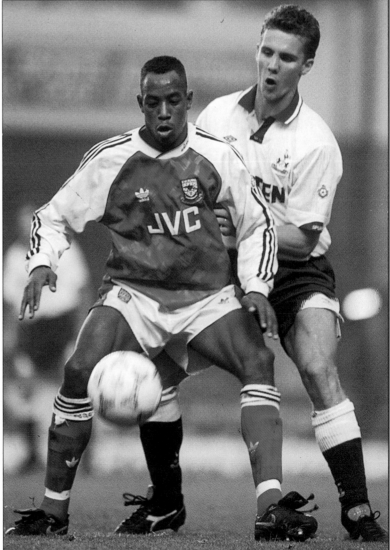

Arsenal scorers Ian Wright (right) and Kevin Campbell (top right) are marshalled by Spurs Gudni Bergsson and Erik Thorstvedt respectively.

110

TOTTENHAM HOTSPUR 1
Stewart

ARSENAL 1
Wright

Tottenham Hotspur

Manager
Peter Shreeves

Arsenal

Manager
George Graham

Tottenham		Arsenal
Erik THORSTVEDT	1	David SEAMAN
Terry FENWICK	2	Lee DIXON
Pat VAN DEN HAUWE	3	Nigel WINTERBURN
Steve SEDGLEY	4	David HILLIER*
David HOWELLS	5	Steve BOULD
Gary MABBUTT	6	Colin PATES
Paul STEWART	7	David ROCASTLE*
Gordon DURIE	8	Ian WRIGHT
NAYIM*	9	Alan SMITH
Gary LINEKER	10	Paul MERSON
Paul ALLEN	11	Kevin CAMPBELL
Paul WALSH(9)	12	David O'LEARY (4)
Justin EDINBURGH	14	Anders LIMPAR (7)

Referee **Mr K P Barrett** (Coventry).

BACKGROUND

After the season's first League meeting Spurs' results improved and a New Year's Day victory at Coventry saw them eighth in the League. From then on their season fell apart. They surrendered their grip on the FA Cup in a third round White Hart Lane replay with Aston Villa, lost four and drew one of their League games. Only in the Rumbelows and European Cup-Winners' Cups could they hope for any consolation. After beating Norwich in the fifth round of the Rumbelows Cup they had drawn at the City Ground in the semi-final first leg but in a week's time were due to face Nottingham Forest in the second leg in London and had not defeated Brian Clough's team at home for six years. In between they were due to meet Feyenoord in Rotterdam in the first leg of their European Cup-Winners' Cup third round tie. Eight days would make or break their season. Vinny Samways had taken on the Paul Gascoigne role and missed only one game all season but Shreeves decided the White Hart Lane pitch did not suit his passing style and left him out with Nayim his replacement. Christmas had proved the turning point for Arsenal. In nine League games they had collected all three points only once and had gone out of the FA Cup to Third Division Wrexham. In their last outing they had, at last, produced a performance of substance, trouncing Sheffield Wednesday 6-1 at Highbury. Colin Pates was given a rare outing as Tony Adams was forced to miss the game with flu and David Rocastle was included even though there were still doubts over an ankle injury which had forced him to miss England's midweek game with France.

BEFORE THE GAME

	P	W	D	L	F	A	Pts
Arsenal	29	11	10	8	50	34	43
Spurs	27	10	4	13	35	35	34

Erik Thorstvedt saves from Steve Bould.

Paul Stewart (pictured here heading Spurs in front).

'DERBY' STAR

Chris Lightbown for 'The Sunday Times' reported...

Spurs bumps prove the great leveller

This will go down as the day Gary Lineker missed two clear-cut chances, both in the six-yard box. Either would have gone in for him on any other day.

Or on any other pitch. Tottenham's has never been the best, but is now appalling. If Premier League membership depended on pitch quality, Tottenham would be out of the forthcoming honeypot. The pitch put an irritating bobble into one of Lineker's missed chances, played a part in at least two of the numerous near-misses during the second half, and led to Peter Shreeves "dropping the best passer in the club - Vinny Samways".

Out with Samways went Spurs' passing game. Shreeves stuck Howells in front of that contradiction in terms, the Spurs defence, and told Stewart to get on with it.

Which was fine. Stewart had a good first half and a great second one. But is there a team less likely to be intimidated by Stewart's roving skills and strength than Arsenal?

Arsenal were concrete. Sometimes silk, too. There was a period in the second half when Rocastle, who was unfit, flitted in, around and through midfield as if he owned it. It was a brief period and, ultimately, probably irrelevant. But when their defence plays like this and Rocastle weaved like only he can, Arsenal are two-thirds of the way back to power.

Back to the pitch. There was a Merson run that it blunted, a Stewart cross it killed and a Durie effort that it wasted, so stuck was the ball in divots and bumps and bounces from hell.

But that didn't stop Durie from nearly gutting Arsenal in his runs from midfield. Neither did it stop Pates dealing, albeit at the death, with most of what Durie tried. But the seven or so goals running pregnant through this game would have been born on even a half-decent pitch.

No matter. Spurs' goal was a peach of a **STEWART** header after Nayim and Allen held a private passing party following a Nayim corner. Allen was pure sweat, guts and near-perfection all afternoon. Arsenal's goal was a safe-cracker, lashed down the field by Merson, slashed to the foot of the post by Campbell, and slotted in by **WRIGHT**. Late, yes. Lucky, no.

And Spurs were committed. Few managers have as difficult a position as Peter Shreeves. Terry Venables, the chief executive, has power. So do the players. But in between, Shreeves is squeezed into a space devoid of money but packed with responsibility. Screaming for his head when some of his players deign to sweat, is unfair.

Even Nayim sweated yesterday, getting back to blunt and distract Wright at one crucial point. The cockerel on the club's crest flapped its wings, did six circuits of the ground and gave birth to twins when it saw that.

The wind was as bad as the pitch, but both keepers were unbowed. There was one Merson shot that Thorstvedt did well to see, never mind save.

Which leaves us with Lineker. Yes, he missed two chances. But he kept at it and gave Durie and Stewart much of the time and space in which they shone. When he was floored as he went to pass to Stewart, he scrambled along the ground to ensure the ball still reached his target. Having seen such shine, the cockerel wants to know why it can't see light every week.

THAT WAS THEN...

★ Seat tickets for this match were priced at £17.50, £16.50 and £13.50. A terrace ticket cost £8.

★ The Spurs programme was 48 pages for £1.50.

★ The official one-day air excursion for Tottenham's forthcoming Cup-winners' Cup tie against Feyenoord in Rotterdam was advertised at £166 with a one-day coach and ferry excursion at £76.

AT THE SEASON'S END

		P	W	D	L	F	A	Pts
4th	Arsenal	38	19	15	8	81	46	72
15th	Spurs	38	15	7	20	58	63	52

111

TOTTENHAM HOTSPUR 1
Allen

ARSENAL 0

Saturday 12th December 1992

FA Premier League

White Hart Lane

Attendance 33,707

Tottenham Hotspur   *Arsenal*

Manager
Terry Venables

Manager
George Graham

Erik THORSTVEDT	1	David SEAMAN
Dean AUSTIN	2	Pal LYDERSEN
Justin EDINBURGH	3	Nigel WINTERBURN
Vinny SAMWAYS	4	David HILLIER
Gary MABBUTT	5	Steve BOULD
Neil RUDDOCK	6	Tony ADAMS
David HOWELLS	7	John JENSEN*
Gordon DURIE*	8	Ian WRIGHT
NAYIM	9	Kevin CAMPBELL
Teddy SHERINGHAM	10	Paul MERSON
Paul ALLEN	11	Ray PARLOUR
Gudni BERGSSON	12	David O'LEARY
Ian WALKER	13	Alan MILLER
Nicky BARMBY (8)	14	Anders LIMPAR (7)

Referee **Mr A N Buksh** (London)

Ian Wright is thwarted by Spurs 'keeper Erik Thorstvedt. Neil Ruddock and Justin Edinburgh are also in attendance.

BACKGROUND

15th in the First Division was Spurs lowest League placing since relegation in 1977, eleven defeats the worst home record ever. It proved a struggle to stay up, and staying in the top flight was essential for the FA Premier League, and all the money it promised, was now in being. In the summer Gary Lineker left for Japan, Paul Stewart went to Liverpool and the sale of Paul Gascoigne to Lazio eventually went through. Peter Shreeves also departed, his contract not renewed. Terry Venables resumed overall control of team affairs with coaches Doug Livermore and Ray Clemence given a greater role. £1.7 million was paid out for Portsmouth's 20 year-old Darren Anderton, another £750,000 to sign Neil Ruddock for the second time and £375,000 for Dean Austin but even before the season began it was obvious a consistent goalscorer was needed. Two goals and two points in the opening three games showed how desperate the need was and when Spurs lost the fourth game 0-5 at Leeds, Venables at last secured long-time target Teddy Sheringham. A draw and two wins followed but the improvement ended as two points in five games left Spurs four off the bottom. When Gary Mabbutt, out of the team since summer surgery, returned, Spurs went six games without defeat but in the two games before Arsenal's visit, Nottingham Forest knocked them out of the Coca Cola Cup and Chelsea inflicted a 1-2 home League defeat. Injuries had forced Venables to give some of Spurs' youngsters a chance but experience was needed against Arsenal and David Howells, Gordon Durie and Paul Allen returned in place of Jason Cundy, Nick Barmby and Kevin Watson. George Graham sprang a surprise just before the start of the season when he allowed the popular David Rocastle to move to Leeds, replacing him with John Jensen who had leapt to prominence with the first goal for Denmark in the summer's European Championship Final against Germany. Jensen became the third Scandinavian at Highbury, joining Anders Limpar and full-back Pal Lydersen who had been signed in November 1991. Lydersen had yet to mark his mark but the arrival of both he and Jensen was to have a far greater impact off the pitch than on it. The season opened with a surprise home defeat by Norwich followed by another at Blackburn. Three victories were followed by two points from four games but Arsenal then embarked on a run of six successive victories and by early November they were top of the table and dreaming of becoming the first winners of the FA Premier League. Those dreams were shattered by the time they arrived at White Hart Lane, goalless and beaten in their last four games, ten points behind leaders Norwich. Jensen was recalled after being dropped for the last game at Southampton, Nigel Winterburn returned after six games out injured but Lee Dixon was now injured and replaced by Lydersen for his first game of the season.

BEFORE THE GAME

	P	W	D	L	F	A	Pts
Arsenal	18	9	2	7	22	19	29
Spurs	18	5	7	6	18	24	22

*Sam Elliott in **"The Independent On Sunday"** reported on...*

Graham objects to referee

George Graham, the Arsenal manager, will contact the FA this week requesting that Alf Buksh, who refereed yesterday's foul-strewn derby at White Hart Lane, not officiate another Arsenal fixture this season.

"We cannot criticise referees," Graham said, "but I will definitely be writing to the FA." The Dollis Hill referee, in fairness, is one of the game's fittest officials and kept up well with the frenetic play, but little vendettas seemed to go unnoticed. Certainly Graham's centre-forward, Ian Wright, was lucky to stay on the field after forcing his palm at speed into David Howells's face midway through the second half.

Howells, who anchored Spurs' midfield admirably throughout, protested vigorously in Wright's direction and Buksh eventually stepped in to administer a quick lecture. The temperature, as ever in derby games, started high up the scale and rose further, particularly after 20 minutes when Paul Allen scored for Spurs and Arsenal were forced to chase the game more forcefully.

Graham's team, desperately searching for a win after three successive defeats, could have been ahead within two minutes on a ground where they have not won since September 1988. Ray Parlour, who started promisingly as Arsenal's most creative player, was brought down by Dean Austin, the Spurs full-back, as he homed in on Erik Thorstvedt's goal. Buksh waved play on to the consternation of the visiting contingent.

Spurs, whose spirits never flagged as they sought to give their fans the win they prize most, settled the game after 20 minutes. Thorstvedt, who gave another outstanding display between the posts, fielded a loose ball with his feet in his six-yard box, adeptly dribbled around Wright before transferring possession to his relieved captain, Gary Mabbutt.

The former England centre-half swept forward and freed Allen, who in turn increased the tempo with a sprint to the halfway line. As Arsenal's midfield scampered about to close him down, Allen flicked the ball wide to Gordon Durie on the right.

The Scottish striker set off, gained some ground before crossing low to where his team-mates were arriving on the edge of the box. Pal Lydersen, Lee Dixon's replacement at right-back, failed to cut out the ball properly, and **ALLEN** nipped in to thread a skimming shot between David Seaman and his left-hand upright.

The home fans, disappointed by the departures of Gascoigne, Lineker and Stewart, had been buoyed by Tottenham's recent form, but this win was the one they wanted. "We're delighted for our fans, who have been magnificent during what is a transitional period," Doug Livermore, the Spurs first-team coach said.

They certainly voiced their delight. "We beat the scum 3-1," came the chant from the home ranks, a cruel reminder to their north London neighbours of that Gazza-driven FA Cup semi-final defeat.

After Allen's moment of composure in the box, the game degenerated slightly with a series of tit-for-tat, over-the-top tackles. Steve Bould, otherwise excellent in Arsenal's back four, was the first of the infamous five to have his name taken by Buksh for his third challenge from behind on Teddy Sheringham. Durie levelled the booking scores in the 27th minute when he tripped Parlour, although the England Under-21 midfielder almost gained revenge seconds later when his low cross from the right was nearly turned in by Paul Merson. Arsenal finished the half on a high, Thorstvedt saving brilliantly from Bould's hard header.

The name of Adams (T) was written down moments after the re-start for a clumsy touchline challenge on Durie. Adams's Essex neighbour Neil Ruddock, who had another solid game, then went into the book for a foul on Parlour. John Jensen completed Buksh's collection of names when he up-ended Vinny Samways.

The lack of a strong hand, pre-empting such incidents rather than reacting to them, disfigured the game and it will be interesting to see Lancaster Gate's reaction to Graham's request. The bookings, and other fractious moments, detracted from the game's better moments, like when 18-year-old Nick Barmby ran from the halfway line to shake Seaman's bar in the final minute. The memory though will be of a game teetering on the brink of lawlessness.

Paul Allen slots home the only goal of the game.

NEVER in the 79 years of north London derbies can there have been a more shameful display of sustained malice, nor a more wretched pretence of words to excuse them from the managers than this. That Spurs had Paul Allen to thank for their victory, that Arsenal, the supposed champions elect, have now gone four consecutive games without a goal or a win, pales into insignificance.

BBC Television last night showed evidence of Ian Wright landing a fist or a hand into the face of Howells. Wright, the volatile England forward, would only comment: "I ain't saying nothing, except we should definitely have had a penalty," while Howells was forbidden to speak to the press.

That after a game in which

AFTER THE GAME

Ian Wright's punch at David Howells may not have been seen by the referee but it was caught by the all-seeing eye of the TV cameras. Charged with misconduct, Wright was found guilty after an FA disciplinary tribunal had viewed the incident on video and suspended for three games. George Graham was also in trouble, fined £500 for comments made to the referee after game.

112

ARSENAL 1
Dickov

TOTTENHAM HOTSPUR 3
Sheringham, Hendry 2

Arsenal | Tottenham Hotspur

Manager **George Graham** | Manager **Terry Venables**

Alan MILLER	1	Ian WALKER
Pal LYDERSEN*	2	David McDONALD
Martin KEOWN	3	Pat VAN DEN HAUWE
Scott MARSHALL	4	Danny HILL
David O'LEARY	5	Gary MABBUTT
Steve BOULD	6	Neil RUDDOCK
Mark FLATTS*	7	Steve SEDGLEY
Ian SELLEY	8	John HENDRY*
Alan SMITH	9	Darren ANDERTON
Paul DICKOV	10	Teddy SHERINGHAM
Neil HEANEY	11	Paul ALLEN
Jimmy CARTER (7)	12	Stuart NETHERCOTT
Gavin McGOWAN (2)	14	Lee HODGES (8)
James WILL	GK	Kevin DEARDEN

Referee **Mr K Cooper** (Pontypridd)

BACKGROUND

The last League game of the season for both clubs with the winners sure to take the higher placing. Normally both would have pulled out all the stops to ensure success but Arsenal had more important things on their mind. Four days later they were due to meet Sheffield Wednesday in the FA Cup Final, the same team they had already beaten in the Coca Cola Cup Final. Graham was not prepared to risk losing any of his probable Cup Final side and despite the possibility of a League fine fielded virtually a reserve side, only Alan Smith and David O'Leary, making what was expected to be his last competitive appearance in an Arsenal shirt, even expected to make the Wembley squad. There were no such problems for Terry Venables in what was to prove his last match in charge of Spurs. After losing to Arsenal in the FA Cup semi-final he had taken the opportunity to blood more of the younger players, Danny Hill, Stuart Nethercott and David McDonald being promoted to follow the earlier successful introduction of Nicky Barmby and Andy Turner. With Highbury's North Bank under reconstruction and few tickets available for Spurs' fans, the game was beamed live to the giant video screen at White Hart Lane.

BEFORE THE GAME

	P	W	D	L	F	A	Pts
Arsenal	41	15	11	15	39	35	56
Spurs	41	15	11	15	57	65	56

AT THE SEASON'S END

		P	W	D	L	F	A	Pts
8th	Spurs	42	16	11	15	60	66	59
10th	Arsenal	42	15	11	16	40	38	56

DEFEAT in the FA Cup semi-final by their deadly rivals was forgotten last night as Tottenham eased through to a Highbury victory that will be celebrated all the way until Saturday afternoon, when Arsenal claim the national spotlight again with their Wembley return against Sheffield Wednesday.

Joking aside, this was no consolation, and Spurs will not consider it as such. The Arsenal support kept ramming home the point by taunting their visitors with their pain refrain "What are you doing Saturday?"

After all, this was virtually the Ar-senal reserve side on parade. The Gunners, with both eyes on the FA Cup final, employed not one player who can realistically hope to be involved in the starting line-up in four days' time.

Still, Spurs can savour the fact that they rise three places in the table to eighth, and especially as they go above Arsenal. It also ensures a last-day bonus of £111,000 because Premier League prize-money is dependent on final placings, while their fans can say they have seen their team gain the most valued double in the season for the first time since 1974.

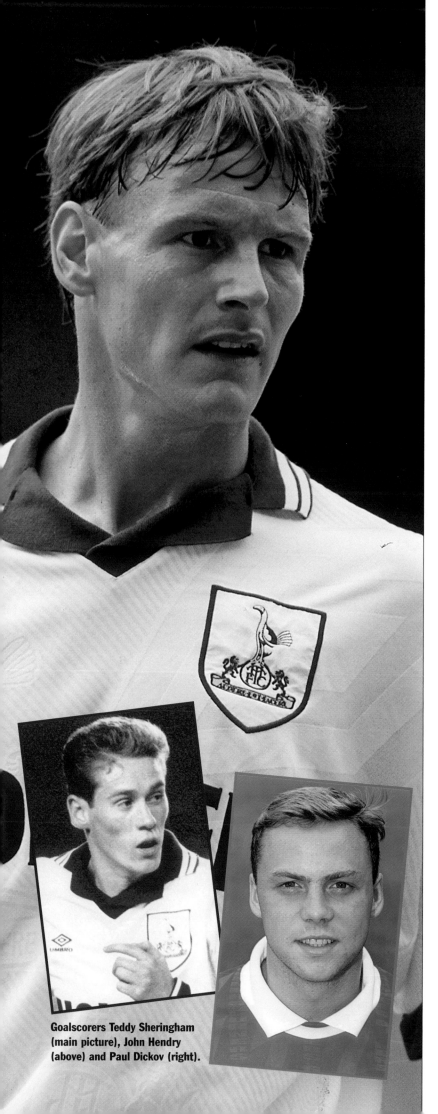

Arsenal's shadow side exposed

Arsenal will go to Wembley on Saturday with their bodies intact but their pride bruised. George Graham, their manager, guaranteed the former by leaving his FA Cup final side in the Highbury stands last night and Tottenham ensured the latter by reaping the benefits of Graham's pragmatism with a conclusive victory and their first derby double for 18 seasons.

Of the team Graham fielded, only Selley and, possibly Carter are likely to be in contention for a place against Sheffield Wednesday in three days time. Much as he may wish otherwise, David O'Leary was almost certainly making his last competitive appearance for a club he has served for 20 years. Captain for the night, he would have wished to bow out on a higher note.

Not that it was a poor game - far from it - just that Tottenham have made all the profits. Having failed to win any of their previous seven games at Highbury, their victory moved them up three places to eighth - above Arsenal in the process - and was worth more than £100,000 in Premier League prize-money.

Graham, for one, will not begrudge Tottenham's glory, tainted as it was. He took his decision - as he had at Hillsborough last Thursday - on the basis that a more important test lies ahead for a club completing its fifth fixture in 11 days and in the knowledge that no punitive action will be forthcoming.

It was hardly surprising that a white tide should flow towards the mural behind Miller's goal in the early stages. Miller stuck out a boot to deny Anderton but needed Lydersen and Keown to rescue him on the line when Hendry powered Anderton's cross past him.

The enthusiasm of Selley and Heaney managed to stem the waves of attacks for a spell. Smith was given two glorious opportunities but headed wide from a cross by Flatts and then scooped the ball almost apologetically into Walker's arms.

McDonald was also forced to make a magnificent saving tackle on Bould at close range but the best chance was missed by Keown, who had been put clean through by Heaney.

Tottenham regrouped and took a stranglehold with goals six minutes before half-time and 60 seconds after it. First, Hill created space for Anderton to direct a header on to the forehead of **SHERINGHAM**, who confirmed his standing as the league's leading scorer with his 22nd of the season; then Hill punished an error by Flatts, crossing low for **HENDRY** to apply the finish.

DICKOV replied immediately after a neat exchange with Smith but Hill, a 19-year-old graduate of the FA School of Excellence, produced a quality pass that set up **HENDRY** for his second.

For Arsenal, short-term priorities had been served. For Tottenham, the prospects in the long term looked particularly promising.

Goalscorers Teddy Sheringham (main picture), John Hendry (above) and Paul Dickov (right).

113

TOTTENHAM HOTSPUR 0

ARSENAL 1
Wright

Tottenham Hotspur

Manager
Ossie Ardiles

Arsenal

Manager
George Graham

Tottenham			Arsenal
Erik THORSTVEDT	1	1	David SEAMAN
Dean AUSTIN	2	14	Martin KEOWN
Sol CAMPBELL	23	3	Nigel WINTERBURN
Vinny SAMWAYS	4	4	Paul DAVIS
Colin CALDERWOOD	5	5	Andy LINIGHAN
Gary MABBUTT	6	6	Tony ADAMS
Steve SEDGLEY	14	7	Kevin CAMPBELL
Gordon DURIE	8	8	Ian WRIGHT
Jason DOZZELL	12	17	John JENSEN
Teddy SHERINGHAM	10	23	Ray PARLOUR
David HOWELLS*	15	11	Eddie McGOLDRICK
Darren CASKEY (15)	20	9	Alan SMITH
Ian WALKER	13	13	Alan MILLER
John HENDRY	25	22	Ian SELLEY

Referee **Mr D Elleray** (Harrow)

BACKGROUND

In the two years since the Sugar/Venables takeover Spurs had looked to be well on the road to recovery, not only financially but also on the pitch. The illusion was shattered almost immediately after the last victory at Highbury with the shock dismissal of Terry Venables as Chief Executive. A High Court injunction re-instated Venables but the reprieve was short-lived and amid allegation and counterclaim which remain the subject of litigation he was forced to concede defeat to the electronics magnate. Ossie Ardiles was appointed manager and, with Steve Perryman his assistant, took on a challenge as difficult as anything he had faced as player or manager. Neil Ruddock had made his position untenable with his outspoken support for Venables and was transferred to Liverpool with Colin Calderwood signed from Swindon as his replacement. Jason Dozzell was also added to the staff and made his debut at newly-promoted Newcastle in the first game of the season when, even without the injured Justin Edinburgh, Nicky Barmby and Darren Anderton, Spurs secured a surprise 1-0 victory. Venables dismissal on the eve of the FA Cup Final grabbed all the headlines, overshadowing Arsenal's subsequent defeat of Sheffield Wednesday and the fifth trophy of George Graham's reign. The only addition to Arsenal's ranks during the summer was Eddie McGoldrick, a £1 million signing from Crystal Palace, but he only made the bench for a disappointing opening day defeat at Coventry. Graham was stung by a performance lacking the commitment that had become Arsenal's trademark and responded by leaving out Paul Merson and Anders Limpar with McGoldrick and Ray Parlour taking their places. Martin Keown came in for injured Lee Dixon. Ian Wright prepared for the match by releasing a record called "Do The Right Thing".

BEFORE THE GAME

	P	W	D	L	F	A	Pts
Spurs	1	1	0	0	1	0	3
Arsenal	1	0	0	1	0	3	0

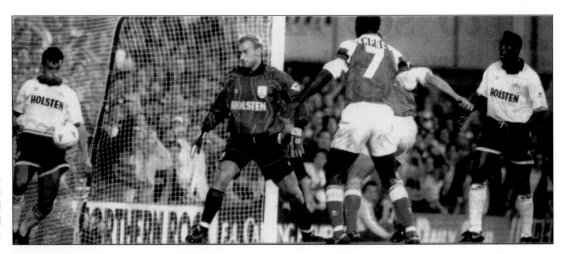

Colin Calderwood clears Tony Adams' goalbound effort, but the Arsenal players claimed the ball was already over the line.

WRIGHT PUTS ARSENAL BACK ON TRACK

Redemption came Arsenal's way last night on the ground where they love to win most of all when, with three minutes remaining, Ian Wright displayed a scoring knack that had been missing from all their earlier attempts to put themselves back in favour with their manager, George Graham.

WRIGHT, the arch penalty box thief, diverted Andy Linighan's prodigious leap at a corner - reminiscent of his FA Cup winning effort last May - to puncture the euphoria that had followed Tottenham back from Newcastle and into Ossie Ardiles' homecoming.

In truth, Alan Sugar's favourite old boy would have been nursing a bigger hangover this morning if Arsenal had not almost succumbed again to the failure to take their chances which continually undermined their attempt last season to put together a decent run in the league.

However, first and foremost last night they had to show that what happened against Coventry on Saturday was only the kind of opening-day disaster that can befall prospective champions. This time the attitude and desire was entirely to Graham's liking, and after a thoroughly entertaining north London derby he was the manager with the smile.

"Tonight we have rolled up our sleeves and won our pride back," he said. "We out-passed a passing team and Arsenal are not meant to do that. The only thing lacking was a killer touch." Graham carried out his threat to "frighten" those culpable against Coventry, and left Paul Merson and Anders Limpar out of the side and with much thinking to do. In Ray Parlour and Eddie McGoldrick , making his full debut after a £1m move from Crystal Palace, he had players more suited to the rigorous demands of this fixture. Parlour worked with hardly a pause for breath while McGoldrick sparkled throughout. It was his late corner from which Arsenal reaped their golden harvest.

With their midfield redesigned and reinforced, the Gunners immediately placed a rigid clamp on the area which would determine victory. Spurs stuck to their principles and tried to pass their way clear from the mass of bodies, but rarely was daylight to be had and from early on the game was going away from them.

The tide was firmly in Arsenal's favour, and television replays showed the should have had the lead in the 35th minute. Another McGoldrick corner was won by Tony Adams, Wright knocked the bouncing ball against a post where Adams appeared to steer the ball home. Not so, said referee David Elleray, even though Colin Calderwood looked to be well behind the line when he made his clearance.

Apart from Wright, Elleray also booked four: Parlour, Martin Keown, Gary Mabbutt and Vinny Samways, but it was never a malicious affair. Compelling, it certainly was.

Arsenal's matchwinner Ian Wright.

Ray Parlour tries to break free from Vinny Samways clutches.

114

ARSENAL 1
Wright

TOTTENHAM HOTSPUR 1
Anderton

Arsenal

Tottenham Hotspur

Manager
George Graham

Manager
Ossie Ardiles

David SEAMAN	1	1	**Erik THORSTVEDT**
Lee DIXON	2	22	**David KERSLAKE**
Martin KEOWN	14	3	**Justin EDINBURGH**
Ian SELLEY	22	4	**Vinny SAMWAYS***
Steve BOULD	12	5	**Colin CALDERWOOD**
Tony ADAMS	6	14	**Steve SEDGLEY**
John JENSEN	17	12	**Jason DOZZELL**
Ian WRIGHT	8	16	**Micky HAZARD**
Alan SMITH*	9	23	**Sol CAMPBELL**
Paul MERSON	10	20	**Darren CASKEY***
Anders LIMPAR	15	9	**Darren ANDERTON**
Kevin CAMPBELL (9)	7	2	**Dean AUSTIN (4)**
Alan MILLER	13	13	**Ian WALKER**
Steve MORROW	21	25	**John HENDRY (20)**

Referee **Mr P Don** (Hanworth Park)

BACKGROUND

Ian Wright's late winner at White Hart Lane set Arsenal off on a run of five wins in six games that took them up to second place before losing to leaders Manchester United at Old Trafford. They bounced back with victory over Southampton but slipped further behind United as October's four League games all ended goalless. Graham shuffled his team looking for consistency but injuries did nothing to help. Knocked out of the Coca Cola Cup by Aston Villa, the European Cup-Winners' Cup was already looking the best bet to add to Highbury's Roll of Honour; Odense and Standard Liege beaten, Torino were waiting in March's semi-final. Two days earlier Coventry had completed the double over Arsenal and Graham again made changes, Limpar and Jensen replacing Davis and McGoldrick. Despite the injury problems that had dogged them from the outset continuing; Dean Austin had broken his leg, Spurs began the season well with only two defeats in the first dozen League games. Teddy Sheringham in particular was flourishing in the short passing game Ardiles advocated so strongly but when he was put out of the game for five months after a typical Bryan Robson tackle at Old Trafford the season fell apart. Nicky Barmby returned after a summer shin operation but with Gordon Durie ignored having made clear his determination to join Glasgow Rangers, Spurs struggled to score goals. Micky Hazard was signed to replace David Howells, another long term injury victim, but eight games without a win saw Spurs plunging down the table. Gary Mabbutt suffered horrendous facial injuries at the elbow of Wimbledon's John Fashanu and a season that had looked so promising now became one of struggle. Ardiles' desperate search for extra firepower was now focussing on Liverpool's Ronny Rosenthal but in the meantime Sol Campbell, a defender, was pressed into service up front. As if Spurs were not in a bad enough state for the game Nicky Barmby suffered a dead leg in morning training so Jason Dozzell, a midfielder who had himself just returned from injury was asked to provide support for Campbell.

BEFORE THE GAME

	P	W	D	L	F	A	Pts
Arsenal	18	8	6	4	17	10	30
Spurs	18	5	7	6	23	20	22

AT THE SEASON'S END

		P	W	D	L	F	A	Pts
4th	Arsenal	42	18	17	7	53	28	71
15th	Spurs	42	11	12	19	54	59	45

Micky Hazard is sent flying by a tackle from Ian Selley.

Right: Spurs No.9 Darren Anderton steers the ball wide of David Seaman to put his side into a 25th minute lead.

Keith Pike in 'The Times' under the headline...

WRIGHT ON THE MARK TO SAVE POINT FOR ARSENAL

Pride remains intact in both the red and white halves of north London after a raucous, riveting derby last night. As much as Tottenham had ruled the Highbury roost for one hour, so Arsenal dominated the next and the contrast in styles kept a near full house living on it's nerves to the death.

If Tottenham's courageous performance could be faulted, it was that, having punctured the meanest defence in the country once, while they were in the ascendancy, they failed to make the game safe. Arsenal's barnstorming display after the interval, as predictable as it was impressive, found a climax in Ian Wright's equalising volley and it was Tottenham who were left hanging on to a precious but deserved point.

Arsenal's ability to captivate one moment, anaesthetise the next, is legendary. When the mood takes them, as it did recently at Carrow Road and in Belgium, they can be breathtaking. More often than not, though, the mood is as dark and depressingly pragmatic as it was for 45 minutes last night: flair is forsaken and all hope diverted down Route One. Seaman becomes play-maker as well as shot-stopper and Wright, darting hither and thither rather like a moving target on an artillery range, is left to pick up the pieces, pop in the goals and justify the means.

His strike last night, his eighteenth of the season and 75th in Arsenal's colours, was out of the George Graham textbook: Seaman's huge punt, Smith's flick, Limpar's clipped pass and **WRIGHT'S** unarguable finish, a flash of the left boot sending a volley past the helpless Thorstvedt.

It had been a long time coming though. The selection of Limpar at McGoldrick's expense had promised much more than it initially achieved and, in any case, what Graham had given with one hand, he had taken away with the other, Jensen's destructive attributes being preferred to the more cultured Davis.

Outplayed, often embarrassingly so, in the first half, Arsenal's greater commitment and more stylish approach after the break had Tottenham stretched to breaking point.

Before his goal, Wright had missed a fine chance, set up by Limpar through an unexpected loss of control, and after it there were any number of close calls in the Tottenham area. Such had been Tottenham's mastery of the first half, though, that their right to a point could not be disputed. Without a win in their eight previous Premiership games, they seemed undeterred by the absence of Barmby, hurt in training, from an already injury-ravaged side.

The strike force of Campbell and Dozzell, with just four goals between them, hardly promised riches but, with Hazard pulling all the strings in midfield, they had regularly cut through to the soft centre of Arsenal's defence in which Adams, in particular, was having an unhappy night.

Kerslake's early shot into Seaman's midriff had been the only shot on target in the opening 25 minutes. But no sooner had Arsenal rectified that, with Limpar duplicating the effort, than Tottenham had taken the lead.

Hazard picked out Dozzell in the centre circle, a flicked header put **ANDERTON** away, and the lanky winger left Adams in his wake before drawing Seaman and rolling a right-foot shot wide of him and inside the far post.

Tottenham might have made it two 12 minutes later. Samways put Campbell through to the byline and his cross just eluded Caskey. Anderton returned the ball from the right and, although Caskey made contact this time, his header flew a foot wide.

Arsenal seemed mesmerised at times, and they nearly paid for Selley's indecision when the youngster allowed himself to be dispossessed by Dozzell on the edge of his area. Samways pounced, shot, and was denied only by Seaman's excellent save.

They were hardly to get in another shot. "We interrupted their passing game in the second half and, had it gone on for another ten minutes, I am sure we would have won." Graham said. "The finish was Ian Wright at his best." Arsenal, too, he might have added.

115

TOTTENHAM HOTSPUR 1
Popescu

ARSENAL 0

Monday 2nd January 1995

FA Carling Premiership

White Hart Lane

Attendance 28,747

Tottenham Hotspur

**Manager
Gerry Francis**

Arsenal

**Manager
George Graham**

Ian **WALKER**	13	1	David **SEAMAN**	
Dean **AUSTIN**	2	2	Lee **DIXON**	
Sol **CAMPBELL**	23	3	Nigel **WINTERBURN**	
Gica **POPESCU***	4	17	John **JENSEN**	
Colin **CALDERWOOD**	5	5	Andy **LINIGHAN**	
Gary **MABBUTT**	6	12	Steve **BOULD**	
Jürgen **KLINSMANN**	18	7	Kevin **CAMPBELL**	
David **HOWELLS**	15	8	Ian **WRIGHT**	
Darren **ANDERTON**	9	15	Stefan **SCHWARZ**	
Teddy **SHERINGHAM**	10	22	Ian **SELLEY***	
Ronny **ROSENTHAL**	11	23	Ray **PARLOUR**	
Justin **EDINBURGH**	3	9	Alan **SMITH** (22)	
Chris **DAY**	30	13	Vince **BARTRAM**	
Stuart **NETHERCOTT** (4)	14	14	Martin **KEOWN**	

Referee **Mr M D Reed** (West Midlands)

BEFORE THE GAME

	P	W	D	L	F	A	Pts
Spurs	22	9	6	7	38	34	33
Arsenal	22	7	7	8	26	25	28

**Gerry Francis
– his first
North London
'derby'.**

BACKGROUND

The fall-out from Terry Venables acrimonious bust-up with Alan Sugar continued to haunt Spurs throughout the summer. An FA inquiry found them guilty of financial irregularities, imposed a 12 point deduction for the new season, banned them from the FA Cup and fined them £600,000. Although the points loss was reduced to six on appeal (at the expense of increasing the fine to £1.5 million) it effectively decreed that no matter what Spurs did the season was going to be one of survival rather than success. Sugar's reaction was to make money available for Ossie Ardiles to buy players who could ensure that, if nothing else, relegation was avoided. £2.8 million was spent on Rumania's Ilie Dumitrescu, another £2 million offered for Brazil's Marcio Santos and when that deal fell through used to sign Jürgen Klinsmann, Germany's World Cup winning striker. The season started with three wins in four games but it was soon apparent that while Ardiles had assembled an array of attacking talent to strike fear into any defence his team had forgotten how to defend. Even the arrival of another Rumanian World Cup star, Gica Popescu, could not stop the rot and when Spurs went out of the Coca Cup Cup to bottom of the First Division Notts County the writing was on the wall for Ardiles. One more game in charge, then he was dismissed. Steve Perryman took over as caretaker-manager for one game before the arrival of Gerry Francis. The former QPR manager immediately set about instilling some discipline and organisation. His first match in charge was lost but eight games without defeat propelled Spurs back up the table. Confidence returned, especially after a special FA Tribunal decided the FA had exceeded it's powers, re-instated Spurs in the FA Cup and cancelled the six point deduction. The last match of 1995 had resulted in a resounding 4-0 win at Coventry and while Nicky Barmby was injured, Ronny Rosenthal was a ready-made replacement. While everything was going well for Spurs the same could not be said of Arsenal. The derby draw of December 1993 started a run of one defeat in 22 League games but half of them were draws and that was not good enough to challenge Manchester United and Blackburn for the title. Bolton dumped them out of the FA Cup but they still had the European Cup-Winners' Cup and even without the suspended Ian Wright, Alan Smith's goal proved enough to beat Parma in Copenhagen. With Stefan Schwarz signed from Benfica to add midfield guile, Manchester City were beaten 3-0 in the season's opening game but a failure to score even once in the next four showed why George Graham had been prepared to spend £5 million on Chris Sutton before the Norwich man joined Blackburn. If Wright was not scoring Arsenal struggled, but to make matters worse Highbury was rocked by stories of off-field activities. First Paul Merson admitted he had drink, drugs and gambling problems, then the Premier League began investigating allegations Graham had taken "bungs" from an agent during the transfers of John Jensen and Pal Lydersen. Arsenal arrived at White Hart Lane with only two wins in twelve games, in the lower half of the table and without Tony Adams, absent for six games. At least David Seaman was fit to resume after also missing six games with a cracked rib while Martin Keown and Alan Smith were dropped and replaced by Andy Linighan and Ian Selley after a 3-1 home defeat by QPR two days earlier.

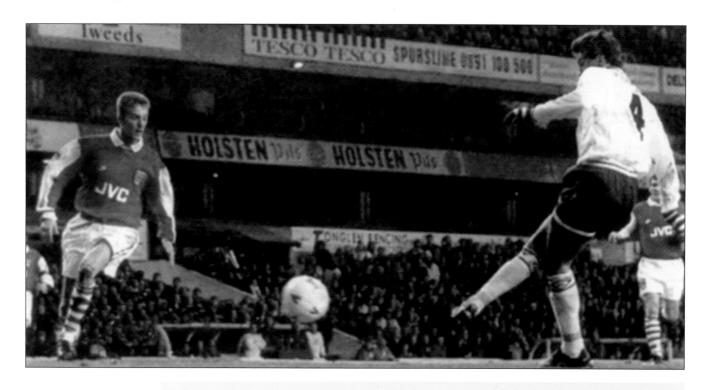

Rob Hughes, Football correspondent of **'The Times'** reported...

Popescu settles north London derby

How the pendulum has swung across north London. Arsenal lost to their neighbours and greatest rivals last night, for only the sixth time in 23 encounters, and illustrated that the reversal of the clubs' fortunes is emphatic indeed. Who would have thought that Tottenham Hotspur would enter 1995 sixth from the top of the FA Carling Premiership, or that Arsenal - pale, aging and unsure of themselves - would be in thirteenth place and falling?

It was a freezing night, yet, from the start, there were occasional flourishes from Tottenham that brought a warming glow to the 28,000 who were shivering at Siberian White Hart Lane. One such led to a wonderful goal after 22 minutes.

Gica Popescu celebrates his 23rd minute goal, seen in the picture above.

David Howells, drafted in to stiffen the sinews of the Tottenham midfield with his ball-winning qualities, turned creator, and, on the halfway line, produced an improvised chip with back spin, rather like a golfer using a sand wedge, that dropped daintily into space for Anderton.

A surge of Anderton's coltish stride unzipped the Arsenal offside trap and defenders' arms went up more in hope than expectation as, too late, Bould and Linighan looked to their right and saw Dixon lurking behind them. He feared that **POPESCU** might be threatening and his fear was justified: Popescu was quicker to the ball and the Romanian had merely to side-foot the ball to score his second goal for the club.

There was no excuse for Arsenal; they had already been warned that Tottenham were dangerous when Klinsmann and Sheringham, both of them working back to prove that defence begins with the front-runners, had linked superbly to release Rosenthal, the Israel international. For an instant, he was clear, his pace too much for Winterburn, but then Bould nudged the Tottenham man, upsetting his balance just enough to allow Seaman to gather when the ball ran loose.

Seaman's presence in goal undoubtedly gave Arsenal more reassurance, but the inclusion of Selley in a five-man midfield at the expense of Smith, a striker, showed clearly the conservative attitude that George Graham, the manager, had adopted from the outset. Twice, Wright was obliged to dash to the vacant wings, turn and attempt centres that should be provided for him. The first was cut out by Mabbutt, the second was missed in the air by Parlour.

Arsenal, though, could not blame Parlour for their problems on the night. He, at least, had the bite, the running and the intention to shoot on sight, even in a team that combined to look rather like a blind man pushing forward with his cane.

Schwarz, the Sweden international, had a little too much bite, even in a by-no-means spiteful derby, receiving a yellow card that was barely sufficient for the way he implanted his studs high into the groin of Howells.

Arsenal strove to get back into the match and thrust Tottenham backwards. Popescu, who played despite suffering the effects of a virus, was fading particularly fast. No matter - his goal remained the winner, largely because of a quite magnificent save in the 52nd minute by Walker, the Tottenham goalkeeper, from Dixon.

The Arsenal right back had burst 70 yards down the right on to a diagonal ball from Selley. His finish was dynamic, but Walker stretched to palm the ball around the near post.

After that, it was a question of whether Wright could somehow conjure something out of nothing. He twice went close, once chipping the ball just behind the crossbar from the tightest of angles, but though Arsenal were incensed not to be given a penalty when the ball struck Campbell on the ground, the last act came at the other end.

Klinsmann had been thrillingly athletic, pacing his game, and, as he advanced towards the penalty area, five minutes from time, Schwarz, with a rush of blood, launched a wild tackle from behind. It earned a second yellow card, then inevitably a red, and all was doomed for Arsenal.

Nevertheless, Graham declared himself very pleased with his team's performance and refused to countenance questions about whether this was acceptable form from Arsenal, or whether two wins out of 12 games also pleased him.

"I'm trying to think positive," he said. "You keep hitting negative questions: I can only talk about tonight, and that was a good performance."

116

ARSENAL 1
Wright (pen)

TOTTENHAM HOTSPUR 1
Klinsmann

Saturday 29th April 1995

FA Carling Premiership

Highbury

Attendance 38,377

Arsenal

Tottenham Hotspur

Manager
Stewart Houston

Manager
Gerry Francis

David SEAMAN	1	13	Ian WALKER
Lee DIXON	2	2	Dean AUSTIN
Nigel WINTERBURN	3	3	Justin EDINBURGH
Martin KEOWN	14	15	David HOWELLS
Steve BOULD	12	5	Colin CALDERWOOD
Tony ADAMS	6	6	Gary MABBUTT
Stefan SCHWARZ	15	7	Nicky BARMBY
Ian WRIGHT	8	18	Jürgen KLINSMANN
John HARTSON	16	9	Darren ANDERTON
Paul MERSON	10	10	Teddy SHERINGHAM
Glenn HELDER*	32	11	Ronny ROSENTHAL
Andy LINIGHAN	5	14	Stuart NETHERCOTT
Vince BARTRAM	13	1	Erik THORSTVEDT
Ray PARLOUR (32)	23	20	Darren CASKEY

Referee **Mr R Hart** (Darlington)

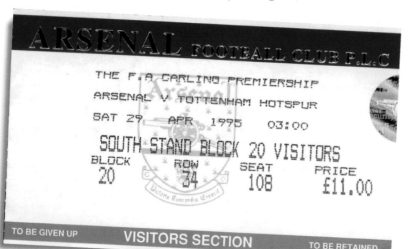

BACKGROUND

After losing at White Hart Lane and drawing at Millwall in the third round of the FA Cup George Graham did what many critics had been advocating for some time, he plunged into the transfer market to secure some support for Ian Wright. Having baulked at the large fees demanded he surprised everyone by laying out £2.5 million for Luton's 19-year old John Hartson and another £1.55 million on Chris Kiwomya from Ipswich. They could do nothing to stop Millwall winning the replay or save Graham's job. Just a week after splashing out another £2 million on Glenn Helder from Vitesse Arnhem, the Premier League enquiry revealed they were satisfied Graham had pocketed over £400,000 from the purchases of John Jenson and Pal Lydersen. He was immediately sacked with Stewart Houston taking over until the end of the season. Arsenal dropped as low as thirteenth in the League but the return of Tony Adams and Paul Merson combined with Graham's last signings settling in kept them on target to retain the European Cup-Winners' Cup. In the three games before meeting Spurs they had beaten Ipswich 4-1 and Aston Villa 4-0 and overcome Sampdoria on penalties to set up a European Cup-Winners' Cup final with Real Zaragoza. Helder was not eligible for the European games but he returned for Spurs' visit with David Hillier standing down. While Arsenal were experiencing the type of front page scandals Spurs had grown to know so well, Gerry Francis was continuing to turn Spurs' season round. Even though there was no money available to bring players in he got the team playing to a system that whilst not as cavalier as under Ardiles was more successful, evidenced by their run to the FA Cup semi-final. Everton's 4-1 victory at Elland Road may have ended hopes of winning a competition they had not even expected to play in when the season began, but Spurs bounced back, beating Manchester City and Norwich at home and drawing at Crystal Palace to take them to Highbury hopeful of qualifying for the UEFA Cup. The only cloud on the horizon came from increasing stories that Jürgen Klinsmann was thinking over a return to Germany with Bayern Munich.

BEFORE THE GAME

	P	W	D	L	F	A	Pts
Spurs	37	16	11	10	59	48	59
Arsenal	39	13	10	16	50	46	49

AT THE SEASON'S END

		P	W	D	L	F	A	Pts
7th	Spurs	42	16	14	12	66	58	62
12th	Arsenal	42	13	12	17	52	49	51

No.18 Jürgen Klinsmann heads Spurs equaliser.

*Frank Clough for **'The Sunday Telegraph'**...*

Klinsmann on target to make Arsenal pay

Jürgen Klinsmann, the brilliant German international striker who was last night voted Footballer of the Year by the members of the Football Writers' Association, celebrated the award a few hours early with a 75th-minute goal that kept alive Spurs' chances of qualifying for European competition next season.

It was his 28th goal in a fantastic season for him and it wiped out a controversial penalty that had been scored by Arsenal sharpshooter Ian Wright some 15 minutes earlier.

e Bould hitches
le with Teddy
ingham.

In a single season, Klinsmann has won over even his fiercest critics by his skill, his touch, his work rate, his sense of humour and his goals.

I was one of the hacks who voted for him and I am delighted that he has won one of the highest awards the game can offer.

His manager, Gerry Francis, was also pleased. He said: "This is a great accolade for Jürgen and for the club. A lot of people wondered how his move here would work out and he has proved everyone wrong."

Klinsmann has now become the inevitable target for some of the biggest clubs in Europe, with Bayern Munich eager to take him back to Germany. The player, the manager and the Spurs chairman, Alan Sugar, are expected to meet shortly to discuss the situation.

Francis said: "He is a World Cup winner and there are not many of those around.

"I am optimistic that we can keep him. He has been a great example to the others by his willingness to work hard, his unselfishness and the goals he has scored."

Francis was disappointed that his team, though finishing the stronger of the two, had not managed to clinch victory. Klinsmann, in fact, had been kept reasonably quite by Arsenal's uncompromising defenders.

He had hooked a good chance wide just before half-time when Darren Anderton put him in and he had set up a couple of reasonable chances for team-mates but, even as Arsenal were congratulating themselves for keeping a world-rated striker quiet, **KLINSMANN** struck.

The Arsenal defence had gone missing when he rose and glanced a delightful header from a cross by Justin Edinburgh past goalkeeper David Seaman.

Tottenham might even have been ahead four minutes later but Seaman produced the sort of save that has made him England's top goalkeeper, diving full length to tip away a ferocious shot by Ronny Rosenthal.

Arsenal escaped again two minutes later when Klinsmann appeared out on the right to fire in a long centre which Sheringham headed wide.

Arsenal had started like a house on fire but their manager, Stewart Houston, admitted afterwards: "We took our foot off the pedal. We had them under a lot of pressure and we made a few chances. But full marks to Spurs for the way they came back at us."

Arsenal had plenty of shots, most of which were high, wide and not particularly handsome.

Paul Merson was the worst offender but Wright also should have scored in the 16th minute when a pass by Nigel Winterburn beat Tottenham's offside trap.

Wright raced into the penalty area but his angled shot was too straight and Ian Walker was able to block it. Wright went close again a moment later, straining valiantly to get a slight touch to a ball that was going away from him but somehow Walker managed to touch it away for a corner.

The commitment from both sides was total and referee Robbie Hart showed the yellow card to Stefan Schwarz, Steve Bould and Winterburn for Arsenal and Austin for Spurs.

John Hartson caused the Tottenham defence problems with his strength in the air and his determination on the ground but his shooting was no more accurate than any of the others.

Arsenal finally broke the deadlock in the 60th minute when Edinburgh up-ended **WRIGHT**, a needless foul as the Arsenal striker was going wide away from goal. He got to his feet and smashed the penalty past Ian Walker.

Unfortunately that goal provoked some violence in the crowd and half-a-dozen Tottenham fans were ejected by the police. A steward was also led off with a cut head and an empty half-bottle of Scotch was also thrown in Wright's direction. Fortunately the angry mood subsided.

TOTTENHAM HOTSPUR 2
Sheringham, Armstrong

ARSENAL 1
Bergkamp

Saturday 18th November 1995

FA Carling Premiership

White Hart Lane

Attendance 32,894

Tottenham Hotspur

Manager
Gerry Francis

Arsenal

Manager
Bruce Rioch

Ian WALKER	13	1	David SEAMAN
Dean AUSTIN	2	2	Lee DIXON
Sol CAMPBELL	23	3	Nigel WINTERBURN
David HOWELLS	4	14	Martin KEOWN
Colin CALDERWOOD	5	5	Steve BOULD
Gary MABBUTT	6	6	Tony ADAMS
Ruel FOX	7	7	David PLATT
Ronny ROSENTHAL*	16	16	John HARTSON
Jason DOZZELL	12	9	Paul MERSON
Teddy SHERINGHAM	10	10	Dennis BERGKAMP
Chris ARMSTRONG	11	11	Glenn HELDER*
Justin EDINBURGH	3	17	David HILLIER (11)
Chris DAY	30	13	Vince BARTRAM
Gerard McMAHON (16)	18	19	John JENSEN

Referee **Mr AB Wilkie** (County Durham)

BEFORE THE GAME

	P	W	D	L	F	A	Pts
Arsenal	12	7	3	2	16	6	24
Spurs	12	5	4	3	19	16	19

Spurs hail their new double act

BACKGROUND

Jürgen Klinsmann's decision to return to Germany for one last tilt at the Bundesliga title was a great disappointment for Spurs, but at least he made his decision early enough for Gerry Francis to seek out a replacement in £4.5 million Chris Armstrong. Gica Popescu also departed having made it known he found the hectic pace of the Premier League too much for him but it was only on the eve of the season that Nicky Barmby resurrected demands to be allowed to return to his native north. His move to Middlesbrough disrupted Francis' plans just as much as a pre-season injury to Darren Anderton. It meant another chance for Ilie Dumitrescu who had spent most of Francis' time in charge on loan to Seville but when two home defeats followed an opening day draw at Manchester City the Rumanian was again left out. Anderton's return coincided with a return to winning ways but when he was injured again the lack of depth in Spurs' squad was exposed. After long negotiations Ruel Fox arrived from Newcastle for £4 million. He could not help as Coventry put Spurs out of the Coca Cola Cup but he got his first goal for the club as revenge was gained in Spurs' last game, a 3-2 win at Highfield Road. Arsenal had broken with the tradition of appointing an old boy as manager when they persuaded Bruce Rioch to leave Burnden Park for the marble halls of Highbury after leading Bolton into the Premiership. Known to favour a more passing game than his predecessor Rioch made his intentions clear with his first signings, £4.5 million England captain David Platt and £7.5 million Dennis Bergkamp. Ian Wright was out through suspension.

Chris Armstrong hits Tottenham's winner.

Arsenal fall to frantic Fox hunt

This was not your average north London derby. Frantic as the pace was, Arsenal started with an extraordinary degree of control, while Spurs produced a second-half display that Gerry Francis said was as good as anything since he began managing the club.

Arsenal's early domination was total. During one period around the 10th minute, they inter-passed across and up and down the pitch as if they were on a training exercise. Bould and Adams brushed the ball into midfield, from where Keown and Platt, among others, swept it on towards Bergkamp. It was almost continental, if you could allow for the slightly faster pace.

At first glance, though, Arsenal were more movement than action in this phase. No meaningful shots or break-throughs came from their interchanging. But Arsenal are gradually adding dimensions to their game and one of these is the way they spend periods probing for openings and hold-ing on to the ball when traditionally they might have lashed it into the penalty area.

This is what was happening in the opening spell and was much assisted by Bergkamp, dropping into midfield, weaving a quick web and then running into the next spot that made sense, be it forwards or backwards.

Meanwhile, Helder put in a couple of dashes down the wing that looked as if they were going to open Spurs up. But Mabbutt and then Calderwood held firm on the edge of their area. Something, you felt, was coming.

It was Merson who led the breakout from Arsenal's half that led to the breakthrough. When he got the ball in the first half, he not so much drifted as ram-raided his way into midfield and it was from one such move, starting in his own half, that he got the ball to **BERGKAMP**. The Dutchman collected it, twisted and shot in one movement and the visi-tors were ahead. It was no more than they deserved.

Spurs snapped back. Rosenthal had a run and cross that Sheringham scooped narrowly over. Howells kept driving through midfield and Fox increasingly had his moments.

None of this even remotely compared to the sight of Keown performing an Ajax-type step-over of the ball on the edge of the Spurs penalty area. Where had he been hiding that?

The crowd gasped in involuntary admiration, but by the time they had regained their breath, Arsenal were moving things on, almost as snappily, in another part of the pitch.

Gradually, though, Tottenham's Fox went hunting. Many of his runs began in his own half and some were smothered at the death. But he was finding room that few other Spurs players seemed able to find. Just as importantly, he was gradually finding his way through to Armstrong and Sheringham.

One of Fox's runs ended with a ball scooped slightly too far ahead of Armstrong. Another led to a Sheringham shot that perhaps was not hit as well as he would have liked. But again, you felt something was coming.

Fox kept hunting, and it was he who set up the equaliser. Down the flank he rushed yet again. The cross seemed to take a deflec-tion but **SHERINGHAM** had it in the net before Seaman could react.

Thereafter, the pendulum swung more in the Spurs direction. They moved far more freely as the second half progressed and their second goal was one result.

Sheringham, dropping back into midfield as readily as Bergkamp, got a precious second on the ball and swept it forward to **ARMSTRONG**. Sandwiched between two Arsenal players, he was quicker than either and strode forward to shoot past Seaman before Adams could descend on him.

Rosenthal just failed to connect with a high ball from Howells; Armstrong and Sheringham almost got each other in on goal. Fox was still the provider, but that was only the visible element of Spurs' resurgence. They subdued Merson more in the second half, reclaimed space they had effectively conceded in the early stages and broke up Arsenal moves before they could get off the launch pad.

Francis's side should not be written off. This won't be a championship season for Spurs, but gradually, powerfully, they are re-emerging and this game may turn out to be a sig-nificant milestone in that process.

Dennis Bergkamp turns and shoots past Ian Walker to put Arsenal in front.

"Fox was really the difference between the sides" admitted Bruce Rioch afterwards.

118

ARSENAL 0

TOTTENHAM HOTSPUR 0

Monday 15th April 1996

FA Carling Premiership

Highbury

Attendance 38,273

Arsenal

Manager
Bruce Rioch

Tottenham Hotspur

Manager
Gerry Francis

David SEAMAN	1	13	Ian WALKER
Lee DIXON	2	15	Clive WILSON
Nigel WINTERBURN	3	3	Justin EDINBURGH
Martin KEOWN	14	4	David HOWELLS
Andy LINIGHAN	12	23	Sol CAMPBELL*
Scott MARSHALL	25	6	Gary MABBUTT
David PLATT	7	7	Ruel FOX
Ian WRIGHT	8	16	Ronny ROSENTHAL
Paul MERSON*	9	12	Jason DOZZELL*
Dennis BERGKAMP	10	10	Teddy SHERINGHAM
Ray PARLOUR	15	11	Chris ARMSTRONG
Glenn HELDER (9)	11	9	Darren ANDERTON (12)
Matthew ROSE	31	30	Chris DAY
John HARTSON	16	14	Stuart NETHERCOTT (23)

Referee **Mr M Reed** *(Birmingham)*

BACKGROUND

With England losing a place in the UEFA Cup because Spurs and Wimbledon had fielded weakened teams in the summer's Intertoto competition, fifth place in the League was essential for qualification. With just four games left Arsenal held the place but Spurs were right behind. Neither had experienced a particularly good season, always up in the chasing pack but never joining the two horse race between Newcastle and Manchester United for the title. Arsenal's cause had not been helped by the continued absence of Tony Adams and Steve Bould, Bruce Rioch shuffling his defensive formation to try and compensate for their loss. With Nigel Winterburn back after missing the Easter Monday defeat at Sheffield Wednesday, Rioch pulled Martin Keown back into the centre of defence alongside Andy Linighan and young Scott Marshall with Winterburn and Lee Dixon expected to operate as wing-backs. It meant no place for John Hartson, Ian Wright left alone up front. For Spurs the FA Cup had always looked their best bet but they had gone out in the fifth round on penalties after a replay with Nottingham Forest. They too were hit by injuries with Dean Austin, injured in training, joining Andy Sinton and Colin Calderwood on the sidelines. More heartening was the return of Gary Mabbutt after missing three games and the reappearance, albeit on the bench, of Darren Anderton who had been out for seven months.

BEFORE THE GAME

	P	W	D	L	F	A	Pts
Arsenal	34	16	9	9	46	30	57
Spurs	34	15	10	9	45	35	55

Justin Edinburgh races clear of Paul Merson.

Ronnie Rosenthal holds off Ray Parlour.

Arsenal waste local authority

Arsenal and Tottenham Hotspur spurned so many opportunities to advance their chances of entering Europe last night that even the most brazen of Euro-sceptics might have blushed at their behaviour. Darren Anderton, the England winger, who has missed so much of the season through injury, came on 12 minutes from the end, but it was too late to break the deadlock in the north London derby.

The teams began the game separated only by the two points that were Arsenal's advantage over their neighbours, with each having four games left to rescue something from their respective seasons. Everton, Nottingham Forest and Blackburn Rovers, the other aspirants to the third and last UEFA Cup place, must have been praying for a stalemate.

Tottenham gained a psychological advantage before a ball had been kicked. Anderton's name appeared on their teamsheet, as substitute, for the first time in seven months, after a season plagued by hernia and thigh problems. His return might be too late for England's game against Croatia next Wednesday, but the winger now has a chance to persuade Terry Venables he can still play a part in the European championship.

In the first half, however, Arsenal ran Tottenham ragged. Playing with three central defenders, and Merson and Bergkamp darting around behind Wright, their formation was too fluid for the visitors to cope with. Bergkamp nearly scored in the second minute, when his shot almost sneaked through Walker's legs.

After a quarter of an hour, Wright was released by a fine through-ball from the Dutchman, but was tripped by Edinburgh, who had already been tricked once by Merson, on the edge of the area. It earned the defender a yellow card, but Arsenal could not profit from the free kick.

Six minutes later, Rosenthal lost the ball in midfield to Parlour, who delayed his pass cleverly before he picked out Merson advancing into the area. Merson shot over the bar and, nine minutes later, he repeated the crime, volleying a fraction too high after Bergkamp's cross. It was all Arsenal, and ten minutes before half-time Platt should have done better than produce a tame header from Wright's cross. Two minutes before the interval, Arsenal spurned perhaps their best chance of all when Winterburn found himself in possession after a suicidal back-heel from Fox, but could only scuff his shot wide from eight yards out.

In the second half, Arsenal's superiority dimmed and they allowed Tottenham to squander some chances of their own. Two minutes after the interval, Parlour and Keown tried to tackle each other in midfield and gave the ball to Howells instead. He released Sheringham, but his low cross-shot rolled just wide of Seaman's left-hand post.

Wright provided the most thrilling moment of the match midway through the half with a glorious cross-field pass to Dixon that dissected the Tottenham defence, but the visitors had their best chance of the game a few minutes later when Sheringham slid a precise pass through to Armstrong on the edge of the Arsenal box. Armstrong looked offside but he was allowed to play on and still managed to pull his shot wide.

Gerry Francis, the Tottenham manager, said he was disappointed with his team's performance but buoyed by Anderton's return. "It is tremendous for him and tremendous for England that someone that talented is back," he said.

AT THE SEASON'S END

		P	W	D	L	F	A	Pts
5th	Arsenal	38	17	12	9	49	32	63
8th	Spurs	38	16	13	9	50	38	61

> **This should have been far more than the meaningless end of season match it became, especially with the final UEFA Cup place in the offing for both sides**
>
> — Rob Shepherd, Daily Mail

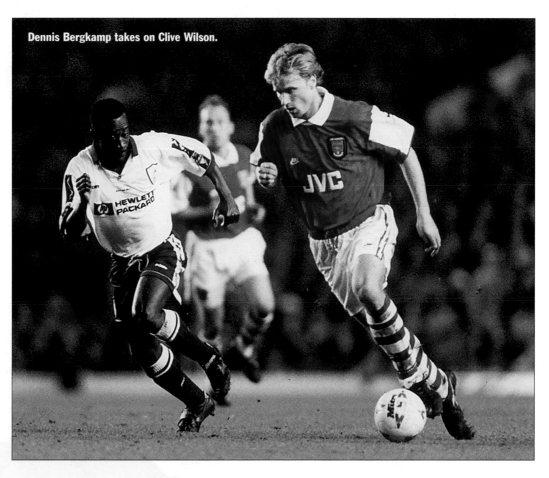

Dennis Bergkamp takes on Clive Wilson.

119

ARSENAL 3
Wright (pen), Adams, Bergkamp

TOTTENHAM HOTSPUR 1
Sinton

Sunday 24th November 1996

FA Carling Premiership

Highbury

Attendance 38,264

Arsenal

Manager
Arsene Wenger

Tottenham Hotspur

Manager
Gerry Francis

John LUKIC	1	13	Ian WALKER
Lee DIXON	2	25	Steve CARR
Nigel WINTERBURN	3	15	Clive WILSON
Patrick VIEIRA	4	4	David HOWELLS
Steve BOULD	5	5	Colin CALDERWOOD
Tony ADAMS	6	23	Sol CAMPBELL
David PLATT*	7	27	Andy SINTON
Ian WRIGHT	8	8	Allan NIELSEN
Paul MERSON	9	9	Darren ANDERTON
Dennis BERGKAMP*	10	10	Teddy SHERINGHAM
Martin KEOWN	14	11	Chris ARMSTRONG
Andy LINIGHAN	12	3	Justin EDINBURGH
Vince BARTRAM	13	13	Espen BAARDSEN
Ray PARLOUR (10)	15	7	Ruel FOX
John HARTSON (7)	16	14	Stuart NETHERCOTT
Steve MORROW	18	29	Rory ALLEN

Referee **Mr D Elleray** (Harrow)

BACKGROUND

Even before the season began Arsenal's renowned team spirit was put to the severest of tests - and it came through with flying colours. Paul Merson's drink, drugs and gambling problems had been well-publicised but did nothing to lessen the shock of Tony Adams' admission to being an alcoholic. Manager Bruce Rioch was sacked only days before the new campaign began and while an open secret former Monaco coach Arsene Wenger would take over, it took two months for the Frenchman to secure his release from Japan's Grampus Eight. Stewart Houston again stood in as caretaker manager but departed before Wenger's arrival to become manager at Queens Park Rangers leaving Pat Rice in temporary control. Such turmoil off the pitch might have shown in results but the players closed ranks and set out to impress the new man, even though he was 6,000 miles away. Not that distance meant Wenger could not influence events at Highbury. He was clearly instrumental in the signings of his compatriots Patrick Vieira from AC Milan and Remi Garde from Strasbourg. The season started well with only one defeat in the opening twelve Premiership games and second place in the table. The one disappointment came in the UEFA Cup, both legs of the first round tie with Borussia Mönchengladbach being lost 2-3. A week before the derby Arsenal were beaten by the only goal of the game at Old Trafford but perhaps worse than the loss of three points was the rib injury that put David Seaman out of Spurs' visit. His replacement was John Lukic, signed on a free transfer from Leeds in the summer six years after leaving Highbury. Spurs, with no summer reinforcements, paid a heavy price for a fine opening day victory at Blackburn; a broken leg putting Gary Mabbutt out for the rest of the season. It was just the first of several injuries that stressed the need for Gerry Francis to move into the transfer market. Denmark's Player of the Year, Allan Nielsen, was signed from Brondby but his arrival was offset by injuries to Darren Anderton, Teddy Sheringham and Chris Armstrong. Long time target Steffen Iversen was close to joining but that would not be until Rosenbourg had completed their Champions League campaign. Already a mid-table position looked the most Spurs could hope for. Four wins in five games was encouraging but with Arsenal clear favourites, Spurs' best hope was the fact that in eleven games as manager of Queens Park Rangers and Spurs, Gerry Francis had yet to finish on the losing side to the Gunners.

BEFORE THE GAME

	P	W	D	L	F	A	Pts
Arsenal	13	7	4	2	24	11	25
Spurs	13	6	2	5	14	11	20

Ian Wright celebrates success from the penalty spot by revealing the message 'I love the lads' on his t-shirt. "It is an appreciation of the team here and what they all mean to me" he explained afterwards.

In *'The Independent'* Trevor Haylett reported...

Bergkamp and Adams break spirited Spurs

Chris Armstrong and Patrick Viera were booked after this second-half flare-up.

The clouds emptied over Highbury yesterday and the wind carried a cutting edge, but for the red half of north London it was to prove, in the end, a wonderful, warming place to be. For a new manager it was also a reminder of the timeless Arsenal virtues of perseverance and pluck.

Only in the last three minutes did Tottenham fall to the winning goals to bring a change to the recent history of this particular fixture, which had seen the Cockerel dominate. Until then a fortunate equaliser, going in off the diving John Lukic, had looked likely to be a source of Arsenal frustration all the way to February and the White Hart Lane return.

Not so. Tony Adams' and Dennis Bergkamp's late sense of drama changed all that and ensured that the game at St James' Park on Saturday will bring together the two leading sides in the Premiership. A victory there against Newcastle and Arsenal will return to the top of the table.

Not since December 1991 have the Tottenham colours been lowered here. One thing that never changes, however, is Arsenal's refusal to give up on any cause, and they were not about to start yesterday. While Tottenham were holding on to a 1-1 scoreline, which in their supporters' eyes would have been an acceptable result, the Gunners decided there was a victory still to be pulled out of the fire.

Standing head and shoulders above the maelstrom was **BERGKAMP**, whose immaculate touch and admirable awareness helped him supply a masterly performance. It was appropriate that the Dutchman should have the final say with a quite exquisite turn inside his defender and a lacerating shot into the far corner of the net for Arsenal's third.

It came just two minutes after **ADAMS** had made excellent use of the license now afforded him under this new, Continental regime, to push forward. Paul Merson's throw was cushioned by Bergkamp, who then delicately lifted the ball in the air for the Arsenal captain to smote his first goal of the season, a left footed volley that diverted off Steve Carr.

It was Bergkamp, using all his wiles and experience, who had helped give Arsenal the lead via the penalty spot midway through the first half. Both he and Clive Wilson found themselves in a heap on the floor, and the Tottenham man appeared to impede his rival as Bergkamp attempted to be first to the loose ball.

The initial feeling was that David Elleray was correct in his decision, though television replays indicated that Bergkamp had considerably

enhanced the contact that had been made with the manner of his fall. Ian **WRIGHT** took three steps back before stroking the penalty head-high to Ian Walker's left for his 160th Arsenal goal.

Before then Spurs had missed the chance to go in front when Allan Nielsen moved in swiftly to challenge Lee Dixon, his diversion putting Teddy Sheringham in the clear. Such opportunities are rarely wasted by the England man but this time he dragged his shot wide.

While Spurs forced a number of corners in the first half, they were finding it hard to penetrate an orderly defence in which Martin Keown gave little change to Chris Armstrong.

After Wright's penalty the controlled nature of Arsenal's one-touch football promised to give them an uncatchable advantage. The easy understanding between Merson and Dixon down the right won them bags of space, and from one such move Bergkamp laid the ball square to Wright, only for Sol Campbell to come in and rescue the situation.

When Colin Calderwood failed to clear Dixon's whipped-in centre, the ball dropped on Wright's left foot but the chance went astray. So did another early in the second half when this irrepressible finisher had stole in ahead of Wilson to gather Merson's subtle chip. Again his left boot was to blame.

Next it was Arsenal's turn to suffer defensive unease and give Lukic the chance to prove that David Seaman's injury absence need not be a critical factor after all. The replacement saved first from Darren Anderton and then, at the second

attempt, from Chris Armstrong. The temperature was rising, Tottenham were glimpsing an equaliser which David Howells' challenge on Adams had appeared to set up. For the second time, however, Armstrong made it easy for Lukic to pull off the save.

Tottenham needed to seize their chances in this period of growing pressure, and, 12 minutes into the second half, they at last found the net even though there was a considerable element of luck about it. Nielsen's long throw found its way to the far side of the goalmouth, where Andy **SINTON** spun and sent in a shot which hit the post and then slipped over the line off Lukic's shoulder.

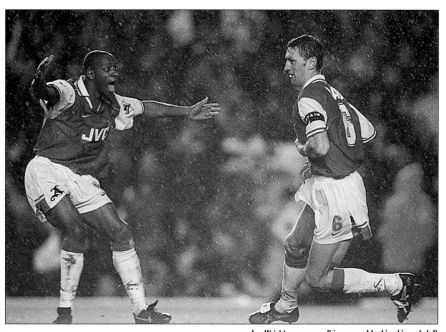

Ian Wright appears well impressed by his skipper's left foot volley which restored Arsenal's lead.

120

TOTTENHAM HOTSPUR 0

ARSENAL 0

Saturday 15th February 1997

FA Carling Premiership

White Hart Lane

Attendance 33,039

Tottenham Hotspur

Arsenal

Manager **Gerry Francis**

Manager **Arsene Wenger**

Ian WALKER	13	24	John LUKIC
Dean AUSTIN	2	2	Lee DIXON
Justin EDINBURGH	3	3	Nigel WINTERBURN
David HOWELLS	4	4	Patrick VIEIRA
Colin CALDERWOOD	5	5	Steve BOULD
Sol CAMPBELL	23	6	Tony ADAMS
Steve CARR	25	14	Martin KEOWN
Andy SINTON	27	8	Ian WRIGHT
Darren ANDERTON	9	9	Paul MERSON*
Ronny ROSENTHAL	16	10	Dennis BERGKAMP
Steffen IVERSEN	18	15	Ray PARLOUR
Ruel FOX	7	18	Steve MORROW
Allan NIELSEN	8	25	Scott MARSHALL
Espen BAARDSEN	13	26	Lee HARPER
Clive WILSON	15	27	Paul SHAW
Rory ALLEN	29	28	Stephen HUGHES (9)

Referee **Mr G Poll** (Hertfordshire)

BEFORE THE GAME

	P	W	D	L	F	A	Pts
Arsenal	25	13	8	4	44	23	47
Spurs	24	9	4	11	27	33	31

AT THE SEASON'S END

		P	W	D	L	F	A	Pts
3rd	Arsenal	38	19	11	8	62	32	68
10th	Spurs	38	13	7	18	44	51	46

BACKGROUND

FA Cup fifth round day. But not for North London. Spurs had, perhaps not unexpectedly, gone out in the third round to Manchester United at Old Trafford; Arsenal, somewhat more surprisingly, to Leeds in the fourth round at Highbury. A miserable 1-6 hammering at First Division Bolton three days after the defeat at Highbury had ended Spurs' interest in the Coca Cola Cup and any hopes of a top six league placing all but vanished when they were thrashed 1-7 at Newcastle in the final game of 1996. Becalmed in mid-table, injuries had done nothing to help their cause with first choice strikers Teddy Sheringham and Chris Armstrong joining Gary Mabbutt as long term absentees. Their loss may have emphasised the lack of depth in Spurs' squad but even when new recruits were secured they were not available for long. John Scales made only two substitute appearances before being struck down with a groin injury and Swiss international Ramon Vega, sent off in his second game, was suspended for Arsenal's visit. Steffen Iversen was more fortunate but pairing the twenty year old with 19 year old Rory Allen merely showed the lack of experience up front. To remedy that shortcoming Ronny Rosenthal was given his first start of the season in place of Allen. At least Darren Anderton was able to begin his first game since the Burnden Park humiliation and both Ian Walker and Sol Campbell had come through England's midweek World Cup clash with Italy without adding to Gerry Francis' injury woes. Four points clear in December, only three wins in nine League games had allowed Manchester United and Liverpool to move ahead of Arsenal but they were still very much in the title race. David Seaman had not recovered from the knee ligament injury that caused him to miss England's Wembley defeat but Tony Adams' ankle had improved sufficiently for him to take his usual place and Dennis Bergkamp was back from suspension. While David Platt was still missing with a hamstring injury, their presence was a great boost as Arsenal looked for the two goal victory that would take them back to the top of the table and set them up perfectly for the visit of leaders Manchester United to Highbury in four days time.

Steffen Iversen, playing in his first North London 'derby', tussles with Paul Merson.

In 'The Sunday Telegraph'
Clive White reported on...

Arsenal miss chance to join United at top

Anyone looking to have their spirits lifted on a return to north London after the depressing lows of Wembley in midweek will have been close to suicide after the first 45 minutes here. But then derbies between Spurs and Arsenal are seldom a great advertisement for the state of the national game. And to think that it had a worldwide audience of 220 million.

Points rather than performance were what mattered more yesterday to Arsenal at White Hart Lane and they did not come away with much of either. A win would have put them level with Manchester United on points at the head of the Premiership table and in the right frame of mind for Wednesday's showdown between the two clubs at Highbury. What with Wimbledon the visitors the following Sunday, this could turn out to be a decisive week in the Gunners' season.

What little they did take away from the match they had the often-maligned John Lukic to thank for. Arsene Wenger, the coach, had encouraged the 'keeper to take more risks around his penalty area, though he seemed to have taken Wenger almost too literally when he saved Arsenal's neck at some risk to his own when diving head first at the feet of the galloping Ronny Rosenthal in the 64th minute to emerge with the ball safely ensnared.

For too many years Arsenal have represented all that is best and bad about English football but the arrival of Wenger this season has added brain to the brawn. Even the psychology of the players appears to be changing. So much so that Paul Merson was quoted as saying on the morning of yesterday's match that he did not care if they lost 10-0 to Spurs so long as they won the title. That amounted to a discernable shift in emphasis.

However, a goalless draw ended up pleasing no-one and Gerry Francis, the Spurs coach, not unreasonably, felt particularly hard done by. "Like the last five or six games, the results have not been what they should have been", he said. To have given more than they got against Arsenal while still seriously depleted by injury was quite an achievement but it will count for little if they do not build on this performance.

They should take heart from the form of Darren Anderton, who, making his first start since November, looked remarkably sharp and self confident. It was probably about the only bit of good news that England coach Glenn Hoddle had all week.

It was different for a midfielder, Wenger argued, attempting to explain the effect that inactivity had had upon his strikers Ian Wright and Dennis Bergkamp, who looked lethargic and uninterested. It is a problem which Francis will face when Teddy Sheringham and Chris Armstrong eventually return to the side after lengthy absences.

How they could have done with even a half-fit version of either yesterday. In their continuing absence, Francis gave Rosenthal his first start of the season and while as usual making every effort, he was all too typically unlucky in his finishing.

The Israeli ought to have given Spurs the lead within the opening 20 seconds but somehow contrived to miss Justin Edinburgh's cross after the full-back, a constant thorn in Arsenal's right flank, had worked a brusque one-two with Steffen Iversen.

As for his bad luck, that came in the shape of a second-half save which Lukic spilled from a fine shot by Anderton which bounced back into the 'keeper's arms as Rosenthal followed up. And then there was the courageous save at his feet.

Not all of Arsenal's resistance was as honourable or as commendable. Wenger may be preaching to them from different text books to that of George Graham these days, but old habits die hard and some of Arsenal's tackling was nothing short of cynical.

How Martin Keown was not booked for manhandling Iversen in the first half beggars belief and when Steve Bould eventually followed Ray Parlour (now suspended for two games) into the referee's book, it could only have been for persistent misconduct.

It needed all of Lee Dixon's "professionalism" to avoid an awkward situation for the Gunners when he accidentally-on-purpose brought down Edinburgh on the edge of the box as he jinked his way into a dangerous position. Something similar happened when Patrick Vieira conveniently got in the way of a Rosenthal run late on.

It was as well for Arsenal that captain Tony Adams had recovered from his ankle injury against all the odds. He provided the sort of steadying influence that England could have done with at the back against Italy.

If goalmouth activity was at a premium in the first half, the game was awash with goal-scoring chances after half-time but neither side were quite smart enough to take full advantage. Parlour came within a whisker of scoring with a first-time volley to Ian Walker's punched clearance and then when Lukic beat out Stephen Carr's shot, which Anderton followed up, it needed a maul on the Arsenal goal-line more in keeping with events at Lansdowne Road to preserve the status quo.

And so it continued until the bitter end with Rosenthal driving the ball across the face of goal with no-one around to provide the necessary touch.

Ray Parlour and Andy Sinton fight for possession.

Justin Edinburgh falls to ground under a challenge from Tony Adams, but it's the Arsenal captain who looks injured as referee Poll has a word in his ear.

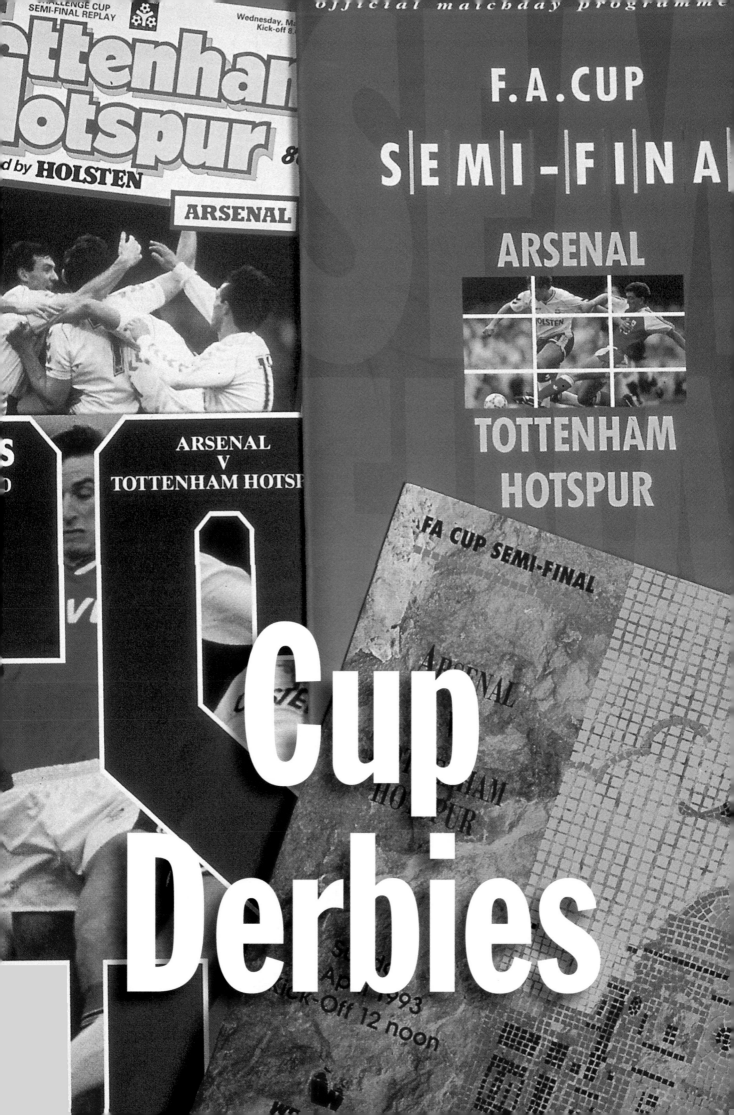

CHALLENGE CUP
SEMI-FINAL REPLAY

Wednesday, Ma
Kick-off 8.

ttenham
otspur

d by HOLSTEN

ARSENAL

official matchday programme

F.A.CUP

S|E|M|I|-|F|I|N|A|

ARSENAL

TOTTENHAM
HOTSPUR

ARSENAL
V
TOTTENHAM HOTSP

FA CUP SEMI-FINAL

ARSENAL

HAM
PUR

Cup
Derbies

Ap 1993
Kick-Off 12 noon

ARSENAL 3
McPherson, Roper, Lishman

TOTTENHAM HOTSPUR 0

Saturday 8th January 1949

F.A. Cup 3rd Round

Highbury

Attendance 47,314

Arsenal		Tottenham Hotspur
Manager **Tom Whittaker**		Manager **Arthur Rowe**
George SWINDIN	1	Ted DITCHBURN
Walley BARNES	2	Sid TICKRIDGE
Lionel SMITH	3	Vic BUCKINGHAM
Archie MacAULEY	4	Bill NICHOLSON
Leslie COMPTON	5	Horace WOODWARD
Joe MERCER	6	Ron BURGESS
Don ROPER	7	Freddie COX
Jimmy LOGIE	8	Harry GILBERG
Ronnie ROOKE	9	Charlie RUNDLE
Doug LISHMAN	10	Les BENNETT
Ian McPHERSON	11	Ernie JONES

Referee **Mr A.E. Ellis** (Halifax)

BACKGROUND

Arsenal had first entered the FA Cup in 1889, Spurs in 1894. They had both entered the competition every year since but had never been drawn against each other. The nearest they had got to a North London FA Cup derby had been in 1922, when, if Arsenal had beaten Preston in a fourth round replay, they would have met Spurs in the semi-final, and 1934, when, if Spurs had beaten Aston Villa they would have met Arsenal in the sixth round. It was perhaps not surprising therefore that interest in the game was truly enormous. With Arsenal deciding not to make the tie all-ticket many people queued all night, which in itself may have put a lot off for the attendance was well below Highbury's 62,000 capacity. Arsenal, the defending League champions, had not got beyond the third round since 1938. Ninth in the First Division, seven points behind leaders Portsmouth, they had won only one of their last eight games and had lost at Derby and Manchester United in their two previous matches. Doug Lishman, signed from Walsall in May 1948, made five disappointing appearances early in the season, was demoted to the reserves to continue his education in the Arsenal style and only returned to the senior team for the game at Old Trafford. Jimmy Logie, injured for that game, returned at the expense of Reg Lewis. Spurs, managed by former Arsenal star Joe Hulme, were third in Division Two, just behind West Brom and Southampton. They had reached the semi-final in 1948 before going out to Blackpool at Villa Park but had also performed poorly in their last two games, drawing with Leicester and losing to Lincoln, both games at home. Horace Woodward had missed the Lincoln game but was fit to return with Vic Buckingham reverting to his usual full-back position and Arthur Willis left out. Inexperienced Charlie Rundle replaced Len Duquemin against Leicester and surprisingly retained his place but the real shock became apparent only when the teams were announced. Eddie Baily, midfield lynchpin, was dropped with his place taken by Harry Gilberg, playing only his third game since the resumption of normal football after the War. Baily was reported to have immediately asked for a transfer although if he did he could not have made that request to manager Hulme. Recovering from illness, he remained at White Hart Lane to watch the reserves play Brentford in the Combination Cup!

Left: Referee Arthur Ellis oversees the pre-match handshake between big friends Ron Burgess and Joe Mercer.
Above: Ted Ditchburn can only help Ian McPherson's shot into the net.

All The Arsenal Line Had A Go - SPURS NEVER KNEW WHAT THEY WERE GOING TO DO

Although both clubs were formed in the late eighties, Arsenal and Spurs had never previously met in the F.A. Cup, and post-match thoughts on the part of the Spurs might have been that they hoped another 62 years would go by before they were called upon to attempt to remove the Arsenal from this most famous knock-out competition.

They never looked like doing so on Saturday; in fact it was always a case of Arsenal knowing far too much for them and for once, at any rate, youth was not served.

Spurs had the physique, the fleetness of foot, but no guile and a palpable inferiority in Soccer science. They back-pedalled in most of their movements whilst apparently waiting for inspiration to tell them what to do with the ball.

Arsenal knew what to do with it and did it, bringing such discomfiture upon the Spurs that the Highbury club could afford to fiddle about once the foundations of success had been laid by their second goal, which came from **ROPER** early in the second half.

ROMAN HOLIDAY

If this match made one thing plain it was that there is a vast difference between First and Second Division soccer. Arsenal enjoyed a Roman holiday, hilarious in its way and such a festive occasion that the forward line was re-arranged every two or three minutes in the last half-hour! They were all having a go.

Roper, Logie, Rooke, Lishman and McPherson, interchanged positions with no to-do at all, and the villain of the piece to the Spurs was Logie. How like James is this fellow developing! He has mastered the art of getting his opponents running the wrong way, can slice the ball with greater delicacy than the grocer doing out the one-ounce bacon ration, and can be about as elusive as the Scarlet Pimpernel, which is what he really is.

Arsenal's vast superiority chiefly lay at inside forward, where Lishman gave us a glimpse of what he is capable of and of dire trouble which he is going to cause a lot more half backs.

Rooke was his imperturbable self, waiting for those through passes which came with regularity, and that he did not score was only because he joined in the second half "festivities" with great abandon.

The biggest mistake that Arsenal's future opponents in the Cup can make is to assume that Anno Domini has laid strong hold upon them. Some of them may be getting on, but above all, they know their way around, as **McPHERSON** indicated when getting past Tickridge and meeting a 30 or 40-yards high ball from Macauley, which he nodded past Ditchburn, after 19 minutes.

MADE AMENDS

Ditchburn ought, perhaps, to have saved this one, for it is questionable if McPherson could have had less room in which to nod the ball between the goalkeeper and the post, but Ditchburn did more than make amends as the game went on.

Macauley will probably do many more good things this season, but that high cross-field pass will be the most valuable. It indicated a way to win the game, and the hint was taken.

Arsenal swung the ball about with far greater freedom than did the Spurs, who never seemed to appreciate that the short-passing game does not pay against defenders who are past masters in the art of marking.

The match was to all intents and purposes over when **LISHMAN** notched Arsenal's third goal after a bout of passing with Rooke and Logie, by which time all were getting a little leg-weary.

Mr A.E.Ellis, of Halifax, contributed in no small measure to the success of the match which could have easily deteriorated. He and his colleagues on the lines exercised rigid control from the start. In fact, the abiding impression of the game was of the officials bringing themselves to the notice of all and sundry. Nor were their intrusions ever out of place.

THE WINNER'S PROGRESS

Date	Rnd	Venue	Att.	Opponents	F-A
29-1-49	Four	Away	31,073	Derby County	0-1

Not this time! Spurs 'keeper Ted Ditchburn saves at the feet of Ian McPherson.

TOTTENHAM HOTSPUR 1
Crooks

ARSENAL 0

Tottenham Hotspur

Manager
Keith Burkinshaw

Arsenal

Manager
Terry Neill

Tottenham Hotspur	No.	Arsenal
Ray CLEMENCE	1	Pat JENNINGS*
Chris HUGHTON	2	Stewart ROBSON
Paul MILLER	3	Kenny SANSOM
Graham ROBERTS	4	Brian TALBOT
Ricky VILLA	5	David O'LEARY
Steve PERRYMAN	6	Chris WHYTE
Ossie ARDILES	7	John HOLLINS
Mark FALCO	8	Alan SUNDERLAND
Tony GALVIN	9	Graham RIX
Glenn HODDLE	10	Peter NICHOLAS
Garth CROOKS	11	Paul DAVIS
Micky HAZARD	12	Raphael MEADE (1)

Referee **Mr N Midgley** (Salford)

BACKGROUND

Spurs had to wait 33 years for the chance to revenge the FA Cup defeat of 1949 and when it came it was their first game in defence of the trophy won seven months earlier with Ricky Villa's great goal against Manchester City. It was Arsenal's first visit to White Hart Lane to meet Spurs in the FA Cup but it was not their first match there in the competition. In 1900 they had drawn with New Brompton (now Gillingham) in a second round third replay, in 1904 they had beaten Bristol Rovers in a qualifying round second replay and in both 1950 and 1952 they had overcome Chelsea in semi-final replays after the first game, on the same ground, had been drawn. Their only FA Cup exit at White Hart Lane had come in 1947 when they lost to Chelsea in a third round second replay. In a season ravaged by atrocious weather Spurs had not played a competitive match since 12th December when they drew at Leeds but they had played a friendly at Plymouth and four days earlier had flown to Portugal for a game with Sporting Lisbon. Arsenal had suffered even more; their last game a League Cup replay at Liverpool on 8th December. They too had managed to arrange a friendly in preparation for the cup-tie although while Spurs had jetted out to Lisbon they had made a short trip to Ireland to meet Glentoran. Steve Archibald, out for a month, was still not fit to play but Spurs were able to welcome back Mark Falco, who himself had not played for almost four months because of an ankle ligament injury. For Arsenal 17-year old Stewart Robson had been called up as replacement for John Devine, injured at the end of November, and retained his place for only his third senior game, all in different competitions; the League, League Cup and now FA Cup.

Celebrations follow the only goal of the game, scored by Tottenham's Garth Crooks (out of picture).

Brian Glanville in *'The Sunday Times'* reported on...

Historic tale of the day Crooks earned his spurs

Matchwinner Garth Crooks.

Tottenham eventually won this Cup-tie, their first against Arsenal for 33 years, by the only goal of the game, but they should have won in a canter. Crooks, their scorer, in fact was engaged for much of the one-sided game in what seemed to be a personal battle with the Arsenal defence, in which he also hit the bar, struck the post, gave Villa an easy chance which was wasted, and finally collided with Jennings, who was obliged to leave the field. By that time, however, the only wonder of it was that Arsenal, with their pathetically under-manned attack, had been allowed to stay in the game so long.

As one who actually saw the last Cup-tie between these teams at Highbury in 1949, and remembers it much more vividly than many a game he has watched this season, I can only say that the contrast was absolute. True, there were rather more spectators at the 1949 game, though not remotely as many as everyone expected, the rumours of swarming streets and a packed house having kept many thousands away.

On that remote afternoon, Tottenham inexplicably dropped their star inside-forward, Eddie Baily, replacing him with an obscure reserve called Harry Gilberg, who did nothing. Ronnie Burgess, their attacking wing-half ran wild, giving the freedom of the park to Arsenal's little inside-right, Jimmy Logie, who ran them ragged. Roper and Lishman, if I remember correctly, ran in to drive ground shots home in the first-half, and Ian McPherson, of all unlikely people, rose on the far post to head the ball past the celebrated Ted Ditchburn in the second.

Yesterday, Arsenal lacked not so much a Logie, though they certainly could have done with him to combat the coruscating skills of Hoddle, as a centre-forward to put beside the lonely Sunderland. Rix was notionally there, but as everybody except Arsenal's obtuse management know, Rix is a midfield player who likes the front line rather as a vampire likes garlic. So it was that he hung deep for most of the game, and even if in the second half he hit the splendid, long, left-footed cross-shot from a free-kick which forced Clemence's only true save of the game, you could never have mistaken him for a striker.

Since we have turned back once into history, let us turn again and say that Arsenal's present desperate lack of a decent centre-forward is reminiscent of the 1930s, when they expensively bought such players as Coleman, Dunne and Halliday, with no successful outcome. Now, they have thrown away their money on Hankin and Hawley, while Meade, who could at least have been relied upon to run vigorously into blind alleys, did not appear till Jennings had gone off with a groin strain, having clashed with Crooks.

It has, sadly, to be said, that Jennings, revisiting his old club was guilty on the goal. Spurs, playing the kind of football Arsenal could never match, advanced through Villa, Hoddle and Ardiles, finally giving **CROOKS** the chance of a right-footed shot, when he had twice failed (once hitting the bar) to score with his more powerful left. This time Jennings seemed to be comfortably capable of saving, but when he dived the ball slipped under his arm, and that was the decider.

Subsequently, Crooks was only just wide, chasing a superbly imaginative long ball from Hoddle (can he ever play for England when he shows such originality?), while subsequently, again set up by Hoddle, Crooks shot against the inside of the right-hand post.

Arsenal had their very first shot a minute earlier, the 44th, through the exceedingly promising right-back, Robson, and soon after half-time Clemence, who had taken that one easily, had to dive among the boots when Talbot turned the ball into the goalmouth. Arsenal's other notable attempt, apart from Rix's fine shot, came when Sansom advanced to find the head of the always resourceful Sunderland, the ball going not far wide. But it was emphatically Tottenham's day.

Referee Neil Midgley keeps a close watch as David O'Leary challenges Tony Galvin.

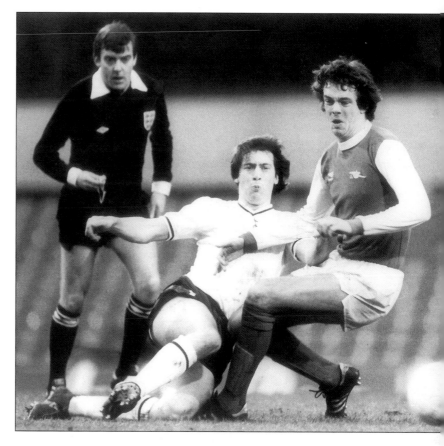

THE WINNER'S PROGRESS

Date	Rnd	Venue	Att.	Opponents	F-A	Goalscorers
23-1-82	Four	Home	46,126	Leeds Utd	1-0	Crooks
13-2-82	Five	Home	43,419	A Villa	1-0	Falco
6-3-82	Six	Away	42,557	Chelsea	3-2	Hazard, Hoddle, Archibald
3-4-82	Semi	Villa Pk	46,606	Leicester C	2-0	Crooks, Wilson (og)
22-5-82	Final	Wembley	100,000	Queens PR	1-1	Hoddle
27-5-82	Replay	Wembley	92,000	Queens PR	1-0	Hoddle (pen)

ARSENAL 1
Smith

TOTTENHAM HOTSPUR 3
Gascoigne, Lineker 2

Sunday 14th April 1991

F.A. Cup Semi-final

Wembley

Attendance 77,893

Arsenal

Tottenham Hotspur

Manager
George Graham

Manager
Terry Venables

Arsenal	No.	Tottenham Hotspur
David SEAMAN	1	Erik THORSTVEDT
Lee DIXON	2	Justin EDINBURGH
Nigel WINTERBURN	3	Pat VAN DEN HAUWE
Michael THOMAS	4	Steve SEDGLEY
Steve BOULD	5	David HOWELLS
Tony ADAMS	6	Gary MABBUTT
Kevin CAMPBELL	7	Paul STEWART
Paul DAVIS	8	Paul GASCOIGNE*
Alan SMITH	9	Vinny SAMWAYS*
Paul MERSON	10	Gary LINEKER
Anders LIMPAR*	11	Paul ALLEN
David O'LEARY	12	Paul WALSH (9)
Perry GROVES (11)	14	NAYIM (8)

BACKGROUND

Arsenal's 17th FA Cup semi-final, Spurs 13th, but for neither had one been as important as this first semi-final to be played at Wembley. The reasons could not have been more different. Despite having two points deducted for their part in the full scale brawl at Old Trafford in October, Arsenal were hot favourites for the League title, five points ahead of Liverpool with five games to play and four of them at Highbury. Beat Spurs and not only would they be favourites to overcome Nottingham Forest or West Ham in the Final, but they would probably never have a better chance of becoming the first club to do the "Double" twice. To Spurs, winning might well prove the difference between survival and extinction. The attempt to diversify from pure football activities had proved a disaster and the club was in severe financial difficulties. Winning the FA Cup would open the door to the riches of European competition again, and might just avoid the sale of Paul Gascoigne and Gary Lineker, Spurs' most valuable assets. The omens and the facts pointed to an Arsenal victory. The omens? There had been only three previous all-London semi-finals and Arsenal had won the lot. The Facts? Top of the table, beaten only once in the League, they had conceded just 25 goals all season, six of them in their Rumbelows Cup defeat by Manchester United and they had no injury worries. Spurs were in a comfortable eighth position but as more news had leaked out about their money troubles, so performances had dipped. Apart from the FA Cup-ties they had won only two of 16 games since Christmas. Their real concern was on the injury front. David Howells had been out for almost three months before playing at Norwich five days before the semi-final. Paul Gascoigne, who had almost single-handedly taken Spurs this far, had played only sixty minutes since a double hernia operation after the sixth round defeat of Notts County. Interest in the game was enormous and the FA had little alternative but to break with tradition and play the game at Wembley. Even then the stadium could have been sold out five times over.

Referee **Mr R Lewis** (Great Bookham)

Old buddies Terry Venables and George Graham share a pre-match joke.

SPURS' PROGRESS

Date	Rnd	Venue	Att.	Opponents	F-A	Goalscorers
5-1-91	Third	Away	9,563	Blackpool	1 0	Stewart
26-1-91	Fourth	Home	31,665	Oxford Utd	4-2	Mabbutt, Lineker, Gascoigne 2
16-2-91	Fifth	Away	26,049	Portsmouth	2-1	Gascoigne 2
10-3-91	Sixth	Home	29,686	Notts C	2-1	Nayim, Gascoigne

ARSENAL'S PROGRESS

Date	Rnd	Venue	Att.	Opponents	F-A	Goalscorers
5-1-91	Third	Home	35,128	Sunderland	2-1	Smith, Limpar
27-1-91	Fourth	Home	30,905	Leeds Utd	0-0	
30-1-91	Replay	Away	27,753	Leeds Utd	1-1*	Limpar
13-2-91	2nd Rep	Home	30,433	Leeds Utd	0-0*	
16-2-91	3rd Rep	Away	27,190	Leeds Utd	2-1	Merson, Dixon
27-2-91	Fifth	Away	12,356	Shrewsbury	1-0	Thomas
9-3-91	Sixth	Home	42,960	Cambridge U	2-1	Campbell, Adams

*After extra-time

One person who did not have a problem getting a ticket was Stuart Jones, football correspondent of 'The Times'. He reported how...

Gascoigne denies Arsenal double

Paul Gascoigne has provoked tears to flow again but yesterday they were not his own. In shaping the destiny of the first FA Cup semi-final to be held at Wembley, he broke the hearts of Arsenal, and especially of their goalkeeper, David Seaman, who left the arena weeping.

Touching heights of brilliance rare even by his elevated standards, Gascoigne blocked Arsenal's path to a historic double and ushered Tottenham Hotspur to the final in which they will meet Nottingham Forest on May 18.

His contribution, though it lasted scarcely an hour, bordered on the sensational.

Show him a spacious stage, turn up the lights, cover the event with television cameras and Gascoigne remains one of the games most enthralling entertainers. As in Italy last summer, he cannot resist taking the starring role during the biggest of occasions.

Throughout his first FA Cup campaign for the club (injury and suspension curtailed his activities in the past couple of seasons) he has been their principal inspiration.

In spite of recently undergoing a stomach operation, he could not be restrained even by the most disciplined defensive organisation in the country.

On the eve of the north London derby he was so overcome by nerves that he could not sleep and required a couple of injections. Within a dozen minutes his natural hyperactive energy was being positively extended and Arsenal's ambitions of winning the Cup as well as the League were in ruins.

After only the third defeat of their extraordinary season, George Graham conceded that "the game was lost" then. **GASCOIGNE**'s first act was outrageous both in conception and execution.

Only he could have considered beating England's goalkeeper with a 35-yard free kick and carried out the undisguised but apparently absurd threat.

His shot, struck with optimum power and rising to the perfect height, brushed Seaman's fingers before nestling in the corner and Tottenham, bristling with purposeful aggression, were ahead. After Gascoigne bemused Thomas with a couple of inventive flicks to release Allen, their lead was extended by a characteristic close-range prod by **LINEKER**.

Tottenham, with their midfield players running from deep to support Lineker, penetrated Arsenal's renowned rearguard with unexpected regularity and might have added another through Samways.

Cautions issued to Dixon, Stewart and Samways punctuated a period of hostility which ended once Gascoigne and Thomas had indulged in their own personal and brief warfare. After the peace had been restored Tottenham's method was temporarily not as convincing. Dixon and Winterburn, full backs who had been forced to concentrate exclusively on their defensive duties, were allowed to augment the attack and Arsenal, for half an hour either side of the interval, came back into genuine contention.

Yet they scored only through an unforced error, perpetrated by the inexperienced Edinburgh, whose misdirected

Paul Gascoigne with plenty to celebrate!

clearance led ultimately to **SMITH** heading in Dixon's cross though surrounded by three opponents.

Arsenal, though encouraged psychologically a few seconds before the change of ends, were unable to increase their momentum.

Winterburn and Smith, who had missed the clearest opportunity of the first half, might have claimed an equaliser before Gascoigne, having scored his sixth goal of the FA Cup, walked off to an ovation from half of the stadium. Almost immediately his replacement, Nayim, gave Tottenham the belief they were seeking.

Within minutes of his incisive run, **LINEKER** made a more profound impact after gaining possession inside the centre circle. Using Samways as a convenient decoy, he accelerated past the comparatively cumbersome Adams and drove across Seaman. Alarmingly, England's goalkeeper could do no more than wave the ball in.

Lineker's fourth goal in two games since returning from Tenerife was more crucial than it seemed at the time. A typically animated Gascoigne watched from the bench as Campbell, who hit the bar, Smith and Merson threatened to belittle his contribution and spoil Tottenham's impending celebrations.

Terry Venables, the Tottenham manager, gave fulsome praise to Gascoigne's goal. "Paul was probably the only player who could do anything like that. To get so much power as well as bend and dip into his free kick was phenomenal. He did a great job, but to be honest, apart from the free kick I don't want to overdo it talking about him because in the end it was a great team effort."

THE WINNER'S PROGRESS

Date	Rnd	Venue	Att.	Opponents	F-A	Goalscorers
18-5-91	Final	Wembley	80,000	Nott'm Forest	2-1*	Stewart, Walker (og)

*After extra-time

Ecstasy at Tottenham's carnival

TRY telling Tottenham that it was not an FA Cup final they won here yesterday. Never has a team and their supporters experienced such ecstacy at the old stadium and left empty-handed.

Top: Tottenham's second goal, frame-by-frame.

Left: Two views of Alan Smith's goal and a tackle from Lee Dixon on David Howells which brought a booking for the Arsenal right-back.

Right: Vinny Samways and Paul Gascoigne celebrate Gazza's stunning free-kick opener.

Below: Dejection for Tony Adams and David Seaman as Spurs celebrate Gary Lineker's second goal.

ARSENAL 1
Adams

TOTTENHAM HOTSPUR 0

Arsenal

Manager
George Graham

Tottenham Hotspur

Manager
Terry Venables

Arsenal	No.	Tottenham Hotspur
David SEAMAN	1	Erik THORSTVEDT
Lee DIXON	2	Dean AUSTIN
Nigel WINTERBURN	3	Justin EDINBURGH
David HILLIER	4	Vinny SAMWAYS
Andy LINIGHAN	5	Gary MABBUTT
Tony ADAMS	6	Neil RUDDOCK
Ray PARLOUR	7	Steve SEDGLEY*
Ian WRIGHT*	8	NAYIM
Kevin CAMPBELL*	9	Darren ANDERTON
Paul MERSON	10	Teddy SHERINGHAM
Ian SELLEY	11	Paul ALLEN
Steve MORROW (8)	12	Nicky BARMBY (4)
Alan SMITH (9)	14	Gudni BERGSSON (7)

Referee **Mr P Don** (Hanworth Park)

BACKGROUND

When Spurs and Arsenal clashed at Wembley in 1991 the FA said a precedent was not being set, Wembley would not host another semi-final. When they were drawn together again only two years later there was no alternative. With so many stadia being re-constructed after the Taylor Report only Wembley could accommodate even a quarter of those anxious to witness the clash. Both clubs had remarkably similar paths to the semi-final, non-League opposition in the third round, Premiership thereafter, they had both pulled off surprising away wins, Arsenal at Leeds and Ipswich, Spurs at Norwich and Manchester City, and both were scoring freely. They each went to Wembley on the back of good performances, Arsenal securing a 0-0 draw at Manchester United and Spurs beating Manchester City 3-2. The other semi-final, an all-Sheffield affair, had taken place at Wembley the previous day. Sheffield Wednesday had prevailed so Arsenal knew that victory over Spurs would set up their second Final against the Owls, for the two were due to meet a fortnight later in the Coca Cola Cup Final.

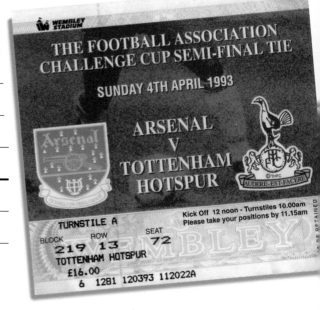

ARSENAL'S PROGRESS

Date	Rnd	Venue	Att.	Opponents	F-A	Goalscorers
2-1-93	Third	Away	8,612	Yeovil Town	3-1	Wright 3
25-1-93	Fourth	Home	26,516	Leeds Utd	2-2	Merson, Parlour
3-2-93	Replay	Away	26,449	Leeds Utd	3-2	Wright 2, Smith
13-2-93	Fifth	Home	27,591	Nott'm Forest	2-0	Wright 2
6-3-93	Sixth	Away	22,054	Ipswich Town	4-2	Adams, Wright (pen), Campbell, Whelan (og)

SPURS' PROGRESS

Date	Rnd	Venue	Att.	Opponents	F-A	Goalscorers
2-1-93	Third	Away*	26,636	Marlow	5-1	Barmby 2, Sheringham, Samways 2
24-1-93	Fourth	Away	15,005	Norwich City	2-0	Sheringham 2
14-2-93	Fifth	Home	26,529	Wimbledon	3-2	Anderton, Barmby, Sheringham
7-3-93	Sixth	Away	34,050	Man City	4-2	Nayim 3, Sedgley

*At White Hart Lane

Ray Parlour halts Justin Edinburgh's progress

Adams leads Arsenal to second final

The north London FA Cup semi-final, following Saturday's Sheffield day of joy, was always a match for drama rather than spectacle yesterday. It was won in controversial circumstances, the referee, Phillip Don, granting Arsenal the free kick from which Tony Adams headed the only goal from almost the identical spot that he had denied Tottenham an even more blatant free kick in the first-half.

For Adams to emerge as the matchwinner, completing a week in which he returned as the hero of Izmir, was an injustice. Adams had reverted to a defender mixing follies with aggression, a man around whom the opposition had seemed likely to win the match long before he claimed the spoils.

We thus have two identical Wembley cup finals - Arsenal versus Sheffield Wednesday in the Coca-Cola Cup on April 18 and the same teams, for even higher glory, on May 15. Lee Dixon, the Arsenal right back, will miss the first final after being sent off for a malicious foul that earned him his second booking of the game and, therefore, a red card. So too will Wednesday's full back, Nigel Worthington, whose yellow card in the 2-1 win over United also disqualifies him.

Yesterday's match was altogether more tight, more cautious, more spiteful than its predecessor on Saturday. Then, after 28 minutes, came the first of two decisions that were to be the crux of the encounter.

Linighan, hopelessly outpaced on the edge of the are by Anderton, tackled from behind. It was an illegal attempt to get at the ball through the legs of the forward and once contact between Linighan's boot and Anderton's trailing leg was established, the only question in the minds of the 76,263 crowd was whether it was inside the area.

The referee abdicated that decision, indicating a corner and leaving Tottenham incensed and bereft of their chance. Disappointingly, this was the hollow reward for a tactical change that had begun to put some flow into the more mobile Tottenham team. They had begun, as expected, with Barmby on the bench, with five across midfield supporting the lone front runner, Sheringham.

However, because Anderton was trying to thread a way through the middle, Tottenham not only lost the width he can supply but also complicated their own approach and denied the space for Samways to spring his forward bursts. It was moments after Anderton had moved wide on the right that Tottenham took the game by the scruff of the neck.

As they continued to press towards half-time, Adams was lucky when his inept attempt at a back pass misfired. Samways preyed on the error but Seaman was able to come off his line and save.

Four men were booked as the temperature rose - Allen for fouling Linighan, Linighan for kicking the heel of Sheringham and then, foolishly, Dixon and Nayim squared up to one another, disputing nothing more than a corner.

Arsenal learnt nothing from these yellow cards, except that the referee had an erratic sense of justice. He did nothing in the fiftieth minute, when Parlour kicked Edinburgh, the foul of a mugger on the New York metro.

Slowly, gradually, Arsenal's muscle and the weight and hunger of their desire began to erode Tottenham's nippier game. This should have brought a goal on the hour; instead, it brought a marvellous double save from Thorstvedt. The Norwegian was lucky that Selley lacked control at his first touch, time enough for the goalkeeper to block the eventual shot; then, from the deflection, the ball fell invitingly to Wright, who stabbed excitedly at the ball as Thorstvedt spread himself.

Twice more Wright should have scored before the second dramatic decision, after 79 minutes. Parlour dashed between Edinburgh and Samways towards the right of the penalty area, a three-way stretch that ended undeniably with Edinburgh's foot bringing down the Arsenal man. Merson floated the ball towards the far post where **ADAMS** lurked and his header, well-timed and accurate, beat Thorstvedt in the bounce.

Dixon was sent off four minutes from time for a disgraceful hack at Edinburgh, a foul in itself worth the red card, and though, by now, Barmby and Bergsson were on instead of Samways and Sedgley, Arsenal held firm.

> "With extra time beckoning for the second successive day, Adams appeared in the Tottenham area to head the winner and wipe away the memories of the 3-1 1991 defeat"
>
> Colin Gibson, Daily Telegraph.

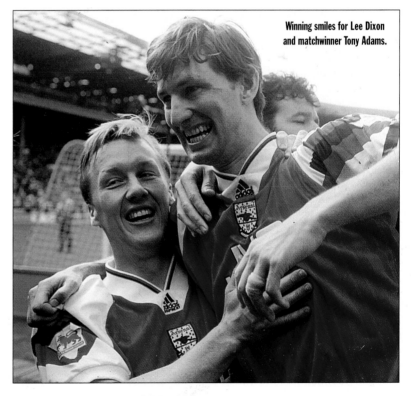

Winning smiles for Lee Dixon and matchwinner Tony Adams.

THE WINNER'S PROGRESS

Date	Rnd	Venue	Att.	Opponents	F-A	Goalscorers
15-5-93	Final	Wembley	79,347	Sheff Wed	1-1	Wright
20-5-93	Replay	Wembley	62,267	Sheff Wed	2-1*	Wright, Linighan

*After extra-time

Left: Tony Adams watches as his header finds its way past Erik Thortsvedt and into the net, then sets off to celebrate his late winner.

Adams ends Arsenal's long wait for revenge

A flying challenge from Steve Morrow blocks Paul Allen's cross.

ARSENAL 1
Radford
TOTTENHAM HOTSPUR 0

Arsenal

Tottenham Hotspur

Manager
Bertie Mee

Manager
Bill Nicholson

Arsenal	No	Tottenham Hotspur
Bob WILSON	1	Pat JENNINGS
Peter STOREY	2	Joe KINNEAR
Bob McNAB	3	Cyril KNOWLES
Frank McLINTOCK	4	Alan MULLERY
Ian URE	5	Peter COLLINS
Peter SIMPSON	6	Phil BEAL
John RADFORD	7	Jimmy PEARCE
David COURT	8	Jimmy GREAVES
Jon SAMMELS	9	Mike ENGLAND
George GRAHAM*	10	Terry VENABLES
George ARMSTRONG	11	Alan GILZEAN
Bobby GOULD (10)	12	Tony WANT

Referee **Mr R V Spittle** (Great Yarmouth)

ARSENAL'S PROGRESS

Date	Rnd	Venue	Att.	Opponents	F-A	Goalscorers
4-9-68	Two	Home	28,460	Sunderland	1-0	Neill
25-9-68	Three	Away	17,450	Scunthorpe	6-1	Jenkins 3, Gould, Court, Sammels
15-10-68	Four	Home	39,299	Liverpool	2-1	Simpson, Radford
29-10-68	Five	Home	32,321	Blackpool	5-1	Radford, Simpson, Gould, Armstrong 2

SPURS' PROGRESS

Date	Rnd	Venue	Att.	Opponents	F-A	Goalscorers
4-9-68	Two	Away	24,775	Aston Villa	4-1	Chivers 3, Jones
25-9-68	Three	Home	25,798	Exeter City	6-3	Pearce 2, Venables, Greaves 3
16-10-68	Four	Home	28,378	Peterboro'	1-0	Greaves
30-10-68	Five	Home	35,198	Southampton	1-0	Collins

BACKGROUND

Like most of the bigger clubs Spurs and Arsenal spurned the League Cup when it was introduced in 1961, feeling they already had enough fixtures to fulfill, a view supported by the fact that both legs of the first final between Rotherham and Aston Villa had to be held over to the following season. The competition gradually grew in stature as more of the top clubs participated and received a tremendous boost in 1966 when it was decided to make the final a one-off, at Wembley and with the winners earning a place in the Fairs Cup. Any route to Europe could not be ignored so Spurs and Arsenal entered for the first time in 1966-67, both going out to West Ham, Spurs in the second round, Arsenal the third. Having won the FA Cup Spurs did not take part in 1967-68 but Arsenal did, reaching Wembley for the first time in 15 years before losing to Leeds. They had a fairly easy passage to the semi-final, the only big name opposition being Liverpool. On paper Spurs progress should not have been too difficult either but they had made hard work of beating Peterborough and Southampton. Arsenal had started the season unbeaten in their first nine League games but won only one of the next eight before a weekend victory over Nottingham Forest. They were at full strength save for Ian Ure replacing Terry Neill. With Martin Chivers a long-term injury victim Spurs lacked punch up front so Bill Nicholson moved Mike England forward. He scored once and helped set up four goals for Jimmy Greaves as Sunderland were beaten 5-1 four days earlier.

Arsenal snatch the winner in injury time

John Radford scores Arsenal's last-minute winner.

Pat Jennings punches clear from the head of Ian Ure.

Arsenal and Tottenham Hotspur were within seconds of making a sad little piece of history at Highbury last night in the first leg of their semi-final tie of the Football League Cup. Never in the history of the 66 matches since their first meeting in 1909 have these two clubs fashioned a goalless draw.

Last night there was all odds on that happening at last, but in the extra seconds allowed for injury time a sad defensive error by Spurs at last let Arsenal in to snatch the goal that for so long had eluded them. Now the Gunners go to White Hart Lane for the second leg a fortnight hence with this slender lead to protect.

Wembley that night will only be a stride away from the men who can suddenly create something out of nothing, and do it rather better than last night. Here we had all the atmosphere of a North London Derby. It attracted a crowd of 55,000 and more, moths enticed out by the lights into a still night. If anyone had constructed a working hypothesis, it was Tottenham, who clearly set out to keep the margin as low as possible for the return tie. And how nearly it worked.

Having lived, and survived, almost all their nine lives, they almost sneaked away like a cat in the dark, only at the end to get their tail caught in an unexpected mousetrap.

The goal for them was a tragedy, although it set Highbury alight as a last gift to an otherwise arid desert of a night.

A long clearance downfield by Wilson from one end to the other was missed in the air by Collins as he went up with Gould, a late substitute in the last 10 minutes for the injured Graham; in desperation Kinnear attempted to head the bouncing ball back towards his own goalkeeper. But Jennings, probably taken by surprise, was that fraction slow in coming out, and in a flash the alert **RADFORD**, so often an Arsenal match winner, had done it again. He was in like a steam engine to blaze his shot into the roof of the Tottenham net.

Beyond that there were few highlights to record. For 99.9 per cent of the time it was Arsenal moving forward in wave after wave of red attack, but being stubbornly met by the tall white defensive cliff of Tottenham. Yet the nearest they came to scoring before at last breaching the barrier arrived from their full back McNab, who three times in the match came from behind his forwards to test Jennings.

The first time was 10 minutes before the interval, when the Tottenham goalkeeper at the second attempt pulled a 30 yards shot down from under his crossbar: and twice later the roar of "goal" was choked in the stands as McNab slashed shots just wide of the posts.

Once, too, a half-chance fell to McLintock only some six yards out from goal. Speed then was the essence, but he could not react quite fast enough, and he saw his shot turned over the bar for a corner. Beyond that, there were no trainers required on the field for nearly an hour, and never a real prospect of a goal. Everyone seemed to be shut in like sardines compressed in a tin can, and all Wilson had really to do was to pick up a number of back passes from his defence. He might as well this night have queued outside an employment agency.

Within the larger battle, too, there was the high duel between the towering England and the towering Ure. Ball after ball was pumped up in the air to them, and like a couple of men with good heads for heights, they climbed the sky like two steeplejacks. Greaves, too, scarcely saw the stray wisp of a chance as Simpson shepherded him out of the match clinically and efficiently. So there it was, a match of tactics and technique, but largely lifeless and without excitement. A match, in fact, largely of negatives.

TOTTENHAM HOTSPUR 1
Greaves

ARSENAL 1
Radford

Tottenham Hotspur

Arsenal

Manager
Bill Nicholson

Manager
Bertie Mee

Tottenham	No.	Arsenal
Pat JENNINGS	1	Bob WILSON
Joe KINNEAR	2	Peter STOREY
Cyril KNOWLES	3	Bob McNAB*
Alan MULLERY	4	Frank McLINTOCK
Peter COLLINS	5	Ian URE
Phil BEAL	6	Peter SIMPSON
Jimmy PEARCE	7	John RADFORD
Jimmy GREAVES	8	David COURT
Mike ENGLAND	9	Jon SAMMELS
Terry VENABLES	10	Bobby GOULD
Alan GILZEAN	11	George ARMSTRONG
Tony WANT	12	George GRAHAM (3)

Referee **Mr W J Gow** (Glamorgan)

Alan Gilzean and Peter Simpson look
on as Jimmy Greaves levels the tie on
aggregate.

BACKGROUND

Between the two legs of the semi-final Arsenal
lost at home to Chelsea and won at Burnley.
Spurs, the visit of Queens Park Rangers postponed, played one game and that resulted in
defeat at Southampton. The only change to the
two teams was Bobby Gould replacing George
Graham up front for Arsenal.

THE WINNER'S PROGRESS

Date	Rnd	Venue	Att.	Opponents	F-A	Goalscorer
15-3-69	Final	Wembley	98,189	Swindon Town	1-3*	Gould

*After extra-time

John Radford pops up
with another last gasp
goal to book Arsenal's
Wembley place.

Radford puts Arsenal in final

A beautifully headed goal by John **RADFORD** as he leapt high to turn in Armstrong's corner in the 87th minute at White Hart Lane last night, put Arsenal through to the final of the Football League Cup at Wembley next March.

A draw was all that Arsenal needed after their 1-0 win over Tottenham in the first leg of this semi-final tie, and that Radford should make the decisive thrust was doubly fitting since his last minute goal at Highbury two weeks ago laid the foundations for their 2-1 victory on aggregate. Luckily last night's game was only a distant relation to the dour defensive first leg.

Arsenal are now in their second League Cup final in successive years - they were beaten 1-0 by Leeds last season - and the manner in which they frustrated Spurs seems a clear pointer to overall victory.

This was only the second cup encounter between these North London giants in more than 70 years, for they have met only once in the F.A. Cup, and that was 20 years ago. And, sad to say, the rarity of their meetings must have been a blessing on last night's evidence, for it was 90 minutes of brutally hard, recklessly fast, intemperate football.

Knowles, the Spurs left back, and England, their centre forward, both had their names taken, the first after a scuffle with Radford, the second for a heavy foul on Wilson, the Arsenal goalkeeper. Nor was it the last bruise Wilson had to take. Mr Gow, the referee, was lenient in not taking stronger action for although tempers were quieter in the second half - when most of the football and both of the goals flowered - the match was shot through with niggly kicking at opponents and deliberately crunching tackles.

But it was all vastly exciting, graceless yet compulsive, crude yet illuminated by some dazzling passes and the two goals. They came too late to redeem the overall quality, but a 55,000 crowd was kept in cruel suspense before **GREAVES** first lashed home a chipped centre by Pearce - set free by a diagonal pass from Mullery - after 68 minutes and then Radford plucked the laurels in those last hectic minutes.

And there was no question that Arsenal were the better side for the third time this season. They came out at the start like greyhounds from traps and in between fouls they chivvied the Spurs defence unmercifully. McLintock and Sammels were masters of the middle, and with Gould charging about like the proverbial bull, and Armstrong teasing with his nimble footwork, Spurs went through a harrowing first half.

Three scorching shots by Venables, all from long range, were the nearest Tottenham got to scoring. They found all their lobs into the centre taken by Ure. The tall Scot gave England painfully few chances.

Spurs moved better in the second half when the indomitable Mullery and Beal took a firmer grip in the middle. When Greaves at last found the mark, his 25th goal of the season, it seemed that they might still break down this closely-knit Arsenal defence. McNab had gone off with a leg injury, to be replaced by Graham, but even re-arranged, the Arsenal defence gave nothing away. Wilson was hurling himself about bravely at the end - though even he can have known little of Gilzean's last shot which spun away off a boot.

TOTTENHAM HOTSPUR 1
Ardiles

ARSENAL 0

Tuesday 4th November 1980

Football League Cup 4th Round

White Hart Lane

Attendance 42,511

Tottenham Hotspur

Manager
Keith Burkinshaw

Arsenal

Manager
Terry Neill

Tottenham	No	Arsenal
Barry DAINES	1	George WOOD
Gordon SMITH	2	John DEVINE
Chris HUGHTON	3	Kenny SANSOM
Paul MILLER	4	Brian TALBOT
John LACY	5	Steve WALFORD
Steve PERRYMAN	6	Willie YOUNG
Ossie ARDILES*	7	John HOLLINS*
Steve ARCHIBALD	8	Alan SUNDERLAND
Ricky VILLA	9	Frank STAPLETON
Glenn HODDLE	10	Steve GATTING
Garth CROOKS	11	Graham RIX
Graham ROBERTS (7)	12	Brian McDERMOTT (7)

Referee **Mr R Challis** (Tonbridge)

SPURS' PROGRESS

Date	Rnd	Venue	Att.	Opponents	F-A	Goalscorers
27-8-80	Two-1	Away	20,087	Orient	1-0	Lacy
3-9-80	Two-2	Home	25,806	Orient	3-1	Archibald 2, Crooks
24-9-80	Three	Home	29,654	Crystal Palace	0-0	
30-9-80	Replay	Away	26,885	Crystal Palace	3-1*	Villa, Hoddle, Crooks

* After extra-time

ARSENAL'S PROGRESS

Date	Rnd	Venue	Att.	Opponents	F-A	Goalscorers
26-8-80	Two-1	Away	17,036	Swansea City	1-1	Stapleton
2-9-80	Two-2	Home	26,399	Swansea City	3-1	Hollins (pen), Walford, Sunderland
22-9-80	Three	Away	11,635	Stockport County	3-1	Hollins, Sunderland, Stapleton

BACKGROUND

Originally scheduled for 27th October, the Republic of Ireland were due to play a World Cup qualifier against France the following day and when they successfully appealed to UEFA for the release of Frank Stapleton and Chris Hughton for 48 hours prior to their game, the derby cup-tie was put back a week. It meant the teams went into the match knowing West Ham awaited the winners in the next round. Neither were at full strength, Spurs with Paul Miller in for Terry Yorath, and Arsenal missing long-term injury victims Pat Jennings and David O'Leary. George Wood, signed three months earlier, was standing-in for Jennings with Steve Walford, who had followed Terry Neill from White Hart Lane to Highbury, wearing the no 5 shirt.

Martin Tyler in **'The Times'**

Tottenham seek old glory on back of a statistical freak

Tottenham Hotspur, winners of the FA Cup in 1901, 1921 and 1961, league champions in 1951 and winners of the League Cup in 1971, gave further notice of their intention to keep the run going in 1981. A first half goal from Osvaldo Ardiles produced their first victory over Arsenal for more than four years to secure a place in the quarter final round against West Ham United.

On a freezing night the temperature of the game was rarely less than equatorial. Tottenham owed much of their early supremacy to the skill and strength of Ricardo Villa, whose appreciation of the demands of English football is now evident on a much more consistent basis. Villa had already had a thundering effort ruled out because of an infringement by Crooks when the two players combined to greater effect for the goal that won the match.

In the twenty-sixth minute, the Argentine finished a powerful run down the left touch line with a precise pass infield. Crooks' dexterity carried him past Young and Wood could only parry out the shot. **ARDILES** solved the problem of two defenders on the line by threading the ball precisely inside the far post.

Immediately Sunderland's header produced a remarkable save from Daines, dropping instantly to his right, and before half time the goalkeeper denied Arsenal an equaliser from Rix in similar style.

Though the quality of football fell away in the second half, no passion was sacrificed. Arsenal's refusal to succumb

Above: Gunners' Steve Gatting keeps his balance
whilst Spurs No.3 Chris Hughton loses his.

Right: The only goal of the game as
Ossie Ardiles beats George Wood.

brought them a greater share of possession, yet Tottenham continued to fashion the more penetrative moments.

Arsenal's persistence in leaving Rix wide on the left instead of allowing him to assume the role of the departed Brady still gives a workmanlike emphasis to their midfield. A superbly angled pass by Stapleton that the willing Talbot could not convert encapsulated their problem, a blunt instrument on a night when a rapier was required.

The roars of Glory, Glory, Hallelujah at the final whistle came as a reminder of past exploits, delivered by supporters well aware that the statistical freak in their club history could be perpetuated after a satisfying victory at the expense of such an old foe.

THE WINNER'S PROGRESS

Date	Rnd	Venue	Att.	Opponents	F-A	Goalscorers
2-12-80	Five	Away	36,003	West Ham U	0-1	

TOTTENHAM HOTSPUR 1
Hoddle (pen)

ARSENAL 2
Nicholas, Woodcock

Tottenham Hotspur

Arsenal

Manager
Keith Burkinshaw

Manager
Terry Neill

Tottenham	No	Arsenal
Ray CLEMENCE	1	Pat JENNINGS
Chris HUGHTON	2	Stewart ROBSON
Danny THOMAS	3	Kenny SANSOM
Paul PRICE*	4	Chris WHYTE
Gary STEVENS	5	David O'LEARY
Steve PERRYMAN	6	Colin HILL
Graham ROBERTS	7	Alan SUNDERLAND
Steve ARCHIBALD	8	Paul DAVIS
Mark FALCO	9	Tony WOODCOCK
Glenn HODDLE	10	Charlie NICHOLAS
Tony GALVIN	11	Graham RIX
Alan BRAZIL (4)	12	Dave MADDEN

Referee **Mr B Stevens** (Stonehouse)

SPURS' PROGRESS

Date	Rnd	Venue	Att.	Opponents	F-A	Goalscorers
5-10-83	Two-1	Home	20,241	Lincoln City	3-1	Galvin, Archibald, Houghton (og)
26-10-83	Two-2	Away	12,239	Lincoln City	1-2	Falco

ARSENAL'S PROGRESS

Date	Rnd	Venue	Att.	Opponents	F-A	Goalscorers
4-10-83	Two-1	Away	20,983	Plymouth Argyle	1-1	Rix
25-10-83	Two-2	Home	22,640	Plymouth Argyle	1-0	Sunderland

THE WINNER'S PROGRESS

Date	Rnd	Venue	Att.	Opponents	F-A	Goalscorers
29-11-83	Four	Home	22,406	Walsall	1-2	Robson

BACKGROUND

In ten games during which they had beaten Feyenoord home and away in the UEFA Cup Spurs had lost only once, at Third Division Lincoln in the second round second leg of the Milk Cup. It was an embarrassing defeat but one that mattered little as they still went through on aggregate. In their last game, a draw at Stoke, Gary Mabbutt had pulled a stomach muscle so Graham Roberts was pushed into midfield with Paul Price coming in at the back. It had not been easy for Arsenal against lower division opposition either, an Alan Sunderland goal proving decisive against Plymouth after a draw in the Home Park first leg. They were at least at full strength with Paul Davis returning in place of Brian Talbot and David O'Leary coming back in for Tony Adams who had made his debut in the weekend defeat by Sunderland at Highbury. Arsenal had won an award for scoring most goals in October, 12 in six games, and two of them goalless, but not one had come from Charlie Nicholas. The Scotland striker had scored only twice all season, and not one in the last 12 games.

Derby chase...
Tony Galvin leads
from Kenny Sansom
and Paul Davis.

Stuart Jones in **'The Times'** *reported...*

Nicholas lights a fire that burns the heart out of Tottenham

Arsenal climbed out of the shadow of their North London rivals and neighbours last night to reach the fourth round of the Milk Cup. For three and a half years, since they last won at White Hart Lane, they have had to watch Tottenham Hotspur take the honours, the spotlight and the praise for a more adventurous style.

In front of a vociferous capacity crowd of over 48,000 they emerged victorious from a tie that crackled with all the crunching ferocity typical of a local derby. They blossomed in a fiery atmosphere and as Keith Burkinshaw later admitted his own Tottenham players merely withered.

In failing to provide adequate support to their front three, Tottenham showed how much they depend upon the industry of Mabbutt, absent for the first time this season. Perryman's aging legs cannot carry him to and fro with any regularity, Roberts was concerned with Rix and Hoddle, usually their leading star, was reduced to playing little more than a bit part by Robson.

If Tottenham's midfield was disappointingly meagre, their back four were as substantial as dampened tissue paper. The list of their errors was surpassed only by the number of occasions they gave away possession, even when under no pressure. Their generosity knew no bounds and both of Arsenal's goals were gifts.

NICHOLAS, denied earlier by the advancing Clemence and also by

Arsenal scorers Tony Woodcock and Charlie Nicholas celebrate.

Stevens' timely intervention, gave Arsenal the lead in the thirty-fourth minute with his first goal since the end of August. He could hardly have missed. When Hill's lob, aimed at Woodcock on the run, bounced off the knees of the distracted Clemence, he was left on the edge of the area and confronted by an empty net.

Arsenal went further ahead five minutes after the interval. This time Stevens was the guilty party. He came across towards the touchline to intercept Sunderland's gentle nudge and succeeded instead in allowing **WOODCOCK** to burst clear. He ran on for 30 yards, with the growing expectation of Arsenal's supporters his only companion, before driving in his eighth goal in five games.

Burkinshaw, not surprisingly, took immediate action and gained an immediate reward. Price, who had been embarrassed by the speed of Arsenal's forwards, was replaced by Brazil as Hoddle prepared to take a corner. When it came over it was met clearly by a stray Arsenal hand, though the identity of the miscreant was not so obvious. **HODDLE** swept home the penalty.

With Roberts caught between falling back to cover for Price and pushing forward to join in the eager search for an equaliser, Tottenham were just as liable to concede another as they were to force a replay. In a frantic close that saw Woodcock, Sunderland and Hoddle added to the name of Roberts in the referee's notebook, Clemence was the busier of the two goalkeepers.

In suffering only their second defeat in a dozen games since the middle of September, Tottenham could scarcely have chosen a worse moment to lose both their confidence and their way. Their opponents at White Hart Lane on Saturday are Liverpool. And who to follow? Luton Town and - away in the UEFA Cup - Bayern Munich.

ARSENAL 0

TOTTENHAM HOTSPUR 1
Allen C.

Sunday 8th February 1987

Littlewoods Cup Semi-final 1st Leg

Highbury

Attendance 41,256

Arsenal

Tottenham Hotspur

Manager
George Graham

Manager
David Pleat

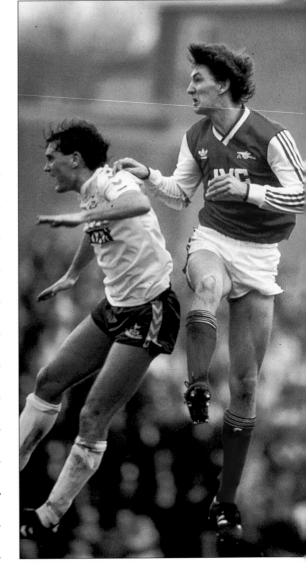

John LUKIC	1	Ray CLEMENCE
Gus CAESAR*	2	Danny THOMAS
Kenny SANSOM	3	Mitchell THOMAS
Steve WILLIAMS	4	Ossie ARDILES
David O'LEARY	5	Richard GOUGH
Tony ADAMS	6	Gary MABBUTT
Perry GROVES	7	Clive ALLEN
Paul DAVIS	8	Paul ALLEN
Niall QUINN	9	Chris WADDLE
Charlie NICHOLAS*	10	Glenn HODDLE
Martin HAYES	11	Nico CLAESEN*
Michael THOMAS (2)	12	Gary STEVENS
Graham RIX (10)	14	Tony GALVIN (11)

Referee **Mr J Martin** (Waterlooville)

BACKGROUND

Arsenal went into their fifth League Cup semi-final the day after being knocked off the top of the First Division by Everton without Viv Anderson and David Rocastle. Both missed their first game of the season through suspension with Gus Caesar and Perry Groves deputising. Confidence was high though after a 6-1 FA Cup thrashing of Plymouth in their last game. Spurs had beaten West Ham 5-0 in a fifth round replay six days earlier with Clive Allen hitting a hat-trick to maintain his record of scoring in every game in the competition and giving him 33 goals in 31 games. December signing Steve Hodge was cup-tied and his place again went to Ossie Ardiles, while Nico Claesen had performed so well against the Hammers that even though Tony Galvin had recovered from injury, he retained his place.

ARSENAL'S PROGRESS

Date	Rnd	Venue	Att.	Opponents	F-A	Goalscorers
23- 9-86	Two-1	Home	15,194	Huddersfield	2-0	Davis, Quinn
7-10-86	Two-2	Away	8,713	Huddersfield	1-1	Hayes
28-10-86	Three	Home	21,604	Man City	3-1	Rocastle, Davis, Hayes (pen)
18-11-86	Four	Home	28,301	Charlton A	2-0	Curbishley (og), Quinn
21-1-87	Five	Home	38,617	Nott'm Forest	2-0	Nicholas, Hayes

SPURS' PROGRESS

Date	Rnd	Venue	Att.	Opponents	F-A	Goalscorers
23- 9-86	Two-1	Away	10,079	Barnsley	3-2	Roberts, C.Allen, Waddle
8-10-86	Two-2	Home	12,299	Barnsley	5-3	Close, Hoddle 2, Galvin, C.Allen
29-10-86	Three	Home	15,542	Birmingham	5-0	Roberts, Hoddle, Waddle, C.Allen 2
26-11-86	Four	Away	10,033	Cambridge Utd	3-1	C.Allen, Close, Waddle
27-1-87	Five	Away	28,648	West Ham Utd	1-1	C.Allen
2- 2-87	Replay	Home	41,995	West Ham Utd	5-0	Hoddle, Claesen, C.Allen 3 (1 pen)

Above: Arsenal fans look on in stunned silence as Clive Allen enjoys his goal.

Left: Tony Adams outjumps Glenn Hoddle.

Patrick Barclay in **'The Independent'** *reported...*

Allen is ready for call-up

Clive Allen broke two records at a stroke yesterday, his first goal against Arsenal, who briefly paid his wages as a teenager, handing the Highbury club the first home defeat since George Graham became manager last summer.

The prolific striker, who is expected to be named in the England squad today for next week's friendly in Madrid, cruelly punished John Lukic for a marvellous, if incomplete, save six minutes before half-time, tilting the balance of an absorbing Littlewoods Cup semi-final firmly in Tottenham's favour.

The second leg at White Hart Lane on Sunday, 1 March may produce even better television, for Arsenal will have to open out again and can only be strengthened by the return of Viv Anderson and David Rocastle from suspension.

Graham, though cautious in the transfer market, must have glanced covetously at David Pleat's substitutes, the internationals Tony Galvin and Gary Stevens.

Tottenham were manifestly stronger in all but the opening stages when Martin Hayes, Niall Quinn and Gus Caesar failed with half-chances. As soon as Spurs found their fluidity, doubts spread through the home ranks.

There was another splendidly competitive performance from Osvaldo Ardiles and when the 34-year-old Argentinian took time out for a breather Glenn Hoddle was only too happy to hog the spotlight.

Twice Hoddle went close to extending Spurs' lead with cunning shots, though this would have been hard on an Arsenal defence in which Tony Adams, another player who has been tipped to travel with Bobby Robson's squad to Spain, displayed customary excellence despite being dragged to the flanks more frequently than usual.

No attacking side can be more difficult to deal with than Spurs at the moment, and it was a typically swift and inventive move by Hoddle and Nico Claesen that gave Clive Allen his first opening. The shot was fierce and dipped alarmingly, but Lukic touched it over the bar.

Paul Davis tried to clear the corner but a bounce found Richard Gough, and then Gary Mabbutt, whose resounding drive Lukic breathtakingly parried at full stretch; almost before the keeper hit the ground, **ALLEN** had the ball in the net for his 34th goal this season.

The celebrations ought to have been repeated two minutes later when the vulnerable Caesar sliced the ball to Clive Allen, who drew Lukic but shot wide from eight yards.

Arsenal's frustration was embodied, predictably, by Steve Williams. His name was already in the book for a silly attack on Mitchell Thomas when, just before half-time, he scuffled with his team-mate, David O'Leary.

In the second half Williams foolishly - to put it at its mildest - indulged in four more illicit challenges. He was lucky not to be sent off by a referee who seemed taken with the idea that this was an occasion when the quiet word, however monotonously repeated, would suffice.

Charlie Nicholas, after a ludicrous attempt to win a penalty at Mabbutt's expense, was taken off but Graham Rix made little difference. Arsenal's best effort came from Perry Groves, who turned quickly and sent a looping volley against the angle of post and bar.

But the harder Arsenal chased forward, the more effectively Tottenham counter-attacked. After Lukic had advanced resolutely to stifle Waddle, the resourceful shooting of Hoddle found first the outside of a post, then the side netting, the latter a remarkable feat with a volley executed from directly in front of the goal.

TOTTENHAM HOTSPUR 1
Allen C.

ARSENAL 2
Anderson, Quinn   (After extra time)

Tottenham Hotspur

Arsenal

Manager
David Pleat

Manager
George Graham

Tottenham		Arsenal
Ray CLEMENCE	1	John LUKIC
Danny THOMAS	2	Viv ANDERSON
Mitchell THOMAS	3	Kenny SANSOM
Ossie ARDILES*	4	Michael THOMAS
Richard GOUGH	5	David O'LEARY
Gary MABBUTT	6	Tony ADAMS
Clive ALLEN	7	David ROCASTLE
Paul ALLEN	8	Paul DAVIS
Chris WADDLE	9	Niall QUINN
Glenn HODDLE	10	Charlie NICHOLAS
Nico CLAESEN*	11	Martin HAYES*
Gary STEVENS (4)	12	Ian ALLINSON (11)
Tony GALVIN (11)	14	Gus CAESAR

Referee **Mr A Gunn** (Burgess Hill)

BACKGROUND

In the three weeks since the first leg, Spurs had beaten Southampton 2-0 and Leicester 5-0 in the League and progressed to the sixth round of the FA Cup at the expense of Newcastle, all the games at White Hart Lane, while Arsenal had drawn at Sheffield Wednesday and Oxford to allow Liverpool to join Everton above them although they had also gone through to the FA Cup sixth round with a 2-0 home victory over Barnsley. Liverpool had overcome Southampton in the other semi-final and were awaiting the winners in the Final. Spurs were unchanged from the first leg but, while Viv Anderson and David Rocastle returned for Arsenal, Steve Williams had been injured at Sheffield, his place going to Michael Thomas.

David O'Leary keeps Clive Allen at bay.

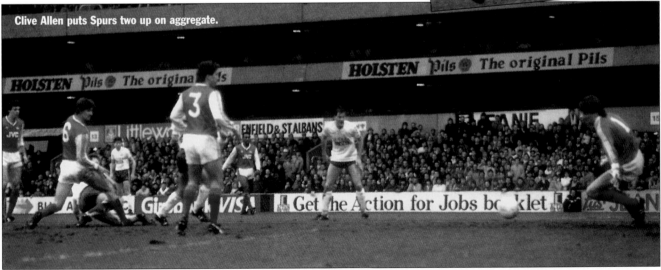

Clive Allen puts Spurs two up on aggregate.

Ray Clemence punches clear as Arsenal put the pressure on.

Patrick Barclay in 'The Independent'...

Allen's misses Spur Arsenal

The assumption that Tottenham would ride to Wembley on the cushion inflated by Clive Allen at Highbury last month was made to look very glib indeed yesterday by an Arsenal side comparatively short of stars but stacked with the resilience on which the club's reputation was built.

A relentless but rancour-free second leg of the Littlewoods Cup semi-final between the north London rivals turned, as the first had done, on Allen. His 38th goal of the season, early and superbly taken, was straight out of Ossie's dream. But his misses early in the second half, both sides of Viv Anderson's reply, proved costly as Niall Quinn took the tie into an inconclusive extra 30 minutes.

The difficulty in separating the contenders to meet Liverpool in the final was then symbolised by the toss to decide the venue of the third match; the coin initially landed on it's side in the mud. When the referee tried the back of his hand, David Pleat called correctly, so the replay will be at White Hart Lane on Wednesday at 8pm. In view of form so far this season, when neither side has won at home in four meetings, the advantage was recognised by both Pleat and George Graham afterwards as somewhat dubious.

Pleat refused to criticise his team, and in particular Allen for allowing the tie to reach a third match. He said. "On about four occasions I thought "this is it", but we missed those chances. That is Clive Allen - I thought he did well with the goal, but he missed a lot as well."

Graham was "quite pleased" with his side's performance, which students of the Scot's determinedly low-key style will understand as high praise. He pointed out that five of his players were under 21, and told the assembled media. "You guys have tried to knock us down, but we keep bouncing back. You did my job for me today, you fired the players up."

Modesty nevertheless demands that Arsenal's players take their share of credit. They were utterly unbowed by adversity, the 19-year-old Michael Thomas meriting special mention for the way he overrode inexperience with industry. Paul Davis was also outstanding in midfield, while Tony Adams shouldered his customary defensive burdens and the gangling Quinn tormented Tottenham's rearguard consistently in the air and occasionally on the ground.

John Lukic began unpromisingly in goal, flapping at rather than punching a lofted free kick from Richard Gough when under challenge from Gary Mabbutt. The loose ball fell to Clive **ALLEN**, who coolly guided it away from the lunging Quinn and Adams before finding the net to equal the League Cup record of 11 goals in a season. But Arsenal's goalkeeper redeemed himself later.

In the interim Charlie Nicholas, who showed immensely encouraging flashes of his best form, had an effort deflected on to the bar, but inevitably Arsenal were leaving gaps as they chased equality. Clive Allen kept catching them square, and had already passed up a couple of chances when Quinn's header let **ANDERSON** bring Arsenal ever closer. He shot wide again, and from Glenn Hoddle's pass was the victim of a particularly resolute save from Lukic, who also blocked Chris Waddle.

Shortly afterwards Arsenal established themselves as the more likely winners when **QUINN** met David Rocastle's cross to stab home at the far post as Tottenham's defence momentarily dropped it's guard. Tottenham threatened briefly when Tony Galvin, belatedly introduced in place of the disappointing Nico Claesen, tried a lob that David O'Leary headed out from under the bar. But Arsenal finished the stronger of two increasingly weary teams.

Both managers indicated afterwards that Wednesday's match was a little too soon after such a strength-sapping encounter. But that will hardly keep the public away after this fine televised advertisement for the vim and vigour of the English game.

TOTTENHAM HOTSPUR 1
Allen C.

ARSENAL 2
Allinson, Rocastle

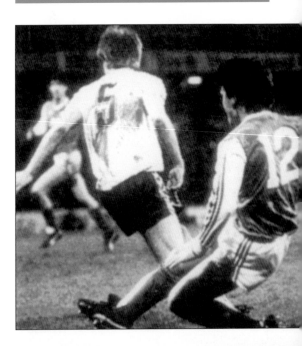

Tottenham Hotspur

Arsenal

Manager
David Pleat

Manager
George Graham

Ray CLEMENCE	1	John LUKIC
Danny THOMAS	2	Viv ANDERSON
Mitchell THOMAS	3	Kenny SANSOM
Ossie ARDILES	4	Michael THOMAS
Richard GOUGH	5	David O'LEARY
Gary MABBUTT	6	Tony ADAMS
Clive ALLEN	7	David ROCASTLE
Paul ALLEN	8	Paul DAVIS
Chris WADDLE	9	Niall QUINN
Gary STEVENS	10	Charlie NICHOLAS
Nico CLAESEN*	11	Martin HAYES
Mark BOWEN	12	Ian ALLINSON (10)
Tony GALVIN (11)	14	Gus CAESAR

Referee **Mr J Worrall** (Warrington)

BACKGROUND

David Pleat won the toss to decide whether the replay should take place at White Hart Lane or Highbury. Despite the energy-sapping extra-time just four days earlier the only absentee was the injured Glenn Hoddle, his place being taken by Gary Stevens.

THE WINNER'S PROGRESS

Date	Rnd	Venue	Att.	Opponents	F-A	Goalscorers
5-4-87	Final	Wembley	96,000	Liverpool	2-1	Nicholas 2

Joe Lovejoy in *'The Independent'*...

Rocastle stars in Arsenal's late, late show

Arsenal scored twice in the last eight minutes of this protracted Littlewoods Cup semi-final, David Rocastle securing a famous victory and his team's first appearance at Wembley for seven years with an injury-time winner.

After five hours of attrition, spread over three invigorating games, George Graham's thrusting young side won through to the final, where they will meet Liverpool on 5 April.

The third match between these traditional rivals followed a similar pattern to the second, and produced the same scoreline.

As on Sunday, the endlessly prolific Clive **ALLEN** shot Tottenham ahead, this time in the 62nd minute, but once again Arsenal responded magnificently to emerge victorious.

They left it perilously late, with the equaliser delayed until the 83rd minute, when a superbly executed turn and strike from close range by Ian **ALLINSON** set the stage for Rocastle's dramatic finale.

Allinson, who came on as substitute for the lame Charlie Nicholas after 64 minutes, played his part here, too, for it was the rebound from his shot, after a David O'Leary free-kick, which presented **ROCASTLE** with his moment of glory.

The 19-year-old midfield player, possibly the best of Graham's unusually gifted crop of youngsters, beat Ray Clemence with an emphatic shot from 12 yards, displaying precocious assurance in the coolness with which he grasped his opportunity.

Arsenal's manager joined in his side's celebrations on the field before expressing his admiration for their achievements.

They remain in contention for a clean sweep of all three major domestic honours, and Graham said: "Of course, I am proud of them. The plat-form for success has been built quicker than I expected when I took over last summer.

"Let us remember, though, that we have won nothing yet, and to be honest when Spurs scored I thought we were out."

Off-side decisions punctuated the game with tiresome regularity, to the irritation of the 41,005 crowd, but for all that there was sufficient drama to satisfy everyone - or the Arsenal fans, at least.

The weather denied Spurs the firm pitch they wanted on which to utilise their skills, and they were further disadvantaged by the loss of Glenn Hoddle, absent injured, and replaced in midfield by Gary Stevens.

Niall Quinn, whose youthful exuberance was in danger of exceeding legal bounds, was fortunate to escape caution in the 28th minute when he led an Arsenal challenge on the grounded Clemence after the goalkeeper had saved a Viv Anderson header.

Clive Allen was then booked for a spiteful foul on Paul Davis, Joe Worrall appreciating the need to assert his authority if fraying tempers were not to spoil the tie.

As the pace became even more frantic the eye was drawn towards Hoddle, the seated figure whose composure was so conspicuously missing. In his absence, there was too much hurrying and scurrying in a midfield which had no authoritative influence.

After a disappointing first half, which failed to do justice to the atmosphere, the tie was given the catalyst it needed by Clive Allen's 39th goal of his endlessly prolific season.

The Football League's leading scorer was as precise as ever from close in, finding the net for the 11th time in his last nine games after Richard Gough had flicked on an Ossie Ardiles free-kick.

Allen's clinical finish appeared to have settled north London's most important domestic dispute of recent years, but Allinson supplied Arsenal with the kiss of life, and the tie turned on it's head in the course of the last eight memorable minutes.

David Rocastle shoots the Gunners to Wembley with this injury-time goal.
Left: Substitute Ian Allinson equalises from close range in the 83rd minute.

ARSENAL 0

TOTTENHAM HOTSPUR 0

Saturday 10th August 1991

Tennents F.A. Charity Shield

Wembley

Attendance 65,483

Arsenal

Tottenham Hotspur

Manager
George Graham

Manager
Peter Shreeves

BACKGROUND

The meeting of League champions Arsenal and FA Cup holders Spurs in the season's traditional curtain-raiser was never going to match the intensity of the clash under the twin towers four months earlier. After the FA Cup semi-final Arsenal had gone on to take the title by seven points from Liverpool, Spurs to beat Nottingham Forest in the Final. Both teams were hit by injuries, Arsenal without Bould and Limpar, Spurs missing Gascoigne.

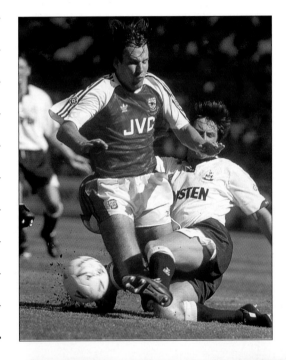

David SEAMAN	1	Erik THORSTVEDT
Lee DIXON	2	Terry FENWICK
Nigel WINTERBURN	3	Pat VAN DEN HAUWE
David HILLIER	4	Steve SEDGLEY
David O'LEARY	5	David HOWELLS
Tony ADAMS	6	Gary MABBUTT
David ROCASTLE*	7	Paul STEWART
Paul DAVIS	8	NAYIM
Alan SMITH	9	Vinny SAMWAYS
Paul MERSON	10	Gary LINEKER
Kevin CAMPBELL*	11	Paul ALLEN
Andy LINIGHAN	12	Paul WALSH
Siggi JONSSON	14	Gudni BERGSSON
Michael THOMAS (7)	15	Justin EDINBURGH
Andy COLE (11)	16	Ian HENDON
Alan MILLER	17	Ian WALKER

Referee **Mr T Holbrook** (Wolverhampton)

Above: A timely tackle
from Terry Fenwick on
Paul Merson.

Right: Shield shared...
No Wembley tears this
time.

Arsenal and Spurs produce little to worry Europe

Why should Europe tremble? Yesterday, neither Arsenal nor Spurs could manage a goal in 90 undistinguished minutes at Wembley. Such a contrast from all the vibrancy of their last meeting here. Spurs came closest with a header by Nayim which Seaman saved, but victory for Spurs would have been as unmerited as a win for Arsenal.

Last time these two north London teams met here at Wembley, it was the semi-final of the FA Cup, and Arsenal were utterly run down by the inspired antics of Paul Gascoigne. Yesterday, tantalisingly, Gascoigne did join in Tottenham's kick-about, but as we all know, strange sad things have happened to him since that memorable Sunday afternoon.

Yesterday, Tottenham decided again to use the tactics, Gazza or no Gazza, which had worked so well against their rivals before. That is to say, they strung five men across the middle, and left Lineker as the Lone Ranger up front.

As for Arsenal, they were obliged to replace Bould, who was injured, with O'Leary, who should never in any case be out of the team. Limpar, injured scoring the winning goal for Sweden against Norway in midweek, was also missing, but Arsenal have plenty of cover for such positions.

Happy to relate, they were not wearing their repugnant new second strip, the kind of thing that seems to have been conjured out of an LSD nightmare. Many years ago, white shirts and black shorts were Arsenal's sober away uniform. Yet dozens of their fans are to be seen wearing the biliousness of the new colours. HL Mencken was plainly right when he said that no one ever went broke underestimating public taste.

Not that Arsenal, without Limpar, are ever as dangerous or as unpredictable. The chorus "Boring, boring Arsenal!" is probably unfair, but without the little Swede, they tend to be predictable. All the more reason why their strikers should put away such chances as are made.

Campbell, who had so far been disappointingly clumsy and wasteful in front of goal, should certainly have done far better, after 19 minutes, with the delightful pass with which Davis released him. His shot was hasty, high and wide.

For a long time, Tottenham's heavily manned midfield, short of Gazza, looked like Hamlet without the Prince. Then, with eight minutes of the first half left, Spurs suddenly broke away to illustrate all my doubts about this supposedly cast-iron Arsenal defence. Samways, largely an obscure figure until now, simply ridiculed Adams out on the left. A clever cross, left-footed, was met by Nayim's head, on the far post. Seaman, who has had his bad moments at Wembley, scrambled across goal for a resourceful one-legged save.

Young though the season is, there is already abundant cause to deplore the wretched eccentricity of our allegedly leading English referees. Last weekend, we had the fiasco of Adams' foul on a Greek defender who had broken through being totally ignored by Mr Worrall.

Last Thursday at Orient, the referee, Mr Ward, allowed the home goalkeeper to haul down an opponent in the box without let or hindrance. And yesterday, we saw the strange, misguided tolerance of Mr Holbrook towards Van den Hauwe.

The Spurs left-back may have been disconcerted by the awful mistake he made early in the sec-

ond half, when he placed his intended back pass straight to Smith, almost conceding a goal.

But this was hardly an excuse for his dreadful elbow-block on Rocastle as the ball was running over the touch-line. Van den Hauwe was not even booked and Rocastle, foolishly trying to take the law into his own hands soon afterwards was. But Van den Hauwe appeared quite unrepentant. Soon, he was painfully bringing down Dixon, and this time, he did get shown a yellow card which could easily have been red.

For what it mattered, Arsenal had somewhat the better of the sunlight but still had a quite mediocre second half. Merson, on the left, did some determined running, and almost forced a goal, when the ball ran to Smith but Thorstvedt was commendably quick to plunge at the feet of Smith. Allen, down the Tottenham right, had a much clearer run, but wantonly wasted a good opportunity to set up something dangerous.

With a dozen minutes left Arsenal brought on their substitutes and it would have been interesting to see young Cole given a longer and larger opportunity. Very different in physique and style from Arsenal's usual big strikers, he had shown promise when he played last Sunday against Sampdoria, a difficult introduction indeed into first-class football. Using him would mean a substantial change in Arsenal's style, but it might in time prove worth the gamble.

In the Tottenham attack, Lineker worked throughout with diligence, intelligence and skill but seldom did he get the response he deserved. It was Allen again, in injury time, who horribly sliced Lineker's deft pass behind the goal.

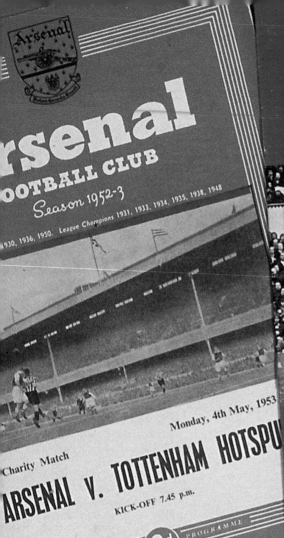

Arsenal
FOOTBALL CLUB
Season 1952-3

League Champions 1931, 1933, 1934, 1935, 1938, 1948
1930, 1936, 1950.

Monday, 4th May, 1953

Charity Match

ARSENAL v. TOTTENHAM HOTSPUR

KICK-OFF 7.45 p.m.

6d PROGRAMME

JOHN PRATT
TESTIMONIAL MATCH
at Tottenham Hotspur Ground
FRIDAY, 12th MAY, 1978
Kick-off 7.30 p.m.

TOTTENHAM HOTSPUR
v ARSENAL

WIN A FOOTBALL TRIP TO EUROPE – For details

Programme 15p   YOUR LU   A

OFF
SOU
PRO
PRIC

TOTTENHAM HOTSPUR
FOOTBALL AND ATHLETIC COMPANY, LIMITED

Official Programme
AND RECORD OF THE CLUB

Secretary: R. S. JARVIS
Team Manager: ARTHUR S. ROWE
Medical Officer: Dr. A. E. TUGHAN

Chairman: FRED. J. BEARMAN
Vice-Chairman: E. DEWHURST HORNSBY
Directors: F. JOHN BEARMAN, Wm. J. HERYET,
FREDK. WALE

PRICE
TWOPENCE

VOL. XLVII.   No. 43   WEDNESDAY, MARCH 2nd, 1955

TOTTENHAM HOTSPUR v ARSENAL

On Saturday, March 5th
MANCHESTER CITY
Football League Div. I   Kick-off 3.15 p.m.

On Wednesday, March 9th
RACING CLUB DE PARIS
Friendly FLOODLIT   Kick-off 7.30 p.m.

Friendly (Floodlit)   March 2nd, 1955   Kick-off 7.30 p.m.
TOTTENHAM HOTSPUR (1) 1
White Shirts, Blue Shorts

RIGHT WING   GOAL   LEFT WING
REYNOLDS
1
BACKS
RAMSEY (Capt.)   HOPKINS
2   3
HALF-BACKS
BLANCHFLOWER   CLARKE   MARCHI
4   5   6   Robb 1
FORWARDS   RELPH
GAVIN   BAILY   DUQUEMIN   BROOKS
7   8   9   10   11

Referee: Mr. A. H. BLYTHE, London
Linesmen: Mr. J. H. BROOKS, London (Red Flag)
Mr. F. M. WILSON, Middlesex (Yellow Flag)

11   10   8   7
MARDEN 5   BLOOMFIELD   ROPER 2   TAPSCOTT 3·4 CLAPTON
6   5   4
FORBES   FOTHERINGHAM   GORING
HALF-BACKS
3   2
EVANS   BARNES (Capt.)
BACKS

PAT JENNING
TESTIMONIAL MA
At Tottenham Hotspur Ground
TUESDAY, 23rd NOVEMBER, 19
Kick-off 7.30 p.m.

TOTTENHAM HOTS
v ARSENAL

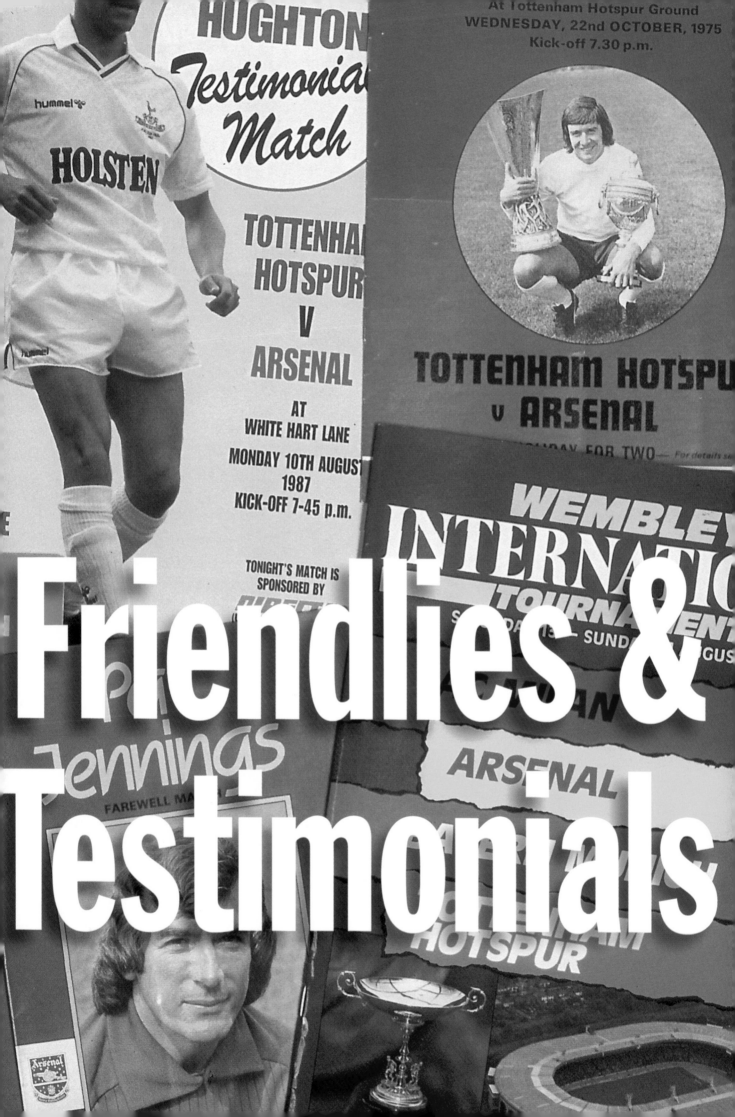

HUGHTON *Testimonial Match*

At Tottenham Hotspur Ground
WEDNESDAY, 22nd OCTOBER, 1975
Kick-off 7.30 p.m.

TOTTENHAM HOTSPUR V ARSENAL

AT WHITE HART LANE
MONDAY 10TH AUGUST
1987
KICK-OFF 7-45 p.m.

TONIGHT'S MATCH IS
SPONSORED BY

TOTTENHAM HOTSPUR v ARSENAL

FOR TWO — For details se

WEMBLEY INTERNATIONAL TOURNAMENT
SUNDAY 13 — SUNDAY
AUGUST

ARSENAL

HOTSPUR

Jennings
FAREWELL MATCH

Friendlies & Testimonials

9th November 1896   **Woolwich Arsenal 2** (Russell 2)
                       Tottenham Hotspur 1 (McElhaney)

Woolwich Arsenal: Fairclough; Buist, Sinclair, Crawford, Steel, Davis, Brodie, Haywood, Boyd, McAvoy, Russell.

Tottenham Hotspur: Ambler; Burrows, Montgomery, Collins, Almond, Crump, McElhaney, Devlin, Newbigging, Clements, Milliken.

Attendance: 2,000

25th February 1897   **Tottenham Hotspur 2** (Devlin, Clements)
                       Woolwich Arsenal 2 (Haywood, Brock)

Tottenham Hotspur: Ambler; Burrows, Montgomery, Collins, Almond, Crump, McElhaney, Milliken, Newbigging, Clements, Payne.

Woolwich Arsenal: Fairclough; Anderson, Caldwell, McAvoy, Crawford, Davis, Brock, Haywood, Caie, O'Brien, Russell.

Attendance: 2,000

25th December 1897   **Woolwich Arsenal 2** (Brock 2)
                       Tottenham Hotspur 3 (Joyce 2, Stormont)

Woolwich Arsenal: Ord, McAuley, Caldwell, Crawford, Farrell, Davis, Brock, Haywood, Devlin, Hannah, White.

Tottenham Hotspur: Cullen; Burrows, Knowles, Hall, Jones, Crump, Hartley, Davidson, Joyce, Stormont, Black.

Attendance: 5,000

8th April 1898   **Tottenham Hotspur 0**
                Woolwich Arsenal 0

Tottenham Hotspur: Cullen; Burrows, Knowles, Hall, Jones, Crump, Hartley, Davidson, Joyce, Stormont, Black.

Woolwich Arsenal: Ord; Caldwell, McConnell, Crawford, Anderson, Davis, Brock, Haywood, Hunt, Hannah, White.

Attendance: 15,000

Scotsman Gavin Crawford was a regular in Arsenal's early meetings with Tottenham.

11th March 1899   **Woolwich Arsenal 2** (Haywood 2)
                 Tottenham Hotspur 1 (Meade)

Woolwich Arsenal: Ord; J Garton, McAvoy, Moir, Dick, Hannah, Hunt, Cottrell, McGeoch, Haywood, Shaw.

Tottenham Hotspur: Cullen; Erentz, Cain, Jones, McNaught, Stormont, Smith, Meade, Rule, Cameron, Bradshaw.

Attendance: 6,000

A Tottenham team group from 1896-97.

Back row (left to right): Ham Casey, J. Campbell (Trainer), Ly Burrows, James Devlin, Charlie Ambler, Stanley Briggs, Harry Crump, F.H. King, Jock Montgomery, Ralph Bullock.
Front row (left to right): Richard McElhaney, Jimmy Milliken, Willie Newbigging, Bob Clements, Ernie Payne.

29th April 1899   **Tottenham Hotspur 3** (Smith, Joyce, Ord (og))
                Woolwich Arsenal 2 (Hunt, Cottrell)

Tottenham Hotspur: Cullen; Melia, Cain, Erentz, McNaught, Stormont, Smith, McKay, Joyce, Cameron, Bradshaw.

Woolwich Arsenal: Ord; Mcconnell, McAvoy, Hannah, Dick, Anderson, Hunt, Cottrell, McGeoch, Haywood, Shaw.

Attendance: 5,000

Woolwich Arsenal's John Caldwell.

SOUTHERN DISTRICT COMBINATION

17th April 1900	**Tottenham Hotspur 4** (Smith, Pratt 2, Kirwan) **Woolwich Arsenal 2** (Gaudie, Tennant)
Tottenham Hotspur:	Haddow; Erentz, Tait, Jones, McNaught, Stormont, Smith, Cameron, Pratt, Copeland, Kirwan.
Woolwich Arsenal:	Hamilton; McNichol, Jackson, Murphy, Dick, Anderson, Lloyd, Logan, Main, Gaudie, Tennant.
Attendance:	4,000

24th April 1900	**Woolwich Arsenal 2** (Logan, Tennant) **Tottenham Hotspur 1** (Pratt)
Woolwich Arsenal:	Hamilton; McNichol, Jackson, Murphy, Dick, Anderson, Hunt, McCowie, Logan, Shaw, Tennant.
Tottenham Hotspur:	Clawley; Erentz, Tait, Jones, McNaught, Stormont, Smith, Cameron, Pratt, Copeland, Kirwan.
Attendance:	500

● *Abandoned after 75 mins due to bad language.*

LONDON LEAGUE

16th September 1901	**Woolwich Arsenal 0** **Tottenham Hotspur 2** (Gilhooley, Brown)
Woolwich Arsenal:	Ashcroft; Cross, Jackson, Coles, Wolfe, J Anderson, Briercliffe, Laidlaw, Swann, Place, Foxall.
Tottenham Hotspur:	Clawley; Erentz, Hughes, Morris, Montgomery, Jones, Smith, Gilhooley, Brown, Copeland, Kirwan.
Attendance:	4,000

4th November 1901	**Tottenham Hotspur 5** (Barlow, Brown 3, Copeland) **Woolwich Arsenal 0**
Tottenham Hotspur:	Clawley; Erentz, Tait, Morris, Hughes, Jones, Smith, Barlow, Brown, Copeland, Kirwan.
Woolwich Arsenal:	Ashcroft; J Anderson, Cross, Coles, Dick, Place, Briercliffe, Edgar, Main, Owens, Foxall.
Attendance:	3,833

17th November 1902	**Woolwich Arsenal 2** (Gooing, Briercliffe) **Tottenham Hotspur 1** (Morris (pen))
Woolwich Arsenal:	Wilcox; Cross, Jackson, Coles, Main, J Anderson, Briercliffe, Connor, Gooing, W Anderson, Lawrence.
Tottenham Hotspur:	Clawley; Erentz, Tait, Morris, Hughes, JL Jones, Gilhooley, Cameron, Barlow, Copeland, Kirwan.
Attendance:	4,000

1st December 1902	**Tottenham Hotspur 1** (Warner) **Woolwich Arsenal 0**
Tottenham Hotspur:	Williams; Erentz, Watson, Brown, Hughes, JL Jones, Gilhooley, Warner, Cameron, Copeland, Kirwan.
Woolwich Arsenal:	Ashcroft; J Anderson, Wolfe, Coles, Main, Ransom, Briercliffe, Connor, Gooing, W Anderson, Lawrence.
Attendance:	3,000

| 1st September 1903 | **Tottenham Hotspur 0** |
| | **Woolwich Arsenal 1** (Coleman) |

Tottenham Hotspur: Williams; Erentz, Tait, Hughes, Morris, JL Jones, Walton, J Jones, Brearley, Copeland, Kirwan.

Woolwich Arsenal: Ashcroft; Thorpe, Jackson, Dick, Theobald, McEarchrane, Briercliffe, Coleman, Gooing, Bellamy, Linward.

Attendance: 7,000

| 14th November 1903 | **Woolwich Arsenal 1** (Briercliffe) |
| | **Tottenham Hotspur 1** (Kirwan) |

Woolwich Arsenal: Ashcroft; Thorpe, Jackson, Dick, Sands, McEarchrane, Briercliffe, Coleman, Gooing, Shanks, Linward.

Tottenham Hotspur: Williams; Hughes, Tait, Morris, McNaught, O Burton, Walton, J Jones, Woodward, Copeland, Kirwan.

Attendance: 16,000

SOUTHERN CHARITY CUP

SEMI-FINAL

| 23rd April 1902 | **Woolwich Arsenal 0** |
| | **Tottenham Hotspur 0** |

Woolwich Arsenal: Ashcroft; McNichol, Jackson, Coles, Dick, J Anderson, Edgar, Main, Gooing, W Anderson, Foxall.

Tottenham Hotspur: Clawley; Erentz, Tait, Morris, McNaught, Hughes, Smith, Barlow, Cameron, Copeland, Kirwan.

Attendance: 3,000

SEMI-FINAL REPLAY

| 29th April 1902 | **Tottenham Hotspur 2** (Copeland, Coles (og)) |
| | **Woolwich Arsenal 1** (W Anderson) |

Tottenham Hotspur: Clawley; Erentz, Tait, Morris, McNaught, Hughes, Smith, Barlow, Cameron, Copeland, Kirwan.

Woolwich Arsenal: Ashcroft; McNichol, Jackson, Coles, Dick, J Anderson, Edgar, Main, Gooing, W Anderson, Foxall.

Attendance: 2,000

1ST ROUND

| 10th October 1904 | **Woolwich Arsenal 1** (Coleman) |
| | **Tottenham Hotspur 3** (Brearley, Woodward 2) |

Woolwich Arsenal: Ashcroft; Cross, Jackson, Dick, Buchan, McEarchrane, Briercliffe, Coleman, Gooing, Hunter, Satterthwaite.

Tottenham Hotspur: Williams; McCurdy, Tait, Morris, Hughes, Bull, Stansfield, Brearley, Woodward, Copeland, Kirwan.

Attendance: 8,000

SEMI-FINAL

| 9th April 1906 | **Tottenham Hotspur 0** |
| | **Woolwich Arsenal 0** |

Tottenham Hotspur: Eggett, Chaplin, Tait, Morris, Bull, Hughes, Berry, Chapman, Woodward, Glen, Murray.

Woolwich Arsenal: Ashcroft; Sharp, Sutherland, Bigden, Theobald, Dick, Garbutt, Coleman, Freeman, Satterthwaite, Templeton.

Attendance: 8,000

Spurs goalkeeper John Eggett kept a clean sheet in the 1906 Southern Charity Cup semi-final but was beaten five times in the replay. He had previously spent half a season with Woolwich Arsenal.

Action from the 1906 Southern Charity Cup semi-final replay at Plumstead... Spurs goalkeeper John Eggett keeps a tight grip on the ball as the Woolwich forwards close in.

Arsenal's Billy Blyth.

SEMI-FINAL REPLAY

28th April 1906	**Woolwich Arsenal 5** (Coleman 2, Sands, Satterthwaite, Ducat) **Tottenham Hotspur 0**
Woolwich Arsenal:	Ashcroft; Cross, Sharp, Bigden, Sands, McEarchrane, Garbutt, Coleman, Ducat, Satterthwaite, Neave.
Tottenham Hotspur:	Eggett, Watson, Chaplin, Morris, Freeborough, Hughes, Stansfield, Woodward, Chapman, Brearley, Whyman.
Attendance:	8,000

LONDON PROFESSIONAL FOOTBALL CHARITY FUND

1st November 1909	**Tottenham Hotspur 3** (Curtis 2, R Steel) **Woolwich Arsenal 0**
Tottenham Hotspur:	Drabble; Wilkes, Harris, Morris, D Steel, Gipps, Woodruff, Curtis, Minter, R Steel, Middlemiss.
Woolwich Arsenal:	H McDonald; Shaw, D McDonald, Dick, Bassett, McEarchrane, Greenaway, Lawrence, Thomson, Lewis, Neave.
Attendance:	5,000
29th September 1919	**Arsenal 0** **Tottenham Hotspur 1** (Minter)
Arsenal:	Williamson; Shaw, Bradshaw, Graham, Butler, McKinnon, Groves, Burgess, White, Blyth, Baker.
Tottenham Hotspur:	Jacques; Goodall, Pearson, Smith, Rance, Grimsdell, Lorimer, Minter, Archibald, Bliss, Dimmock.
Attendance:	10,000
25th October 1920	**Tottenham Hotspur 2** (Wilson 2) **Arsenal 0**
Tottenham Hotspur:	Jacques; Clay, McDonald, Smith, Rance, Grimsdell, Walden, Banks, Wilson, Findlay, Dimmock.
Arsenal:	Williamson; Shaw, Bradshaw, Baker, Pattison, McKinnon, Rutherford, White, Walden, Hardinge, Blyth.
Attendance:	17,436

LONDON FA CHARITY CUP

SEMI-FINAL AT STAMFORD BRIDGE

10th November 1913	**Tottenham Hotspur 2** (Fleming, Cantrell)
	Woolwich Arsenal 1 (Devine)
Tottenham Hotspur:	King; Hobday, Webster, Weir, R Steel, Grimsdell, Tattersall, Fleming, Cantrell, Bliss, Heggarty.
Woolwich Arsenal:	Lievesley; Shaw, Fidler, Jobey, Thomson, Graham, Lewis, Flanagan, Devine, Hardinge, Burrell.
Attendance:	7,800

SECOND ROUND

1st November 1920	**Tottenham Hotspur 3** (Grimsdell, Walden, Banks)
	Arsenal 1 (White)
Tottenham Hotspur:	Jacques; Clay, McDonald, Smith, Rance, Grimsdell, Wilson, Seed, Wilson, Banks, Dimmock.
Arsenal:	Williamson; Buckley, Peart, Baker, Pattison, Whittaker, Greenaway, White, Pagnam, Blyth, Toner.
Attendance:	14,500

SEMI-FINAL AT STAMFORD BRIDGE

14th November 1921	**Arsenal 0**
	Tottenham Hotspur 0
Arsenal:	Williamson; Bradshaw, Hutchins, Baker, Butler, Whittaker, Creegan, Blyth, Henderson, Hopkins, Toner.
Tottenham Hotspur:	French; Forster, McDonald, Skinner, Walters, Grimsdell, Banks, Seed, Lindsay, Bliss, Dimmock.
Attendance:	11,000

● *Abandoned after 5 mins of extra-time.*

SEMI-FINAL REPLAY AT HOMERTON

21st November 1921	**Arsenal 2** (Henderson, Butler)
	Tottenham Hotspur 1 (Clay (pen))
Arsenal:	Williamson; Bradshaw, Turnbull, Baker, Butler, Milne, Rutherford, Blyth, Henderson, Hopkins, Toner.
Tottenham Hotspur:	Hunter; Clay, McDonald, Archibald, Walters, Skinner, Banks, Thompson, Lindsay, Bliss, Dimmock.
Attendance:	9,028 After extra-time.

FIRST ROUND

23rd October 1922	**Arsenal 3** (Patterson, Roe, Graham (pen))
	Tottenham Hotspur 2 (Handley 2)
Arsenal:	Dunn; Mackie, Turnbull, Milne, Graham, John, Rutherford, Young, Roe, Baker, Paterson.
Tottenham Hotspur:	Blake; Clay, McDonald, Skinner, Lowe, Grimsdell, Lindsay, Seed, Dimmock, Thompson, Handley.
Attendance:	11,207

FINAL AT STAMFORD BRIDGE

4th May 1931	**Arsenal 2** (Cope, Brain)
	Tottenham Hotspur 1 (Lyons (pen))
Arsenal:	Preedy; Robinson, Cope, Seddon, Haynes, Male, W Warnes, Brain, Parkin, Thompson, Williams.
Tottenham Hotspur:	Taylor; Lyons, Poynton, Rowe, Cable, T Evans, Bellamy, Hunt, Howe, Smy, W Evans .
Attendance:	10,160

Above: Action from Park Royal in the Daily Telegraphic Titanic Fund match with Spurs defending. Note the flags at half mast!

Right: Spurs line-up prior to the above game...
(left to right) Curtis, D.Steel, Webster, Minter, R.Steel, Lightfoot, Collins, Lunn, Bliss, Darnell, Middlemiss.

DAILY TELEGRAPHIC TITANIC FUND

PLAYED AT PARK ROYAL

29th April 1912	**Tottenham Hotspur 0** **Woolwich Arsenal 3** (Hanks, Greenaway, Thomson)
Tottenham Hotspur:	Lunn; Webster, Collins, Lightfoot, D Steel, Darnell, Curtis, Bliss, Minter, R Steel, Middlemiss.
Woolwich Arsenal:	Crawford; Shaw, Peart, McKinnon, Thomson, McEarchrane, Greenaway, Common, Hanks, Flanagan, Lewis.
Attendance:	5,000

WAR RELIEF FUND

22nd August 1914	**Tottenham Hotspur 1** (Minter) **Woolwich Arsenal 5** (King 2, Flanagan 2, Rutherford)
Tottenham Hotspur:	Jacques; Clay, Webster, Fleming, R Steel, Grimsdell, Walden, Minter, Cantrell, Woodger, Crowl.
Woolwich Arsenal:	Lievesley; Shaw, Benson, Grant, Buckley, Graham, Rutherford, Flanagan, King, Bradshaw, Lewis.
Attendance:	13,564

LONDON FOOTBALL COMBINATION

4th September 1915   **Arsenal 2** (Thompson, Lewis)
Tottenham Hotspur 0

Arsenal: Beale; Shaw, Liddell, Fordham, Buckley, Graham, Rutherford, Groves, Thompson, Bradshaw, Lewis.

Tottenham Hotspur: Joyce; Clay, Chaplin, Darnell, Rance, Barton, Fricker, Minter, Banks, Bliss, Morris.

Attendance: 14,879

13th November 1915   **Tottenham Hotspur 3**
(Travers, Bliss, Steel)
Arsenal 3 (King 3)

Tottenham Hotspur: Joyce; Clay, Ralston, Darnell, Rance, Barton, Morris, Bassett, Travers, Bliss, Steel.

Woolwich Arsenal: Kempton; Sands, Shaw, Ducat, Buckley, Bradshaw, Wallace, Groves, King, Norman, Thompson.

Attendance: 7,000

4th March 1916   **Arsenal 0**
Tottenham Hotspur 3
(Barton, Banks, Bliss)

Arsenal: Kempton; Shaw, Bradshaw, Mason, Buckley, McKinnon, Thompson, Tyler, King, Cockle, Lewis.

Tottenham Hotspur: Jacques, Clay, Steel, Elliott, Rance, Barton, Morris, Bassett, Banks, Bliss, Wilson.

Attendance: 6,000

8th April 1916   **Tottenham Hotspur 3** (Clay (pen), Bassett, Bliss)
Arsenal 2 (Lees, Chipperfield)

Tottenham Hotspur: Jacques, Clay, Steel, Elliott, Rance, Barton, Morris, Bassett, Banks, Bliss, Hopkins.

Arsenal: Kempton; Bradshaw, Bourne, Morris, Buckley, Madge, Broderick, Cockle, Chipperfield, Lees, Thompson.

Attendance: 7,000

9th September 1916   **Arsenal 1** (King)
Tottenham Hotspur 1 (Bassett)

Arsenal: Williamson; Shaw, Bradshaw, Allman, Stapley, Knowles, Rutherford, King, Weaver, Chipperfield, Elkington.

Tottenham Hotspur: Jacques; Clay, Ralston, Thwaites, Elliott, Barton, Morris, Bassett, Travers, Bliss, Lloyd.

Attendance: 6,000

2nd December 1916   **Tottenham Hotspur 4** (Bassett, Banks 3)
Arsenal 1 (Williams)

Tottenham Hotspur: Jacques; Clay, Ralston, Elliott, Rance, Barton, Walden, Bassett, Banks, Bliss, Smith.

Arsenal: Williamson; Bradshaw, Hutchins, Hardinge, Liddell, Stapley, Weaver, Hibbert, King, Williams, Baker.

Attendance: 11,000   *Played at Highbury*

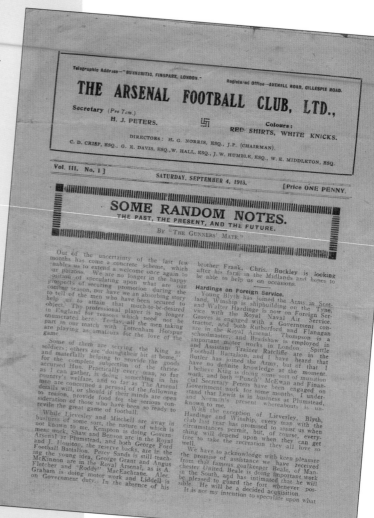

The programme from the first
London Combination meeting
between the sides.

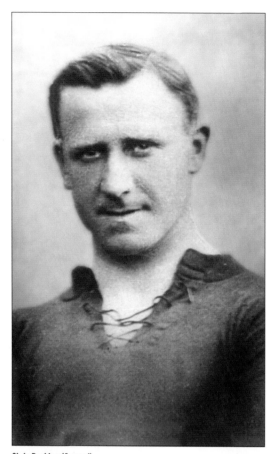

Chris Buckley (Arsenal).

Arthur Hutchins (Arsenal).

6th April 1917

Tottenham Hotspur 0
Arsenal 0

Tottenham Hotspur: Jacques; Clay, Ralston, Elliott, Rance, Barton, Walden, Bassett, Banks, Bliss, Hawkins.

Arsenal: Williamson; Shaw, Hutchins, Cockerill, Stapley, McKinnon, Rutherford, Groves, Elkington, Allman, Wilkins.

Attendance: 5,000   *Played at Homerton*

9th April 1917

Arsenal 3 (Cockerill, Wilkins, Sanderson)
Tottenham Hotspur 2 (Rance, Banks)

Arsenal: Williamson; Shaw, Hutchins, Cockerill, Stapley, McKinnon, Rutherford, Groves, Sanderson, Hardinge, Wilkins.

Tottenham Hotspur: Jacques; Ralston, Barton, Elliott, Rance, Darnell, Walden, Bassett, Banks, Bliss, Middlemiss.

Attendance: 12,000

22nd September 1917

Tottenham Hotspur 1 (Potter)
Arsenal 2 (Rutherford, Pagnam)

Tottenham Hotspur: Jacques; Clay, Ralston, Elliott, Rance, Coomber, Walden, Bassett, Potter, A Lindsay, Hawkins.

Arsenal: Williamson; Bradshaw, Hutchins, McKinnon, Plumb, Chipperfield, Rutherford, Groves, Pagnam, Grant, Lewis.

Attendance: 10,000   *Played at Highbury*

17th November 1917

Arsenal 0
Tottenham Hotspur 1 (Nuttall)

Arsenal: Williamson; Bradshaw, Hutchins, Johnson, Grant, Chipperfield, Broderick, Groves, Pagnam, Tyler, Lewis.

Tottenham Hotspur: Jacques; Clay, Ralston, Elliott, Rance, Darnell, Walden, Banks, Nuttall, Lightfoot, Hawkins.

Attendance: 10,000

12th January 1917

Tottenham Hotspur 4
(Walden, Chipperfield (og), Banks, Peake)
Arsenal 1 (Tyler)

Tottenham Hotspur: Jacques; Clay, Elliott, Tomkins, Rance, Darnell, Walden, Banks, Nuttall, Peake, Hawkins.

Arsenal: Williamson; Groves, Hutchins, Webber, Liddle, Chipperfield, Rutherford, Tyler, Rayner, Relfe, Lewis.

Attendance: 9,000   *Played at Highbury*

9th March 1918

Arsenal 4 (Hardinge, Ralston (og), Rutherford, Chipperfield)
Tottenham Hotspur 1 (Minter)

Arsenal: Williamson; Shaw, Hutchins, Ducat, Stapley, McKinnon, Rutherford, Groves, Hardinge, Chipperfield, Lewis.

Tottenham Hotspur: Jacques; Clay, Ralston, Tomkins, Rance, Barton, Walden, Banks, Minter, Peake, Hawkins.

Attendance: 15,000

12th October 1918

Arsenal 3 (Hardinge 2 (1 pen), Groves)
Tottenham Hotspur 0

Arsenal: Williamson; Shaw, Hutchins, Ducat, Gregory, Liddell, Groves, Thompson, Hardinge, Bradshaw, Spittle.

Tottenham Hotspur: D Lindsay, Hawkins, Ralston, Thomas, Rance, Darnell, Hadyn-Price, Banks, Blake, A Lindsay, Dockray.

Attendance: 19,900

| 7th December 1918 | **Tottenham Hotspur 1** (McCalmont) |
| | **Arsenal 0** |

Tottenham Hotspur:	D Lindsay; Clay, Worrall, Elliott, Rance, Tomkins, Banks, Goldthorpe, McCalmont, Peake, Freeman.
Arsenal:	Williamson; Shaw, Hutchins, Ducat, Liddell, Gregory, Groves, Dominy, Hardinge, Spittle, Chipperfield.
Attendance:	12,000 *Played at Highbury*

| 1st February 1919 | **Arsenal 2** (Miller, Hardinge) |
| | **Tottenham Hotspur 3** (Bennett, Minter, Jack) |

Arsenal:	Williamson; Bradshaw, Hutchins, Ducat, Plumb, Gregory, Groves, Dominy, Miller, Hardinge, Wilkins.
Tottenham Hotspur:	Jacques; Clay, Worrall, Tomkins, Rance, Darnell, Bennett, Minter, Elliott, Banks, Jack.
Attendance:	16,000

| 29th March 1919 | **Tottenham Hotspur 0** |
| | **Arsenal 1** (Hardinge) |

Tottenham Hotspur:	Jacques; Clay, Barton, Tomkins, Rance, Grimsdell, Bennett, Minter, Elliott, Banks, Dockray.
Arsenal:	Williamson; Shaw, Bradshaw, Ducat, Voysey, McKinnon, Rutherford, Robson, Hughes, Hardinge, Lewis.
Attendance:	33,000 *Played at Highbury*

JUBILEE TRUST FUND

| 20th August 1938 | **Arsenal 0** |
| | **Tottenham Hotspur 2** (Morrison, Lyman) |

Arsenal:	Swindin; Male, Hapgood, Crayston, Male, Copping, Griffiths, L Jones, Drake, B Jones, Bastin.
Tottenham Hotspur:	Hooper; Sproston, Whatley, Howe, Page, Buckingham, Spelman, GW Hall, Morrison, AE Hall, Lyman.
Attendance:	41,997

| 19th August 1939 | **Tottenham Hotspur 0** |
| | **Arsenal 1** (Drury) |

Tottenham Hotspur:	Hooper; Ward, Nicholson, Burgess, Hitchins, Buckingham, Sargent, GW Hall, Ludford, Dix, Lyman.
Arsenal:	Marks; Male, Hapgood, Crayston, Joy, L Jones, Kirchen, Drury, Lewis, B Jones, Nelson.
Attendance:	32,702

FOOTBALL LEAGUE SOUTH

18th November 1939	**Arsenal 2** (D Compton, Nelson) **Tottenham Hotspur 1** (Howe)
Arsenal:	Marks; Male, Hapgood, Crayston, Joy, Jones, Kirchen, Nelson, L Compton, Lewis, D Compton.
Tottenham Hotspur:	Hooper; Dorling, Whatley, Howe, Hitchins, Spelman, Sargent, GW Hall, Morrison, Duncan, Medley.
Attendance:	15,000

25th January 1940	**Tottenham Hotspur 0** **Arsenal 1** (Bastin)
Tottenham Hotspur:	Hooper; Ward, Howe, Burgess, Hitchins, Spelman, McCormick, GW Hall, Morrison, Dix, Lyman.
Arsenal:	Platt; Male, Hapgood, L Jones, Joy, Collett, Bastin, Bremner, L Compton, Curtis, D Compton.
Attendance:	9,054

30th March 1940	**Tottenham Hotspur 1** (Medley) **Arsenal 1** (Nelson)
Tottenham Hotspur:	Hooper; Ward, Dorling, GW Hall, Hitchins, Howe, Cox, Duncan, Ludford, Dix, Medley.
Arsenal:	Swindin; Male, L Compton, Bastin, Joy, L Jones, Nelson, Platt, Lewis, B Jones, D Compton.
Attendance:	15,000

24th April 1940	**Arsenal 2** (Drake, Bastin) **Tottenham Hotspur 4** (Duncan, Morrison 2, Dix)
Arsenal:	Wilson; Male, Hapgood, Pryde, Joy, L Jones, Drake, Lewis, L Compton, Curtis, Bastin.
Tottenham Hotspur:	Hooper; Ward, Whatley, Burgess, Hitchins, Howe, Cox, Duncan, Morrison, Dix, Medley.
Attendance:	4,455 *Played at White Hart Lane*

12th October 1940	**Tottenham Hotspur 2** (Skinner, Medley) **Arsenal 3** (Kirchen 2, L Compton)
Tottenham Hotspur:	Flack; Ward, Whatley, Henley, Hitchins, Buckingham, K Bennett, Skinner, Ludford, Duncan, Medley.
Arsenal:	Dean; Male, Scott, Bastin, Joy, Collett, Kirchen, Curtis, L Compton, L Jones, D Compton.
Attendance:	4,568

● *Abandoned after 47 mins due to Air Raid Warning*

16th November 1940	**Arsenal 1** (Drake) **Tottenham Hotspur 1** (Burgess)
Arsenal:	Marks; Male, Scott, Crayston, Joy, Collett, Drake, Henley, L Compton, Bastin, D Compton.
Tottenham Hotspur:	Saunders; Ward, Whatley, White, Hitchins, Buckingham, Paton, O'Callaghan, Burgess, Duncan, Ludford.
Attendance:	1,916 *Played at White Hart Lane*

7th November 1942	**Tottenham Hotspur 1** (Beasley) **Arsenal 0**
Tottenham Hotspur:	Ditchburn; Ward, Whatley, White, Chisholm, Burgess, Beasley, Martin, Gibbons, Hall, Pattison.
Arsenal:	Marks; Scott, Hapgood, Henley, Joy, Male, Kirchen, Drake, Lewis, Bastin, D Compton.
Attendance:	21,551

Action from the Jubilee Trust Fund...

HIGHBURY 1938

Above: Spurs' Percy Hooper saves from Leslie Jones as Bill Whatley looks on.

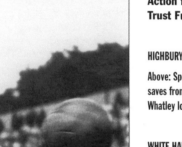

WHITE HART LANE 1939

Left: Ex-England international Ronnie Dix, making his Spurs debut, gets in a shot despite the close attentions of Jack Crayston.

Far left: Percy Hooper saves a penalty from Arsenal's Alf Kirchen.

13th February 1943   **Arsenal 1** (Kirchen)
Tottenham Hotspur 0

Arsenal: Marks; Male, L Compton, Copping, Joy, Collett, Kirchen, Nelson, Drake, Bastin, D Compton.

Tottenham Hotspur: Hooper; Ward, Whatley, Ludford, Chisholm, Howe, Beasley, Martin, Gibbons, Broadis, Pattison.

Attendance: 30,690   *Played at White Hart Lane*

18th December 1943   **Tottenham Hotspur 2** (Beasley, Rowley)
Arsenal 1 (Briscoe)

Tottenham Hotspur: Ditchburn; Ward, Whatley, Ludford, Chisholm, Burgess, Beasley, Martin, O'Donnell, Rowley, Jones.

Arsenal: Marks; Scott, Barnes, Male, Joy, Collett, Briscoe, Flavell, Lewis, Bastin, D Compton.

Attendance: 22,683

22nd April 1944   **Arsenal 3** (Drake, Alexander, Bastin)
Tottenham Hotspur 3
(Burgess, Beasley, Martin)

Arsenal: Marks; Male, Scott, Farquhar, Joy, Hamilton, Alexander, Collett, Drake, Bastin, Barnes.

Tottenham Hotspur: Ditchburn; Ward, Whatley, White, Buckingham, Burgess, Beasley, Martin, O'Donnell, Wilson, Gilberg.

Attendance: 26,330   *Played at White Hart Lane*

2nd September 1944   **Tottenham Hotspur 4** (Broadis 2, Ludford 2)
Arsenal 0

Tottenham Hotspur: Hughes; Ward, Willis, White, Pryde, Page, Walters, Broadis, Ludford, Beasley, Goodman.

Arsenal: Swindin; A Jones, Ferrier, Collett, Bradley, Hamilton, Briscoe, Henley, Horsmann, Bastin, Nelson.

Attendance: 13,625

9th December 1944   **Arsenal 2** (Drake, Farquhar)
Tottenham Hotspur 3 (Gibbons 3)

Arsenal: Swindin; Male, Mennie, Bastin, Joy, Collett, Farquhar, Drake, Steele, Nelson, Wrigglesworth.

Tottenham Hotspur: Hughes; Ward, Willis, White, F Hall, Burgess, Walters, Flavell, Gibbons, Beasley, Ludford.

Attendance: 29,432   *Played at White Hart Lane*

9th February 1946   **Arsenal 1** (Bastin)
Tottenham Hotspur 1 (Blair)

Arsenal: Swindin; Scott, Collett, Male, L Compton, Patterson, Cartwright, Nelson, Barnard, Bastin, Cumner.

Tottenham Hotspur: Hughes; Willis, Buckingham, White, F Hall, Burgess, AE Hall, Skinner, Blair, Dix, Whitchurch.

Attendance: 38,927   *Played at White Hart Lane*

16th February 1946   **Tottenham Hotspur 2** (AE Hall, Whitchurch)
Arsenal 0

Tottenham Hotspur: Hughes; Willis, Buckingham, White, F Hall, Burgess, AE Hall, Skinner, Blair, Dix, Whitchurch.

Arsenal: Swindin; Male, Collett, Nelson, Waller, Cartwright, Cumner, L Jones, Barnard, Bastin, D Compton.

Attendance: 44,510

Arsenal and Spurs War-time 'derby' programmes.
Arsenal also played their home games at White Hart Lane.

David Nelson's goal helped Arsenal overcome Spurs in the Football League War Cup.

Ralph Ward netted a penalty for Spurs in the 3-3 London War Cup draw.

FOOTBALL LEAGUE WAR CUP

FOURTH ROUND FIRST LEG

5th April 1941	**Arsenal 2** (Nelson, Bastin)
	Tottenham Hotspur 1 (Howe)
Arsenal:	Marks; Scott, Hapgood, Henley, Joy, Collett, Kirchen, Lewis, L Compton, Bastin, Nelson.
Tottenham Hotspur:	Hooper; Ward, Whatley, White, Hitchins, Burgess, Howe, Hall, Gibbons, Broadis, Ludford.
Attendance:	22,107 *Played at White Hart Lane*

FOURTH ROUND SECOND LEG

12th April 1941	**Tottenham Hotspur 1** (Ludford)
	Arsenal 1 (L Compton)
Tottenham Hotspur:	Hooper; Ward, Whatley, White, Hitchins, Burgess, J Sperrin, Hall, Gibbons, Broadis, Ludford.
Arsenal:	Hapgood; Male, Scott, Crayston, Joy, Collett, Kirchen, Henley, L Compton, Bastin, D Compton.
Attendance:	25,258

LONDON WAR CUP

3rd May 1941	**Tottenham Hotspur 3** (Ward (pen), K Bennett, Gibbons)
	Arsenal 3 (Kirchen, L Compton 2)
Tottenham Hotspur:	Hooper; Ward, Howe, White, Hitchins, Hall, W Sperrin, K Bennett, Gibbons, Duncan, Ludford.
Arsenal:	Boulton; Drake, Scott, Henley, Joy, Collett, Kirchen, Lewis, L Compton, Beasley, Nelson.
Attendance:	9,651

21st May 1941	**Arsenal 0**
	Tottenham Hotspur 3 (Gibbons, Duncan 2)
Arsenal:	Boulton; L Compton, Hapgood, Pryde, Joy, Collett, Beasley, Henley, Drake, Bastin, D Compton.
Tottenham Hotspur:	Hooper; Ward, Howe, White, Hitchins, Hall, W Sperrin, Broadis, Gibbons, Duncan, Ludford.
Attendance:	6,673 *Played at White Hart Lane*

LONDON WAR LEAGUE

20th September 1941	**Arsenal 4** (Cumner 2, Lewis 2)
	Tottenham Hotspur 0
Arsenal:	Platt; Male, Hapgood, Bastin, Joy, Collett, Kirchen, Nelson, Lewis, Curtis, Cumner.
Tottenham Hotspur:	Hooper; Tickridge, Ward, White, Hitchins, Burgess, W Sperrin, Broadis, Gibbons, Hall, Ludford.
Attendance:	17,446 *Played at White Hart Lane*

27th December 1941	**Tottenham Hotspur 1** (Ludford)
	Arsenal 2 (Drake, D Compton)
Tottenham Hotspur:	Ditchburn; Ward, Tickridge, White, Hall, Whatley, W Sperrin, Broadis, Gibbons, Duncan, Ludford.
Arsenal:	Platt; L Compton, Hapgood, Male, Joy, Collett, Kirchen, Drake, Lewis, Bastin, D Compton.
Attendance:	16,777

FRIENDLIES

19th November 1887	**Tottenham Hotspur 2** **Royal Arsenal 1**

Tottenham Hotspur: Team unknown

Royal Arsenal: Beardsley; rest of team unknown

● *Abandoned after 75 mins due to bad light*

4th February 1888	**Royal Arsenal 6** (Connolly 4, Unknown 2) **Tottenham Hotspur 2**

Royal Arsenal: Weeks; Brown, Danskin, Wells, Hartland, Lucas, Creighton, Ridgwell, Connolly, Hill, Morris.

Tottenham Hotspur: Team unknown but Spurs fielded only nine players

22nd September 1888	**Royal Arsenal 0** **Tottenham Hotspur 1** (Baldock)

Royal Arsenal: Team unknown but included Hill

Tottenham Hotspur: Team unknown but included Jull, Casey and Baldock

Attendance: 500

9th March 1889	**Tottenham Hotspur 0** **Royal Arsenal 1** (Scott)

Tottenham Hotspur: Team unknown

Royal Arsenal: Beardsley; rest of team unknown but included Wilson, McBean, Morris, Charteris, Connolly and Scott.

21st September 1889	**Royal Arsenal 10** (Horsington, Barbour 2, Robertson 3, Meggs 4) **Tottenham Hotspur 1** (Parker)

Royal Arsenal: Beardsley; Offe (or Offer? see addendum), McBean, Howat, (or Howatt? see addendum), Bates, Julian, Horsington, Meggs, Barbour, Robertson, Crichton.

Tottenham Hotspur: Anderson; Griffith, Jull, Baldock, Pracey, Ayres, Cottrell, Cadman, Tyrell, Buckle, Parker.

Attendance: 1,500

1st October 1892	**Tottenham Hotspur 3** (Jull, Harston 2) **Royal Arsenal Athletic 0**

Tottenham Hotspur: Monk; Moody, Welham, Jull, Briggs, Simpson, Sykes, Lomas, Cottrell, Harston, Ellis.

Royal Arsenal Athletic (Woolwich Arsenal's reserve team): team due to be Ambler; Burrows, Rankin, George, McKenzie, Stacey, Calmar, Connolly, Barber, Pell, Kirk, but only Ambler, Rankin, Connolly and Brown known to have played.

16th March 1896	**Woolwich Arsenal 1** (Boyd (pen)) **Tottenham Hotspur 3** (Hunter, Brown, Gilmer (og))

Woolwich Arsenal: Gilmer; Caldwell, Murdoch, Davis, Jenkyns, Crawford, Duff, O'Brien, Boyd, Mortimer, Hare.

Tottenham Hotspur: Ambler; McGahey, Montgomery, Collins, Briggs, F Markham, Lanham, Hunter, Brown, Clements, Logan.

Attendance: 1,000

26th March 1896	**Tottenham Hotspur 1** (Clements) **Woolwich Arsenal 3** (O'Brien, Haywood 2)

Tottenham Hotspur: Ambler; Hay, Montgomery, Collins, Almond, F Markham, Logan, Hunter, Brown, Clements, Payne.

Woolwich Arsenal: Fairclough; Powell, Caldwell, Gordon, Jenkyns, Davis, Crawford, Haywood, Buchanan, O'Brien, Mortimer.

Attendance: 3,000

30th April 1896	**Tottenham Hotspur 3** (Almond, Clements, Payne)

Stanley Briggs played for Tottenham against his former club Woolwich Arsenal in 1896.

Henry Boyd scored from the penalty spot for Arsenal against Spurs in March 1896.

Tottenham's Jimmy Dimmock.

Ted Drake played for the Gunners against Spurs at Colchester.

Woolwich Arsenal 2 (Hare, Jenkyns)

Tottenham Hotspur:	Ambler; McGahey, Montgomery, Collins, Almond, Crump, Lanham, Logan, Brown, Clements, Payne
Woolwich Arsenal:	Fairclough; Ward, Powell, Davis, Jenkyns, Gordon, McEvoy, O'Brien, Johnson, Hare, Hills.
Attendance:	1,500

28th April 1898

Woolwich Arsenal 5 (Brock 2, White 2, Murphy)
Tottenham Hotspur 0

Woolwich Arsenal:	Hamilton; Caldwell, McConnell, Crawford, Anderson, Davis, Brock, White, McGeoch, Murphy, Hannah.
Tottenham Hotspur:	Cullen; Burrows, Montgomery, Hall, Jones, Downie, Hartley, Davidson, Joyce, Stormont, Crump.
Attendance:	2,000

1st February 1908

Tottenham Hotspur 0
Woolwich Arsenal 1 (C Satterthwaite)

Tottenham Hotspur:	Manning; Chaplin, Burton, Morris, Bull, Gray, McNair, Pass, Woodward, Reid, Middlemiss.
Woolwich Arsenal:	Ashcroft; Gray, Sharp, Ducat, Dick, McEarchrane, Freeman, Lewis, Kyle, Satterthwaite, Mordue.
Attendance:	10,000

24th May 1912

Tottenham Hotspur 0
Woolwich Arsenal 4 (Calder 3, Winship)

Tottenham Hotspur:	Team unknown but included Lightfoot
Woolwich Arsenal:	Unknown

24th May 1919

Arsenal 0
Tottenham Hotspur 0

Woolwich Arsenal:	Unknown
Tottenham Hotspur:	Jacques; Pearson, Clay, Tomkins, Rutherford, Barton, Dimmock, Innes, Minter, Powell, Furr.
Attendance:	4,000

MAYOR OF COLCHESTER'S CUP

17th April 1939

Arsenal 2 (Drury 2)
Tottenham Hotspur 1 (Duncan)

Arsenal:	Marks; Male, L Compton, L Jones, Field, Collett, Drake, Drury, Lewis, B Jones, Cumner.
Tottenham Hotspur:	Hooper; Ward, Whatley, Burgess, Hitchins, Buckingham, Cox, GW Hall, Ludford, Duncan, Medley.
Attendance:	6,000 *Played at Colchester*

8th May 1943

Tottenham Hotspur 1 (Ludford)
Arsenal 2 (Bastin (pen), Kirchen)

Tottenham Hotspur:	Hooper; Ward, Howe, Jones, Chisholm, Buckingham, Beasley, Hall, Ludford, Clayton, Burley.
Arsenal:	Marks; Male, Delaney, Collett, Joy, Hamilton, Briscoe, Henley, Vaughan, Bastin, Kirchen.
Attendance:	8,560

19th May 1945

Tottenham Hotspur 4 (Walters, Flavell, Dix, Howe)
Arsenal 0

Tottenham Hotspur:	Roberts; Ward, Willis, Ludford, Burke, Burgess, Walters, Flavell, Lyman, Dix, Howe.
Arsenal:	Marks; Collett, Chenhall, Woodford, Wade, Farquhar, Nelson, Whent, Harris, Stanley, Taylor.
Attendance:	10,450

25th January 1947   **Tottenham Hotspur 2** (Woodward, AE Hall)
Arsenal 0

Tottenham Hotspur: Hughes; Tickridge, Whatley, Woodward, Chisholm, Trailor, AE Hall, Bennett, Duquemin, Dix, Whitchurch.

Arsenal: Dingley; Jones, Chenhall, Sloan, Fields, Edlington, Clelland, Gudmundsson, Lewis, Curtis, Rudkin.

Attendance: 16,537

LORD MAYOR OF LONDON'S NATIONAL FLOOD DISASTER FUND

4th May 1953   **Arsenal 0**
Tottenham Hotspur 2 (Bennett, Duquemin)

Arsenal: Kelsey; Wade, Chenhall, Forbes, Daniel, Bowen, Cox, Oakes, Holton, Goring, Marden.

Tottenham Hotspur: Ditchburn; Baker, Hopkins, Wetton, King, Burgess, Walters, Bennett, Duquemin, Baily, McClellan.

Attendance: 21,778

2nd March 1955   **Tottenham Hotspur 1** (Robb)
Arsenal 4 (Roper, Tapscott 2, Marden)

Tottenham Hotspur: Reynolds; Ramsey, Hopkins, Blanchflower, Clarke, Marchi, Gavin, Baily, Duquemin, Brooks, Robb.

Arsenal: Kelsey; Tapscott, Evans, Goring, Fotheringham, Forbes, Clapton, Tapscott, Roper, Bloomfield, Marden.

Attendance: 14,350

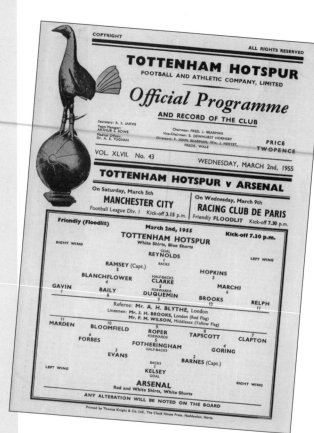

The programme from the 1955 friendly.

Geoff Strong heads Arsenal's goal in the 1963 White Hart Lane friendly.

Cyril Knowles equalises for Spurs in his Testimonial, watched by brother Peter (left of the ball).

26th January 1963	**Tottenham Hotspur 3** (Greaves 2, Jones) **Arsenal 1** (Strong)
Tottenham Hotspur:	Brown; Baker(Dennis), Henry, Marchi, Norman, Mackay, Medwin, Clayton, R Smith, Greaves, Jones.
Arsenal:	McClelland; Magill, McCulloch, Barnwell, Brown, Sneddon, Court, Strong, Baker, Eastham, Macleod.
Attendance:	19,893

CYRIL KNOWLES TESTIMONIAL

22nd October 1975	**Tottenham Hotspur 2** (McAllister, C Knowles) **Arsenal 2** (Nelson, Kidd)
Tottenham Hotspur:	Jennings(Daines); McAllister(Smith), C Knowles, Conn, Young, Osgood, McNab, Coates, Chivers, Jones(P Knowles[Naylor]), Neighbour.
Arsenal:	Rimmer(Parker); Rice(Powling), Nelson, Kelly, Mancini(Storey), Simpson(Matthews), Armstrong, Cropley, Stapleton, Kidd, Brady.
Attendance:	17,346

PETER SIMPSON TESTIMONIAL

9th October 1976

Arsenal 1 (Macdonald)
Tottenham Hotspur 2 (Conn, Duncan)

Arsenal:	Rimmer(Parker); Storey, Radford(Rostron), Matthews, O'Leary(Howard), Simpson, Ball, Brady, Macdonald, Stapleton, Armstrong(Gatting)
Tottenham Hotspur:	Daines; Naylor, Young, Hoddle, Pratt, Osgood(Keeley), Conn, Perryman, Moores, Duncan(Jones), Coates.
Attendance:	19,456

A crowd of just under 20,000 saw Tottenham win 2-1 at Highbury in a Testimonial for Peter Simpson (right).

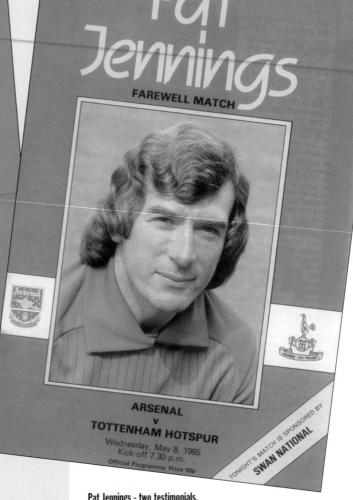

PAT JENNINGS TESTIMONIAL

23rd November 1976   **Tottenham Hotspur 3** (Taylor, Greaves 2)
Arsenal 2 (Nelson, MacDonald)

Tottenham Hotspur: Jennings(Daines); Osgood, Knowles(Gorman), McNab, Young(McAllister), Naylor, Taylor, Perryman(Pratt), Moores, Greaves, Coates.

Arsenal: Rimmer; Rice, Nelson, Ross, Howard, Simpson, Ball, Brady, MacDonald, Stapleton, Armstrong.

Attendance: 28,582

PAT RICE TESTIMONIAL

22nd November 1977   **Arsenal 1** (Stapleton)
Tottenham Hotspur 3 (Heffernan, Coates, Duncan)

Arsenal: Jennings; Rice, Nelson, Walford(Simpson), O'Leary, Young, Brady, Sunderland(Heeley), Macdonald, Stapleton, Rix.

Tottenham Hotspur: Daines; Naylor, Holmes(Heffernan), Coates, Osgood, Perryman, Pratt, McNab, Lee(Armstrong), Duncan(Moores), Taylor.

Attendance: 17,154

JOHN PRATT TESTIMONIAL

12th May 1978   **Tottenham Hotspur 3** (Perryman, Moores 2)
Arsenal 5 (Fuccillo 3, Radford, Sunderland)

Tottenham Hotspur: Daines(Kendall), Naylor(Stead), Holmes, Hoddle, McAllister, Perryman, Pratt, McNab(Coates), Moores, Greaves, Cliff Jones(Taylor).

Arsenal: New; Stead, Roeder, Sunderland(Heeley), O'Leary(Gatting), McLintock, Fuccillo, Rix, Radford, Stapleton, Hudson.

Attendance: 23,044

Pat Jennings - two testimonials, nine years apart, same scoreline!

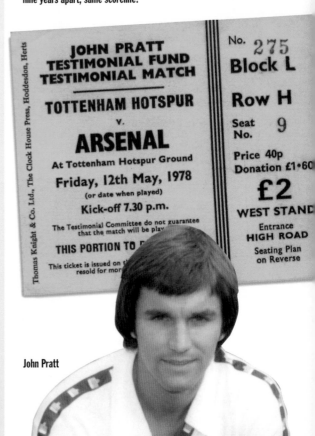

John Pratt

Above: Glenn Hoddle's Testimonial, one of the few occasions when Arsenal have worn a change strip against Tottenham. Hoddle is pictured jumping with David O'Leary.

Below: A Wembley derby watched by only 30,000 in August 1988.

PAT JENNINGS TESTIMONIAL

8th May 1985	**Arsenal 2** (Brady, Hayes) **Tottenham Hotspur 3** (Crook, Falco 2)
Arsenal:	Jennings(Still), Anderson(Hill), Sansom, Talbot, Mariner, Brady, Williams, Allinson(Hayes), Woodcock, Rix, Nicholas.
Tottenham Hotspur:	Clemence(Parks); Thomas, Mabbutt, Roberts, Miller(Galvin), Perryman, Crook, Falco, Leworthy, Hoddle, Dick.
Attendance:	25,252

GLENN HODDLE TESTIMONIAL

4th August 1985	**Tottenham Hotspur 1** (Leworthy) **Arsenal 1** (Robson)
Tottenham Hotspur:	Clemence; Thomas, Hughton, Roberts, Culverhouse, P Allen, Ardiles(Crook), Hazard(Chiedozie), Leworthy, Hoddle(Samways), Waddle.
Arsenal:	Lukic, Anderson, Sansom, Williams, O'Leary, Caton, Allinson, Robson, Mariner(Nicholas), Woodcock, Rix.
Attendance:	13,567

CHRIS HUGHTON TESTIMONIAL

10th August 1987	**Tottenham Hotspur 3** (Thomas, C Allen, Claesen) **Arsenal 1** (Adams)
Tottenham Hotspur:	Clemence(Parks); Stevens(Polston), Thomas, Gough, Fairclough, Mabbutt, C Allen, P Allen, Waddle(Galvin), Hodge, Claesen.
Arsenal:	Lukic; Thomas, Sansom(Winterburn), Williams, O'Leary, Adams, Rocastle, Davis, Smith(Merson), Nicholas(Groves), Hayes.
Attendance:	17,826

MAKITA TOURNAMENT AT WEMBLEY

13th August 1988

Arsenal 4 (Marwood 2, Merson, Smith)
Tottenham Hotspur 0

Arsenal:	Lukic; Dixon, Winterburn, Thomas, O'Leary(Bould), Adams, Rocastle, Davis, Smith, Merson(Hayes), Marwood.
Tottenham Hotspur:	Mimms; Allen, Stimson, Fenwick, Fairclough, Mabbutt, Walsh, Gascoigne, Waddle, Stewart(Gray), Samways(Howells).
Attendance:	30,104

GRAHAM RIX TESTIMONIAL

13th October 1990

Arsenal 2 (Smith, Merson)
Tottenham Hotspur 5 (Stewart 3, Samways, Walsh)

Arsenal:	Montanei(Will); Thomas(Brady), Sansom(Caesar), Rocastle, Bould(Pates), Linighan, Petrovic(Davis), Brady(Hillier), Smith, Merson, Rix(Groves).
Tottenham Hotspur:	Mimms; Bergsson(Edinburgh), Van den Hauwe(Statham), Sedgley, Thomas, Tuttle, Stewart, Moncur, Nayim, Samways, Walsh(Van den Hauwe).
Attendance:	14,806

Anyone for cricket?

In the summer of 1973 of crowd of around 5,000 turned up at Finsbury Park to see a North London Derby with a difference. It was a whole new ball game as Arsenal and Tottenham footballers competed for the Austin Morris Empire Trophy... at cricket!

Arsenal 178 *(after 30 overs)*
Geoff Barnett 67, Jeff Blockley 21, Bob McNab 22.
Ralph Coates and Roger Morgan took 2 wickets each.

Tottenham 160
Cyril Knowles 45, Roger Morgan 35, Martin Peters 19, Martin Chivers 12.
Bob McNab 2-19.

Approximately £1,500 was raised in aid of the Woodberry Down Boy's Club, Manor House.

Pictured above are Umpires Bill Nicholson and Bertie Mee.

SUNDAY 29th JULY at 2 p.m.

AUSTIN MORRIS EMPIRE TROPHY
at
Finsbury Park, London, N4
ARSENAL F.C.
v.
TOTTENHAM HOTSPUR F.C.

Charity Cricket Match in aid of the Woodberry Down Boys Club

Woodberry Down Boys Club is situated in North London and has a membership of about 150 local boys, aged from about eight to seventeen years, and the emphasis is mainly on sports activities such as cricket, football, table tennis, billiards, athletics, judo, swimming and chess with qualified leaders and instructors from ILEA.

Today's match, which will provide the spectacle of North London's Football Stars in a different role, should prove to be most entertaining, for both Arsenal and Tottenham Hotspur can boast of some cricketers of no mean ability. We thank them for appearing today and making this occasion possible. Both Clubs have also given considerable help in the organisation of the event, also the G.L.C. and, in particular, Mr. Cyril Wilding (The Park Manager) and his very helpful staff.

Our thanks are also extended to the sponsors of today's competition which will be the Austin Morris Empire Trophy for which we are extremely grateful.

We hope that you have an enjoyable day at Finsbury Park, and we thank you for your generosity in providing the financial support essential to allow our club to continue and expand.

JOHN FORDYCE
Chairman
Woodberry Down Boys Club

ADMISSION BY PROGRAMME 20p

DERBY FACT FILE

Aggregate Derby Results

	Played	Spurs Won	Arsenal Won	Drawn	Spurs Goals	Arsenal Goals
League	120	44	49	27	168	176
FA Cup	4	2	2	0	4	5
League Cup	7	2	4	1	6	8
Charity Shield	1	0	0	1	0	0
Total	132	48	55	29	178	189

Highest Individual Team Scores
Arsenal: 6 at White Hart Lane on 6-3-35
Spurs: 5 at White Hart Lane on 25-12-11 and 4-4-83

Widest Victory Margin
Spurs 0 Arsenal 6 on 6-3-35
Spurs 5 Arsenal 0 25-12-11 and 4-4-83

Highest Aggregate Derby Score
Arsenal 4 Spurs 4 on 22-2-58
Spurs 4 Arsenal 4 on 6-10-62
Arsenal 4 Spurs 4 on 16-10-63

Largest Home Win
Spurs 5 Arsenal 0 on 25-12-11 and 4-4-83
Arsenal 4 Spurs 0 on 7-2-53 and 16-9-67

Largest Away Win
Spurs 0 Arsenal 6 on 6-3-35
Arsenal 0 Spurs 3 on 27-2-54

Longest Derby Sequence Without A Win
Arsenal: 5 games between 5-9-59 and 26-8-61, 6-10-62 and 10-10-64 and 4-11-80 and 12-4-82
Spurs: 7 games between 27-12-76 and 30-8-80

Longest Derby Sequence Without Scoring
Spurs: 4 games, 11-4-77 to 26-12-79.
Arsenal: 3 games, 13-10-73 to 19-10-74, 4-11-80 to 2-1-82, and 1-1-86 to 6-9-86.

Most Derby Appearances
Spurs: Gary Mabbutt - 31
First: 27-12-82 (in a 0-2 defeat at Highbury)
Last: 15-4-96 (in a 0-0 draw at Highbury)
Steve Perryman - 31
First: 5-9-70 (in a 0-2 defeat at Highbury)
Last: 1-1-86 (in a 0-0 draw at White Hart Lane)
Arsenal: David O'Leary - 33(2)
First: 27-9-75 (in a 0-0 draw at White Hart Lane)
Last: 11-5-93 (in a 1-3 defeat at Highbury)

Most Derby Goals
Spurs: Bobby Smith - 10 in 13 games.
Arsenal: Alan Sunderland - 8 in 11(1) games.

The First League Derby Goal
Walter Lawrence in Woolwich Arsenal's 1-0 victory in the first "Derby" at The Manor Ground on 4-12-09.

The First Substitute Used In A Derby
Roy Low for Spurs at White Hart Lane on 11-9-65 replacing Derek Possee.

First Floodlight Derby
The first derby to be played entirely under floodlights was the League meeting at White Hart Lane on 13th March 1957 when Arsenal won 3-1.

First "Live" Television Derby
The first derby to be shown live on TV was the 100th League meeting at White Hart Lane on 4th January 1987 when Arsenal won 2-1.

Own Goals
Four own goals have been scored in derby matches, all by Spurs' players:

Player	Date	Derby number
Tom Evans	20-10-1934	27
Ron Henry	22-2-1958	44
Laurie Brown	11-9-1965	59
Phil Beal	10-8-1968	65

Sendings-Off
Despite the intense rivalry only seven players have been sent off in North London derbies:

Player	Date	Derby number
Len Julians	31-1-1959	46
Willie Young	27-12-1976	81
Chris Hughton	29-3-1982	89
Alan Sunderland	29-3-1982	89
Stewart Robson	27-12-1982	91
Lee Dixon	4-4-1993	FA Cup semi-final
Stefan Schwartz	2-1-1995	115

The First Player Sent Off In A Derby
Len Julians for Arsenal at White Hart Lane on 31-1-59

Derby Hat-Tricks

Player	Derby no.	Date	Goals	Result
Ted Drake	27	20-10-1934	3	Arsenal 5 Spurs 1
Terry Dyson	51	26-8-1961	3	Spurs 4 Arsenal 3
Alan Sunderland	83	23-12-1978	3	Spurs 0 Arsenal 5

One Hundred Up
● The 100th goal in derby League contests was scored by Jimmy Logie. It was the last goal in Arsenal's 4-0 success at Highbury in derby no.34 on 7th February 1953.
● The 100th goal in all League and Cup derby contests was scored by Cliff Holton. It was Arsenal's first goal in their 4-0 victory in derby no.34 on 7th February 1953.
● The 100th Spurs' goal in League and Cup derby contests was scored by Jimmy Greaves. It was Spurs' second goal in derby no.57 on 10th October 1964 which saw Spurs win at 3-1 at White Hart Lane.
● The 100th Arsenal goal in League derby contests was scored by Joe Baker. It was Arsenal's second goal in derby no.58 on 23rd February 1965 which saw Arsenal win 3-1 at Highbury.
● The 100th Arsenal goal in all League and Cup derby contests was scored by Geoff Strong. It was Arsenal's goal in their 1-3 defeat at White Hart Lane in derby no.56 on 22nd February 1964.

Derby Doubles
While Spurs have managed to win both League games the clubs have played in a season only six times, Arsenal have pulled off the feat twelve times.

Spurs			Arsenal		
1955-56	1960-61	1966-67	1934-35	1952-53	1954-55
1969-70	1973-74	1992-93	1956-57	1958-59	1968-69
			1970-71	1978-79	1979-80
			1983-84	1987-88	1988-89

In the 60 seasons the clubs have played in the same division Spurs have been placed above Arsenal 29 times, vis:

1909-10, 1912-13, 1920-21, 1921-22, 1923-24, 1924-25, 1950-51, 1951-52, 1954-55, 1956-57, 1957-58, 1959-60, 1960-61, 1961-62, 1962-63, 1963-64, 1964-65, 1965-66, 1966-67, 1967-68, 1969-70, 1975-76, 1981-82, 1982-83, 1984-85, 1986-87, 1989-90, 1992-93, 1994-95

and Arsenal above Spurs 31 times, vis:

1910-11, 1911-12, 1922-23, 1925-26, 1926-27, 1927-28, 1933-34, 1934-35, 1952-53, 1953-54, 1955-56, 1958-59, 1968-69, 1970-71, 1971-72, 1972-73, 1973-74, 1974-75, 1976-77, 1978-79, 1979-80, 1980-81, 1983-84, 1985-86, 1987-88, 1988-89, 1990-91, 1991-92, 1993-94, 1995-96, 1996-97

Derby Appearances for Arsenal - The Top Fifty Six

The seasons given cover both the first and last season in which the player appeared in a derby game; eg 1969-86 covers seasons 1969-70 and 1985-86.

Player	Seasons	League	FA Cup	Lge Cup	Charity Shield	Total
David O'LEARY	1975-93	27+2s	1	4	1	33+2s
George ARMSTRONG	1962-82	25	-	2	-	27
Tony ADAMS	1984-97	17	2	3	1	23
John RADFORD	1964-76	21	-	2	-	23
Paul DAVIS	1979-94	14+2s	2	4	1	21+1s
Kenny SANSOM	1979-88	15	1	5	-	21
Peter SIMPSON	1964-77	18	-	2	-	20
Nigel WINTERBURN	1987-97	16	2	-	1	19
Graham RIX	1976-87	15+1s	1	2+1s	-	18+2s
John LUKIC	1983-97	15	-	3	-	18
Peter STOREY	1965-77	16	-	2	-	18
Pat RICE	1967-80	17+1s	-	-	-	17+1s
Lee DIXON	1988-97	14	2	-	1	17
Paul MERSON	1988-97	13+1s	2	-	1	16+1s
David ROCASTLE	1985-92	13	-	2	1	16
Frank McLINTOCK	1964-73	13+1s	-	2	-	15+1s
Steve BOULD	1988-97	14	1	-	-	15
Bob McNAB	1966-74	13	-	2	-	15
Alan SMITH	1987-95	12+1s	1+1s	-	1	14+2s
Jack KELSEY	1952-62	14	-	-	-	14
David SEAMAN	1990-96	11	2	-	1	14
Billy BLYTH	1920-28	13	-	-	-	13
Brian TALBOT	1978-85	11	1	1	-	13
Billy McCULLOUGH	1959-66	12	-	-	-	12
Charlie NICHOLAS	1983-87	8	-	4	-	12
Jon SAMMELS	1965-70	10	-	2	-	12
Bob WILSON	1968-74	10	-	2	-	12
George GRAHAM	1966-72	10+1s	-	1+1s	-	11+2s
Michael THOMAS	1987-91	8	1	2+1s	1s	11+2s
Alan SUNDERLAND	1978-83	8+1s	1	2	-	11+1s
Alf BAKER	1920-28	11	-	-	-	11
Jack BUTLER	1920-28	11	-	-	-	11
Danny CLAPTON	1955-61	11	-	-	-	11
George EASTHAM	1960-66	11	-	-	-	11
Dennis EVANS	1953-60	11	-	-	-	11
Bob JOHN	1924-35	11	-	-	-	11
Doug LISHMAN	1948-55	10	1	-	-	11
Stewart ROBSON	1981-86	9	1	1	-	11
Ian URE	1963-69	9	-	2	-	11
Len WILLS	1953-61	11	-	-	-	11
Ian WRIGHT	1991-97	10	1	-	-	11
Liam BRADY	1973-80	10+2s	-	-	-	10+2s
David HERD	1956-61	10	-	-	-	10
Eddie KELLY	1969-76	10	-	-	-	10
Martin KEOWN	1985-97	10	-	-	-	10
Jimmy LOGIE	1948-55	9	1	-	-	10
Terry NEILL	1960-69	10	-	-	-	10
Walley BARNES	1948-56	8	1	-	-	9
Jimmy BLOOMFIELD	1955-61	9	-	-	-	9
David COURT	1962-69	7	-	2	-	9
Alex FORBES	1950-56	9	-	-	-	9
John HOLLINS	1979-83	7	1	1	-	9
Pat JENNINGS	1978-84	7	1	1	-	9
Don ROPER	1948-56	8	1	-	-	9
Jock RUTHERFORD	1920-25	9	-	-	-	9
Frank STAPLETON	1975-81	8	-	1	-	9

Derby Goalscorers for Arsenal

The seasons given cover both the first and last season in which the player appeared in a derby game; eg 1969-86 covers seasons 1969-70 and 1985-86.

Player	Seasons	League	FA Cup	Lge Cup	Charity Shield	Total
Alan SUNDERLAND	1978-83	8	-	-	-	8
David HERD	1956-61	7	-	-	-	7
John RADFORD	1964-76	5	-	2	-	7
Joe BAKER	1962-66	6	-	-	-	6
Ian WRIGHT	1991-97	6(2p)	-	-	-	6(2p)
Ted DRAKE	1934-35	5	-	-	-	5
Jimmy LOGIE	1948-55	5	-	-	-	5
Charlie NICHOLAS	1983-87	4	-	1	-	5
Tony ADAMS	1984-97	3	1	-	-	4
Jimmy BRAIN	1924-28	4	-	-	-	4
Cliff HOLTON	1951-58	4	-	-	-	4
Don ROPER	1948-56	3	1	-	-	4
Geoff STRONG	1962-65	4	-	-	-	4
Tony WOODCOCK	1982-87	3	-	1	-	4
Mel CHARLES	1959-62	3	-	-	-	3
David COURT	1962-69	3	-	-	-	3
Jackie HENDERSON	1958-62	3	-	-	-	3
Doug LISHMAN	1948-55	2	1	-	-	3
Malcolm MACDONALD	1976-77	3	-	-	-	3
Jock RUTHERFORD	1920-25	3	-	-	-	3
Alan SMITH	1987-95	2	1	-	-	3
Frank STAPLETON	1975-81	3	-	-	-	3
Michael THOMAS	1987-91	3	-	-	-	3
George ARMSTRONG	1962-82	2	-	-	-	2
Cliff BASTIN	1933-35	2(1p)	-	-	-	2(1p)
Dennis BERGKAMP	1995-97	2	-	-	-	2
Reg BOREHAM	1921-23	2	-	-	-	2
Dave BOWEN	1954-59	2	-	-	-	2
Jackie CHALMERS	1910-12	2	-	-	-	2
George EASTHAM	1960-66	2(1p)	-	-	-	2(1p)
Alex FORBES	1950-56	2(1p)	-	-	-	2(1p)
Joe HAVERTY	1956-61	2	-	-	-	2
Ray KENNEDY	1969-74	2	-	-	-	2
Alf KIRCHEN	1934-35	2	-	-	-	2
Raphael MEADE	1982-84	2	-	-	-	2
Arthur MILTON	1951-55	2	-	-	-	2
Gordon NUTT	1955-59	2	-	-	-	2
David ROCASTLE	1985-92	1	-	1	-	2
Jon SAMMELS	1965-70	2	-	-	-	2
Alan SKIRTON	1961-66	2	-	-	-	2
Peter STOREY	1965-77	2	-	-	-	2
Reg TRICKER	1926-27	2	-	-	-	2

The following players have each scored one goal in League derby matches:
Colin Addison, Alf Baker, Walley Barnes (pen), John Barnwell, Pat Beasley, Ray Bowden, Liam Brady, Jack Butler, Kevin Campbell, Danny Clapton, Alf Common, Paul Davis, Paul Dickov, Peter Dougall, Peter Goring, Alex Graham (pen), George Graham, George Grant, Perry Groves, Vic Groves, John Hawley, Sid Hoar, Brian Kidd, Walter Lawrence, Tommy Lawton, Charlie Lewis, John MacLeod, Charlie McGibbon, Brian Marwood, Paul Merson, Terry Neill (pen), David Price, Charlie Randall, Jimmy Robertson, Stewart Robson, Brian Talbot, Derek Tapscott, Frank Townrow, Paul Vaessen, Gerry Ward, Henry White, Tom Winship, Nigel Winterburn, Phil Beal (og), Laurie Brown (og), Tom Evans (og), Ron Henry (og).

The following players have each scored one goal in Cup-tie derby matches:
Ian Allinson, Viv Anderson, Ian McPherson, Niall Quinn.

LEADING DERBY APPEARANCES & GOALSCORERS FOR SPURS

Derby Appearances for Tottenham - The Top Fifty Four

The seasons given cover both the first and last season in which the player appeared in a derby game; eg 1969-86 covers seasons 1969-70 and 1985-86.

Player	Seasons	League	FA Cup	Lge Cup	Charity Shield	Total
Gary MABBUTT	1982-96	25	2	3	1	31
Steve PERRYMAN	1969-86	28	1	2	-	31
Glenn HODDLE	1976-87	18	1	4	-	23
Pat JENNINGS	1964-77	21	-	2	-	23
Cyril KNOWLES	1964-76	20	-	2	-	22
Paul ALLEN	1985-93	14	2	3	1	20
Alan GILZEAN	1964-74	17	-	2	-	19
Maurice NORMAN	1955-65	18	-	-	-	18
Phil BEAL	1963-75	16	-	2	-	18
Jimmy GREAVES	1961-70	15	-	2	-	17
Ossie ARDILES	1978-88	11+1s	1	4	-	16+1s
Danny BLANCHFLOWER	1954-64	16	-	-	-	16
Ray CLEMENCE	1981-87	11	1	4	-	16
Mike ENGLAND	1966-75	14	-	2	-	16
Alan MULLERY	1964-72	14	-	2	-	16
David HOWELLS	1987-97	13+2s	1	-	1	15+2s
John PRATT	1968-80	15+2s	-	-	-	15+2s
Peter BAKER	1956-64	15	-	-	-	15
Tony GALVIN	1979-87	12+1s	1	1+3s	-	14+4s
Graham ROBERTS	1980-87	12	1	1+1s	-	14+1s
Jimmy DIMMOCK	1920-28	14	-	-	-	14
Ted DITCHBURN	1948-58	13	1	-	-	14
Cliff JONES	1957-67	14	-	-	-	14
Martin CHIVERS	1967-76	13+1s	-	-	-	13+1s
Harry CLARKE	1950-57	13	-	-	-	13
Arthur GRIMSDELL	1912-28	13	-	-	-	13
Bobby SMITH	1955-64	13	-	-	-	13
Mitchell THOMAS	1986-91	9+1s	-	3	-	12+1s
Tommy HARMER	1951-60	12	-	-	-	12
Ron HENRY	1955-65	12	-	-	-	12
Chris HUGHTON	1979-86	9	1	2	-	12
Tony MARCHI	1953-65	12	-	-	-	12
Jimmy SEED	1920-27	12	-	-	-	12
Bert SMITH	1920-28	12	-	-	-	12
Erik THORSTVEDT	1989-94	9	2	-	1	12
Vinny SAMWAYS	1987-94	8+1s	2	-	1	11+1s
Bill BROWN	1959-66	11	-	-	-	11
Tommy CLAY	1913-27	11	-	-	-	11
Dave MACKAY	1959-68	11	-	-	-	11
Matt FORSTER	1923-28	10	-	-	-	10
Joe KINNEAR	1966-75	8	-	2	-	10
Alex LINDSAY	1922-28	10	-	-	-	10
Paul MILLER	1978-86	8	1	1	-	10
Terry NAYLOR	1972-79	10	-	-	-	10
Alf RAMSEY	1950-55	10	-	-	-	10
George ROBB	1952-59	10	-	-	-	10
Steve SEDGLEY	1989-94	7	2	-	1	10
Chris WADDLE	1985-89	7	-	3	-	10
Chris JONES	1974-82	9+1s	-	-	-	9+1s
Steve ARCHIBALD	1980-84	7	-	2	-	9
Eddie BAILY	1950-56	9	-	-	-	9
Terry MEDWIN	1956-63	9	-	-	-	9
Teddy SHERINGHAM	1992-97	8	1	-	-	9
Sonny WALTERS	1950-56	9	-	-	-	9

Derby Goalscorers for Tottenham

The seasons given cover both the first and last season in which the player appeared in a derby game; eg 1969-86 covers seasons 1969-70 and 1985-86.

Player	Seasons	League	FA Cup	Lge Cup	Charity Shield	Total
Bobby SMITH	1955-64	10	-	-	-	10
Alan GILZEAN	1964-74	7	-	-	-	7
Jimmy GREAVES	1961-70	6(1p)	-	1	-	7(1p)
Les ALLEN	1959-63	6	-	-	-	6
Steve ARCHIBALD	1980-84	6	-	-	-	6
Cliff JONES	1957-67	6	-	-	-	6
Martin CHIVERS	1967-76	5	-	-	-	5
Billy MINTER	1909-13	5	-	-	-	5
Clive ALLEN	1984-88	1	-	3	-	4
Jimmy CANTRELL	1912-22	4(1p)	-	-	-	4(1p)
Garth CROOKS	1980-85	3	1	-	-	4
Jimmy DIMMOCK	1920-28	4	-	-	-	4
Terry DYSON	1960-65	4	-	-	-	4
Terry MEDWIN	1956-63	4	-	-	-	4
George ROBB	1952-59	4	-	-	-	4
Mark FALCO	1982-87	3	-	-	-	3
Tommy HARMER	1951-60	3(1p)	-	-	-	3(1p)
Chris HUGHTON	1979-86	3	-	-	-	3
Alex LINDSAY	1922-28	3	-	-	-	3
Dave MACKAY	1959-68	3	-	-	-	3
Taffy O'CALLAGHAN	1926-34	3	-	-	-	3
Frank SAUL	1960-68	3	-	-	-	3
Jimmy SEED	1920-27	3	-	-	-	3
Sonny WALTERS	1950-56	3	-	-	-	3
Eddie BAILY	1950-56	2	-	-	-	2
Jabez DARNELL	1909-12	2	-	-	-	2
John DUNCAN	1974-77	2	-	-	-	2
Jack ELKES	1923-27	2	-	-	-	2
Willie EVANS	1933-35	2(1p)	-	-	-	2(1p)
Paul GASCOIGNE	1988-91	1	1	-	-	2
John HENDRY	1992-94	2	-	-	-	2
Gary LINEKER	1989-92	-	2	-	-	2
Frank OSBORNE	1924-28	2	-	-	-	2
John PRATT	1968-80	2	-	-	-	2
Jimmy ROBERTSON	1964-69	2	-	-	-	2
Teddy SHERINGHAM	1992-97	2	-	-	-	2
Alfie STOKES	1955-58	2	-	-	-	2

The following players have each scored one goal in League derby matches:

Paul Allen, Darren Anderton, Chris Armstrong, Danny Blanchflower (pen), Bert Bliss, Alan Brazil, Ron Burgess, Nico Claesen, Eddie Clayton, Ralph Coates, John Curtis, Bill Felton (pen), Arthur Grimsdell, Charlie Handley, Mike Hazard, Les Howe, Percy Humphreys, George Hunt, Chris Jones, Jurgen Klinsmann, Chris McGrath, John McTavish, Tony Marchi, Bert Middlemiss, Alan Mullery, Peter Murphy, Steve Perryman, Martin Peters, Gica Popescu, Derek Possee, Graham Roberts, Vinny Samways, Andy Sinton, Bert Smith, Bobby Steel, Gary Stevens, Paul Stewart, Mitchell Thomas, Andy Thompson, Chris Waddle, Paul Walsh, John White, Willie Young.

The following players have each scored one goal in Cup-tie derby matches:

Ossie Ardiles, Glenn Hoddle.

The following players all made their full first team debuts for Spurs in the North London League derby:

Player	Date	Derby number
BROOKS, Sammy	30-9-1922	14
BROWN, Laurie	22-2-1964	56
COLLINS, Peter	10-8-1968	65
DUNMORE, Dave	27-2-1954	36
EVANS, Ray	24-3-1969	66
JONES, Cliff	22-2-1958	44
LEWORTHY, David	17-4-1985	96
McGRATH, Chris	13-10-1973	75
MILLER, Paul	10-4-1979	84
PEARCE, Jimmy	10-8-1968	65
PHYPERS, Ernie	6-3-1935	28
PRATT, John	24-3-1969	66
TATE, John	19-4-1913	8
WALDEN, Fanny	19-4-1913	8
WEBSTER, Fred	25-12-1911	5

The following players all made their full first team debuts for Arsenal in the North London League derby:

Player	Date	Derby number
BRADY, Liam	13-10-1973	75
BRAIN, Jimmy	25-10-1924	17
BUCHAN, Charlie	29-8-1925	19
CRAWFORD, Harry	25-12-1911	5
DAVIS, Paul	7-4-1980	86
DICKOV, Paul	11-5-1993	112
DUNCAN, David	14-12-1912	7
KIRCHEN, Alf	6-3-1935	28
McCLELLAND, John	21-1-1961	50
McGOLDRICK, Eddie	16-8-1993	113
SNEDDEN, John	16-1-1960	48
WEBSTER, Malcolm	16-9-1969	67
WILLS, Len	10-10-1953	35
WILLIAMS, Steve	1-1-85 (as sub)	95

The only player to make his first team debut in a North London Cup derby was THOMAS, Michael when he went on as a substitute in the first leg of the Littlewoods Cup semi-final on 8-2-87.

The two major awards which are available to Spurs and Arsenal players within the domestic game are the Football Writer's Association "Footballer of the Year" (first awarded for the 1947-48 season) and the Professional Footballers' Association "Footballer of the Year" (first awarded in 1974).

The following Spurs and Arsenal players have won these awards:

Spurs

Danny Blanchflower	1957-58	(Football Writers award)
Danny Blanchflower	1960-61	(Football Writers award)
Pat Jennings	1972-73	(Football Writers award)
Pat Jennings	1976	(P.F.A. award)
Steve Perryman	1981-82	(Football Writers award)
Clive Allen	1986-87	(Football Writers award)
Clive Allen	1987	(P.F.A. award)
Gary Lineker	1991-92	(Football Writers award)
Jurgen Klinsmann	1994-95	(Football Writers award)

Arsenal

Joe Mercer	1949-50	(Football Writers award)
Frank McLintock	1970-71	(Football Writers award)
Liam Brady	1979	(P.F.A. award)

The following Spurs and Arsenal players have won the P.F.A. Young Player of the Year award:

Spurs		*Arsenal*	
Glenn Hoddle	1980	Tony Adams	1987
Paul Gascoigne	1988	Paul Merson	1989

**Danny Blanchflower -
twice voted 'Footballer
of the Year'.**

PLAYERS WHO HAVE PLAYED FOR BOTH ARSENAL AND SPURS

● Even allowing for the intense rivalry there have been remarkably few direct transfers between the two clubs. Seven players have moved from Spurs to Arsenal, four of them following Terry Neill, while only three have gone in the opposite direction.

The first was **JIMMY BRAIN**. Bristol born he was playing for the Welsh club, Ton Pentre, when he had the chance to join both Spurs and Arsenal in 1923. He chose Highbury and made his debut in October 1924 scoring the only goal of the game against Spurs! An inside or centre-forward he proved a prolific scorer becoming the first Gunner to net 100 League goals. A member of the 1927 FA Cup final side and top scorer for four seasons from 1924 he picked up a championship medal in 1931 but by then was only a reserve for David Jack and Jack Lambert. With Spurs struggling to escape the Second Division and Brain unable to make Arsenal's first eleven, he made the short trip across North London in September 1923 having netted 139 goals in 232 senior games for Arsenal. A regular in his first season at Spurs, he scored ten goals in 47 games before moving on to the coaching staff and was later manager of Kings Lynn and Cheltenham and finished his career in football scouting for Arsenal.

GEORGE HUNT became the first player transferred from Spurs to Arsenal in October 1937. Rejected by Port Vale and Sheffield United, he turned down the chance to join Barnsley because he did not consider the terms offered good enough and instead signed for Chesterfield. Herbert Chapman was keen to take him to Highbury but when he decided to leave his move for a while Percy Smith nipped in to sign him for Spurs in September 1930. Competing with Ted Harper, Hunt did not find it easy to start with, but within a year replaced the former England centre-forward and began to hit the target with amazing regularity. His goals took Spurs back into the top flight in 1933 and to third place the following season but persistent injuries restricted his effectiveness as Spurs were relegated in 1935. Those problems continued for the next two years and with the emergence of Johnny Morrison Hunt found himself out of favour. It was still a huge shock though when Spurs allowed him to move to Highbury in October 1937 after netting 138 goals in 198 matches. He was needed to replace the injured Ted Drake and played his part in helping Arsenal capture another League title with 3 goals in 21 League games and three FA Cup-ties. With the return of Drake, Hunt was allowed to move to Bolton in March 1938 and had just over a season with Sheffield Wednesday after the Second World War before returning to Burnden Park where he served on the coaching staff for over 20 years.

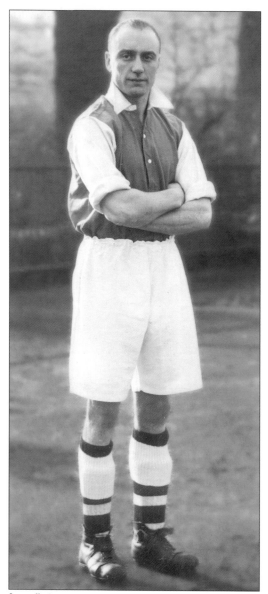

George Hunt

After joining Spurs as an amateur **FREDDIE COX** played for their nursery club at Northfleet before signing professional in August 1938. Like so many of his generation he lost valuable years to the Second World War but on the cessation of hostilities made the outside-right berth his own until new manager Arthur Rowe made it clear he preferred the somewhat more direct style of Sonny Walters. Arsenal immediately stepped in to sign Cox for £12,000 and he moved to Highbury in September 1949 with a Spurs record of 17 goals in 105 senior competitive games. 16 goals in 94 matches were added to his total in four years at Highbury during which he played in the FA Cup finals of 1950 and 1951, his goals having taken Arsenal through to Wembley each time. In 1950 he scored once in a 2-2 semi-final draw with Chelsea and notched the winner in the replay. He went one better in 1952 scoring Arsenal's goal in the first meeting with Chelsea and two in the replay. All four games took place at White Hart Lane. Cox moved on to West Brom in July 1953 as player/coach and later enjoyed a lengthy career in management with Bournemouth, Portsmouth, Gillingham and Bournemouth again.

An England and Great Britain amateur international centre-forward, **LAURIE BROWN** made his name with Bishop Auckland before joining the professional ranks at Northampton Town in October 1960 but less than a year later moved to Arsenal for £35,000. Switched to centre-half he scored twice in 109 games but lost his place with the arrival of Ian Ure. He joined Spurs in February 1964 for £45,000 to replace England centre-forward Bobby Smith making his debut against Arsenal only 24 hours after his transfer. Not up to First Division standard as a front line striker he reverted to centre-half but with the signing of Mike England was allowed to move to Norwich in September 1966 having scored three goals in 65 appearances. He later played for and managed Bradford PA before moving into management in non-League circles.

A member of Arsenal's 1968 League Cup final team, **DAVID JENKINS** joined Spurs in October 1968. He had made his Arsenal debut two years earlier and was just beginning to establish himself in the first team with nine goals to his credit from 25 matches. He proved a poor signing by Bill Nicholson making just 17 appearances, four as a substitute, in four years and scoring only two goals. In July 1972 he moved to Brentford and later played for Hereford, Newport, Shrewsbury, Workington and in South Africa.

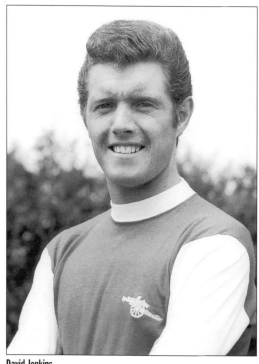

David Jenkins

Jimmy Robertson

As part of the deal that saw Jenkins move to Spurs, **JIMMY ROBERTSON** made the switch to Highbury. A former Cowdenbeath amateur he had joined Spurs from St Mirren in March 1964 for £25,000 and gone on to win one Scottish cap. Included in his 31 goals in 177 games (plus four as a substitute) was the first goal in the 1967 FA Cup final. He scored eight goals in his 59 appearances for Arsenal, moved on to Ipswich in March 1970 following the arrival of Peter Marinello, and later played for Stoke, Seattle Sounders, Walsall and Crewe.

Big **WILLIE YOUNG** was the first of the quartet to follow Terry Neill from White Hart Lane to Highbury. Signed by Neill for Spurs from Aberdeen in March 1975, Young was not the most attractive of footballers but he had an enthusiasm for the game that compensated for his lack of finesse. He was not, though, the type of central defender Keith Burkinshaw wanted but with Terry Neill looking to replace Peter Simpson was just what his former manager was looking for and left Spurs in March 1977 for £80,000 with 64 matches and four goals to his credit. Young's attitude and obvious pleasure at playing football at the highest level were well appreciated at Highbury and he became a cult figure to Arsenal supporters, playing in the three successive FA Cup finals between 1978 and 1980. After 237 appearances and 19 goals he moved to Nottingham Forest in December 1981, later turning out for Norwich, Brighton and Darlington.

KEVIN STEAD was a young centre-forward with Spurs who had failed to make the breakthrough when given a free transfer in May 1977. He joined Arsenal two months later but fared little better at Highbury appearing in just two League games, one as a substitute, before moving to Oxford City on a free transfer in September 1979.

The last two transfers between the clubs were in August 1977 and there could not be more of a difference in experience between the two players.

PAT JENNINGS M.B.E, O.B.E, at 32 still regarded as one of the world's best goalkeepers and the perfect example of how 'keepers only get better with age, had seen it all and done it all. Signed from Watford in June 1964 just a year after moving to England from Newry Town he took a little time to settle in at White Hart Lane, but when he did proved the rock upon which so much success was built. A member of the teams that won the FA Cup in 1967, League Cup in 1971 and 1973, UEFA Cup in 1972 and reached the final of the same competition in 1974 he collected 66 caps for Northern Ireland and made a record number of appearances for Spurs, subsequently beaten only by Steve Perryman. Injury sidelined Jennings for much of the 1976-77 season and when it came to re-assessing his playing staff for Spurs' first season back in the Second Division Keith Burkinshaw decided to release Jennings and rely on the younger Barry Daines. Made available for a nominal £45,000, several clubs were keen to acquire his services but Jennings chose to join his former international team-mate Neill. He left Spurs with 590 senior games under his belt and the never to be forgotten record of having scored in the 1967 FA Charity Shield at Old Trafford. If anyone thought Jennings would quietly wind down his career at Highbury they could not have been more mistaken. For eight years he remained first choice, setting new standards of consistency and performance and helping Arsenal to the FA Cup finals of 1978 to 1980 and European Cup-Winners' Cup final of 1980. He made a total of 327 senior appearances and picked up another 42 caps. Eventually displaced by John Lukic, Jennings returned to Spurs in the summer of 1985 to keep fit for the 1986 World Cup finals, after which he eventually called it a day. He now assists Spurs as specialist goalkeeping coach, and there could not be one better.

At the same time as Jennings moved to Highbury so did **STEVE WALFORD**, a young Islington born defender who had been given little chance to show what he could do for Spurs. Signed as an apprentice in April 1974 and upgraded to professional status twelve months later he made only two senior outings, one as a substitute. £25,000 may seem a lot for an inexperienced 19 year old but it proved a bargain. Happy at centre-half, full back or in midfield he gave Arsenal almost four years valuable service, playing 78 full games, 20 as a substitute (including the 1978 FA Cup final) and scoring four goals before moving to Norwich for £175,000 in March 1981. After two years in Norfolk he spent four years with West Ham and played on loan for West Brom, Huddersfield and Gillingham before short spells in Turkey and Hong Kong. He finished his career with Wycombe Wanderers where he moved into coaching.

Laurie Brown, Freddie Cox, David Jenkins, Pat Jennings, Jimmy Robertson and Willie Young all played for both clubs in North London derbies but only Jimmy Robertson scored for both. Willie Young scored for Spurs and Laurie Brown for Arsenal, although he managed to do that while playing for Spurs!

Pat Jennings

● In the late 1890s and early 1900s players were usually signed on one year contracts and if not renewed were free to move to another club without a fee being paid. The following players were not directly transferred between the clubs but immediately after being released by one joined the other.

Diminutive winger **DAVID BLACK** had won a Scottish cap in his days with Hurlford after starting his football career with Rovers FC. He then played for Grimsby, Middlesbrough, Wolves and Burnley, scoring Wolves goal in the 1893 FA Cup final. Spurs secured his signature in May 1897 and it was a surprise when they released him after one season in which he had been almost ever-present. He signed for Woolwich Arsenal in May 1898 but failed to make an outing in their colours before returning to Scotland, and Clyde, in September that year.

WALTER BUGG had gained experience with West Norwood and Millwall reserves when he joined Woolwich Arsenal as a 19-year old but in his one year at the Manor Ground failed to make the first eleven and was released. He joined Spurs in September 1901, played three senior games in the next two years but was released after medical advice to give up playing. In fact he did try to play again, with Norwich, but after five games retired.

Goalkeeper **TOM HATFIELD** joined Woolwich Arsenal as an amateur in January 1895, being upgraded to professional status three months later in time for his Football League debut. He added one more game to his League total in 1895-96, was released at the end of that season and signed for Spurs in September 1896 as cover for Charlie Ambler. Ten senior outings followed and after his release in April 1897 he joined Royal Engineers.

Bustling centre-forward **PETER KYLE** was a football nomad with something of a rebellious nature. He joined Spurs in the summer of 1905 from Larkhall Thistle and proved a big success with 17 goals in 39 senior games but was suspended in March 1906 for a breach of training rules and did not play for the club again before joining Woolwich Arsenal at the end of the season. 23 goals in 60 games over the next two seasons followed before a transfer to Aston Villa in March 1908. Seven months later he moved to Sheffield United and later played for Royal Albert and Watford.

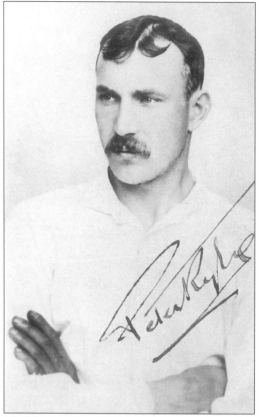

Peter Kyle

Plumstead born **TOM MEADE** was a prolific scorer in his three years with Woolwich Arsenal despite most of his appearances being in friendly games or at reserve level. He only played 17 senior matches but still managed to score 10 goals. With the promise of regular first team football he joined Spurs in May 1897 but a dispute between Spurs and Arsenal restricted his outings in his first year in North London and left him playing mostly reserve games again. Released in the summer of 1899 he later spent four years with Fulham.

Clive Allen

● There have been several other players who have played for both clubs, although not always at senior level.

CLIVE ALLEN joined Arsenal from Queens Park Rangers in June 1980 for £1.25 million but played in only three pre-season tour games before moving to Crystal Palace in exchange for Kenny Sansom two months later. After another spell at Loftus Road he signed for Spurs in August 1984 and spent almost four years at White Hart Lane before moving to Bordeaux.

BOBBY BUIST was one of the first players to join Royal Arsenal after their decision to turn professional, being lured down from Clyde in September 1891. Regular centre-half for three years he returned to Scotland to play for Leith Athletic but was with Royal Ordnance when he played three games for Spurs in March and April 1896 as they looked to sign professional players for their first season in the Southern League. Spurs did not take him on but he must have impressed Gravesend who provided the opposition in two of those games as later signed for them.

JIMMY CALDWELL was a goalkeeper who joined Spurs from East Stirling in the summer of 1908, spent the whole season in the reserves and moved to Reading a year later. He did well in Berkshire and in June 1912 joined Everton where he spent one season as first choice before arriving at the Manor Field a year later. He had just a season in South London as reserve to Joe Lievesley and made few senior appearances before going back to Reading just before the outbreak of War.

JIMMY CHIPPERFIELD signed for Luton in June 1914 but had few chances until the Great War when he turned out regularly for Arsenal, impressing enough to play in an international trial match in April 1919. With the resumption of normal football several clubs were keen to sign him but he chose Spurs and started the 1919-20 season as first choice outside-left. He lost his place to Jimmy Dimmock because of a cartilage injury and was never able to get

Jimmy Caldwell

George Payne

back in. In Decemeber 1921 he was allowed to move to Notts County and later played for Northfleet and Charlton.

JAMES DEVLIN joined Spurs in the summer of 1896 from Airdrie having been playing on loan for Hereford Thistle. A regular in Spurs' first season in the Southern League, he signed for Millwall in October 1897, quickly moved on to Sunderland and by December that year was back in London with Arsenal. Illness curtailed his appearances at the Manor Ground and in August 1898 he went back to Airdrie.

JOHN EGGETT joined Woolwich Arsenal in the summer of 1903 having made his name with Doncaster Rovers but was transferred to West Ham in January 1904 without playing a senior game for the Gunners. He left the East End for North London in May 1904 making over a hundred appearances in the next three years before joining the newly-professionalised Croydon Common club.

ARTHUR ELLIOTT gained experience with Gainsborough Trinity and Accrington before joining Royal Arsenal in the summer of 1892. In two years he made over 100 senior appearances but on being released, just like Arsenal colleague Bill Julian, applied to be re-instated as an amateur so he could turn out for Spurs. Unlike Julian, though, he played just one game, in October 1894, before returning to his native Nottingham and signing for Nottingham Forest.

VIC GROVES was on the books of Leytonstone when he signed amateur forms for Spurs in June 1952. He made four League appearances but preferred to play for Leytonstone and Walthamstow Avenue before joining the professional ranks at Leyton Orient in October 1954. A little over a year later he was transferred to Arsenal and made over 200 senior appearances before joining Canterbury City in September 1964.

BILL JULIAN so impressed Arsenal playing against them for Boston Town in April 1889 that they immediately fixed up a job at the Royal Arsenal armaments factory so he could turn out for them. He captained the first professional club in London in his four years there, had a year as player-coach of Luton and in September 1894 was re-instated as an amateur so he could play for Spurs. After two years with Spurs he had a year at Dartford and later became a sports coach in Holland.

Inside-forward **JIMMY MEGGS** made his name with City Ramblers, at one time north London's premier amateur outfit and one that with the right guidance might have gone on to great things. He joined Royal Arsenal in September 1889, making his debut that month against his former team-mates, and spent two years as regular in Arsenal's pre-League days before returning to the Ramblers. In April 1893 he first turned out for Spurs, City Ramblers again providing the opposition, and over the next couple of years helped them out on rare occasions, but never on a regular basis.

Woolwich born **BILLY MINTER** spent four months as an amateur on the books of Woolwich Arsenal in 1906 but failed to make the first team and tried his luck with Reading. Top scorer for two years he joined Spurs in March 1908 and went on to give them 32 years service as player, trainer, manager and assistant secretary until his death in 1940.

GEORGE PAYNE joined Spurs from Barnet Alston in November 1906 but made few appearances before moving to Crystal Palace in May 1909. 25 Southern League goals in one season persuaded Sunderland to invest in him in April 1911 but after only a couple of League appearances he returned to London with Leyton in January 1912. Six months later he joined Arsenal and played three League games before the outbreak of the First World War during which he was badly wounded and unable to play again.

RON PIPER was another who spent a short spell as an amateur with Arsenal but later went on to play for Spurs. Signed as a professional in September 1960 after a month in the amateur ranks he made only one League appearance, in May 1963 before being released and moving into non-League football.

TOM PRATT was a big signing when he joined Spurs from Preston in April 1899 having previously played for Fleetwood Rangers and Grimsby Town. He helped Spurs win the Southern League title but after a year returned to Preston. Two years at Deepdale were followed by one at Fleetwood before Pratt joined Arsenal in August 1903. He had little success at the Manor Field, moved to Fulham in August 1904 and a year later went to Blackpool.

ANDREW SWAN made his name with Lincoln City and spent a year with both New Brompton and Barnsley before arriving at Arsenal in May 1901. He started the season as first choice but soon fell out of favour and by Christmas 1901 had moved to Stockport. Five months later he was on his travels again joining Mexborough United and in May 1904 signed for Spurs. He made only six senior appearances, was released at the end of the season and later played for Plymouth.

Kent born goalkeeper **CHARLIE WILLIAMS** began his career with local junior clubs before joining Arsenal in Nov 1891. He settled to top flight football well but with the signing of Harry Storer in May 1894 was allowed to move to

Manchester City where he enjoyed the best days of his career, a regular for eight years and playing for the Football League. With City relegated from the First Division in 1902 Williams was released and joined Spurs as understudy to George Clawley. He spent three years at White Hart Lane, then played for Norwich and Brentford before coaching and managing in France, Holland and Brazil where he eventually settled.

● With the exception of the 1892-93 season, when they played in the Southern Alliance, Spurs played only friendly and local cup-ties until joining the Southern League in 1896. It was not until 1908 that they were elected to the Football League, a competition in which Arsenal had carried the banner for London football since 1893. As a player signed forms to play for a club in a particular competition it meant there were several players who were able to turn out for both clubs in the different competitions.

CHARLIE AMBLER was first associated with Royal Arsenal in 1891, initially as an amateur but later, when they had dropped Royal in favour of Woolwich, as a professional. He played regularly for their reserve side, with few first eleven outings, between 1891 and 1893 when he threw in his lot with Dartford. A year in Kent and a month with Luton followed before he joined Spurs in October 1894, almost immediately becoming first choice between the posts. In November 1895 Woolwich Arsenal suspended their regular custodian Harry Storer and Ambler signed Football League forms for them but conceded five goals in his one Football League game at Newton Heath. Arsenal then turned to Tom Hatfield while they looked for a permanent replacement for Storer. Ambler stayed with Spurs until 1900 going on to serve Gravesend, New Brompton, West Ham and Millwall.

Centre-half **STANLEY BRIGGS** first played for Spurs in January 1892 and went on to establish himself as one of the top amateurs in London, if not the country. He received many offers to take up the paid game but resisted them all, preferring to remain true to his amateur principles. However he did sign Football League forms for Woolwich Arsenal in November 1893 and played two games for them that month. With Spurs turning professional in 1895 Briggs preferred to play for Clapton and later served the well-known West London amateurs, Shepherds Bush.

LY BURROWS was playing for Woolwich Polytechnic when he first caught the eye of Woolwich Arsenal and signed for them in January 1892. Basically a reserve, he accepted an offer to play for Spurs in October 1894 and gave them three years service although he continued to make himself available for Arsenal when it came to Football League games and he played ten games for them in that competition. In December 1897 work took him to Sheffield and he signed for Sheffield United.

TOM FITCHIE was one of those players from the early years of the century who turned down numerous invitations to play full-time, preferring to make a career in business and play for pleasure. Moving to London as a schoolboy he first came to prominence with the West Norwood club and signed Football League forms for Woolwich Arsenal in November 1901. He played more than sixty senior matches over the next eight years, and won three Scottish caps, but was often unavailable due to business commitments. Arsenal had first call on his services for Football League games but he also played for London Caledonians, Fulham, Norwich and, when working in Glasgow, Queen's Park. His association with Spurs was very brief, just two games in April 1902. In 1909 he threw in his lot with Glossop North End where he played for three years before ending his playing days at Fulham.

● With Arsenal playing their home games at White Hart Lane for most of the Second World War it might be expected that players of one club guesting for the other would have been a common occurrence. In fact it happened very rarely. Percy Hooper, Les Stevens, Ralph Ward and Bill Whatley were the only Spurs' players to assist Arsenal; Les Henley, David Nelson and Albert Young the only Arsenal players to turn out for Spurs.

There were more players, though, who guested for both clubs, vis:-. Pat Beasley (Huddersfield and ex-Arsenal), Frank Boulton (Derby and ex-Arsenl), Harry Brown (QPR), Bernard Bryant (Walthamstow), Harry Ferrier (Barnsley), Len Flack (Norwich), Bobby Flavell (Airdrie), Fred Hall (Blackburn), H Harris (Distillery), Archie Hughes (Huddersfield and later Spurs), Eric Jones (WBA), Phil Joslin (Torquay) and Albert Sibley (Southend). Ex- Spurs defender Wally Alsford made one appearance for Arsenal and Fulham's former Arsenal reserve James Evans played once for Spurs.

Guest players were not so common during the First World War. No Spurs player turned out for Arsenal and the only Arsenal player to don a Spurs' shirt was goalkeeper Tim Williamson, whose one appearance cost Spurs a five guinea fine because they did not have Arsenal's permission to play him.

Tom Fitchie

Wally Alsford

DERBY MANAGERS

Note: To enable a fair comparison of a manager's derby record 2 points are given for a win and one for a draw. Those who were not at the helm for a derby match are not included.

Spurs Managers

Manager	Seasons	Played	Won	Drawn	Lost	Points
Directors	1909-13	7	3	1	3	7
Peter McWilliam	1913-27	14	7	3	4	17
Billy Minter	1927-28	3	1	1	1	3
Percy Smith	1933-35	4	1	1	2	3
Joe Hulme	1948-49	1	0	0	1	0
Arthur Rowe	1950-55	10	2	2	6	6
Jimmy Anderson	1955-59	7	3	1	3	7
Bill Nicholson	1958-75	33	15	8	10	38
Terry Neill	1974-76	4	2	1	1	5
Keith Burkinshaw	1976-84	17	5	2	10	12
Peter Shreeves	1984-86	4	2	1	1	5
	1991-92	3	0	2	1	2
David Pleat	1986-88	6	1	1	4	3
Terry Venables	1988-91	8	2	2	4	6
	1992-93	3	2	0	1	4
Ossie Ardiles	1993-95	2	0	1	1	1
Gerry Francis	1994-97	6	2	3	1	7

Arsenal Managers

Manager	Seasons	Played	Won	Drawn	Lost	Points
George Morrell	1908-13	8	3	2	3	8
Leslie Knighton	1919-25	10	4	1	5	9
Herbert Chapman	1925-34	7	1	3	3	7
George Allison	1933-35	3	2	0	1	4
Tom Whittaker	1947-56	14	8	2	4	18
Jack Crayston	1956-58	3	1	1	1	3
George Swindin	1958-62	8	3	1	4	7
Billy Wright	1962-66	8	1	4	3	6
Bertie Mee	1966-76	22	8	4	10	20
Terry Neill	1976-83	15	8	2	5	18
Don Howe	1983-85	5	3	1	1	6
Steve Burtenshaw	1985-86	1	0	0	1	0
George Graham	1986-95	23	11	6	6	28
Stewart Houston	1994-95	1	0	1	0	1
Bruce Rioch	1995-96	2	0	1	1	1
Arsene Wenger	1996-97	2	1	1	0	3

Tom Whittaker outside the Highbury entrance.

MANAGERS AND PLAYERS

The only person to manage both Arsenal and Spurs, **TERRY NEILL**, a native of Belfast, joined Arsenal from Bangor as a 17-year old in December 1959. He slowly developed into a first team regular, playing as the defensive wing-half along the centre-half or in the centre of defence himself. Winning his first cap when still only 18 he soon rose to captain his country, an almost ever-present in the green jersey, collecting a total of 43 caps whilst at Highbury. In July 1970 he was transferred to Hull for £40,000 as player-manager, a role he occupied for his country in taking his total of caps to 59. Articulate and media friendly his four years with Hull were expected to be his apprenticeship for taking over Arsenal but when he returned to north London it was with Spurs. His appointment as successor to Bill Nicholson was a considerable surprise and he never had an easy time in his two years at White Hart Lane. Resigning in June 1976 he almost immediately succeeded Bertie Mee at Arsenal. In taking over from two of the most successful managers in the game he certainly showed he was not afraid of anybody's shadow! Always an advocate of attacking football he never shirked paying out big transfer fees for the players he wanted and, if only for his attitude, deserved more success than he achieved. He led Arsenal to three successive FA Cup finals between 1978 and 1980 and the Cup-Winners' Cup final in 1980 but the only trophy he won was the FA Cup in 1979. Dismissed in December 1983 after Walsall had knocked Arsenal out of the Milk Cup he went into media work where his wit and easy-going style of commentary has made him very popular.

JOE HULME is the only ex-Arsenal player to have managed Spurs. Starting with York, Hulme had three years with Blackburn before Herbert Chapman laid out £3,500 to sign him in February 1926. For the next twelve years he was the almost automatic choice on the right wing, one of the biggest names in a team of stars that took Arsenal to heights hardly dreamed of. In almost four hundred senior appearances he scored over one hundred goals, collected three championship medals, played in four FA Cup finals, picking up winners medals in 1930 and 1936, and won nine England caps. In January 1938 he joined Huddersfield and at the end of the season played in his fifth FA Cup final. Returning to London, Hulme joined Spurs as assistant secretary in February 1944 and in January 1946 took over as manager. In the three years he was in charge he was unable to get Spurs out of the Second Division but laid the basis for the "Push and Run" team that was to bring so much credit to his successor, Arthur Rowe. After Spurs Hulme was a journalist for many years.

HERBERT CHAPMAN was little more than a journeyman footballer around the turn of the century, but as a manager he was a football genius. Starting with his home club Kiveton Park, Chapman played for Ashton North End, Rochdale, Grimsby, Swindon, Sheppey United, Worksop, Northampton, Sheffield United, Notts County and Northampton again before arriving at Tottenham in March 1905 for £70. For two years he proved a competent if not spectacular footballer, certainly not in the same class as his brother Harry, before returning to Northampton as player-manager in April 1907. Northampton had just finished bottom of the Southern League; two years later they won the title. It was just a foretaste of Chapman's managerial talents, of the way he could take a club going nowhere and turn it into champions. In May 1912 he returned to his native Yorkshire taking on the task of turning round the fortunes of Leeds City, his first job to help them gain re-election to the League. That achieved, two years later he had taken them to within two points of promotion to the First Division but any hopes of doing better were ruined by the First War. Chapman spent most of the war helping manage a munitions factory and was not party to, although quite possibly aware of, illegal payments made to players. When Leeds refused to open their books for inspection in October 1919 they were expelled, Chapman, perhaps harshly as he had not even been at Elland Road when the alleged payments were made, suspended. It took Chapman nearly a year to get his suspension lifted but when he did he soon found a job as Huddersfield secretary. It was September 1920 and Huddersfield had just embarked on their first season in Division One. Appointed manager in March 1921, Chapman led Huddersfield to FA Cup success in 1922, the League title in 1924 and 1925. They completed a hat-trick in 1926 but by then Chapman had accepted Sir Henry Norris' offer of £2000 a year to take over at Highbury. Chapman had said it would take five years to win anything for Arsenal. He was right, although he very nearly proved himself wrong taking them to second in the League in 1926 and the FA Cup final a year later. It was 1930 when Chapman's team provided Arsenal with their first major silverware, the FA Cup. The League title followed twelve months later, the FA Cup again in 1932 and the Championship again in 1933. Chapman had firmly established Arsenal as the greatest club in the country and they were on the way to the second of what was to be three successive titles when, in January 1934, what had started as a simple cold developed into pneumonia and Chapman died. Football was robbed of the most successful manager the game had known but he left a mark on history that can never be removed.

Terry Neill

Joe Hulme

Herbert Chapman

Stars of the Seventies

As a prelude to a match played in memory of Cyril Knowles in November 1991, a Spurs 1970-71 side faced an Arsenal 1970-71 team.

Tottenham's line-up (above). Back row (left to right): Terry Naylor, Jimmy Neighbour, Phil Beal, Mike England, Joe Kinnear, Pat Jennings, Martin Peters, Martin Chivers. Front: Cliff Jones, John Pratt, Ralph Coates, Phil Holder, Frank Saul.

Arsenal (below). Back: Frank McLintock, Jon Sammels, Paul Barron, Eddie Kelly, Peter Storey, Willie Young, David Court, Sammy Nelson. Front: Pat Rice, George Armstrong, John Radford, George Graham.

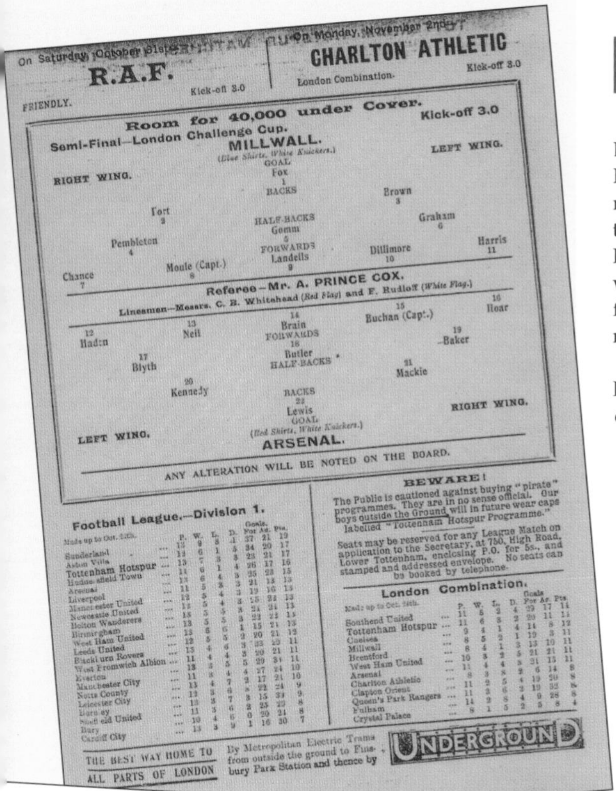

On Saturday, October 31st

R.A.F.

Kick-off 3.0

FRIENDLY.

On Monday, November 2nd

CHARLTON ATHLETIC

London Combination.

Kick-off 3.0

Room for 40,000 under Cover.

Kick-off 3.0

Semi-Final—London Challenge Cup.

MILLWALL.

(Blue Shirts, White Knickers.)

RIGHT WING. LEFT WING.

GOAL
Fox
1

BACKS
Fort 2 — Brown 3

HALF-BACKS
Pembleton 4 — Gomm 5 — Graham 6

FORWARDS
Chance 7 — Moule (Capt.) 8 — Landells 9 — Dillimore 10 — Harris 11

Referee—Mr. A. PRINCE COX.

Linesmen—Messrs. C. B. Whitehead (Red Flag) and F. Rudloff (White Flag.)

FORWARDS
12 Haden — 13 Neil — 14 Brain — 15 Buchan (Capt.) — 16 Hoar

HALF-BACKS
17 Blyth — 18 Butler — 19 Baker

BACKS
20 Kennedy — 21 Mackie

GOAL
22
Lewis

LEFT WING. RIGHT WING.

(Red Shirts, White Knickers.)

ARSENAL.

ANY ALTERATION WILL BE NOTED ON THE BOARD.

Football League.—Division 1.

Made up to Oct. 25th.

	P.	W.	L.	D.	Goals For	Goals Ag.	Pts.
Sunderland	13	9	3	1	37	21	19
Aston Villa	12	6	1	5	34	20	17
Tottenham Hotspur	13	7	3	3	23	21	17
Huddersfield Town	11	6	1	4	26	17	16
Arsenal	13	6	4	3	25	23	15
Liverpool	11	5	3	3	21	13	13
Manchester United	12	5	4	3	19	16	13
Newcastle United	11	5	4	3	15	24	13
Bolton Wanderers	13	5	5	3	21	21	13
Birmingham	13	5	5	3	22	22	13
West Ham United	13	6	6	1	15	21	13
Leeds United	12	5	5	2	20	21	12
Blackburn Rovers	13	4	6	3	23	20	11
West Bromwich Albion	11	4	4	3	20	21	11
Everton	13	3	5	5	29	31	11
Manchester City	11	3	4	4	27	24	10
Notts County	13	4	7	2	17	21	10
Leicester City	12	3	6	3	23	24	9
Burnley	13	3	7	3	15	31	9
Sheffield United	11	3	6	2	23	23	8
Bury	10	4	6	0	20	21	8
Cardiff City	13	3	9	1	16	30	7

BEWARE!

The Public is cautioned against buying "pirate" programmes. They are in no sense official. Our boys outside the Ground will in future wear caps labelled "Tottenham Hotspur Programme."

Seats may be reserved for any League Match on application to the Secretary, at 750, High Road, Lower Tottenham, enclosing P.O. for 5s., and stamped and addressed envelope. No seats can be booked by telephone.

London Combination.

Made up to Oct. 24th.

	P.	W.	L.	D.	Goals For	Goals Ag.	Pts.
Southend United	11	5	2	4	29	17	14
Tottenham Hotspur	11	6	3	2	20	11	14
Chelsea	9	4	1	4	14	8	12
Millwall	8	5	2	1	19	8	11
Brentford	8	4	1	3	13	10	11
West Ham United	10	3	2	5	21	21	11
Arsenal	11	4	4	3	21	15	11
Charlton Athletic	9	3	8	2	6	14	8
Clapton Orient	11	2	5	4	19	20	8
Queen's Park Rangers	11	3	6	2	19	32	8
Fulham	14	2	8	4	9	28	8
Crystal Palace	8	1	5	2	5	8	4

THE BEST WAY HOME TO ALL PARTS OF LONDON

By Metropolitan Electric Trams from outside the ground to Finsbury Park Station and thence by

UNDERGROUND

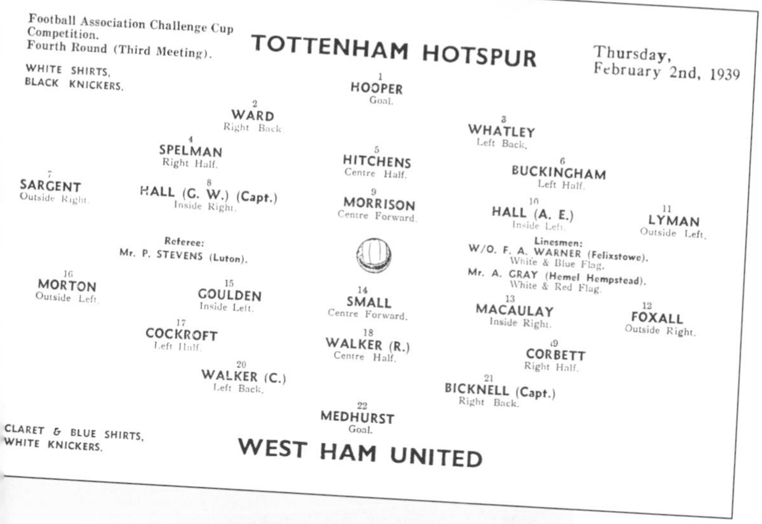

Football Association Challenge Cup Competition.
Fourth Round (Third Meeting).

TOTTENHAM HOTSPUR

Thursday, February 2nd, 1939

WHITE SHIRTS, BLACK KNICKERS.

1 HOOPER, Goal.

2 WARD, Right Back. — 3 WHATLEY, Left Back.

4 SPELMAN, Right Half. — 5 HITCHENS, Centre Half. — 6 BUCKINGHAM, Left Half.

7 SARGENT, Outside Right. — 8 HALL (G. W.) (Capt.), Inside Right. — 9 MORRISON, Centre Forward. — 10 HALL (A. E.), Inside Left. — 11 LYMAN, Outside Left.

Referee: Mr. P. STEVENS (Luton).

Linesmen: W/O. F. A. WARNER (Felixstowe). White & Blue Flag. Mr. A. GRAY (Hemel Hempstead). White & Red Flag.

16 MORTON, Outside Left. — 15 GOULDEN, Inside Left. — 14 SMALL, Centre Forward. — 13 MACAULAY, Inside Right. — 12 FOXALL, Outside Right.

17 COCKROFT, Left Half. — 18 WALKER (R.), Centre Half. — 19 CORBETT, Right Half.

20 WALKER (C.), Left Back. — 21 BICKNELL (Capt.), Right Back.

22 MEDHURST, Goal.

CLARET & BLUE SHIRTS, WHITE KNICKERS.

WEST HAM UNITED

HOME FROM HOME

During the First World War White Hart Lane was taken over by the Ministry of Munitions. With the terraces and pitch area converted into a factory for the manufacture of gas-masks, Spurs played about half their home matches in war-time competition at the Homerton ground of Clapton Orient. Arsenal made Highbury available for the rest. Spurs reciprocated during the Second World War when Highbury was requisitioned as an ARP centre. White Hart Lane was home for all but one of their matches during this period including their famous meeting with Dynamo Moscow in November 1945.

Apart from these times, when greater forces than football were dictating events, Highbury and White Hart Lane have also played host to their owners' closest rivals on several occasions when a neutral venue was required.

■ In November 1899, two months after Spurs' new headquarters had been opened, Woolwich Arsenal made their first visit to White Hart Lane. In the third qualifying round of the FA Cup they had already met New Brompton three times, drawing 1-1 at the Manor Ground, 0-0 at New Brompton's Gordon Road ground and 2-2 at Millwall's old East Ferry Road ground on the Isle of Dogs. The third replay was again inconclusive, another 1-1 draw, and a fifth meeting at Gravesend was needed before New Brompton triumphed by the only goal.

■ Woolwich Arsenal began their 1903-04 season winning 1-0 at White Hart Lane in the London League. With Spurs still in the Southern League they were not scheduled to visit Tottenham again but after two one-all draws with Bristol Rovers in the last qualifying round before the FA Cup competition proper began a neutral venue was required for a second replay in December 1903. Spurs were asked to play hosts and a lone goal from Tom Briercliffe was enough to see the Gunners through to a first round meeting with Fulham. A month later they were back to record their third victory of the season at White Hart Lane beating Reading 3-1 in the semi-final of the Southern Professional Charity Cup.

■ Inaugurated in 1908, The London Charity Cup was competed for by the capital's professional and leading amateur outfits. By 1930 both Arsenal and Spurs had relegated it to reserve team status but originally they treated it seriously, fielding the strongest elevens available.

■ In the first year of the competition, Woolwich Arsenal met Leyton at Spurs in the semi-final, losing 1-2 in February 1909. They went on to play two further semi-finals at White Hart Lane before the competition was devalued, beating Crystal Palace 2-0 in November 1914 before losing to Millwall in the final, and beating Millwall 3-1 in October 1925 before losing to West Ham.

■ It was in the London FA Charity Cup that Spurs made their only visit to the Manor Field for a game that was not against Woolwich Arsenal, losing 1-2 to Crystal Palace in the final in December 1913. After Arsenal's move to North London, Highbury hosted three games in the competition in which Spurs participated. In both April 1921 and November 1924 they lost 1-2 to Clapton Orient at the semi-final stage, and in May 1929 beat Millwall 5-1 in the final.

■ Highbury has only been used as a neutral venue for games involving Spurs on two other occasions, each time in the FA Cup. In February 1939, Spurs met West Ham in a fourth round second replay, having drawn the first game 3-3 at Upton Park and the first replay 1-1. West Ham won 2-1. In April 1981 Spurs were given a distinct advantage with the choice of Highbury for the semi-final replay as their fans heavily outnumbered those of Wolves to see Spurs triumph 3-0.

■ Since the Second World War White Hart Lane has been used as a neutral venue for five matches involving Arsenal, all of them in the FA Cup and all against Chelsea. The first was in January 1947 when Chelsea won 2-0 in the third round after two 1-1 draws.

■ In 1950 they met in the semi-final and after a two-all draw Arsenal won through by the only goal of the game to meet, and beat, Liverpool in the final. Two years later they again needed two games to overcome Chelsea in the semi-final, this time winning 3-0 after a 1-1 draw. Freddie Cox, who had spent thirteen years on Spurs' books after signing as an amateur in 1936, scored in all four of the semi-final clashes back on his old stamping ground.

Freddie Cox (left) returned to his old ground to score in four FA Cup semi-finals for Arsenal.

Many words have been spoken and written by players, supporters and managers of both clubs across the years of derby rivalry. Here are just a few that capture the flavour of football life in North London.

▼ **Ron Burgess:** *'Football - My Life'* talking about Arsenal's 3-0 FA Cup victory in January 1949:

"Arsenal beat us 3-0, beat us well and truly for we never looked like making a game of it .... I was up against my 'bogey-man' that afternoon - that great-hearted, brilliant little Scot, Jimmy Logie. He and I are the best of friends, but he gives me more trouble on the field than any other inside-forward. I rate him as the modern Alex James, he's like a will-o'-the-wisp. When you think you've got him covered, you find he isn't there. He certainly gave me a tiring afternoon in that Cup-tie."

▼ **Bernard Joy:** *'Forward Arsenal'* talking about the same match:

"What was hailed as the tit-bit of the season and the greatest Cup-tie North London had seen, ended as a flop. Spurs made a last-minute change, dropping effervescent inside-right Eddie Baily in favour of Harry Gilberg, and the team work suffered. When McPherson squeezed a header from a narrow angle past Ted Ditchburn early on, Spurs seemed to crumble. The half-time score was still 1-0, but with little fight in their opponents, Arsenal went further ahead through Roper and Lishman. The size of the crowd was just as great a fiasco. So many people were frightened off by anticipating a huge attendance, that there was only 47,314, over 15,000 below capacity."

▼ **Mel Stein:** *'Ha'way The Lad'* - The Authorised Biography of Paul Gascoigne talking about Gascoigne's first derby on 10th September 1988:

"In the build-up to the match wherever he went he was urged on by Spurs supporters, jeered by Arsenal fans .... The Arsenal game was not the perfect build-up (to England's game with Denmark four days later), with tackles flying in from all directions. Played at 150 miles an hour ..... "

▼ **Pat Jennings:** *'An Autobiography':*

"The tremendous rivalry between the fans is only matched at places like Liverpool and Manchester. Feelings were much fiercer on the terraces than in the respective dressing rooms - but, to be fair, that is only to be expected. Most supporters live in the same area all their lives, while players come and go. Usually they haven't grown up in the middle of Arsenal-Spurs arguments.

"Footballers know in their hearts that all supporters have the same attitude. If you are doing your stuff they back you all the way. If not ...... Where I have been lucky is that I have played for two clubs where the fans are particularly warm-hearted when things are going well, and I have enjoyed a fair degree of success at both Highbury and White Hart Lane."

Pat Jennings

Dennis Bergkamp tussles with Sol Campbell during Arsenal's 3-1 win at Highbury in November 1996.

Terry Neill

▼ **Terry Neill:** *'Revelations of a Football Manager'*.

"Even though I spent most of my career at Arsenal, I have a deep affection for Tottenham. I would have been happy to have spent the rest of my life giving my all for them. Nothing would prevent me from admiring and respecting Tottenham and I am still proud to have been their manager, even though it was for only two seasons."

▼ **Irving Scholar:** *'Behind Closed Doors':*

"It always means so much to beat Arsenal. It is much more than just three points, it is a case of pride and achievement. This rivalry will never die, and that is why a game between the two sides is a high or a low point of the season. If you win, you can hold your head high; if you lose, you are dreading meeting the next Arsenal supporter".

▼ **Charles Buchan:** *'A Lifetime in Football'* talking about the first meeting under the new offside law in August 1925:

"When Arsenal held their meeting before the first League game of the season with Tottenham Hotspur at Highbury I proposed that Jack Butler, our centre-half who really deserved, but did not get, an international cap, should take over a defensive role. I was overruled. We opened the programme with the old methods.

"We did not make a good start. Spurs beat us 1-0. I ran up against Arthur Grimsdell, one of the best all-round half-backs I ever met, in his finest form.

"He did not let me have many kicks at the ball. I did my best, but it was not good enough, Arthur was the master."

▼ **Tom Watt:** *'The End':*

"The local derby is the most intense, if not the most crucial, of the season's fixtures. A victory can be enjoyed for years, entering the private arcane of the rivals involved. A particularly ignominious defeat can hang around supporters' necks for even longer.

" .... Arsenal-Spurs games, however, tend to be fired by a bitterness all their own. This may be due, in part, to the peculiarly harsh and unforgiving edge that North Londoners enjoy in their sense of humour. This is the natural home of the wind-up, after all, and the appetite for mockery is not tempered, in the metropolitan sprawl, by any sense of regional solidarity or fellow-feeling. There is little hint of celebration, of a local occasion to be proud of, here. The games - and the rivalry between supporters - are unremittingly competitive, and victory is the only satisfactory outcome."

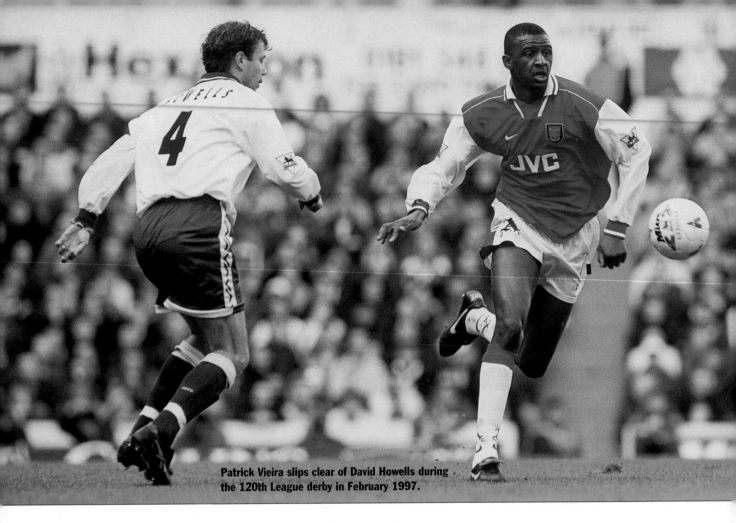

Patrick Vieira slips clear of David Howells during the 120th League derby in February 1997.

Subscribers

1	JOHN HARRIS, Southgate, London		28	RAY MURPHY, Bournemouth, Dorset
2	CAROLYN TINGAY, Cheshunt, Herts		29	JOHN PRICE, Erith, Kent
3	LES GOLD, Palmers Green, London		30	PAUL & SARAH COGGIN, Broxbourne, Herts
4	JOE BAKER, Edinburgh, Scotland		31	DAVID KEATS, Thornton Heath, Surrey
5	BOBBY SMITH, Palmers Green, London		32	T.J. WALTON, Moredon, Swindon, Wilts
6	ANDY PORTER, Billericay, Essex		33	ANDREW JANKO, Cheshunt, Herts
7	JOHN BETAMBEAU, Aston Clinton, Bucks		34	MARK MERRIMAN, Edmonton, London
8	GRAHAM BETTS, Aston Clinton, Bucks		35	JOHN MACAULAY, Chelmsford, Essex
9	BARRY CHARLES, Hornchurch, Essex		36	JOHN CROCKETT, Newtownabbey, Co. Antrim
10	FRED DOWRY, Chelmsford, Essex		37	DAVID DICKENS, Braunton, Devon
11	KEITH GREENHALF, Romford, Essex		38	ERIC BROWNE, London W10
12	MARK HAMMOND, Romford, Essex		39	CHARLIE PILAKOUTAS, Nicosia, Cyprus
13	STEVE MARTIN, Cheshunt, Herts		40	MARK HAYSOM, Western Mail & Echo, Cardiff
14	JULIAN BASKCOMB, Leicester		41	ANDREW MOXHAM, Woodford Green, Essex
15	GERALD TOON, Leicester		42	CHRIS SMITH, Wanstead, London
16	DAVID GASK, Rothley		43	IWAN JONES, Porthmadog, Gwynedd
17	RUSSELL STANDER, London		44	DARREN GALE, Southend-on-Sea
18	TONY PRINCE, London		45	DAVID BOSHER, Haynes, Beds
19	IAN GUILDFORD, Derby		46	MAL & LOIS PHILP, Mitcham, London
20	NEIL FOWLER, Cardiff		47	MIKE LYONS, East Grinstead, West Sussex
21	DAVID WHITTON, Cheltenham		48	COLIN BEWLEY, Bardwell Suffolk
22	ROGER R. DAVIES, Cwmcarn, Gwent		49	PETER BEWLEY, Edmonton, London
23	J. RINGROSE, Romford, Essex		50	GEORGE PAINTER, Castle Cary, Somerset
24	IAN GRIFFITHS, Saltney, Chester		51	ANDY CRADOCK, Cherry Hinton, Cambridge
25	JOHN A. VYVYAN, Greenford, Middlesex		52	PAUL LUNNEY, Glasgow
26	ALAN PARKE, Hanworth, Middlesex		53	BRIAN J. ADAMS, Herne Bay, Kent
27	MARK O'CONNOR, Gants Hill, Ilford		54	MARTIN WEILER, Exeter, Devon